FOURTH EDITION

Research Design in Clinical Psychology

Alan E. Kazdin

Yale University

Allyn and Bacon

Boston • London • Toronto • Sydney • Tokyo • Singapore

Series Editor: Rebecca Pascal
Editorial Assistant: Kate Edwards
Editorial-Production Service: Matrix Productions Inc.
Compositor: Publishers' Design and Production Services, Inc.
Composition Buyer: Linda Cox
Manufacturing Buyer: JoAnne Sweeney
Cover Administrator: Linda Knowles

Copyright © 2003 by Allyn & Bacon
A Pearson Education Company
75 Arlington Street
Boston, MA 02116

Internet: www.ablongman.com

Between the time Website information is gathered and then published, it is not unusual for some sites to have closed. Also, the transcription of URLs can result in unintended typographical errors. The publisher would appreciate notification where these occur so that they may be corrected in subsequent editions.

Library of Congress Cataloging-in-Publication Data

Kazdin, Alan E.
   Research design in clinical psychology / Alan E. Kazdin. — 4th ed.
     p. ; cm.
   Includes bibliographical references and index.
   ISBN 0-205-33292-7
    1. Clinical psychology—Research—Methodology. I. Title.
  [DNLM: 1. Psychology, Clinical. 2. Research Design. WM 105 K23r 2002]
  RC467.8 .K39 2002
  616.89′007′2—dc21   2001053993

Printed in the United States of America
10 9 8 7 6 5 4 3   06 05 04

To Nicole and Michelle

Contents

Preface

The purpose of this book is to describe and explain methodology and research design in clinical psychology. The focus is on clinical psychology, but the issues and methods are relevant to other areas as well, such as counseling, education, school psychology, psychiatry, social work, and nursing. The topics within each of these areas span theory, research, and application. Consequently, many of the methodological challenges are shared. The book elaborates the methods of conducting research and the broad range of practices, procedures, and designs for developing a sound knowledge base.

Many available texts on methodology elaborate fundamental practices and methods of research design. Often research methods are presented by describing idealized conditions of laboratory studies or in abstract discussions removed from investigations within the field. In clinical, counseling, and educational psychology, as well as related disciplines, a great deal of research is conducted outside of the laboratory. Essentials of research design are no less important. Indeed, an in-depth understanding of methodology is of even greater importance because of the range of influences in such research that can obscure the results. These influences cannot be used as an excuse for poorly designed research. On the contrary, the subject matter requires grasp of the underpinnings and nuances of design so that special arrangements, novel control conditions, and methods of statistical evaluation can be deployed to maximize clarity of our findings. Methodology, including the underlying tenets and specific practices, permit the combination of rigor and ingenuity as a defense against the multitude of influences that can obscure the relations among variables.

The scope and challenges of research that spans laboratory and applied contexts make research design a rich topic. For example, clinical psychology has embraced a variety of topics, including the study of personality; assessment and prediction of psychological functioning and adjustment; etiology, course, and outcome of various forms of psychopathology; the impact of interventions (treatment, prevention, education, and rehabilitation); and cross-cultural studies of personality and behavior. Many issues of contemporary life have added to the range of topics, as witnessed by the strong role that clinical psychology plays in research on health, violence, crime, homelessness, and substance abuse. Also, family life and demographic characteristics of the population have changed (increases in teenage mothers, single-parent families, blended families, and elderly who are physically active), and these have spawned rich areas of study (child care and elder care arrangements). Diversity of cultural and ethnic issues and understanding the bases of cultural variation further add to the richness of the field.

The topical breadth of clinical psychology also has been accompanied by a diversity of research methods. Consider a few of the dimensions that convey the methodological diversity of the field. Research in clinical psychology encompasses large-scale, multisite investigations involving groups of subjects as well as experiments with the single case (individual subject); methods of data evaluation that use inferential statistical techniques as well as nonstatistical and clinical criteria to assess change; and experiments that are conducted in laboratory settings as well as observational studies in hospitals, clinics, schools, and the community. The diversity of topics and types of research require coverage and appreciation of the full range of methodological weapons that can be deployed to combat ambiguity.

This book is designed to address methodology in the contexts in which clinical psychologists are called upon to work and in relation to the very special demands that these contexts may place. Although specific methodological practices and procedures are covered in detail, the book focuses on their underpinnings, rationales, and purposes as well. After all, methodology is not merely a compilation of practices and procedures. Rather, it is an approach to problem solving, thinking, and acquiring knowledge. An investigator in clinical and counseling psychology, for example, frequently is called upon to resolve questions related to evaluation when the usual practices cannot be used and to maximize the knowledge yield from the demonstration.

The content of the book encompasses experimental design, assessment, sources of artifact and bias, data evaluation and interpretation, and ethical and professional issues raised by research. Issues are traced as they emerge in the planning and execution of research from developing the research idea through selecting methods, procedures, and assessment devices, to analyzing and interpreting the data, and finally to preparing the written report of the results. At each stage of research, various principles, pitfalls, artifacts, biases, alternative strategies, and guidelines are presented. Attention also is devoted to quasi-experiments, case-control studies, case studies and single-case experiments for clinical use, qualitative research, assessment methods, and diverse approaches to data evaluation.

Five themes pervade the book. First, methodology is a way of thinking, problem solving, and approaching substantive questions. To be sure, many specific practices and design options central to methodology (random assignment, use of control groups) exist, and these are elaborated. Yet, it is as or more important to understand why these practices are central. Once understood, the options for designing research and for overcoming seeming constraints increase. Understanding the underlying issues can greatly expand the options for designing research and the quality and creativity of the products.

Second, methodology cannot be divorced from substance or content. The ways in which we design and evaluate our studies include and embrace substantive views about how we conceptualize the phenomena we study. Our selection of levels of the independent variable, of subjects, and especially of statistical analyses says something important, even if implicit, about how we view the world, our theories, and hypotheses. Drawing these connections encourages novel methods as a way of developing or testing theories.

Third, methodology is not merely a tool to evaluate ideas, but in many ways it shapes the ideas. Precisely what methods are used, how we frame the question, the groups we include, and the ways we decide to measure key constructs directly affect the answers we obtain. It is not the case that every answer to every question will change depending on our methods. Even so, it is important to understand that different answers can be readily achieved with different methodological tools and decisions. It is important to understand how methodology affects the yield from research, both for our own studies and for interpreting the research of others.

Fourth, methodology is evolving within psychology and the sciences more generally. Of course, one can find stability in methodology. Random assignment of subjects to groups or conditions, when possible, is still wonderful. Yet, much of methodology continues to change. Examples include what constitutes a "good" or "well-controlled" study; what measures ought to be used in a given area; how participants in research studies ought to be informed, treated, and protected; and what constitutes conflict of interest among investigators. The book covers many of the changes and the broader point that methodology is not at all static.

Finally, research has multiple methodologies, and the focus, yield, and contributions of these vary. We usually learn in our training the importance of experiments based on groups, comparison of group differences, statistical evaluation, and so on. This is the emphasis of the present book. Other approaches—such as single-case experimental designs and qualitative research—overlap in goals (demonstrating causal knowledge, testing and generating theory). These other methodologies are mentioned because they are important in their own right in relation to topics studied in clinical, counseling, educational, and other areas of psychology. Also, the methodologies convey and place into sharper focus many research practices we currently take for granted as the only paradigm for empirical science. The five themes, stated nebulously here, become more concrete throughout the text.

This revised edition includes several additions to reflect the evolving nature of methodology and salience of many research issues in both public and professional sources. Two new chapters have been added. Chapter 11 on assessment and evaluation in clinical practice focuses on methodological practices that can be used to evaluate the individual case in clinical work. User friendly and methodologically informed practices are presented to strengthen the inferences that can be drawn about interventions in clinical work and the basis for decision making about patient care. Chapter 14 focuses on assessment and evaluation issues that emerge in the context of intervention research (treatment, prevention, education, and enrichment programs). Special issues—such as evaluating the impact of the intervention and mechanisms of change, and strategies to assess follow-up—are considered.

Apart from additions, each chapter was revised and updated. Among the revisions are greater attention to tenets of science and how these affect methodology, ways of generating ideas for research, the need for and importance of theory in research, types of relations that can be studied (e.g., risk, causal factors), the study of mediators and moderators, modalities of psychological assessment, measurement development, contributions of different methodologies (e.g., qualitative research), and ethical issues. Throughout the book examples are provided to illustrate key points. The examples draw from classic (old) and new studies and from clinical and other areas of psychology.

Also, as in the previous editions, I have drawn examples from other disciplines including epidemiology, public health, and medicine.

The purpose in drawing on diverse examples is threefold. First, psychology is a scientific discipline and many of the central issues and concerns specific to areas of this book (clinical, counseling) are characteristics of many disciplines. Seeing an issue in these different contexts can lead to better understanding as well as increase options for how we address the matter in our studies. Second, disciplines often approach topics somewhat differently. For example, there are currently new and evolving guidelines regarding the use of placebos in medicine. The ethical issues and new guidelines developed to address those issues raise critical points for psychological research in relation to the various control and comparison groups we use. Third, many fascinating examples from diverse areas can illustrate key points. For example, methodology is illustrated with examples on such topics as the effects of wine and religion on health. In my career I have worked very hard to make sure my writings are *not* interesting. I trust the reader will see how regrettably well I have achieved this. However, some of the examples from the latest advances in science are simply fascinating, and I cannot take responsibility for the fact that including some of them runs the occasional risk of making the book interesting.

Apart from research, examples also draw from everyday experience and topics in the news. Science and scientists are interested in such topics (e.g., violence, depression). Although there is an ivory tower feature of methodology, as scientists we are in the world in many ways, and it is important to keep the relevance of what we do in mind as we design, complete, and write up our research.

This edition includes teaching aids for the reader. First, throughout the book, I have added tables to provide summaries and aids. When there are multiple points that require discussion (how to increase power, types of relations the investigator may wish to study), it is easy to lose sight of the key points. The tables are useful study guides once the individual entries have been elaborated. Second, outlines are provided at the beginning of each chapter to help organize the content and scope of the issues that each topic entails. Third, the end of each chapter has a summary, a list of key concepts, and a list of readings that directs the interested reader to more in-depth presentations of topics raised in the chapter. Fourth, a glossary is included at the end of the book to centralize and define briefly terms introduced throughout the chapters. Special terms italicized within the text are usually covered in the glossary as well. Although the book is not overabundant in terminology, there is value to providing a quick reference to terms and practices. Finally, for the instructor a test-item manual is available to develop exams, projects, and study guidelines for the course.

Several persons have contributed to the thrust and focus of this book over the last several years. It is usually gracious for an author to convey to the reader that any errors that remain in the book after extensive input from others are his or her responsibility alone. I do not like to be shackled by accountability and personal responsibility, so permit me to depart from tradition. Unlike authors of most other books, I hold the people who contributed to this book personally responsible for limitations, errors, and oversimplifications. This is the fourth edition of the book, and you would think that colleagues would have caught the problems by now. Of course, to the extent that anything in the pages that follow is helpful, interesting, or inspired, I am pleased to share the credit.

Actually, the list of mentors, colleagues, and graduate students who deserve credit would be lengthy; the net effect of enumerating all of them would be to diffuse the special gratitude I feel toward each person. Permit me to mention a few by name. Lee Sechrest has had significant impact on the book in this edition and prior ones as well. He has been a constant source of guidance on the topic and has been generous in suggesting what I ought to know and know better. His specific suggestions for this edition were stellar; prior suggestions made by his students in a graduate course also proved quite useful. Professors Thomas Bowers, The Pennsylvania State University, John Horan, Arizona State University, and Kathleen Schiaffino, Fordham University are other reviewers who provided comments, and I am grateful for their extremely helpful suggestions. Graduate students at Yale University who have taken the course on the topic of this book also have provided detailed input and comment. I am especially grateful to those students who did not demand refunds for the book halfway into the course.

Finally, although many years have passed since my dissertation, I owe a special debt of gratitude to my dissertation committee. Many of their comments at my dissertation orals linger in their influence on me and on the topic of this book (e.g., "Alan, find another career." "Research isn't for everyone." "A 50% rate of attrition in a control group starting with 2 subjects is problematic." "When we said, 'Use a pretest,' we did not mean omit the posttest.") These pithy, even if subtle, comments raised the prospect that understanding methodology may be rather important. (Not wanting to be identified with my study, all my committee members entered the Dissertation Committee Witness Protection Program immediately after my oral exam, and unfortunately cannot be identified by name. I am grateful to you all wherever you are.)

Several sources of research support were provided during the period in which this book was written. I am pleased to acknowledge grants from the Leon Lowenstein Foundation, the William T. Grant Foundation (98-1872-98), and the National Institute of Mental Health (MH59029). Support from the John D. and Catherine T. MacArthur Foundation is also gratefully acknowledged. Participation in the Network on Psychopathology and Development of the John D. and Catherine T. MacArthur Foundation has been enormously influential because colleagues in the Network have shaped my views about science and evaluation more generally. Needless to say, the views expressed in this book do not reflect the views of any agency that has provided research support nor, for that matter, the agencies that have not provided support.

Alan E. Kazdin

About the Author

Alan E. Kazdin, Ph.D., is the John M. Musser Professor of Psychology at Yale University, Professor in the Child Study Center (Child Psychiatry), and Director of the Yale Child Conduct Clinic, an outpatient treatment service for children and their families. He received his Ph.D. in clinical psychology from Northwestern University (1970). Prior to coming to Yale, he was on the faculty of The Pennsylvania State University and the University of Pittsburgh School of Medicine. He has been a fellow of the Center for Advanced Study in the Behavioral Sciences, President of the Association for Advancement of Behavior Therapy, recipient of awards for research from the American Psychological Association and the Association for Advancement of Behavior Therapy, and Chairman of the Psychology Department at Yale. He has been editor of various journals (*Journal of Consulting and Clinical Psychology, Psychological Assessment, Behavior Therapy,* and *Clinical Psychology: Science and Practice*). Currently, he is Editor of *Current Directions in Psychological Science*. His research focuses primarily on the development, treatment, and clinical course of aggressive and antisocial behavior and depression in children; child, parent, family, and contextual influences that contribute to child dysfunction; and processes and outcome of child therapy. He has authored or edited over 35 books primarily in the areas of methodology and research design, child and adolescent disorders, and treatment interventions. Some of his recent books include

The Encyclopedia of Psychology

Psychotherapy for Children and Adolescents: Directions for Research and Practice

Conduct Disorders in Childhood and Adolescence (2nd ed.)

Methodological Issues and Strategies in Clinical Research (2nd ed.)

Single-Case Research Designs: Methods for Clinical and Applied Settings

Behavior Modification in Applied Settings (6th ed.)

Cognitive Behavioral Interventions (with L. Craighead, W.E. Craighead, & M.J. Mahoney)

Chapter 1

Introduction

CHAPTER OUTLINE

Methodology and Research Design
    Overview
    Tasks of Research

Key Concepts Underlying Methodology
    Parsimony
    Plausible Rival Hypotheses
    Findings versus Conclusions

Philosophy of Science, Research Methodology, and Statistical Inference

Characteristics of Research in Clinical Psychology

The "Psychology" of Research Methodology

Overview of the Book

The general purpose of science is to establish knowledge. Although many areas of scientific investigation, such as the study of the stars, weather, plants, and animals, are familiar to us, the systematic methods of investigation in scientific research and how these methods improve upon casual observation are not widely appreciated. Indeed, occasionally the public is skeptical about scientific research and frustrated with the yield of individual studies. For example, the seemingly frequent findings that various foods or food additives may cause cancer in animals have raised public disenchantment with scientific research. The list of things that may cause or contribute to cancer (cigarettes, cigars, fatty foods, asbestos, radon) becomes longer and longer with each passing week. The disenchantment is reflected in the quip "the only thing that causes cancer is scientific research!"

Public frustration with research also results from conflicting findings. For example, various foods (e.g., eggs, butter, meat, coffee) have been shown at various points in time to be harmful, helpful, and neutral in relation to particular health outcomes (forms of cancer, heart disease). Moreover, nuances and qualifiers often sabotage the simple findings or rules we would like (e.g., x is "bad" for us). The fact is that some of the findings are complex. Thus, we have learned that a little wine is good for us but a lot is bad and that some wines (e.g., red) seem to be better than others. Also, chocolate, a mild but notable vice of many people, maybe is not such a vice. Chocolate, especially dark chocolate, is filled with antioxidant compounds (polyphenols) that are considered to be quite healthful in controlling cholesterol and free radicals that contribute to heart disease (Bearden et al., 1999; Waterhouse, Shirley, & Donovan, 1996). A candy bar can provide the equivalent of a day's worth of fruits and vegetables. Of course, there is the other side of chocolate, namely, saturated fats and calories. (Merely for health benefits, as I write these words I am sipping wine and finishing the last few pieces of a box of chocolates.)

Even when the scientific verdict seems relatively clear and has broad consensus (e.g., cigarette smoking contributes to many untoward health outcomes), many of us seem to know someone who is an exception (a 90-year-old uncle who is very healthy and smokes 2 packs a day, immediately after eating his favorite breakfast—lard soufflé). Inconsistencies in scientific findings and counterinstances of a given finding in everyday life often reflect the complexities of empirical relations. It is not the scientist's fault, for example, that high cholesterol at once is associated with an increased risk for heart disease but a decreased risk for cancer (West, 1995).

Even though many findings are incomplete, and there are complexities we would prefer not to have, enormous advances have been made that we take for granted in everyday life (vaccines for diseases, predictions of weather, medications and psychotherapies for depression, books on methodology). The complexities of many scientific findings and the relevance of many findings to the public place special responsibilities on the researcher. Among the responsibilities, research ought to be conceived, designed, conducted, and interpreted in such a way as to maximize clarity of the findings and conclusions. This book is devoted to the many practices that can fulfill these responsibilities, that is, to the design, conduct, and interpretation of research.

Scientific research is essential for understanding natural phenomena and for advancing knowledge. Although a number of research methods are available, they have in common careful observation and systematic evaluation of the subject matter under varying conditions. The diverse methods constitute special arrangements and plans of observation that are designed to uncover relations between variables in a relatively unambiguous fashion. The relations may seem apparent in nature when a particular phenomenon is observed casually. Yet, the complex interrelations and combinations of many variables obscure many relations as they normally appear. Scientific research seeks to describe and to explain these relations. The challenges of describing and explaining relations among variables are compounded by the characteristics and limits of our perception. Among complex relations, it is easy and natural for us to connect variables perceptually and conceptually and to then integrate these into our belief systems. The relations can be firmly entrenched in our belief systems and perceptions, independently of whether the variables genuinely go together and are related in fact.

Scientific research attempts to simplify the complexity of nature and to isolate a particular phenomenon for careful scrutiny. The phenomenon is examined by manipulating or varying values of the variable of interest while controlling extraneous factors that might otherwise influence the results. By controlling or holding constant sources of influence that might vary under ordinary circumstances, the relation between the variables of interest can be examined. In addition to arranging features of nature, science also provides methods to aid perception. The methods consist of diverse practices, procedures, and decision rules to aid in drawing conclusions and in reaching a consensus about relations observed in research. Among the interesting features of scientific research is that the methods used to reveal nature can contribute significantly to the results. That is, how a study is conducted, the measures that are used, and how the data are analyzed are just a few of the aspects of methodology that influence the specific conclusions the investigator will draw. Consequently, the study of methodology and the underpinnings of decision making is essential.

In this book I discuss impediments to knowledge and methodological practices to combat them. It is important to understand these impediments because they foster an appreciation of the reasons why various methodological practices are used and foster improvisation when such practices may not be feasible. For example, random assignment of subjects to conditions or groups is important for all sorts of reasons and is to be encouraged whenever feasible. Yet, often such assignment is not feasible, and that does not in any way doom a study to weak inferences. But the how and why of random assignment are critical to discuss to ensure that if substitute procedures are selected, they address those factors that can impede clear conclusions.

In clinical psychology, psychiatry, counseling, social work, educational and school psychology, and other areas of research and disciplines that span theory, research, and application, major challenges derive from addressing questions outside of the laboratory. Drawing valid inferences is not sacrificed when one leaves the methodological comforts of the laboratory. Thoughtful and creative application of design strategies assumes greater importance as the complexity of the subject matter and the situations in which it is studied increases.

METHODOLOGY AND RESEARCH DESIGN

Overview

Methodology refers to the diverse principles, procedures, and practices that govern research. Within that general domain is the concept of *research design*, which refers to the plan or arrangement used to examine the question of interest. These terms tend to focus on the specific practices and options that characterize research. The focus of the present book is on methodology and research design and hence covers diverse practices and procedures. Yet, the focus on concrete methods and practices has the danger of emphasizing ingredients of research and perhaps conjuring up a cookbook for the design of experiments. Methodology is not merely a compilation of specific practices, procedures, or strategies. Even highly revered practices (random assignment of subjects or participants, use of large sample sizes) may be unnecessary to reach valid inferences in a given study.[1] Moreover, even when a study includes several practices, this does not necessarily mean the findings are sound or even true. Mastery of methodology requires understanding the rationale for key methodological practices as well as knowing the practices themselves.

Methodology refers to a *way of thinking*, and this is another reason to avoid overemphasis of concrete practices involved in the research process. Methodology alerts us to the issues that affect how we examine and interpret phenomena. Consider an example of the type of thinking that methodology fosters. Sir Francis Galton (1822–1911), the British scientist, investigated the extent to which prayer increases how long people live. Specifically, he was interested in whether praying for the health and longevity of other persons in fact added years to the lives of those persons. The hypothesis would be one of great theoretical and applied interest, to say the least. Galton reasoned that if prayer were effective, then kings, queens, and other royalty would live longer than others. After all, their health and longevity are consistently the objects of prayer (as attested to by frequent exhortations, "Long live the Queen," in contrast to the no doubt rare and less familiar, "Long live the beggar").

Galton selected and compared different groups who were presumed to vary in the extent to which people prayed for their health and longevity (Galton, 1872). The results indicated that royalty died at an earlier age than nonroyalty. Specifically, the mean (average) age at the time of death of royalty was 64.0 years, a number lower than other groups, including men of literature and science (67.6 years) and the gentry (70.2 years). Clearly, royalty died at a younger age. Does this study show that prayer was ineffective in increasing the longevity of royalty? Not at all.

Methodology teaches us ways to think about the relations between variables, about causes and effects, and about conclusions drawn from theory, research, and experience. In the case of Galton's study, methodology draws our attention to the hypothesis, how the hypothesis was tested, the findings, and the conclusions one is entitled to draw. Consider the following. It might well be that at the time of Galton, royalty without the benefit of other people's prayers would have died at an earlier age

---

[1]Throughout the book the terms subjects, participants, and clients will be used to delineate those persons who are being studied, i.e., those who participate in research and provide the data. The usage warrants comment because there has been a change in recommended terminology to use "participants" instead of "subjects" (American Psychological Association [APA], 2001). The change is intended in part to recognize that the participant is not merely an "object" of study but rather a person with special rights and privileges (e.g., as represented by providing informed consent) and hence has more than a passive role in research. In this book, the term subject is retained and used interchangeably with the other terms (participant, client, patients). The term subjects is important because it has been adopted in key topics related to methodology (e.g., subject selection, subject artifacts). Also, participants in research include investigators (who design the study) and experimenters (who administer the conditions) and, in an important sense, consumers of research (other professionals, the public at large). These distinctions are elaborated later. It will be important to be clear at all times about who provides the data (the subjects).

than the mean of 64.0 years. Perhaps the sedentary schedule; rich food; weighty responsibility; frequent guest appearances; tight-fitting, heavy, and jewel-laden clothes, and riding in coaches with neither seat belts nor airbags would have conspired to produce a much earlier death. Let us say, for hypothetical purposes, that royalty during the time of Galton would normally live to be 55 years of age, on average. It is quite possible that prayer did in fact increase longevity from, say, 55 to 64 years of the royalty included in Galton's study. The data show only that royalty died at a younger age than comparison groups. Yet, the hypothesis was not whether royalty live *longer* than nonroyalty but whether prayer increases longevity. It is quite possible that prayer increases longevity (number of years of living) without making one group of persons actually live longer than another group. *The original hypothesis remains unscathed and, in that study, not really tested.*

All sorts of studies might be planned to clarify the results. We might, for example, wish to examine the extent to which royalty are prayed for and the impact on longevity. Presumably "more might be better" and not all royalty are prayed for equally. Groups within the overall "royal class" might be matched on health characteristics related to longevity (age, sex, blood pressure, family history of disease, and longevity) but vary in the extent to which they are the objects of prayer. To ensure that they differed in the extent to which they were prayed for, perhaps we could survey the public to identify the persons about whom their prayers are directed. Also, it is possible that members of royalty themselves engage in more (or less) praying than others. Perhaps praying rather than being prayed for is critical. In general, we would wish to control for or assess several variables that plausibly relate to longevity to ensure that these did not vary between groups or were taken into account when comparing groups. It is important not to belabor the example. At the same time, how a study is designed and conducted determines how the findings can be interpreted. Methodology is a way of thinking about phenomena because it alerts us to the types of questions to ask and, as important, to the practices we need to obtain enlightened answers.

Incidentally, there has been further testing of the relation of prayer to longevity and more generally to physical and mental health. Actually, the research focuses primarily on participation in religion and physical and mental health. Among the findings are studies showing that participation in religion (belief in God, attending church regularly, being committed to religion, engaging in Bible or Scripture study) is associated with reduced rates of suicide, death from heart disease, and depression, and with higher levels of overall well being (Levin, 1996; McCullough, 1995). These findings hold even while controlling for obesity, alcohol consumption, and cigarette smoking, which might be confounded with participation in religion. Closer to the Galton study, participation in religion is related to longevity, at least among the elderly (Koenig et al., 1999). Longitudinal research has shown that individuals who participate in religion live longer. The effect is partially, but only partially, accounted for by the better physical condition and health practices among individuals who participate in religion. These findings are intriguing and important; they do not directly test the Galton hypothesis about being prayed for (in case the reader is looking for a dissertation topic).

Tasks of Research

Designing research often is presented as a straightforward enterprise. At the most rudimentary level, an investigation may include an experimental and a control group. The experimental group receives some form of the experimental condition or intervention and the control group does not. Differences between groups are considered to reflect the effect of the experimental manipulation. Alternatively, there may be no experimental manipulation in the sense that something is done by the investigator to the subjects. Rather, subjects may be selected because of their special characteristics (meeting criteria for a particular psychiatric or medical disorder or not meeting such criteria; having experienced abuse versus no such experience), as in the above study by Galton. In either case a comparison is usually made between groups. Although research inherently involves some comparisons, the bulk of research is more intricate than simple comparisons. Research may be based on hypotheses varying in complexity as the investigator attempts to explain, predict, and explore specific relations.

Studies in psychology usually are designed to test specific hypotheses. When hypotheses are formulated, they represent "if-then" statements about a particular phenomenon. The "if" portion of the hypothesis often refers to the independent variable that is manipulated or varied in some other way, whereas the "then" portion refers to the dependent variable or resulting data. Findings consistent with an experimental hypothesis do not necessarily prove that hypothesis. Data can be taken as proof of a hypothesis only if no conceivable alternative hypothesis can account for the results or if the predicted relations would be obtained if and only if the hypothesis were true. Yet, these requirements are more likely to be met in logic and deductive reasoning than in scientific research. Whether another hypothesis conceivably could account for the results may be a matter for future investigators to elaborate. Also, whether a finding would result only from a particular hypothesis cannot be known with any certainty. The confidence of certainty provided in logical deductions is not available in science. Of course, this fact refers to the logical bases of scientific conclusions. As scientists we often *feel* quite certain about our conclusions. The experience or feeling of certainty is quite separate from the logical status and truth-value of scientific propositions.

Not all investigations are conducted to test a particular prediction or "if-then" relations. Many investigations explore the relations of variables and are not formulated as tests of hypotheses. Yet, the tenuous nature of the conclusions still applies. The findings, however systematic, do not necessarily reflect the effects of the independent variables. The findings may be a function of unspecified factors extraneous to the independent variable itself. A number of these factors may be uncontrolled variables within or outside of the experiment and serve as explanations of the findings.

Although many extraneous factors can be recognized and controlled in advance of an experiment, others cannot. It may even take years of research to recognize that something in the experiment other than the variable of interest contributed to the original findings. For example, in human drug research, a routine practice is to keep the hospital staff or investigators naive so that they do not know who is receiving the experimental (treatment) drug and who is receiving a placebo. Keeping staff naive is now recognized to be important because staff beliefs and expectancies can influence patients' responses to treatment, even without an active medication. In years past, many drug studies lacking this precaution were completed and can now be regarded only as inconclusive.

KEY CONCEPTS UNDERLYING METHODOLOGY

A few key concepts help place the goals and tasks of methodology in context. These concepts reflect broader characteristics of science and reflect a way of interpreting research. These concepts are considered briefly here but will be woven into comments of several methodological practices discussed throughout the book.

Parsimony

Parsimony reflects an accepted principle or heuristic in science that guides our interpretations of data and phenomena of interest. Typically, a given finding or phenomenon may be explained in many different ways. Parsimony directs us to select the simplest version or account of the data among the alternatives that are available. There are other names for the guideline, and they convey the thrust that is intended. Among the other terms are the principle of economy, principle of unnecessary plurality, principle of simplicity, and Occam's razor. The last term is the most familiar and is a useful place to begin. William of Ockham (ca 1285–1349) was an English philosopher and Franciscan monk. He applied the notion (plurality [of concepts] should not be posited without necessity) in the context of writing on epistemology, in which he advocated that concepts ought not to be added (plurality) if they are not needed (necessity) in accounting for phenomena. Supposedly, his frequent and sharp invocation of the principle allegedly accounts for why the term "razor" was added to his (Latinized) name to form Occam's razor.

In the context of science, parsimony means that if competing views or interpretations of any phenomenon can be proposed, one adopts the simplest one that can explain the data or information. The presumption of parsimony is not tantamount to saying that things are simple or can be explained simply but rather that the simplest account of the data or phenomenon is the one we adopt, until there is a need to move to more complex interpretations. Applications in everyday life and other areas of science convey the pervasive impact and use of parsimony as well as the thought processes involved.

In everyday life there might be a sighting of an unidentified flying object (UFO) in the evening sky. Let us assume several people report the sighting. What was this, or stated another way, how ought we to explain the data (reports of many people)? One explanation is that the UFO is a spaceship (flying saucer) from another galaxy. The explanation might continue by noting that the life forms or beings (often called Martians no matter where they are from) on the flying saucer are visiting to find a way to inhabit Earth because their planet is dying. Oy vey. Needless to say, this is one of the most unparsimonious interpretations that could be given. Note, however, the comments are not at the point of evaluating whether the hypothesis is true. It might well be.

Parsimony begins the other way, namely, can we explain the data with concepts and phenomena we already know. First, most such sightings are "shooting stars" or rather meteorites across the sky. Could this explain what was seen? Second, our own military often experiments with advanced flying machines. Could this explain what was seen? No doubt other interpretations could be advanced, but the key question inherent in parsimony is, Must we introduce new concepts to explain the data and, if so, let us adopt the fewest concepts to account for the data. Maybe we have to add new concepts (spaceship, Martians), and it is easy to add a hypothetical bit of data to move us to more complex explanations. Say the UFO was sited as crashing and, in fact, there was evidence of the crash. Parsimony still teaches simplicity and skepticism along with that. Could this be a flying saucer that crashed or a hoax?

Let us add more details. At the crash scene we might find that the ship was of an odd shape and composed of a seemingly new and unfamiliar metal or plastic. These features increase the likelihood that extraterrestrial sources are involved. On the other hand, as we examine the accident site, we notice a decal (bumper sticker) on the remnants of the door of the space ship that says, "I ♥ Galaxy #2555," intended to identify the putative home of the spaceship occupants. With the bumper sticker, hoax may be the more parsimonious interpretation. There are so many precedents for hoax as an explanation in the context of UFO sightings that this interpretation is likely to emerge early in the search for explanations. The example is a good place to start because we all want to know whether there really are flying saucers (leaving aside cups, plates, or serving dishes) from other galaxies. But this is a distracting feature and in many ways is beside the point. Parsimony alerts us to the questions, what are the data or facts, and what are the minimal concepts that can explain the data?

Throughout history of science there is an unending array of instances where one view replaced or expanded on another. The instances are such that among competing views, one provided a better or simpler account of the data. If the data can be explained equally well by two views, the more parsimonious one is adopted. In science often two views might explain one phenomenon equally well, but a second view makes other predictions or provides a better or more reasoned account of other phenomena. In either case parsimony is invoked. Among the many instances that are commonly cited is the view within cosmology advocated by Nicolas Copernicus, a Polish scientist and astronomer (1473–1543). Copernicus's view was that the planets orbited around the sun (heliocentric view) rather than around the earth (geocentric view). This latter view had been advanced by Claudius Ptolemy (ca. 85–165), a Greek astronomer and mathematician, whose view had dominated for hundreds of years. There is more to the general comment noting the significance of the Copernican Revolution. Copernicus's view was able to account for the orbits of the planets as well as or better than Ptolemy's view and was able to do so more simply (parsimoniously).

Parsimony is usually discussed at the level of broad theory or after several years of study of a phenomenon, as in the case of the Copernican Revolution or in more contemporary discussions in astronomy, such as how the universe was formed. At the level of methodology of individual studies parsimony plays a central role too. At the end of a study the investigator may wish to say that the findings can be attributed to some experimental manipulation or intervention. Parsimony reins here as well. Is it true that the investigator's interpretation is the most parsimonious among the possible explanations? If the study is poorly designed and many confounding influences might be present, then all sorts of interpretations might be available and parsimonious.

Even if the study is well designed or seemingly well designed, parsimony may dictate an explanation that departs from the one proposed by the investigator. For example, two "new and improved" cognitively based therapies might be compared for the treatment of anxiety disorder. Let us say subjects in both treatments greatly improve, and the treatments seem to be equally effective. The investigator discusses cognitions, how important they are, and how therapies alter them. Is there a more parsimonious account of the findings? That is, in deference to parsimony, do we really need the investigator's interpretation of the data and new or more complex constructs (cognitions) to explain the effects, or can we explain them with concepts already available? Although the next chapters will detail many parsimonious interpretations that could be applied to this study, consider two briefly here. Expectations on the part of the subjects and the mere participation in a systematic form of treatment (even if not cognitively based) could readily explain the findings. Is the investigator's view of cognitive processes wrong? This is not the appropriate question. Rather, for this study as presented, there is no need to invoke the concepts of cognition. From a methodological standpoint, we can say that this study was poorly designed in relation to the conclusions the investigator wished to reach. Specifically, we would want a study in which changes in cognitive process is a very, if not *the most*, parsimonious account of the findings. It is not so difficult to design a study to accomplish this, and later chapters will discuss many strategies the investigator can adopt to carry out such a study.

Plausible Rival Hypotheses

The nature of scientific inquiry is such that in principle and often in practice the results of any single investigation may be the result of influences other than the intervention or experimental manipulation. For example, it could be that "chance" explains the result of a particular experiment or there was something very special about the sample that on this one occasion led to a particular finding. Research cannot really prove a hypothesis. A hypothesis gains support by being tested, hopefully on multiple occasions. The test yields results that are consistent with the hypothesis and more than that the explanation of the finding is a plausible account of what happened.

At the end of a study, an investigator wishes to conclude that the results are due to the influence of the independent variable. For example, an investigator may wish to compare individuals with a history of some form of abuse (e.g., parents deprived their children of methodology books early in life) versus no abuse (e.g., lots of methodology books and bedtime stories about well-designed studies during childhood). The findings indicate that quality of life, happiness, health, and wealth are much better for the nonabused group. Methodology is all about the conclusions that can be reached from a study and making one interpretation of the findings more likely (plausible) than other interpretations. It may be difficult to establish that the one difference between the groups was based on the abuse experience, such as psychopathology of the parent, the presence of other types of abuse than just deprivation of methodology books, and an endless array of many etceteras. One can use many strategies, but the brief description of the study leaves open many other ways to explain the data.

Central to methodology and conclusions in a particular study is the notion of *plausible rival hypotheses* (Campbell & Stanley, 1963; Cook & Campbell, 1979). A plausible rival hypothesis refers to an interpretation of the results of an investigation on the basis of some other influence than the one the investigator has studied or wishes to discuss. The question to ask at the completion of a study is whether there are other interpretations that are plausible to explain the findings. This sounds so much like parsimony that the distinction is worth making explicit. Parsimony refers to adopting the simpler of two or more explanations that account equally well for the data. The concept is quite useful in reducing the number and complexity of concepts that are added to explain a particular finding.

Plausible rival hypothesis as a concept is related to parsimony but has a slightly different thrust. At the end of the investigation are there other plausible interpretations we can make of the finding than one advanced by the investigator? Simplicity of the interpretation (parsimony) may or may not be relevant. At the end of the study there could be two or ten equally complex interpretations of the results, so parsimony is not the issue. For example, an investigator wishes to see whether ethnicity contributes to how healthfully people eat and how healthy they are (instances and duration of illnesses, operations, and hospital visits in the past year). Let us say that two different ethnic groups are shown to differ on each of these measures. At the end of the study the investigator discusses ethnic differences and how these explain the findings. A plausible rival hypothesis might be socioeconomic status (family income, occupational status, and education). That is, if socioeconomic status (SES) was not controlled in this study, then SES becomes a plausible rival hypothesis. Is SES more parsimonious? Maybe, maybe not. The findings might be equally accounted for by posing one influence versus another (a key SES or ethnic difference), so whether one is simpler than another is arguable. Parsimony (the more simple explanation that can account for the data) and plausible rival hypotheses (other interpretations of the data that could readily explain the effect, whether simple or not) often overlap. Yet, a plausible rival hypothesis does not necessarily invoke simplicity as a key feature but rather asks only whether some other interpretation is plausible. Plausibility derives from whether there is a reasonable basis to say that the findings could be explained in some other way. Often plausibility stems from the fact that other, prior studies have shown that a particular influence has an effect very much like the one produced in the study and explained by the investigator in some other way.

As an example, a recent study compared St. John's wort with medication for the treatment of mild to moderate depression (Woelk, 2000). St. John's wort is a plant that has been used as an herbal remedy for all sorts of problems (depression, anxiety, cramps, arthritis, and bedwetting, to mention a few).[2] In this study the extract of St.

---

[2] St. John's wort has been used as an herbal remedy since the Middle Ages. Among the many uses, the herb was considered to ward off evil, in part due to the fact that the smell is rather obnoxious and would make evil spirits flee. The herb was named after John the Baptist; it has been used as anointing oil, and because it yields a red color, it has symbolized the blood of Christ in such uses. As a treatment the herb has been used in very many ways. Research has looked at many facets due in part to chemistry of the herb; many components of the herb are likely to interact with and affect neurotransmitters of the brain.

John's wort (hypericum perforatum) and medication (imipramine) were compared in a few hundred outpatients. The results indicated that patients who received either St. John's wort or medication improved equally well by the end of treatment. The author discussed the benefits of St. John's wort and how this is a treatment of choice for depression because it is more natural and has fewer side effects.

I mention one facet of the study at this point to convey the notion of how plausible rival hypotheses are central to methodology. Alas, at the end of this study there is a critical plausible rival hypothesis to explain the findings. It is possible that patients improved equally because of placebo effects—that is, the extra attention they received and the fact that they participated in a treatment. Placebo effects, discussed in further detail later, are a plausible rival hypothesis because there is vast evidence that great improvements in many mental and physical diseases are evident in controlled treatment trials. Because of this rather vast evidence, we say that in this study it is quite plausible that placebo effects accounted for improvements rather than therapeutic effects of the drug or St. John's wort. (Placebo effects may be especially plausible in part because the imipramine was provided at a much lower dose than usual and hence the therapeutic benefit of the medication itself is in question.)

An investigator (the person who designed the study) and consumers of research (us) might debate whether placebo effects are a plausible interpretation of the findings. This argument and some variant is why methodology is so important. A high-quality investigation is one in which key plausible rival hypotheses that might be proposed are made to be implausible. In the prior study, for example, a placebo control group ought to have been included. The results might have shown that medication and St. John's wort were better than placebo, in which case our rival hypothesis would have been ruled out.

Methodological practices are intended to rule out or to make implausible competing interpretations of the results. At the completion of a study the explanation one wishes to provide ought to be the most plausible interpretation. This is achieved not by arguing persuasively, but rather by designing the study in such a way that other explanations do not seem very plausible or parsimonious. The better designed the experiment, the fewer the alternative plausible explanations that can be advanced to account for the findings. Ideally, only the effects of the independent variable could be advanced as the basis for the results. Subsequent chapters discuss the many ways to maximize clarity of the findings.

Findings versus Conclusions

A critical distinction that underlies remaining chapters pertains to the findings and the conclusions of a study. The findings refer to the results that are obtained. This is the descriptive feature of the study or what was found. A statement of a finding might be that one group was better or worse than another. The conclusions refer to the explanation of the basis of the finding. This is where parsimony and plausible rival hypotheses come in. The investigator may wish to make one conclusion, but from the design of the study he or she is not really entitled to that conclusion. The reason: There are more parsimonious and plausible explanations than the one the investigator has in mind. Artifact and bias in experimentation constitute common plausible rival interpretations, and we design and execute studies carefully to make interpretations implausible so that our conclusions adhere closely to our findings. Two examples given above—the hypothetical one about cognitive behavior therapy for anxiety and the real example about St. John's wort for depression—suffer from a major discrepancy between findings and conclusions. No doubt is cast here on what was obtained, but in each case there is no reason to accept the investigator's interpretation of the study and there are strong reasons to pose alternative interpretations.

Methodology is about designing all the facets of the study so that if a particular finding is obtained, we can reach a conclusion that is relatively free from ambiguity. Features of the findings themselves—such as how the data are collected and analyzed and possible problems in how the study is executed—raise questions that methodology addresses. But even before these issues emerge in a study, consideration of the conclusions of the study is important. Perhaps it is counterintuitive, but one is concerned with the conclusions at the planning stages of a study. That is, we design and plan a study in light of what we wish to say when the study is completed. Careful experimental controls, selection of subjects, and use of various control groups are planned to rule out rival hypotheses and to permit conclusions we would like to reach.

PHILOSOPHY OF SCIENCE, RESEARCH METHODOLOGY, AND STATISTICAL INFERENCE

Empirical research encompasses three broad interrelated topics: philosophy of science, methodology, and statistical inference. Philosophy of science considers the logical and epistemological underpinnings of the scientific method in general. Historically, experimentation has been closely tied to philosophical thought. Topics such as the basis of knowledge, the organization and limitations of perception, the nature and perception of "causal" relations, methods and limitations of inductive reasoning, the conditions required for testing and verifying predictions, and indeed the very notion of a "hypothesis" all derive from philosophy. The philosophy of science reveals, among other things, fundamental limitations in the logical underpinnings of observational and experimental methods. Experimental methods rely on several presuppositions and assumptions about the nature of the world and our knowledge of that world; the presuppositions and assumptions cannot be logically derived or justified. The philosophical challenge points to the tenuous nature of empirical knowledge. Yet, the challenge has not deterred research from progressing to elaborate natural phenomena.

The day-to-day business of the researcher requires planning investigations so that conceptual, interpretive, and practical problems are minimized. Research methods, rather than philosophy of science, enter at this point to provide options that maximize the clarity of the results. Broadly conceived, methodology encompasses the procedures and practices of conducting and designing research so that lawful relations can be identified. Results of research by their very nature are tentative because any particular finding may depend on unique features of the setting and experimental arrangement in which the finding was obtained. Findings may also be ambiguous because the relations could be due to influences that the investigator did not know, acknowledge, or identify. Tentativeness and ambiguity of research findings can never be completely eliminated. At the same time, the accumulation of multiple investigations can increase the clarity of the findings.

Statistical inference is integrally related to experimentation because of the extensive reliance upon statistical tests in research to draw conclusions from the data. Also, statistical techniques can be used to focus the interpretation of the findings of a particular study. Statistical controls or analyses of variables within the study that might contribute to or be confounded with the independent variable can help to reduce the plausibility of rival interpretations of the results. For example, socioeconomic disadvantage (poverty, receipt of social assistance) is related to many variables of interest in psychological research (physical and mental health, child-rearing practices, stress). Data-analytic strategies can play a major role in examining the separate and combined influences of socioeconomic disadvantage and these other variables and hence facilitate inferences about substantive issues. Thus, statistical analyses often work in concert with methodology.

Statistical evaluation provides agreed-upon decision rules so that there is some uniformity in the criteria used to draw conclusions. Ironically, the criteria for making statistical inferences themselves often are based on arbitrary decisions. For example, the precise point that a finding is called statistically reliable or significant is purely a matter of convention, rather than being a statistically or logically justifiable criterion or, in a given situation, even well advised. The manner in which experimental data ought to be analyzed statistically, and the advantages and disadvantages of different analyses, are widely discussed and debated. Developments in mathematics and statistics have made the area of statistical inference extremely important in its own right in understanding how data are to be interpreted and how experiments are to be designed to maximize interpretability.

The philosophy of science, research methodology, and statistical inference overlap considerably. This book focuses primarily on research methods. This focus will require little excursions to issues related to the basis of knowing and interpretation, but clearly not into epistemological discussions. Similarly, I address selected statistical issues in which research design is inextricably bound, but eschew the underpinnings of data analysis. There are major advances in statistical analyses and all sorts of analyses that can be applied to a given data set. Unfortunately, these advances and methods could not be covered without sacrificing basic methodology. The excursions into other topics are all designed to serve the central goal, namely, to examine research methodology.

CHARACTERISTICS OF RESEARCH IN CLINICAL PSYCHOLOGY

Several standard features of scientific research will be covered, such as defining the research idea, generating and testing hypotheses, designing investigations, and collecting and analyzing data. Yet, in clinical, counseling, educational psychology, and other disciplines in which laboratory, clinical, and applied studies are conducted, the methodological acumen of the investigator is challenged. The challenges derive from the many topics that are studied, the diverse conditions under which they are studied, and the range of methods that can be used.

Consider a sample of the content areas that research in clinical psychology encompasses. Clinical psychology includes the study of diverse populations as illustrated by investigations of all age groups from infancy through the elderly. Indeed, the field extends beyond these age limits, in some ways, by studying processes before birth (e.g., prenatal characteristics of mothers and families) and after death (e.g., the impact of death on relatives, treatment of bereavement). Also, a variety of special populations are studied, such as those with special experiences (e.g., the homeless, divorced, prisoners of prior wars), with psychological or psychiatric impairment (e.g., children, adolescents, or adults with depression, anxiety, posttraumatic stress disorder, autism, schizophrenia, to mention only a few), and with medical impairment and disease (e.g., cancer, Acquired Immune Deficiency Syndrome [AIDS], spinal cord injury, diabetes). Persons in contact with special populations are often studied (e.g., children of alcoholics, spouses of depressed patients, siblings of physically handicapped children).

Examples of a few of the populations in clinical research merely begin to convey the breadth of foci. Consider a few other dimensions that might be mentioned. Research in clinical psychology is conducted in diverse settings (e.g., laboratory, clinics, hospitals, prisons, schools, and industry) and in the absence of structured settings (e.g., runaway children and homeless families). Clinical psychology research is also conducted in conjunction with many other areas of research and with different disciplines (e.g., criminology, health psychology, neurology, pediatrics, psychiatry, public health). In addition, central areas of research within the field have remarkable breadth in the topics they encompass. For examples, the study of personality characteristics; the assessment, diagnosis, treatment, and prevention of clinical dysfunction; and cross-cultural differences in personality, adjustment, and maladjustment are rich and broad areas of research.

Understandably, diverse methods of study are required to meet the varied conditions in which psychologists work and the special challenges in drawing valid scientific inferences from situations that are often complex. The methodological diversity of research can be illustrated in many different ways. Studies vary in the extent to which the investigator can exert control over the assignment of subjects to conditions or administration of the intervention (e.g., true experiments and quasi-experiments) and the selection of preexisting groups and how they are followed and evaluated (e.g., case-control designs, cross-sectional and longitudinal studies). Also, designs (e.g., group and single case), methods of data evaluation (e.g., statistical and nonstatistical) and approaches to the study of clinical phenomena (quantitative and qualitative) further convey the methodological richness of the field. The book discusses and illustrates diverse methodological practices and options.

The purpose in highlighting the diversity and richness of the content areas of psychological research is to underscore the importance of facility with the methods of research. Special demands or constraints are frequently placed on the researcher working in applied settings or on topics that extend beyond the laboratory. Ideal methodological practices (e.g., random assignment) are not always available. Also, restrictions (e.g., a control group might not be feasible, only small sample sizes are available) may limit the researcher's options. The task of the scientist is to draw valid inferences from the situation and to use methodology, design, and statistics toward that end. In science, a problem-solving approach (generating ideas, possible options, views) characterizes how we address substantive questions (why do some people drive recklessly, what are the long-term effects of abuse, does reading methodology really increase sexual appeal?). The scientist considers how the phenomenon comes about and designs an investigation to reveal critical facets. Methodology requires a problem-solving approach as well. What is the best way to test the idea, and how can the study be designed in such a way as to provide a clear answer? Constraints and restrictions on what can be done constitute a challenge. The investigator must be able to draw on a wide range of options of methodology, design, and statistics to identify creative solutions.

Occasionally, research on topics that may have application (education, treatment, prevention) is considered as a soft science where inferences are fuzzy because of the nature of the topic. Part of the difficulty is that loose testimonials often get passed to the media and are not distinguished from scientific knowledge. For example, it is not difficult to find a mental health professional commenting on what makes a good marriage based on his or her experience with couples or why he or she feels children are violent in the schools. Of course, all of these opinions may have little or no relation to what is known based on the latest research findings on the topic. Research in clinical, counseling, and other areas that include nonlaboratory studies is not soft science at all. Indeed, the processes involved reflect science at its very best precisely because of the thinking and methodological ingenuity required to induce nature to reveal its secrets. Deploying strategies to accomplish this requires an appreciation of the purposes of research and the underpinnings of research strategies that serve as the means to achieve these ends.

THE "PSYCHOLOGY" OF RESEARCH METHODOLOGY

In discussing methodology and the goal toward which methodological practices are directed, I fear I have depersonalized science and the research enterprise. Concepts such as parsimony, rival hypotheses, and findings versus conclusions explain how we approach research. These concepts, while central, may suggest that science is purely deliberative, rational, and intellectual. Such an account would be incomplete at best. It is critical to underscore that research design, and science more generally, are basically human enterprises. This does not mean that the methods and findings are subjective or that science is guided by whim. Yet, researchers are "people" first. This obvious statement has broad implications for the design, execution, and interpretation of research. As people, we have ideas, beliefs, ambitions, and individual histories and experiences. These natural human characteristics do not seep into science; they are central to it. Throughout the book different facets of how the human condition (ambition, conflict of interest) influences scientific findings and their interpretation are shown. At this point, consider only one facet, namely, how we view and interpret findings.

Consider, for example, the goal of research, namely, to draw clear inferences about the relations among variables. In subsequent chapters I shall spend a great deal of time on ways to design investigations to maximize the clarity of the findings. Yet, "clarity of the findings" is not a property of the results of a study. Rather, it has to do with the consensus among those who read the report of the study. Reaching a consensus extends beyond epistemology or that branch of philosophy that addresses how we come to know things. Of relevance as well are the substantive findings from psychology (research on perception, learning, attitudes, beliefs, and persuasion). That is, at what point are people (we) convinced, willing to give up some view to which we adhere, or believe that a threshold has been passed to say what is true or probably true?

In most research, findings are not unequivocally clear, especially those that break new ground. Usually, research must accumulate for years to elaborate a phenomenon and to clarify the circumstances and contexts in which the effects are evident. Our individual thresholds for stating that the findings are established or clear assume an important role. At what point shall we believe that a particular finding is sound or true? The threshold varies as a function of the specific area of research, strength of our beliefs, prior training and experiences, and no doubt many other factors. A finding may more readily be embraced as "clear" or "valid" to the extent it is compatible with what we believe, think we already know, or take as givens.

Considering our own research versus the research of others conveys an amusing illustration of how the threshold for believability and persuasiveness of findings can vary. The language with which we refer to our own research and the research of others may belie our varied thresholds for evaluating a study. For example, when *I* use weak measures in my studies and have an inadequate control group, I may regard and refer to the study as "somewhat weak," the "best that could be done under the circumstances," and clearly "better than prior work" in the area. Also, when I conduct many statistical analyses that seem to depart from the hypotheses of the original study, I am doing "exploratory analyses" and "generating hypotheses for future research."

All this changes when this is someone else's (e.g., your) investigation. When *you* conduct an experiment with identical characteristics, I may view this a bit more harshly. Your measure may be "homemade" and "not validated"; the lack of essential controls may represent a "serious or fatal design flaw" and may "preclude conclusions" about the phenomenon of interest. Also, the bunch of extra statistical analyses you have performed is clearly a "fishing expedition" that is likely to come up with "chance findings." Indeed, perhaps as a general rule, my research is more believable than yours, or at least to me. Of course, if your study replicates key findings of my study, then the entire picture changes. I am likely to describe your study with the same endearing terms used to describe my own study. In fact, now that you have replicated *my* findings, you have gone from a bumbling investigator who could not tell the difference between a statistical analysis and a urinalysis to an inspired scientist who does relevant, important, and cutting-edge research.

We need not lament the different standards that individuals may apply to a given study or pattern of results among many studies. I mention the point here to provide an important context for the topic at hand. Methodology has to do in part with the believability and persuasiveness of findings. We engage in specific strategies and practices to persuade ourselves and the scientific community at large. Often findings are so clear and repeated so often that consensus is great. Even here, clarity is a matter of degree, and individual preference is not entirely erased. For example, for many years data on the dangers of cigarette smoking varied in their credibility to scientists and the public. At first, individuals may have doubted the main finding that cigarettes are hazardous to one's health. As the evidence accumulated and entered the mass media, more people were persuaded and acknowledged this as "true." Some still are not persuaded; others are persuaded but retain their original belief by stating that there are special circumstances in their case that mitigate the dangers of smoking. Their belief is retained, not by denying the finding (a main effect), but by noting that the danger is not applicable given their special circumstances (an interaction). The specific hypothesis under which such persons operate might well be accurate, namely, that in their cases some other variable may reduce the danger. Yet, that hypothesis probably is untrue, is unlikely to be well tested, and probably is inadvisable to believe from the standpoint of physical health. (Of course, nonmethodologically based interpretations of why people completely ignore warnings about the hazards of smoking are readily available. From clinical psychology, defense mechanisms may explain this—remember, "Denial is not just a river in Egypt.")

The example is mentioned here to convey crucial aspects about beliefs and how they influence the clarity and impact of research findings. The task for an individual study and for psychological research as a whole is to develop tests of hypotheses that are convincing. "Convincing" in this context does not mean that the results show a particular pattern, "prove" the hypotheses, or demonstrate that the investigator is "right." Rather, "convincing" relates to the quality of the research design and those features that permit sound inferences to be drawn. A well-designed study provides a convincing test so that the results, whatever their pattern, would be persuasive to the investigator as well as to others in the scientific community.

The fact that research depends on beliefs and persuasion is not a weakness of the scientific enterprise. It is, however, important to accept this as a given and as a critical point of departure. The task before us is to uncover the secrets of nature. We adopt strategies of all sorts—theory construction, research methodology, and statistical evaluation—to aid in our task. Each strategy involves decision points that may affect the clarity of the conclusions we draw. Reasonable people not only can disagree about the conclusions of individual studies but do so routinely. Thus, there are inherent limits to what we can expect from an individual study, not merely from the complexity of the subject matter, but because of the diversity of human characteristics on which inferences and interpretation depend. At the same time, we can do a great deal to maximize the information from research and to accumulate knowledge in spite of these limitations.

OVERVIEW OF THE BOOK

Research methodology can be viewed as a decision-making process. Decisions are made at all stages of the process of an investigation, beginning with the decision of what to study and how to move from the idea to the investigation, and ending with interpretation of the findings. It is not always possible to specify how each decision should be made in advance of considering a particular study. Each decision has its own implications and tradeoffs in terms of the final product. Also, the decisions may depend upon how the phenomenon examined in the experiment is conceptualized. This book describes and evaluates different methodological, design, and assessment options and the rationale for their use. The book focuses upon many of the complexities of design by emphasizing the problems that arise in experimentation and techniques designed for their control. Advantages, limitations, and other considerations in using particular design practices are elaborated.

The purpose of research is to draw valid inferences about the relations between variables. Methodology consists of those practices that help to arrange the circumstances so as to minimize ambiguity in reaching these inferences. Many of the factors that can interfere with drawing clear conclusions from research can be readily identified. These factors are referred to as threats to validity and serve as the basis for why and how we conduct research. Types of experimental validity and the factors that interfere with drawing conclusions serve as the basis for Chapters 2 and 3.

Many sources of artifacts and bias can interfere with drawing valid inferences from an experiment. These may derive from the investigator who designs and analyzes the experiment, the experimenter who actually runs the subjects, demand characteristics of the experimental situation, the roles that subjects adopt as they participate in the study, and subject-selection biases prior to and during the experiment. Chapter 4 examines these influences, the manner in which they are likely to affect the results, and methods to minimize, assess, or eliminate their impact.

The investigation begins with an idea that becomes translated into a specific question or statement. A particular subset of variables is selected for manipulation or scrutiny. The study may be designed to test specific hypotheses, to generate hypotheses, or some combination of both. Sources of research ideas, types of variables, diverse questions, and the conditions under which these are investigated are described in Chapter 5.

An initial decision in research is selecting among the many different design options. The range of questions, topics, and foci of research in clinical psychology has led to use of a large variety of designs. Advantages and potential limitations of several types of designs, problems that are likely to arise in their use, and control techniques to improve the designs are presented. Group designs used in experimental research in which variables are manipulated by the investigator are detailed in Chapter 6. Questions that are addressed in experimental research depend heavily on the control and comparison groups included in the design. Chapter 7 discusses several types of control and comparison groups and the considerations that dictate their use.

A crucial aspect of experimental research is ensuring that the independent variable was effectively manipulated and delivered as intended. Checking on the experimental manipulation can greatly enhance the conclusions drawn from research. The procedures to assess the implementation of the experimental manipulation, the interpretation of the results of these techniques, and the problems that may arise are elaborated in Chapter 8.

A great deal of research is based on understanding variables that cannot be manipulated directly, as illustrated, for example, in the study of individuals with different characteristics (clinical disorders, experiences, exposure to events). Observational designs (case-control and cohort designs), in which individuals are selected and evaluated concurrently or longitudinally, are presented in Chapter 9. These designs are quite powerful in identifying antecedents (e.g., risk factors) and even causal relations even though the investigator does not manipulate the independent variables.

The study of the individual—or the case study—is a methodology that spans many disciplines. In Chapter 10 two methods are discussed that are used in clinical psychology, counseling, and psychiatry. These include the anecdotal or uncontrolled case study and single-case experimental designs. Anecdotal case studies serve as a useful backdrop because of their place in the history of psychological and medical treatments, but do not serve as a sound basis for drawing conclusions. In contrast, single-case designs permit experimentally valid conclusions to be reached. This chapter presents special design and data evaluation strategies that characterize single-case experimental research.

Chapter 11 discusses evaluation of the single case in clinical work. The discussion focuses on quasi-experimental designs that are clinically feasible and sensitive to the demands of therapy and the priorities of clinical care. Steps for developing a plan for assessment and evaluation of the individual case are presented and illustrated. The methodology provides an alternative to anecdotal case studies and single-case experiments.

The vast majority of research within psychology is within the quantitative tradition involving group designs, hypothesis testing, assessment on standardized scales and inventories, and statistical evaluation. From a different tradition and approach, qualitative research methods are enjoying increased use in psychology and social sciences more generally. The topic is not usually covered in research design books within the quantitative tradition. Qualitative research is a scientifically rigorous approach and makes a special contribution to knowledge. Chapter 12 provides an overview of the qualitative research, conditions to which the designs are suited, and illustrations to convey the contribution to developing the knowledge base. Qualitative research with its unique methods also place into perspective quantitative research and the assumptions we often make that the dominant research paradigm (quantitative research) is the only path toward empirical knowledge.

Selection of the measures to use in research raises a number of conceptual and assessment issues. The requirements for "appropriate" and useful measures in a particular investigation are manifold. Different modalities of assessment may be selected and, within these, vast options are available for specific measurement techniques. Usually more than one assessment modality is incorporated into the design. Chapter 13 discusses basic assessment considerations that dictate selection and use of measures in research and also highlights commonly used assessment modalities.

A considerable amount of research in psychology (clinical, counseling, educational) and other disciplines (psychiatry, social work, nursing) focuses on interventions. Several assessment and evaluation topics emerge in the context of intervention research, and these serve as the basis of Chapter 14. Among the topics are assessment of the clinical significance of intervention effects, measures to evaluate treatment beyond the usual outcome foci, methods to evaluate mechanisms of change, and strategies and methods for follow-up assessment.

Evaluating the results of an experiment raises many options in psychology. Clearly, statistical methods of data evaluation, particularly significance testing, are commonly used in empirical research. Chapter 15 focuses on the rationale and requirements of statistical evaluation and controversies associated with testing for statistical significance. Various strategies for data analyses and the conditions that dictate their use are discussed. In addition, recommendations for replacing or supplementing significance testing are provided.

Analyzing the data quantitatively is only part of the task of making sense of the results. Data interpretation and factors that facilitate and impede interpretation are no less significant. Special topics related to data evaluation and interpretation are covered in Chapter 16. Different types of effects produced by independent variables, no-difference findings (so-called negative results), and replication of research are presented.

Conducting psychological research raises ethical issues that bear directly upon design considerations. The manner in which a hypothesis is examined may entail the use of deception, invasion of privacy, violation of confidentiality, and withholding of treatment. One reason the ethical issues are essential to consider is that they frequently specify the confines in which design options must be selected. Ethical issues in relation to the protection of subject rights, dilemmas of clinical research, guidelines for research, and responsibilities of the investigator in relation to the research enterprise and the scientific community are presented in Chapter 17.

Completion of an experiment is often followed by preparation of a written report intended for publication. Communication of the results is not an ancillary feature of research methodology. The thought and decision-making processes underlying the design of a study and the specific methods that were used have direct implications for the conclusions that can be drawn. Preparation of the report is the investigator's opportunity to convey the interrelation of the conceptual underpinnings of the study and how the methods permit inferences to be drawn about those underpinnings. Chapter 18 discusses the written report and its preparation in relation to methodological issues presented in previous chapters. The special role that methodological issues and concerns play in the communication and publication of research is highlighted. Questions are provided to help guide the write-up of research on a section-by-section basis.

The book ends with closing comments (Chapter 19) that discuss the interplay of substantive and conceptual issues and methodology and how advances in the latter enrich the former. The reader who has completed and mastered the book will not need any simple, summary, nutshell rendition of how to develop and design the almost perfect study. Even so, at the very end are simple guidelines for applying all that has been learned in a format that, hopefully, will assist any person designing his or her first study, or planning a project or grant proposal.

KEY CONCEPTS AND TERMS

Methodology   Plausible Rival Hypotheses

Parsimony   Findings versus Conclusions

FOR FURTHER READING

Klee, R. (1997). *Introduction to the philosophy of science: Cutting nature at its seams.* New York: Oxford University Press.

Kuhn, T.S. (1996). *The structure of scientific revolutions* (3rd ed.). Chicago: University of Chicago Press.

Nagel, E. (1961). *The structure of science.* New York: Harcourt.

Polkinghorne, J. (1996). *Beyond science: The wider human context.* New York: Cambridge University Press.

Popper, K. (1959). *The logic of scientific discovery.* New York: Basic Books.

Scheffler, I. (1967). *Science and subjectivity.* Indianapolis: Bobbs-Merrill.

Note: The early works cited here are among classics in scientific method and philosophy of science.

Chapter 2

Drawing Valid Inferences I

Internal and External Validity

The purposes of empirical research are to uncover relations between variables that otherwise could not be readily detected and to verify relationships that have been hypothesized. Without research, potential relations between variables must be viewed in their full complexity as they appear in nature. Research design and statistical evaluation help simplify the situation in which the influence of many variables, often operating simultaneously, can be separated from the variable(s) of interest to the investigator. Without such simplification and isolation of variables, many—if not an unlimited number of—interpretations could explain a particular phenomenon. The special contribution of research is that it helps rule out or make implausible different factors that might explain a particular phenomenon. An experiment does not necessarily rule out all possible explanations. The extent to which it is successful in ruling out alternative explanations is a matter of degree. From a methodological standpoint, the better the design of an experiment, the more implausible it makes competing explanations of the results. One of the reasons that there are differing views about the quality of a given study is that what constitutes a competing explanation of the results is a matter of debate.

TYPES OF VALIDITY

The purpose of research is to reach well-founded (i.e., valid) conclusions about the effects of a given intervention and the conditions under which it operates. Four types of experimental validity address these purposes in different ways: internal, external, construct, and statistical conclusion validity (Cook & Campbell, 1979). These types of validity serve as a useful way to convey several key facets of research, to give the rationale for many methodological practices, and to delineate the types of problems that can emerge in designing and interpreting a study. Table 2.1 lists each type of validity and the broad question each addresses. Each type of validity is pivotal. Together they

TABLE 2.1.   Types of Experimental Validity and the Questions They Address

Type of Validity	Questions Addressed
Internal validity	To what extent can the intervention, rather than extraneous influences, be considered to account for the results, changes, or group differences?
External validity	To what extent can the results be generalized or extended to people, settings, times, measures, and characteristics other than those in this particular experimental arrangement?
Construct validity	Given that the intervention was responsible for change, what specific aspect of the intervention or arrangement was the causal agent, that is, what is the conceptual basis (construct) underlying the effect?
Statistical conclusion validity	To what extent is a relation shown, demonstrated, or evident, and how well can the investigation detect effects if they exist?

convey many of the considerations that investigators have before them when they design an experiment. These considerations then translate to specific methodological practices (e.g., random assignment, selection of control groups).

It is not difficult to argue in any given instance that one type of validity is the most important. Indeed, I provide examples where the very nature of the investigator's interest dictates the priority of one over another. In designing an experiment, it is critical for investigators to identify their purposes and specific questions quite clearly at the outset and to emphasize validity issues within the design that these entail. The reason is that it is impossible to design and execute an experiment that addresses each type of validity perfectly. Investigators prioritize types of validity and management of threats, where decisions are needed, to ensure that their hypotheses are well tested. A weak experiment is one in which the inferences the investigator wishes to make are not carefully addressed within the design. This chapter discusses internal and external validity. These types are presented first because they are relatively straightforward and reflect fundamental concerns. Also, failures to consider internal validity often represent the most blatant flaws in research. External validity is virtually always relevant to a study and hence can be cogently raised as a concern.

INTERNAL VALIDITY

An investigation cannot determine with complete certainty that the independent variable accounted for change. However, if the study is carefully designed, the likelihood that the independent variable accounts for the results is high. When the results can be attributed with little or no ambiguity to the effects of the independent variable, the experiment is said to be internally valid. *Internal validity* refers to the extent to which an investigation rules out or makes implausible alternative explanations of the results. Factors or influences other than the independent variable that could explain the results are called *threats to internal validity.*

Threats to Internal Validity

Several types of threats to internal validity have been identified (Cook & Campbell, 1979). An investigation ought to be designed to make implausible the influences of these threats. To the extent that each threat is ruled out or made relatively implausible, the experiment is said to be internally valid.

History.   This threat to internal validity refers to any event—other than the independent variable—occurring in the experiment or outside of the experiment, that may account for the results. History refers to the effects of events common to all subjects in their everyday lives (at home, school, or work). The influence of such historical events might alter performance and be mistaken for an effect resulting from the intervention or treatment. It is important to be able to distinguish the effect of events occurring in the lives of the subjects from the effect of the experimental manipulation or intervention.

The events that happen to subjects may vary greatly depending on their individual situations and daily lives, so how could historical events explain the results of an experiment? If the experiment takes a short or a long time (e.g., over a period of two days or several years), historical events would include events in the news (national, local), weather, or common experience that might explain or contribute to the results. For example, an episode of school violence in the national news and all the associated publicity might be relevant to an experiment and the reactions that subjects have to an experimental manipulation. For historical factors one looks for influences that could affect all or most of the subjects. Examples are provided in the discussion of the next threat (maturation), which often accompanies history as a threat to internal validity.

Although history usually refers to events outside of the experiment, it may include events that take place during the experiment as well. When subjects are run in a group, unplanned events (e.g., power blackout, medical emergency of one of the participants, fire drill) may disrupt administration of the intervention and reduce or enhance the influence that the intervention normally would produce. Insofar as such events provide plausible explanations of the results, they threaten the validity of the experiment.

Maturation.　　Changes over time may result not only from specific events but also from processes within the subjects. Maturation refers to processes changing over time and includes growing older, stronger, wiser, and more tired or bored. Maturation is a problem only if the design cannot separate the effects of maturational changes from the intervention.

History and maturation often, but not invariably, go together as threats to internal validity. In any given case it may not be easy to determine whether historical events or maturational processes accounted for change. Yet, in pointing out flaws of a study, it may not be important to make this distinction as long as one or the other or both are plausible explanations of the results. For example, the problem of history and maturation can be seen in a study of childbirth among expectant mothers (Klusman, 1975). The study examined whether two different training courses reduce self-reported anxiety during childbirth. This is an important focus, not only in its own right but also because level of maternal anxiety is related to the amount of pain experienced during labor. One of the courses trained expectant mothers to engage in special exercises that would facilitate delivery (Lamaze method); the other course merely provided information about labor, delivery, and child care (Red Cross course). In general, both groups of expectant mothers showed reduced anxiety and were not different from each other.

The conclusion that both interventions worked cannot really be made. There is no clear basis for asserting that either training program was responsible for change. Quite possibly and quite plausibly, historical events occurring over time in the life of expectant mothers (reading about children, labor, and delivery; chatting with other expectant or new mothers about their experiences, enlisting greater support from one's spouse) or maturational processes (becoming less concerned about the anxieties of delivery over time, hormonal changes over the course of pregnancy) could explain the results. Special training programs may not be necessary for reductions in anxiety over the course of pregnancy. To help rule out the possible influence of history and maturation, the investigator could have evaluated mothers who did not undergo training (a no-treatment group). This group would have helped to separate treatment effects from naturally occurring events or processes extraneous to treatment.

One does not have to sift carefully through the literature to identify examples in which history and maturation are plausible explanations for the results. As another example, cognitive behavior therapy and a nonspecific control condition (discussion of activities and one's "mental state") were compared for the treatment of depression in clinically referred children and adolescents (Vostanis, Feehan, Grattan, & Bickerton, 1996). By the end of treatment, both groups significantly improved on a variety of measures (e.g., mood, anxiety, and social adjustment) but were not different from each other. It might well be that both interventions were effective. However, history and maturation are plausible explanations of these findings. People often change over time, and if one is interested in the study of an intervention or experimental manipulation, the task is to show that the intervention surpasses or differs from these changes.

History and maturation are fundamental and almost always must be ruled out by the design. It is not true that "time heals all wounds," but the expression does capture the fact that processes associated with time often lead to changes. Thus, history and maturation are plausible explanations of change over time. In an experiment, the investigator must rule out that these changes associated with passage of time, whatever their basis (history, maturation), can be distinguished from the changes associated with an intervention (psychotherapy, an experimental manipulation in a lab study).

Testing.   This threat to internal validity refers to the effects that taking a test one time may have on subsequent performance on the test. In an experiment pre- and postintervention tests might be given to evaluate how much an individual improves or deteriorates over time on a particular measure. Practice or familiarity with the test may influence performance at the second testing. That is, changes at the second testing might not be due to an experimental manipulation or intervention but to the effects of repeated testing. In the prior examples for treatment of anxiety related to childbirth (Klusman, 1975) and for child and adolescent depression (Vostanis et al., 1996), improvements with repeated testing alone might also account for the pattern of results. Merely repeating the assessments, without an intervention, can significantly improve performance on measures of adjustment and personality (Frank, Nash, Stone, & Imber, 1963; Knowles, Coker, Scott, Cook, & Neville, 1996; Windle, 1954). A group that receives repeated testing without the intervention, such as a no-treatment control group, can help rule out testing as an explanation of changes evident in the intervention group. The no-treatment group would be expected to show the effects of testing; the treatment group shows the impact of the intervention over and above any effects of testing alone.

Instrumentation.   This refers to changes in the measuring instrument or measurement procedures over time. For example, in many clinical studies therapists or clients rate client improvement or observe overt behaviors. The standards or scoring criteria that the therapists or clients use in rating or observing behaviors may change over time. Changes in the dependent variable over the course of treatment may result from changes in scoring criteria, rather than changes in actual behavior. Whereas the threat of testing refers to changes in the individual over time (due to experience and practice on the measure), instrumentation refers to actual changes in the measuring device or how it is used. For example, in athletic competition such as gymnastics and ice skating, judges rate performance of individuals in a given event. Instrumentation would refer to any changes in the scoring criteria that might occur, unwittingly or otherwise, over time. For example, assume for a moment that a very superb gymnast performs and receives perfect ratings (a score of 10.0 from each of the judges). Will the criteria or standards for making judgments be any different for the next person who is to be rated, or if the next person performs identically, will she or he receive all perfect ratings? It is conceivable that the standards for ratings change a little over time. (Friendly advice—the next time you are in national or international competition for events where judges make ratings, walk over and explain instrumentation to the judges in a constructive fashion before you perform to make sure they do not unfairly change the standards. I think my failure to do so has been the reason why I never win medals.)

Instrumentation can greatly affect substantive conclusions about changes over time in clinically and socially relevant domains. For example, a major social concern is teenage substance use. Annual surveys track changes in use over time. A difficulty is that the surveys (the measure itself) change periodically as questions are reworded, dropped, and otherwise refined. Some of the seeming changes in the level of drug use—both increases and decreases—are the result of changes in the measure, i.e., instrumentation. These changes have been evident by comparing old and new variations of the instrument in a given year and showing that differences are related to the measure rather than to actual drug use (Moss, 1996). Data gathered longitudinally, as in the case of teen drug use, are often subject to instrumentation. Investigators, administrators, or those responsible for policy may refine or even make major changes in the instruments to better assess current concerns (use of new drugs, new opportunities for deviance, new activities that were not performed previously very much).

Instrumentation is usually not considered as a problem when standardized paper-and-pencil tests are administered or when automated devices are used to score a response. The measuring devices, instruments, and scoring procedures are the same for each administration. Even so, it is conceivable that casual remarks by the experimenter at the time of the test administration might affect the subject's response and effectively alter the nature of the test and how the responses are obtained. For example, in a laboratory experiment on the reduction of arousal, stress, and anxiety, the experimenter might well say, "I'll bet you're really relieved now that the film (story, task) is over. Please complete this measure again." These different instructional sets or attitudes on the part of the experimenter are part of the measurement procedures. Conceivably, the different instructions preceding the measure could alter the assessment in systematic ways and lead to the report of less anxiety. The reduction may result from assessment changes, rather than from the experimental manipulation or changes over time due to other influences (history, maturation).

I was not going to mention a more subtle variation of instrumentation, but I can tell that the reader is thinking of a situation I have neglected. Yes, it is possible that the instrument can change and be the same at the same time, even though this sounds contradictory. It is possible that the items remain the same (absolutely no change in the instrument, wording, or ways in which the instrument is administered). Yet, the items may have different meaning because of the social context of a given point in time. *Response shift* refers to changes in a person's internal standards of measurement. The shift reflects a change in values, perspective, or criteria that lead to evaluation of the same or similar situations, behaviors, states, in a different way (see Schwartz & Sprangers, 2000). For example, questions such as, Do you spend much time with your . . . (partner, spouse, or children)? Are you happy with your . . . (standard of living, apartment, or car)? Is your . . . (relationship, sexual activity, or income) where you would like it to be? These questions can be the same as printed on a sheet, but are not the same in their meaning over time. Social mores, expectations, and practices can change how the questions are interpreted. In relation to the specific questions noted here, changes in acceptable or normative standards for spending time with loved ones, the status of the economy (unemployment, income), and period of one's life (age 20-something vs. 40-something) may affect how one responds.

Response shift might well occur in other contexts of research. In psychotherapy research, for example, one could easily envision all sorts of ways in which response shift could influence the results. It could be that clients do not change after treatment, but have altered their standards in defining what a problem is. That is, their clinical problem has not changed (e.g., tics, anxiety, depression all at the same level), but the clients may see themselves as better because they know now that relative to what they thought before or relative to other people, their problems are minor. Here the actual functioning of the client and the measure itself (e.g., items, format) have not changed, but the standards for rating one's own functioning may have changed. Response shift reflects a change in threshold for answering a particular way. The threshold may be influenced by historical and maturational changes in the individual or the context (e.g., after treatment) in which the instrument is embedded.

Statistical Regression.   As a threat to internal validity, regression refers to the tendency for extreme scores on any measure to revert (or regress) toward the mean of a distribution when the measurement device is readministered. If individuals are selected for an investigation because they are extreme on a given measure, one can predict on statistical grounds that at a second testing the scores will tend to revert toward the mean. That is, the scores will tend to be less extreme at the second testing. A less extreme score is, of course, one closer to the mean.

For example, in the investigation on child and adolescent depression noted earlier, youths were selected because they met criteria for depression (Vostanis et al., 1996). Both groups improved and did not differ from each other on outcome measures at the end of the treatment phase. The authors suggest that both conditions were effective. Yet, statistical regression could also have explained the results. Subjects were selected for the study because they were initially extreme on the measure of dysfunction. One would expect that, on retesting, the group would become less extreme in their scores. Thus, the group may improve (decrease in depression) on the measure without any treatment. A no-treatment or waiting-list control would have helped because we could then discern whether the changes in the two treatment conditions were any greater than changes without treatment. Any changes due to statistical regression would have been evident in the no-treatment group as well and would provide a base for evaluating incremental changes associated with treatment. In general, regression is a threat to internal validity if the change due to the intervention cannot be distinguished from the effect of scores reverting toward the mean. (Regression will be discussed in greater detail in Chapter 6.)

Selection Biases.   A selection bias refers to systematic differences between groups before any experimental manipulation or intervention on the basis of the selection or assignment of subjects to groups. Obviously, the effects of an independent variable between groups can be inferred only if there is some assurance that groups do not systematically differ before the independent variable is applied. Random assignment of subjects is the procedure commonly used to minimize the likelihood of selection biases.

In many ways selection bias is the most obvious threat to internal validity. Investigators routinely assign subjects to conditions in a way that is intended to disperse subject characteristics (age, sex, and diagnosis) that may introduce a selection bias. Yet, selection bias often arises in clinical, counseling, and educational research where intact groups are selected, such as patients from separate clinics or hospitals and students from different classes and different schools. In prevention programs, for example, comparisons often are made among classes, schools, or school districts that receive or do not receive the intervention. Random assignment of classes or schools may not be possible for practical reasons (e.g., proximity of the schools in relation to the investigator, willingness of the school to have the intervention program). Also, of course, random assignment of the children to different classes or schools is definitely not an option as a general rule. Groups are preformed and cannot be rearranged for research purposes. Thus, the project begins with special responsibility of the investigator to make implausible that selection might account for any group differences.

Even when groups are not already formed, practical demands may interfere with randomly assigning subjects to groups. For example, in a classic study designed to evaluate processes and outcomes of client-centered therapy, clients were assigned either to a treatment or waiting-list control group (Rogers & Dymond, 1954). The treatment group received client-centered therapy; the control group received no treatment for 60 days and was measured before and after this waiting period to provide comparison data for the treatment group. If clients were assigned randomly to these conditions, subject selection would not serve as a threat to internal validity. Yet, subjects were assigned on the basis of whether it seemed that they could wait for treatment (serve in the waiting-list control group) without serious harm or discomfort. Thus, clients assigned to treatment and control groups might differ in terms of severity of their psychological state and many other variables as well. Group composition changed further once treatment began. Clients assigned to the waiting-list group occasionally were reassigned to the treatment group if, during the waiting period, they became anxious or were advised by someone else (e.g., the student's college advisor) to receive treatment. The main *conclusion* was that therapy was superior to no treatment. Yet, the *finding* is that the group assigned to treatment was better than the group not assigned to treatment. A difference in group composition—that is, selection—is a threat to internal validity. It is plausible that subjects in treatment and waiting-list groups were quite different even without treatment in light of the way they were assigned to groups. In other words, this study does not provide evidence that treatment is better than no treatment. The conclusion is not supported or justified by the findings.

Attrition.   Attrition or loss of subjects may serve as a threat to internal validity. Loss of subjects occurs when an investigation spans more than one session and hence lasts days, weeks, months, or longer. Intervention studies and longitudinal investigations that track individuals over time are primary examples. Some of the subjects may leave the investigation after the initial session or assessment, refuse to participate further, move to another city, or die. In clinical research, studies spanning multiple settings, populations, and types of treatments have shown that loss of subjects is a direct function of time (Phillips, 1985). Most subjects or cases are lost early and a decreasing proportion is lost as time progresses. More contemporary analyses indicate that in the context of psychotherapy 40–60 percent of children, adolescents, and adults drop out of treatment early (Kazdin, 1996b; Wierzbicki & Pekarik, 1993). Thus, loss of subjects and the bias this may introduce in drawing valid inferences are significant problems.

As a threat to internal validity, consider the simple case first. In a study of one group an investigator may propose that the group will get better (change in means) over time. Attrition is a threat to validity if there is any loss of subjects. Changes in overall group performance on the measures may be due to the loss of those subjects who scored in a particular direction, rather than to the impact of an experimental manipulation or intervention. That is, the mean of the dropouts may be different from the mean of the rest of the sample, so that changes in the mean may result from the loss of a select group of subjects.

In a study in which there are two or more groups, attrition can also be a threat to internal validity if there is a differential loss of subjects between groups or if the number of subjects lost is similar but there is some reason to believe that the characteristics of subjects who dropped out differ between groups. Attrition can introduce selection biases into the study, even though the investigator may have randomly assigned all cases to conditions. As subjects drop out, the remaining subjects cannot be assumed to represent the original sample that was recruited and assigned, nor can the groups within the study (treatment, control) be assumed to be equivalent. Differential attrition across conditions within a study is likely in investigations in which conditions are differentially attractive or effective or vary in their side effects. Subjects are more likely to remain available and cooperative during and after treatment if they are receiving a treatment that is interesting, has little or no cost or adverse side effects, seems plausible, and is effective, than if they are receiving a treatment that is less desirable on these and related dimensions.

For example, in a classic study on the treatment of adult depression, the effectiveness of medication (imipramine) and cognitive therapy were compared (Rush, Beck, Kovacs, & Hollon, 1977). Cognitive therapy was found to be more effective. The study was the first randomized study to show that cognitive therapy was more effective than a standard medication treatment for depression. Did cognitive therapy lead to better outcomes than medication? Interestingly, drug therapy led to significantly greater attrition during treatment than did cognitive therapy. The differential effects of treatment on outcome measures of depression might be the result of comparing groups of subjects at posttreatment that are no longer comparable in the way they were prior to treatment. Differences between groups might be due to the different treatments or to the different types of subjects remaining in each of the groups. From this study, there remains ambiguity about the relative effectiveness of cognitive therapy and medication. Attrition has implications for each type of experimental validity and for data analyses. Hence, I shall return to the topic on a few occasions.

Combination of Selection and Other Threats.   Most of the prior threats refer to conditions that apply to all groups within the study (history, maturation, testing, regression) and that could explain the pattern of findings. Attrition was an exception in which differential loss of subjects across two or more groups is a potential problem. History, maturation, and the other threats may affect groups differently in a study. Thus, for example, group differences might be accounted for by, say, different histories or maturation, for the treatment group versus the control group. Whenever threats to internal validity vary for the different groups within the study, these are referred to as *combinations of selection and that other threat*. Another way to refer to this is to say that the threat interacts with (differentially applies to) groups (experimental and control conditions). An example is selection × history, which means that one of the groups has a historical experience (exposure to some event in or outside of the investigation) that the other group did not have and that experience might plausibly explain the results. The threat is referred to as selection × history because the threat (history) was selective and applies to only one (or some but not all) of the groups.

For example, one study was designed to compare the effects of behavioral-milieu therapy with routine ward care for the treatment of chronic psychiatric patients (Heap, Boblitt, Moore, & Hord, 1970). The behavioral-milieu therapy consisted of providing an incentive system on the ward for developing individualized self-care and social behaviors. Patients were assigned to either the experimental ward or the control ward that received routine custodial care. The main *finding* was that the behavioral-milieu therapy was much better on various outcomes in comparison to the routine care group. The conclusion was that behavioral-milieu therapy improves on the usual hospital care. The finding stands but the conclusion—well, not so fast.

The experimental group was moved to a special ward that was made available especially for this study. This ward included amenities such as drapes, bedspreads, rugs, clocks, and similar improvements not available in the control ward. Both the move and the addition of amenities to the ward constitute historical events within the experiment that were provided only to the behavioral-milieu therapy subjects. Thus special historical events applied to one of the groups. That is, there is a combined selection × history threat to internal validity. (If the move were provided to all subjects, there would be no threat of history or selection × history. History would have been constant across all subjects, and any difference might more reasonably be credited to the treatment.)

Concern with the historical events and related experiences may seem awfully picky and purely academic. Threats to validity, to be threats at all, must be plausible alternative hypotheses that could reasonably explain the pattern of results. Thus, one does not pose frivolous differences (what experimenters were wearing on a given day, weather) between experimental and control groups in a study. To pose a threat to validity, two conditions must be met, namely, that the difference systematically varied between experimental groups (or conditions) *and* that the difference could plausibly explain the results. In this case of the study on the hospital ward, how plausible is it that merely moving to another ward with more livable household conditions could alter the behavior of seriously impaired psychiatric patients? Actually, the impact of a move and amenities is quite plausible. Other studies have shown that merely moving to another ward, independently of whether a new treatment is given, can lead to durable therapeutic improvements in psychiatric patients (Gripp & Magaro, 1971; Higgs, 1970). Thus, historical differences (experiences, events) between groups could plausibly account for the differences the authors attribute to the different treatments.

Selection × history and selection × maturation are likely to be the most frequent confounds involving selection, but other combinations are possible. For example, if the participants in different groups are not assessed at the same time, the results might be due to changes in the assessment procedures or criteria for scoring behavior over time (i.e., selection × instrumentation). As a general statement, if any single influence (e.g., history, testing) applies to only one of the groups or applies in different ways to the groups, the threat involves selection as an interaction. Some practices we regard as routine—such as carefully supervising implementation of an intervention and ensuring subjects are treated in identical ways except for the experimental manipulation—are conducted in part to control for selection × history threats.

Diffusion or Imitation of Treatment. It is possible that the intervention given to one group may be provided accidentally to all or some subjects in a control group as well. At first blush this threat would seem to be something of academic interest with absolutely no real examples. Obviously, one does not give the treatment to a control condition (unless treatment is delayed in a waiting-list control condition). And certainly, if a subject is assigned to treatment, he or she receives the treatment rather than the control condition. Yet, this is a real threat that is much more common than one would imagine.

Clearly, administration of treatment to the control group may be inadvertent and, of course, opposite from what the investigator has planned. Yet, when this occurs, the effect will be to attenuate the effects of treatment (since both groups received some treatment) and alter what the investigator concludes about the efficacy of treatment. Rather than comparing treatment and no-treatment conditions or two or more distinct treatments, the investigator is actually comparing conditions that are more similar than intended. As a threat to internal validity, the effect of a diffusion of treatment is to equalize performance of treatment and control groups and thus reduce or distort effects of the intervention obtained in the study.

An example of a diffusion of treatment as a threat to internal validity was reported in an investigation that compared two treatments for psychiatric patients in a day (rather than residential) hospital program (Austin, Liberman, King, & DeRisi, 1976). Day hospital treatment, where patients do not sleep over, is distinguished from and much less costly than residential treatment and is used when extensive care is needed but the patients can be maintained in other living situations (at home or a community residence). One treatment was a behaviorally oriented program that included multiple techniques (incentive program, social skills training) to develop adaptive behaviors that would facilitate community adjustment. The other program, conducted at a different facility, had an eclectic-milieu therapy approach where group interaction, patient–staff planning meetings, and other forms of therapy were offered. (Yes, yes, it is wonderful that the reader instantaneously thought of the possibility of selection bias because two different intact groups were used that could not be randomly assigned to treatment. However, let us leave that prospect alone for this example.) The results, evaluated 3 and 6 months after treatment, showed a slight superiority of the behavioral program in the extent to which patients improved on their individualized treatment goals, but this did not attain statistical significance. Strictly speaking, there was no evidence to say that one treatment led to better effects than the other.

At the end of the study, it was discovered that one of the therapists in charge of the eclectic-treatment condition used behavioral techniques extensively in her group—that is, techniques of the other treatment condition. This therapist had a close friend who was a behavioral psychologist and had taken workshops for further professional training in behavior therapy during the course of this project. So it was understandable but lamentable from the standpoint of the design that this therapist might administer behavioral treatments to patients she saw. Because the patients treated by this latter therapist really did not receive the eclectic-milieu treatment, their data were withdrawn and the results were reanalyzed. The reanalyses showed that the behavioral treatment was significantly better than eclectic-milieu treatment. The threat to internal validity is clear in this example only because the authors were able to detect that the treatment for subjects in one condition was inadvertently provided to some subjects in the other condition. Because the treatments were not as distinct as originally planned, the net effect was to diffuse the apparent treatment effect upon subsequent statistical analyses.

Diffusion of treatment is not a trivial or infrequent problem and affects a range of areas. For example, years ago a special program was designed to decrease heart attacks among men ($N = 13,000$, ages 35–57) at risk for coronary disease (Multiple Risk Factor Intervention Trial Research Group, 1982). The intervention included personal dietary advice, drugs to control hypertension, advice to stop smoking, and exercise. Random assignment permitted comparison of this group with a control group that received testing (physical exams) but no special intervention (routine care). A follow-up 6 years after the program showed that the intervention reduced risk factors for heart disease but death rates due to heart disease were not statistically different between intervention and control groups. The absence of group differences has been interpreted to reflect a diffusion of treatment because subjects in the control group adopted many health-promoting practices on their own and also decreased their risk factors (Farrington, 1992). Actually, history and maturation, as well as diffusion of treatment, could explain the absence of differences.

Another facet of diffusion, no less significant, is that some cases do not receive the intervention. In this situation a diffusion of the no-treatment condition occurs— that is, no treatment "spreads" to cases (e.g., individuals in a therapy study, classes in a prevention study) assigned to receive the intervention. The net effect is the same, namely, where there is a diffusion of the conditions, the conclusions at the end of treatment are likely to be misleading. In many psychotherapy studies the effectiveness of treatment has been underestimated or inaccurately estimated because participants in the intervention group were unwittingly treated like controls and did not receive the special treatment, or because controls received some of the intervention (Feldman, Caplinger, & Wodarski, 1983; Land, McCall, & Williams, 1992; Patterson, Chamberlain, & Reid, 1982).

Special Treatment or Reactions of Controls.   In an investigation in which the intervention, treatment, or program is administered to the experimental group, the no-treatment control group may also be accorded special attention. This is likely to occur in applied settings such as schools, hospitals, and industry rather than in laboratory studies with college students. One group receives the special program that is viewed as generally desirable. Participants in the no-treatment control group may not receive the specific intervention of interest, but they may receive other services such as more money, more monitoring of their well being, or special privileges. The services provided to the control group are usually intended to redress the apparent inequality and to compensate for not providing the intervention. From the standpoint of internal validity, however, the no-treatment group may be receiving an "intervention" in its own right that obscures the effect of the program provided to the experimental group.

Even if no special compensation in attention or money is provided to no-treatment control subjects, the absence of treatment may lead to special performance. When participants are aware that they are serving as a control group, they may react in ways that obscure the differences between treatment and no treatment. Control subjects may compete with the intervention subjects in some way. For example, teachers at control schools who learn they are not receiving the intervention (e.g., to improve academic performance) may become especially motivated to do well and to show they can be just as effective as those who receive the special treatment program. On the other hand, rather than trying extra hard, controls may become demoralized because they are not receiving the special program. The controls may have experienced initial enthusiasm when the prospect of participating in the special intervention was announced, but their hopes may be dashed by the fate of random assignment. As a consequence, their performance deteriorates. By comparison, the performance of the intervention group looks better whether or not the intervention led to change.

Awareness of participating in an experiment can influence both intervention and control groups. From the standpoint of internal validity, a problem arises when this awareness differentially affects groups so that the effects of the intervention are obscured. At the end of the study differences between treatment and control subjects, or the absence of such differences, may be due to the atypical responses of the control group rather than to the effects of the intervention. The atypical responses could exaggerate or attenuate the apparent effects of treatment.

General Comments

Ideally, it would be instructive to select a single study that illustrated each of the threats to internal validity. Such a study would have failed to control for every possible threat and would not be able to attribute the results to the effects of the independent variable. A study committing so many sins would not be very realistic and would not represent most research efforts in which flaws are committed only one or a few at a time. Thus, detailing such an ill-conceived, sloppy, and uncontrolled study would have little purpose. (It would, however, finally give me a forum to present the design and results of my dissertation in detail.)

In most research the minimal experimental conditions include one group that receives an intervention and another group that does not. The purpose of using a no-intervention (or no-experimental manipulation) control group, of course, is to rule out or make implausible the threats to internal validity. History, maturation, testing, and so on could not account for group differences because both groups presumably would share the effects of these influences. Any group differences due to the intervention are superimposed on changes occurring for these other reasons. One might hypothesize that groups differed systematically in history, maturation, regression, and so on. But this is the combined threat of selection × history (or selection × some other factor). However, if participants were assigned randomly to groups, it may be difficult to explain how there were differences between groups on one of these dimensions. (Possible differences arising from random assignment are discussed in Chapter 6.)

In the course of an investigation, groups that are initially similar might become different for reasons other than the effects of the intervention. For example, it may well be that subjects in a no-treatment group of a psychotherapy study drop out in higher numbers than those who remain in treatment. If one group loses more subjects than another group with scores that are better or worse than the rest of the sample in that group, subsequent group differences might be a function of who dropped out of the study rather than a function of the independent variable. Similarly, participation in a control condition may generate reactions such as compensatory performance or demoralization. Treatment and control group differences emerge from reasons other than the intervention provided to the treatment group.

Threats to internal validity are the major category of alternative explanations of the conclusion that the intervention (manipulation or experimental condition) was responsible for group differences or changes. If a threat to internal validity is not ruled out or made implausible, it becomes a rival explanation of the results. That is, whether the intervention or particular threat to validity operated to cause group differences cannot be decided, and the conclusion about the intervention becomes tentative. The tentativeness is a function of how plausible the threat is in accounting for the results, given the specific area of research. Some threats may be dismissed based upon findings from other research that a particular factor does not influence the results. The degree to which a rival interpretation can be dismissed may be a matter of debate and may require subsequent research to resolve.

From a practical standpoint it is important and useful for an investigator to decide in advance whether the investigation, when completed, would be open to criticism to any of the threats and, if so, what could be done to rectify the situation. In the examples cited where history, maturation, and regression were plausible, a no-treatment condition to rule out each of these threats might have been included. Not all threats to internal validity can be considered and completely averted in advance of the study. Problems may arise during the study that later turn out to be threats (e.g., instrumentation or attrition). Even so, with many problems in mind prior to the study, specific precautions can be taken to optimize the clarity of the results.

EXTERNAL VALIDITY

External validity refers to the extent to which the results of an investigation can be generalized beyond the conditions of the experiment to other populations, settings, and circumstances. External validity encompasses all of the dimensions of generality of interest. Characteristics of the experiment that may limit the generality of the results are referred to as *threats to external validity*.

Threats to External Validity

Threats to external validity constitute questions that can be raised about the limits of the findings. It is useful to conceive of external validity as questions about the boundary conditions of a finding. Assume that a study has addressed the issues of internal validity and establishes a relation between an intervention and outcome. One is then likely to ask, does this apply to other groups of persons (the elderly, nonhospitalized persons, diverse ethnic or racial groups), to other settings (clinics, day-care centers), or to other geographical areas (rural, other countries)? What are the boundaries or limits of the demonstrated relationship? Stated another way, one can discuss external validity in terms of statistical interactions. The demonstrated relation between the independent and dependent variables may apply to some people but not others or to some situations but not others; that is, the independent variable is said to interact with (or operates as a function of) these other conditions. For example, if the finding is obtained with women but not men, we say that the intervention interacts with subject gender. Also, one could say the effects of the treatment are moderated by gender. We shall return to the concepts here apart from external validity.

The factors that may limit the generality of an experiment usually are not known until subsequent research expands upon the conditions under which the relationship was originally examined. The manner in which experimental instructions are given, the age, ethnicity, race, and sex of the subjects, whether experimenters are from the general population or college students, the setting in which the experiment is conducted, and other factors may contribute to whether a given relationship is obtained. Threats to validity are often used as superficial criticisms of an investigation. That is, one can always criticize a study by saying, "The finding may be true, but the investigator did not study subjects who . . . ." (Dear Reader—this is a fill-in example; please select your favorite one of the following: were much older or younger, were of that ethnicity, were from that country, had this rather than that clinical problem, had multiple clinical problems, were from this rather than that socioeconomic class.) These tend to be superficial criticisms when they are posed cavalierly without stating why one would expect findings to be different as a function of the characteristic selected. In fact, the generality of experimental findings may be a function of virtually any characteristic of the experiment, and the subject characteristics noted previously might well be plausible. There is some responsibility of the individual who poses the concern to explain in a cogent way why it is a threat. Recall, for a threat to be a threat it must be a plausible factor that restricts generality of the results. Several characteristics, or threats to external validity, can be identified in advance of a particular study that might limit extension of the findings.

Sample Characteristics. The results of an investigation are obtained with a particular sample. A central question is the extent to which the results can be generalized to others who vary in age, race, ethnic background, education, or any other characteristic. In research there are different types or levels of concern in generalizing from one sample to another.

One concern is the extent to which findings from animal research can be extended to humans. For example, this concern has emerged in laboratory animal research where experimental manipulation of diet (e.g., consumption of soft drinks or a particular food) in rats is shown to cause cancer. Assume that the findings are unequivocal. We, as humans, want to know whether the results generalize from this sample to us. No doubt, *non*laboratory rats share our concern. Sample differences are quite plausible because the multiple cancer-related factors may vary between laboratory rats and humans. The laboratory rats are given a heavy diet of a soft drink, and humans normally consume some significantly lower proportion of their diet as soft drinks. The results may not generalize to subjects (humans) whose diets, activities, metabolism, longevity, and other factors differ. Also, special features of the subjects (rats of a particular species) may have made them differentially responsive to the intervention and hence restrict generality across species. Medical researchers, of course, are well aware of this threat and often select species where the mechanism or process of interest parallels the species to which one would like to generalize.

Generality is not an inherent problem in the leap from animal to human research. Just the opposite, many of the major advances in psychology (e.g., learning), biology (e.g., brain functioning, genetic transmission, understanding HIV), and medicine (e.g., vaccination effects) have derived from the fact that there *is* considerable generality across species. Also, animal research often looks closely at identifying mechanisms that might be involved in a problem where applicability of key findings with humans is already known. For example, exposure to low levels of lead among children is associated with hyperactivity, deficits in neuropsychological functioning (verbal, spatial ability), distractibility, lower IQ, and overall reduced school functioning and these effects continue to be evident several years later (Needleman, Schell, Bellinger, Leviton, & Alldred, 1990). Ingestion of leaded paint (children eating paint chips), fumes from leaded gasoline, and residue of leaded pipes from which water is consumed have been key sources of exposure, before changes in each of these sources has been made (e.g., shift to unleaded gasoline). Lead collects in the bones and is concentrated in the blood, and in high doses can cause seizures and significant brain damage. Several studies with humans have established the deleterious and enduring effects of lead exposure among children. Apart from several studies of humans, animal research has elaborated critical processes involved. Experimentally induced exposure to low lead levels in rats and monkeys influences brain activity and structure (neurotransmitter activity, complexity in dendrite formation, inhibition of the formation of synapses) and hence elaborates how learning and performance are inhibited (Needleman, 1988). There is likely to be great generality of these findings in terms of the brain structures and functions affected.

The lead example conveys areas where animal research has been helpful in elaborating findings immediately pertinent to humans. It would be a disservice to animal research and the issue of generality of findings to leave the matter here. The value of animal research among several scientific disciplines including psychology does not stem from immediate generality. Much of the understanding of basic processes (e.g., brain functioning) stems from animal research. Also, animal research often conveys what can happen in principle and raises questions about mechanisms of action. For example, research on worms (nematodes) has enormous implications for aging (Melov et al., 2000). These worms normally live about 21 days. In an intervention vs. control (no-intervention) study, an antioxidant drug was shown to extend the lives of the worms by approximately 50 percent. The results convey that life can be extended with medication, in this case a powerful antioxidant. In principle, this is quite significant. The public will immediately want to know if this relates to humans; for those of us who are aging rapidly, we may even want to know sooner than immediately. However, this is far from the point and indeed the importance of the research. A demonstration of this type is important apart from generality of the results. The findings show what can happen and possible mechanisms through which aging might occur.

In psychology a frequently voiced concern about generalizing results from one sample to another is based in the extensive use of college students as subjects. Much of psychological research includes laboratory studies of critical topics (aggression, depression, memory) where students are brought into the laboratory for a brief experiment. How could the results be generalizable? In fact, comparisons of laboratory and field studies show quite similar effects, and the worry of generality of findings may be exaggerated (Anderson, Lindsay, & Bushman, 1999). College students are often participants in clinical psychology studies to evaluate treatment, or correlates of a clinical or subclinical disorder (e.g., depression), or they are persons who have had a particular traumatic experience (e.g., date rape). The research questions, samples, and findings are of interest in their own right. Will the findings from such research extend to others whose age, education, motivation, and other characteristics differ? The use of college student samples does not necessarily restrict generality of a finding in clinical studies. However, college students represent a very special sample in terms of subject and demographic characteristics, socioeconomic class, level of intelligence, experience, and other attributes. It may be plausible that some of these special characteristics relate to the independent variable of interest.

Consider as an example an investigation designed to change beliefs about child rearing and whether some techniques (spankings) ought to be used. An investigator may give a pretest to college students on their propensity toward spankings and then randomly assign half of the students to receive a persuasive appeal not to spank. All subjects take the test again and, as predicted, the persuasive appeal decreased propensity to spank when the appeal and no-intervention controls are compared. Interesting demonstration? Very hard to tell from the absence of the rationale. Are the results likely to generalize to parents? This can plausibly be challenged. Unmarried college students (most students) without children, compared to the general population, as a group are more educated, are less invested in childrearing on a daily basis, and may not have as firm or crystallized beliefs about this or that discipline practice that rearing children may foster. Consequently, whether the findings generalize to parents is iffy and worthy of noting as a threat to external validity. The findings with college students may be important because of some critical theoretical question that was addressed about persuasive messages or beliefs. Generality may or may not have been high among the investigator's priorities and not necessarily critical. For our purposes it is plausible to question the generality to parents in light of multiple characteristics of the subjects.

Another concern about the generality of findings from one sample to another pertains to the limited inclusion of underrepresented and minority groups as research participants. Women and various ethnic groups have not been extensively studied in the context of many topics within the biological, behavioral, and social sciences (Guthrie, 1997; Sue, 1999). Ironically, many studies (approximately 40 percent) do not even report ethnicity of the sample, so the scope of the problem is not easily assessed (Case & Smith, 2000). Even so, it is clear that many groups have not been routinely included in research. In relation to proportion of the population in the census (in the United States), some groups have been overrepresented in research (e.g., African Americans) and others have been quite underrepresented (e.g., Hispanic Americans). A critical issue is the extent to which findings may be restricted to those groups included in research.

The focus on underrepresented and ethnic minority groups in the United States raises broader research issues. As psychologists we are not concerned merely with findings of one group and then the extension of findings to other groups that have been neglected and underrepresented. To be sure, we are concerned with this, but the scientific agenda is much broader. We are interested in many peoples of the world, in many cultures, and many subgroups within a culture. We wish to know the extent to which findings extend to these peoples, and principles or processes that can explain how culture influences affect, cognition, behavior, development, the family, and so on. We would like to know about processes that explain generality of findings or lack of generality of findings among diverse groups and cultures, in part because every key or major finding could not be studied with all different ethnic groups and indigenous populations in the world. This is not a reason to restrict research to one or a limited number of groups. Quite the opposite. However, the comments also convey that extending research to different groups is not an end in itself. Rather, the goal is to understand the processes, sources of influence, and factors that might dictate why or how a finding is one way in this context but another way in a different context. As these comments suggest, external validity is not just a topic of methodology, but raises important substantive questions about research findings and the factors that may influence them.

When the study of the generality of findings across groups or samples serves as the basis for research, it is important to go beyond the basic question of whether or the extent to which prior results also apply to a new group. As a basis for new research, it is very useful to identify theoretical issues or to propose mechanisms or processes, which would lead one to expect differences in the findings across previously studied and to-be-studied samples. For example, if differences are expected as a function of sex, ethnicity, social class, country of origin, or type of personality style, it is advisable for the investigator to specify *why* this would be expected and to measure the processes or hypothesized basis for group differences in the investigation. This type of study is a much more significant contribution than merely assessing whether effects of prior research generalize to a new set of subjects who vary in some way from the original sample.

Process is important merely for the reason of understanding why generality varies, but there is also a practical side. There are many more groups than can ever be studied, to test the generality of all or all major findings, whatever these findings would be. For example, the most recent census in the United States recognizes 126 different racial and ethnic identities (detailed further in Chapter 6).[1] Some African countries can distinguish over 200 ethnic groups (see www.infoplease.com/ipa/A0855617.html.) Not all psychological, biological, health, and other findings could be tested among these different groups. Moreover, characteristics and responses of a given ethnic group can vary considerably as a function of where they are currently living (e.g., country) and how recently they have immigrated, if they have changed countries (Lin, Poland, & Nakasaki, 1993). Add to these other important characteristics (age and gender identity of the subjects) and the research agenda becomes infinitely large.

The importance of studying different groups and coupling this with conceptualization of critical processes sounds so important in principle. Can this be done? An example that provides helpful insight has focused on the effects of medication for various psychiatric disorders (depression, anxiety). Responsiveness to psychotropic medication varies as a function of ethnicity (Lin et al., 1993). There are important reasons to expect ethnic differences, in part because diverse groups differ in concentrations of various enzymes that influence metabolization of drugs. Many of the enzyme concentrations seem to be genetically controlled and perhaps emerged in defense to toxins (exposure to plants, pollen, and infection) in the environment that vary in respective areas of origin for the different ethnic groups. Absorption and rate of metabolization of drugs that in some way utilize these enzymes can vary significantly and hence serve as the basis for expecting ethnic differences in response to medication (among African-American, Asian, Caucasian, Hispanic, and Saudi Arabian adults). From a clinical perspective this means that a recommended dose (of some antidepressant and antianxiety medications) for members of one group can be an overdose or underdose for members of another group. From a methodological perspective this means that findings from a study with one ethnic group might not generalize to another group whose enzyme profile in relation to processes involved in a particular medication are known to differ from the profile of the sample included in the study. In passing, it is important to note that the ethnic differences in medication response and metabolization include genetic, environmental, and cultural influences beyond the purposes of this illustration so that, for example, a particular subgroup may respond differently as a function of where they live (if they have immigrated to another country or reside in their country of origin) and presumably what they eat.

---

[1]Ethnicity and race are inconsistently defined, distinguished, and assessed in research, and these inconsistencies raise substantive and methodological issues in science, including but well beyond psychology. Definitions of ethnicity usually emphasize cultural characteristics shared by a group of people and that reflect commonalities in history, values, language, attitudes, and behaviors. Definitions of race usually emphasize biologically transmitted characteristics. Many more concepts that can be delineated, and each of these has problems in how they are defined and measured (see Demo, Allen, & Fine, 2000).

Stimulus Characteristics and Settings.   Although the usual concern in generality of results has to do with sample characteristics and whether the findings extend across different subjects, equally relevant but less commonly discussed is the extent to which the results extend across the stimulus characteristics of the investigation (Brunswik, 1955). The stimulus characteristics refer to features of the study with which the intervention or condition may be associated and include the setting, experimenters, interviewers, or other factors related to the experimental arrangement. Any of these features may restrict generality of the findings (Maher, 1978a).

Consider a number of examples in which generality of findings from one setting or context to the next has been questioned. Reviews of psychotherapy research consistently conclude that treatment is effective for a variety of clinical problems (Kendall & Chambless, 1998; Nathan & Gorman, 1998). Some analyses suggest that the effectiveness of treatment in controlled studies is greater than the effects obtained in clinical settings (Weisz, Weiss, & Donenberg, 1992).[2] Clearly, generality of results from controlled clinic/laboratory settings to "real-life" clinics raises a critical issue. As an aside, other reviews suggest that in fact treatment effectiveness is similar in controlled studies and in clinical work and across a range of settings (Shadish, 1996; Shadish, Navarro, Matt, & Phillips, 2000). The discrepant conclusions and paucity of treatment outcome research in clinic settings make this an area ripe for further research.

An example from medicine may be better because the influence of the locale or setting has been isolated in some studies and reflects findings that might not be expected at first blush. For medical interventions we tend to consider interventions to be fairly applicable across settings and contexts. Yet, the external validity threat is no less relevant to medical than to psychological interventions. For example, consider the effectiveness of vaccinations for pertussis (whopping cough). This disease is a highly contagious respiratory condition that affects more than 50 million people worldwide and kills approximately 350,000 people annually (Winslow, 1995). In the United States vaccination is effective in 70–95 percent of the cases; that is, those vaccinated do not contract the disease. In randomized controlled trials in other countries the effectiveness of the vaccination has been much lower (36 percent in Italy, 48 percent in Sweden). Thus, different conclusions have been reached about the effectiveness of the vaccination. One explanation is that, compared to people in the United States, people in other countries have much higher exposure to the bacteria causing the disorder and hence require much stronger protection than the usual vaccination

---

[2]Contemporary discussions of psychotherapy outcome research make a distinction between efficacy and effectiveness (Hoagwood, Hibbs, Brent, & Jensen, 1995). *Efficacy* refers to treatment outcomes obtained in controlled psychotherapy studies that are conducted under laboratory and quasi-laboratory conditions (cases are recruited who are homogeneous and who may show a narrow range of problems, treatment is specified in manual form, and treatment delivery is closely supervised and monitored). *Effectiveness* refers to treatment outcomes obtained in clinic settings where the usual control procedures are not implemented. Efficacy and effectiveness studies can be conceived as a continuum or multiple continua because several dimensions can vary across clinic and laboratory settings that affect generality of the results (Hoagwood et al., 1995; Kazdin, 1978a). I use the term effectiveness here generically to mean having impact on the problem that has been treated.

provides. In any case, findings on the effectiveness of vaccinations in the United States do not automatically generalize to the other countries.

These examples convey that generality across settings cannot be automatically assumed. A difficulty in research is identifying what facets of the different settings may be responsible for (moderate, interact with) the intervention and account for the different effects. For example, in the case of psychotherapy as conducted in the laboratory versus clinical settings, there are many differences in the clients (as to who is seen in treatment, what types of problems they present), in who provides treatment, and in how carefully treatment integrity is monitored (Kazdin, 2000). If these were controlled, setting may or may not make a difference in the effects of psychotherapy. An excellent line of research is to test why an effect does not generalize and then what can be done to promote generalization.

The setting is only one example of the stimuli conditions that may be relevant. The general concern is that some feature of the stimulus conditions within the investigation may restrict generality. From the standpoint of designing an investigation, it is hazardous to use *one* experimenter or therapist, to show *one* videotaped vignette to present stimuli to the subjects, or to embed the manipulation in any *one* set of stimuli. That is, the narrow range of stimuli may contribute to the findings, and the results may not extend beyond these stimuli. The implications of including a narrow range of stimuli in an investigation extend beyond a threat to external validity. Hence, I address and elaborate the issue again in the context of construct validity in the next chapter. At this point it is important to note that the stimulus conditions of the experiment and settings in which research is conducted may very much relate to, and hence limit, generality of the results.

Reactivity of Experimental Arrangements.   As a threat to external validity, reactivity of an experimental arrangement refers to the influence of the subjects' awareness that they are participating in an investigation. The results of an experiment may be influenced by the fact that subjects know they are being studied or that the purpose is to examine a particular relationship between variables. The external validity question is whether the results would be obtained if subjects were not aware that they were being studied.

In evaluating treatment in an outpatient clinic, investigators may find that the results may differ depending upon whether subjects know they are participating in an experiment. Participation in an experiment may elicit reactions such as trying to please the experimenter or avoiding responses that might lead the experimenter to evaluate the subject adversely. These influences presumably would not be present if subjects believed they were merely attending the clinic for the usual care and were unaware of their participation in a special experiment. Awareness of participation in a study may lead to changes in how individuals respond that would not carry over to other situations.

In the vast majority of studies, subjects must be made aware that they are participating in an investigation. Among the exceptions are those studies that examine records (e.g., medical records, school files) that are routinely available in a setting and where the individual subject cannot be identified. In these studies informed consent may not be required, and subjects then will not be told that they are in a study. Even here, there is no firm rule. If it is possible that the records might be used in ways that could affect the individual subject (e.g., showing that alcoholism is rampant among parents in a particular school district), consent may still be required.

If virtually all experiments are likely to be arranged so that subjects are aware that they are participating in a study, why even discuss reactivity? The answer is that we want to reveal relations that are not necessarily restricted to the particular settings in which the relations are demonstrated. For many types of experiments (e.g., animal studies), we can be assured that reactivity is not likely to be a problem. But for human studies in laboratory paradigms, participants have their own motivation and interpretation of what is transpiring. If they are aware of participation, the effect of the experimental manipulation can be affected by these motives and interpretations. Reactivity can be a matter of degree. The fact that the subject is aware of participating in an experiment does not mean that the results will be altered. Subjects can vary in the extent to which their performance is altered, and experimental arrangements can vary in the extent to which they are likely to foster special reactions. I shall discuss the effect of awareness in different contexts in Chapter 13 to elaborate reactive influences on subjects' responses and what can be done to minimize the impact.

Multiple-Treatment Interference. In some experimental designs subjects are exposed to more than one experimental condition. Subjects might receive two or more interventions or alternate between intervention and no-intervention conditions. Multiple-treatment interference refers to drawing conclusions about a given treatment when it is evaluated in the context of other treatments. The conclusion drawn about one treatment or intervention might be restricted by the administration of prior treatments. Stated another way, the effects obtained in the experiment may be due in part to the context or series of conditions in which it was presented.

The problem of multiple-treatment interference can be illustrated in a study designed to treat marital discord (Azrin, Naster, & Jones, 1973). Twelve married couples interested in marital counseling were seen for treatment. The study examined a technique referred to as "reciprocity counseling," which consists of a multifaceted program that helps spouses express mutual appreciation, provide feedback about areas of behavior that could be improved, and fulfill each other's fantasies to increase marital satisfaction, along with other procedures designed to enhance communication and sensitivity to the needs of the partner. Prior to receiving 4 weeks of reciprocity counseling, all couples received 3 weeks of "catharsis" counseling, where the couples met with a therapist and talked about their problems and feelings. This was a reasonable initial focus with the goal of ruling out that merely talking about one's problems might explain any therapeutic effects the investigators wished to attribute to reciprocity counseling.

The results showed that reciprocity counseling was associated with marked improvements in marital satisfaction, whereas catharsis counseling did not improve satisfaction. Does reciprocity counseling improve marital satisfaction? From the study we can infer that it does, at least when preceded by the opportunity to discuss problems in a more traditional therapy format (catharsis). The external validity of the reciprocity counseling may be restricted to those individuals who receive catharsis counseling. That is, the context or prior history of the catharsis treatment may be critical for reciprocity counseling to be effective. The results may not be applicable to participants who do not have a similar set of prior experiences within the experiment or when treatment is presented without the opportunity to cathart.

Novelty Effects. As a threat to external validity, novelty effects refer to the possibility that the effects of an intervention may in part depend upon their innovativeness or novelty in the situation (Bracht & Glass, 1968). It is possible that the effects of the intervention depend upon the fact that it is administered under conditions where it is particularly salient, infrequent, or otherwise novel in some way. Consider an example of novelty effects well outside of psychology. In the United States thousands of accidents occur each year between fire trucks and other vehicles. Research has shown that yellow fire trucks, compared to more traditional red fire trucks, have significantly fewer accidents with cars (Christian, 1995). The usual interpretation of this finding is that the human eye has greater difficulty in perceiving red relative to many other colors, including yellow. Because drivers more readily see yellow trucks, they can avoid the trucks more easily, and hence fewer accidents are likely. (Incidentally, notwithstanding this finding, most fire trucks continue to be red, in part to maintain a long tradition.)

Consider the role novelty might play as a threat to external validity, that is, the generality of the finding that yellow trucks will reduce accidents across many situations. Quite possibly, the reduced accident rate associated with yellow fire trucks was due in part to the fact that such trucks are quite novel—that is, they depart from the vast majority of red trucks that still dominate the United States. The reduced accident effect could be restricted to the *novelty* of introducing a new color of truck. Perhaps if most fire trucks were yellow, the benefits would be lost. Indeed, against a sea of yellow trucks, red trucks might be associated with reduced accidents because of *their* novelty. As a matter of safety, it may be prudent to change the color of fire trucks to yellow with the hope that there is no novelty effect. As part of this change, it would be important to evaluate the effects to ensure that the reduced accident rates are maintained. This research would be easy to do in naturalistic studies; many firehouses refuse to change colors of their trucks because red is the traditional color, so some carefully devised comparisons could provide the necessary data.

As an aside, the importance of understanding why an intervention has an effect can be readily seen in this simple example. If the color of fire trucks were the critical issue, then changing to yellow trucks would be the obvious strategy. If novelty accounts for the effect, this leads to a different strategy. One would encourage changes in fire trucks. Whenever trucks are replaced or repainted, perhaps their color ought to change, and the color (from red to yellow and perhaps back to red) might not be too important. The research may sound silly, but without understanding why reduced accidents occur, it is easy to adopt a strategy that will have little impact. For example, a change to all yellow or mostly yellow fire trucks may have no enduring impact on accidents if novelty is responsible for the effect. (My master's thesis on polka-dotted fire trucks shed interesting light on this matter. Unfortunately, ongoing vituperative exchanges with a journal editor over publication of this study preclude a preview of the findings here.)

The presence of novelty effects is difficult to evaluate. Thus, a new treatment when first introduced may seem to be effective because of its special therapeutic procedures or because of its novelty (or some combination). Effects due to novelty would wear off over time as the treatment is extended to more and new therapists and patients. That is, the treatment will move from novel to mainstream. It may be that treatments that are novel to the public and are "new and improved" —very much like the soaps, cereals, automobiles, and shampoos we purchase—will be effective in part because of their novelty. Indeed, telling people that the treatment is new and improved increases expectancies that the treatment will lead to therapeutic change, at least in college student samples (Kazdin & Krouse, 1983). When a new treatment is introduced, we may not know whether it is the "new" (novelty effect) or the "improved" (putatively better procedures or techniques) that accounts for the change. In such cases, novelty becomes a threat to external validity.

It is possible that treatment loses its effectiveness over time for reasons other than novelty. In the case of psychotherapy, early applications might prove to be more effective than later ones. Early applications develop often in a laboratory where treatment is very carefully conducted and monitored, or in a clinic with a charismatic therapist whose beliefs and passion about the treatment are unique. As treatment is extended to other research settings and clinics, it may be carried out less faithfully, be more diluted, be combined with other procedures, or be applied to more complex clinical cases. Treatment may work less well, and it is not a novelty effect but one of these other reasons that effectiveness is diminished. (It would be worth trying to study experimentally the role beliefs, passion, and charisma play in changing behavior or effecting therapeutic change by holding treatment constant but varying these other conditions.)

Reactivity of Assessment.   In most psychology experiments, subjects or clients are aware that some facet of their functioning is assessed. If subjects are aware that their performance is being assessed, the measures are said to be *obtrusive*. Obtrusive measures are of concern in relation to external validity because awareness that performance is being assessed can alter performance from what it would otherwise be. If awareness of assessment leads persons to respond differently from how they would usually respond, the measures are said to be *reactive*.

In clinical research, the fact that clients are aware of the assessment procedures raises an important question about the generality of the findings. If the results of a treatment study are evident on paper-and-pencil inventories or on interviews by a therapist in the clinical setting, one might question the generality of treatment effects. That is, to what extent do treatment effects demonstrated on reactive measures within the laboratory or clinic setting extend to measures that are not reactive and administered outside of the setting? Treated clients may show great reductions in anxiety on various questionnaires, but has their anxiety decreased and are they functioning any better in their everyday lives? An exceedingly important question is whether the changes carry over to actual experience of the clients in their ordinary everyday settings, a question of external validity of the results. The question is not an esoteric methodological issue. Among the thousands of controlled studies of various forms of therapy, few show that performance in everyday life (beyond various questionnaires and inventories) or on unobtrusive measures improves.

A deceptively simple solution is to include in studies one or two measures that the subjects are not aware of—that is, use some unobtrusive measures. Then one could examine whether the results (e.g., treatment is effective) vary as a function of the awareness of being assessed. This solution raises both critical ethical issues (e.g., informed consent) and measurement issues (e.g., are the unobtrusive measures as valid as the more studied self-report questionnaires and inventories?). I discuss these topics in greater detail in the chapters on assessment. At this point it is important to note that results may not necessarily generalize to situations (reactive experimental arrangements already mentioned) and measures (reactive measures) in the study.

Test Sensitization.   In many investigations, particularly in therapy research, pretests are administered routinely. The purpose is to measure the client's standing on a particular variable before receiving the experimental manipulation or treatment. There are many methodological and statistical benefits in using a pretest, as belabored in a later chapter. At the same time, administration of the pretest may in some way *sensitize* the subjects so that they are affected differently by the intervention, a phenomenon referred to as *pretest sensitization*. Individuals who are pretested might be more or less amenable or responsive to an intervention (treatment, persuasive message) than individuals who are not exposed to a pretest merely because of the initial assessment.

As an example, consider an investigator who wishes to examine people's views toward violence. The hypothesis may be that viewing violent movies leads to an increase in aggressive thoughts and a positive evaluation of violence. The investigator may wish to evaluate views of people after they see a violent gangster film at a movie theater and asks patrons to complete a questionnaire before and after they see the film. As participants enter the lobby, they complete the measure right before viewing the film, and then on their way out of the theater, they complete the measure again.

It is possible that administration of a test before the film is shown—that is, the pretest—makes people view and react to the film somewhat differently from their usual reaction. Perhaps the questions heighten sensitivity to certain types of issues or to the entire topic of violence, which may not have otherwise been raised. At posttest performance, how subjects respond is not merely a function of seeing the movie but also may be due in part to the initial pretest sensitization. Hence, a possible threat to external validity is that the results may not generalize to subjects who have not received a pretest. Administering a pretest does not necessarily restrict generality of the results. It does, however, raise the question of whether nonpretested individuals, usually the population of interest, would respond to the intervention in the same way as the pretested population. As with other threats to external validity, there is no challenge here about the finding itself, but there is a question of whether the relationship between viewing a violent movie and attitudes about violence would be evident without some sensitization experience that immediately precedes the movie.

Even when a pretest is not used, it is possible that assessment may influence the results. The posttest might sensitize subjects to the previous intervention that they have received and yield results that would not have been evident without the assessment. This effect, referred to as *posttest sensitization* (Bracht & Glass, 1968), is very similar to pretest sensitization where test administration may crystalize a particular reaction on the part of the subject. With posttest sensitization, assessment constitutes a necessary condition for treatment to show its effect. Essentially, treatment effects may be latent or incomplete and appear only when an obtrusive assessment device is administered. Subjects can tell they are being assessed (obtrusive assessment) and prompted to think of violence in a way they might not have otherwise thought (sensitized). As a threat to external validity, posttest sensitization raises the question of whether the results would extend to measures that subjects could not associate with intervention or measures that were completely out of their awareness. The effect of posttest sensitization is slightly more difficult to assess and control than is pretest sensitization because it requires the use of unobtrusive measures of treatment effects and a comparison of the results across measures varying in whether or not they are obtrusive or in the degree of their obtrusiveness.

In passing, it is important to note that sensitization effects are not always viewed as artifacts or threats to external validity. Occasionally, interventions are designed in such a way as to capitalize on sensitization effects to increase the impact of a subsequent intervention. For example, one study demonstrating the importance of sensitization evaluated the impact of a television advertising campaign designed to reduce alcohol consumption among persons who had been identified as drinkers (Barber, Bradshaw, & Walsh, 1989). Large-scale media campaigns (via television, radio, newspapers) designed to reduce substance abuse are not usually very effective. The investigators evaluated whether sending a letter to persons in advance of the campaign would sensitize community members to the television commercials that followed. Interestingly, persons who were sent the letter alerting them to the upcoming campaign and who then received the advertising on television showed significant reductions in alcohol consumption and were significantly lower in consumption than those who received the advertising campaign without the letter or the letter without the advertising campaign. Thus, in this study sensitization enhanced the impact of the intervention. The finding is important insofar as it suggests that some presensitization experience might augment the impact of an otherwise weak intervention.

Timing of Measurement. In some research, measures are administered on multiple occasions over time. For example, longitudinal research may study a sample spanning many years. In other research the measures may be administered over a shorter period even though we are interested in conclusions over time (psychotherapy outcome or prevention studies with postintervention and some follow-up assessment). The results of an experiment may depend on the point in time that assessment devices are administered. An external validity question that can be raised is whether the same results would have been obtained had measurements been taken at another time, say, several months later.

A prime area where this threat emerges is in the context of psychotherapy outcome research. The effectiveness of treatment usually is evaluated immediately after the last therapy session (posttreatment assessment). It is possible that the conclusions at this time would not extend to a later period. For example, in one study, separate treatments were implemented at school to alter the behavior of maladjusted children (Kolvin et al., 1981). Two of the interventions (group therapy, behavior modification) yielded different effects depending on the point in time that assessment was completed. Immediately after treatment, relatively few improvements were evident. At follow-up, approximately 18 months later, improvements in these groups, relative to controls who had not received treatment, were marked. The effects evident at one time (posttreatment) were different from those at another time (follow-up). Other treatment studies with adults and children occasionally show that the conclusions reached about a particular treatment or the relative effectiveness of different treatments in a given study vary from posttreatment to follow-up assessment. In some cases treatments are no different at posttreatment but are different at follow-up (e.g., Meyers, Graves, Whelan, & Barclay, 1996); in other cases treatments are different at posttreatment but no different at follow-up (e.g., Newman, Kenardy, Herman, & Taylor, 1997). In short, conclusions about the effectiveness of treatment may depend on when the assessments are completed. Stated as a threat to validity, one might say, "Yes, this treatment is more effective, but would this conclusion apply to another time period (e.g., in a year from now)?"

Methodological concerns connect with substantive issues all of the time, and it is useful to mention the connection here beyond the context of findings on the effects of psychotherapy. A given relation between two (or more) variables (sex and problem-solving skills; responsiveness to persuasive appeals and peer pressure) may be studied in a sample of college students in their early 20s. Does the finding generalize to other periods in which the relation would be assessed? For example, if this sample or indeed another sample were assessed in their 40s would the relationship be the same? Common sense and experience convey that our beliefs, values, and views change over time due to historical events (getting married, having children) and maturation (gaining experience, learning). Presumably, these would be reflected in the relations among variables assessed in a psychological experiment. The point is to note that time of measurement can affect conclusions quite broadly. Of course, describing and understanding changes in relations among variables over time is part of developmental psychology and life span research. This is a case where the concern of external validity has important substantive (developmental) implications.

General Comments

The previously discussed threats to external validity only begin to enumerate those conditions that might restrict the generality of a finding. Not all of the conditions that are relevant to the generality of a finding can be specified in advance. In principle, any characteristic of the experimenters, subjects, or accouterments of the investigation might later prove to be related to the results. If one of the threats applies, this means that some caution should be exercised in extending the results.

One way of conceiving many of the threats that were mentioned and others that might be raised is the notion of context. It might be that the experimental manipulation or intervention achieved its effects because of something about the context in which it was studied or demonstrated. If the intervention occurred after some other intervention (multiple-treatment interference), under arrangements in which subjects knew they were being studied (reactive arrangements), under conditions in which the experimental intervention might seem quite novel in light of one's usual experience (novelty), or with assessments that may be especially prone to show effects (reactive assessments, test sensitization, right after the manipulation but not months or years later), one could raise questions of external validity. The effects may be carefully demonstrated (internal validity was well handled), but perhaps the findings would not be obtained or obtained to the same extent without one of these contextual influences. The degree of caution in generalizing the results is a function of the extent to which special conditions of the study depart from those to which one would like to generalize *and* the plausibility that the specific condition of the experiment might influence generality.

One cannot simply discount the findings of a study as a very special case by merely noting that participants were pretested, that they were aware that they were participating in an experiment, or by identifying another characteristic of the experiment. Enumerating possible threats to external validity in principle is insufficient to challenge the findings. The onus is on the investigator who conducts the study to clarify the conditions to which he or she wishes to generalize and to convey how the conditions of the experiment represent these conditions. The onus on those skeptical of how well this has been achieved is to describe explicitly how a particular threat to external validity would operate and would be plausible as a restriction of the findings.

Many conditions might be ruled out as threats to external validity on seemingly commonsense grounds (hair or eye color of the experimenter, season of the year, birth weight of participants). In any given area these seemingly remote factors might well be important. The task of the reviewer or the consumer of research (other professionals, lay persons) is to provide a plausible account of why the generality of the findings may be limited. Only further investigation can attest to whether the potential threats to external validity actually limit generality and truly make a theoretical or practical difference. Of course, there is no more persuasive demonstration than several studies conducted together in which similar findings are obtained with some consistency across various types of subjects (patients, college students), settings (university laboratory, clinic, community), and other domains (different researchers, countries). Replication of research findings is so important to ensure that findings from an initial study are not likely to be due to various threats to internal validity or to chance. Replication is also important for external validity because further studies after the original one are likely to vary some conditions (geographical locale, investigator, and type of subject) that extend the generality of the findings.

PERSPECTIVES ON INTERNAL AND EXTERNAL VALIDITY

Plausibility and Parsimony

Internal and external validity convey critical features of the logic of scientific research. Internal validity is addressed by experimental arrangements that help rule out or make implausible factors that could explain the effects we wish to attribute to the intervention. Everyday life is replete with "demonstrations" that do not control basic threats to internal validity. For example, almost any intervention that one applies to oneself or a group can appear to "cure" the common cold. Consuming virtually any vitamin or potion from assorted animal parts, reading highly arousing material (on methodology and research design, of course), or surfing the Web for 50 minutes each day in a few days will be followed by a remission of cold symptoms. Pre- and postassessments with one of the above interventions would no doubt show a reduction in cold symptoms (on a checklist of cold symptoms), improved feelings of well being, and changes in various biological indices (body temperature, swelling of the sinuses). Did our intervention lead to improvement? Probably not. We can muse at the example because we know that colds usually remit without the above interventions. The example is relevant because maturation (immunological and recuperative processes within the individual) is a threat to internal validity and can readily account for changes. For areas we do not understand as well and where the determinants and course are less clear, a host of threats can compete with the variable of interest in accounting for change. Control of threats to internal validity becomes essential.

Mentioned previously was that for a threat to be a genuine concern, it ought to be plausible. We can expand beyond plausibility as a basis for posing threats, namely, the principle of parsimony. As mentioned in the previous chapter, parsimony refers to selecting the least complex interpretation that can explain a particular finding or set of findings. Key threats to internal validity (history, maturation, repeated testing) are threats in part because they are likely to be parsimonious interpretations of the data and often more parsimonious than the interpretation proposed by an investigator. For example, consider a study in which all subjects with a particular problem receive psychotherapy and improve significantly from pre- to posttreatment assessment. The investigator claims that therapy was effective and then foists upon us all sorts of explanations that mention the latest in cognitions, family processes, and brain functions to explain treatment (done rather well, I might add, in the second Discussion section of my dissertation). However, basic threats to internal validity are quite plausible as the basis for the change and are as (or more) parsimonious as (than) an investigator's interpretation. History, maturation, and the other internal validity threats show broad generality across many areas of research and hence can account for more findings than those obtained in this particular study. Consequently, as a matter of principle, the scientific community adopts the threats to internal validity as the more likely basis for explaining the findings if these threats are not addressed specifically by the design. This does not mean history, maturation, and so on *did* cause the changes or that psychotherapy did *not* work. However, in light of parsimony as a basic tenet, there is no reason to resort to some specific explanation of the changes in this study, when we have as plausible alternatives changes that can be pervasive across many areas of study.

If the investigator has in the study a control group, and subjects were assigned randomly to psychotherapy or control conditions, then history, maturation, and the other threats are no longer very plausible or parsimonious. The skeptic must pose how history or maturation applies to one group rather than another (selection × history, selection × maturation) to explain the differential changes. This is often possible, but rarely parsimonious or plausible. The simpler explanation of the finding is that the therapy was responsible for the differences between groups.

Parsimony applies equally to threats to external validity. It is not reasonable to look at a finding and say, in a knee jerk way, "Yes, but does the finding apply to this or that ethnic group, older or younger people, people of a different gender, or subjects without a pretest?" Parsimony begins with the assumption that most humans are alike on a particular process. This does not mean that most humans *are* alike on any particular process or characteristic. Parsimony is a point of departure for developing interpretations and not an account of the world. Absent evidence or theory, one does not merely propose differences. One needs a reason to suggest that generality is restricted beyond merely noting that the study did not sample all conceivable populations or circumstances in which this independent variable could be tested. There *are* restrictions in findings, and a given finding does not invariably generalize. That said, this does not mean all findings are suspect or limited unless broad generality is shown. Parsimony moves us in a more sympathetic direction, namely, the finding is the best statement of the relationship unless there are clear reasons to suspect otherwise.

Priority of Internal Validity

As a priority the internal validity of an experiment is usually regarded as more important than, or at least logically prior in importance to, external validity. One must first have an unambiguous finding before one can ask about its generality. Given the priority of internal validity, initial considerations of an investigation pertain to devising those conditions that will facilitate demonstrating the relation between the independent and dependent variables. A well-designed experiment maximizes the opportunity to draw valid inferences about the intervention.

By emphasizing internal validity, there is no intention to slight external validity. For research with applied implications—as is often the case in clinical psychology, counseling, and education—external validity is particularly important. A well-conducted study with a high degree of internal validity may show what *can* happen when the experiment is arranged in a particular way. Yet it is quite a different matter to show that the intervention would have this effect or in fact does operate this way outside of the experimental situation. For example, as mentioned already, experiments on cancer may show that a soft drink or food additive caused cancer in laboratory animals fed very high doses. Internally valid experiments of this sort are informative because they show what can happen. For this initial demonstration, external validity is actually irrelevant. The issue is whether a causal relation can be shown, whether a possible mechanism of action might be feasible, or whether a particular theory (e.g., about carcinogenic effects) can be supported. The findings may have important theoretical implications for how and why cancers develop, and these are important ends in themselves.

In addition, we may also be interested in the immediate utility of the findings for applied purposes such as whether cancers develop in this way outside of the laboratory. Do the findings extend from mice and rats to humans, to lower doses of the suspected ingredients, or to diets that may include potentially neutralizing substances (e.g., water and assorted vitamins and minerals)? All these questions pertain to the external validity of the findings. We tend to focus heavily on external validity, in part because findings in the public domain (e.g., new reports of advances in science) usually move quickly to generality of effects. Generality is what we might care about the most. Hence, a laboratory study with an important advance that has theoretical significance is less likely to be picked up or promoted. This is all reasonable—the public is interested in the question, "So what is really different or new that will affect me, my life, or the people I care about?"

However, it is very important for the researcher to keep in mind that some of the best and most helpful research begins with understanding the phenomenon of interest, and studies with that focus may have very little external validity (Mook, 1983). Studies in physics represent a broad class of such work. The findings often will have generality to conditions well beyond the lab as principles developed in research with seemingly little external validity eventually are used to improve space travel or to improve surgery (control and understanding of lasers). I have mentioned other examples (aging).

The goal of research is to understand phenomena of interest. Internal validity is obviously relevant because it pertains to many potential sources of influence, artifact, and bias that can interfere directly with the inferences drawn as to why a finding was obtained. In the context of understanding phenomena, external validity has a very important role that goes beyond merely asking, "Yes, but do the findings generalize to other . . . (people, places, settings, and so on)?" When findings do not generalize, there is a very special opportunity to understand the phenomenon of interest. Failure to generalize raises questions of "why." In the process a deeper level of understanding of the phenomenon of interest is possible. It may be that the relation depends on the presence of some third variable (personality, sex, education of the subjects) or some artifact in the experiment (e.g., a threat to internal validity). Either way, establishing when the finding does and does not hold can be a conceptual advance.

A contemporary public health example conveys the importance of external validity issues in relation to understanding a phenomenon of interest. As we know, contracting the human immunodeficiency virus (HIV), through sexual contact or injection of infected needles, leads to acquired immunodeficiency syndrome (AIDS) and death. This finding has broad external validity insofar as it generalizes across people, places (countries), settings, and so on. However, a small proportion of individuals who contract the infection do not progress to AIDS. In the context of the present discussion, the finding that HIV leads to AIDS does not generalize to everyone. The importance of external validity does not end in just noting that the finding is not universal. Rather, the failure to generalize immediately prompts questions about why, and in this case these questions focus on characteristics of individuals to whom the finding does not apply. This has led to important work on immune systems and genetics to understand the mechanism(s) that stop HIV from progressing to AIDS (see Balter, 1996; Waldholz, 1997). Identification of a protective inborn gene mutation, the suspected mechanism, has led to interventions that can mimic the inborn protective factor and stop the progression from HIV to AIDS. In short, failure of a finding to generalize is critically important to progress in research and application because it promotes questions about the mechanisms involved and hence fosters a much deeper understanding of the phenomenon.

Issues of external validity sometimes emerge or at least ought to when there is a failure to replicate a finding. Failures to replicate a finding sometimes are viewed as reasons to be suspicious about the original finding. Either the original finding was an artifact (due to threats to internal validity or other biases we shall consider later), or the finding was veridical but restricted to very narrow conditions of the original investigation (limited external validity). It is possible that some other variable provides the boundary conditions under which a finding can be obtained. Theory and research about that variable (or variables) can promote highly valuable and sophisticated research. As researchers, we often search for or believe we are searching for general principles that have widespread, if not universal and intergalactic, generality. Yet, the value of a finding does not necessarily derive from its generality. Knowledge of a phenomenon entails identifying the conditions under which the findings may not apply and the reasons for seeming exceptions to what we thought to be a general rule. External validity issues are not mere afterthoughts about whether the findings "generalize," but get at the core of why we do research at all.

Considerations pertaining to external validity often serve as the initial attraction of persons beginning in psychological research. Students early in their research careers often wish to study something relevant. Thus, research questions in such settings as a treatment clinic, psychiatric hospital, homes where families reside, or schools may be very enticing because of their obvious relevance to applied questions that may motivate research. As one becomes involved in research, sometimes one moves to more narrowly framed questions and away from the applied settings or problems that were initially enticing. Perhaps part of the influence is due to the obstacles that research in applied settings often raises and the difficulties in drawing valid inferences. Another part of the influence no doubt is realization that the goal is to understand and that some of the best applications can come from understanding the phenomenon of interest in ways that are difficult to obtain from research in applied settings. Consequently, lines of research develop and laboratory paradigms are devised to study a phenomenon in a very special way. All of this is to the good. In addition, direct tests of generality of the findings remain important to ensure that what we understand is not completely restricted in its applicability to the situations about which we wish to speak.

SUMMARY AND CONCLUSIONS

The purpose of research is to understand phenomena peculiar to a discipline or specific area of study. This translates concretely to the investigation of relations between independent and dependent variables. The value of research derives from its capacity to simplify the situation in which variables may operate so that the influence of many variables can be separated from the variable of interest. Stated another way, an investigation helps to rule out or to make implausible the influence of many alternative variables that might explain changes on the dependent measures.

The extent to which an experiment rules out as explanations those factors that otherwise might account for the results is referred to as internal validity. Factors or sources of influence other than the independent variables are referred to as threats to internal validity and include history, maturation, testing, instrumentation, statistical regression, selection biases, attrition, selection in combination with other threats (e.g., selection × history), diffusion of treatment, and special treatment or reactions of controls.

Aside from evaluating the internal validity of an experiment, it is important to understand the extent to which the findings can be generalized to populations, settings, measures, experimenters, and other circumstances than those used in the original investigation. The generality of the results is referred to as the external validity. Although the findings of an investigation could be limited to any particular condition or arrangement unique to the demonstration, a number of potential limitations to the generality of the results can be identified. These potential limitations are referred to as threats to external validity and include characteristics of the sample, the stimulus conditions or setting of the investigation, reactivity of experimental arrangements, multiple-treatment interference, novelty effects, reactivity of assessments, test sensitization, and timing of measurement.

Internal and external validity address central aspects of the logic of experimentation and scientific research more generally. The purpose of research is to structure the situation in such a way that inferences can be drawn about the effects of the variable of interest (internal validity) and to establish relations that extend beyond the highly specific circumstances in which the variable was examined (external validity). A natural tension often arises in attempts to meet these objectives. Occasionally, the investigator arranges the experiment in ways to increase the likelihood of ruling out threats to internal validity. In the process, somewhat artificial circumstances may be introduced (videotapes to present the intervention, scripts that are memorized or read to the subjects). This means that the external validity may be threatened. The purposes of the investigation, both short- and long-term, ought to be clarified before judging the extent to which the balance of threats is appropriate. Sometimes external validity is not a major concern, especially in the context of testing theoretical predictions to determine whether something can occur under even rather special circumstances. The next chapter turns to the notions of construct and statistical conclusion validity and then discusses the interrelations and priorities of all four kinds of validity.

KEY CONCEPTS AND TERMS

External Validity

Internal Validity

Reactivity

Threats to Validity (and each of the threats)

FOR FURTHER READING

Anderson, C.A., Lindsay, J.J., & Bushman, B.J. (1999). Research in the psychological laboratory: Truth or triviality? *Current Directions in Psychological Science, 8,* 3–9.

Case, L., & Smith, T.B. (2000). Ethnic representation in a sample of the literature of applied psychology. *Journal of Consulting and Clinical Psychology, 68,* 1107–1110.

Cook, T.D., & Campbell, D.T. (Eds.) (1979). *Quasi-experimentation: Design and analysis issues for field settings.* Chicago: Rand McNally.

Council of National Psychological Associations for the Advancement of Ethnic Minority Interests (2000). *Guidelines for research in ethnic minority communities.* Washington, DC: American Psychological Association.

Mook, D.G. (1983). In defense of external invalidity. *American Psychologist, 38,* 379–387.

Reichardt, C.S., & Gollob, H.F. (1989). Ruling out threats to validity. *Evaluation Review, 13,* 3–17.

Shadish, W.R., Cook, T.D., & Campbell, D.T. (2002). *Experimental and quasi-experimental designs for generalized causal inference.* Boston: Houghton Mifflin.

Shadish, W.R. (1995). The logic of generalization: Five principles common to experiments and ethnographies. *American Journal of Community Psychology, 23,* 419–428.

Sue, S. (1999). Science, ethnicity, and bias: Where have we gone wrong? *American Psychologist, 54,* 1070–1077.

Chapter 3

Drawing Valid Inferences II

Construct and Statistical Conclusion Validity

CHAPTER OUTLINE

Construct Validity
> Threats to Construct Validity
>> Attention and Contact with the Clients
>> Single Operations and Narrow Stimulus Sampling
>> Experimenter Expectancies
>> Cues of the Experimental Situation
> General Comments

Statistical Conclusion Validity
> Overview of Essential Concepts
>> Statistical Tests and Decision Making
>> Effect Size
> Threats to Statistical Conclusion Validity
>> Low Statistical Power
>> Variability in the Procedures
>> Subject Heterogeneity
>> Unreliability of the Measures
>> Multiple Comparisons and Error Rates
> General Comments

Experimental Precision
> Holding Constant versus Controlling Sources of Variation
> Tradeoffs

Summary and Conclusions

Internal and external validity are fundamental to research and nicely convey the rationale for many methodological practices (use of control groups, random assignment) that are detailed in later chapters. Two other types of validity, referred to as construct validity and statistical conclusion validity, must also be addressed to draw valid inferences. These types of validity are no less central to research design. Yet, they are less familiar to researchers and consumers of research and reflect slightly more complex concepts and design considerations than do internal and external validity. They are also more likely to be neglected in the design of research. When studies are designed and when the findings are eventually written for publication, we as authors often praise ourselves if the concerns raised by internal validity have been carefully addressed. Our peers and those who evaluate research usually assume that internal validity threats are controlled, which is why being able to generate examples where the threats have been neglected is so surprising. The quality of a study often is judged on the extent to which construct and statistical conclusion validity issues are also addressed. Construct validity often addresses subtler-than-usual questions that guide research; statistical conclusion validity takes into account many factors about how well the study was conducted, well beyond "mere" statistical issues. (In retrospect, I can see now that I should never have said to my dissertation committee that I did not want my study to be bogged down with construct or statistical conclusion validity or, for that matter, control groups.) This chapter considers construct and statistical conclusion validity and the interrelations and priorities of the different types of validity. As in the previous chapter, the goal is to describe the nature of these types of validity and the threats they raise.

CONSTRUCT VALIDITY

Construct validity has to do with interpreting the basis of the causal relation demonstrated in an investigation. The meaning requires careful delineation of construct from internal validity. Internal validity, as you recall, focuses on whether an intervention or experimental manipulation is responsible for change or whether other factors (history, maturation, testing) can plausibly account for the effect. Assume for a moment that these threats have been successfully ruled out by randomly assigning subjects to treatment and control groups, by assessing both groups in the same way and at the same time, and so on. We can presume now that the group differences are not likely to have resulted from the threats to internal validity but rather to the intervention. It is at this point that the discussion of construct validity can begin. What *is* the intervention, and why did it produce the effect? *Construct validity* addresses the presumed cause or the explanation of the causal relation between the intervention or experimental manipulation and the outcome. Is the reason for the relation between the intervention and behavior change due to the construct (explanation, interpretation) given by the investigator? For example, let us say that an experiment shows that psychotherapy is better than no treatment in reducing anxiety. Why did this difference occur? What was responsible for the superiority of treatment versus no treatment? The answer to these questions focuses specifically on construct validity.[1]

---

[1]Construct validity is a more familiar term in the context of test development and validation (Braun, Jackson, & Wiley, 2000). An investigator may develop a psychological test to measure anxiety. Several types of studies are completed to establish the construct validity, that is, that it is anxiety that the scale measures, rather than some other construct (intelligence, deviance, honesty, altruism) (see Chapter 13). Thus, in the use of test development, construct validity refers to the explanation of the measure or the dimension that it assesses. In a parallel way, construct validity of an experiment refers to the explanation of the findings (see Cook & Campbell, 1979).

Several features within the experiment can interfere with the interpretation of the results. These are often referred to as *confounds*. We say an experiment is confounded or that there is a confound to refer to the possibility that a specific factor varied (or co-varied) with the intervention. That confound could, in whole or in part, be responsible for the results. Some component other than the one of interest to the investigator might be embedded in the intervention and account for the findings.

For example, consider a familiar finding about the effects of moderate amounts of wine on health. Consuming a moderate amount of wine (one or two glasses with dinner) is associated with increased health benefits (e.g., reduced risk of heart attack). In studies of this relation, consumption of wine is the variable of interest. The basic test comes from a two-group comparison, namely, those who consume a moderate amount of wine and those who do not. Assume for the moment that threats to internal validity are ruled out. Alas, the findings indicate consuming a moderate wine is associated with health benefits. The construct validity question is, "Yes, but is it the consumption of wine or something else?" For example, maybe people who drink wine are generally more mellow and easy going (even without the wine), more social, and less obese than nonwine drinkers. Indeed, maybe while wine drinkers are sipping wine, their nonwine drinking controls are stuffing themselves with nacho chips and cheese and watching television. That is, wine drinking may be confounded with diet or some other variable(s), and these other variables, rather than the wine drinking, may account for the finding. Thus, we say, "Yes, the finding is correct insofar as the wine-drinking group may be healthier and threats to internal validity are not plausible. But what is the variable 'wine drinking'?" It may be a package of characteristics, and the wine part may not be related to heart disease and mortality from other causes. It makes a huge difference in knowing the answer. If it is not wine drinking, encouraging people to drink may have no impact on heart disease and health more generally and, indeed, may even have some deleterious side effects associated with increased alcohol consumption. This question and similar concerns here pertain to construct validity.

In passing, the benefits of drinking moderate amounts of wine seem to hold—that is, wine plays a role. But wine drinking is associated with (confounded by) other characteristics. People who drink wine, compared to those who drink beer and other alcohol (spirits), tend to live healthier life styles and to come from higher socioeconomic classes (Wannamethee & Sharper, 1999). They tend to smoke less, to have lower rates of obesity, and to be lighter drinkers (total alcohol consumption). Each of these characteristics is related to mortality. Controlling these other factors reduces, but does not eliminate, the contribution that wine makes to lower mortality rate. (Only because of these research findings, guess what I am sipping while I ~~right~~ write this?)

The comments here are helpful in making another point. Methodology and statistics are often taught independently from substantive issues. That is, they are presented as tools to accomplish a task. As illustrated throughout the book, methodology and statistics are embedded in, central to, and influence substantive findings. In the case of the wine example, the construct validity question is not about methodology alone, but about understanding the independent variable—and this is what theory, hypotheses, and predictions are about. In research it is invariably useful for the investigator to ask, "What might be going on here to cause the effects I am observing or predicting? Is there any way I can isolate the influence more precisely than gross comparisons of groups?" The gross comparison of groups (e.g., wine drinkers versus nondrinkers) is an excellent point of departure, but only a beginning in the effort to understand.

Back to construct validity. In one's own studies (and even more so in everyone else's studies!) it is meaningful to challenge the findings with the questions, "What is the intervention?" and "Does the intervention include other components than those discussed by the investigator?" Those features associated with the intervention that interfere with drawing inferences about the basis for the difference between groups are referred to as *threats to construct validity*.

Threats to Construct Validity

Construct validity illustrates and exemplifies the connections between methodology and substantive questions. That is, the reason why the independent variable has an effect raises fundamental questions about the construct the variable is designed to reflect. The independent variable may be a package of factors that ought to be broken down into components. Maybe the independent variable (wine drinking) is a proxy (stands for) a bunch of characteristics that go together (all sorts of healthful behaviors). Theory and research often focus on evaluating such characteristics, their relative contribution, and how they are related to each other and to some outcome of interest (health, adjustment). One cannot identify all the competing constructs that might be pertinent to explain a finding. Yet, a number of factors emerge in research that can have a pervasive influence in many different areas of research. These are threats to construct validity.

Attention and Contact with the Clients.   Attention and contact accorded the client in the experimental group or differential attention across experimental and control groups may be the basis for the group differences and threaten construct validity. The intervention may have exerted its influence because of the attention provided, rather than because of special characteristics unique to the intervention. A familiar example from psychiatric research is the effect of placebos in the administration of medication. Suppose investigators provide a drug for depression to some patients and no drug to other patients. Assume further that groups were formed through random assignment and that the threats to internal validity were all superbly addressed. At the end of the study, patients who had received the drug are greatly improved and significantly different from those patients who did not receive the drug. The investigator may then discuss the effect of the drug and how this particular medication affects critical biological processes that control symptoms of depression. We accept the *finding* that the intervention was responsible for the outcome (internal validity). Yet, on the basis of construct validity concerns, we may not accept the *conclusion*.

The intervention consists of all aspects associated with the administration of the medication in addition to the medication itself. We know that taking any drug might decrease depression because of expectancies for improvement on the part of the patients and on those administering the drug. Merely taking a drug and undergoing treatment, even if the drug is not really medication for the condition, can lead to improvement. This is called a *placebo effect*. A *placebo* is a substance that has no active pharmacological properties that would be expected to produce change for the problem to which it is applied. A placebo might consist of a pill or capsule that is mostly sugar (rather than antidepressant medication) or an injection of saline solution (salt water) rather than some active medication for the problem of interest. Placebo effects are "real," powerful, and important. They are studied in research and used clinically to make people better (Spiro, 1998). For example, medications for depression are effective (lead to recovery, significantly reduce symptoms) in approximately 50–60 percent of the adult patients; placebos are effective for 30–35 percent of the patients (Agency for Health Care Policy and Research, 1999). While research supports the superiority of active medication to placebos, the potency of placebo effects is dramatic. In general, expectancies for improvement can exert marked therapeutic effects on a variety of psychological and medical dysfunctions (Shapiro & Shapiro, 1998; Spiro, 1998). In relation to construct validity, expectancies for improvement generated by placebos must be controlled if an investigator wishes to draw conclusions about the specific effects of the intervention (medication, psychotherapy).

To examine the basis for the effects (construct validity), it would be essential to include a third group that received a placebo on the same schedule of administration. A placebo might be a pill, capsule, or tablet of the same size and shape and perhaps share other characteristics of the active medication. These other characteristics may try to mimic taste of the medication and even some of the side effects (dry mouth, blurred vision, nausea, sleep disruption). Occasionally, the placebo is a real medication that is inert or not effective in relation to the problem of interest. This is not a contradiction; a placebo is defined as a substance that is inert with respect to the symptoms or disorder being treated. The purpose of using a medication rather than an inert substance is to produce some side effects and provide a more convincing placebo control group. An active medication conveys to patients and staff that the person is in a medication condition. (Until later in the book, let us leave aside ethical issues raised by all of this.) But as for findings, active placebos (with some side effects) produce even more potent effects than the placebos that are totally inert substances (Kirsch & Sapirstein, 1998).

Placebo effects are not merely reactions in the patients. Those who administer the drug (physicians or nurses) can exert influence in patient responses by their expectations and comments. Consequently, physicians and nurses as well as patients ought to be naive ("blind") to the conditions (medication or placebo) to which patients are assigned. This is sometimes referred to as a *double-blind study* because both parties (e.g., staff, patients) are naive with regard to who received the real drug.[2] (The word

---

[2]Sometimes the concept of a triple-blind study is used, in which case the subjects, doctors who administer the drugs, and those who oversee the study (e.g., experimenters who monitor drug administration, or investigators responsible for the study) do not know precisely which subjects receive the medication. Which subjects are to receive the medication or placebo is coded (by patient number, "drug" number for that day), and these codes are stored. When all the results are in and no bias can be conveyed through interactions with the subjects or the doctors, the codes are revealed so the data can be analyzed. (I think the reader would want to know that among the innovations of my dissertation was the use of a quadruple-blind procedure where no one—and I mean no one—knew what condition anyone received. This meant that I could never decide who was in the intervention or control group and hence could not make statistical comparisons. I liked the innovation because it eliminated all sorts of potential biases, maybe even some that have not been invented yet. My dissertation committee thought the inability to report any results was too large a price to pay.)

masked is sometimes used to replace *blind* to eschew any reference to visual impairment. However, use of blind and double blind in the medication and methodology literature and their databases is still much more pervasive. Consequently, blind is retained here.) The goal of using a placebo, of course, is to ensure that expectations for improvement might be constant between drug and placebo groups. With a placebo control group, attention and contact with the client and expectations about clients on the part of experimenters become less plausible constructs to explain the effects the investigator wishes to attribute to the medication.

In a somewhat parallel fashion, treatment and no treatment are often compared in psychotherapy research. The treatment may, for example, focus on cognitive processes (negative self-statements, attributions of helplessness) that the investigator believes to be critical to therapeutic change. Assessment completed after treatment may reveal that the treatment group is significantly better than the no-treatment group on various outcome measures. If the investigator explains the finding as support for the importance of altering cognitions or using this particular treatment, there is a construct validity problem. We must question whether there are plausible features associated with the intervention that ought to be ruled out.

In fact, the treatment and no-treatment groups differ on several characteristics. The treated subjects, but not the untreated subjects, received regular meetings with a therapist, some palpable effort to improve their problems. No doubt participating in a treatment—any treatment perhaps—generates stronger expectations for improvement than not participating in treatment. Might these differences plausibly account for the benefits attributed to the treatment? Some writers about psychotherapy answer affirmatively (Eysenck, 1995; Frank & Frank, 1991); in addition, evidence suggests that when control subjects are led to expect improvement, they often improve whether they received a veridical treatment or not (Bootzin, 1985). Hence, if the investigator wishes to explain the findings in terms of specific mechanisms or processes of the treatment (changes in cognitions, therapeutic alliance), attention and expectations associated with the treatment ought to be controlled, or measures of these processes ought to be obtained in the study and shown to be a plausible cause of the change. Otherwise, these other constructs could plausibly explain the findings. I shall discuss this further when control groups are examined in Chapter 7.

In general, there is a threat to construct validity when attention, contact with the subjects, and their expectations might plausibly account for the findings and were not controlled or evaluated in the design. A design that does not control for these factors is not necessarily flawed. The intention of the investigator, the control procedures, and the specificity of the conclusions the investigator wishes to draw determine the extent to which construct validity threats can be raised. If the investigator presents the *findings* as the therapy group led to a better outcome than the control group, we cannot challenge that. If the investigator wishes to *conclude* why the intervention achieved its effects, attention and contact ought to be ruled out as rival interpretations of the results. Attention and participation generate expectations for improvement, and these expectations serve as a parsimonious explanation of the results. Expectations are parsimonious because the construct provides an explanation of the effects of many studies in which treatment (some form of psychotherapy or medication) is better than a control condition.

Single Operations and Narrow Stimulus Sampling.   Attention and contact with the client and the expectations they engender are not the only features that can threaten construct validity. Sometimes an experimental manipulation or intervention includes features that the investigator considers as irrelevant to the study, but these features may introduce ambiguity in interpreting the findings. The construct validity is the same as we have discussed so far, namely, was the intervention (as conceived by the investigator) responsible for the outcome, or was it some seemingly irrelevant feature with which the intervention was associated?

For example, two different treatments might be compared. Let us say we recruit therapists who are experts in treatment A to administer that treatment and other therapists skilled in treatment B to administer that treatment. Thus, different therapists provide the different treatments. This is reasonable because we may wish to use experts who practice their special techniques. At the end of the study, assume that therapy A is better than B in the outcome achieved with the patient sample. Because therapists were different for the two treatments, we cannot really separate the impact of therapists from treatment. We might say that treatment A was better than treatment B. Yet, a colleague who suffers from OCMD (Obsessive-Compulsive Methodological Disorder) and is overly concerned with construct validity might propose that therapists who administered treatment A may have simply been much better therapists than those who administered treatment B and that therapist competence may account for the results. The confound of treatment with therapists raises a significant ambiguity. Another way of saying this is to describe the independent variable. The investigator pitched the study to us as treatment A vs. treatment B, but our OCMD colleague cogently points out that the study really examined treatment-A-as-practiced-by-therapist-team 1 versus treatment-B-as-practiced-by-therapist-team 2. As with any other threat, the plausibility of considering this as a competing interpretation is critical. During the study the investigator may collect data to show that somehow therapists were equally competent (in adhering to their respective treatments, in training and initial skill, and in warmth). Equivalence on a set of such variables can help make the threat to construct validity less plausible. Even so, some overall difference—including therapist competence—that is not assessed might, in a given study, continue to provide a plausible threat to construct validity.

A more subtle variation may emerge as a threat to construct validity. Say we are comparing two treatments and we use one therapist. This therapist provides both treatments and sees clients in each of the treatment conditions. At the end of the investigation suppose that one treatment is clearly more effective than the other. The investigator may wish to discuss how one technique is superior and explain on conceptual grounds why this might be expected. We accept the finding that one intervention was more effective than the other. In deference to construct validity we ask, what *is* the intervention? The comparison consisted of this therapist giving treatment A versus this same therapist giving treatment B. One might say that the therapist was "held constant" because he or she was used in both groups. But it is possible that this particular therapist was more credible, comfortable, competent, and effective with one of the techniques than with the other. Perhaps the therapist believed in the efficacy of one technique more than another, performed one technique with greater enthusiasm and fidelity than the other, or aroused patients' greater expectancies for improvement with one of the techniques. The differential effects of treatment could be due to the interaction of the therapist × treatment, rather than a main effect of treatment. The study yields somewhat ambiguous results because the effect of the therapist was not separable in the design or data analyses from the different treatment conditions.

The history of psychotherapy outcome research provides many examples where one therapist has administered two or more treatments (Ellis, 1957; Lazarus, 1961; Shapiro, 1989). In these cases the more or most effective treatment was the one developed by the therapist/investigator and predicted to be more effective. We tend to be skeptical of the results until they are replicated because the particular therapist in combination with one of the treatments (therapist × treatment effect) may have been responsible for the effects, rather than the treatment alone. Our skepticism is based on the concern that therapists of a particular conceptual persuasion are more likely to achieve effects favoring their treatment (Luborsky et al., 1999). Our skepticism is reduced if the results are replicated. We use two or more therapists or experimenters in a single investigation to see if an effect is "replicated" across stimulus conditions. And, of course, replications across different investigators and settings bolster our confidence in the finding even more. When replications show similar effects, the plausibility that a particular therapist contributed the effects is reduced.

In general, construct validity could be improved by sampling across a wider range of conditions associated with treatment delivery (i.e., therapists and experimenters) so the effects of treatment can be evaluated in the design. Two or more therapists could be included; each would administer both treatments. At the end of the study the impact of therapists could be separated from the impact of treatment (e.g., in an analysis of variance). If the effectiveness of treatment varied between the therapists, this could be detected in the statistical interaction (treatment × therapist) term.

Consider, as another example, a laboratory experiment designed to evaluate opinions held about mental illness. The purpose is to see if people evaluate the personality, intelligence, and friendliness of others differently if they believe these other persons have been mentally ill. College students serve as subjects and are assigned randomly to one of two conditions. In the experimental condition the students see a slide of a 30-year-old man. They then listen to a tape that describes him as holding a factory job, and living at home with his wife and two children. The description also includes a passage noting that the man has been mentally ill, experienced strange delusions, and was hospitalized two years ago. In the control condition, students see the same slide and hear the same description except for those passages that talk about mental illness and hospitalization. At the end of the tape, subjects rate the personality, intelligence, and friendliness of the person in the slide. Alas, the hypothesis is supported—subjects who heard the mental illness description showed greater rejection of the person than did subjects who heard the description without reference to mental illness.

The investigator wishes to conclude that the content of the description that focused on mental illness is the basis for the group differences. After all, this is the only feature that distinguished experimental and control groups. Yet, there is a construct validity problem here. The use of a single case in the slide (the 30-year-old man) is problematic. It is possible that rejection of the mental illness description occurred because of special characteristics of this particular case presented on the slide. The difference could be due to the manipulation of the mental illness description or to the interaction of this description with characteristics of this case. We would want slides of different persons varying in age, sex, and other characteristics so that mental illness status could be separated from the specific characteristics of the case. Even two slides rather than one would make a rather large difference for improving the methodology of this study. With two slides the investigator could show with data analyses that the slide does not make a difference (assuming that it does not). That is, the effect of the experimental manipulation does not depend on unique characteristics of the case description. In general, it is important to represent the stimuli in ways so that potential irrelevancies (the case, unique features of the task) can be separated from the intervention or variable of interest. Without separating the irrelevancies, the conclusions of the study are limited (Maher, 1978a).

The use of a narrow range of stimuli and the limitations that such use imposes sound similar to external validity. They are. Sampling a narrow range of stimuli as a threat can apply to both external and construct validity. If the investigator wishes to *generalize* to other stimulus conditions (other therapists or types of cases in the above two examples, respectively), then the narrow range of stimulus conditions is a threat to *external validity*. To generalize across stimulus conditions of the experiment requires sampling across the range of these conditions, if it is plausible that the conditions may influence the results (Brunswik, 1955). If the investigator wishes to *explain why* a change occurred, then the problem is one of *construct validity* because the investigator cannot separate the construct of interest (treatment or types of description of treatment) from the conditions of its delivery (the therapist or case vignette).

As this example shows, the same problem in a study may serve as a threat to more than one type of validity. I have discussed narrow stimulus sampling as one example. Some problems (e.g., attrition) serve as threats to all types of validity. Also, the types of validity themselves are not all mutually exclusive. Construct and external validity, for example, can go together, and which one to invoke in evaluating a study has to do with the particular conclusion one wishes to make or to challenge. In the previous example, if the investigator wishes to say that the description led to the change, the skeptic can cogently say, "I don't think so because of construct validity." If the investigator wishes to say that the findings apply to adults in general (women, the elderly, different ethnicities), the skeptic can cogently say, "I don't think so because of external validity."

Experimenter Expectancies.   In both laboratory and clinical research, it is quite possible that the expectancies, beliefs, and desires about the results on the part of the experimenter influence how the subjects perform.[3] The effects are sometimes re-

---

[3]For purposes of discussion, we shall consider the *investigator* as the person who has responsibility for planning and designing the study and the *experimenter* as the person who is actively running the subjects and carrying out the procedures. This distinction is helpful despite the fact that the investigator and experimenter are occasionally the same person and that multiple persons in a project may vary in the extent to which they share these roles. We focus here on the experimenter to emphasize the person in direct contact with the subjects.

ferred to as *unintentional expectancy effects* to emphasize that the experimenter may not do anything on purpose to influence subjects' responses. Depending on the experimental situation and experimenter–subject contact, expectancies may lead to changes in tone of voice, posture, facial expressions, delivery of instructions, and adherence to the prescribed procedures and hence influence how participants respond. Expectancy effects are a threat to construct validity if they provide a plausible rival interpretation of the effects otherwise attributed to the experimental manipulation or intervention.

Expectancy effects received considerable attention in the mid-1960s, primarily in the context of social psychological research (Rosenthal, 1966, 1976). However, it is not difficult to imagine their impact in clinical research. In treatment research the expectancy effects might be suspected in situations where the experimenter has a strong investment in the outcome and has contact with subjects in various treatment and control conditions. For example, in therapy outcome studies cited earlier, the treatment invented by the investigator surpassed the effectiveness of other conditions to which that treatment was compared. In each case the investigator served as the therapist for all conditions. It is plausible that expectancies of the investigator might be quite different for the treatments and perhaps these were conveyed to the individuals during the course of treatment or assessment. Expectancies might be much less plausible if the treatment preferred by the investigator were less effective than one of the other treatments. Yet, because the investigator served as experimenter and had direct and sole contact with the subjects and because the findings were perfectly consistent with the investigator's preferences, expectancy as a possible threat to construct validity cannot be easily dismissed. We would very much want to see the study replicated with more and different therapists and perhaps even assess therapist expectancies at the beginning of the study to see if these predicted therapeutic changes in the clients.

The notion of *experimenter expectancies*, as a threat to validity, is infrequently invoked for at least two reasons. First, both the construct and the ways through which it achieves its effects are unclear. Second and related, more parsimonious interpretations than expectancies can be invoked. For example, differential adherence of the experimenter to the conditions or changes in the measurement criteria if therapist ratings were used to assess the outcome (treatment × instrumentation) might explain why two conditions differ in their effects. Nevertheless, in a given situation, expectations on the part of the experimenter may plausibly serve as a source of ambiguity and threaten the construct validity of the experiment.

Cues of the Experimental Situation.   Cues of the situation refer to those seemingly ancillary factors associated with the intervention that may contribute to the results. These cues have been referred to as the *demand characteristics* of the experimental situation (Orne, 1962). Demand characteristics include sources of influence such as information conveyed to prospective subjects prior to their arrival to the experiment (rumors about the experiment, information provided during subject recruitment), instructions, procedures, and any other features of the experiment. These other features may seem incidental, but they may lead to changes or results that the investigator mistakenly attributes to the experimental manipulation.

The influence of cues in the experiment distinct from the independent variable was dramatically illustrated in a study that examined the role of demand characteristics in a sensory deprivation experiment (Orne & Scheibe, 1964). Sensory deprivation consists of minimizing as many sources of sensory stimulation as possible for the subject. Isolating individuals from visual, auditory, tactile, and other stimulation for prolonged periods has been associated with distorted perception, visual hallucinations, inability to concentrate, and disorientation. These reactions usually are attributable to the physical effects of being deprived of sensory stimulation. Orne and Scheibe suggested that cues from the experimental situation in which sensory deprivation experiments are conducted might contribute to the reactions. That is, the cues themselves might evoke or foster precisely those reactions mistakenly attributed to deprivation. This is an interesting hypothesis, but testing it requires separating real sensory deprivation from the cues associated with the deprivation.

Orne and Scheibe completed an experiment where subjects were exposed to the accouterments of the procedures of a sensory deprivation experiment but actually were not deprived of stimulation. Subjects received a physical exam, provided a short medical history, were assured that the procedures were safe, and were exposed to a tray of drugs and medical instruments conspicuously labeled "Emergency Tray." Of course, any of us would be alerted to all sorts of potential issues and problems with such procedures. (Indeed, in life one learns rather quickly that reassurances can have a meaning that is opposite from their face value. For example, a warning that "this will not hurt" often means that it will; and a comment from a friend that begins, "I do not want to criticize you, but. . . ." is a warning that a criticism is approaching at relativistic speeds; and, of course, a big one is when your partner says, "Before I say what I am about to say, I want you to know I love you very much. . . ." which usually means that a huge relationship issue is just around the corner.) In the Orne and Scheibe study, subjects were told to report any unusual visual imagery, fantasy, or feelings, difficulties in concentration, disorientation, or similar problems. They were informed that they were to be placed in a room where they could work on an arithmetic task. If they wanted to escape, they could do so by pressing a red "Emergency Alarm." In short, subjects were given a variety of cues to convey that strange experiences were in store.

The subjects were placed in the room with food, water, and materials for the task. No attempt was made to deprive subjects of sensory stimulation. They could move about, hear many different sounds, and work at a task. This arrangement departs from true sensory deprivation experiments in which the subjects typically rest, have their eyes and ears covered, and cease movement as much as possible. A control group in the study did not receive the cues preparing them for unusual experiences and were told they could leave the room by merely knocking on the window. At the end of the "isolation" period, the experimental group showed greater deterioration on a number of measures, including the report of symptoms characteristically revealed in sensory deprivation experiments. In this experiment the cues of the situation, when provided without any deprivation, led to reactions characteristic of deprivation studies. By implication the results suggest that in prior research, deprivation experiences may have played little or no role in the findings.

Demand characteristics can threaten the construct validity if it is plausible that extraneous cues associated with the intervention could explain the findings. The above demonstration conveys the potential impact of such cues. Whether these demand characteristics exert such impact in diverse areas of research is not clear. Also, in many areas of research, the independent variable may include cues that cannot be so easily separated from the portion of the manipulation that is considered to be crucial. For example, different variations of treatment or levels of an independent variable (high, medium, and low) may necessarily require different cues. Perhaps different demand characteristics are inherent to or embedded in different variations of the experimental manipulation. In such cases, it may not be especially meaningful to note that demand characteristics accounted for the results.

When several conditions provided to one group (treatment) differ from those provided to a control group (no-treatment), one might weigh the plausibility of demand characteristics as an influence. Perhaps an implicit demand conveys to control subjects that they are not expected to improve from one test occasion to another. That is, demand may not operate only on experimental subjects, but also may be in a direction of limiting changes that otherwise might occur in a control group. Presumably, if cues were provided to convey the expectation of no change for the control group, treatment and no-treatment differences might well be due to different demand characteristics between groups. The means of evaluating demand characteristics and ruling out their plausibility as explanations of the findings are discussed in Chapter 4.

General Comments

The discussion has noted common threats to construct validity. However, a complete list of construct validity threats cannot be provided. The reason is that the threats have to do with interpretation of the basis for the results of an experiment. Thus, theoretical views and substantive knowledge about how the experimental manipulation works or the mechanisms responsible for change are also at issue, apart from the issue of experimental confounds. The questions of construct validity are twofold: What *is* the intervention? and why did this intervention lead to change? The first question emphasizes the fact that the intervention may be confounded with other conditions that influence and account for the findings. The second question emphasizes the related issue of interpretation of what led the intervention to change performance. Here we do not speak of confound as much as better understanding of the mechanism, process, or theory to explain the change. The questions encompass construct validity because they affect interpretation of the basis of a given finding.

STATISTICAL CONCLUSION VALIDITY

Internal, external, and construct validity and their threats codify many of the concerns to which methodology is directed. The list of these concerns is long; what more can remain? Actually, a great deal. Assume we have designed our wonderful experiment to address the bulk of those threats already highlighted. Shall we find reliable (statistically significant) differences between the groups? Even if the intervention and control conditions really would produce differences in their outcomes, whether we find such differences depends on multiple considerations. *Statistical conclusion validity* refers to those facets of the quantitative evaluation that influence the conclusions we reach about the experimental condition and its effect.[4]

Statistical evaluation often is viewed and taught from two standpoints. The first of these pertains to understanding the tests themselves and their bases. This facet emphasizes what the tests accomplish and the formulae and derivations of the tests. The second and complementary facet pertains to the computational aspects of statistical tests. Here application of the tests to data sets, use of software, and interpretation of the findings are emphasized. Another facet might be considered as a superordinate level, namely, the role of statistical evaluation in relation to research design and other threats to validity. Statistical conclusion validity reflects this level of concern with quantitative evaluation and is often the Achilles' heel of research. Because this type of validity is often neglected when studies are planned and executed, statistical issues at this broader level, rather than the specific analyses selected, commonly undermine the quality of an investigation. Several facets of the results and statistical evaluation can obscure interpretation of the experiment. These are referred to as *threats to statistical conclusion validity*.

It is important to note at this point that the discussion makes critical assumptions that are not fully agreed on in science in general or psychological research in particular. The assumptions are that statistical tests and probability levels (alpha), at least as currently practiced, are a good and reasonable basis for drawing inferences. These assumptions are a matter of debate (see Schmidt, 1996; Thompson, 1996). Many of these issues will be addressed in Chapter 15. The present discussion skirts these issues in recognition of the fact that the bulk of research in psychology is based on drawing inferences from statistical evaluation. As such, common weaknesses of research can be identified under the rubric of statistical conclusion of validity.

Overview of Essential Concepts

Statistical Tests and Decision Making.   Before discussing the threats to validity, it is important to review a few of the essential concepts of statistical evaluation. As the reader well knows, in most psychological research, the conclusions in an experiment depend heavily on hypothesis testing and statistical evaluation. The *null hypothesis* H_0 specifies that there are "no differences" between groups (e.g., treatment versus control group). Statistical tests are completed to evaluate whether the differences that are obtained are reliable or beyond what one is likely to find due to chance fluctuations. We can reject the null hypothesis of no difference if we find a statistically significant

---

[4]Statistical conclusion validity is a term the reader ought to know and use as a category for classifying the threats related to quantitative data evaluation (Cook & Campbell, 1979; Shadish et al., 2002). The term is reasonable because the vast majority of psychological research uses statistics to make inferences about the impact of an experimental condition or manipulation. A preferable term, from my perspective, would be *data evaluation validity*, because not all data evaluation in psychology is based on inferential statistics. Two examples discussed later include qualitative research and single-case experimental designs, methodologies that depart from the usual group research used in psychology. In these methodologies statistical evaluation can be, but usually is not, used to draw inferences from the data.

difference, or accept this hypothesis if we do not. The rejection and acceptance of hypotheses are weighty topics, only part of which we can treat here. The decision-making process is based on selecting a probability level that specifies the degree of risk of reaching a false conclusion. If the statistical difference between groups surpasses this probability level, we state that the difference is reliable and represents an effect of the intervention. If the difference fails to pass the threshold, we say that the difference is not statistically significant and that the groups are not different.

Figure 3.1 notes the outcomes of an investigation based on the conclusions we might draw from statistical evaluation. The four cells represent the combination of *our decision* (there is a difference versus there is no difference) and the *true state of affairs in the world* (there really is a difference, or there is no difference). Our goal in experimentation is to draw conclusions that reflect the true state of affairs in the world. That is, if there is a difference (e.g., in means) between two or more conditions (i.e., if the intervention is truly effective), we wish to reflect that in our decision (Cell B). If there is no difference between the conditions in the world, we would like to conclude that as well (Cell C). Occasionally, there is a clear effect in our study, when in fact there really is no effect in the world (Cell A), or no effect in our study, when in fact there is one in the world (Cell D). We specify our probability level (alpha) as the criterion for our decision making, that is, concluding the difference we obtain is significant. By doing so, we also fix the risk of concluding erroneously that there is a

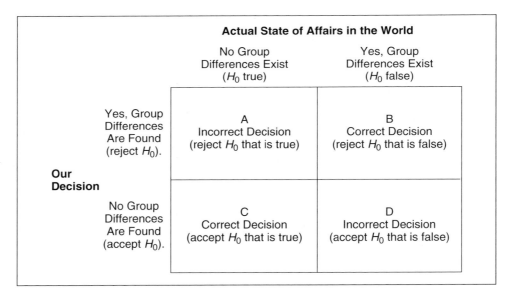

	Actual State of Affairs in the World	
	No Group Differences Exist (H_0 true)	Yes, Group Differences Exist (H_0 false)
Yes, Group Differences Are Found (reject H_0).	A Incorrect Decision (reject H_0 that is true)	B Correct Decision (reject H_0 that is false)
No Group Differences Are Found (accept H_0).	C Correct Decision (accept H_0 that is true)	D Incorrect Decision (accept H_0 that is false)

Our Decision

FIGURE 3.1. A 2×2 matrix that conveys the decisions we reach based on our statistical evaluation of the results and in relation to the true state of affairs in the world. If H_0 (the null hypothesis) is true, there really are no group differences in the world. If H_0 is false, there really are group differences. (The cells have other names as discussed in the text.) In particular, it is worth noting here that Cell A is also known as alpha (α) or Type I error; Cell D is known as beta (β) or Type II error.

TABLE 3.1.   Important Concepts in Relation to Statistical Conclusion Validity

Concept	Definition
Alpha (α)	The probability of rejecting a hypothesis (the null hypothesis) when that hypothesis is true. This is also referred to as a Type 1 error (Cell A).
Beta (β)	The probability of accepting a hypothesis (the null hypothesis) when it is false. This is also referred to as a Type II error (Cell D).
Power	The probability of rejecting the null hypothesis when it is false or the likelihood of finding differences between conditions when, in fact, the conditions are truly different. This probability is $1 - \beta$ (Cell B).
Effect size	A way of expressing the difference between conditions (e.g., treatment vs. control) in terms of a common metric across measures and across studies. The method is based on obtaining the difference between the means of interest on a particular measure and dividing this by the common (pooled) standard deviation.
Standard deviation	A measure of variation or variability about a mean. The standard deviation (also the square root of the variance) of a sample is given by the formula:

$$S = \sqrt{\frac{\Sigma(X_{i-n} - \overline{X})^2}{N - 1}} \quad \text{or} \quad \frac{SS}{df}$$

where X_{i-n} = individual observations of subjects i through n (all subjects)
$\overline{X}$ = mean of the sample
N = sample size
SS = sum of squared deviation
df = degree of freedom

difference when in fact there is none in the world, and of concluding that there is no difference when in fact there is. The cells in Figure 3.1 have well-established names that reflect critically important statistical concepts to refer to the decision-making process, outcomes of our experiment, and risk of reaching a false conclusion. Table 3.1 lists these and other concepts that we draw on later to elaborate the threats to statistical conclusion validity and to discuss statistical evaluation more generally.

Effect Size.   Among the concepts listed in Table 3.1, effect size is especially critical because it underlies several issues we shall consider. *Effect size* (*ES*) refers to the magnitude of the difference between two (or more) conditions or groups and is expressed in standard deviation units. For the case in which there are two groups in the study, effect size equals the differences between means, divided by the standard deviation:

$$ES = \frac{m_1 - m_2}{s}$$

where m_1 and m_2 are the sample means for two groups or conditions (e.g., treatment and control groups), and s equals the pooled standard deviation for these groups.

For example, in a two-group study that evaluates treatment for clients who worry excessively, assume clients are assigned to treatment or no-treatment conditions.

After the study, clients complete a measure (a happy-go-lucky scale) in which higher scores equal greater freedom from worry, a more relaxed attitude, and resignation to the stressors, hassles, and woes of life. Suppose that treated subjects show a post-treatment mean of 16 on the scale, whereas control subjects show a score of 10. That is, the treated subjects have a higher happy-go-lucky score. We shall also suppose that the standard deviation is 8. Effect size equals .75 (derived from 16 minus 10 divided by 8). This means that in standard deviation units, the mean of the treatment group was .75 higher than the mean of the control group.

Effect size is often assumed to reflect the magnitude of the difference, as that difference exists in nature. Thus, if an investigator is exploring a truly effective technique or variable, this will produce a marked effect size and statistically significant results. However, effect size is very much dependent on the design and methodology of the study. A poorly planned or executed study can produce small and nondetectable effects even when the effect size in nature is rather large. Flagrant methodological flaws, sloppiness, and error within the experiment—but also more subtle nuances related to heterogeneity of procedures, subjects, and conditions—can increase variation (the standard deviation) and dilute, diminish, and negate any differences between groups.

We can influence effect size by considering the relation between different levels of the variable of interest and the outcome and selecting those levels (very high versus very low) that are likely to show the greatest difference between groups. In testing a particular set of hypotheses, it is not only fine to select conditions that will maximize the likelihood of showing effects but also prudent to do so. With a very strong test, positive or negative results may then be more likely to be interpretable. For example, if we hypothesize that cholesterol is related to heart disease, we could compare two groups, individuals with "normal" levels versus individuals with slightly elevated levels of cholesterol, and examine the proportion of individuals who have heart disease. The effect size is likely to be lower, and a statistically significant difference (in heart disease) is more difficult to demonstrate, than if the study compared "normal" (or even low) levels and very elevated levels of cholesterol. Also, with logic that is often but not invariably correct, if really high levels of cholesterol produce no effect, then it is less likely that low levels will. (The logic depends in part on a linear relation between the variables, in this case cholesterol and heart disease. A linear relation happens to characterize the relation of cholesterol and heart disease, but such relations are not always the case.)

Assuming a given or fixed effect size in nature, we can do much to determine whether this is detected within our experiment. We can greatly influence the effect size obtained in our study by reducing variability in the procedures to minimize the error term (standard deviation) that is used in the effect size equation. Many efforts to control features of the experiment are designed to minimize "error" variance, that is, variability, in the formula for effect size. The larger the variability (denominator), the smaller the effect size for a constant difference between means (numerator).

Threats to Statistical Conclusion Validity

Low Statistical Power.   Central to statistical evaluation is the notion of statistical power, which refers to the extent to which an investigation can detect differences between groups when differences exist within the population (see Table 3.1). *Power* is the probability of rejecting the null hypothesis (i.e., there are no differences) when that hypothesis is false. Stated differently, power is the likelihood of finding differences between conditions when, in fact, the conditions are truly different in their effects. Certainly, if there is a difference between groups and if the intervention or experimental manipulation is effective, we wish to detect this difference in our statistical tests.

The central and probably most common threat to statistical validity in studies is relatively weak power or a low probability of detecting a difference if one truly exists. When power is weak, the likelihood that the investigator will conclude there are no differences between groups is increased. There might well be no differences in the world, and the intervention may in fact be no different in the effects it produces from those of a control condition. However, the conclusion of "no difference" might be due to low power, rather than to the absence of a difference between groups. The study must be designed so as to detect a difference if there is one.

Power is not an esoteric concept of relevance only to researchers in the confines of their studies, but can also influence decision making about practices that affect our daily lives and physical and mental health. For example, studies of treatments for cancer occasionally have been unable to demonstrate differences due to weak statistical power (see Freiman, Chalmers, Smith, & Kuebler, 1978). Indeed, a review of medical research for a variety of diseases and conditions revealed that over 25 percent of the published studies (from 1975–1990) surveyed revealed no differences between the treatments that were studied. In the majority of these studies power was very weak (Moher, Dulberg, & Wells, 1994). That is, there may have been treatment differences, but the power was insufficient to tell. While we are waiting for effective treatments for many types of cancer, we do not want to hear that viable treatments might work, but one could not tell because power was low within the studies! More central to clinical psychology, the majority of comparisons of different psychotherapy techniques show no differences in treatment outcome. Studies comparing two or more treatments have far too little power to detect "real" differences, given the relatively small samples and small effect sizes that characterize this research (Kazantzis, 2000; Kazdin & Bass, 1989). Unfortunately, weak power characterizes studies in many areas of research (Rossi, 1990; Sedlmeier & Gigerenzer, 1989). Weak power has broad implications insofar as it slows theoretical and empirical advances (by misguiding us in the conclusions that are reached) and utilizes resources (subject and investigator time, tax dollars from grants) that might be more wisely used elsewhere. There are ethical implications as well; is it ethical to subject participants to any procedures as part of an investigation if that investigation has very little likelihood of detecting a difference, even if there is one? Understandably, many funding agencies require that grant applications include estimates of power.

Statistical power of an experiment is a function of the criterion for statistical significance (alpha), the size of the sample (N), and the differences that exist between groups (effect size). The most straightforward method of increasing power is to increase sample size. Yet, this is not always possible. Fortunately, there are number of other options that I address in more detail in Chapter 15.

Variability in the Procedures.   The notion of effect size is useful as a way of introducing other threats to statistical conclusion validity. Consider, as a hypothetical experiment, a comparison of two treatments (A and B), which are administered to different groups. Ordinarily, effect size is considered to be a function of the true differences in the effects of these treatments. That is, if treatment A is more effective than treatment B in the "real world," this will be evident in our experiment and be shown in our statistical evaluation. Reconsider the formula for effect size. The denominator includes a measure of variability (standard deviation). Thus, whatever the outcome difference (on the dependent measures) between treatment A and B in our study, that difference will be influenced by variability in our experiment. This variability includes individual differences among the subjects, random fluctuations in performance on the measures, differences in experimenters or therapists in how they administer the intervention, and other sources, not all of which are easily specifiable.

Standard deviation (or the variance, which is the standard deviation squared) is a familiar statistical concept that harbors all sorts of influences. One source of variation has to do with how the interventions or experimental procedures are carried out. Ideally, the procedures will be held relatively constant and implemented in a way so as to minimize variation among subjects. This means that the procedures will be applied consistently and experimenters will be highly trained to administer the instructions and other procedures in a constant way. Rigor in the execution of the procedures is not a methodological nicety for the sake of appearance. Consistency in execution of the procedures has direct bearing on statistical conclusion validity. A given difference between groups may or may not be statistically significant or produce an effect size of a given magnitude. Variation cannot be eliminated, especially in relation to those aspects of research involving human participants (as subjects, clients, experimenters, therapists) and in settings outside of the laboratory. However, in any experiment, extraneous variation can be minimized by attention to details of how the study is actually executed. If variability is minimized, the likelihood of detecting a true difference between the treatments or treatment and control conditions is increased. In terms of our formula for effect size, the differences between groups will be divided by a measure of variability; this measure will be larger when there is more, rather than less, uncontrolled variation. The larger the variability, the lower the effect size evident for a given difference between groups.

Sometimes one can tell from the way an experiment is designed that there will be relatively high levels of variability and consequently great difficulty in demonstrating a difference between conditions. For example, several years ago, a now classic study compared behavior therapy and psychodynamically oriented psychotherapy for the treatment of adults who came for treatment (Sloane et al., 1975). Shortly after its appearance, this study was cited as one of the best therapy outcome studies by some authors (Bergin & Lambert, 1978; Marmor, 1975; Strupp, Hadley, & Gomes-Schwarz, 1977) and one of the worst studies by other authors (Bandura, 1978; Rachman & Wilson, 1980). Discrepancies this large certainly drew attention to the study. Clearly, the quite positive and negative evaluations focused on different aspects of the study. Among the praiseworthy components was the effort to test treatment with "real" patients, in a real clinic without many of the seeming artificialities of controlled research. Stated another way, the investigators gave the highest priority to external validity. The blameworthy components of the study pertained to internal validity (e.g., diffusion of treatment), construct validity (e.g., what each of the interventions was, sampling of therapists), and statistical conclusion validity, which I take up here.

Clients were assigned to behavior therapy, psychotherapy, or a waiting-list control. The way in which the two treatments were designed and implemented provided the opportunity for relatively large variability. Specifically, treatment guidelines were provided to behavior therapists ($n = 3$) and psychotherapists ($n = 3$). Each therapist was selected because of special expertise and considerable experience in the practice of one of the two approaches. Consequently, great latitude was given to what was done in the treatment sessions; therapists could treat the cases as they wished within these broad guidelines. In short, what they actually did in treatment varied greatly within a given condition. In seeing this feature of the design, one is immediately alerted that large within-group variability is likely. Such variability could diminish the obtained effect size and the likelihood of obtaining statistical significance between conditions. In an important sense, reading the methodology of the write-up conveyed that the results were not likely to show very much.

In general, the results showed few statistically significant differences in the outcomes between behavior therapy and psychotherapy. The findings led to some conceptual relief among psychotherapy researchers and practitioners. To the traditional therapists, psychodynamic therapy remained viable and seemed to be just as good as behavior therapy, which at the time was sort of the new kid on the block. To behavior therapists, the results were rather disappointing, but reaffirmed the effectiveness of an odd mix of behavioral interventions. Methodologists jumped out of their basement windows. Common features in the notes they left mentioned that the categories "behavior therapy" and "traditional therapy," as applied to diverse problems, did not constitute a real test of anything and that variability in how the study was run and low power undermined the demonstration.

It would be an oversimplification to state that this one aspect of the study, namely, high within-treatment variability led to no differences. First, there were other large sources of variation, including heterogeneous subject characteristics (very diverse clinical problems and a wide age range). Also, we do not know that high variability was responsible for no differences. Yet, the multiple sources of variability in how the study was designed (what defined the two treatments) and implemented (selection of cases, guidelines of treatment) make extremely plausible the rival hypothesis that low power would account for few or no differences. On the basis of the results we are hard pressed to tell whether the absence of differences is due to the equivalent effects of treatment or the manner in which the treatments were implemented. This latter point might always be raised in a study were few or no differences are found. However, the design of this study heightens the concern because variability, usually controlled by specifying and administering treatment in a relatively standardized way, was given rather free reign.

Subject Heterogeneity.   Subjects in an investigation can vary along multiple dimensions and characteristics such as sex, age, background, race and ethnicity, and marital status. In the general case, the greater the heterogeneity or diversity of subject characteristics, the less likelihood of detecting a difference between conditions.

Critical to the statement is the assumption that subjects are heterogeneous on a characteristic that is related to (or correlated with) the effects of the independent variable. For example, clients who are recruited for a psychotherapy study may vary widely (and "lengthily") in shoe size. Is this heterogeneity of great concern? Probably not. It is unlikely for most forms of psychotherapy that treatment effectiveness and performance on the outcome measures would be correlated with shoe size. On the other hand, clients may vary widely in their severity or duration of the clinical problem, socioeconomic class, and the presence of other problems (substance abuse, depression, chronic medical disease) not of interest in the study. The impact of treatment and performance on the dependent measures might well be influenced by these factors. That these factors influence outcome is not inherently problematic or undesirable. However, heterogeneity of the sample means that there will be greater variability in the subjects' reactions to the measures and to the intervention. This variability will be reflected in the denominator for evaluating effect size. As mentioned before, the greater that variability (denominator), the lower the effect size for a given difference between means (numerator) and the less likely the difference in means will be statistically significant.

Consider, as an example, treatment research in which individuals are recruited because they are depressed. Screening criteria are invoked to ensure that subjects meet criteria for a psychiatric diagnosis of major depression. Some of these subjects may also meet criteria for other psychiatric disorders as well (anxiety disorder, antisocial personality disorder). (*Comorbidity* is the term used to refer to instances when an individual meets criteria for two or more disorders.) One source of heterogeneity of the subjects is whether cases meet criteria for multiple disorders. At the end of a study treatment A may be compared with no treatment or another treatment, and the effects may appear weak or nonexistent (effect size is small or zero). One possible reason for this result might be that all subjects were considered as representing a single group that included both subjects with depression and those with depression and a comorbid disorder. Treatment may have worked only for the former; hence, including all subjects in one overall comparison will dilute the effect size. Variation among subjects in relation to comorbidity enters into the denominator as within-group variability and attenuates the likelihood of showing group differences. Although the example is stated hypothetically, treatment research has shown that individuals with comorbid disorders often respond less well to treatment than those without a comorbid disorder (Brown, Antony, & Barlow, 1995; Kazdin, 1995; Ryan et al., 1986).

Heterogeneity of the subjects, as a threat to statistical conclusion validity, can be addressed in different ways. The first, of course, is to choose homogeneous samples. Homogeneity is a matter of degree. One might wish to limit the age range, type of clinical problem, educational level, and other variables within some reasonable boundaries. Ideally, the decision of what variables to consider and how to limit the variation in the sample is based on theory or research on the effects of these and related variables on the measures of interest. If in doubt, one might select a relatively homogeneous set of subjects on diverse factors as a conservative way of addressing this threat.

A second alternative is to choose heterogeneous samples but to ensure that the impact or effect of selected subject characteristics can be evaluated in the design. For example, in the above hypothetical example, comorbidity could be taken into account in the analyses by evaluating the effects of treatment separately for cases with and without a comorbid disorder. More than one variable may be analyzed in this way if it makes sense to do so on conceptual grounds. For example, the data can be analyzed by including subjects of different ages and presence of a comorbid disorder. In the data analysis, the effects of age (above vs. below the median) and depression (with and without a comorbid disorder) are included as separate factors (e.g., in an analysis of variance or a regression analysis). When these factors are analyzed as separate effects, they no longer become within-group or error variance and do not serve to increase the denominator in evaluating treatment differences. In principle and practice, it is possible to analyze the data to death to explore an indefinite set of characteristics that might contribute to the results. Psychological studies typically have too few subjects to analyze very many factors, and such fishing expeditions have other problems (increase in the likelihood of chance findings). If a heterogeneous sample is selected, it is useful to begin the study with specific hypotheses about the subanalyses that will be completed to ensure that these subanalyses can be conducted with adequate power. I shall return to these points in Chapter 15.

Unreliability of the Measures.   Reliability refers to the extent to which the measures assess the characteristics of interest in a consistent fashion (and will be taken up again in chapters on assessment). Reliability is, of course, a matter of degree and refers to the extent of the variability in responding. Variability has many sources. One of them pertains to characteristics of the measure as applied to a particular population or sample. The measure may have characteristics that foster error or variability. Performance on the measure may vary widely from item to item within the measure because items are not equally clear or consistent in what they measure and hence performance may vary widely from occasion to occasion. To the extent that the measure is unreliable, a greater portion of the subject's score is due to unsystematic and random variation. Other variation not of interest for the moment is worth distinguishing nevertheless. Performance is variable from occasion to occasion as a function of mood, experience, context, and many other unspecifiable influences. Thus, even if a measure is perfectly reliable from internal analyses of the scale, as humans we are likely to respond differently to it from one occasion to the next because performance is multiply determined, and the measure is only one contributing factor. Even so, one wants to limit extra, unneeded, and unsystematic variation from the measure. This variation means that in statistical evaluation, relatively large variability can be introduced. In studies with relatively unreliable measures, the obtained effect size is likely to be lower. Selection of assessment devices in designing a study is more than a quick shopping trip to the literature (see Chapter 13). Selection of poorly designed measures in which reliability (and validity) are in doubt can threaten statistical conclusion validity.

It is useful to be wary in one's own research or the research of others about using measures that "seem" to get at the construct, that are homemade, that have no background evidence in their behalf, and that are used in ways that depart from the uses that have supporting data on the validity of the scale (with a sample quite different in age from the usual use, of a different ethnicity). More generally, we need to ask at the beginning of the investigation, "Is there any evidence that the measure is consistent internally?" This means that the items go together the way they are supposed to. If the scale measures one construct, trait, and characteristic, it is likely that the items ought to be interrelated. In addition, from one occasion to the next over at least a brief period, does performance behave on the measure the way one would expect? If the measure is a trait type of measure, one expects the relation (correlation) between time one and time two (e.g., spanning weeks or months) to be rather high. It is difficult here to give firm and fast rules because how a measure ought to behave depends on the construct it is supposed to measure. Some constructs are expected to be stable over time (traits, personality characteristics) and others less so (states, moods). The general point: An unreliable measure increases variability and can reduce power. Sometimes multiple measures can be combined statistically in an effort to devise a more stable estimate of the characteristic of interest. From a power standpoint this is a useful strategy.

Multiple Comparisons and Error Rates.   Not all of the threats to statistical conclusion validity pertain to variability. Statistical evaluation of the results can be hindered by other problems that directly influence whether the investigator concludes that groups differed. In an investigation several different measures are likely to be used to evaluate the impact of the intervention. For example, in a treatment study, the clients, clinician, and perhaps relatives of the clients are likely to complete a few measures (e.g., depression, symptoms in diverse areas, social functioning). At the end of the investigation, treatments A and B will be compared statistically on each of the measures.

    Some separate but interrelated problems reflect a threat to statistical conclusion validity. The main problem to note at this point pertains to the number of statistical tests that will be completed. The more tests that are performed, the more likely a chance difference will be found, even if there are no true differences between conditions. Thus, the investigator may conclude mistakenly that there is a difference between groups and that this is a true effect of the intervention (Type I error). The possibility of this occurring is evident in any experiment. The risk of such an error is specified by alpha or the probability level that is used as a criterion for statistical significance. Yet, this risk and its probability level apply to an individual test. When there are *multiple comparisons,* alpha is greater than .05, depending on the number of tests. The risk across several statistical tests, sometimes referred to as *experiment-wise error rate,* is much greater. The number of tests within a study can lead to misleading conclusions about group differences. At this point it is useful to note that multiple statistical tests serve as a threat to statistical conclusion. Strategies to address statistical issues and multiple comparisons within an experiment are discussed in Chapter 15.

General Comments

The threats to statistical conclusion validity refer to the features of the study that affect the quantitative evaluation of the results. When the threats are made explicit, they may appear obvious. Yet, they often serve as the tacit downfall of an experiment. Excellent ideas conducted in carefully controlled tests routinely have weak power, a topic we shall take up further. Perhaps even more pervasive is the hidden variability that can emerge in all facets of experimentation and can obscure differences between conditions.

The notion of experimental control, when first introduced into the discussion of research, is usually raised in the context of control groups and threats to internal validity. However, a deeper understanding of the notion of control stems in part from its relation to statistical conclusion validity. The control and evaluation of variability in research, to the extent possible, are critical. The initial question of interest in designing a study is, "Are the groups or conditions different?" This question emphasizes the means on some measure or set of measures. The next question is, "If there is a difference, will this study be able to detect it?" This latter question raises concerns over statistical conclusion validity. Whether a difference can be detected is influenced by several features of the design (subject selection, sample size) and procedures (implementation of the intervention, training of the experimenters or therapists). Many facets of research—including recruitment of subjects, preparation and delivery of experimental instructions, and methods of scoring and checking data—all become potential sources of uncontrolled variation and can introduce ambiguity into the results. Error and sloppiness each has its own consequences (as my dissertation committee was overly fond of stating), but they unite in a final common pathway of increased within-group variability. This variability dilutes the obtained effect size and diminishes the likelihood of statistical significance when there is a real effect to detect.

We have discussed variability and variation as if they were enemies. There is some sense in which this might be true, but great care is needed in making this point. The goal of our research is not to eliminate variability but rather to understand it, which means we wish to elaborate the full range of factors that influence affect, cognitions, behavior, personality, and other domains of interest. These factors include our interventions (e.g., a new treatment), those interventions of "nature" not under our experimental control (childhood experiences, past and present stress, and any historical and maturational influence), and individual differences (temperament, generic predisposition, and personality style). When any one or more of these serves as the focus of our study, we need to control other sources of variation because the source of variation that is of interest in our study may be obscured by allowing free fluctuation of all other sources of variation. Research design, various methodological practices, and statistical evaluation are tools that help to separate and evaluate these different sources of variation.

EXPERIMENTAL PRECISION

In the present and previous chapters we have covered internal, external, construct, and statistical conclusion validity. At the design stage all of the threats to validity ought to be considered. Not all of the problems that can interfere with valid inferences can be predicted or controlled in advance (e.g., loss of subjects over time). However, most can be addressed in planning the experiment and its execution. Also, even those that cannot be resolved in advance are worth considering at the design stage.

Addressing each type of validity, leaving aside all of their constituent threats, is not possible. The reason is that addressing one type of validity often compromises another type of validity. This is not really a problem. The problem emerges when an investigator gives more attention to one facet of validity that was probably of lower priority than another. For example, in the study (Sloane et al., 1975) cited earlier, comparing behavior therapy and psychotherapy, enormous attention was given to external validity. The investigators wanted to recruit "real" therapists and "real" patients and to take all comers, that is, virtually all patients coming to a clinic. The goal was to be able to generalize to a broad sample. This seems like such an apple pie, motherhood idea that who can criticize this? Hopefully, now you can. Actually, there is no criticism of the goals but rather some of the means elected to achieve them. Too many facets were allowed to vary so that within-group variability was likely to be large. In the design and execution of this study, there was such heterogeneity of the sample that within-group variability starts out rather high. If one wants to retain this feature of the study, all sorts of other sources of variability (treatment procedures, therapists) that could be controlled should be. In that study other sources were allowed to vary and hence the absence of statistical differences on most comparisons was fairly predictable. In one's own research it is not an idle exercise to consider, before a study, which threats are likely to haunt one when the study is completed. Of course, apart from considering the threats it is important to plan how to address them in the design or subsequent data analyses.

Holding Constant versus Controlling Sources of Variation

Threats to internal validity generally can be ruled out or made implausible as rival hypotheses by allocating subjects randomly to conditions and controlling potential sources of bias (e.g., instrumentation, diffusion of treatment) that might arise during the experiment. Yet, in designing experiments, researchers usually are interested in more than ruling out threats to internal validity; they also are interested in providing the most sensitive test of the independent variable possible. Maximizing the likelihood of detecting the relationship raises issues of statistical conclusion validity. The investigator wishes to minimize extraneous influences and sources of variation in how subjects respond in the experiment.

Increased precision is achieved by *holding constant* the potential sources of influence on subjects' behavior other than the independent variable. Conditions are held constant if they are identical or very close to that across subjects and experimental conditions. Of course, one cannot realistically expect to implement an experiment in which all conditions are the same except for the independent variable. To cite an obvious problem, all subjects in the study vary because of their differences in genetic make-up, childhood experiences, physical capabilities, intelligence, age, ethnic background, and familiarity with research. These factors and many others introduce some variation into the experiment in terms of how subjects respond to the intervention.

The manner in which the independent variable is implemented may introduce extraneous variation into the experiment. Ideally, the conditions of administration among subjects within a given condition would not vary at all. Some features of the experimental manipulation might be held constant, such as administering instructions or showing materials to the subjects by using audio or videotapes. If an experimenter interacts with the subjects, this interaction may vary slightly across different subjects; if several experimenters are used in the study, even greater variation may be introduced. Other extraneous factors of the experiment, such as the time of the day, weather, and how the independent variable is implemented all may contribute to sources of variation. These factors can be *controlled* by letting them vary unsystematically across groups. Control is achieved by dispersing these factors equally across groups by assigning subjects randomly to groups and by running subjects in each condition over the course of the experiment (instead of running all subjects in the experimental condition in the first half of the study then all subjects in the control condition in the second half of the study). These and other practices, discussed in later chapters, eliminate the bias such influences might exert. If there is no systematic bias with these sources of variation, the experiment is controlled. However, these factors can be *held constant,* which may even be better from the standpoint of demonstrating the relationship between the independent and dependent variables. By reducing or removing sources of variation, a more sensitive (powerful) test of the independent variable is provided.

Tradeoffs

At first glance it may seem that experimenters should automatically maximize the sensitivity of all experimental tests by making the experiment as precise as possible in terms of minimizing extraneous sources of variation. Yet, experimental precision has a potential cost, namely, limited generality of the experimental results. *As a general rule, design features that make an experiment more sensitive as a test of the independent and dependent variables tend to limit the generality of the findings. Conversely, features of an experiment that enhance generality of the results tend to increase variability and to decrease the sensitivity of the experimental test.*

Careful experimental control does not always restrict the generality of a finding in clinical research, but there seems to be a relationship so that a gain in either experimental precision or generality may be associated with a sacrifice in the other. Once a finding has been established through well-controlled and internally valid studies, research emphasis can extend to external validity. External validity is evaluated by systematically broadening samples of subjects, the types of settings in which treatment is administered, the variations of treatment that are attempted, and the types of measures and constructs used to evaluate outcome.

The relevance of research for clinical practice is a central concern in psychotherapy research. Salient among the issues is the fact that, in research, several practices are conducted to minimize variability, including selection of homogeneous subjects and therapists and careful control and monitoring of treatment administration. The investigator is wise to carry out these and related practices to provide a sensitive test. At the same time, the question is raised regarding the extent to which the effects, once demonstrated in well-controlled research, can be extended to situations in which many of the controls over variability are not easily carried out (Hoagwood & Hibbs, 1995). In other words, the control over the intervention and extraneous sources of variability (e.g., homogeneous subject sample) may bear a cost in terms of the external validity of the results. Conditions of tightly controlled research may deviate so markedly from the ordinary situation that the plausibility of producing generalizable findings is commensurately decreased. Research is required to address the matter by extending studies to these other situations and by evaluating their impact.

SUMMARY AND CONCLUSIONS

Construct validity pertains to interpreting the basis for the causal relation between the independent variable (intervention, experimental manipulation) and the dependent variable (outcome, performance). The intervention of interest may be one of many factors that distinguishes intervention and control conditions or two or more intervention conditions. The investigator may conclude that the intervention (e.g., some new and improved form of therapy) was responsible for change, but the study may not permit this conclusion because of other factors embedded in the intervention that alone, or in combination with the intervention, might account for the findings. Factors that may interfere with or obscure valid inferences about the reason for the effect are threats to construct validity. Major threats include attention and contact with the clients, single operations and narrow stimulus sampling, experimenter expectancies, and cues of the experimental situation.

Statistical conclusion validity refers to those aspects of the study that affect the quantitative evaluation and can lead to misleading or false conclusions about the intervention. Several concepts basic to statistical evaluation were mentioned because of their role in statistical conclusion validity. These concepts included the probability of accepting and rejecting the null hypothesis, the probability of making such decisions when they are false, and effect size. Major factors that commonly serve as threats to statistical conclusion validity operate by influencing one or more of these concepts and include low statistical power, variability in the procedures of an investigation, subject heterogeneity, unreliability of the measures, and multiple statistical comparisons and their error rates.

All four types of validity—internal, external, construct, and statistical conclusion validity—need to be considered at the design stage of an investigation. It is not possible in any one experiment to address all threats well or equally well, nor is this necessarily a goal toward which one should strive. Rather, the goal is to address the primary questions of interest in as thorough a fashion as possible so that clear answers can be provided for those specific questions. At the end of that investigation, new questions may emerge or questions about other types of validity may increase in priority. The need for further information is not necessarily a flaw, but rather the continued line of inquiry to which an important study invariably leads.

The obstacles in designing experiments emerge not only from the manifold types of validity and their threats, but also from the interrelations of the different types of validity. Factors that address one type of validity might detract from or increase vulnerability to another type of validity. For example, factors that address statistical conclusion validity might involve controlling potential sources of variation in relation to the experimental setting, delivery of procedures, and homogeneity of the subjects. In the process of maximizing experiment control and making the most sensitive test of the independent variable, the range of conditions included in the experiment becomes increasingly restricted. Restricting the conditions, such as the type of subjects or measures, and standardization of delivering the intervention or independent variable may commensurately limit the range of conditions to which the final results can be generalized.

In this and the previous chapter we have discussed different types of validity and their threats. The primary purpose has been to describe these threats and how they operate. In remaining chapters I raise several of these areas again and more concretely discuss strategies to address threats and to strengthen the inferences drawn from research.

KEY CONCEPTS AND TERMS

Construct Validity

Power

Effect Size

Statistical Conclusion Validity

Placebo Effect

FOR FURTHER READING

Lipsey, M.W. (1990). *Design sensitivity: Statistical power for experimental research*. Newbury Park, CA: Sage.

Schmidt, F.L. (1996). Statistical significance testing and cumulative knowledge in psychology: Implications for training of researchers. *Psychological Methods, 1*, 115–129.

Shadish, W.R., Cook, T.D., & Campbell, D.T. (2002). *Experimental and quasi-experimental designs for generalized causal inference*. Boston: Houghton Mifflin.

Wampold, B.E., Davis, B., & Good, R.H., III (1990). Hypothesis validity of clinical research. *Journal of Consulting and Clinical Psychology, 58*, 360–367.

Chapter 4

Sources of Artifact and Bias

CHAPTER OUTLINE

Sources of Bias
> Rationales, Scripts, and Procedures
> Experimenter Expectancy Effects
> Experimenter Characteristics
> Situational and Contextual Cues
> Subject Roles
> Data Recording and Analysis

Subject-Selection Biases
> The Sample: Who Is Selected for the Study?
> Attrition: Who Remains in the Study?

Summary and Conclusions

The threats to validity to research represent key concepts and serve as the reason why we design experiments rather than merely rely on opinions and unsystematic observations. The focus of the threats has been primarily on alternative interpretations of the results. Artifacts and biases in experimental research direct attention to specific practices and procedures within an experiment that can interfere with drawing inferences, that is, threaten the validity of an experiment. The specific practices convey more concretely how validity is threatened and what can be done in an experiment to limit the influence of artifact and bias.

An *artifact* or extraneous influence includes all those variables that the experimenter is not interested in examining. The factors that can give rise to conclusions in an experiment are virtually unlimited. Which ones are artifacts and biases depend upon the focus of the investigation. For example, one investigator may wish to study the effects of therapist beliefs on treatment efficacy and view beliefs as the independent variable. Another experimenter may be interested in the efficacy of different treatments and regard therapist beliefs as a potential source of artifact. Thus, a given source of influence may be viewed at times as an artifact and at other times as an independent variable.

Influences commonly identified as artifacts evolve through stages (McGuire, 1999). The first stage is *ignorance*. During this stage, investigators are unaware that an extraneous variable is operative in an experiment and may account for the results.

When such a source of artifact is posed, it may be denied. The next stage is *coping*. In this stage the existence and possible importance of the artifact are recognized. Investigators increasingly recognize the potential influence of the artifact in their experiments and implement control procedures to detect, estimate, reduce, or prevent its impact. The final stage is *exploiting* the source of artifact in its own right, rather than trying to minimize or eliminate the effect. The "artifact" becomes an area of research, and studies attempt to examine the source of influence as an independent variable. The influence is maximized in experiments, and variations are examined to establish the way in which it operates. At this stage substantive knowledge accrues, and the variable is more widely understood as a source of influence. Placebo effects, discussed in the previous chapter in the context of construct validity, represent a good example of the evolution through these stages.

This chapter examines several sources of influence often regarded as artifacts in psychological research. Conceptualization of many of these influences has evolved, and they are recognized as important independent variables in their own right. From a methodological standpoint, however, it is important to consider methods of coping with these influences in research and hence to look at different influences as potential contaminants of experimental results. Several influences are discussed that may interfere with drawing conclusions about a given independent variable. These include biases stemming from those who conduct research, demand characteristics, subject roles, and subject selection.

SOURCES OF BIAS

In delineating some of the sources of bias, it is useful to distinguish between the individual(s) designing the investigation (referred to as the investigator) and the individual(s) actually executing it (referred to as the experimenter), as noted in the previous chapter. Distinguishing between investigator and experimenter may oversimplify the different roles because the same person may serve as investigator and experimenter. And, of course, there may be multiple investigators and experimenters, or, in automated and mechanized experiments, no real experimenter in the usual sense. However, the different roles or functions of investigator and experimenter help delineate a number of problems that may contribute to the results of an experiment.

Rationales, Scripts, and Procedures

Nature of the Problem.　　Potential sources of bias in an experiment include the instructions and experimental material or procedures to which subjects are exposed. The source of bias varies depending precisely on what the experimenter and subject are supposed to do. A major source of bias may result from imprecision in the script or protocol that the experimenter should follow in the experiment. The script refers to the specific activities, tasks, and instructions that the experimenter administers. Depending upon the investigation, this may entail delivering a rationale, providing a brief interview, answering questions, assisting the subject, and performing a task or implementing the experimental manipulation. The experimenter's script must be well specified by the investigator. Failure to specify in detail the rationale, script, and activities of the experimenter has been referred to as the *loose protocol effect* (Barber, 1976).

Several problems may result from failing to specify how the experimenter should behave. First, the lack of specificity of the procedures means that the investigator does not know what actually was done with the subjects and hence cannot convey the procedures to other investigators. The study cannot be repeated either by the original investigator or by others because of the lack of important details.

A second problem from not specifying the script is inconsistency among different experimenters when two or more experimenters are used to run the experiment. The procedures may vary systematically from experimenter to experimenter in terms of what is said to the subject, the general atmosphere that is provided, and other features. This variation in experimenter behavior is more likely when details of implementing the procedures are not well specified. For example, in one study interviewers obtained different sorts of data when the procedures they conducted were not well structured and when they had latitude in devising the questions for the subjects (Feldman, Hyman, & Hart, 1951). On the other hand, very similar data were obtained when the procedures were structured and the questions were specified in advance. Interactions that can be, or by design are, somewhat unstructured or free flowing (interviews, psychotherapy sessions), unlike many laboratory arrangements, might maximize the influence of the experimenter (interviewer, therapist) because of the nature of the interaction.

Inconsistencies among experimenters may readily obscure the effects of an independent variable. When the experimenters perform differently, this introduces "noise" into the data. Within-group variability (error variance) is increased; this can reduce the obtained effect size and power of an experiment and threatens the statistical conclusion validity. The effect of the independent variable may need to be extremely potent to overcome this variability. For this reason alone, it is advisable to standardize the performance of the experimenters so that the experimenters perform alike and so that a given experimenter performs consistently over time.

Standardizing the rationales, procedures, and experimenter's script is a matter of degree. In treatment, prevention, and educational research in applied settings such as clinics and schools, it may not be possible or desirable to codify all statements and types of comments made by the experimenter. For example, in the context of therapy, specifying the procedures requires delineating those aspects of treatment considered to be important for change. Treatment manuals are commonly used in research to specify in varying degrees of explicitness what procedures are to be followed over the course of the intervention. Yet in light of fluid interactions of the client and therapist, not all statements made by the therapist can be specified in advance. Additional comments and extended dialogues may arise as distressed clients report events in their lives over the course of treatment. In many areas of research other than therapy, the interactions between an experimenter and subject can be completely specified, and the experimenter may not have to deviate from a carefully detailed script except for an occasional and unpredicted question from the subject.

Even if the investigator specifies the procedures in careful detail, another problem that can arise is the failure of experimenters to adhere to these procedures. There is no guarantee that the experimenter will carry them out as specified. The experimenter may alter the procedures to suit his or her own personality or may neglect specific aspects that appear irrelevant, awkward, or redundant. Over time, experimenters may become increasingly divergent in how they run subjects, and hence they may deviate from the original procedures. The task of the investigator therefore is not only to specify the experimenter's script in detail but also to ensure that the script is executed as specified.

Recommendations.   To ensure that the experimental procedures are conducted in a consistent fashion, the procedures should be explicit and standardized for the experimenters. For laboratory research, and in varying degrees in applied research, many aspects of the procedures can be automated or taped in advance. Tape recordings of instructions to the subjects, videotapes of visual material, and the use of computers for instructions and tasks to be presented to the subject can ensure standardization. When these options are unavailable or seem undesirable by virtue of the goals of the intervention, the statements to be made by the experimenters may be spelled out verbatim. Detailed specification of the rationale or instructions guarantees a certain amount of consistency. Experimenters may vary some of the words used and introduce their own statements but these do not necessarily compete with the overall consistency of the script.

One source of variation among experimenters is how they respond to sensitive questions on the part of the subject ("Am I just a guinea pig?," "Is this the control group?"). Depending upon the experiment, it may be useful to try to anticipate the range of questions that may arise and to provide guidelines or particular statements for answering them. Of course, variations in handling an occasional question may reflect inconsistencies among experimenters but are not likely to be as serious as basic differences in how subjects are routinely run.

Another recommendation is to train experimenters together. During training, experimenters can practice conducting the experiment on each other or the investigator to see how the procedures are to be performed. By having experimenters practice and receive feedback together, relatively homogeneous behavior during the actual experiment is more readily assured. Homogeneity in performance can be sustained by conducting training sessions periodically with all experimenters as a group while the experiment is actually being run. One procedure to examine and sustain consistency of performance among experimenters is to include "subjects" in the study who are working for the investigator. These subjects, referred to *confederates,* enter the study as if they were completing the experiment. However, their task is to discuss with the investigator what was done, how it was done, and so on after they participate in the experiment. In my own work, occasionally I have utilized as confederates persons who know the procedures well because of their prior work as experimenters. Perhaps the most useful facet of the procedure is to tell experimenters at the beginning of the project that individuals will be coming through the experiment as fake subjects. These confederates are unannounced and interspersed with other subjects. Probably, the most interesting aspect of this procedure is that it may increase vigilance of the experimenters, as they ponder who is working as a confederate and remain especially careful in adhering to the experimental script.

Another procedure to evaluate the consistency in performance among experimenters is to interview the subjects after the experiment. Subjects can be interviewed by someone not involved with the experimental manipulation to reduce the bias conveyed to subjects to respond in a particular way during the interview. An alternative is a questionnaire administered to the subject after the experiment that asks questions about the experimenter's behavior and the manner in which the procedures were executed. A problem with a questionnaire is that the answers are based upon the subjects' perceptions and recall and hence may not reflect accurately what the experimenter actually did. Also, questionnaire responses based upon an individual subject's perceptions may not be sensitive enough to reveal inconsistencies in how different subjects were treated by different experimenters. On the other hand, if subjects' responses differ systematically among different experimenters, this may provide important clues about the procedures. If there is some reason why the experimenter's behavior needs to be very closely monitored, video or audio tape recordings can be made of all experimenter–subject interactions. This might be completed as part of the experiment as in the case of studying process variables in psychotherapy research. Yet, even if the interaction is not of interest, occasional and perhaps even unobtrusive recordings of an experimental session may be desirable.

Experimenters ought to be encouraged to report sessions in which they have deviated from the script. Experimenters should not be expected to perform consistently beyond a certain point and to be entirely free from error. For example, subjects may be run in a condition other than the one to which they were assigned, receive a portion of some other condition, or through some unusual event receive a diffuse or interrupted version of their condition. Ideally, the investigator establishes a climate where high standards of performance are expected, yet errors are readily acknowledged and reported to serve the goals of the research, namely, to provide a meticulous test of the hypotheses. Encouraging experimenters to report instances where they inadvertently deviated from the script or were forced to deviate by virtue of the subject's behavior will help the investigator monitor the sorts of inconsistencies that transpire. Gross deviations from the procedures may require excluding subjects from data analysis.

Although it is important to specify the script of the experimenters, this requirement must be placed in context. A considerable amount of research, usually laboratory based, includes straightforward procedures on the part of the experimenter where deviation from the script may not be very serious. Experimenters frequently provide simple instructions, play tape recordings, show slides, administer questionnaires, and explain the tasks and benefits of treatment. Presumably, loose protocols are less likely than in more complex social interaction or intervention studies involving more intricate manipulations.

In some studies, it may be important not to standardize heavily what experimenters do. For example, in some forms of therapy, treatment manuals consist of general guidelines to direct the therapist in making decisions about the focus of treatment and how to implement various techniques to effect change (Henggeler et al., 1998). Replications of the treatment and of outcome studies attesting to the effects suggest that the guidelines can be implemented across settings. Occasionally, studies have evaluated treatments and have provided such broad guidelines as to make individual treatments amorphous and diffuse. As mentioned in the previous chapter, broad guidelines can lead to amorphous, highly variable, and diffuse treatments that threaten both construct validity and statistical conclusion validity (e.g., by guaranteeing no statistically significant differences, even when true differences exist). Even general guidelines must be well specified and perhaps illustrated with examples. If two or more treatments are to be evaluated, keeping the treatments distinct requires especially great clarity in the guidelines.

Experimenter Expectancy Effects

Nature of the Problem.   One source of potential bias in experimental research is *experimenter expectancy effects,* a topic discussed in the previous chapter. These effects refer to the influence of the experimenter's beliefs and desires about the results on how the subject performs. The effects are considered to be unintentional because the experimenter may not do anything on purpose to influence subjects' responses. Rather, through tone of voice, posture, facial expressions, and other cues, the experimenter may influence how the subject responds. Leading experimenters to expect certain results can also influence how the subjects actually perform. Indeed, expectancy effects have been demonstrated with human and animal research (Rosenthal, 1966, 1976). The research on unintentional expectancy effects has been critically reviewed by noting such problems as inappropriate statistical analyses and selective omission of data in many of the studies. Nevertheless, some evidence has shown that experimenters' expectancies influence what the subjects do (see Barber, 1976). In addition, characteristics of experimenters and how they behave (those who act more professional, competent, and relaxed) systematically relate to the magnitude of the expectancy effects (Rosenthal, 1976).

In treatment research, the problem of expectancy effects might be particularly acute in situations where the experimenter may have a strong investment in the outcome and is completely responsible for running subjects in the various treatment and control conditions. This is rarely the experimental arrangement used in treatment studies. Yet, if an investigator has a special interest or commitment to one of the conditions in the study, and this commitment is conveyed to the experimenter, it is conceivable that group differences might be explained by expectations conveyed to the subjects. The use of multiple experimenters (e.g., therapists) and manualization of treatment are designed to reduce the uncontrolled influences, such as expectancies, or at least limit the ways in which they can be conveyed to influence subject performance.

Expectancies can threaten the construct validity of the experiment. Features of the experimenter considered to be irrelevant to the experimental manipulation (expectancies, enthusiasm, suggestions for improvement) may vary systematically with the conditions. Expectancies alone or in combination with the manipulation may be responsible for the pattern of results. Whether expectancies of the experimenter represent a plausible account of the results is difficult to say. For example, in the context of psychotherapy research, the results of a study tend to support the effectiveness of the treatments to which investigators seem to be conceptually committed (Luborsky et al., 1999). There are all sorts of interpretations of this finding, but one possibility, even if remote, is that expectancies of the investigator may play a role in research findings.

Recommendations.   Current evidence suggests that the experimenter's expectancies can influence results, although the pervasiveness of this influence among different areas of research is not known. How experimenter expectancies exert their influence is unclear. It is important to know the different ways in which experimenter expectancies operate because this will influence the type of control procedures needed. For example, expectancies operating through loose protocols or systematic errors in calculating data would lead the investigator to control some features, whereas expectancies operating through subtle verbal or nonverbal cues would lead the investigator to control entirely different procedures.

Currently, the most conservative practice would be to keep experimenters naive or "blind" with respect to the purpose of the experiment and to evaluate the extent to which this is accomplished.[1] As mentioned in the previous chapter, in research on medications for psychiatric disorders, this practice is commonly employed. Experimenters (physicians, nurses, others who may be involved in administration of treatment) are kept "blind," that is, they are not informed as to which conditions or treatments subjects receive. Different drugs might be administered in coded capsule form. Although experimenters may be involved in the administration of the capsules, they are not informed who receives the active drug (or which active drug) and who receives a placebo; moreover, they have no way of telling from the capsules themselves.

In psychological research keeping the experimenters naive usually refers to withholding the hypotheses of the experiment. However, the experimenters who administer the different treatments cannot always be kept "blind" in the sense of not knowing who receives treatment or who receives one variation of treatment rather than another. Thus, even though experimenters are not told about the hypotheses, they are likely to guess what the study is about and to make plausible estimates about those conditions that are likely to effect greater change. In treatment research, for example, therapists are likely to develop hypotheses about what treatments should produce more change than others and what treatments actually are control procedures for the investigation. The hypotheses that are formulated among different experiments in a study may be quite similar because of some of the obvious differences among treatment and control conditions. For example, occasionally I have conducted treatment studies in which two (or more) conditions are compared. One condition consists of a treatment (e.g., problem-solving skills training), and the other consists of that treatment plus another treatment (e.g., parent management training). In all likelihood therapists expect the combined treatment to be better, and this expectancy probably is consistent among multiple therapists. More of anything (in this case treatment) is assumed to be better and may lead to an expectancy of superior outcomes for patients who receive more of something. If the combined treatment is better (it is), expectan-

---

[1]As I mentioned in the previous chapter, other terms than "blind" (such as experimentally naive or masked conditions) are sometimes used to refer to procedures in which the investigator, experimenter, and others (staff, assessors) are kept naive with respect to the hypotheses and alternative experimental or control conditions of the study. These alternative terms would be quite preferable because they avoid the pejorative reference to loss of vision that the term "blind" might entail. In this latter context, too, "blind" has often been replaced (visually impaired). "Blind" is retained here because the term has a well-established meaning and continues to have wide usage in research.

cies may become a possible hypothesis to explain the results. In the general case, whether the investigators' hypotheses are accurately guessed may depend upon the complexity of the hypotheses (e.g., whether complex interactions among conditions are predicted), the similarities among different conditions, and whether the individual experimenter has access to all the relevant information delineating treatments. If expectancies are likely to be a plausible explanation of the results, they can be assessed directly to provide evidence either way.

Even if experimenters are "blind" to the hypotheses or conditions to begin with, the effects of the interventions may well develop expectancies and hypotheses that are fairly accurate. In treatment research, for example, not telling experimenters or clinicians what drug conditions are administered does not always really keep them "blind." Studies have repeatedly shown that experimenters and clinicians kept "blind" can readily guess correctly who received active medication versus placebo, who received which medication (Margraf et al., 1991; Weiss et al., 1971), and who received psychotherapy, medication, or placebo (Carroll, Rounsaville, & Nich, 1994). In this latter study, seeing through the blind also influenced clinical ratings of patients treated for cocaine dependence. Evaluators who accurately guessed who received a placebo rated those cases as more severe in their symptoms during the treatment phase compared to cases they had accurately guessed to have received medication. In short, clinical ratings of treatment outcome varied as a function of whether the evaluator had accurately guessed the condition to which cases were assigned. More objective measures (days of drug use, money spent on drugs) were not so influenced by whether the clinical evaluator had correctly guessed the treatment condition.

Occasionally, those experimenters in charge of data collection (assessors, observers) differ from those who administer the experimental manipulation or treatment conditions. Keeping the assessors naïve is very important, if expectancies or bias is likely to be a plausible rival hypothesis for any group differences. The success in keeping assessors naive can be determined empirically. A relatively simple procedure has been proposed (Beatty, 1972). Specifically, observers are asked to guess which of the specific treatments subjects have received. If the observers guess among the available alternatives, the investigator can compare the frequency of correct identifications obtained with those expected by chance. If observers correctly identify a larger proportion than expected by chance, this suggests that they were not naive. If the observer can distinguish conditions, the bias and expectancies during assessment might well have influenced the results.

The above method of estimating whether experimenters can identify the conditions to which subjects are exposed does not solve the problem of keeping experimenters naive. However, it provides information that can greatly enhance the interpretation of the findings. At present, researchers routinely say that the experimenters are "blind" merely because they were not explicitly told what the hypotheses are. Yet, whether experimenters are "blind" can be evaluated empirically. This may mean assessing experimenter expectancies about the outcome of different conditions or assessor ability to correctly identify the conditions to which subjects are exposed, depending upon the role of the experimenter. In either case, information about the actual expectations of the experimenters would be very useful.

Experimenter Characteristics

Nature of the Problem.   Several different characteristics of the experimenters may influence subject behavior. Characteristics of the experimenter—such as age, gender, race, ethnic identity, level of anxiety, friendliness, and prestige—have been known for decades to affect responses given by the subjects on self-report and projective tests, measures of intelligence, and various laboratory tasks (Barber, 1976; Masling, 1960). These characteristics may interact with the independent variable or characteristic of the subjects to produce the results.

Under most circumstances the influence of experimenter characteristics may only restrict the external validity of the findings. Conceivably, the relationship between the independent and dependent variables may hold up only with experimenters who have specific characteristics. In most experiments this is not likely to be a problem. Two or more experimenters may be used and run subjects across all conditions. The results can be analyzed to determine whether experimenters affected subjects differently. If no differences are obtained, this suggests that the results are not restricted to a particular characteristic of the experimenter. Of course, it is possible that all experimenters share a characteristic (e.g., are college students) that contributes to the results. However, this becomes less plausible as the number of experimenters and the heterogeneity of experimenters increase and as the amount of interaction between the experimenter and subject in the experiment decreases.

Characteristics of the experimenter could threaten the construct validity of the results. This is possible where one experimenter administers one experimental condition and another experimenter administers another condition. When experimenters are confounded with conditions, the characteristics of the experimenters rather than the independent variable may account for the pattern of results. The confounding of experimenters with conditions occasionally arises and raises the prospect that experimenter characteristics accounted for or contributed to group differences.

The characteristics of experimenters as a source of influence are not well studied in psychology in general. In clinical psychology an important exception is research in psychotherapy, where characteristics of persons who administer the interventions (therapists) are often studied (Beutler, Machado, & Neufeldt, 1994). A variety of therapist characteristics that can play an important role in treatment outcome include level of empathic understanding, amount of experience, and degree of openness and directiveness, to mention a few. In some cases therapist characteristics in relation to client characteristics may be of central interest and importance. For example, matching of the therapist with the client on ethnicity or background (history of the clinical problem for which the client has sought treatment) may influence treatment outcome. In the case of treatment delivery, therapist characteristics can make a difference in the results of a study.

Recommendations.   The range of experimenter attributes that may influence the results and the pervasiveness of this influence across experimental paradigms and areas of research are not known. Many tests of experimenter characteristics have been reported in interview, testing, or therapy situations where the amount of interaction between subjects and experimenter is relatively great and where the subjects may be placed in a situation where they might be evaluated. The literature would not seem to justify the potentially great experimental effort of routinely sampling a broad range of experimenter characteristics in an investigation. Experimenter characteristics are not easily balanced across conditions or groups in an experiment because so many different characteristics (sex, ethnicity, race, age) might easily be identified.

It would be useful if investigators more carefully specified the characteristics of experimenters in their reports of research. This would at least allow other investigators to examine these characteristics in subsequent research and to evaluate whether the characteristics are important for a particular area of inquiry. Also, many investigators could analyze their data for experimenter characteristics (therapist sex, experience) that might provide additional information about the generality of the results. If particular characteristics cannot be examined, data at least can and should be analyzed for differences among experimenters. Within a given investigation, there may be too few experimenters to permit careful evaluation of experimenter effects. However, if experimenters were described better in published reports, and data associated with different types of experimenters were available, meta-analyses would be able to elucidate the nature of these effects within a given area of research.

Situational and Contextual Cues

Nature of the Problem.   *Demand characteristics,* discussed in the context of construct validity, refer to cues in the experimental situation that may influence how subjects respond. Their significance derives from the possibility that these cues rather than or in conjunction with the experimental manipulation account for the pattern of results. The range of cues that may contribute to subject behavior is difficult to specify. Any facet of experimenter behavior, the setting, experimental materials, and context of the research that are irrelevant conceptually to the variables of interest and that might foster certain types of performance could contribute to demand characteristics.

Of course, all experiments include multiple characteristics that are unique to the study. These cues do not necessarily contribute to demand characteristics. Those cues that are plausibly related to the pattern of results (e.g., differences between groups) and are confounded with the groups can be considered as demand characteristics. Demand characteristics may be a plausible rival interpretation of results attributed to a particular independent variable. For example, in a study described earlier, the extraneous cues of sensory deprivation research were shown to lead to effects resembling those attributed to diminished sensory input, even when sensory input was not reduced in the group in which demand characteristics were maximized (Orne & Scheibe, 1964). The research design allowed for a rather clear separation of the extraneous cues and the independent variable (reduced sensory input).

In many areas of research the independent variable may include cues that lead subjects to behave in ways that cannot be so easily separated from the portion of the variable that is considered crucial. The cues that may give subjects hints on how to perform may be part and parcel of the manipulation itself. In such cases, it is not particularly meaningful to say that demand characteristics accounted for the results. For example, in psychotherapy research the intervention usually carries with it a strong expectation for the desired change on the part of the subject. Many of the cues associated with treatment (a convincing therapist, a coherent treatment rationale, office decor suggesting a qualified and competent professional) may lead subjects to expect change. The impact of these cues could be studied in laboratory research, but they are also central to routine applications of treatment. It is not clear that we would want to remove or alter these cues because they may be central to treatment and may facilitate, enhance, or otherwise augment the impact of other influences (e.g., the treatment technique) that are provided.

Recommendations.   In an investigation there may be special cues associated with the experimental condition, or cues may vary greatly between different conditions. Special equipment or arrangements (e.g., unusual activities) that vary across conditions would be examples. If it is plausible or perhaps conceivable that different cues across experimental conditions could affect the dependent measures in systematic ways, the role of demand characteristics may be worth evaluating. However, conceptually this requires clarifying how the critical difference between experimental conditions can be separated or distinguished from a particular task or set of demands.

Three procedures have been suggested to evaluate the influence of demand characteristics (Orne, 1969). Table 4.1 highlights each of the procedures. Each assesses whether the cues of the experimental situation alone would lead to performance in the direction associated with the independent variable. If the cues of the situation do

TABLE 4.1.   Procedures for Evaluating Whether Demand Characteristics May Account for the Results

Procedure	*What Is Done*	*How to Interpret*
Postexperimental inquiry	Ask subjects at the end of an experiment about their perceptions as to the purpose, what was expected, how they were "supposed" to perform.	If subjects identify responses that are consistent with expected performance (the hypothesized performance), this raises the possibility that demand characteristics may have contributed to the results.
Preinquiry	Subjects are exposed to the procedures (told what they are), see what subjects would do, hear the rationale and instructions, but not actually run through the study itself. They are then asked to respond to the measures.	If subjects respond to the measures consistent with predicted or hypothesized performance, this raises the possibility that demand characteristics could contribute to the results.
Simulators	Subjects are asked to act as if they have received the procedures and then to deceive assessors (naive experimenters) who do not know whether they have been exposed to the actual procedures. Similar to preinquiry except that subjects actually go through that part of the experiment, if there is one, in which experimenters or assessors evaluate subject performance.	If simulators can deceive a naive experimenter—that is, make the experimenter believe they have actually been exposed to the experimental procedures—this is consistent with the possibility that demand characteristics could contribute to the results.

not lead subjects to perform in the way that they would when exposed to the experimental manipulation, this suggests that demand characteristics do not account for the results.

The *postexperimental inquiry* focuses on asking subjects about the purposes of the experiment and the performance that is expected of them. Presumably, if subjects are aware of the purpose of the experiment and the performance expected of them, they can more readily comply with the demands of performance. Hence, their responses may be more a function of the information about the experiment than the manipulation itself. The postexperimental inquiry of subjects may convey useful information but has unique restrictions. The inquiry may generate its own set of demands, so subjects will not tell all they know or will feign their motivation for responding. Also, subjects may not have perceived the demand characteristics but still have responded to them in the experiment. The cues of the experiment that dictate performance may be subtle and depend upon behaviors of the experimenter or seemingly irrelevant procedures. The subject may not necessarily integrate all of these and be able to verbalize their net effect. Even if the subjects respond in a way that indicates awareness of the purpose of the experiment, it is possible that the inquiry itself, rather than the experiment, stimulated this awareness. The questions may stimulate insights that were not present while they were responding to the manipulation.

With the *preinquiry*, subjects are not actually run through the procedures in the usual way. Rather, they are asked to imagine themselves in the situation to which subjects would be exposed. These subjects may see the equipment that will be used, hear the rationale or instructions that will be provided, and receive all of the information that will be presented to the subject short of actually going through the procedures. Essentially, the procedures are explained but not administered. After exposing the subjects to the explanations of the procedures and the materials to be used in an experiment, the experimenter asks subjects to complete the assessment devices as if they actually had been exposed to the intervention. The task is to respond as subjects would who experienced the procedures. Preinquiry research can inform the investigator in advance of conducting further investigations whether demand characteristics operate in the direction of expected results derived from actually running the subjects. Preinquiry data also may be useful when compared with data from actually conducting the investigation and running subjects through the procedures. If the preinquiry data and experimental data are dissimilar, this suggests that the cues of the experimental situation alone are not likely to explain the findings obtained from actually being exposed to treatment.

The use of *simulators* also can evaluate demand characteristics. Subjects who serve as simulators are asked to act as if they received the experimental condition or intervention even though they actually do not. These simulators are then run through the assessment procedures of the investigation by an experimenter who is "blind" as to who is a simulator and who is a real subject (a subject run through the procedures). Simulators are instructed to guess what real subjects might do who are exposed to the intervention and then to deceive a "blind" experimenter. If simulators can act as real subjects on the assessment devices, this means that demand characteristics could account for the results.

If data from postinquiry, preinquiry, or simulators and from "real" subjects who completed the experiment are similar, the data are consistent with a demand-characteristics interpretation. The consistency does *not* mean that demand characteristics account for the results. Both demand characteristics and the actual effects of the independent variable may operate in the same direction. The consistency raises issues for construct validity and interpretation of the basis for the findings. If the data from evaluation of demand characteristics and real subjects do not correspond, this suggests that the cues of the situation do not lead to the same kinds of effects as actually running the subjects. Yet, even here there is some ambiguity. Being exposed to an explanation of treatment (as in preinquiry or simulator techniques) is not the same as actually undergoing treatment and could generate different demand characteristics. Thus, differences between these subjects do not completely rule out demand characteristics.

Efforts to evaluate the role of demand characteristics are to be actively encouraged if demand is a plausible and conceptually interesting or important threat to construct validity. If demand characteristics generate results different from those generated by subjects who completed the experimental conditions, interpretation of the findings can be clarified. If demand characteristics can threaten construct validity, it is useful to design experiments so that merely exposing subjects to the cues (irrelevancies) of the experiment is not plausible as an explanation of the results. This can be accomplished by controlling or holding fairly constant all of the cues or designing experiments so the predicted results are counterintuitive, that is, go in a direction opposite from what experimental demands would suggest.

Subject Roles

Nature of the Problem.   Demand characteristics draw attention to the cues of the experiment that may influence subject behavior. Subjects are assumed to respond to these cues in such a way as to give the experimenter what he or she wants in the way of results. Yet, exposure of subjects to a particular set of cues does not invariably result in certain responses. The discussion of demand characteristics glosses over the fact that subjects may interpret cues differently and respond as a function of their own perceptions and purposes rather than the purposes of the investigator (Kihlstrom, 1995).

Subjects may adopt different ways of responding to the experimental cues of the experiment. These different ways of responding are referred to generally as *subject roles* and reflect how the subject intends to respond to the task or problem of the experiment. Several different roles have been distinguished, including the good, negativistic, faithful, and apprehensive subject roles (see Greenberg & Folger, 1988; Weber & Cook, 1972). These are described in Table 4.2. The adoption and impact of different subject roles have been difficult to evaluate, in part because the different roles can lead to similar predictions in how subjects will behave. Also, subjects often need information (e.g., knowledge of the experimenter's hypothesis) to enact a particular role. Studies rarely provide evidence that this condition is met (see Greenberg & Folger, 1988).

The apprehensive subject role may be the most applicable across areas of research within clinical, counseling, or educational psychology. Subjects frequently at-

TABLE 4.2.   Roles That Subjects May Adopt when Participating in an Experiment

Good Subject

This refers to the attempt of subjects to provide responses in the experiment that will corroborate the investigator's hypotheses. This role may reflect a subject's concern that his or her responses provide information that is useful to science. To adopt this role, the subject must identify the hypotheses and then act in a fashion that would be consistent with these hypotheses.

Negativistic Subject

This refers to the attempt to refute the investigator's hypotheses. The negativistic subject is assumed to provide evidence for some alternative, perhaps opposing, hypothesis, or to provide information that will be of no use. This role may result from the subject's concern over being controlled, predictable, or in a position where he or she is somehow forced to respond.

Faithful Subject

This refers to the attempt of subjects to follow carefully the experimental instructions and to avoid acting on the basis of any suspicions that they might have about the actual purpose of the investigation. This role may be performed passively if subjects apathetically follow the instructions of the experiment or actively if subjects are highly motivated to help science and take special care in not letting their suspicions or preconceptions enter into their responses.

Apprehensive Subject

This final role is adopted when subjects are concerned that their performance will be used to evaluate their abilities, personal characteristics (e.g., adjustment), or opportunities (e.g., employment). Subjects often are motivated to present themselves favorably to psychologists, who presumably are regarded as experts in evaluating one's psychological adjustment and other characteristics. When subjects respond in a socially desirable fashion and hence place themselves in a desirable light, such responding may reflect the apprehensive subject role.

tempt to place themselves in a desirable light. Adoption of the apprehensive role might be expected, given the stereotypes and suspicions that subjects have about research. Research may foster the apprehensive role if subjects assume the focus is designed to assess psychological adjustment and psychopathology or to provide information that will be used for some end (employment, placement).

Subject roles can threaten the validity of an experiment in different ways. If roles are likely to vary systematically with conditions or groups within the experiment, construct validity of the study may be threatened. If a particular condition fosters diverse roles, variability of performance among the subjects may be increased and threaten statistical conclusion validity. External validity might be threatened if the results apply only to subjects who adopt a particular role (e.g., are apprehensive about being evaluated). One of the issues of concern in human laboratory research is that subjects are almost always participating in reactive arrangements, as mentioned in the preceding chapter. Such arrangements allow subjects to adopt specific roles and indeed may foster such roles because subjects know they are participating in an experiment. If such roles can lead to special behavior, findings from such research may not generalize to the real world.

Such artifact and bias as subject roles are relevant to many areas of clinical work. If adults are asked as part of a study the extent to which they engage in spouse abuse, they are likely to adopt an apprehensive role. The investigator is likely to want to delineate those who engage in one type of abuse rather than another or those who do versus those who do not engage in spouse abuse. If subjects adopt an apprehensive role, it is likely that responses will be quite distorted and some number of subjects in the nonabuse group will in fact be abusers. Adopting the apprehensive role will lead to a diffusion of the manipulation. That is, the abuse versus nonabuse groups constructed by the investigator will not be so clear because apprehensive subjects distorted their answers (lied) and many falsely cast themselves as nonabusers. The results may show no differences between abusers and nonabusers on some other measures, but this could be due to many misclassifications of subjects that result from adoption of the apprehensive subject role.

Recommendations.   Several different procedures might be implemented to minimize the influence of subject roles in an experiment. Perhaps the greatest attention should be paid to the apprehensive subject role because evidence suggests this is the most pervasive role that subjects select. If subjects are apprehensive that their behavior is to be evaluated, attempts might be made to reduce these concerns. The procedures may assure the subjects that their performance will not be used to infer psychological adjustment or mental health or used for any purposes other than those about which they were informed. It may be useful to convey that there are no right or wrong answers or correct responses to the task and that their responses will be valuable and important no matter what they are. In practice, this is difficult to do in situations where questions included in the measures (about presence of deviant behaviors) arouse apprehensiveness about being evaluated.

Any inducements for performance normally included as part of the experiment, such as money or course credits, might be given prior to the subject's performance. Subjects otherwise might believe that the rewards for participating in some way depend upon how well they do or the impression they convey. Despite disclaimers at the beginning of an experimental session, subjects often seem to associate the rewards for participating in the session with how well they perform.

Apprehensiveness may be minimized by conveying to subjects that their responses are anonymous and confidential. Presumably, subjects who believe that their responses cannot be identified are less motivated to convey a specific image. In addition, feedback from the experimenter about how well subjects are doing should be minimized. The feedback, unless part of the independent variable, conveys which responses are highly valued and provides guidelines on how subjects are to perform if they wish to appear in a favorable light.

Subject roles might be minimized by ensuring that the subjects do not perceive the hypotheses of the experiment. When subjects know what the hypotheses are (by speaking to a confederate or receiving the hypotheses as part of the procedures), their responses may be altered (see Weber & Cook, 1972). Subjects are less readily able to respond in a manner consistent with the role they may have adopted if they are unaware of the specific hypotheses.

Subjects might always be said to adopt some role or specific reaction to the experiment. They have perceptions about the experiment and expectations about what is likely or not likely to happen. These perceptions and expectations can readily influence how they perform (Kihlstrom, 1995). Exceptions would be when subjects do not realize they are participating in research, because of the type of study (e.g., in naturalistic or field settings) and the assessment is unobtrusive (e.g., archival records). In studies when subjects are aware of their participation, the experimenter may wish to foster a set that encourages candid and honest responding. The task is to convey to subjects that their participation, honesty, and candor, rather than the direction of the results, are critical. This is a set that may be fostered to the subjects directly from experimenter to subjects. The set may be equally important to convey from investigator to experimenter, namely, that accurate information, rather than support for a specific hypothesis, is critical.

Data Recording and Analysis

Nature of the Problems.   Several different kinds of problems pertain to the data obtained in an experiment. These include making errors in recording or computing the data, analyzing select portions of the data, and fabricating or "fudging" the data. Errors in recording or calculating the data include inaccurately perceiving what the subject has done, arithmetic mistakes, errors in transposing data from one format to another (questionnaires to data sheets or computer files), and similar sources of distortion. These errors are not necessarily intentional or systematic.

Evaluation of recording and arithmetic errors across several studies has yielded a rate of approximately one percent. This refers to the percentage of data points incorrectly recorded or scored. Errors tend to be in the direction of the investigator's or experimenter's hypotheses (see Barber, 1976; Rosenthal, 1984). Errors in scoring or calculating data obviously are important because they may lead the investigator to make unwarranted conclusions. Systematic errors in the data may alter the affirmative conclusions; unsystematic or random errors in the data may negate or obscure group differences because the errors add variability to the data.

The heavy reliance on computers might seem to aid in reducing computational errors. To be sure, there are obvious advantages in the use of computers in scoring and checking data and computing or transforming scores based on operations that previously would be completed by calculator or by hand. A main advantage is evident when subjects respond directly on a computer (keyboard, touch screen) and the data are automatically scored and entered on a spread sheet or database. Intervening steps (scoring the data, entering the data) are reduced or eliminated, along with the opportunity for errors.

Needless to say, computers do not necessarily reduce or eliminate data errors, if for no other reason than humans are still involved in the data processes somewhere. For example, a subject's condition, sex, age, or other characteristic may be coded incorrectly as data are entered. The fact that computers play a critical role in data entry and scoring of measures does not reduce the importance of checking the data. Computers can facilitate verification of the data because of the relative ease of entering the data independently on separate occasions and checking to ensure the numbers are correct. It is likely that many investigators check their data, particularly data that depart from the expected findings. In fact, if data are not routinely checked, investigators are likely to assume that data supporting a hypothesis are accurate and are more likely to check data that are discrepant with a hypothesis. The biases resulting from selective checking are obvious and are likely to apply to published studies that have yielded data consistent with their predictions.

Biases in the data analyses may refer to a host of problems. Many of these problems stem from biased selection on the part of the investigator of those data that should be analyzed or reported. An investigator may select data from the experiment that appear most promising and subject them to extensive analyses. Alternatively, all of the data may be analyzed, but only select portions are reported. The implication for these selective uses of the data is that the predicted results were achieved. The conclusions will be misleading because they fail to include all of the data and all of the analyses that were completed.

The problem may be relatively common when many different dependent measures are used and only a small number are reported. The reader of the published account of the investigation may not know that a particular percentage of the analyses would be expected to be statistically significant on the basis of "chance." The percentage of statistically significant differences expected on the basis of chance often is much higher than the frequently cited five percent (for analyses conducted at the .05 level of confidence). The percentage of chance differences may increase depending upon the nature of the tests, independence of the sets of data included in the tests, and other factors, discussed later (Chapter 15). Without knowing how many analyses are expected to be significant, the results might be attributed to nonchance differences.

A related issue pertains to the specific statistical tests and the implications their selection may have for the conclusions. Often the investigator has many choices of different methods of analyzing the data. The different analyses may lead to different conclusions (Nich & Carroll, 1997; Speer & Greenbaum, 1995). The different analyses do not always refer to choosing between alternative statistical tests (e.g., analysis of variance or multiple regression). Within a given type of analysis, changes in seemingly minor decisions can generate a different set of significant results and lead to different conclusions (Matt, 1989; Weisz et al., 1995). The problem is exacerbated by the use of a fixed threshold calling effects statistically significant ($p < .05$) at one point but not at another ($p < .06$). As such, seemingly minor decisions such as adoption or alteration of default criteria or the treatment of missing data within the analysis can alter the findings regarded as statistically significant. Default criteria refer to decisions that are made in software programs regarding assumptions of the data analysis, underlying statistical model, or criteria for proceeding or stopping within the analysis. For example, in using factor analysis to identify the internal structure of the scale, selecting among alternative multiple comparison tests to compare means, deciding criteria for entry and removal of variables from discriminant analysis to predict group status, using multivariate versus univariate tests, and conducting cluster analyses to identify typologies, all can produce very different results from the same data set, depending on decisions made within the analysis. A bias can occur if the results are analyzed in several different ways and then selectively reported based on the pattern of statistically significant findings.

The selective reporting of data and data analyses raises a broader issue. Many experiments are completed and yield findings that are not statistically significant. The results of such experiments usually are not reported but merely allocated to a file drawer. The *file-drawer problem* (Rosenthal, 1979), as this is sometimes called, refers to the possibility that the published studies represent a biased sample of all studies that have been completed for a given hypothesis. Those that are published may be the ones that obtained statistical significance, that is, the five percent at the $p < .05$ level. There may be many more studies, the other 95 percent, that did not attain significance. Methods can be used to estimate how many studies with no-difference findings would be needed to place reasonable doubt on a finding that has attained significance (see Rosenthal, 1984). Thus, the bias can be addressed. For present purposes the broader point is critical, namely, findings must be viewed in a broader context of other findings and other studies that attempt to replicate the research.

Certainly, the most misleading type of bias in data analysis is reporting fraudulent data. If the investigators have sole access to the data, systematic fudging on a large scale may be difficult to detect. Instances of making up the data instead of running the investigation, or changing aspects of the results, are difficult to detect, but many dramatic instances across diverse areas of scientific research have been documented (see Bell, 1992; Miller & Hersen, 1992; National Academy of Sciences, 1989). Efforts to monitor research and to underscore the responsibilities of the researcher to the broader scientific community are responses to such instances. We shall discuss this matter further in the context of ethical issues that guide research (Chapter 17).

Recommendations. The recommendations for handling various biases that may enter into the data vary greatly depending upon the precise source of error. Misrecording and miscalculating the data are relatively easily controlled, although they may be difficult to eliminate entirely in very large databases. Obviously, individuals who record the data should be kept uninformed of the experimental conditions so that the possibility of directional (biased) errors in favor of the hypotheses is removed. Scoring and entry of the data can include a variety of steps that may vary as a function of the nature of the data, such as whether the dependent measures (e.g., questionnaires) are scored by hand or by computer, whether data are entered directly from scored forms or are first entered onto data sheets, and others. Whenever possible, it is preferable to have subjects enter their responses directly on a computer (keyboard, touch screen). If the data are self-report and direct entry is not possible, the score sheets ought to be scanned and entered directly onto the computer database through this procedure. The use of computers in these ways is not only efficient in moving from data collection to data analyses, but also omits a number of steps that can lead to errors.

It is still the case that use of computers in these ways is the exception rather than the rule. The scoring of data and transposition to data sheets or computer should be checked at each stage. The very beginning step is ensuring that the subject has completed all the measures (all items, all assessments) and that the marks or subject responses can be unambiguously scored. Interim steps vary but are determined by places where error could reasonably enter the process. Checking data is a process that one can integrate into routine activities of the research team. It is helpful to convey to all research assistants that errors can be expected, but that they need to be found and corrected.

Eventually, the data are usually entered on computer files for analyses. Here editing of the data can be completed to check accuracy for the number of subjects in each condition, on each assessment occasion, and for each measure, whether the range of scores for a given measure represents a legitimate (possible) score, whether there are outliers, and so on. Compulsive checking may be time-consuming, but it involves a relatively small cost considering the amount of time that goes into the planning and implementation of the experiment. If not all of the data can be checked, certainly a generous proportion from all conditions should be randomly sampled to provide an idea of whether errors occurred and what their influence on the results might be. Checking is important for the obvious reason of detecting and correcting errors. Perhaps as well the checking conveys to all those involved in the research process the importance of accuracy and integrity of the data.

It is more difficult to address the problems of selectively reporting data or data analyses. Presumably, instructing investigators about the need to plan analyses in advance, conveying their responsibilities in the reporting of data and their analyses, and noting the consequences of selectively reporting data may help. Yet, the problems here extend beyond the individual investigator. Publication practices continue to emphasize investigations that find statistically significant differences. The message is clearly conveyed to most investigators to find significance, rather than to report whatever results come from their experiments. When significance is obtained for some dependent variables but not others, journal editors occasionally require authors to delete portions of their results that did not obtain significance. (This is allegedly the main reason I was asked to delete the entire Results section when writing up my dissertation— I have to say "allegedly" until the trial is completed.) The pressure for journal space may lead editors and authors to delete details and qualifications about the results, such as different patterns across different analyses. The intent is to save journal space, but the effect is that the conclusions the readers may draw from the published report misrepresent the findings. Of course, it takes years to straighten all of this out, so journal space is probably spent in the process.

The problem of fudging is also difficult to control directly. The threat of expulsion from the scientific community, the strong demands for accurate reporting in science, and improved efforts to educate scientists during training are intended to hold data fabrication in check, important topics to which we shall return (Chapter 17). Cases of fudging may be difficult to detect if data are kept secret. Conveying the purposes and goals of research and modeling responsible practices in the training of researchers, requiring investigators to make raw data available, and encouraging investigators to replicate each other's work are possible solutions. Probably one of the best checks is to replicate work that has been reported. This not only addresses the veridical nature of the findings but serves many other functions in the accumulation of scientific knowledge, as discussed later in the book.

SUBJECT-SELECTION BIASES

Subject-selection biases refers to influences attributable to types of subjects who participate in experiments. Different selection biases may operate at different points in the experiment, beginning with the type of person who is recruited for participation and ending with those who finally complete the experiment. Two major sources of selection biases are the use of special samples and the loss of subjects during an experiment.

The Sample: Who Is Selected for the Study?

Nature of the Problem. A pervasive concern about psychological research is the restricted range of subject populations that are sampled. I mentioned already the frequent criticism of psychological research because of the heavy reliance on college students, particularly students enrolled in psychology courses. Typically, students are enticed into participation in an experiment by receiving credit toward an undergraduate psychology course, by being given monetary incentives, or by being solicited as volunteers by experimenters who circulate among psychology classes. An issue of concern is whether the findings obtained with college students will generalize to other samples. As mentioned in the discussion of external validity, the issue may be significant in areas of clinical research. For example, psychotherapy research has occasionally utilized student samples whose subject and demographic characteristics and types and severity of dysfunction depart from those of persons who are referred for treatment. The generality of findings of such samples to persons who are referred for treatment might plausibly be challenged because subject, demographic, and problem-related characteristics (severity, chronicity, comorbidity) are likely to influence the effect of treatment and who responds to treatment.

Apart from college students, occasionally there is concern about the using of *samples of convenience*. This refers to the selection and use of subjects merely because they are available. Obviously, a sample of subjects must be available. However, occasionally subjects are selected because they are present in a convenient situation (waiting room, hospital ward) or are available for a quite different purpose (e.g., participation in another experiment that requires a special population). An investigator may use an available sample to test a particular idea or to evaluate a measure he or she has just developed, but the sample may not be appropriate or clearly the one best suited to the test.

The most common use of samples of convenience is in situations in which a sample is recruited for and well suited to one purpose. As that study is begun, the original investigators or other investigators realize that the data set can be used to test other hypotheses, even though the original sample may not be the sample that would have been identified originally if these other, new purposes were the central part of the study. When samples of convenience are used, the onus is on the investigator to evaluate whether unique features of the sample may contribute to the results. The use of a highly specialized population that is selected merely because it is convenient raises concern. The specialized population and the factors that make them particularly convenient may have implications for generalizing the results. As an extreme case, the sample may be recruited because of meeting criteria related to clinical dysfunction (e.g., use of illicit drugs, excessive consumption of alcohol) in keeping with the goals of a study. Another study is added on to that by perhaps adding a measure or two to evaluate depression, personality style, or some other domain not part of the original study. Utilization of the sample in novel ways is fine and often creative. However, it may be appropriate at the end for the reader of the report to ask, "Why this sample? How will the results pertain to the sample one cares about (e.g., people not recruited for some very special purpose)?" Samples of convenience appropriately raise these concerns.

A more pervasive way of delineating subjects that can lead to selection biases has to do with *volunteer status*. In most research all subjects are volunteers in some sense. Informed consent procedures require subjects to agree to participate voluntarily, rather than to participate under duress of any kind. One can define volunteer status in a more restricted sense. From a large group of available subjects (college students, samples of convenience, community members), participants may be solicited through newspapers, notes posted on kiosks on college campuses, and public radio or television announcements. Some individuals agree to serve (volunteers) and participate in the study; others do not (nonvolunteers). The subjects determine whether they will participate. The possibility that those who volunteer to participate may differ in important ways from those who do not can restrict the generality of experimental findings.

Obviously, an important question is whether volunteer subjects differ in any important ways from nonvolunteer subjects. Considerable research has been conducted comparing individuals who volunteer to participate with those nonvolunteers whose responses can also be assessed within the experiment (through routine administration of test batteries, or by pursuing contact with nonvolunteers to induce their participation). Several variables have been related to volunteering for experiments. Major variables and their relation to volunteering are listed in Table 4.3. The literature is equivocal in many areas and, no doubt, the impact of volunteer status may vary greatly among areas of research and type of experiment. For most purposes it is important to note that sufficient evidence is available indicating that individuals who volunteer for psychological experiments differ on a number of dimensions from nonvolunteers. Thus, findings obtained with volunteer subjects may be limited in their generality across certain subject characteristics.

It is important not to cast aside too quickly the potential significance of volunteer status as an influence on findings of research and indeed on clinical research specifically. It is quite possible that those who volunteer differ in ways that are systematically related to the hypotheses of interest and hence lead to conclusions that might not represent the population. For example, in a study on social relations and behavior among school-age children, data were obtained on how peers and teachers rated the children (Noll et al., 1997). Parent consent was sought to have children included in the ratings by peers and by the teacher. Data were obtained for children whose parents provided consent and for children whose parents did not. (The authors and school personnel felt that excluding children from peer rating lists might present its own stigma and hence all children ought to be included as part of routine assess-

TABLE 4.3.   Relationship between Subject, Demographic, and Personality Variables and Volunteering for Experiments

Variable	Volunteers Relative to Nonvolunteers
Education	Better educated
Socioeconomic status	Higher occupational status
Intelligence	Higher in intelligence
Need for approval	Higher in need for social approval
Sociability	More social
Arousal seeking	More sources of stimulation
Conventionality	Less conventional in their behavior
Sex	Female
Authoritarianism	Less authoritarian
Religious affiliation	Jewish more likely than Protestant and Protestant more likely than Catholic
Conformity	Less conforming
Town of origin	From a smaller town
Religiosity	More interested in religion
Altruism	More altruistic
Self-disclosure	More self-disclosing by providing information about their beliefs, aspirations, and preferences
Adjustment	More maladjusted when volunteering for unusual situations
Age	Younger

Note: The variables are ordered according to the confidence that has been placed in the relation indicated on the basis of available evidence (Rosenthal & Rosnow, 1975). The material presented here is a guideline; volunteer status and its correlates can vary as a function of the type of task and experiment.

ment.) The results showed systematic differences among children as a function of whether their parents provided consent. Volunteer children (those with consent) were more sociable, less aggressive, and more athletically competent than nonvolunteer children. Clearly, volunteer status made a considerable difference.

In a different context, tests of treatment (psychotherapy, medication) require that patients agree to participate, that is, volunteer. Prospective patients are informed of the treatment and any control conditions that are included in the study. Yet, patients may or may not volunteer based on the specific treatments included in the study. Even if patients are randomly assigned to conditions after they do agree, the study must begin with those who agree to participate, and this may very much be influenced by the very conditions that are offered (Bradley, 1997, 1999). That is, a very select group may volunteer to begin with or volunteer once they learn the precise conditions included in the study.

The key question is whether volunteers and nonvolunteers differ in the ways that affect generality of the findings. Stated another way, within the sample of volunteers in the study, any relations that are demonstrated (correlations, interactions with other variables, or the absence of correlations and interactions) might be quite different from what the larger population would show. The people who do not volunteer are not randomly drawn from the distribution of scores on the dependent variables of interest. By representing a particular part of the distribution (e.g., a more extreme group, a more varied group), the quantitative findings within the study and the inferences drawn from them are likely to be quite different from those that would be reached if the entire population were included.

In clinical research, a cautionary note is important to raise whenever one investigates clinically referred samples (at an outpatient or inpatient treatment service, crisis center). Individuals who are referred often have significant other factors (impairment, concerned relatives, insurance coverage) that separate them from the larger population of individuals with similar problems but who are not referred. This is not necessarily a sampling problem; we are quite interested in groups who come to clinics, hospitals, and medical health services. For example, it is important to study patients with psychiatric disorders, individuals who have committed crimes and are incarcerated, homeless families or runaway children who come to a shelter, women who solicit help at a rape crisis center, and individuals who see therapists for abuse. Yet most of the individuals who have the target characteristic of interest (psychiatric disorders, criminal behavior) are not referred or in contact with various agencies. It is important to be cautious about the conclusions that are drawn from special samples that seek help, are part of a system where most individuals with the characteristic are not participating, and who volunteer to participate or are volunteered, recommended, or referred by others to participate.

Recommendations. Perhaps the most obvious recommendation that might be made is to increase the range of persons from among whom volunteers are sought. Certainly, as behavioral scientists, psychologists should be able to devise techniques to encourage individuals to volunteer when solicitations are made. More intense efforts at recruiting presumably would bring into experiments individuals who would not usually volunteer. Also, better understanding of the determinants of subject participation may be helpful. Many variables influence the rate of volunteering, such as aversiveness of the task, the magnitude of incentives for participation, and apparent importance of the subject's participation to the experimenter. Structuring the situation so that the research actively fosters greater participation and serves a need or interest of the subjects is likely to increase the rate of volunteering.

The differences between volunteers and nonvolunteers do not necessarily restrict the generality of the results obtained with volunteer subjects. It is likely that some findings are not influenced by whether subjects were volunteers, and other findings are influenced in varying degrees. In cases where findings are influenced by the volunteer status of the subjects, the research conclusions may vary merely in terms of the magnitude of performance on the dependent variables. For other findings the volunteers may behave in a fashion diametrically opposed to that of nonvolunteer subjects. Research is needed to assess the impact of volunteer status on external validity across a variety of independent and dependent variables and experimental arrangements and tasks. This research would be of great benefit if guided by conceptual models about key processes that might mediate volunteer status so that our understanding about the basis of these effects could advance.

There are situations in clinical work in which volunteer status can be readily studied. For example, in treatment and institutional programs, occasionally within the same program some persons vary in the extent to which they "volunteer" to participate (self-referred for treatment, court referred). The difficulty in evaluating volunteer status is that it often covaries with other characteristics (such as clinical problem, demographic variables), as illustrated previously. In laboratory research, volunteers might be examined and compared with persons who initially did not volunteer. Further attempts to recruit these latter subjects would provide an opportunity to evaluate the impact of volunteer status on the measures of interest.

In clinical research it is sometimes helpful to consult findings from population studies. For example, epidemiological studies of clinical disorders are based on sampling from the population at large and include more representative samples than a sample obtained from a clinical service (Regier et al., 1984). One can compare characteristics of a clinic sample with characteristics of those studied in community-based samples to identify differences in subject and demographic variables as well as other characteristics possibly related to the clinical focus of the study (e.g., comorbidity). Census data, too, can be useful if one is interested in whether a study sample represents or reflects characteristics of a larger population. Such comparisons can examine the extent to which a clinic sample departs from the population or at least from a sample where an effort was made to represent the population.

In general, the plausibility and relevance of volunteer status in contributing to the results must be considered in relation to the specific area of research. The concern emerges in those circumstances where the investigator draws sweeping conclusions about the effect of a manipulation without acknowledging that how subjects were recruited might well contribute to generality of the findings. In advance of information about the generality of findings with volunteer subjects, it is essential to specify how subjects are recruited and any factors that may operate to select some subjects over others. In treatment research, selection factors often refer to screening requirements used to select clients who are reasonably homogeneous (e.g., with respect to psychiatric diagnosis). In experimental research, variables related to subject selection—such as year or major in college and circumstances of solicitation—might warrant specification because they may relate to who volunteers to participate and who does not. If recruitment and subject-selection practices relate to the results, the failure of findings to be replicated among separate studies may be accounted for by these variables.

Attrition: Who Remains in the Study?

Nature of the Problem. Whether subjects volunteer for research constitutes a potential selection bias that operates prior to the experiment. Yet, there is a continuation of the selection process during the experiment. If there is repeated assessment of the subject over time, as in the case of follow-up assessment, the selection process continues. The loss of subjects during the course of an investigation can affect virtually all facets of experimental validity by altering random composition of the groups and group equivalence (internal validity); by limiting the generality of findings to a special group (e.g., those subjects who are persistent) (external validity); by raising the prospect that the intervention, combined with special subject characteristics, accounts for conclusions the investigator would like to attribute to the intervention (external and construct validity); and by reducing sample size and power (statistical conclusion validity).

In laboratory research with one or two sessions to complete the experiment, loss of subjects is not likely to be a major problem. In clinical research in the context of treatment, prevention, and longitudinal studies, loss of subjects is common. In psychotherapy research attrition has been the subject of considerable study and hence offers examples of some of the major problems. First and most obvious, subjects who drop out of a treatment outcome study are likely to differ from those who remain in the study. Dropouts may differ on a range of variables (type, severity, or chronicity of dysfunction; family history; past treatment experiences) that could interact with the intervention (see Kazdin, 1996b). Conclusions about the effect of treatment may be restricted to a highly select group, depending on the proportion of subjects lost.

Second, the number of subjects who drop out may vary significantly between or among groups. For example, in a study showing that cognitive therapy was more effective than medication (imipramine) in treating depression, the medication condition led to more dropouts before posttreatment assessment (Rush et al., 1977). Differences in rates of attrition between groups themselves result in an interesting outcome but also raise questions about the comparisons at posttreatment. Were the two treatments differentially effective on measures of depression, or were group differences due to differential selection? These questions are not easily resolved.

Third, it is possible that the type of person who drops out varies among conditions or groups within the study. That is, the people who drop out from one condition may differ systematically from those who drop out from another condition. For example, if 5 subjects drop out of a psychotherapy condition and 5 other subjects in the study drop out of a medication condition, it is not necessarily the case that these persons are "the same." There may be systematic differences in the conditions leading to attrition in ways that affect different types of people. Perhaps those psychotherapy subjects who did not wish to chat about their past and never considered their therapists to be like a father or mother (transference) tired of psychotherapy and left; those medication subjects who were discomforted by a dry mouth and heart palpitations (side effects) may have quit their treatment. The subjects remaining in each of the groups and included in statistical comparisons may be different kinds of subjects in terms of subject, demographic, and personality characteristics; this cannot be easily tested given the small sample sizes and absence of available information on a vast range of possible differences in these characteristics. Usually, the number of attrition cases is too small to compare groups in a statistically sensitive way. Indeed, investigators may show no statistically significant differences between dropouts from two or more groups. This could provide illusory comfort that attrition did not lead to any selection biases that would favor one group.

Finally, it is possible that so many cases drop out that valid conclusions about treatment cannot be made. For example, in one large-scale investigation noted earlier, youth ($N = 450$) received one of three treatment or control conditions designed to reduce antisocial behavior (Feldman et al., 1983). The design evaluated several factors (therapist experience, type of treatment, type of group) in a factorial design ($2 \times 3 \times 3$ or 18 groups). A one-year follow-up was conducted. Almost 90 percent of the cases

(396/450) who completed treatment were lost one year later. The small sample (n = 54) divided among the set of experimental conditions precluded evaluation of the effects of treatment. The loss of a large number of studies in intervention research is not at all rare. Indeed, between 40–60 percent of children, adolescents, and adults drop out of treatment studies (Kazdin, 1996b; Wierzbicki & Pekarik, 1993). In such cases, selection biases are readily plausible. Moreover, the large number of lost cases has dire consequences for sample sizes and hence statistical conclusion validity. Studies of treatment in clinical research usually begin with samples that are relatively small (see Kazdin & Bass, 1989; Rossi, 1990). Attrition further weakens the sensitivity of statistical tests.

The problem of subjects dropping out or terminating their participation may be exacerbated greatly by investigators. Investigators may use subjects who drop out in such a way as to obfuscate further the conclusions that might be drawn by reassigning subjects to conditions in the investigation on the basis of whether they have dropped out. For example, occasionally investigators use those who drop out as no-treatment control subjects to evaluate the treatment condition (Beneke & Harris, 1972). The obvious rationale is that these subjects were in the original subject pool and did not receive treatment, and hence ought to provide a suitable control. Yet, the random assignment of conditions is violated if subjects who drop out are reassigned to some other condition. Even if dropouts are shown not to differ from nondropouts at pretreatment assessment on subject and demographic variables, the extent to which the dropouts and nondropouts are *likely* to improve may be quite different. Threats to internal validity (selection × history, selection × maturation) may be plausible as rival hypotheses in explaining group differences or the absence of differences.

Recommendations.   Several options are available to address the problem of attrition. Special orientation (pretreatment) interviews, various mailings during the course of treatment, reminders and methods of scheduling appointments, and monetary incentives have been effective (see Baekeland & Lundwall, 1975; Flick, 1988). For example, one technique to decrease attrition in treatment research is to request clients to provide a deposit that will be refunded after treatment. Clients are told that the deposit will be refunded if they attend all or a specified percentage of sessions. Requesting and holding a deposit has been found to reduce attrition, and larger deposits (e.g., $20.00) have been more effective in this regard than smaller ones (e.g., $5.00) (Hagen, Foreyt, & Durham, 1976). The use of a deposit has its own problems. For one, it may actually be or be viewed by clients, investigators, or research evaluation committees as a form of coercion. On the other hand, it may be reasonable to ask clients at the beginning of treatment to make a commitment to participate.

Another strategy for minimizing attrition is to identify variables correlated with attrition and utilize the information to decide who participates in subsequent research. For example, in a study of antisocial children seen for outpatient treatment, several variables (family socioeconomic disadvantage, level of parent stress, number of child symptoms) reliably predicted who remained in and who dropped out of treatment (Kazdin, Mazurick, & Bass, 1993; Kazdin, Stolar, & Marciano, 1995). From this type of information one might identify cutoff scores or a profile of families at risk for attrition and use this as the basis for selecting clients for research. Such a strategy raises other compromises. With more stringent selection, a larger number of subjects will need to be recruited and screened. Also, there may be greater restrictions on the generality of the results with more exclusions.

An additional strategy is to try to understand the reasons why people drop out (Kazdin, Holland, & Crowley, 1997) and to devise specific procedures to combat attrition (Prinz & Miller, 1994). For example, in the latter study, personal issues and problems of the parents were proposed as the basis of children dropping out of therapy. Providing parents with opportunities to discuss personal problems and issues significantly lowered dropout rates. Thus, much can be done on the part of investigators to retain cases in treatment.

Attrition is likely to occur in studies that extend beyond more than one or a few sessions. In studies of several months or years, researchers understand at the outset that attrition will occur. Several statistical approaches to attrition have been developed and provide useful strategies to complement active efforts to minimize attrition. Statistical methods allow researchers to identify the likely bias that attrition introduces into the data and the conclusions that would be warranted if the lost subjects had improved, remained the same, or became worse (see Howard, Krause, & Orlinsky, 1986; Little & Rubin, 1987; Nich & Carroll, 1997). The most common approach for analyzing the data from cases who drop out utilizes the last available data point from such cases to draw conclusions about treatment. This will be discussed later (Chapter 15).

SUMMARY AND CONCLUSIONS

Sources of artifact and bias in an experiment are a function of what the investigator is interested in studying. That is, what is a bias in your research may be the phenomenon to which I devote my career. Even so, a number of influences can be identified that usually serve as artifacts rather than the basis of investigation and as such threaten experimental validity. The loose protocol effect refers to sources of artifact and bias that emerge when the investigator does not carefully specify the rationale, script, and activities of the experimenter. Departures from the intended procedures may influence the results by systematically biasing one condition or by introducing variability that obscures group differences.

Experimenter expectancy effects refer to those unintentional influences that stem from beliefs of the experimenter about what ought to happen, that is, what would support the hypotheses. Situational and contextual influences refer to cues of the experiment that can influence the results. Demand characteristics were described as those extraneous cues that prompt subjects to behave within the experiment. The results may reflect responses to these cues rather than the different experimental manipulations the investigator intended to evaluate. Subject roles refer to ways that subjects may respond to the experiment and can introduce biases in the results. Evidence suggests that subjects are most likely to be concerned with evaluation of their performance in an experiment and hence adopt the apprehensive subject role. Adoption of subject roles can be minimized by attempting to reduce subject concern about being evaluated, dissociating any inducements for participation in the experiment with the results or responses that the subject produces, informing subjects that their responses are confidential and anonymous, and keeping subjects "blind" about the specific hypotheses to be tested.

Subject-selection biases encompass different types of considerations. First, the use or overuse of specific populations (e.g., college students), samples selected merely because they are available (samples of convenience), and persons who are asked to volunteer often raise major concerns of generality of the results (external validity). Second, selection biases may emerge over the course of the investigation. The advantage of random assignment at the beginning of the investigation is to distribute potential sources of bias equally or in an unbiased way across groups. Attrition eliminates this advantage; whether it interferes with the results of any particular investigation is not always clear. Yet, loss of subjects over time raises special problems. Differential attrition in terms of number or types of cases may lead to bias in groups that can threaten each type of experimental validity.

KEY CONCEPTS AND TERMS

Apprehensive Subject Role

Demand Characteristics

Experimenter Expectancy Effects

File-Drawer Problem

Loose Protocol Effect

Sample of Convenience

Subject Roles

Subject-Selection Biases

FOR FURTHER READING

Greenberg, J. & Folger, R. (1988). *Controversial issues in social research methods.* New York: Springer-Verlag.

Kihlstrom, J. (June, 1995). *From the subject's point of view: The experiment as conversation and collaboration between investigator and subject.* Keynote address presented at the meeting of the American Psychological Society, New York, New York.

Kruglanski, A. W. (1975). The human subject in the psychology experiment: Fact and artifact. In L. Berkowitz (Ed.), *Advances in experimental social psychology* (Vol. 8, pp. 101-147). Orlando, FL: Academic Press.

Rosenthal, R., & Rosnow, R.L. (1969). *Artifact in behavioral research.* New York: Academic Press.

Rosenthal, R., & Rosnow, R.L. (1975). *The volunteer subject.* New York: Wiley.

Chapter 5

Selection of the Research
Problem and Design

The prior chapters identified the considerations that influence rather directly how the study is planned, including the design, methods, participants, and other features. Although I shall say more about design options, at the outset the investigator must have in mind the central concerns that underline why we carefully design and plan studies at all. Of course, a key ingredient for research has been left out, namely, what will be studied? That is, what will be the focus of the research or the problem I am trying to solve, and how does one either get an idea or move from idea to an actual study?

Selection of the research problem refers to the idea that serves as the impetus or focus for investigation. Perhaps the general idea expresses the relation to be studied (e.g., between stress and perception of other people) or specific hypotheses of what will happen when certain conditions are varied (e.g., if positive cognitions are planted in the subjects, these subjects will rate their quality of life more highly?). The general idea must be reexpressed in concrete terms that specify the precise way in which the general concepts will be studied. The concrete terms refer to what will be done in the investigation and how performance will be measured. This chapter discusses the initiation of research and specification of the idea. The chapter also previews many of the design options from which the investigator can select.

RESEARCH IDEAS

Developing the research idea can be addressed in several ways. This discussion presents the task in different and somewhat overlapping ways to convey the task, how it can be conceived and approached, and broad types of research. The focus is on developing the idea for an investigation. Progression of research and levels of understanding about a particular topic can also help guide what to study and how.

Sources of Ideas

The research investigation begins with an idea or question that serves as the basis of a study. The question may arise from many sources and from efforts to think about a phenomenon in novel ways (see McGuire, 1997). Table 5.1 samples both several ways in which the idea for a study emerges and the sources of many studies. The ideas or sources of research are not necessarily independent and do not necessarily reflect an ordering of the level of sophistication of the research idea. The sources listed in the table are a useful place to begin to see what kinds of ideas can be tested and what the impetus may be for an investigation. Some elaboration may be useful.

First, many ideas arise out of simple curiosity about a phenomenon. Curiosity is no explanation of why a particular course of research is pursued, but it helps convey that the motive for asking particular questions in the context of experimentation need not always germinate out of complex or highly sophisticated theoretical notions. This research may seek to describe how people are or how they will perform in a particular situation. The more the study seeks to generate and test ideas about why people behave in a particular way, the better for research, but just beginning with a demonstration that they do or do not behave in a particular way may be interesting by itself.

Second, in several areas of research (clinical, counseling, and educational psychology; psychiatry; medicine), a prominent source of hypotheses has been the case study. A case study usually consists of the intensive evaluation of an individual over time. Close contact with an individual case provides unique information because of observation of many variables, their interactions over time, and views about the bases of personality and behavior. Cases can generate many hypotheses about all facets of functioning (impact of special events in childhood, why one relates to others in particular ways). The case study has played a special role in clinical psychology and in research and hence is treated further in a separate discussion (Chapter 10).

TABLE 5.1.   Selected Sources of Ideas for Studies

Source of Idea	Defined	Hypothetical Empirical Questions
Simple curiosity	Special interest from observation, belief, experience not necessarily theoretically or empirically driven.	Are musicians (or leaders, psychiatric patients, Nobel Laureates) more sensitive (or eccentric, motivated, clumsy) than nonmusicians (etc.)?
Case study	Seeing what seems to be a relation among features within an individual and examining whether the relation in fact exists and has any generality.	Does therapy A (which seemed to make this patient better) lead to greater change than no treatment or some competing treatment? Do people who seem to . . . (love, despise, or both) their parents have similar views toward their children?
Studying special populations	Research that isolates a special group for close analysis of characteristics.	What are the cognitions of individuals with depression? Does the presence of a particular personality characteristic predict other characteristics of interest (later success, dysfunction, and drug use)?
Studying exceptions	A variant of the above in which a small subpopulation that violates the general rule is identified and investigated or where a particular principle or relationship is likely to depart from the usual one.	What are the characteristics of children who are abused (or who come from seemingly horrible environments, or who eat horribly unhealthful foods) and have wonderful life outcomes (or experience no deleterious effects)? Or what are the characteristics of people who come from seemingly perfect environments and have disastrous outcomes?
Studying subtypes	Also a variant of the above but one in which an overall group that has been studied is evaluated to predict critical distinctions or subtypes.	Can one distinguish in meaningful ways those individuals who are clinically depressed (or who show agoraphobia, high levels of achievement)?
Extending and translating findings from animal research	Drawing from findings on basic processes or patterns of functioning.	Can exposure to anxiety-provoking stimuli (flooding in animal research) be used to develop a parallel treatment for anxiety among adults? Are there parallels in courtship (or communication, dominance, interactions with newborns) between a specific mammal species and humans, or does the animal research lead to a prediction in one of these areas?
Measurement development and evaluation	Efforts to assess a concept (self-esteem, anger) and to evaluate aspects of the measure.	Studies of the reliability and validity of the measure; utility of a measure in predicting an outcome.
Resolving a specific issue from prior research	Addressing a question stimulated or unresolved by a specific prior study or area of research.	Can the construct be divided to separate the influence of multiple factors that may be present (construct validity)? Can a competing interpretation be provided that better accounts for the original finding and makes new predictions?

TABLE 5.1. *(continued)*

Source of Idea	Defined	Hypothetical Empirical Questions
Extending the dependent variables or outcomes	Efforts to see if the relation affects other areas of functioning or domains not originally studied.	Studies to see if other areas are influenced or affected. Psychotherapy alters symptoms of adults (e.g., anxiety); does the therapy also affect the marital relations or child–parent contacts of the treated patients? Treatment A helps depression; can it also be used for eating disorders?
Extending external validity	Efforts to see if the relation applies to new populations, settings, and context.	Does a prior finding or theory apply to a different ethnic group or under varied circumstances? Can the treatment be delivered by . . . (parents, college students, computer)?
Studying moderators	Investigation of a variable (sex, age, culture) that influences the relation of two variables. A relation may vary as a function of some other condition.	Does the effect of exposure to violence vary for boys and girls (i.e., is sex a moderator)? Does the effectiveness of therapy depend on whether subjects have expectations that they will get better (i.e., is type or level of expectations a moderator of therapeutic change)?
Studying mediators	Investigation of why some-thing has the effect it does, the mechanisms or processes involved.	Does cognitive behavior therapy for eat-ing disorders work because cognitions are altered in treatment, that is, are changes in cognitions the reason for the outcome?
Testing theory	Predictions derived from a conceptual model or set of concepts that suggest what contributes to a particular relation or how some process works.	From a cognitively based theory of depression, can one predict interactions in marital relations and child rearing? in novel situations?

Third, the study of special populations is encompassed by a few of the entries in Table 5.1 (study of special populations, exceptions, subtypes, extending external va-lidity). A great deal of research focuses on a special group of individuals and com-pares them with others who do not have the special status. Common among such studies are comparisons of individuals with and without a particular clinical disorder (depression versus no disorder or some other disorder) or the search for subtypes among all individuals who might be designated as having a particular problem or dis-order. A particular clinical problem (e.g., posttraumatic stress disorder), style of func-tioning (e.g., risk taking), or population (e.g., first-born children, spouses who are violent with each other) may be of interest, and the investigator asks, "What are the key and associated characteristics, or how do individuals with the characteristic differ from those without the characteristic?" The correlates (in personality style, family background) and similarities and differences among varied clinical problems encom-pass a wide range of investigations. The special population might be selected because of a particular experience in their past (sexual abuse, exposure to violence, being an orphan, last-born child) or because of a current experience (victim of trauma such as a natural disaster, becoming a new parent).

Noted in the table is the study of exceptions, and this invariably is an interesting line of work. We expect or indeed know from prior research that individuals with some experiences or exposure to some factors will have a particular outcome but there might be exceptions. For example, people exposed to horrible experiences (sexual and physical abuse, extreme poverty, serving as a prisoner of war) or adversity (their parents were criminals, alcoholics, or methodologists) often function quite well in everyday life. Research that identifies and describes such groups and begins to shed light on processes involved can be very informative. Of course, the opposite of this example is interesting too. People exposed to seemingly nurturing conditions (high levels of warmth and involvement of both parents, wonderful sibling relations, opportunities and competencies early in life, methodology bedtime stories every night) may turn out horribly. In adulthood, they turn to crime, drugs, and yes, methodology. What "went wrong?" Can research begin to identify what these exceptions are like? In my own work, for example, our group has taken interest in clinically referred children and families who drop out of treatment very early but get a lot better (Kazdin, Mazurick, & Siegel, 1994; Kazdin & Wassell, 1998). How could this be? Understanding who and why would be a major breakthrough in psychotherapy research. (I stopped studying this quickly because I avoid major breakthroughs whenever I can.)

Fourth, research often derives from extending or translating findings from animal research to a clinical phenomenon. In psychology and basic sciences generally, extensions from animal to human research move in both directions. For example, human studies of lead poisoning and cigarette smoking were elaborated by animal studies looking at processes and mechanisms that could explain how these toxins damaged various organs (dendrite formation in the brain and lungs, respectively). In clinical psychology more pertinent is the extrapolation of findings from animal research to human behavior as a basis for a study. For example, can some process related to development, social interaction, parent–child interaction, or conflict resolution demonstrated in basic animal research be used to inform and to study human interaction? Of course, to extend animal research to humans does not mean or imply that there are no unique features of a particular species (us). Also, sometimes the public is loath to learn of continuities if there is the implication that we are "no different from animals." This latter implication is rarely, if ever, the research agenda. Continuities and discontinuities are important to demonstrate and understand because they have broad biological, psychological, and social implications. So, for example, when we learn that dolphins in the wild seem to call (signal) each other by name—that is, they have names sort of like us (Janik, 2000)—or that elephants seem to communicate by producing sounds (through the air) but also by vibrations through the ground from foot stomping (O'Connell-Rodwell, Arnason, & Hart, 2000), this has fascinating implications in relation to language, brain development, and socialization that may transcend any particular species. Research that draws these connections can be extremely informative because much can be brought to bear in understanding by showing the ways in which species are and are not similar.

Fifth, a considerable amount of research focuses on the development or elaboration of measures. This research may merge with one of the other sources of research, such as studying a particular population. Developing assessment devices is central because measurement is a precondition for other research. An investigator may be interested in studying empathy, risk taking, hopelessness, adjustment, psychopathology, love, bereavement, altruism, propensity toward violence, and extraversion, in relation to other constructs. As psychologists we are interested in a vast range of constructs and how they operate with many different populations. Research is begun to develop a new measure and to establish various types of reliability and validity of the measure. In the process of this research the relations of the measure and underlying construct to other domains of functioning are elaborated. In my own work, for example, our group has had interest in measuring hopelessness in children and perceived barriers that families experience that are associated with coming to treatment (Kazdin et al., 1983; Kazdin, Holland, & Crowley, 1997). Each line of work requires developing the measure, collecting validity information, and then testing hypotheses for which the measures were developed. In clinical psychology, the presence of a number of journals devoted to assessment attests to the importance of assessment issues as a line of research.[1]

Sixth, research is often stimulated by other studies. This is encompassed by a few other sources of ideas, including resolving a specific issue from prior research, extending the focus (outcomes, dependent variables), and evaluating external validity (populations, settings). These overlap, but the emphasis is one that guides different types of studies. Research may evaluate the interpretation of a relation provided by the original investigator or test the generality of conditions across which the relation holds. A very large portion of the published research is directed at building upon, expanding, or reexplaining the results of other studies. The study may redress ambiguities from prior research or elaborate a relation that has been proposed. It is difficult to state what the questions are in any general way because the precise focus is determined by the prior studies.

Replications and extensions of prior work are obviously important. Extending an intervention to new domains (different clinical problems or consequences beyond those originally studied) is one variation that can be an interesting line of work. One sees this in drug studies quite often—that is, if a drug treats depression effectively, can it also be used for anxiety or eating disorders? In psychotherapy studies, if treatment leads to improvement in the client, does this affect others (e.g., spouses) who interact with that client? Fleshing out the broad impact of interventions or exposure to an undesirable experience (e.g., abuse) can provide an important line of work. This, too, is familiar. Cigarette smoking has been shown to have all sorts of deleterious consequences well beyond lung cancer. Research has extended the scope by elaborating

---

[1]Investigations of assessment devices can appear in many journals. However, some journals focus exclusively or almost exclusively on measures and their investigation. Prominent examples include *Psychological Assessment, Journal of Personality Assessment,* and *Behavioral Assessment.*

the range of impact on individuals and others with whom they have close contact. Tests of external validity, also noted in the table, usually focus on different populations. Here it is usually important to make a strong case of why it would be interesting or worthwhile to extend a finding to different conditions. Because the extensions are limitless, any research is advised to convey why any one is of special interest— that is, whether there are compelling reasons beyond "this has not been done before."

Table 5.1 includes as sources of ideas the focus on moderators, mediators, and theory. They are not last in the table or in my mention here because they are minor. Just the opposite. Much of research focuses on moderators, mediators, and theory— or at least ought to. Consequently, these are addressed further below to elaborate their role and importance in research more generally.

Needless to say, the source of an idea for psychological experimentation is not restricted to the options listed in Table 5.1. The value of the idea is determined by the empirical and conceptual yield. Ideas that are derived from everyday experience, common cultural wisdom, or stereotypic or counterstereotypic notions about behavior may be as useful in generating hypotheses as more complex psychological theories. It is, of course, the quality of the idea that is ultimately evaluated. Quality of the idea is based upon subjective evaluation, theoretical predilection, and ultimately by its empirical yield. Despite the difficulty in judging the quality of ideas, professionals are called upon to make these judgments all of the time in the context of reviewing research reports for possible journal publication or grant applications that seek funding. Professionals are asked to determine whether a completed or proposed study addresses an important question, adds to existing knowledge, and focuses on an agreed-upon problem in an area of research. (I successfully petitioned to get out of these criteria for my dissertation.)

An idea that may be viewed as a contribution to the literature often involves focusing on a problem area or unresolved issue in the specific research area of interest to the investigator. To develop a study on a problem or unresolved aspect of a given literature, detailed knowledge of that literature is extremely helpful. There is simply no substitute for knowing the area thoroughly. Reading incisive reviews and individual studies from the relevant literature is helpful; writing such a review may even be better. Although there is no substitute for expertise to generate a research idea that takes an important "next step," mastery of the literature can be delimiting as well. The literature in a given area reflects a set of agreed upon assumptions and methods, many of which are accepted on faith. Drawing upon areas outside of the content area to be researched frequently adds new dimensions that might not have been pursued otherwise (McGuire, 1997). Thus, the advantage of novice researchers often is that their thinking is not confined by the standard topics, procedures, and methods that have come to be rather fixed—some for good reason, but others from tradition.

Levels of Understanding and the Focus of the Study

The overall goal of research is to understand the phenomenon of interest, which means that we know its characteristics, the factors with which it is associated, how it operates, and how it can be controlled. Sometimes the goal of research is stated to identify causal relations, and that is a useful point of departure. Once causal relations are known, we know a great deal. However, there is more to know about relations among variables than their causal connection and also a great deal of important information to know even if we do not know about cause. Levels of understanding of the phenomena can better be described as a process in moving from description to explanation, where both description and explanation can vary in how much is known. In both description and explanation, there is an interplay between theory and evidence. A source of ideas for research is considering where a given area of research might be with respect to levels of understanding, and developing a study to move the evidence further along. Examples will illustrate studies to convey these levels and also some of the next questions or steps that could serve as a basis for a new study.

Key Questions and Concepts.   Several key questions and concepts with which they are associated convey the different levels of understanding and different methodological issues and strategies. Table 5.2 presents key questions and concepts that pertain to the relations among variables of interest and that often serve as the impetus for an investigation. Research in clinical, counseling, and educational pyschology and other areas of psychology often focuses on identifying *correlates* among variables. Subjects are tested on several measures at a particular point in time to relate such variables as symptoms (depression, anxiety), cognitive processes, personality, stress, family functioning, or physical health, and correlations predicted from theory or another

---

TABLE 5.2.   Sample Questions and Concepts that Serve as the Impetus for Research

1. What is the relationship between (among) the variables of interest?

Correlate—The two (or more) variables are associated at a given point in time in which there is no direct evidence that one variable precedes the other.

Risk Factor—A characteristic that is an antecedent to and increases the likelihood of an outcome of interest. A "correlate" in which the time sequence is established.

Cause—One variable influences, either directly or through other variables, the appearance of the outcome. Changing one variable is shown to lead to a change in another variable (outcome).

2. What factors influence the relationship between variables, that is, the direction or magnitude of the relation?

Moderator—A variable that influences the relationship of two variables of interest. The relationship between the variables (A and B) changes or is different as a function of some other variable (sex, age, ethnicity).

3. How does the phenomenon work, that is, through what relation or mechanism or through what process does A lead to B?

Mediator—The process, mechanism, or means through which a variable produces a particular outcome. Beyond knowing that A may cause B, the mechanism elaborates precisely what happens (psychologically, biologically) that explains how B results.

4. Can we control or alter the outcome of interest?

Intervention—Is there something we can do to decrease the likelihood that an undesired outcome will occur (prevention) or decrease or eliminate an undesired outcome that has already occurred (treatment)? Although these questions are usually framed as focusing on some undesirable outcome, they often promote positive, prosocial outcomes to achieve their end.

Note: These terms and the relations they reflect are detailed elsewhere (see Holmbeck, 1997; Kazdin et al., 1997; Kraemer et al., 1997).

source are examined. Identifying characteristics of affect, cognition, behavior, and the contextual environment (e.g., characteristics of others) that are or are not correlated with a particular problem can be important for elaborating the nature of a problem and for testing or developing theories about onset or course of a problem. For example, there is a relation between seasons and emotions among adults. Among adults depression (as well as anger, anxiety, and irritability) is highest in the winter, lowest in the summer, and in between for the other two seasons (Harmatz et al., 1999). A correlation between season and affect is very interesting indeed and prompts questions that, when studied, will move toward a deeper level of understanding. The obvious general question, of course is, why is there a relation? All sorts of studies can address this more concretely; is the relation due to greater physical activity, exposure to light (longer days), or more vacations during the summer months? Perhaps there is a theory or hypothesis to guide the next step. At some point the description will move to explanation by ruling out some explanations and making others more plausible.

Beyond correlation, the notion of *risk factor* represents a deeper level of understanding because the time line is established. That is, an experience, variable, or event (abuse, exposure to religion) is correlated with a characteristic that emerges at a later point in time (e.g., marital happiness). Risk factor, as a concept, emerged from public health and in the context of studying disease (morbidity) and death (mortality). The term and common foci in that context refer to "risky" practices (eating high-fat diets, smoking cigarettes, not taking methodology courses) and deleterious outcomes (heart disease, death). However, the term refers more broadly to events, experiences, or practices that increase a particular outcome of interest (see Kraemer et al., 1997). The experiences (meditating, exercising) and the outcomes (coping well with stress, donating to charity) can be quite positive. Consequently, the term is used to reflect characteristics that are correlated with and antecedent to a later outcome, no matter what that outcome is.

The difference between a correlate and a risk factor is critically important. For example, some evidence suggests that harsh discipline is related to lower intelligence among young children (1–3 years of age), that is, these variables are correlated (Smith & Brooks-Gunn, 1997). Stated another way, two variables (discipline practices and IQ) when examined at a specific point in time, are related. It is not clear that discipline practices precede lower intelligence. Maybe lowered IQ precedes discipline practices. That is, perhaps children with lower IQs on the whole have other disadvantages (cry more, have more illnesses) that lead to more harsh punishment—quite plausible. On the other hand, perhaps children who are abused have lower IQ because abuse changes brain functioning or is associated with some other variable (speaking less to one's child, poverty) that could explain the relation. This, too, is quite plausible; abuse can alter brain functioning. Risk factors require a time line to show one variable is present before the other and is predictive of that other variable. In any case, an excellent source of studies is trying to sort out the order and influence of variables.

Risk factors are not to be confused with causes. For example, risk factors for heart disease include elevated cholesterol; cigarette smoking; lack of exercise; and being short, bald, and male, to mention a few. None of these necessarily causes a heart attack, although all combine to increase risk. With a risk factor, we know that some early experience or exposure, for whatever reason, increases the likelihood that the later outcome will occur. Demonstrating cause means, of course, that we have established that the relation is not merely in a temporal ordering of events but rather some direct influence. Demonstration of causality is a high level of understanding and, as noted previously, a goal of research. I shall return to this in a few moments. I mention this here because an excellent idea for research is moving from demonstration of a risk factor to a cause, by asking, "If this risk factor is changed, would there be a change in the outcome?"

Research often focuses on *moderators,* that is, variables that influence the direction, nature, and magnitude of the relation. We may show, for example, that the relation holds for women but not for men, for individuals with a particular history, or for some ethnic groups but not others. Identification of moderators is an important advance in understanding, because knowing what other factors influence the relation between variables often prompts theory and research to explain why the moderator has an influence. We know, for example, that the rate of sudden infant death varies greatly (is moderated by) another variable (whether anyone is a cigarette smoker in the home). This finding does not mean that sudden infant death is caused by cigarette smoking. It could be something about homes where cigarette smoking is going on that accounts for or contributes to the relation (more abuse of the child, poor child nutrition). However, knowing that smoking plays a role prompts further theory and research. How do the homes differ and what of these differences is *the* or *a* likely explanation?

Causal relations can refer to many different types of cause and to causes that bear varied temporal relations to an outcome (see Haynes, 1992). In the usual case in clinical research, cause refers to knowing how to change a phenomenon. For example, a great deal of research focuses on interventions (treatment, prevention, and educational programs) to reduce clinical dysfunction, to prevent the onset of dysfunction, and to promote learning and adaptive functioning. These studies focus on causal relations—that is, making a change at the level of the individual, school, or community, for example, will lead to change in the outcome(s) of interest.

Intervention research focuses on causes of change, which may be different from, and not necessarily related to, the original causes that led to the development of the problem. For example, psychotherapy and surgery can "cause" change and eliminate a problem (anxiety and cancer, respectively), although, of course, the absence of psychotherapy or surgery were not the causes of the dysfunctions to which they were applied. Related to this concept, in referring to a causal relation, it is important to bear in mind that there may be many causes. For example, to say that a causal relation has been shown between smoking and lung cancer is not the same thing as saying that smoking is *the* cause of lung cancer. There may be many causes of lung cancer, and smoking is one of them. Indeed, many people who have lung cancer have never smoked cigarettes.

We may know how to produce change (cause) even if we are not sure of the mechanisms involved. For example, successful prevention programs (e.g., for young children at risk for school failure and behavior problems) often rely on multimodal interventions, that is, programs that entail several techniques (counseling and medical care for the parents, special day care for the child, changes at home for the child such as reading, and others) (see Mrazek & Haggerty, 1994). If such an intervention produces reliable change, we can say that a causal relation was demonstrated, even though we may not know how change was produced, precisely what facet of the intervention produced change, or what intervening steps (affect, cognition, behavior) led to the change in the target domain. This was discussed in the context of construct validity, that is, knowing that the intervention was responsible for the outcome but not knowing what aspect of the intervention was responsible.

The focus on *mediators* or *mechanisms* represents a deeper level of understanding beyond the relations noted previously, because this means we know *how* the problem unfolds, through what *processes,* and what precisely are the *ways* in which one variable leads to another. For example, research on the relation of cigarette smoking and lung cancer has spanned the range of concepts included in Table 5.2. That is, studies involving both human and animal research have shown that cigarette smoking is correlated with, a risk factor for, and a cause of lung cancer. For example, longitudinal data with humans revealed that those who smoke but do not have lung cancer are much more likely to have lung cancer later (risk factor); animal research showed that inducing smoking in some animals but not others leads to (causes) lung cancer. There is much more work here, but let me return to the main point. All such demonstrations, even those showing a causal relation, still leave open the question of *how* cigarette smoke leads to the disease. Science is never satisfied with "it just does."

Research has elaborated the mechanism involved in the causal relation. A chemical (benzo[*a*]pyrene) found in cigarette smoke induces genetic mutation (at specific regions of the gene's DNA) that is identical to the damage evident in lung cancer cells (Denissenko, Pao, Tang, & Pfeifer, 1996). This finding conveys precisely how cigarette smoking leads to cancer at the molecular level. Thus, beyond the demonstration of a causal relation, a fine-grained analysis of mechanisms is important as well. Knowing the mediator of a relation between variables obviously does not require knowing the biological substrates. The mechanism or process through which two variables are related may involve all sorts of psychological constructs, as illustrated with later examples.

The study of *subtypes* or *variations of a problem* is one area that stimulates research. An investigator may believe that what seems to be one type of person or clinical problem ignores an important distinction. The goal of research is to show that there are subtypes and that characteristics of the subtypes (correlates, risk factors) vary. For example, children who are antisocial engage in such behaviors as fighting, stealing, lying, and running away. Research has suggested that it is meaningful to delineate children as primarily those who are aggressive (engage in fighting) versus those who primarily are delinquent (engage in stealing, vandalism) (and a third group that apparently engages in both). Correlates, risk factors, histories, and long-term outcomes vary as a function of these subtypes (e.g., Hill & Maughan, 2001; Stoff, Breiling, & Maser, 1997). Another way of subtyping such children is distinguishing those who begin antisocial behavior in childhood versus those who begin in adolescence. Evidence suggests that those who begin early tend to be more aggressive and are disproportionately boys; those who begin in adolescence engage more in vandalism. The proportion of boys and girls is about equal among those with adolescent onset. These subtypes are far from resolved, and there are many opportunities to elaborate these and other subtypes to identify the most meaningful and useful way to delineate among such youths.

Identifying subtypes is an important focus of research in part because the results can have broad implications. If there are, say, two different subtypes of a problem, this might be quite useful in preventing or treating the problem. The different subtypes may suggest different causal paths and allow one to target the intervention to influences that will make a difference for one, both, or more of the subtypes. For example, some patients respond to chemotherapy for brain cancer and others do not. Is there a subtype here that can be meaningfully delineated and used as a basis for improved treatment? Apparently, yes. A gene that is active in some individuals, but not others, can undo the effects of chemotherapy by repairing the cancer cells that chemotherapy breaks down (Esteller et al., 2000). This is quite important because if individuals can be typed in advance of treatment, those who will respond will be known and those who would not ordinarily respond might be given some other agent (e.g., to block the genetic influence that undermines chemotherapy) or treatment.

Research on subtypes can be very important. In subtyping individuals there is no need to explain all variations of the problem or to place all individuals into one of the categories or types. Showing that there is one (or two) type(s) that have a distinct pattern and can be reliably delineated can be very important. Later research can advance to explain more of the population, but delineating a small portion of the group can still be very worthwhile.

Essentially, research on subtypes focuses on a moderating variable, namely, a key characteristic that influences the relations obtained among other variables. Research on moderating variables can be informative because it suggests that the relationship depends on some other variable. Indeed, two variables may look unrelated because the effect applies to some individuals (girls, young people) but not to others (boys, the elderly).

Another type of research focuses on *paths* or *course of a problem*. In this case the investigator is interested in the order, unfolding, phases, or sequence of events related to a particular problem or phenomenon. The investigator identifies individuals in a particular stage or state and then hypothesizes how changes occur. As an example, we have learned from psychotherapy research with adults that there are phases through which individuals go as they improve in psychotherapy. Clients tend to change first in their subjective well being, followed by reductions in symptoms, followed by changes in life functioning or more enduring characteristics (Howard, Lueger, Maling, & Martinovich, 1993). One type of change is likely to occur before the other, and a later phase of change is not likely to occur unless changes in a prior phase have occurred. Needless to say, this is not the way all changes occur, nor phases through which all patients must pass, nor necessarily the only way of characterizing phases or stages of psychotherapy. A broader lesson we have learned from much research is that there are often many paths (progressions, causal relations) that lead to a particular outcome. In the context of phases of psychotherapy, research can begin to identify the persons and situations to which this phase model applies (moderators), the reasons or bases for movement within the phases (mediators), factors that influence progress at a given stage, and so on. In any case, impetus for research may stem from hypotheses about how the phenomenon of interest unfolds or progresses over time.

Some Examples.   An investigator may select one level of understanding to begin a study and over time move toward deeper levels. Our understanding is optimal, of course, when we know all of the above in great detail about a particular phenomenon of interest, that is, correlates, risk factors, moderators, causes, and mediators. Fortunately, we can make enormous theoretical and practical advances well before having the complete answers. There are several lines of work where one can see the progression in level of understanding. Consider briefly two examples from clinical psychology (on parenting and child rearing) and one example from public health (HIV and AIDS).

The first illustration focuses on parenting practices and the development of aggressive and antisocial behavior in children. Inept parental discipline practices have been shown to foster aggressive and antisocial behavior at home (see Dishion, Patterson, & Kavanagh, 1992; Patterson, Reid, & Dishion, 1992). These discipline practices include parental attention to deviant and even increasingly aggressive child behavior, inattention to prosocial behavior, coercive punishment, poor child supervision, and failure to set limits. Initial studies showed that inept discipline practices correlated with child antisocial behavior—as measured by parent, teacher, and peer ratings—in both community and clinic samples of boys and girls (Dishion et al., 1992; Forgatch, 1991). Cross-sectional and longitudinal studies helped to establish the time line of inept child-rearing practices (risk factor) and child antisocial behavior. In addition, intervention studies were conducted in which parents were randomly assigned to various treatment and control conditions. Those conditions involving direct alteration of parent discipline practices, compared to treatment and control conditions without this focus, led to decreases in child antisocial behavior (Dishion & Andrews, 1995; Dishion et al., 1992). Several well-controlled studies have shown similar results, namely, changes in parenting skills lead to changes in child behavior, thus showing a causal relation (see Brestan & Eyberg, 1998; Kazdin, 1997). From multiple studies we know that adverse (especially harsh) parenting practices lead to aggressive and antisocial child behavior, even though this does not imply such practices are *the* cause of aggressive behavior, the *only* cause of these behaviors, or even a *necessary or sufficient* cause of the behaviors. Yet, from the progression of research we know a great deal about parenting practices, their impact, and what we can do about them.

A second example also illustrates the progression of understanding and pertains to the relationship between reading among children (ages 6–8) and subsequent school attainment. In an initial set of three studies parents were interviewed to identify background factors (e.g., attitudes toward play, discipline, activities, use of leisure time, and attitudes toward school) in the home that were associated with reading achievement of the children (Hewison & Tizard, 1980). Reading achievement is one of the best measures of current school achievement and the best single predictor of subsequent attainment for this age group. The first study showed that among many characteristics examined, child reading in the home emerged as a significant influence (correlate) of reading achievement. Specifically, parents who reported that they listened regularly to their children read at home had children who were significantly higher in reading and school achievement, as measured by standardized tests. Similarly, in a second and larger-scale study, listening to children read at home on a regular basis, in relation to a number of other family characteristics, had the strongest correlation (among those factors studied) with child reading achievement and standardized intelligence test performance. This finding was robust across boys and girls and multiple samples and schools and could not be explained by several potentially confounding influences (child IQ, parental attitudes, mother language ability). A third study replicated the finding but also examined whether there was a dose–response relation between reading at home and reading attainment.[2] Parents were classified by the extent to which they listened to their child read (3-point scale—regular, occasional, none). The results supported a dose–response relation; more frequent reading was associated with higher levels of child achievement.

The prior studies, however interesting, were correlational, so the antecedent relation of listening to children read on a regular basis and a later outcome (reading and school achievement) was not demonstrated. An intervention study was conducted to evaluate whether there was a causal relation between reading and academic achievement (Tizard, Schofield, & Hewison, 1982). A home-reading program was evaluated in which parents listened to their children read. Classrooms from several schools (with multiracial, inner-city children ages 6–7) were randomly assigned to one of three conditions: (1) parent-intervention condition in which parents were available to assist and to listen to their children read on a regular basis; (2) teacher- reading condition (reading at school to control for increased exposure to reading materials), and (3) no special intervention (classroom practices as usual). In the parent-intervention condition reading by the child at home was directly monitored, and teachers sent home reading material for the child to read. After 2 years of the intervention, reading achievement of the children in the parent-intervention condition improved on standardized measures of reading and school achievement, was significantly higher than the other two conditions, and surpassed the reading achievement level of their respective schools in prior years before the intervention. The effects were maintained at a 1-year follow-up after the intervention had been terminated. Overall, the results demonstrated that parents' listening to the children read at home plays a causal role in subsequent school achievement. The sequence of studies conveys the progression from correlate to causal factor and the interplay of research strategies in this progression.

A final example can be drawn from research on HIV and AIDS. Early research identified several factors associated with contracting HIV—these were correlates of

---

[2]Dose–response relation—a term frequently used in medicine, epidemiology, and public health—refers to a gradient in the relation between a proposed antecedent and outcome. For example, there is a dose–response relation between cholesterol and heart disease, between cigarette smoking and cancer, between severity of accidental head injury early in life and rates of later psychiatric impairment. In each case the greater the level of the antecedent (e.g., more cigarette smoking), the greater (more severe, more prevalent) the outcome. Each of these findings comes from longitudinal studies in which the antecedent (e.g., cholesterol levels, smoking) occurred before the outcome. Demonstrating a dose–response relation between an antecedent variable and a later outcome is consistent with a causal relation between the antecedent and outcome. The relation makes less plausible that some other antecedent variable is responsible for the outcome, but by itself does not firmly establish a causal role per se.

HIV. For example, one factor was intravenous drug use, that is, individuals who engaged in such use had higher rates of HIV. This was an important but early step in terms of levels of understanding. One hypothesis about the mediator, that is, process relating drug use to HIV, was that heavy drug use impaired one's immune system and led to increased vulnerability to the virus. From years of research we know much more about HIV, and among other things, that the basis for the relation of drug use and HIV lies elsewhere. The mechanism relating these variables is sharing of needles for intravenous injection, which spreads the virus directly. This level of understanding is obviously greater than the mere connection of the two variables—drug use and HIV. Knowing the mechanism can be used to alter the spread of AIDS by decreasing the sharing of needles or by making "clean" needles available.

As is common knowledge now, research has elaborated other paths for contracting HIV (direct sexual contact, contact with blood) and has shown rather clearly that the virus plays a direct role in relation to disease and death (the higher the level of the virus in the body, the shorter the period of survival) (Mellors et al., 1996). Further research has shown that most people, but not everyone, exposed directly to HIV are infected or proceed to AIDS. That is, there is some "natural" subtyping that has emerged, those that do and those that do not progress to AIDS. This has been an important breakthrough. The HIV virus is a necessary but not sufficient condition for contracting AIDS. Substances found within human cells influence the likelihood that an exposed person will contract HIV and AIDS (Cohen, 1996). Most people have these cofactors (as they are called), but not everyone. Such work can have implications for treatment and prevention. Obviously, although much remains to be known about HIV, the level of understanding about the disease is considerable.

THEORY AS A GUIDE TO RESEARCH

Such concepts as correlate, risk factor, moderator, and others do not convey the full range of foci of investigations, but they illustrate overarching ways of identifying research problems and sources of ideas. More generally, the concepts show the important movement from merely establishing a relation to elaborating critical features about that relation. The progression of research from description to explanation and from correlation to cause, as described to this point, may inadvertently imply a crass empiricism: One merely tests different types of relations among variables to see what role they play, if any. Underlying the concepts that guide research (and material in Table 5.2) is the investigator's theory, which focuses the research idea.

Definition and Scope

Theory, broadly defined, refers to a conceptualization of the phenomenon of interest. The conceptualization may encompass views about the nature, antecedents, causes, correlates, and consequences of a particular characteristic or aspect of functioning. Also, the theory may specify the relations of various constructs to each other. There are different levels of theory. In clinical and counseling psychology, theories of personality have been a central topic in which diverse facets of human functioning are explained. Psychoanalytic theory illustrates this well by posing a variety of constructs, mechanisms that are designed to explain intrapsychic processes and performance in everyday life, psychopathology, development, and so on. More circumscribed theoretical views characterize contemporary research in an effort to develop specific models, or integrated sets of findings and relations among variables. The models may explain the relation between specific characteristics and a disorder (e.g., hopelessness and helplessness in relation to depression) and how these characteristics lead to other features of dysfunction.

Many related terms seem to serve as theory or conceptual underpinnings of a phenomenon of interest. Prime examples are terms such as approach, conceptual view or model, theoretical framework, and working model. Theory and these other concepts are used with great variability; they also tend to be fuzzy and overlap. For example, in the context of treatment research, much of so-called theory reflects an approach or orientation toward therapy (psychodynamic, cognitive–behavioral, and family based). An approach refers to an overall orienting view with rather global concepts. For example, a cognitive-behavioral approach to therapy invariably focuses on some broad properties of behavioral or cognitive repertoires such as deficits or distortions. Typically, an approach is applied to many clinical problems and treatment techniques. In fact, an approach may encompass scores of constituent theories, not all of which are compatible.

Conceptual view and model often are slightly sharper versions of approaches. They relate to approaches insofar as they often present broad orienting views that encompass the constructs on which the investigator focuses. They tend to be more specific than an approach. For example, there may be a cognitive model of therapy for a particular type of problem (depression, anxiety). This is more specific than approaches of yesteryear in which a given label, such as behavior therapy, encompassed a large set of treatments for a large set of clinical problems. Even so, conceptual views and models often serve in the same role as approaches. They direct attention to the orientation and key constructs of treatment.

The focus of theory can be broad or narrow. The investigator may wish to explain how and why variables are related. For example, mother postpartum depression and child adjustment and social functioning are related (Miller, 1999). A theoretical statement may propose and test how and why these are related. It may be that the link is genetic in some simplistic way (the biological propensity in the parent is passed on in the infant), or biological in some other way (hormonal abnormalities perhaps induced by stress during pregnancy that had enduring effects in structure and functioning of parent and child), or child–parent interaction (poor bonding and attachment). These are all important to pose and test. Broader theories may be proposed that account for different types of disorders and how multiple variables come together and operate. One might include the interplay of biological (e.g., temperament), psychological (e.g., social relations), and contextual (e.g., living conditions) factors into a network or larger model that explains how depression comes about.

Apart from scope of theory, the focus may vary. Consider three examples. First, theory may focus on the nature of a clinical dysfunction or behavioral pattern. Here the theory would consider conceptual underpinnings and hypotheses about the likely factors leading to the clinical problem or pattern of functioning, the processes involved, and how these processes emerge or operate. Perhaps the theory would consider various risk and protective factors, paths and trajectories, and how early development results in subsequent dysfunction. Second, the theory might focus on factors that maintain a particular problem or pattern of behavior. Here the theory could consider the factors that might operate to influence, sustain, or shape the way in which the problem is continued, long after onset is established. Perhaps the theory would focus on how, why, or when relapse occurs, that is, why a pattern is not maintained. Third, the theory might focus on change as in therapeutic change or changes in development. In the context of therapy the theory might consider the necessary, sufficient, and facilitative conditions on which change depends. There are many other areas where theory would be relevant. In each case, of course, the reasons or explanations are proposed to explain how and why the relations of interest occur.

Why Theory Is Needed

To understand human functioning, we do not merely accumulate facts or empirical findings. Rather, or in addition, we wish to relate these findings to each other and to other phenomena in a cohesive way. For example, an investigator may demonstrate that there is a sex difference regarding a particular disorder, personality characteristic, or cognitive style. However, by itself a sex difference is not necessarily interesting. A theoretical understanding would pose how this difference develops and what implications the difference may have for understanding biological or psychosocial development. Inevitably, there will be many exceptions to the theory, and these will require posing moderators and new lines of work. From the standpoint of research, theoretical explanations guide further studies, and the data generated by the studies require emendations of the theory. This is an important exercise because theory moves us to implications beyond the confines of the specific empirical relations and the restricted conditions in which these relations may have been demonstrated.

One can be more specific about why theories are needed and the benefits that derive from them. First, theory can bring order to areas where findings are diffuse or multiple. For example, consider the area of psychotherapy. There are hundreds of various forms of psychotherapy, and the number continues to grow (e.g., Kazdin, 2000). Theory could bring unity to this area. Perhaps there is a small set of common mechanisms or processes that could be identified that span several treatments. It is unlikely that all the treatments work (assuming for a moment the generous thought that many of them work at all) for the same reasons. Yet, there might be a few theories that account for how change comes about and that unite the disparate treatments and their findings.

Second, theory can explain the basis of change and unite diverse outcomes. Again, using therapy as an example, all sorts of changes occur in treatment. Of course, therapy changes various social, emotional, and behavioral problems for which individuals often seek treatment (depression, anxiety). In addition, therapy improves symptoms of physical health, increases survival rates among terminally ill cancer patients, and increases fertility among infertile couples (Domar, 1998; Luborsky, Crits-Christoph, Mintz, & Auerbach, 1988; Spiegel, Bloom, Kraemer, & Gottheil, 1989). How can these effects occur? The answer entails a theoretical statement. Such a statement, when elaborated empirically, could greatly improve our understanding of many facets of human functioning, beyond psychotherapy.

Third, theory can direct our attention to which moderators to study. In any area an infinite number of moderators might be proposed. The standard litany would be sex, age, gender, socioeconomic class, and the list could continue to encompass all characteristics of people and the conditions and contexts in which they live. For example, marital satisfaction could be influenced by scores of characteristics of each partner (early childhood, sibling relations, histories of their parents, current living conditions, personality of each person, education, similarity of each partner on any one of the above characteristics, and an endless so on). We do not want research merely to catalogue what factors do and do not serve as influences. Not all studies can be completed, and hence focused attention and prioritization of what to study is very important. Theory points to what we might or indeed ought to look at.

Fourth, application and extension of knowledge to the world beyond the laboratory is invariably a goal of clinical, counseling, educational, organizational, and other areas of psychology where theory, research, application, and practice are all important. The best way to advance application is through understanding how something operates, that is, identifying the critical mechanisms. Understanding how and why something works can be used to optimize the effects of a particular influence. For example, there is now a keen interest in seeing if various forms of treatment, well studied in the laboratory, can be effective in clinical practice. Unfortunately, there is very little knowledge of why and how treatment works, so we really do not know precisely what to extend to clinical practice, what ingredients of therapy are necessary, sufficient, and facilitative. Without understanding, interventions are going to be difficult to extend in a way that will be very effective.

In vastly different context, security blankets, small stuffed animals, and parents can comfort very young children in stressful situations. For example, in one experiment with 3-year-olds undergoing medical procedures, security blankets and moms were equally effective (compared to no supportive agent) in reducing stress, and providing blankets and moms did not surpass the benefits of the separate support source (Ybarra, Passman, & Eisenberg, 2000). It would be very informative to understand the range of processes (biological and psychological) that are involved. It may be that people in general, or perhaps just children, can be comforted in several ways, and understanding the different ways and commonalties in how they operate would require theory and research. The knowledge, once gained, might well have broad implications for allaying fear, addressing loneliness, and teaching coping.

Overall, the goal of science is to understand, and this entails connecting empirical relations with statements of mechanisms and process. We do not want only to know that the universe is expanding but to understand how and why. We do not want only to know that most crime among adolescents is committed while youths are under the influence of an illicit substance (alcohol, drugs), but why. It may be simply that inhibitions and restraints that thwart lawbreaking are reduced, but it may be other influences as well, such as selection (those who abuse illicit substances are more likely to commit crime whether they use the substances or not, or peer relations in which substance use occurs foster crime, and so on). The value of understanding is critically important, in this case, to intervene to reduce the problem.

Generating versus Testing Hypotheses

In beginning a study or research career, investigators are often encouraged to start with a theoretical statement or model of the variables of interest and then to test the model empirically. Testing hypotheses based on a conceptual view is sometimes seen as the better and indeed only way to develop and conduct research. However, this emphasis raises an immediate dilemma, namely, where does one get a conceptual view to begin with? Clearly, there is no substitute for brilliance and merely generating explanations for why things are the way they are. There is also no substitute for close-up observations and contact with the phenomenon of interest. Meeting, working with, and participating in the situations or contexts one wishes to understand generate reams of ideas about what needs to be studied and what processes are involved.

In a later chapter I provide an overview of qualitative research, a methodology not taught very much in graduate programs in psychology. A characteristic of qualitative research is to interview extensively individuals and groups who experience a particular situation or show a special characteristic. From intensive interviews one can develop, in systematic ways, ideas about what are key dimensions of a problem and what needs to be studied. In qualitative research the term *grounded theory* is used to denote that hypotheses emerge from intensive observations of the phenomenon—that is, theory comes from and is grounded in observation. Examples of qualitative research and the move from observation to understanding will be elaborated in Chapter 12. I mention the issue because it is easy to say here that ideas will flow once one works with the phenomenon of interest. It is likely that this is too nebulous to be of much help. However, qualitative research offers systematic ways to speed this process by meeting with individuals and groups with special experiences of interest to the investigator and to move from description to explanation.

Within psychology, purely descriptive research that is not guided by a strong conceptual view is often looked at negatively at worst or ambivalently at best. There is some basis for concern about research that might merely study the relation of any two (or more) variables, whether or not the case is made that these variables and the relation are important or have implications for anything. For example, one could study length of one's hair and propensity for depression, blood pressure and shoe size, and attitudes toward government and one's toothbrushing habits (this last one was my undergraduate thesis, I might add). The rationale might be that one is merely describing a relation to generate a conceptual view. In the extreme, any line of work can be made to seem odd. Clearly, there needs to be some basis that the phenomenon of study has some interest and that the study, if not based on theory, might well be useful in generating relations that would be informative.

Some examples might make the point. What happens to individuals when they drop out of therapy very early? In my own work there was no strong theory to pursue this question or to make predictions. It turns out many people who leave therapy early are doing poorly, that is, they have not changed appreciably in the clinical problems that brought them to treatment. Describing who leaves early and improves and who leaves early and does not might well generate some interesting data about therapeutic change and attrition. This is not a theory-based line of work but could lead, and has led, to some theory about dropping out of treatment (e.g., Kazdin, Holland

& Crowley, 1997). As another example, among individuals who have a heart attack, those who experience depression are more likely to have another heart attack and to die from it (Honig, 2000; Seiner & Mallya, 1999). Descriptive information about those who have a heart attack and depression but do not have a second heart attack or those who have a heart attack, no depression, and who do have a second heart attack could be quite informative. Moreover, such research beginning purely at a descriptive and correlational level can readily prompt hypotheses that go beyond the data and build theory. For example, mechanisms (biological processes, coping processes) that connect depression and heart attack are likely to emerge from such studies.

In some areas of research more than others, descriptive research that does not immediately move to theory still can be regarded as quite important. For example, a significant risk factor for suicide among adolescents and young adults is the presence of a gun in the home (Brent et al., 1991). All sorts of supportive and interesting findings further elaborate this finding by showing, for example, that purchasing a gun increases the risk of suicide by handgun over the subsequent years, that most firearms suicide victims do not purchase a gun to commit suicide, and that restrictive gun legislation appears to reduce subsequent suicide rate (see Brent et al., 2000). There is not much in this literature that would be regarded as theory, but the research has gone very far to identify the role that guns can play in risk and who (what types of families) are likely to purchase guns among families with an adolescent who is already at risk for suicide. The findings have moved beyond merely a correlation here or there and suggest that the presence and absence of firearms can greatly influence suicide.

The goal of research is to understand, and theory plays a central role in bringing together multiple variables and processes. Although it is important we end up after several studies with an explanation of what is operating, and why, with a given topic, we need not start with a conceptual view. Stated another way, we demand of most researchers that they begin their articles with a conceptual statement (a model or theory) followed by predictions. It would be equally useful perhaps to expand this demand so that researchers must either begin or end their articles in that way. Research that attempts to describe and generate hypotheses for further research might not begin with a theoretical statement and predictions. However, at the end of the article (Discussion section) the study might well connect what has been found with some theory and make predictions that are followed in a second study.

Good data on a topic are a great basis for developing theory and a key to understanding. Indeed, it is easy to see occasional examples of theory-based research where the information on which the theory was based was removed from reality or where the person derived the theory in his or her office with quite little contact with the world. The interplay between theory and empirical research and between explanation and description is reciprocal. I have denoted this section as generating *versus* testing hypotheses to indicate a tension in the field. However, a good study can do either, and often a superb study does both. That is, a hypothesis (theory prediction) may be tested, but the data gathered are used to extend the description of the phenomenon in ways that beg for further theory. Alternatively, a study may begin with a careful description and end with a model or conceptual view that can be tested in subsequent studies.

FROM IDEAS TO OPERATIONS

Operational Definitions

Whatever the original idea that provides the impetus for research, it must be described concretely so that it can be tested. It is not enough to have an abstract notion or question. For example, one might ask at a general level such questions as, "Do anxious people tend to withdraw from social situations?" or "Are college students put to sleep by the lectures of their instructors?" These and similar notions are adequate for initial leads for study but require considerable work before empirical research could be executed.

The concepts included in the abstract notion must be operationalized, that is, made into operational definitions. *Operational definitions* refer to defining a concept on the basis of the specific operations used in the experiment. For example, an operational definition of anxiety could be physiological reactions to a galvanic skin response measure of skin resistance and an individual's self-report of being upset, nervous, or irritable in several situations. Greater specificity may be required than noting the measure. For example, a study might require operational criteria for designating anxious and nonanxious individuals. "Anxious" may be operationalized by referring to persons who attain relatively high scores (at or above the 75th percentile) on a standardized measure of anxiety. Nonanxious or low anxious persons might be defined as those who attain relatively low scores (at or below the 25th percentile) on the same scale. Specifying the measure and the cut-off criteria to define anxious and nonanxious groups would clearly satisfy the requirements of an operational definition.

Although operational definitions are essential for research, such definitions bear limitations. To begin with, the investigator starts with an abstract notion (concept or construct) that must be operationalized. An operational definition may greatly simplify the concept of interest or focus only on a part of that construct. For example, an operational definition of romantic love might be based upon the expression of love on a self-report measure or overt physical expressions of affection. Although each of these measures is part of what people often mean by love, the measures, either separate or combined, are not the full definition that people usually have in mind when they talk about or experience love. From the standpoint of research, the purpose is to provide a working definition of the phenomenon. Yet, the working definition may not be complete and all-encompassing or even bear great resemblance to what people mean in everyday discourse.

A second limitation is that the operational definition may include features that are irrelevant or not central to the original concept. For example, anxiety might be operationalized by including persons who attend a clinic and complain of various symptoms of anxiety. Yet, this definition includes components other than anxiety that can influence the conclusions of the study. Attending a clinic is determined by many factors other than experiencing a problem, including the availability of clinic facilities, ethnic or cultural views about attending treatment, concern over possible stigma, encouragement by relatives and friends, and insurance to cover the cost. There may be many persons in the community who are equally anxious as, or more anxious than, those who seek treatment, and hence studies that define anxiety as those individuals who are anxious and attend treatment may yield different conclusions from those that define anxiety but do not also require attending treatment. In general, there is always a concern that an operational definition may include components irrelevant or ancillary to the original concept.

A third limitation of operational definitions pertains to the use of single measures to define a construct. There are limitations to all measurement devices due to special features of the device itself. Performance of the subject on a single measure is determined by more factors than the construct that is being measured. For example, although self-report of anxiety on a questionnaire is likely to be related to the experience of anxiety in everyday life, the extent to which anxiety is reported is likely to be a function of such other factors as the purposes for which the test will be used (e.g., receiving free therapy versus obtaining a job), how the subject feels on that day, how the questions are worded, the characteristics of the individual administering the test, and the subject's general likelihood of admitting socially undesirable characteristics. Simply stated, any one method of operationalizing a construct is fallible because it may depend on specific and unique characteristics of the measure and method of assessment.

Investigators usually wish to describe general relationships that go beyond single and narrowly circumscribed operations. For example, if possible, it is important to be able to make general statements about anxiety and its relation to other phenomena independently of the many different ways in which anxiety can be operationalized. Using a single measure to define a construct may impede drawing general relationships among concepts.

Multiple Operations to Represent Constructs

The inadequacies of defining a concept with a single measure or operation (referred to as *single operationism*) had led to use of multiple measures or operations (*multiple operationism*). Although a concept may be imperfectly measured by individual operations, the commonalties among several measures may converge on the concept of interest. Thus, self-report of anxiety, physiological responsiveness in anxiety-provoking situations, and overt behavioral performance together may help estimate a person's anxiety. Combined measures that attempt to explore a concept with different operations may allow an investigator to place more confidence in capturing the concept of interest.

Most investigations in clinical, counseling, and educational psychology utilize a set of measures to operationalize different constructs. For example, an effective treatment might be expected to improve three domains of client functioning: client symptoms, work adjustment, and family interaction. Each domain of interest represents a construct. Ideally, each of these constructs would be represented in any investigation by two or more measures. The reason is that individual measures are fallible and unlikely to capture the construct of interest. Also, if the results are obtained (or not obtained), it is possible that the result is restricted to the specific way in which the construct was measured. It is better to have two or more measures to evaluate whether the conclusion was restricted to any particular way of operationalizing the construct. Whenever possible, as investigators, we look for consistency among measures of a given construct, but if there is not consistency, we wish to know that as well.

Advances in design and statistical analyses have expanded the methods of evaluating constructs and combining multiple measures. Within a given study multiple measures (two or more) can be used to define a construct. The relations of the measures to each other and to the overall construct as well as to other measures or outcomes can be examined. The notion of *latent variable* has been used to reflect the idea of a construct represented by several measures. The specific measures are referred to as *observed variables* and represent the construct of interest. Correlational analyses can evaluate the associations among observed variables and the extent to which they represent a single latent variable of interest. Because that latent variable is defined by several different measures, it is not confounded by the measurement error of a single measure.

Consider an example of the methods of operationalizing latent variables in the context of research on adolescent drug use (Newcomb & Bentler, 1988). The investigators were interested in identifying critical paths toward deviance over the course of adolescence and young adulthood, with particular focus on the role of early drug use. They assessed youths over a period spanning 4 years to understand the factors that predict outcomes in young adulthood and to identify causal paths toward deviance. Several constructs or domains of functioning (latent variables) were assessed during adolescence, each represented by multiple measures. The domains included drug use, social conformity, criminal activity, deviant peer networks, and others. Three separate measures were used to operationalize drug use: frequency of alcohol use (beer, wine, liquor), cannabis use (marijuana and hashish), and hard drug use (tranquilizers, sedatives, barbiturates, heroin, cocaine, and several others). The three measures were assumed to reflect a general tendency toward drug use, that is, an overall latent variable or construct. Specific data-analytic techniques (e.g., confirmatory factor analyses) demonstrated that the observed variables were highly related and reliably reflected the construct of interest. In passing, it is worth noting that during adolescence, heavy teenage drug use was significantly related to lower levels of social conformity, greater criminal activity, and having a deviant friendship network. Early drug use was related years later to reduction in academic pursuits (less involvement in college), job instability (unemployment, being fired), and increased psychoticism (disorganized thought processes). Although the latent variable, drug use, was associated with untoward long-term outcomes, the analyses permitted separate evaluation of different observed variables or operational definitions. That is, the different measures and types of drug use were analyzed separately. As might be expected, among drug use measures in adolescence, hard drug use had particularly untoward outcomes in young adulthood.

Generally, use of multiple measures to operationalize a construct (both the independent variable and dependent variable) is to be encouraged. If our study shows that the predicted relation between two constructs (e.g., anxiety and social behavior) holds when each is measured in more than one way, this greatly strengthens the demonstration and its interpretation. When the finding holds for more that one measure, we have greater assurance that the finding is not unique to one special type of measure (e.g., a self-report questionnaire). The advantages of using multiple measures stem from overcoming the problems of narrow stimulus sampling discussed previously.

There are some measures in psychology (Minnesota Multiphasic Personality Inventory-2, Wechsler Adult Intelligence Scale) that have been studied extensively, and their relation to other measures and many other facets of behavior are well known. When one of these measures is used by itself to define a construct, there is less of an objection than would be the case if a less well-established measure or questionnaire were used. The underlying principle here is that if the construct validity of a measure is well established, greater faith can be placed in subsequent research that invokes the construct when interpreting the results of that measure. Yet, any measure, however well established, is restricted by adopting a specific assessment method (self-report, or other report, or direct observation), and the results may be restricted to that method.

In an investigation, researchers often wish to include many different constructs. This is reasonable, in part because an investigation may be so difficult to do that one wants to take advantage of the situation and opportunity, or the conceptual view may simply require multiple constructs. At the same time it is important to measure a given construct in more than one way whenever possible for all the reasons discussed here. As a general guideline for research it is usually better to examine multiple measures and few constructs, rather than multiple constructs and few measures. (My dissertation was one measure and one construct, which, in retrospect could have been improved, but the study was not "a blemish on the entire institution of science" that some members of my committee stated.)

Discrepancies among Definitions

While it is useful to operationalize a construct in more than one way, investigators who do this may subsequently feel they were punished by an unwanted dose of reality. Different operational definitions can lead to different conclusions about the phenomenon of interest. For example, in the study of child psychopathology, psychiatric disorders (depression, conduct disorder, anxiety disorder) are often operationalized by using different measures and different raters (child, parent, teacher, peers) to define disorders of the child. A difficulty is that when different measures and raters are used, there is little overlap among the children who are identified as showing a particular problem (Offord et al., 1996). Thus, children identified as clinically depressed by one operational criterion are not the same children as those defined as depressed by another criterion. This is not a minor annoyance. Because once one examines the correlates or features associated with a particular problem (cognitive processes, social behavior, and self-esteem), the results can vary as a function of which method is used to operationalize the problem (Kazdin, 1989). The point here is not to suggest that every different method of operationalizing a construct leads to a specific and unique result. However, differences are quite possible among varied ways of operationalizing constructs, and these, too, need to be examined.

One might challenge the entire research enterprise if different ways of defining a construct lead to different findings. Yet, different definitions do not invariably lead to differences. Also, we wish to understand discrepancies that might emerge. For example, one investigator may operationalize happiness based on the number of smiles and positive statements a person makes in an interview; another investigator may operationalize the construct by having persons complete a scale in which they report the degree to which they are happy. Differences or discrepancies in these methods of operationalizing the construct are not "problems." We wish to understand as part of the elaboration of human functioning what accounts for the fact that not all persons who smile frequently report themselves to be happy, and not all persons who say they are happy smile frequently.

General Comments

Research usually begins with an abstract notion or concept that reflects the construct of interest. For purposes of experimentation the concept is operationalized through one or more procedures or measures. The constructs that constitute both the independent and dependent variables are translated into specific procedures and measurement operations. The experiment demonstrates a relation between the independent and dependent variables, which are specified very concretely. After the experiment the investigator usually wishes to go beyond the specific operations and back to the more abstract level of concepts. Thus, an experiment may demonstrate a particular relation under specific environmental conditions with concrete operational definitions of the independent and dependent variables; however, to go beyond the very specific demonstration requires assuming a broader relation. There are an infinite number of ways that a construct might be operationalized. In a given study it is valuable to utilize multiple measures of the construct of interest to evaluate the generality of findings among different concrete measures or operations and sources of measurement error.

VARIABLES TO INVESTIGATE

Types of Variables

Defining the research idea in operational terms is an important step in moving toward the investigation itself. Another way to consider the initial stage of the research process is in terms of the types of variables that are studied. The specific idea or hypothesis is expressed in such a manner that some independent variable can be altered and evaluated. The independent variable of a study refers to the conditions that are varied or manipulated to produce change or, more generally, to the differences among conditions that are expected to influence subject performance. Three types of independent variables that will be distinguished here include environmental or situational variables, instructional variables, and subject variables.

Environmental or Situational Variables.   Many variables of interest consist of altering the environmental or situational conditions of an experiment. An *environmental variable* consists of varying what is done to, with, or by the subject. A given condition or task may be provided to some subjects and not to others (treatment versus no treatment). Alternatively, different amounts of a given variable may be manipulated (more treatment to some subjects than to others). Finally, the environmental variable may consist of providing qualitatively different conditions to the subjects (one type of feedback or message versus another type within the experiment). The following questions illustrate the type of manipulations that require varying an environmental or situational variable.

1. Does a prenatal care program for pregnant women increase the birth weight and decrease birth complications of their newborns? Here the special intervention (home visits, counseling in diet, monthly physical exams) is an environmental variable.

2. Are some forms of psychotherapy more effective than others with depressed clients? Here the type of treatment given is the environmental variable.

3. Does recording one's calorie consumption and weight after each meal alter eating habits? The environmental variable here would be the task of self-observation and might be invoked for some subjects but not for others.

Instructional Variables.   These variables refer to a specific type of environmental or situational manipulation. *Instructional variables* refer to variations in what the participants are told or are led to believe through verbal or written statements about the experiment and their participation. In the simplest situation, when instructional variables are manipulated, other environmental variables are held constant. Instructional variables usually are aimed at altering the participant's perception, expectation, or evaluation of a situation or condition. The following experimental questions consist of manipulations of instructional variables.

1. Does telling clients that they are participating in a "treatment project that should alter their behavior" enhance the effects of a veridical treatment technique relative to telling clients they are participating in an "experiment that is not expected to alter their behavior"? Here, the treatment procedure is constant across groups. However, different instructions are compared to examine the influence of client expectancies on treatment outcome.

2. Do therapists interpret psychological test results differently when they are told that the test responses were produced by "disturbed patients" rather than from people functioning adequately in everyday life? The sample test responses given to different therapists might be identical, but the instructions to the therapists about who completed them would vary.

3. Does telling participants that their responses on psychological tests will be anonymous rather than identifiable influence their admission of socially undesirable behaviors? The task presented to the subject consists of a set of questions or items. Completion of the test is preceded by instructions that lead subjects to believe that their scores are anonymous or not.

Subject or Individual Difference Variables.   *Subject variables* refer to attributes or characteristics of the individual subjects. A term occasionally used is organismic variables, and this conveys nicely that some characteristic of the person or organism is to be studied. The way in which the term is used in psychology also encompasses characteristics to which subjects may be exposed (environmental contexts, living conditions). Subject variables are not usually manipulated directly. Rather, they are varied in an experiment by selecting subjects with different characteristics, experiences, attributes, or traits. Subject variables may include such obvious characteristics as age, education, social class, sex differences, exposure to trauma, or scores on some personality measure. In clinical psychology special samples are frequently studied, such as depressed adults, physically or sexually abused children, families of patients with a diagnosis of schizophrenia, couples in conflict, twins, only children, individuals who are identified as intellectually gifted, and persons of various cultural or ethnic backgrounds. In such studies, persons with or without the characteristic of interest or persons with varying degrees of that characteristic are compared.

The fact that the variables usually are called subject variables does not mean that the attributes only of individuals who usually serve as subjects are studied. Characteristics of therapists, interviewers, and experimenters also are subject variables and may be studied as such in experiments. Subject variable research may seek to elaborate differences and similarities among varied groups. For example, depressed and nondepressed parents may be identified and then compared in the manner in which they interact with their newborn infants, children, or spouses. Also, subject-variable research may evaluate the differential responsiveness or reactions of some persons to other variables (psychotherapy, efforts to manipulate mood). The following questions illustrate the subject variable research approach.

1. Do clients with more formal education gain more from psychotherapy than do clients with less education? Here education is the subject variable. Participants may be categorized in the study as college versus no college degree or baccalaureate versus postbaccalaureate education.

2. Do persons who have tested positive for HIV have increased stress relative to those untested or who have tested negative? Here groups are selected to evaluate the potential impact of diagnostic information.

3. Does birth order of the individual (position of birth among one's siblings) influence the professional accomplishments achieved in later life? Here adults who have, say, two siblings will be included. The adults might be placed into one of three groups according to whether they were born first, second, or third in relation to their two siblings. Individuals who vary in birth order are considered to be treated differently from each other in their families and this may be evident in later personality.

Subject variables often apply to broader characteristics that are related to living circumstances or situations. For example, socioeconomic status is frequently studied, in part because one's occupational, educational, and income level predict all sorts of mental and physical health outcomes. Lower socioeconomic status is associated with worse outcomes. Grouping individuals according to income or education would be subject-variable research as conceived here. Also, one might investigate special circumstances of the home (e.g., presence of guns in the home, single-parent families, parents who do versus do not share child-rearing responsibilities). None of these variables is manipulated by the experimenter and falls into this category.

Investigation of Multiple Variables

This discussion might imply that a given investigation is restricted to studying only one type of variable. Yet, an investigation can examine multiple variables of a particular type or different types of variables within a single study. Indeed, combining variables across categories in a given study is an excellent research strategy and may address a host of important questions. For example, for research in psychotherapy we do not wish merely to examine the effectiveness of varied treatments (an environmental variable). It is likely that the effects of a given treatment depend on a variety of other factors such as client characteristics (diagnosis, severity of problems) and therapist characteristics (competence, experience, warmth) (subject variables). To understand treatment as well as to identify optimally effective applications, studies that at once evaluate environmental variables in the context of subject variables can make a special contribution.

In general, a study that manipulates a single variable or single class of variables addresses a rudimentary question. This does not mean that the question is trivial. The importance of the question cannot be evaluated in the abstract; it is determined by the relation of the study to the existing literature, theory, practice, and other considerations. However, the complexity of the question is increased by combining variables, including variables from separate classes (subject and environmental variables). The question now addresses the impact of a given manipulation under varied conditions and hence represents a deeper understanding of how the variables of interest operate.

RESEARCH DESIGN OPTIONS

The initial stages of research entail development of the research idea and operationalization and selection of the specific variables of interest, as already highlighted. There remain a variety of options for research related to how the idea is evaluated and the conditions in which the study is conducted. The options have implications for diverse threats to validity and hence the conclusions that can be drawn. The different ways in which the study might be designed are detailed in subsequent chapters. As a way of an overview, it is useful to consider major design options in which the variables of interest may be evaluated.

Types of Research

Research in psychology actively draws upon three major types of studies: true experiments, quasi-experiments, and case-control designs. *True experiments* consist of investigations in which the arrangement permits maximum control over the independent variable or manipulation of interest. The investigator is able to assign subjects to different conditions on a random basis, to vary conditions (treatment and control conditions) as required by the design, and to control possible sources of bias within the experiment that permit the comparison of interest. From the standpoint of demonstrating the impact of a particular variable of interest, true experiments permit the strongest basis for drawing inferences.

True experiment is a generic term applied to studies with an intervention or experimental manipulation and random assignment of subjects to conditions. When true experiments are conducted in the context of an intervention, they are referred to as *randomized controlled clinical trials* (RCT or *randomized controlled trial*). The term is used in many disciplines (e.g., epidemiology, medicine) and refers to an outcome study in which clients with a particular problem are randomly assigned to various treatment and control conditions. In clinical psychology these are usually referred to as treatment outcome studies, the vast majority of which in fact are based on random assignment. Yet, an RCT leaves no doubt that the study uses random assignment and that the treatment or intervention is evaluated in the context of a clinical sample. It is useful to be familiar with this term because of its widespread use and because this type of study is recognized to be the best and most definitive way of demonstrating that an intervention is effective.

Occasionally, an investigator cannot control all features that characterize true experiments. Some facet of the study—such as the assignment of subjects to conditions or of conditions to settings—cannot be randomized. *Quasi-experiment* refers to those designs in which the conditions of true experiments are approximated (Campbell & Stanley, 1963). For example, an investigator may be asked to evaluate a school-based intervention program designed to prevent drug abuse or teen pregnancy. The investigator wishes to use a nonintervention control group because the passage of time, and influences that occur during that time (history, maturation, testing, and other internal validity threats), can lead to change. However, for practical reasons a control condition is not permitted within the school that wishes the program. The investigator seeks other schools that will serve as nonintervention control groups and uses students in these control schools for comparison purposes. These other schools might be similar (in population, size, geography). We have lost the central feature of true experiment, random assignment to groups, and a host of factors (e.g., motivation for change among administrators) may differ greatly across conditions. Already the design is less ideal than one would like. Yet, there are many design options and methods of drawing valid inferences. Quasi-experiments can provide very strong bases for influences and ought not to be ruled out. More later on this point.

True and quasi-experiments refer primarily to studies where an independent variable is manipulated by the investigator, as illustrated by providing treatment or an experimental condition to some persons but not to others. A great deal of clinical research focuses on variables that "nature" has manipulated in some way, as mentioned in the discussion of subject variables earlier in the chapter. *Case-control designs* refer to studies in which the variable of interest is studied by selecting subjects (cases) who vary in the characteristic or experience of interest. For example, the investigator might wish to study differences between cigarette smokers and nonsmokers in relation to some personality traits or background characteristics; between marital partners who are in the same occupation versus those who are not; between males and females; between persons who were former prisoners of war and those who were not. Of course, the investigator does not manipulate the independent variable, but does identify groups that vary in the characteristic of interest. A comparison group or groups must also be identified to control for factors that may interfere with drawing conclusions. Case-control studies can provide critical insights about the nature of a problem, characteristic, or experience, as I shall discuss at greater length later.[3]

It is often the case that true experiments, as compared to case-control studies, are considered as the only firm basis for drawing "causal" inferences in science, a clear demonstration that the independent variable led to the effects on the dependent variable. The strength of true experiments is without peer in demonstrating the impact of an in-

---

[3]Case-control design, as a term, is used frequently in epidemiology and public health but much less frequently in psychology. The type of research to which this term is used *has* been used frequently and has a long history in psychology. The terms in psychology related to case-control studies have been referred to as "correlational research" (see Cronbach, 1957, 1975) or "passive-observational studies or designs" (Cook & Campbell, 1979; Shadish et al., 2002) in which the relations among variables are observed but not manipulated. These designs are distinguished from "experimental research" in which variables are manipulated directly by the investigator.

dependent variable, given the control afforded and the ways in which that control rules out a variety of explanations that might account for the results. Even so, true experiments are not flawless. A true experiment, however well controlled, does not provide the basis for certainty of the finding. Also, case-control studies are not merely diluted experiments, invariably flawed, nor inherently incapable of yielding causal information. Ingenuity of the investigator in relation to selecting cases, and advances in methodology and statistics (path analyses, causal modeling, structural equation modeling, cross-lagged panel correlations) permit strong inferences to be drawn from case-control studies. Interests of clinical research involve many questions about "nature's" interventions. Theory, methodology, and statistical evaluation can be used to help separate the impact of different variables when the phenomenon of interest is not experimentally manipulated. It is worth noting that important breakthroughs come from sciences in which experimental manipulation and true experiments are not used or are used relatively infrequently. For example, empirical advances in economics, sociology, meteorology, and epidemiology often come from careful observation and analysis without experimental manipulation.

I have emphasized the importance of understanding the underlying rationale of methodological practices in addition to the practices themselves. A case in point is using designs in which one cannot manipulate the independent variable or assign subjects randomly. The purposes toward which these practices are directed are important to understand because designs such as quasi-experiments and case-control studies can be very powerful by making explicit efforts to rule out rival interpretations that true experiments easily accomplish. Chapters on various designs will convey and illustrate this more concretely.

Design Strategies

Research in clinical, counseling, and many other areas of psychology draws upon different types of designs. Group designs and single-case designs highlight the diversity of methods employed in clinical research. In *group designs* several subjects are studied. In the usual experiment, groups are formed by the investigator who assigns subjects to conditions, and each group usually receives only one of the conditions. Occasionally, the general class of designs is referred to as *between-group research* because separate groups of subjects are formed and ultimately compared. A between-group design includes at least as many groups as there are experimental conditions or treatments. In addition, depending on the precise question or hypothesis of interest, control groups add to the number of groups in the study.

The effects of different experimental and control conditions among groups are evaluated statistically by comparing groups on the dependent measures. Preliminary assignment of subjects to groups is usually determined randomly to produce groups equivalent on factors possibly related to the independent variable (intervention) or that might also account for group differences on the measures (dependent variables). If groups are equivalent on such factors *before* the experimental manipulation or treatment, any differences among groups *after* the manipulation are assumed to result from the effects of different experimental conditions. In clinical research a wide range of group designs are used, and the diversity of this general type of research alone raises a plethora of methodological issues.

In addition to group designs, clinical research also entails *single-case experimental designs*. These designs are characterized by investigation of a given individual, a few individuals, or one group over time. The underlying approach toward research for group and single-case designs is identical, namely, to implement conditions that permit valid inferences about the independent variable. However, in single-case research this is accomplished somewhat differently. Typically, one or a few subjects are studied. The dependent measures of interest are administered repeatedly over time (days or weeks). The manner in which the independent variable is implemented is examined in relation to the data pattern for the subject or group of subjects over time. Single-case designs can play a special role in clinical work where the focus is, of course, on the individual client. Single-case designs can be used to experimentally evaluate the impact of a given intervention or multiple interventions. As with group designs, there are many different single-case designs, with their own requirements, advantages, and obstacles.

Conditions of Experimentation

The conditions under which the investigation is conducted to test the ideas of interest can vary widely. Three distinctions can capture key differences in the conditions of the experiment and are noted in Table 5.3. The distinctions are relevant in any scientific discipline where there is interest in both basic questions (processes, mechanisms, structure, function) and applied questions (how can the information be used to make something work better, help people, enhance life?). Within many areas of

TABLE 5.3.   Conditions of Experimentation: Commonly Made Distinctions

Distinction/Terms	Bases for the Distinction
Laboratory versus applied (or field) research	The extent to which research is conducted under highly controlled conditions that depart from the conditions of everyday life and often the questions that are studied (e.g., basic process questions); applied is more likely to focus on real-world settings with the goal of establishing or showing what can be accomplished in actual conditions of everyday life or of direct clinical relevance.
Analogue versus clinical studies	The extent to which the research studies a phenomenon that is intended to resemble something that occurs in everyday life. The study of experimental neuroses induced in animals as a model to evaluate anxiety would be an example of an analogue study of human anxiety. The analogue–clinical distinction has been used in clinical psychology to encompass the issues discussed in efficacy versus effectiveness (see below).
Efficacy versus effectiveness	A distinction that has been reserved for intervention trials (treatment, prevention). Efficacy refers to research that is directed more toward the controlled conditions of the laboratory. An efficacy trial evaluates the impact of treatment under such conditions. Effectiveness refers to intervention research that is in applied settings and under the conditions in which treatment is actually administered (patients, therapists, and settings).

Note: The distinctions are often discussed as qualitatively different; as noted in the discussion, the conditions of research can vary along multiple dimensions that may vary in the extent to which the research falls more toward one side of the dimension (e.g., laboratory) versus the other (e.g., applied). This means that a great deal of research falls within the middle.

psychology (clinical, counseling, educational) and among many disciplines (medicine, social work, education, rehabilitation, nursing) these distinctions often emerge. The distinctions in the table are often discussed as if they were sharp and categorical. So, for example, one can read about laboratory *versus* applied research. In fact, as noted below, one can view each as a bipolar continuum, that is, with one label on the right (e.g., laboratory) and one label on the left (e.g., applied.). Two studies from each extreme side may look completely dissimilar, but it is easy to blur each of the distinctions by pointing to research somewhere in the middle.

Laboratory research, in contrast to *applied research,* usually refers to investigations conducted in a special research setting (psychology department, research space where subjects are brought to engage in some laboratory procedure). Laboratory research usually is devoted to basic questions under conditions that are highly controlled. For example, laboratory research may consist of evaluation of the performance of college students who receive instructions designed to alter their mood, perform a task, or evaluate videotape of another person. The researcher is not likely to be interested only in the moods of college students in the laboratory, but rather in how moods operate in general. In contrast, research in an applied setting may be at a clinic where patients are seen for treatment. The research may evaluate different types of treatment or evaluate different populations (persons referred for one type of problem versus another type of problem). In laboratory and applied research, the differences encompass more than merely the settings. The research questions, characteristics of the subjects, nature of the dependent variable, and research problems that emerge can vary greatly as well.

Analogue and *clinical research* are related to laboratory and applied, but the terms have been used slightly differently. An analogue study usually focuses on a carefully defined research question under well-controlled conditions. The purpose of the research is to illuminate a particular process or to study treatment that may be important in clinical applications. The process or topic studied in the laboratory is considered to closely resemble or to provide a model for some phenomenon that is more difficult to study or to isolate in everyday life. Table 5.3 mentions experimental neurosis as an example. Experimental neurosis is a laboratory-induced emotional reaction that was discovered in the context of animal conditioning experiments. Under special circumstances during conditioning, an animal may become very agitated and show reactions (irritability, escape, avoidance, and disturbances in physiological activity) that suggest extreme anxiety. The phenomenon had theoretical implications related to learning and psychopathology. Experimental neurosis also served as a basis for developing a number of treatments for human anxiety disorders. Experimental neurosis is not like anxiety disorders in humans, which are not experimentally induced reactions. However, this served as a useful analogue of anxiety reactions (see Kazdin, 1978b).[4]

---

[4]This phenomenon emerged in the study of discriminations in Pavlov's laboratory in 1912–13. Animals were trained to make a discrimination. When the discrimination became difficult to make, the animals showed a reaction that evidenced great agitation and disruption. This later came to be known as experimental neurosis and also became a topic of experimental research. Different ways of inducing the reaction were developed and studied across several species (goats, sheep, pigs, rabbits, cats, and dogs).

Analogue research refers to a wide range of studies beyond those involving animal research. For example, analogue research has consisted of interpersonal interactions in laboratory studies where interviews or personal exchanges resemble in varying degrees the interactions of a therapist and patient in psychotherapy. The distinction of analogue and clinical research has emerged in the context of psychotherapy research (e.g., Kazdin, 1978a). Studies of therapy or therapeutic processes were completed with college students under well-controlled conditions that bore little or no resemblance to clinical work.

Although analogue research is clear when one tries to capture a particular process (social interaction, cognitions induced by stress) in a laboratory setting, the concept may be considered more broadly. In a sense virtually all experimental research with human subjects is analogue research insofar as it constructs a situation in which a particular phenomenon can be studied. Informing subjects that they are participating in research, evaluating controlled and time-limited interventions or experimental manipulations, using as outcome measures specific psychological assessment devices (e.g., questionnaires), and similar conditions make the situation analogous to one to which the investigator might wish to generalize. Although all or most research is an analogue in some way, clearly research can vary in the extent to which it isolates the phenomenon of interest and departs from the phenomenon as it exists in nature.

As mentioned in Chapter 2, efficacy and effectiveness research is a distinction that focuses on intervention research and specifically psychotherapy outcome research (Hoagwood et al., 1995). *Efficacy research* refers to treatment outcomes obtained in controlled psychotherapy studies that are conducted under laboratory and quasi-laboratory conditions (subjects are recruited, they may show a narrow range of problems, treatment is specified in manual form, and treatment delivery is closely supervised and monitored). *Effectiveness research* refers to treatment outcomes obtained in clinic settings where the usual control procedures are not implemented (patients seek treatment, many present multiple clinical problems). Efficacy and effectiveness studies can be conceived as a continuum or multiple continua because several dimensions can vary across clinic and laboratory settings that affect generality of the results (Hoagwood et al., 1995; Kazdin, 1978a). Table 5.4 conveys many of these dimensions and points on the continuum that vary from a clinical setting (effectiveness type of research) versus laboratory setting (efficacy). A given psychotherapy study can vary along the different dimensions. The closer one moves toward the *right side* of the table, where conditions of the experiment do not resemble very well clinical or applied settings, the greater the ability of the investigator to control facets of the investigation and hence rule out many threats to internal validity. Studies characterized by features toward the right of the table are more likely to be labeled as efficacy studies. The closer one moves toward the *left side* of the table, where conditions resemble applied settings, the greater the external validity, but also the more difficulty in controlling many facets of the study. Studies characterized by features toward the left of the table are more likely to be labeled as effectiveness. The extent to which a study has generalizable results that apply to the clinical setting cannot be decided by merely looking whether the study departs from

TABLE 5.4.   Select Dimensions along Which Studies May Vary and the Degree of Resemblance to the Clinical Situation

	Resemblance to the Clinical or Nonresearch Situation		
Dimension	*Identity with or Great Resemblance*	*Moderate Resemblance*	*Relatively Low Resemblance*
Target problem	Problem seen in the clinic, intense or disabling	Similar to that in clinic but less severe	Nonproblem behavior or experimental task
Population	Clients in outpatient treatment	College students with nontreatment interest	Infrahuman subjects
Manner of recruitment	Clients who seek treatment	Individuals recruited for available treatment	Captive subjects who serve for course credit
Therapists	Professional therapists	Therapists in training	Nontherapists or nonprofessionals
Client set	Expect treatment and improvement	Expect "experimental" treatment with unclear effects	Expect experiment with nontreatment focus
Selection of treatment	Client chooses therapist and specific treatment	Client given choice over few alternative procedures in an experiment	Client assigned to treatment with no choice for specific therapist or condition
Specification of treatment	What to do is at the discretion of the therapist	General guidelines, goals, and themes to direct focus of the session	Treatment manual specifies means and ends of each treatment session, including, maybe, even many of the statements of the therapist
Monitoring of treatment	Little or no monitoring of what is done with the client	Case supervision or discussion to review what was done, how it was done, and client progress	Careful assessment of how treatment was delivered (audio, videotape; direct observation, case supervision)
Setting of treatment	Professional treatment facility	University facility that may not regularly offer treatment	Laboratory setting
Variation of treatment	Treatment as usually conducted	Variation to standardize treatment for research	Analogue of the treatment as in infrahuman equivalent of treatment
Assessment methods	Direct unobtrusive measure of the problem that the client originally reported	Assessment on psychological devices that sample behaviors of interest directly	Questionnaire responses about the behaviors that are a problem

the left side of the table on various dimensions. Many of the dimensions listed may not influence external validity, even though the study departs from the conditions of applied settings.

External validity is not the only issue to consider in deciding what experimental conditions to use. In some cases there is no interest in generalizing to other settings as, for example, when basic research is conducted to test theory or to understand a particular process (communication between couples, changes in cognitions as a function of special kinds of communication). A problem in research emerges when the setting or type of research is not well suited to the focus. For example, well-controlled laboratory (efficacy) studies of therapy have focused on whether treatment produces therapeutic change. This is fine but quite limited. The advantages of the laboratory are that one can study mechanisms, processes, and how therapy works. Fine-grained analyses of treatment can be made. Very few laboratory studies of therapy have this focus (Kazdin, 2001). The concern for effectiveness studies is a reminder to researchers that outcome questions need to incorporate subjects (patients) and conditions (real clinics and therapists) where these questions matter. It is not that laboratory studies of therapy are unimportant. Just the opposite; they are needed to ask the questions that cannot be easily asked in real-world settings.

Time Frame for Research

Research often varies in the time frame for investigation. The bulk of research is conducted in a concurrent time frame in which the experimental manipulation (independent variables of interest) and the measures to evaluate the impact of the manipulation (dependent variables) are administered and completed within a relatively brief period. An example would be a laboratory experiment in which subjects are exposed to an independent variable and complete the measures within one or two laboratory sessions. In contrast, the investigation may be conducted over an extended period of, say, several years. A frequent distinction is made between cross-sectional and longitudinal studies. *Cross-sectional studies* usually make comparisons between groups at a given point in time. *Longitudinal studies* make comparisons over an extended period, often involving several years. The results from cross-sectional and longitudinal studies can be quite different even when similar questions are addressed.

For example, over the course of child development, many behaviors bothersome to children or parents (stuttering, anxiety, destroying objects, lying) are relatively common. The different problems wax and wane over the course of development, peak at different periods, and usually diminish to a very low rate among nonclinic samples. The pattern of behavior can be assessed concurrently by evaluating children of different ages (e.g., Achenbach, 1991). This would be a cross-sectional study and would show a pattern of behavior at different ages. This type of study *suggests* a developmental pattern, that is, how behaviors change in frequency over time. This is not the same as the yield from a longitudinal study in which a group is identified in infancy or childhood and repeatedly assessed (e.g., every few years) over the course of childhood, adolescence, and adulthood (Werner & Smith, 1992). The longitudinal study portrays how behaviors actually *change* in a given sample because the same children are studied over time.

One type of study is not inherently superior. Indeed, they have different strengths and limitations. For example, a cross-sectional study may suggest that children show different characteristics at different ages. Yet, there is a possible *cohort effect*. This refers to the possibility that different age groups of subjects (cohorts) may have unique characteristics because of their different histories. Thus, for example, 2-year-olds may not have the pattern of behavior of the 8-year-olds when they mature; possibly something about how the 2-year-olds are growing up (nutrition, different parenting styles with more or fewer parents in the home) influences their performance in ways not evident in the other group(s), and in 6 years, when they are 8 years old, they will not look like the 8-year-olds included in the cross-sectional study.

In a longitudinal study differential history of the group is controlled because a group or more than one group is followed over time. We know that the 2-year-olds matured into 8-year-olds with a particular pattern. There is a cohort effect as well within the longitudinal study because it is possible that 2-year-olds, who were followed over time, might differ from other 2-year-olds who were selected at a different point in time. Also, in longitudinal studies it is often difficult to follow the subjects. Attrition or loss of subjects over time can limit the conclusions because of selection biases if the sample is increasingly depleted. Longitudinal and cross-sectional design strategies are often combined by selecting a few groups (4-, 6-, and 8-year olds), assessing them cross-sectionally, and then following them for a few years (2–4 years). The strategy speeds up the design a bit from merely following one sample and permits one to assess whether cohorts differ when they reach a given age, as discussed further in a later chapter.

Evidence from different time frames can be used to address different questions or even the same question differently. For example, the investigator may be interested in the correlates of viewing violence on television among children, a topic that has received considerable attention. Within a current time perspective, the investigator might compare children who view violent television versus those who watch as much television but who do not view violent programs. Children might be matched on diverse subjects (age, sex, IQ) and demographic characteristics (socioeconomic status, type of neighborhood). Comparisons might then be made on some other measures such as personality characteristics of the child or parents or perhaps aggressive behavior of the child at home or at school. The purpose would be to elaborate the features associated with television viewing. As an alternative, a more longitudinal focus might include following (assessing) children over time. Among the questions that might be asked is, "What are the correlates of early television viewing later in life?" Both cross-sectional and longitudinal studies indicate that viewing violence on television is associated with aggressive behavior and that the relation is influenced by a variety of factors (sex of the child, success of children in school) (see Strasburger, 1995). In general, the time frame is important to consider in designing research because, as we shall see later, conclusions often vary as a function of when assessment is conducted over time.

SUMMARY AND CONCLUSIONS

The research idea that serves as a basis for experimentation may be derived from any of several sources, including curiosity about a particular phenomenon, case studies, interest in special populations (those who meet criteria for a particular disorder, those with a special history or experience), extrapolation of findings from other types of research (e.g., processes studied in animal research), development of measurements, and many others. Research may also seek to illuminate whether variables or characteristics are related as reflected in such concepts as correlates, risk factors, causes, moderators, and mediators. When possible it is useful to draw on theory to guide a research study. Theory refers to a conceptual view about the relationship, that is, how the variables of interest relate to each other and to the extent possible, why, and under what conditions.

Not all research needs to be driven by theory. Research that carefully describes phenomena, too, can contribute greatly. The distinction was made between testing hypotheses (usually theory driven) and generating hypotheses (describing phenomena so as to generate theory). The goal of research is to understand the phenomenon of interest, and one can begin the path toward this by generating or testing hypotheses.

Whatever the initial impetus for research, ultimately it needs to be specified in operational terms. Specific experimental operations, procedures, and measures define the independent and dependent variables. When the experiment begins, it is not the overall concept that is manipulated but rather the specific operationally defined variable. Characteristics, strengths, and limitations of operational definitions were discussed.

The variables that comprise clinical investigations usually include environmental, instructional, and subject variables. Environmental variables usually consist of manipulating what is offered, presented, or done to the client. Instructional variables, actually a subcategory of environmental variables, refer to what the client is told. Subject variables consist of attributes, traits, or characteristics of the subjects, experimenters, or therapists, or others. Subject variables are examined by selecting subjects with specific characteristics rather than by manipulating specific conditions.

Developing the research idea and operationalizing and selecting the specific variables are initial stages of the study. A variety of design options emerge in relation to how the effect of the variables is actually examined. True experiments, quasi-experiments, and case-control studies were highlighted to define major types of research. Randomized controlled clinical trial is a term that is often used to delineate a true experiment in the context of treatment research. Varied design strategies were noted by distinguishing group and single-case research.

The conditions under which research is conducted were also discussed. Distinctions often made in research—including laboratory versus applied, analogue versus clinical, and efficacy versus effectiveness studies—were highlighted. These distinctions are related insofar as one end of the spectrum (laboratory, analogue, and efficacy) emphasizes experimental control whereas the other side (applied, clinical, effectiveness) focuses more on extensions to the real world. Studies can vary along multiple dimensions to reflect these different ends of the pole.

Finally, the time frame of research was discussed as a condition that can vary among experiments. Cross-sectional and longitudinal research were noted to convey strategies that vary in the time frame. Design and method options vary in the advantages and disadvantages they provide. In the next chapters I elaborate designs in clinical research and the issues they address and raise in relation to drawing valid inferences.

KEY CONCEPTS AND TERMS

Mediator

Moderator

Operational Definitions

Quasi-Experiments

Randomized Controlled Clinical Trial

Risk Factor

True Experiment

FOR FURTHER READING

Adams, J.L. (1990). *Conceptual blockbusting: A guide to better ideas* (3rd ed.). Cambridge, MA: Perseus.

Baron, R.M., & Kenny, D.A. (1986). The moderator-mediator variable distinction in social psychological research: Conceptual, strategic, and statistical considerations. *Journal of Personality and Social Psychology, 51,* 1173–1182.

Haynes, S.N. (1992). *Models of causality in psychopathology: Toward dynamic, synthetic, and nonlinear models of behavior disorders.* Needham Heights, MA: Allyn & Bacon.

Holmbeck, G.N. (1997). Toward terminological, conceptual, and statistical clarity in the study of mediators and moderators: Examples from the child-clinical and pediatric psychology literatures. *Journal of Consulting and Clinical Psychology, 65,* 599–610.

Kazdin, A.E., Kraemer, H.C., Kessler, R.C., Kupfer, D.J., & Offord, D.R. (1997). Contributions of risk-factor research to developmental psychopathology. *Clinical Psychology Review, 17,* 375–406.

Kraemer, H.C., Kazdin, A.E., Offord, D.R., Kessler, R.C., Jensen, P.S., & Kupfer, D.J. (1997). Coming to terms with the terms of risk. *Archives of General Psychiatry, 54,* 337–343.

McGuire, W.J. (1997). Creating hypothesis generating in psychology: Some useful heuristics. *Annual Review of Psychology, 48,* 1–30.

Chapter 6

Experimental Research

Group Designs

By far the most common research designs within psychology compare groups of subjects who are exposed to different conditions that are controlled by the investigator. The general strategy can entail a variety of different arrangements depending on the groups included in the design, how assessment is planned, and when and to whom the intervention is presented. This chapter considers fundamentals of group designs and various options when the investigator manipulates or systematically varies conditions and controls the assignment of subjects to different conditions.

SUBJECT SELECTION

A fundamental issue in group designs is the selection of participants for research, that is, who will serve as subjects in the study. This topic is underdiscussed in psychological methods because the task of subject selection seems obvious. If one wants to do animal research, then the sample (rats, mice) usually is dictated by tradition and subject matter; if one wants to conduct a laboratory study with humans (e.g., in social or clinical psychology), then college students enrolled in introductory psychology are probably just fine. Yet, there are many issues about subject selection that have great implications for methodological concerns, beyond the obvious matter of external validity or generalizing to a population.

Random Selection

Randomness is discussed frequently in scientific research. When investigators discuss randomization in experimentation, they usually are concerned with one of two concepts, namely, random selection of subjects from a population and random assignment of subjects to experimental conditions. In group designs within psychology, random assignment and related procedures to form groups are the central topics and are taken up later in this chapter. Random selection is an independent issue that is not necessarily related to the particular design but warrants mention.

Random selection of subjects refers to the equal probability that subjects within the population can be selected. That is, there is no bias in who is selected for the study based on all of the cases from which the sample might be drawn. Random selection enhances the generality (external validity) of experimental results. If we wish to generalize results from a sample of subjects in the experiment to a population of potential subjects, usually it is essential to select a representative sample of the population. For example, if we wish to draw conclusions about depressed patients in general, we would not want to restrict selection to patients in a particular hospital or clinic in a particular city, state, or country but would want to sample from all available persons. If subjects can be drawn from the entire population, it is more likely that the sample will represent that population. Generality of experimental results (external validity) depends upon the representativeness of the participants in the experiment to those individuals who were not included, that is, the rest of the population. Random selection refers to drawing from the total population of interest in such a way that each member of the population has an equal probability of being drawn. If that is accomplished and the sample is relatively large, one can assume there is no special bias in who was selected.

There is an obvious restriction in principle as well as practice to random selection. Subjects in an experiment cannot be selected from a population unless that population is very narrowly defined. For example, for a population defined as "all introductory psychology students currently enrolled in a given term at this university," a random sample might be obtainable. However, a random sample of "introductory psychology students in general" could not be readily obtained. To sample this latter population would require being able to select from all individuals who have had introductory psychology already, including those no longer living, all those currently enrolled, and all who are yet to enroll (including unborn individuals) across all geographical settings. Sampling from all subjects in the population including those who are deceased or yet to be born, of course, is not possible. If generality of the experimental results to a population depends upon having randomly sampled from a population, conclusions would seem to be restricted to the narrowly confined groups of subjects.

Random selection from a population is often central to research. For example, epidemiological research identifies the distribution of various conditions (diseases, mental disorders) within a population. In such studies, special sampling procedures are used to ensure that the sample represents the current population of interest. Usually, different segments or subgroups of a population (households, blocks within a neighborhood) are identified to reflect such demographic variables of interest as geography, social class, ethnicity, and religion. Within such groups persons are selected randomly so that the final sample reflects this distribution. In survey and opinion poll research as well, sampling from the population in this way is also critically important to ensure generality of the findings to the larger population, within some margin of error. Also, it may be of interest to divide the data by the various subgroups in the sample and report data separately. For example, in surveys, often women versus men, younger versus older, and other subgroups are presented separately.

In psychological research—whether in clinical, social, counseling, or other areas—random sampling from a population is not usually invoked. A representative sample is not considered as essential, nor is its absence viewed as an issue. There are exceptions. For example, one study was designed to evaluate and to treat cigarette smokers and to sample from two communities in a way that the results would represent the population within these communities (Killen et al., 1996). The selection began with calling segments of the population to represent the larger communities; this included random-digit dialing (because many residents had unlisted phone numbers). Once a home was called, all adults who were smokers were identified and asked to be interviewed, and eventually invited (with an opportunity to win $100) for treatment. This is a complex procedure and, of course, includes several hurdles in obtaining the final sample. The final sample (who agrees to participate) may not represent the population perfectly (e.g., excludes those without phones). As discussed in the previous chapter, volunteer subjects can be quite different from nonvolunteer subjects. Even so, the effort to recruit in this study is likely to represent the community fairly well and much better than a study that recruits a sample from one or two sources.

Who Will Serve as Subjects and Why?

Diversity of the Sample.   If selection is not random, then much further thought needs to be given to who *is* selected and why. A few critical issues ought to be considered explicitly when beginning a study. The most salient one is that much of research in the United States (psychological, biological) has been conducted primarily with European American males (see Graham, 1992; Guthrie, 1997). Underrepresented and minority groups are less frequently studied. Important scientific, social, and policy issues underlie this concern. For example, minority groups represent multiple and significant segments of the population, and there is no compelling scientific rationale for their exclusion. Indeed, insofar as findings from research have immediate as well as long-term implications for physical and mental health or well being in general, the absence of research on the various groups might even be considered as discriminatory. Any benefits directly stemming from a specific research project (e.g., diagnostic and intervention studies) or policy decisions that might result from a series of studies could be limited to or influenced by the restricted groups of subjects who were studied.

In psychology add to the limited sampling of ethnicity, the extreme reliance on college students, and the very narrow range of citizens is even more restricted. As researchers we usually do not want to restrict research to one group. Sex, ethnic identity, and socioeconomic status are three categories for consideration that illustrate the issue. These variables could moderate all sorts of relations of interest. For example, in clinical psychology such topics as the family, stress and coping, social support, child-rearing practices, bereavement, and participation in or seeking treatment enter into many areas of research with multiple tributaries. There are ethnic group differences in relation to each of these areas and one ought to ensure that these differences are addressed, revealed, and eventually understood in research. Mentioned previously (Chapter 2) were studies of biological differences among diverse ethnic and cultural groups that have significant influence on the effects and side effects of medication for psychological problems (depression, anxiety).

Similarly, socioeconomic status is a variable that has pervasive influences on all sorts of mental and physical health outcomes (Adler et al., 1994; Luthar, 1999). It is very likely that socioeconomic status (occupational status, education, income) will moderate many relations and findings in psychological research. Indeed, on a priori, rather than empirical, grounds one can conclude that socioeconomic differences will play a major role in some areas of research. The base rates of some characteristics psychologists study (high levels of stress, illness, early mortality) differ as a function of socioeconomic status, and this can influence the correlations of these variables with other influences that are studied.

There has been direct neglect of many populations. In addition, a general operating assumption has been that lawful relationships from experiments with a given sample (European American males, college students) are likely to hold for other individuals as well. Many variables across which one wishes to generalize may be irrelevant to the lawful relation discovered in the initial experiment. For example, assume we have developed an effective psychotherapy to treat agoraphobia (fear of open spaces) among young adults. It seems parsimonious to assume initially that this treatment will be effective for males and females, young and old adults, and various ethnic and racial groups. As a general rule, the variables across which the results of a given finding can be extended must be determined empirically. The justification of generalizing results can come from direct experimental extensions to these other samples or from inferences about the likelihood that basic processes demonstrated in research vary, or are not likely to vary, as a function of different subject or other variables. Yet, it is quite possible, and in a given case maybe even likely, that generality might not hold.

A dilemma is that we do not want to study whether a particular empirical relation or finding generalizes across all possible conditions (any subject or group characteristic). For example, the most recent United States Census recognized over 60 different racial options including 6 single races (White, Black, Asian, American Indian or Alaska Native, Native Hawaiian or Other Pacific Islander, and Some Other), 15 possible combinations of 2 races, 20 combinations of 3 races, 15 combinations of 4 races, 6 combinations of 5 races, and one grand combination of all 6. Moreover, these racial categories were further combined with two ethnic categories (Hispanic or non-Hispanic), which led ultimately to 126 different combinations of race and ethnicity. Even at that it is obvious that many of the groupings (e.g., the 6 single races) gloss over distinctions that are important. The number (126 combinations) itself is not significant for present purposes except to convey the point that it would not be possible—or, I believe, desirable—to evaluate whether particular findings extended across each of the recognized populations. Of course, race and ethnicity leave out many other grouping variables (gender identity and preference, country of origin) that delineate us and can make a difference in psychological and biological domains.

Theory is very relevant as a way of suggesting what dimensions might influence generality of the finding and generating hypotheses about why the phenomenon would be evident in one set of circumstances or for some subjects but not others. When there is no theory, it still can be quite useful to test whether the results obtained in the study (main effect) vary as a function of such other variables as sex, race, ethnicity, or social class. Although such comparisons may not initially be based on theory, differences that are found can be used to generate possible ideas for research as to why there might be such differences. A difficulty is that much research is based on just testing a novel group without even moving to suggest or explain why there might be differences. For example, a given effect may vary among different ethnic groups as a function of perception of the task, cultural meaning, context in which such influences ordinarily occur, accessibility to language use in the experiment, and other such influences (see Council of National Psychological Associations, 2000).

In some research, selecting a very restricted sample is fine for several reasons. First, the goal of the study may dictate a restricted sample. For example, studies of postpartum depression and breast cancer focus on women who experience the problem. The main interest is in women, although each of these disorders is also evident in men (at a very minute rate in men). Including men would not be feasible and would be likely to be outside the goals of most research. Also, it is quite likely that different processes are involved for males and females in the onset and course of the disorders.

Second, the investigator may view the sample as not particularly relevant or critical. The demonstration may focus on a phenomenon that is of theoretical significance. Ivan Pavlov's (1849–1936) research on classical conditioning with dogs is of this ilk. It is fortunate for us that Pavlov did not start worrying immediately if dogs of different sizes, temperament, color, age, and weight—not to mention dog socioeconomic status—would also show the effects of conditioning. Fortunately as well, there was no naive and annoying methodologist who was peppering Pavlov with questions about external validity. Years later we learned of the amazing generality of the phenomenon, but this was not the initial import of the finding.

Third, even when generality is interesting and important for the initial finding, a broad and diverse sample is not always available for study. In most settings not all the racial and ethnic groups from which one might like to sample are available. For example, my own research is conducted at a clinic for the treatment of children and families.[1] The clinic draws from local communities and hence includes European American, African American, Hispanic American, Asian, and combinations. The first two groups comprise over 90 percent of the sample, and only these groups can be examined in the data analyses. The small numbers have never permitted data analyses of other groups because of inadequate power.

Samples of Convenience.   It is often the case that a sample is selected because it is around or available. A *sample of convenience* is a set of subjects that is studied because they are present in a convenient situation (waiting room, hospital ward) or is available for a quite different purpose (participation in another experiment that requires a special population). An investigator may use an available sample to test a particular idea or to evaluate a measure he or she has just developed. However, in a sample of convenience, often there is no clear rationale as to why this sample is important, useful, or relevant to the study.

College students who serve as subjects constitute the main instance of this. Few researchers are really interested in specifically how college students behave, but they are selected because they are captive and in many cases are required to complete experiments as part of their participation in a course. Samples that are used merely because they are available are referred to as samples of convenience. Perhaps because college students are used so frequently, the term is not usually applied to students. That is, in many areas of research, college students are the standard subject population and hence not viewed as special or select. However, it is useful to view this as a sample of convenience because in most studies, the hypotheses, focus, or research design rarely calls for the use of a young, educated, bright, sexually active, and often tired and stressed human sample.

The typical situation in which the term sample of convenience is used is one in which a project is conducted to evaluate a special population (parents of children who visit a clinic for their diabetes, a sample of psychiatric patients). As that study is begun, the original investigators or other investigators realize that the data set can be used to test other hypotheses, even though the original sample may not be the sample that would have been identified originally if these other, new purposes were the central part of the study. When samples of convenience are used, the onus is on the investigator to evaluate or at least discuss whether unique features of the sample may contribute to the results. The use of a highly specialized population that is selected merely because it is convenient raises concern. It is not clear that the sample is well

---

[1]Occasionally in this book, I make reference to a clinic in which I work. This is the Yale Child Conduct Clinic, an outpatient treatment service for children and families. Children seen at the clinic are between the ages 2–13 and are referred for oppositional, aggressive, and antisocial behavior. Treatments provided at the clinic include variations of cognitive problem-solving skills training and parent management training (see Kazdin, Siegel, & Bass, 1992; Kazdin & Wassell, 2000).

(or for that matter poorly) suited to the question. The specialized population and the factors that make them particularly convenient may have implications for generalizing the results.

The entire issue of sample of convenience raises a broader question that is pertinent to all research. Some rationale ought to be provided why the sample (college students, people of one ethnicity, a particular age) was selected for any research project. More thought about the sample could enrich the hypotheses and yield as well. The thought might prompt more hypotheses to test or generate predictions about characteristics (moderators) that influence the findings. On the other hand, the investigator may feel that the population is not relevant. That would be a rather strong claim and would be worth making and explaining.

SUBJECT ASSIGNMENT AND GROUP FORMATION

Selection of the sample—that is, who will serve as subjects—is, of course, quite different from how subjects, once selected, are allocated to various groups or conditions in the study. A fundamental issue of research is ensuring that subjects in different groups or conditions are not different before the experimental manipulation or intervention is provided. Indeed, in an earlier discussion, selection (group differences) was a fundamental bias or threat to internal validity. Selection in this sense does not refer to who the subjects are but rather whether groups may differ because subjects selected to serve in one group (e.g., treatment) differ from those selected to serve in another group. A goal of research is to equalize groups except for the one variable (or multiple variables) that the investigator wishes to study or evaluate.

Random Assignment

Once the group of subjects has been selected for the study, it is critical to assign them to groups in an unbiased fashion. *Random assignment* consists of allocating subjects to groups in such a way that the probability of each subject appearing in any of the groups is equal. This is usually accomplished by determining the group to which each subject is assigned by a table of random numbers. Typically, such tables are available in many statistics books and Web sites.[2] For example, if there are three groups in the

---

[2]There are Web sites that can provide random numbers to be used for research (e.g., Random.org; randomizer.org; fourmilab.ch/hotbits; lavarand.sgi.com). I am almost certain that the reader is eager to learn that many—probably most or even almost all—random-numbers tables or computer-generated sequences of numbers are not truly random. (These are the topics often discussed at late-night methodology parties [they usually end by 10:00 pm].) For example, computers follow algorithms, and any particular algorithm influences—or, rather, dictates—the next number in the sequence. Technically, this is not purely random. The Web sites noted previously give numbers that are random or better approximations. For example, Random.org generates numbers in the following way. A radio is tuned to an unused frequency. Static is generated from the atmosphere on that station (as one hears static on a radio). The fluctuating static is converted into numbers that are unpredictable and random (from one to the next). Just using a random-numbers table is fine.

experiment, a random-numbers table can be consulted to draw numbers 1, 2, and 3 that correspond to each of the groups several times in random order. The numbers would be listed in the order in which they are drawn from the table (1, 1, 3, 2, 3, 3, etc.). (Numbers other than 1, 2, or 3 in the table, of course, are ignored.) As the subjects arrive to the experiment, they are assigned to the groups in the order according to the number that was drawn. So the first two subjects in our study would be assigned to group 1, the third to group 3, and so on in order. With such assignment, subjects are effectively assigned to groups randomly, according to the predetermined schedule.

Drawing random numbers to determine group assignment does not guarantee that an equal number of subjects would be assigned to each group. In the above example, the number 3 may have been drawn from the table more times than the numbers 1 and 2, and thus more subjects would be assigned to this group than to the other groups. For power of statistical tests (statistical conclusion validity) and convenience in conducting several statistical analyses, it is better to have equal, rather than unequal, group sizes. This can be accomplished without violating random assignment by grouping subjects into blocks. Each block consists of the number of subjects that equals the number of groups in the experiment. If there are three groups, the first three subjects who appear in the experiment can be viewed as one block. One subject from this block of three would be assigned to each of the three groups. Importantly, the group to which any individual is assigned within a block is random. Assignment is accomplished by drawing numbers 1, 2, and 3 in any order as long as each block encompasses each number (1,2,3) only once. Assigning subjects based on numbers drawn in this way ensures that, as the experiment progresses, groups will not differ in size and that subjects in each group are run over the course of the experiment.

Random assignment obviously is important and seems too basic to warrant comment. However, the simplicity of random assignment as a procedure—that is, how it is accomplished—belies greater complexities. As I discuss later, random assignment does not necessarily guarantee that groups are equivalent. Even so, random assignment is the best guarantee of making implausible various threats to internal validity (selection × history, selection × maturation) and for addressing the range of unintended influences (e.g., different subject characteristics in the groups) that might contribute to group differences.

Random assignment is obviously important on a priori grounds, but does it make a difference in any palpable way? Few studies have looked at the impact of random assignment on the results. As an example, a review of marital and family therapy research compared studies in which individuals were randomly assigned to conditions with those in which they were not (Shadish & Ragsdale, 1996). The strength of the effects (effect size) was greater and less variable for those studies that used random assignment. This is interesting indeed. The primary rationale for using random assignment is to facilitate interpretation of the effects we obtain, apart from any impact that assignment may have on the results themselves.

Although randomly assigning cases to conditions is the preferred method of assigning subjects, in many situations in which researchers work (clinics, hospitals, schools) this is not possible. This does not in any way doom the study to weak inferences. Indeed, one's knowledge of principles and practices of methodology becomes more important in this context to ensure that valid and strong inferences can be reached. A later discussion of different designs (quasi-experimental and case-control studies) will illustrate this point further.

Group Equivalence

Random assignment is important as a means of distributing characteristics of the sample among groups. There are several subject characteristics (age, sex, current historical events, motivation for participation), circumstances of participation (order of appearance or entry into the study), and other factors that might, if uncontrolled, interfere with interpretation of group differences. In some studies, evaluating the impact of these variables may be the central purpose. In other studies, they might be regarded as nuisance variables that, if uncontrolled, will obscure interpretation. *Nuisance variables* essentially are those characteristics in which one is not interested but that, in principle, could influence the results. Random assignment is a way of ensuring that such nuisance variables will be distributed unsystematically across groups. An advantage of random assignment is that it does not require the investigator to be aware of all of the important variables that might be related to the outcome of the experiment. Over a sufficient number of subjects, the many different nuisance variables can be assumed to be distributed evenly among groups.

Random assignment sometimes is viewed as a dependable way of producing equivalent groups. Yet, random assignment refers only to the method of allocating subjects to groups and, in a given experiment, has no necessary connection with a particular outcome. Randomly assigning subjects can produce groups that differ on all sorts of measures. Group differences are more likely when sample sizes are small and when there are extreme scores in the sample. (When I say group differences, I do not necessarily mean statistically significant differences, but rather genuine differences in characteristics of the sample. The small sample size might not permit detection, for reasons noted below.) As an extreme example, if 15 subjects are to be allocated to three groups and the subjects vary widely in age, level of anxiety, and other subject variables, it is quite possible that groups may differ significantly on these variables even after random assignment.

It is important to underscore that random assignment does not necessarily produce equivalent groups. With random assignment, the likelihood that groups are equivalent increases as a function of the sample size. This means that with small samples, group equivalence cannot be assumed. This is especially relevant to clinical research, as for example in studies of psychotherapy, where sample sizes may be relatively small (10–20 subjects per group) (see Kazdin & Bass, 1989). When the total sample (N) is in this range (e.g., 20–40 subjects total in a two-group study), the likelihood that groups are not equivalent across a number of nuisance variables is relatively high (see Hsu, 1989). The net effect is that at the end of the study, the difference between groups due to the intervention may be obscured or misrepresented because of the nonequivalence of groups. An effect of therapy may be diminished or hidden (no statistically significant differences) because of the impact of such variables on outcome. For example, some unknown characteristic more evident among subjects in the treatment group may have made them less likely to change with treatment, or that characteristic may have made the group look better at posttreatment even if no treatment had been administered.

Investigators wish to establish that the groups are equivalent by comparing groups after their random assignment on such variables as age, sex, IQ, years of institutionalization, and pretest performance on the measure of interest. The absence of differences (nonsignificant *t* or *F* tests) may provide false comfort that the groups are equivalent. When the samples are relatively small, statistical power (sensitivity) to detect differences is weak. Thus, the situation in which random assignment is least likely to obtain equivalence (small samples) is also one in which such differences may be the most difficult to detect. Investigators may feel that the absence of significant differences will satisfy others (reviewers and advisors), and it usually does. However, the systematic variation that was not detected between groups can still obscure the findings and generate misleading results. With larger samples the absence of differences between groups on subject variables and pretreatment measures provides greater assurance of group equivalence. Even so, such results do not establish absolutely that the groups are equivalent. Groups still may differ on some variable, relevant or irrelevant to the experimental manipulation and performance on the dependent measures, that the investigator did not assess. In general, random assignment remains vitally important as a concept and procedure. However, there is a belief that the procedure guarantees group equivalence in situations when this is not likely, that is, when the sample size is relatively small (Hsu, 1989; Tversky & Kahneman, 1971). Use of larger-than-usual sample sizes (> 40 subjects in each group) can increase the confidence in the equivalence of groups.

Matching

Often the investigator does not wish to leave to chance the equivalence of groups for a given characteristic of the sample. If a specific subject variable is known to relate to scores on the dependent measure, it is important to take this variable into account to ensure that groups do not differ prior to treatment. For example, it is possible that randomly assigning clients seeking treatment for anxiety could result in one of the treatment groups having participants who were more anxious prior to treatment than those in one of the other groups. Group differences after treatment could be directly influenced by severity of anxiety of the groups before treatment began. It is undesirable to allow groups to differ prior to the intervention on a variable that is highly related to performance on the dependent measure. The best way to ensure equivalence of groups on a particular dimension is to match subjects on the dimension and then to assign subjects randomly to groups.

Matching refers to grouping subjects together on the basis of their similarity on a particular characteristic or set of characteristics. By matching, subjects at each level of the characteristic appear in each group, and the groups will not differ on that characteristic prior to treatment. Matching can be accomplished in different ways. Consider, for example, a two-group experiment designed to investigate the effectiveness of treatments for depression. Prior to treatment, subjects complete a measure of depression. One way to match subjects is to look for pairs of subjects with *identical pretreatment scores.* When two subjects are found with the same scores, each is assigned to one of the two groups in an unbiased fashion (using a random-numbers table or coin toss). This is continued with all pairs of subjects with identical scores. If enough pairs of subjects are available and are assigned to groups, pretreatment mean depression scores for the groups would be identical. Yet, looking for sets of identical scores to match subjects is usually prohibitive because it means that most subjects who did not have a score identical to another subject's score would not be used. Thus, large numbers of subjects would need to be assessed to find enough subjects to fill the groups.

A more commonly used procedure is to *rank all of the subjects,* in this case from high to low depression scores. If there are three groups in the experiment, the first three subjects with the highest scores form the first block. These three subjects are assigned randomly, so that one member of this block appears in each group. The three subjects with the next highest scores form the next block and are assigned randomly to each group, and so on until all subjects are assigned. This method of assignment utilizes all of the subjects by drawing them from the ranks in blocks of three (or whatever number of groups there are) and assigning them randomly to each of the groups. Matching, when followed by random assignment, can equalize groups on the characteristic of interest. The advantage of this procedure is that it does not leave to chance the equivalence of groups on the characteristic(s) of interest.

In some cases the investigator may wish to ensure that the groups are equivalent on a categorical variable such as subject sex or ethnicity. Random assignment may not ensure that the proportion of subjects assigned to each group will be the same. One way to avoid this problem is to develop the random order of assignment of cases to conditions, as already discussed, but to have separate lists for, say, males and females. If the first two subjects who arrive at the experiment are males, they are assigned (randomly) to each of the two groups (treatment, control) of the experiment. If the next person to arrive is a female, she is assigned randomly to the first condition on a separate list for female subjects. Assignments continue in this fashion based on the separate lists. Since each list includes a long stream of 1s and 2s (to indicate assignment to group 1 or 2), the proportion of subjects of each sex will be equal or close to equal no matter how many males or females come into the study. If the overall ratio of males to females who participate in the study is 3:1, this ratio will be reflected in each of the groups. One refers to this in describing the procedure as random assignment with the restriction that an equal number of cases of each sex was assigned to each condition.

Implicit in the discussion is interest in the nature of the variables that are used for purposes of matching. Subjects are matched on those variables that are either known or assumed to be related to performance on the dependent measure. For example, in a treatment study, matching on initial severity of dysfunction, as measured by a pretest, is reasonable because pretest performance is likely to be related to posttest performance, and one may not want to leave group equivalence to chance (assume that random assignment will take care of this). Other variables may be expected to relate to the outcome (diagnosis, age, birth order, and self-concept) and serve as the basis of matching. Matching is not essential or inherently valuable in its own right. An investigator matches groups when he or she knows or suspects that the characteristic relates to performance on the dependent measures.

Mismatching

The critical component of matching is random assignment. Subjects are matched first and then randomly assigned to groups. Occasionally, matching has been used in an attempt to equalize groups where random assignment is not possible. For example, consider a treatment study in which the investigator wishes to compare two forms of psychotherapy administered to clients who come for outpatient treatment. Two different clinics are used in a particular city, and each clinic will receive one or the other form of treatment. Cases referred to the clinics are not under the control of the investigator, that is, they cannot be randomly assigned. So it is possible that at the end of the study, treatment A (at clinic 1) and treatment B (at clinic 2) will appear differentially effective because groups at the different clinics were not similar to begin with. The investigator might reasonably wish to evaluate treatment on clients who are equal in severity of impairment. Assume that the investigator assesses severity of symptoms from intake clinician ratings or a self-report measure from the clients. Assume further that the scores on the measures can vary from 0 to 100, with a higher score indicating greater severity of symptoms.

The clients at the two clinics may differ in overall severity of symptoms because they come from somewhat different populations (segments of the city). Yet, there is likely to be some overlap of scores. The scores of clients from each of the clinics in this hypothetical example are illustrated in Figure 6.1. Each normal distribution in the figure represents the distribution of scores for that clinic. It is obvious from the figure that clients at clinic 2 generally have higher scores. However, the distributions of scores of the clinics overlap, as reflected in the scores that fall within the shaded area that crosses both distributions. The investigator may equalize severity of the cases in the study by drawing cases with similar scores (only those cases within the shaded area). In some sense, the clients have been matched because those used in each clinic have equal or approximately equal mean symptom severity scores. Unfortunately, this matching procedure is problematic.

Each client's score is made up of a true level of symptoms plus error associated with such factors as the unreliability of the assessment device, daily fluctuations in client behavior, and other factors. The error in measurement is reflected in the fact that scores from one testing to another are imperfectly correlated. Scores that are extremely high on one day are likely to be slightly lower on the next day or assessment occasion. Conversely, scores that are extremely low one day are likely to be slightly higher on the next testing. As a general rule, the more extreme the score, the more likely it is to revert in the direction of the group mean on subsequent assessment. Not every high score will become lower and not every low score will become higher, but on the average the scores at each of these extremes will revert or regress toward the mean.

Regression toward the mean is a statistical phenomenon that is related to the correlation between initial test and retest scores. *The lower the correlation, the greater the amount of error in the measure, and the greater the regression toward the mean.* The problem with matching subjects who are in preassigned groups is that scores in each of the groups may regress toward a different mean. Even if subjects across groups are selected because their scores are equal, the groups may come from populations with different means and be at different places in the distribution of scores in their

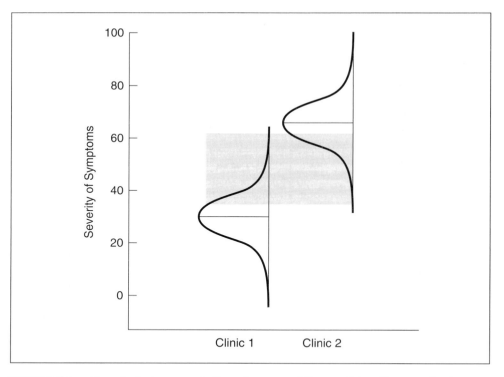

FIGURE 6.1.   Hypothetical scores of clients from two different clinics. The two distributions represent all of the scores for the clients at the respective clinics. The shaded area reflects those cases with similar scores across the two clinics and cases that might be matched across the clinics. At clinic 1 those cases are individuals with the highest scores (more symptoms, above their group mean); at clinic 2 those cases are individuals with the lowest scores (few symptoms, below their group mean). To the extent there is error in measurement, at a second assessment, the cases will regress to the means of their respective distributions.

respective groups. Hence, subsequent testing might lead to group differences merely because the groups regress toward their respective means.

Regression can lead to posttreatment differences even when treatment has no effect. In this example, the clients selected for the experiment from the two different clinics might be reassessed at some later point. One would expect merely on the basis of regression that certain changes would take place in symptom scores. Clients from clinic 1 would be expected to show a *decrease* in their scores on reassessment because cases from this group were above their group mean of symptom severity. In contrast, clients from clinic 2 would be expected to show an *increase* in severity of symptoms because their scores tended to be below their group mean. In short, upon reassessment each of the samples will revert toward its group mean. If different treatments were administered at the clinics, the investigator might conclude that the treatment at clinic 1 really helped the clients (reduced symptoms), whereas the treatment at clinic 2 made clients worse (increased symptoms). Unfortunately, this change on reassessment may well have occurred independently of the interventions merely on the basis of regression.

In general, regression is of concern when subjects are selected because of their extreme scores. In such cases, depending on the test–retest correlation, subjects at the extreme levels are likely to revert toward the mean. The error that contributed to their extreme scores on one occasion is less likely to operate in the same direction on the next assessment occasion. Thus, upon retesting, their scores are likely to revert toward the mean.

There are two problems to bear in mind. The first regression problem I have discussed was differential regression (or selection × regression)—that is, subjects in different groups show regression but they regress to different means. This is possible in situations in which intact groups are used (students in different classrooms or schools, patients from clinics) and by definition random assignment to groups is not possible. When random assignment *is* possible, then differential regression is not likely to be a plausible explanation for group differences at the end of the study. Any regression toward the mean would be equally evident and in the same direction for both groups due to the random composition of the groups.

The second regression problem is the one I discussed when threats to internal validity were presented. In this variation all groups show an improvement from pre- to posttreatment, and no differences are evident between groups or in the amount of improvement at the second assessment. In such cases, regression might explain why everyone improved, namely, cases were selected because they were extreme (on a screening criterion) and assigned randomly to groups. However, all subjects as a group were likely to regress (show lower scores), and when they do, this could be a result of treatment or simply statistical regression. This version of regression, as a threat to internal validity, is relatively common among studies in which two or more interventions are compared and no control group is included in the design (Ouimette, Finney, & Moos, 1997; Vostanis et al., 1996). Subjects in all treatment groups, selected because they were high on some measure on the one assessment occasion (pretest), are likely to "show improvements," that is, score lower on the next assessment occasion, which happens to be called posttreatment. When the treatment appears to be working, it may not really be having any effect. Statistical regression is quite plausible.

SELECTED GROUP DESIGNS

Assigning subjects to groups in an unbiased fashion is one of the major defining characteristics of group experiments. Again, by experiments we are referring to those studies in which the investigator is manipulating conditions, that is, controls the delivery of some procedure, intervention, or experimental manipulation. Subject allocation, of course, refers merely to how the groups are formed and not to the experimental design. There are several experimental designs. This section discusses different designs commonly used in clinical psychology along with their strengths and weaknesses. To illustrate the designs, the sequence of events in the design (assessment, intervention) for each group will be presented symbolically using the following notation: *R* stands for random assignment of subjects to conditions; *O* for observation or assessment; and

X for the experimental manipulation or treatment (Campbell & Stanley, 1963). The symbols are presented in temporal order so that, for example, $O_1 X O_2$ signifies that the first observation or pretest (O_1) was followed by an intervention (*X*) followed by the second observation or posttest (O_2).

Pretest–Posttest Control Group Design

The *pretest–posttest design* consists of a minimum of two groups. One group receives treatment and the other does not. The essential feature of the design is that subjects are tested before and after the intervention. Thus, the effect of the intervention is reflected in the amount of change from pre- to postintervention assessment. In this design, subjects are assigned randomly to groups either prior to or after completion of the pretest. (Again, the *R* denotes that subjects are assigned randomly; *O* denotes an observation or assessment; and *X* denotes the intervention.) The design can be diagrammed as follows:

$$R \quad O_1 \quad X \quad O_2$$
$$R \quad O_3 \quad\quad O_4$$

This design enjoys wide use in clinical, counseling, and educational psychology. The administration of a pretest and posttest allows assessment of the amount of change as a function of the intervention. Although all experimentation is interested in change, assessment of the amount of change is particularly important in intervention research. For example, treatment research is designed to determine how much change was made and how many clients made a change of a particular magnitude. Also, severity of impairment prior to treatment may be an important source of information for predicting whether clients are likely to profit from certain kinds of treatment. For these reasons a pretest is essential.

Considerations in Using the Design.   The design has several strengths. To begin with, the design controls for the usual threats to internal validity. If intervening periods between pre- and posttreatment assessment are the same for each of the groups, threats such as history, maturation, repeated testing, and instrumentation are controlled. Moreover, random assignment from the same population reduces the plausibility that group differences have resulted from either selection bias or differential regression (to different means). Attrition is not an inherent problem with the design, although—as in any experiment—differential loss of subjects could interfere with drawing a conclusion about the intervention.

The use of a pretest provides several advantages, as listed in Table 6.1. First, the data obtained from the pretest allow the investigator to match subjects on different variables and to assign subjects randomly to groups. Matching permits the investigator to equalize groups on pretest performance. Second and related, the pretest data permit evaluation of the effect of different levels of pretest performance. Within each group, different levels of performance (high and low) on the pretest can be used as a variable in the design to examine whether the intervention varied in impact as a function of the initial standing on the pretested measure. Third, the use of a pretest

TABLE 6.1.   Advantages of Using a Pretest in Research

- Allows the investigator to match (equalize) subjects on one of the variables assessed at pretest (e.g., level of anxiety) that may influence the result
- Permits evaluation of that matched variable in the results (e.g., as a separate factor in an analysis of variance or regression analysis)
- Increases statistical power of the test
- Allows the investigator to examine who changed and what proportion of individuals changed in a particular way (show a clinically significant change)
- Allows evaluation of attrition (what were the subjects like who dropped out and did not complete the posttreatment measures?)

affords statistical advantages for the data analysis. By using a pretest, within-group variability is reduced and more powerful statistical tests of the intervention, such as analyses of covariance or repeated measures analyses of variance, are available than if no pretest were used (see Chapter 15). This advantage alone is a strong reason to use a pretest because so many studies have insufficient statistical power to detect differences between groups.

Fourth, the pretest allows the researcher to make specific statements about change, such as how many clients improved. In clinical research where individual performance is very important, the pretest affords information beyond mere group differences at posttreatment. One can evaluate the persons who did or did not change and generate hypotheses about the reasons. The pretest permits identification of the persons who changed. Finally, by using a pretest, one can look at attrition in a more analytic fashion than would be the case without a pretest. If subjects are lost over the course of the study, a comparison can be made among groups by looking at pretest scores of those who dropped out versus those who remained in the study. If only a few subjects dropped out, a comparison of dropouts and completers may not be very powerful statistically. Yet, the comparison may show differences, may generate hypotheses about who drops out and why, or may suggest that even with very lenient criteria (e.g., $p < .20$) dropouts and completers do not seem to differ on the variables evaluated. The pretest allows examination of the plausibility of these alternatives.

There are some weaknesses to the pretest–posttest treatment control group design. The main restriction pertains to the influence of administering a pretest. A simple effect of testing, that is, repeatedly administering a test, is controlled in the basic design. What is not controlled is the possibility of an interaction of testing × treatment or a pretest sensitization effect. Possibly the intervention had its effect precisely because the pretest sensitized subjects to the intervention. A pretest sensitization effect means that the results of the study can be generalized only to subjects who received a pretest.

Whether there is a pretest sensitization effect cannot be assessed in this design. The likelihood of sensitization depends upon several factors. If assessment and the intervention are not close together in time or are unrelated in the perceptions of the subject, sensitization probably is less likely. Therefore, a pretest administered immediately prior to an intervention in the context of the experiment is more likely to lead to sensitization than is assessment in a totally unrelated setting (in class or in a door-to-door survey at the subject's home) several weeks prior to treatment. Yet the more remote the pretest from the posttest in time and place, the less adequate it may be as a pretest. Intervening events and processes (history, maturation) between pretest and posttest obscure the effects that can otherwise be more readily attributed to the experimental manipulation. In general, the strengths of the design clearly outweigh the threat that pretest sensitization will obscure the findings. The information about subject status prior to intervening, the use of this information to match cases and to evaluate change, and the statistical advantages are compelling.

Posttest-Only Control Group Design

The *posttest-only design* consists of a minimum of two groups and essentially is the same as the previous design except that no pretest is given. The effect of the intervention is assessed on a postintervention measure only. The design can be diagrammed as follows:

$$R \quad X \quad O_1$$
$$R \quad \quad O_2$$

The absence of the pretest makes this design less popular in clinical research. There are at least two reasons for this. First, in clinical research, it is often critical to know the level of functioning of persons prior to the intervention. For example, in studies designed to treat or prevent various disorders, it is important to establish that the clients were dysfunctional or at risk for dysfunction prior to the intervention. When screening criteria are used to identify subjects, pretest assessment is critical to examine whether clients begin at the intended level of functioning. Second, the lack of a pretest raises the discomforting possibility that group differences after the intervention might be the result of differences between groups prior to the intervention. Of course, random assignment of subjects, particularly with large numbers of subjects, is likely to equalize groups. And there is no more likelihood that random assignment will produce different groups prior to treatment with this design than in the previous design. Admittedly, however, there is no assurance that groups are similar on key measures prior to treatment, a luxury afforded by the previous design.

Considerations in Using the Design.   The design controls for the usual threats to internal validity in much the same way as the previous design. The absence of a pretest means that the effect of the intervention could not result from initial sensitization. Hence, the results could not be restricted in their generality to only those subjects who have received a pretest.

Often a pretest may not be desirable or feasible. For example, in brief laboratory experiments, the investigator may not wish to know the initial performance level or to expose subjects to the assessment task before they experience the experimental manipulation. Also, large numbers of subjects might be available and randomly assigned to different conditions in such experiments. With large numbers of subjects and random assignment to the groups, the likelihood of group equivalence is high. Assurances of equivalent performance on premeasures may be of less concern to the investigator.

Certainly another feature that must be considered is that a pretest is not always available in clinical research. In many cases the assessment effort is very costly, and a pretest might be prohibitive. For example, an extensive battery of tests might serve as the outcome measures. The time required to administer and interpret an assessment battery may be several hours, which might make the pretest not worth the cost or effort. Indeed, from a practical standpoint, there may be no alternative but to omit the pretest. Ethical considerations also may argue for omission of the pretest, if for example, a pretest might be stressful or invasive (taking blood samples, asking sensitive personal questions).

The weaknesses of the posttest-only control groups design derive from the disadvantages of not using a pretest. Thus, the inability to ensure that groups are equivalent on the pretest, to match subjects on pretest performance prior to random assignment, or to study the relation between pretest standing and behavior change; the lack of pretest information to evaluate differential attrition across groups; and reduced statistical power are all consequences of forgoing a pretest. Apart from these disadvantages, demonstration of the equivalence of groups at pretest and, of course, prior to any intervention is often comforting both to the investigator and to those who examine or review the work. As already noted, with small samples "no differences" on pretreatment performance does not necessarily mean that the groups are equivalent. Even so, it is more assuring to have data in favor of equivalence than to omit a pretest altogether. In general, several of the advantages of a pretest may not be of interest to the investigator. The statistical advantage of repeated observations that the pretest provides remains a decided advantage of the pretest–posttest design.

Solomon Four-Group Design

The effects of pretesting (pretest sensitization) were discussed in each of the above designs. The purpose of the *Solomon four-group design* is to evaluate the effect of pretesting on the effects obtained with a particular intervention (Solomon, 1949). That is, does administering a pretest, in fact, influence the results? To address this question, a minimum of four groups is required. These four groups in the design are the two groups mentioned in the pretest–posttest control group design plus the other two groups of the posttest-only control group design. The Solomon four-group design can be diagrammed as follows:

$$
\begin{array}{cccc}
R & O_1 & X & O_2 \\
R & O_3 & & O_4 \\
R & & X & O_5 \\
R & & & O_6
\end{array}
$$

Considerations in Using the Design.   The design controls for the usual threats to internal validity. The effects of testing per se can be evaluated by comparing two control groups that differ only in having received or not received the pretest (comparison of O_4 and O_6). More important, the interaction of pretesting and the intervention can be assessed by comparing pretested and unpretested groups (comparison of O_2 and O_5). Actually, the data can be analyzed to evaluate the effects of testing and the testing × treatment interaction. To accomplish this, the posttreatment assessment data for each group are combined into a 2×2 factorial design and analyzed with a two-way analysis of variance. Only the following observations are used: O_2, O_4, O_5, and O_6. The factors in the analysis are testing (pretest versus no pretest) and treatment (treatment versus no treatment). Other methods of analyzing the data from the design are available (see Braver & Braver, 1988).

Another feature of the design is that it includes replication of treatment and control conditions. The effect of treatment (X) is replicated in several different places in the design. The effect of treatment can be attested to by one within-group comparison (O_1 versus O_2) and several between-group comparisons (O_2 versus O_4 or O_6; O_5 versus O_6 or O_4; O_5 versus O_3 or O_1). If a consistent pattern of results emerges from these comparisons, the strength of the demonstration is greatly increased over designs that allow a single comparison. Yet, there is a price for the gain in elegance and strength of inferences this design provides. As noted earlier, the experiment can be conceptualized as two smaller experiments. Twice the effort and costs are involved in the number of subjects run, the amount of data collected, and so on. To justify the extra effort, the investigator usually would want to be primarily interested in evaluating pretest sensitization.

The design may appear to be somewhat esoteric because sensitization effects rarely enter into theoretical accounts of clinical phenomena. Yet, sensitization occasionally has important implications beyond design considerations. For example, in one study, a Solomon four-group design was used to evaluate the impact of a suicide-awareness program for high-school students (Spirito et al., 1988a). The intervention consisted of a school curriculum designed to increase knowledge about suicide and to prevent or decrease the likelihood of suicide. Some students received the curriculum; others did not. Within these groups, some were pretested on measures related to knowledge about and attitudes toward suicide and hopelessness. The curriculum increased positive attitudes and reduced hopelessness. The finding is noteworthy because hopelessness is related to suicide, and altering the former will hopefully have impact on the latter. The effects of the intervention were more marked for those who received the pretest—a pretest sensitization effect. Replication of these findings would be very important because they suggest a way to augment the effects of intervention programs.

Additional research efforts probably should be directed at studying the effects of pretesting. The pretest–posttest control group design is used extensively, and the influence of pretesting is rarely studied in the contexts of clinical research. A few studies using the Solomon four-group design in well-researched areas might be very valuable. Demonstrations across dependent measures might establish that in clinical research with widely used measures or interventions, pretest sensitization is restricted to a narrow set of conditions or may not occur at all.

Factorial Designs

The above designs consist primarily of evaluating the impact of a single independent variable. The independent variable (e.g., treatment) may be given to one group but withheld from another group. Alternatively, different versions of treatment might be provided across several groups. Whatever the variations, the studies basically evaluate one independent variable.

The main limitation of single-variable experiments is that they often raise relatively simple questions about the variable of interest. The simplicity of the questions should not demean their importance. In relatively new areas of research, the simple questions are the bedrock of subsequent experiments. However, more complex and refined questions can be raised. For example, a single-variable experiment might raise the question of which treatment works better for a particular clinical problem or whether experienced therapists exert more impact than nonexperienced therapists. A more complex question might be raised by including more than one variable. For example, are certain treatments more effective with certain types of therapists or clients? The latter type of question is somewhat more specific and entails evaluation of the separate and combined effects of two or more variables.

Factorial designs allow the simultaneous investigation of two or more variables (factors) in a single experiment. Within each variable two or more conditions are administered. In the simplest factorial design two variables (e.g., therapist experience and type of treatment) would each consist of two different levels (experienced vs. inexperienced therapists and treatment A vs. treatment B). In this 2 × 2 design, the four groups represent each possible combination of the levels of the two factors, as shown in Figure 6.2.

Of course, a factorial design is not a single design but rather a family of designs that vary in the number and types of variables and the number of levels within each variable. The variation of factorial designs also is influenced by whether or not a pretest is used. If a pretest is used, testing can become one of the variables or factors (time of assessment) with two (pretest versus posttest) or more levels. The data can be analyzed to assess whether subjects changed with repeated assessment, independently of a particular intervention.

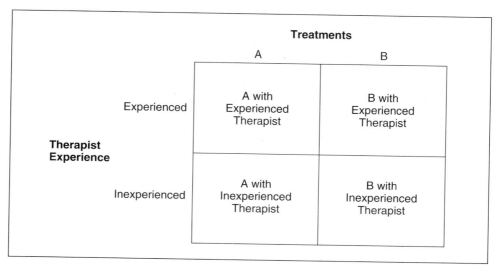

FIGURE 6.2.   Hypothetical factorial design comparing two independent variables (or factors): therapist experiment and type of treatment. Each factor has two different levels of conditions making this a 2 × 2 factorial design.

In single-variable experiments one manipulation is of interest, and all other variables that might influence the results are controlled. In a factorial experiment multiple variables are included to address questions about separate and combined effects of different variables. The variables that are included in the factorial design are not merely controlled, their effect is evaluated as distinct variables in the design. For example, a factorial design might evaluate the influence of characteristics of the subject (e.g., sex of the client), the therapist (e.g., degree of warmth during the therapy session), variations of treatment (treatments A, B, or C), and duration of therapy (number of sessions). These general classes of variables may be combined in a single study to ask pointed questions about the conditions under which variables exert their effects.

A major reason for completing a factorial experiment is that the combined effect of two or more variables may be of interest—that is, their interaction. An *interaction* means that the effect of one of the variables (e.g., treatment A or B) depends on the level of one of the other variables (e.g., sex of the patient). Earlier we discussed interactions in terms of external validity. In this light the interaction means that the effect of one variable may or may not be generalized across all conditions. Rather, the impact of that variable occurs only under certain conditions or operates differently under those conditions (with men rather than women, with younger rather than older persons).

Considerations in Using the Design.   The strength of a factorial design is that it can assess the effects of separate variables in a single experiment. The feature includes one of economy because different variables can be studied with fewer subjects and observations in a factorial design than in separate experiments for the single-variable study of each of the variables, one at a time. In addition, the factorial design provides unique information about the combined effects of the independent variables.

The importance of evaluating interactions cannot be overestimated in conducting research. Essentially, interactions provide the boundary conditions of independent variables and their effects. For example, in the context of treatment, a given intervention may not simply be effective or ineffective but rather may depend upon a host of qualifiers such as who administers treatment, what type of client problem, under what conditions of administration, and for how long. These qualifiers refer to variables with which treatment is likely to interact. Another way to refer to these qualifiers is to raise the notion of moderators, mentioned earlier. Interactions identify those variables that moderate (influence) the effects of other variables. Results that reveal a significant interaction may be of interest because of the information about the generality of the effect across conditions as well as theoretical implications.

The concerns about using the factorial designs are both practical and interpretive. On the practical side one must remember that the number of groups in the investigation multiplies quickly as new factors or new levels of a given factor are added. For example, a design in its conceptual stages might simply begin as a 2 × 3 by looking at type of treatment (meditation training versus biofeedback) and severity of anxiety (high, moderate, and low). This design already includes 6 (i.e., 2 × 3) groups. Yet, it also might be interesting to study whether the treatment is administered by a live therapist or simply by prerecorded taped instructions. This third variable, manner of administering treatment, includes two levels, so the overall design now is a 2 × 2 × 3 and has 12 groups. Also, while we are at it, perhaps we could explore a fourth variable, instructions to the subjects. This variable might have two levels in which half of the subjects are told that the treatment was "discovered by a guru" and the other half that it was "discovered by a scientist engaged in basic laboratory research." We might expect meditation subjects who receive the "guru instructions" and biofeedback subjects who receive the "scientific researcher instructions" to do better than their counterparts. Now we have a $2 \times 2 \times 2 \times 3$ design or 24 groups, a formidable doctoral dissertation, to say the least. Instead of a study, we have a career. As a general point, the number of groups in a study may quickly become prohibitive as factors and levels are increased. This means that the demand for subjects to complete each of the combinations of the variables will increase as well. In practice there are constraints in the number of subjects that can be run in a given study and the number of factors (variables) that can be easily studied.

A related problem is interpreting the results of multiple-factor experiments. Factorial designs are optimally informative when an investigator predicts an interactive relationship among two or more variables. Simple interactions involving two or three variables often are relatively straightforward to interpret. However, when multiple variables interact, the investigator may be at a loss to describe the complex relationship in a coherent fashion, let alone offer an informed or theoretically plausible explanation. A factorial design is useful for evaluating the separate and combined effects of variables of interest when these variables are conceptually related and predicted to generate interactive effects. The inclusion of factors in the design is dictated by conceptual considerations of those variables and the interpretability of the predicted relations.

Quasi-Experimental Designs

The previous designs constitute basic between-group experimental designs and are true experiments because several facets of the study can be adequately controlled to eliminate threats to internal validity. The strength of the designs derives from the investigator's ability to control what treatment is administered to whom and at what point in time. Most important, subjects can be assigned randomly to conditions, thereby reducing the plausibility of potential threats to validity. There are, however, many situations in which the investigator cannot exert such control over subjects and their assignment or the administration of treatment to particular groups. In clinical, counseling, and educational research, investigators often are unable to shuffle clients or students to meet the demands of a true experiment but must work within administrative, bureaucratic, and occasionally even anti-research constraints. As noted earlier, research designs in which the investigator cannot exert control required of true experiments have been referred to as *quasi-experimental designs* (Campbell & Stanley, 1963). For investigators who are genuinely bothered by less well-controlled studies, these can also be called *queasy-experimental designs*. No matter what they are called, very strong inferences can be drawn from quasi-experimental designs. However, the designs often require greater ingenuity in selecting controls or analyzing the data to make implausible various threats to validity (especially, selection × . . . threats to internal validity).

Pretest–Posttest Design.   There are many between-group quasi-experimental designs, the most common of which parallel the pretest-posttest and posttest-only experimental designs. For each of the quasi-experimental equivalents of these designs, the control group is not demonstrably equivalent to the experimental group, usually because subjects have been assigned to groups prior to the inception of the investigation. Because the groups are already formed, they may differ in advance of the intervention. This explains why the designs have also been referred to as *nonequivalent control group designs* (Campbell & Stanley, 1963).

The most widely used version of a nonequivalent control group design is the one that resembles the pretest–posttest control group design. The design may be diagrammed as follows:

$$\text{non}R \quad O_1 \quad X \quad O_2$$
$$\text{non}R \quad O_3 \quad\quad O_4$$

In this version nonrandomly assigned subjects (subjects who already may be in separate hospitals, clinics, or classrooms) are compared. One group receives the treatment and the other does not. The strength of the design depends directly upon the similarity of the experimental and control groups. The investigator must ask how the assignment of subjects to groups originally might have led to systematic differences in advance of the intervention. For example, two high schools might be used to evaluate a drug-abuse-prevention intervention in which the intervention is provided at one school but not at the other. Youths in the schools may vary on such factors as socioeconomic status, IQ, or any number of other measures. Possibly, initial differences on the pretest measures or different characteristics of the groups, whether or not they are revealed on the pretest, account for the findings. The similarity of youths across schools can be attested to partially on the basis of pretest scores as well as on various subject variables. Pretest equivalence on a measure does not mean that the groups are comparable on all dimensions relevant to the intervention, but it increases the confidence one might place in this assumption.

In the version of the design diagrammed previously, the results could not easily be attributed to history, maturation, testing, regression, mortality, and similar factors that might occur across both groups. However, it is possible that these threats might differ *between* groups (selection × history or selection × maturation). These interactions mean that particular confounding events may affect one group but not the other, and hence might account for group differences. For example, one group might experience historical events (within the school) or differ in rate of maturation (improvements without treatment). These influences might account for group differences even if the subjects were equivalent on a pretest. At the same time the design can yield strong inferences based on what the investigator does to make implausible those threats that random assignment normally handles.

As an illustration a nonequivalent quasi-experimental design was used to evaluate the effects of participating in a group awareness training (Fisher et al., 1989). Such training includes experiences that individuals sought to improve their daily life, personal effectiveness, decision-making skills, and interpersonal awareness. Adults ordinarily seek such training on their own and cannot easily be assigned to a control group. Thus, the authors began with a task of evaluating the impact of an intervention wherein treatment and control groups cannot easily be formed by random assignment of cases to groups. The investigators devised a nonrandomly assigned control group to assist in reducing the plausibility of various threats to internal validity. The authors used a peer-nominated, no-intervention group. Specifically, persons who sought and participated in awareness training (intervention group) were asked to nominate other persons not in their household who were the same sex, approximately the same age, from the same community, and whom they considered to be like themselves. These nominated persons (control group) were recruited and asked to complete the assessment battery at different points in time, to coincide with the pre–post interval for subjects who received awareness training.

This control group clearly is not equivalent to a group comprised from random assignment of subjects to intervention and nonintervention groups. Was the group equivalent to the group that received awareness training? Data analyses revealed that at pretest, experimental and control subjects were no different in age, education, sex, income, and a variety of psychological measures of interest (e.g., social functioning, self-esteem). There was one initial preintervention difference on a measure of perceived control; training subjects attributed more internal control to themselves than did nonintervention subjects. However, across a very large number of variables and statistical tests the groups were not different prior to the intervention. There might well have been differences on some variables related to self-selection and interest in group awareness training in addition to the initial difference in perceived control on one of many measures. Yet, the onus is on us as readers to pose a relevant difference that might plausibly influence the results. This nonequivalent group controls reasonably well for threats to internal validity (testing, history), even though our confidence would have been augmented with equivalent and randomly comprised groups. In passing, the results indicated that group awareness training and control subjects were not different on virtually all of the measures at posttreatment and a one-year follow-up.

Posttest-Only Design.   A nonequivalent control group design need not use a pretest. The posttest-only quasi-experimental design can be diagrammed as follows:

$$\text{non}R \quad X \quad O_1$$
$$\text{non}R \quad \quad\;\; O_2$$

Of course, the problems with this design, as with its true experimental counterpart, is that the equivalence of groups prior to the intervention cannot be assessed. In the posttest-only experimental design, discussed earlier, the absence of a pretest was not necessarily problematic because random assignment increases the likelihood of group equivalence, particularly for large sample sizes. However, in a posttest-only quasi-experiment, the groups may be very different across several dimensions prior to treatment. Hence, attributing group differences to the intervention may be especially weak. Aside from problems of probable group nonequivalence prior to treatment and the absence of a pretest to estimate group differences, this version of the nonequivalent control group design suffers from each of the possible threats to internal validity of the same design with a pretest.

Although the posttest-only quasi-experiment is weak, occasionally this may be the most viable design available. For example, one study focused on the evaluation of an inpatient treatment program for chemically dependent adolescents (dependent primarily on alcohol, marijuana, speed, downers, and cocaine) (Grenier, 1985). The intervention consisted of a multidisciplinary program in the hospital (individual, group, and family therapy; an Alcoholics Anonymous model toward complete abstinence; and other procedures). The investigator examined whether those who completed the program were any more improved than those who had not received the program. Random assignment was not possible. Consequently, the investigator completed an assessment of former patients and of persons on the waiting list. The abstinence rates of the groups were 65.6 percent of the youth who received the program and 14.3 percent for those who had yet to receive the program. The results are compatible with the view that the program improves outcome. Clearly, several questions remain unanswered. At the same time, this initial test provides critical information to suggest that the program may offer some benefit. A quasi-experiment provides an excellent beginning, particularly when viewed against the alternative of little or no evaluation, which characterizes most institutional programs.

Variations.   Before completing the discussion on nonequivalent control group designs, it is important to mention variations of the above designs that also might be used. A variation of the nonequivalent control group design with a pretest might be diagrammed as follows:

$$
\begin{array}{ccccc}
\text{non}R & O_1 & X & O_2 & \\
\text{non}R & & O_3 & & O_4
\end{array}
$$

(The version of the design without the pretest can be illustrated simply be omitting O_1 and O_3.) The diagram indicates that groups received the pre- and posttreatment assessments at different points in time. Obviously, such a design has more problems than designs in which measures are administered to groups at the same time. With this version, pretest equivalence of groups cannot really be determined because when one group is tested, there is no basis to infer the standing of the other group on the same measures at that time. In addition, different historical events, maturation, and instrument decay across groups become increasingly plausible as rival hypotheses of the results as the time of assessment of different groups becomes disparate.

Occasionally, the experimental and treatment groups are assessed at different times, as diagrammed above, but staggering the conditions does not necessarily compete with the conclusions that can be drawn. Treatment and control conditions in institutional experiments often are staggered to keep patients in different conditions from interacting. For example, one quasi-experiment of this sort evaluated the effects of teaching problem-solving skills to male hospitalized alcoholic patients (Intagliata, 1978). Treated patients received 10 one-hour group-therapy sessions, during which they were trained to recognize and define problems, to generate solutions, and to select alternatives. The purpose was to train persons to handle real-life problems after discharge. The assignment of subjects was staggered; groups were not run or assessed at the same time. The first 32 admissions were assigned to the control group. The next 32 admissions were designated as the treatment group. This violation of random assignment was based on the author's interest in keeping controls (receiving routine ward treatment) from having direct contact with experimental patients. Indeed, the experimental patients did not begin their treatment until control patients had been discharged. The results showed that training in problem solving enhanced these skills on paper-and-pencil measures and in helping individuals plan for their postdischarge community adjustment.

Given the design, it is possible to raise rival hypotheses such as the nonequivalence of groups or differential history, maturation, or instrumentation. However, these are not very plausible despite the quasi-experimental nature of the study, in part because pretest information showed the groups did not differ in age, verbal IQ, marital status, and other variables and because the assignment to groups differed only by three or four weeks. Hence, this quasi-experiment staggered assessment and evaluation of the different groups, but the plausibility of rival interpretations resulting from that were minimal. Despite the disadvantages of using control groups that are assessed at different points in time from the experimental group, the addition of the control group makes these designs better than using only one group that receives the intervention. If only one group were used with pre- and postintervention assessment—or, even worse, merely the postintervention assessment—not much more than an uncontrolled case study remains, and most threats to internal validity cannot be ruled out.

Although the nonequivalent control group designs already mentioned constitute the most frequently used variations, all of the possible quasi-experimental designs cannot be enumerated. (A rather unique design variation was pioneered by my dissertation, which was a *pre*test-only quasi-experimental design. Through a rather embarrassing oversight, I forgot to administer the posttest. Although omission of a posttest precluded evaluation of the experimental manipulation, I hasten to add that there was absolutely no possibility of any bias due to posttest sensitization with this design.) The general characteristic of these designs is that constraints inherent in the situation restrict the investigator from meeting the requirements of true experiments. In such cases, ingenuity is required to mobilize methodological weapons against ambiguity. Various control groups can be used to weaken one or more threats to internal validity and patch up an otherwise imperfect design. Indeed, groups added to designs to rule out various rival explanations of the results have been referred to as *"patched-up" control groups* (Campbell & Stanley, 1963) and are discussed in the next chapter.

MULTIPLE-TREATMENT DESIGNS

The defining characteristic of the *multiple-treatment design* is that each of the different treatments under investigation is presented to each subject. Although the evaluation of treatments is "within subjects," separate groups of subjects are usually present in the design. In most multiple-treatment designs in clinical research, separate groups are used so that the different treatments can be balanced across subjects, that is, so that treatments can be presented in different orders. Because separate groups are used in the multiple-treatment designs, points raised about random assignment and matching are relevant for constructing different groups for multiple-treatment designs.

Different versions of multiple-treatment designs depend upon the number of treatments and the manner in which they are presented. All of the designs might be called *counterbalanced designs* because they try to balance the order of treatment across subjects. However, it is worth distinguishing both the commonly used version of the multiple-treatment design as well as the general method for balancing treatments.

Crossover Design

A specific multiple-treatment design that is used in treatment research is referred to as the *crossover design*. The design receives its name because partway through the experiment, usually at the midpoint, all subjects "cross over" (i.e., are switched) to another experimental condition. The design is used with two different treatments. Two groups of subjects are constructed through random assignment. The groups differ only in the order in which they receive the two treatments. The design can be diagrammed as follows:

$$R \quad O_1 \quad X_A \quad O_2 \quad X_B \quad O_3$$
$$R \quad O_4 \quad X_B \quad O_5 \quad X_A \quad O_6$$

The design is relatively straightforward. Essentially, each group is formed through random assignment (R). A pretest may be provided to assess performance prior to any intervention. The pretest (designated in the diagram as O_1 and O_4) is not mandatory but is included because it is commonly used and provides the benefits of a pretest, discussed earlier. The crucial feature of the design is that the groups receive the interventions (X_A and X_B) in a different order. Moreover, the subjects are assessed after each intervention. Thus, there is an assessment halfway through the study at the crossover point as well as after the second and final treatment is terminated.

The design is used frequently in evaluating the effects of medication on various symptoms or disorders. For two (or more) medications, a comparison can be made within the same patients if there is an intervening "washout" period during which all medication is stopped. The second medication can then be administered with little or no concern over lingering effects of the first medication. In psychological experiments two or more treatments can be provided this way, too, but it is difficult to continue to show increments of change as one treatment builds on another on outcome measures, for reasons discussed later.

The crossover design is nicely illustrated in a comparison of two conditions (treatment, control) provided to each subject. In this example the design was used to evaluate the impact of exposure to light for the treatment of seasonal affective disorder among children and adolescents, ages 7–17 (Swedo et al., 1997). The youths were diagnosed with the disorder because of their repeated episodes of depression during winter months. The treatment condition was exposure to light (exposure to 2 hours of simulation of the dawn plus 1 hour of bright light) and was compared to a placebo condition (exposure to 5 minutes of simulation of the dawn and 1 hour of wearing clear glasses while doing a sedentary activity such as reading or watching television). Cases were assigned to receive the treatment or placebo condition first followed by the other condition. Treatment led to significant reductions in depression, based on weekly parental ratings of symptoms. This is an important demonstration in showing that light can lead to change. A logical next step would be to provide treatment in a between-group design and for a longer or more intense period to see if depression can be influenced in ways that do not reverse as soon as treatment is withdrawn.

Multiple-Treatment Counterbalanced Design

The crossover design as discussed here is a simple design, usually with two treatments, in which each client receives the different treatments but in a different order; that is, the treatments are counterbalanced. With an increase in the number of treatments, however, counterbalancing becomes more complex, and the order in which the treatments are given is more difficult to balance. For example, consider the hypothetical experiment in which four treatments (A, B, C, and D) are to be compared. Each subject will receive each of the treatments. An important issue is deciding the order in which the subjects should receive treatment. One method is to determine the sequence of treatments randomly for each subject. Thus, the sequence for each subject will vary depending upon "chance." This procedure would be adequate with a large number of subjects. However, it is possible, particularly with a small number of subjects, that one of the four treatments may appear at some point in the sequence (e.g., the first treatment) but not at the other points. More likely, the different treatments will not appear at each point in the sequence for an equal or approximately equal number of times. This inequality could interfere with the conclusions about treatment effects. For example, one treatment may appear to be more effective because it happened to appear more often as the first treatment given to subjects. Obviously, if multiple treatments are evaluated within subjects, the order of the individual treatments must be distributed or varied (the first, second, or third treatment) across subjects.

A useful procedure for ordering the treatments in a multiple-treatment design is to select a set of sequences in advance and to assign subjects randomly to these sequences as they arrive to the experiment. For example, suppose that there are four groups of subjects and each subject receives each of the four treatments. A few specified arrangements or sequences of treatments could be preselected in advance to which the subjects are randomly assigned. If there were four arrangements of the treatments, the design might be summarized as presented in Table 6.2. The characteristic of this ordering is that each group has a different sequence that includes each

TABLE 6.2. Order of Four Treatments (A, B, C, D) in a Latin Square Design

Sequence	Order			
	1	*2*	*3*	*4*
I	A	B	C	D
II	B	A	D	C
III	C	D	A	B
IV	D	C	B	A

Each subject is assigned randomly to one of four groups (I, II, III, or IV), which constitutes a different sequence of the four treatments. Sequence refers to the set of treatments in a given order (the rows in the table); order refers to the position of a given treatment or whether it appears 1st, 2nd, 3rd, or 4th (the columns).

of the four treatments (A, B, C, and D). Moreover, each of the treatments is administered once in each of the available positions. The arrangement of treatments in such a way that each occurs once and only once in each position and in each group is referred to as a *Latin square*. In a Latin square the number of groups (represented by rows in the table), orders or positions (represented by columns), and treatments (represented by A through D) are equal. (The table represents only one way of ordering the treatments. Actually, for a given number of treatments, there are several Latin squares.) At the end of the investigation, analyses can compare different treatments and can assess whether there were any effects due to groups (rows), to order (columns), or to treatment (A's vs. Bs vs. Cs vs. D).[3]

One effect not completely controlled is the sequence in which the treatment appears. The sequence of treatments in the table (the rows) does not represent all possible sequences. Not every treatment is preceded and followed by every other treatment. For example, treatment B never immediately follows treatment D, nor does treatment C follow treatment A, and so on. Hence, it is not really possible with the above design to rule out the influence of different sequences as a contributor to the data for a given treatment. There may be an interaction between the effects of treatment and when treatment appears in the sequence. This interaction can be avoided as a source of confound by using all possible orders of treatment with separate groups of subjects. In a completely balanced design each treatment occurs equally often in each order and each treatment precedes and follows all others. The problem with such a design is that the number of groups and subjects required may be prohibitive. (The number of subjects for complete counterbalancing would be *k* factorial, where *k* equals the number of treatments in the experiment.)

In general, the administration of multiple treatments to the same subject is rare. When treatment studies use multiple-treatment designs, two treatments are more commonly compared, as illustrated with the crossover design. Conducting additional treatments may require a relatively long period of continuous treatment so that each treatment has an opportunity to influence behavior. Moreover, the problem of reflecting change with multiple treatments, discussed below, makes testing for effects of several treatments a dubious venture. Consequently, several treatments are evaluated within subjects infrequently; when they are, the designs usually are not completely balanced to include all possible sequences of treatment.

Considerations in Using the Designs

The utility of multiple-treatment designs depends upon several factors, including the anticipated effects of juxtaposing different treatments, the type of independent and

---

[3]Although main effects of treatment, order, and groups can be extracted from Latin square analyses, interactions among these effects present special problems that are beyond the scope of the present chapter. For a discussion of procedures to select or to form Latin squares for a given experiment and for a table of various squares, the interested reader is referred to other sources (Fisher & Yates, 1963; Kirk, 1994); for a discussion of strategies for data analyses, the seminal paper on the topic (Grant 1948) or more recent discussions (Winer, Brown, & Michels, 1991) are quite useful.

dependent variables that are studied, and the measurement of cumulative treatment effects with the same subjects.

Order and Sequence Effects. Perhaps the most important consideration in using a multiple-treatment design relates to the problem of ordering treatments. Actually different problems can be distinguished. To begin with, if an experiment consisted of one group of subjects that received two different treatments (A and B) in a particular order, the results would be completely uninterpretable. For example, if treatment B led to greater change than treatment A, it would be impossible to determine whether B was more effective because of its unique therapeutic properties or because it was the second treatment provided to all subjects. Treatment B may have been more effective because a continuation of treatment, independently of what the treatment was, may have led to greater change. Thus, the order in which the treatments appeared in this single group study might have been responsible for treatment differences and hence serves as a plausible alternative explanation of the results.

When the order of treatments might account for the results, this is referred to as an *order effect*. The effect merely refers to the fact that the point in time in which treatment occurred, rather than the specific treatment, might be responsible for the pattern of results. In most multiple-treatment designs, order effects are not confounded with treatments because of counterbalancing, as illustrated in the discussion of crossover and Latin square designs. Although order is not confounded with treatment where counterbalancing is used, it still may influence the pattern of results. We have known for some time that order effects may be important. Usually, treatments presented earlier in the sequence are more effective independently of what the treatment is (Crowe et al., 1972; Hackmann & McLean, 1975). Quite possibly, the reason for this is related to ceiling and floor effects, discussed later, in that by the time the final treatment is provided in a series of treatments, the amount of change that can be reflected on the dependent measures is small.

There is another way that the specific order of treatments may influence the results. Specifically, the transfer from one treatment to another is not the same for each treatment. Receiving treatment A followed by treatment B may not be the same as receiving treatment B followed by treatment A. The order in which these appear may partially dictate the effects of each treatment. When the arrangement of treatments contributes to their effects, this is referred to as *sequence effects*. The nature of the problem is conveyed by other terms that are sometimes used, such as *multiple-treatment interference* or *carryover effects*. The importance of the sequence in which different events appear in dictating their effects is obvious from examples of everyday experience. For example, the taste of a given food depends not only on the specific properties of the food but also upon what food or liquid has immediately preceded it.

As a general statement, multiple-treatment designs are quite susceptible to the influence of sequence effects. Whether these effects are viewed as nuisances depends upon the purposes of the investigator. Sequence effects represent complex interactions (e.g., treatment *x* order of appearance) and may be of interest in their own right. All events in one's life occur in the context of other events. Hence, sequence effects embrace questions about the context in which events occur and the effects of prior experience on subsequent performance. Depending upon one's purpose, the fact that sequence effects occur may be central. However, for treatment evaluation, sequence effects are rarely sought. The purpose is to produce therapeutic change and to determine which among alternative treatments effectively accomplishes this.

Restrictions with Various Independent and Dependent Variables.   Considerations pertaining to the variables that are to be studied may dictate whether a multiple-treatment design is likely to be appropriate or useful for the experiment in question. Certain variables of interest to the investigator are not easily studied in a multiple-treatment design. For example, the experimental instructions or subject expectancies may present particular problems, depending upon the precise experimental manipulations. The problem is in providing to the subject separate interventions that may present conflicting information or procedures. For example, individual therapy and family therapy may be difficult to compare within a particular set of subjects. The respective treatment rationales may present conflicting information to the subjects about the appropriate focus of intervention (on either the individual or the family). The second treatment might seem odd if it would contradict the theoretical basis and actual operations of the first treatment. Hearing the rationale and receiving one of these procedures first might influence the client's belief in the other one. The problem of potentially conflicting information among the different treatments can sometimes be resolved. The solution may lie in the intricacy of the rationales that the experimenter provides so that the different treatments will not appear to conflict. Thus, the creativity of the investigator argues against any absolute rules about which treatments can and cannot accompany another in a multiple-treatment design.

Discussing potentially conflicting interventions raises another side of the issue. It is possible to select interventions that are very similar. For example, the "different treatments" presented to the subjects may vary only in subtle characteristics. These "different" treatments may produce few detectable effects in a multiple-treatment design because clients do not distinguish the conditions. The first intervention may lead to a certain degree of change. The second intervention, or variation, may not be perceived as any different from the first one and hence may produce no differences within subjects; essentially, the second intervention is perceived as a continuation of the first. Although intervention differences would not be revealed by changes within subjects, a comparison between groups for the first treatment conditions administered might yield a difference.

Personality, demographic, physical, and other stable characteristics are not studied within subjects because they do not vary within the same subject for a given experiment. Obviously, participants are not both male and female or a psychiatric patient and not a patient within the same experiment. However, it is possible to provide experiences within the experiment (instructions, expectancies, incentives to perform in one way rather than another) that change how a subject reacts to certain variables. A participant could be given a success or failure experience in an attempt to assess the impact of these experiences on dependent measures. Stable subject characteristics can be readily studied in factorial designs that combine group and multiple-treatment features. For example, a subject can be classified by one variable (sex, age, level of anxiety) and receive each of the different levels of another variable (treatments A and B). This combined design can examine whether treatment effects differ according to subject characteristics.

Aside from restrictions on independent variables, restrictions on dependent measures can be readily evaluated in a multiple-treatment design. Dependent measures involving such skills as cognitive or motor abilities may not readily reflect treatment effects within subjects. When one treatment alters a skill (e.g., bicycle riding or reading), the effects of other treatments are more difficult to evaluate than when transient changes in performance are made.

Ceiling and Floor Effects.   A possible problem in evaluating different interventions within the same subjects is that ceiling or floor effects may limit the amount of change that can be shown. *Ceiling* and *floor effects* refer to the fact that change in the dependent measures may reach an upper or lower limit, respectively, and that further change cannot be demonstrated because of this limit. The amount of change produced by the first intervention may not allow additional change to occur.

Assume, for example, that two treatments are presented in a multiple-treatment design and evaluated on a hypothetical measure of adjustment that ranges in scores from 0 to 100. Here, a score of 0 equals "poor adjustment," which means the individual is constantly depressed, anxious, drunk, suicidal, and apathetic—and this is on the good days. Assume that 100 equals the paragon of adjustment or that the individual is perfectly adaptive, content, and self-actualizing even in the face of recent loss of family, possessions, job, fortune, and memory. In pretreatment assessment, subjects are screened and selected based on their poor adjustment on the scale; say, scores lower than 25. Then two treatments are provided, in counterbalanced order, to two groups of subjects. Suppose the initial treatment increases adjustment to a mean of 95. With this initial change, a second treatment cannot provide evidence of further improvements. For example, the data might show the pattern illustrated in Figure 6.3, in which it can be seen that the first treatment (A or B) led to marked increments in adjustment, and administering the second treatment did not produce additional change. The conclusion would be that the treatments are equally effective and that one does not add to the other.

A different pattern might emerge if there were no ceiling on the measure. That is, if even higher scores were allowed and a greater amount of change could be shown, different conclusions might be reached. For example, if the adjustment scale allowed scores beyond 100 and additional degrees of adjustment, different results might have been obtained. The treatments might have been different at their first presentation. Treatment A might have led to a mean score of 95 but treatment B to a score of 150. In that case, when the other (second) treatment was applied to each group, additional changes may have been detected, at least in going from A to B.

In general, the problem of ceiling or floor effects is not restricted to multiple-treatment comparisons. The absence of differences between groups on a measure may result from limits in the range of scores obtained on that measure. If scores for the different groups congregate at the upper and lower end of the scale, it is possible that differences would be evident if the scale permitted a greater spread of scores. For example, in a child treatment outcome study, we evaluated treatment acceptability,

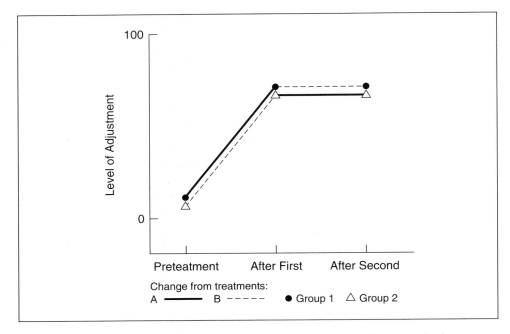

FIGURE 6.3 Hypothetical data for a crossover design wherein each group of subjects receives treatments but in a counterbalanced order.

that is, the extent to which treatment was viewed as appropriate, fair, and reasonable (Kazdin, Siegel, & Bass, 1992). At the end of the study, parents and children rated the treatment they received. The three treatments in the study were rated quite positively and did not differ in level of acceptability. It is possible that the treatments were equally acceptable. Yet, the means for the treatments were close to the upper limit of possible scores on the scale. Thus, it remains possible that acceptability would differ if the ceiling of the scale had not been so limited.

There are obvious and subtle problems to be aware of with regard to floor and ceiling effects. The obvious one which I have been discussing, is that there may be a numerical limit to the scale that will not allow changes to be found. That is, the first intervention leads to a mean score of 95 on a scale of 100, so the second intervention has not much of a place to show further increments; the numerical limit of the scale will limit what can be found.

The more subtle version is that toward the upper (or lower) ends of a scale (ceiling and floor, respectively), the amount, level, or magnitude of change needed to move one's score at one point on the scale or measure may be much greater than what is needed to change when at a less extreme point on the scale. Let me say this in a way to convey the point, even though it is not quite accurate. When dieting, the first 10 pounds (4.53 kilograms) is easier to lose than the second 10 pounds. The point is that an increment or decrement of 10 is not equally easy at all points on the measure (in losing weight). For a measure of psychological adjustment or some other construct used in a multiple-treatment design, the first intervention may move people to a mean score of 75 on a scale that goes to 100. The investigator may say there is no ceiling effect because the next treatment still has a lot of room (25 points) to get to the maximum score, so there is no ceiling effect problem. There may be a ceiling problem. Changes in these last 25 points (from 75–100) points may be more difficult to make than changes from 50–75. There may be a de facto ceiling that the numerical limit does not necessarily reflect. To obtain a score of 90–100, for example, this really requires amazing adjustment that few people would have. How can one tell if this more subtle version of ceiling effects is likely? Does other research show that people, in fact, can or often do score at the extremes of the scale? Is there evidence that the end points provide useful and usable data? If yes, then ceiling (or floor) effects are not likely to be a problem. Most of the time, it is useful just to worry about the obvious way in which ceiling and floor effects are evident, but the subtle way is not trivial.

Although the problem of ceiling and floor effects can occur in any design, it is exacerbated by multiple-treatment designs because different treatments operate toward continued increases (or decreases) in scores. With repeated treatments the limit of the scores may be approached with one or two treatments and not allow differentiation of later treatments. Thus, one consideration in using a multiple-treatment design is whether the different measures provide a sufficient range of scores to allow continued increments in performance from a purely measurement standpoint.

From multiple-treatment designs, ceiling and floor effects are readily avoided when behavior change is transient. For example, interventions based upon administration of drugs or incentives for performance may produce effects only while the interventions are in effect. Assessment of behavior can be made while these interventions are in effect. After withdrawal of the intervention—perhaps with an intervening period so that drug or incentive effects are completely eliminated—the second intervention can be implemented. If the effects of an intervention are transient and evident only when the intervention is in effect, the improvements resulting from one treatment will not limit the scores that can be achieved by the second treatment. The study of interventions with transient effects resolves the problem of ceiling and floor effects in the dependent measures. However, in areas of clinical or applied research as in psychotherapy, counseling, and educational interventions, the purpose is to produce a nontransient change. It is not reasonable to select interventions with transient effects for purposes of design if the goal is protracted change.

SUMMARY AND CONCLUSIONS

Fundamental issues in research include the selection of subjects and their assignment to conditions within the experiment. Random selection was discussed as one possible way of selecting subjects; this is very rare in psychological research. Subjects are selected from available samples or those with a particular characteristic (clinical disorder). Critical sampling issues were discussed, including the heavy reliance on a narrow range and type of subjects. Males, college students, and subjects who are of European American descent and of middle socioeconomic status are disproportionately represented in many areas of psychological research, relative to their proportion in the population at large. Not every way of delineating people can be studied in research. At the same time, sample characteristics (sex, ethnicity, socioeconomic status) often are likely to serve as moderators of many relations. In selecting subjects, samples of convenience were also mentioned. These are subjects identified merely because they are available and usually because they are serving some other purpose. An investigator ought to make the case in any study why the sample used is appropriate to the hypotheses.

Assignment of subjects to groups or conditions is obviously critical. Careful attention must be given to the assignment of subjects to groups. In experimental research, subjects are assigned in an unbiased fashion so that each subject has an equal probability of being assigned to the different conditions. Typically, random assignment is employed. As an adjunctive procedure, subjects may be matched on a given variable at the beginning of the experiment and randomly assigned in blocks to conditions. Matching followed by random assignment is an excellent way to ensure equivalence of groups on a measure that relates to the dependent variable.

Several different designs were discussed, including the pretest–posttest control group design, posttest-only control group design, Solomon four-group design, factorial designs, and quasi-experimental designs. In these designs each subject receives one condition (treatment, control), and groups are compared to evaluate the impact of the intervention or manipulation. The pretest–posttest control group was noted as particularly advantageous because of the strengths that the pretest provides for demarcating initial (preintervention) levels of functioning, evaluating change, and increasing power for statistical analyses.

Multiple-treatment designs were also discussed. In these designs each subject receives all of the conditions (more than one treatment, or treatment and control conditions). Separate groups of subjects are used so that the different treatments can be counterbalanced. Counterbalancing is designed to ensure that the effects of the treatments can be separated from the order in which they appear. In the simplest multiple-treatment design, referred to as the crossover design, two treatments are given to two groups of subjects but in different order. In more complex versions several treatments may be delivered and presented either in a randomized or a prearranged order to randomly comprised groups of subjects. A Latin square design refers to ways of arranging multiple treatments within subjects where the number of treatments is equal to the number of groups and where each treatment appears once in each position in the sequence in which treatments are arranged.

There are several considerations in using multiple-treatment designs. Order and sequence effects can emerge and must be controlled by ensuring whenever possible that each treatment is administered at each point in the order of treatments (first, second, third, etc.). Also, ceiling and floor effects are more likely in multiple-treatment designs, that is, upper or lower limits on the response measure that will not allow subsequent interventions to reflect further change in performance.

KEY CONCEPTS AND TERMS

Ceiling Effects	Random Assignment
Matching	Random Selection
Multiple-Treatment Designs	Sample of Convenience
Order Effects	

FOR FURTHER READING

Campbell, D.T., & Kenny, D.A. (1999) *A primer on regression artifacts.* New York: Guilford Press.

Cook, T.D. & Campbell, D.T. (1979*). Quasi-experimentation: Design and analysis issues for field settings.* Chicago: Rand McNally.

Council of National Psychological Associations for the Advancement of Ethnic Minority Interests (2000). *Guidelines for research in ethnic minority communities.* Washington, DC: American Psychological Association.

Guthrie, R.V. (1997). *Even the rat was white: A historical view of psychology.* Needham Heights, MA: Allyn & Bacon.

Hsu, L.M. (1995). Regression toward the mean associated with measurement error and the identification of improvement and deterioration in psychotherapy. *Journal of Consulting and Clinical Psychology, 63,* 141–144.

Kisker, E.E., & Brown, R.S. (1997). Nonexperimental designs and program evaluation. *Children and Youth Services Review, 19,* 541–566.

Rosenthal, R., & Rosnow, R.L. (1991). *Essentials of behavioral research: Methods and data analysis* (2nd ed.). New York: McGraw-Hill.

Shadish, W.R., & Ragsdale, K. (1996). Random versus nonrandom assignment in controlled experiments: Do you get the same answer? *Journal of Consulting and Clinical Psychology, 64,* 1290–1305.

Chapter 7

Control and Comparison Groups

In discussions of research we are often taught that an experiment requires a control group. Of course, the notion of *a* control group is mildly misleading because it implies that the addition of a single group to a design may provide a general control for diverse biases, artifacts, and rival hypotheses that might plague the research. In fact, all sorts of groups may be added or included in a design, depending on the potential influences other than the intervention, that may account for the results (threats to internal validity) and the specificity of the statements the investigator wishes to make about what led to change or group differences (threats to construct validity). Indeed, a more in-depth understanding of research design might be pursued by discussing the broader concept of comparison groups. *Comparison groups* refer to any group included in design beyond the primary group or groups of interest. Comparison groups permit the investigator to draw various conclusions; the groups differ in the types of conclusions they permit. There might be multiple-treatment groups, for example, that differ on one or two ingredients or components because the investigator wishes to dissect treatment or make claims about a particular ingredient. Here the comparison groups all include treatment and in some sense are not "control" groups as this is usually discussed.

Control groups are merely one type of comparison group. Some control groups (e.g., no-treatment, waiting-list) primarily address the threats to internal validity; other control groups (e.g., nonspecific treatment) address threats to construct validity in the sense that they aid in interpreting the basis for the impact of the intervention. The investigator may wish to make any number of statements about the intervention and what accounted for the change. Because the range of possible conclusions varies widely with content area and investigator interest, not all groups of interest can be catalogued. Nevertheless, comparison groups often used in clinical research can be identified and illustrated. This chapter discusses groups that are often used in clinical research, the design issues they are intended to address, and considerations that dictate their use.

CONTROL GROUPS

Control groups are usually used to address such threats to internal validity as history, maturation, selection, and testing. Control of these threats is accomplished by ensuring that one group in the design shares these influences with the intervention group but does not receive the intervention or experimental manipulation. If the intervention and control groups are formed by random assignment and assessed at the same time(s), internal validity threats are usually addressed. In clinical research several control groups are often used.

No-Treatment Control Group

Description and Rationale.   In evaluating a particular therapy or experimental intervention, a basic question can always be raised, namely, to what extent would persons improve or change without treatment? The question can be answered by including a *no-treatment control group* in the experimental design. This group is so fundamental to intervention research that it was included in the basic descriptions and diagrams of the pretest–posttest control group and posttest-only control group designs discussed in the previous chapter. This is the group that is assessed but otherwise receives no intervention. By including a no-treatment group in the design, the effects of history and maturation as well as other threats to internal validity are directly controlled.

The performance of persons in a no-treatment control group can change significantly over time, which underscores the importance of this group in providing a baseline level for purposes of comparison. For example, in psychotherapy research, improvements often occur among clients who are in the no-treatment control condition. Historically, these improvements have been referred to as *spontaneous remission*. The term is not extremely informative because the reason for the change ("spontaneous") and the extent to which change has improved client functioning ("remission") are arguable. Actually, spontaneous remission refers to changes made without receiving formal treatment in a given investigation. The term embraces history, maturation, and statistical regression, but is usually not discussed as such in evaluations of therapy. In some cases clear historical events are possible explanations. For example, people who are assigned to no treatment may seek other treatments at another clinic. Even if another type of treatment is not formally sought, clients may improve as a function of more informal means of "treatment" such as talking with relatives, neighbors, members of the clergy, or general-practice physicians. Improvements over time may also result from changes in the situations that exacerbated or precipitated the problem (e.g., adjustment after a death of a loved one) and other maturational influences that affect one's mood, outlook, and psychological status. Individuals who come for treatment may be at a particularly severe point in their problem. Hence, one would expect that reassessment of the problem at some later point would show improvement. It may not be true that "time heals all wounds," but ordinary processes occurring with the passage of time certainly are strong competitors for many therapeutic techniques. In view of the multiple influences that may impinge on clients who are in a no-treatment group, it is difficult to specify whether changes over time are "spontaneous," whatever that means. From a methodological standpoint, the important issue is to control for the amount of improvement that occurs as a function of these multiple, even if poorly specified and understood, influences. A no-treatment control group assesses the base rate of improvement for clients who did not receive the treatment under investigation.

Ideally, one would know in advance what the level of improvement is for clients with a particular problem so that treatment could be evaluated without using no-treatment control procedures. Yet, even if improvement rates for various client disorders were well known, a no-treatment group is required in treatment research for other reasons. Changes in behavior may result from repeated assessment on the various dependent measures used to evaluate treatment, as discussed in Chapter 2. A no-treatment group is exposed to the same assessment procedures of the treatment group, thus making implausible the effects of testing and instrument decay as possible explanations of the results.

It is important to use as a no-treatment group clients who have been randomly assigned to this condition. Violation of random assignment erodes the interpretability of any between-group differences after treatment has been completed. For example, some individuals for one reason or another may choose not to participate in the program after pretreatment assessment or may withdraw after a small number of treatment sessions. Persons who have withdrawn from treatment would, of course, not be appropriate to consider as part of, or additions to, the no-treatment control group. While these clients might be considered to have received no treatment, they are self-selected for that status. Their subsequent performance on any measures might well reflect variables related to their early withdrawal, rather than to the absence of treatment.

Special Considerations.   Using a no-treatment control group presents obvious ethical problems. When clients seek treatment, it is difficult to justify withholding all attempts at intervention. Providing an experimental or exploratory treatment that is reasonable, even if unproved, is more ethically defensible than providing no treatment at all. When it comes to withholding treatment in a clinical situation, ivory tower pleas for experimental elegance, control groups, and the importance of scientific research may be unpersuasive to prospective clients. Actually, the ethical issue is usually circumvented by conveying at the outset of a study that one could be assigned to a no-treatment condition and that individuals ought to participate in the study only if this possibility is acceptable. Solicitation of consent to participate in advance of the study conveys the options to the prospective participants and allows them to decide if participation is reasonable. Even this is by no means a great solution. Clients may agree to participate but then end up dropping out if they are not assigned to the treatment group. This is reasonable or at least quite understandable from the standpoint of a client. Leaving this issue aside, for clients who are suffering significant impairment or dysfunction and indeed who are in crisis, it is unclear whether assignment to no treatment would be ethically defensible even if they agreed to participate and remained in the condition.

Aside from ethical issues, there are obvious practical problems in utilizing a no-treatment control group. Difficulties are encountered in explaining to clients who apply why treatment is unavailable or why there is a no-treatment condition. When the study begins, persons who are assigned to the no-treatment condition, may seek treatment elsewhere, or they may resent not receiving treatment and fail to cooperate with subsequent attempts to administer assessment devices.

If a no-treatment group of clients is successfully formed, it is likely that there will be time constraints on the group. As a general rule, the longer that clients are required to serve as no-treatment controls, the more likely they will drop out of the study. The investigator may wish to know the effects of the intervention over an extended period (1, 5, or 10 years of follow-up). However, continuation of a no-treatment condition usually is not feasible over an extended period (e.g., months). Few no-treatment subjects are likely to remain in the study over an extended period; those who do may be a select group whose data are difficult to interpret. A partial solution to withholding treatment and meeting the requirements of a no-treatment control group is to use a waiting-list control group.

Waiting-List Control Group

Description and Rationale.   Rather than withhold treatment completely, one can merely delay treatment. A *waiting-list control group* withholds treatment for a period of time, after which treatment is then provided. The period for which treatment is withheld usually corresponds to the pre-to-posttreatment assessment interval of clients in the treatment condition. Thus, treatment and wait-list cases are assessed at the beginning of the study (before any treatment is given) and at that point that the treatment group has completed treatment. The waiting-list group will not have received the intervention during this period but will have completed all of the pre and "post" assessments (it is really a second pretreatment assessment for them because they have not received treatment). As soon as the second assessment battery is administered, these subjects receive treatment.

When clients originally apply for treatment, they can be asked whether they would participate even if treatment were delayed. Only those subjects who agree would be included in the study. These clients would be assigned randomly to either treatment or waiting-list control conditions. The control clients are promised treatment within a specified time period and in fact are called back and scheduled for treatment. Although it is tempting to assign those clients who indicate they could wait for treatment to the control group and those who could not wait to the treatment group, circumventing random assignment in this way is methodologically disastrous. Treatment effects or the absence of such effects could be the result of subject selection in combination with history, maturation, regression, and other threats to internal validity.

Three rudimentary features characterize a waiting-list control group. First, if a pretest is used, there must be no treatment between the first and second assessment period for the waiting-list control group. During this period, the group is functionally equivalent to a no-treatment control group. Second, the time period from first to second assessment of the waiting-list control group must correspond to the time period of pre- and posttreatment assessment of the treatment group. This may be easily controlled if treatment consists of a particular interval (e.g., 2 months) and the pre-to-posttreatment assessment period is constant across treated subjects. Then waiting-list control subjects can return for reassessment after that fixed interval has elapsed. If treatment duration varies, a waiting-list subject might be reassessed at the same interval of the treatment subject to which he or she has been matched. For example, a waiting-list control subject can be scheduled for reassessment at the same time that a treated subject returns for posttreatment assessment. The waiting-list control and experimental subjects are grouped in this way on the basis of having taken the pre- and posttreatment assessment devices over the same time interval (e.g., within one week), or perhaps even on the same days. It is important to keep the time interval constant to control for history and maturation over the course of the assessment interval.

Third, waiting-list control clients complete pretest or posttest assessments and then receive treatment. An important practical question is how to have the waiting-list subjects return for reassessment immediately prior to providing them with treatment. Actually, this is not particularly difficult. Clients usually are required to complete the assessment again before receiving treatment. Essentially, reassessment is connected with the promise of scheduling treatment and serves as an immediate antecedent to the long-awaited intervention.

Special Considerations.   There is an obvious limitation of the waiting-list control condition, particularly in comparison to a no-treatment group. Because subjects in the waiting-list group receive treatment soon after they have served their role as a temporary no-treatment group, the long-term impact of such processes as history, maturation, and repeated testing cannot be evaluated. Even if waiting-list subjects did not change very much in the time interval in which they waited for treatment, they may have improved or deteriorated greatly by the time of follow-up assessment even without treatment. One can follow the treatment group to see how they are doing one or two years later. Yet, the waiting-list control group is no longer available for comparison; by this time this group will be another treatment group.

Although rare, in some instances, wait-list control cases are informed that they will receive treatment after an extended period. For example, in one study, two 12-week treatments were compared to a waiting-list control condition (Cunningham,

Bremner, & Boyle, 1995). To their credit, the investigators wished to obtain 6-month follow-up data. Wait-list cases were told that they could begin treatment after the 6-month follow data were obtained. This was an excellent strategy from the standpoint of design, but would not be feasible in the vast majority of cases in which clients experience mild-to-significant clinical impairment.

The use of a waiting-list control group has much to recommend it. From a practical standpoint, it usually is not as difficult to obtain waiting-list control subjects as it is to obtain no-treatment subjects. The difficulty partially depends upon how long the controls are required to wait for treatment, the severity of the problem, their perceived need for treatment, and the availability of other resources. From the standpoint of experimental design, there is a decided advantage in the use of a waiting-list control group. This group allows careful evaluation of treatment effects at different points in the design. Because treatment eventually is provided to the waiting-list control subjects, its effects can be evaluated empirically. Essentially, a waiting-list control study using a pretest can be diagrammed as follows:

$$R \quad O_1 \quad X \quad O_2$$
$$R \quad O_3 \quad \quad O_4 \quad X \quad O_5$$

The effect of treatment (X) is replicated in the design. Not only can the treatment be assessed by a between-group comparison (comparison of O_2 and O_4) but also by within-group comparisons as well (comparison of change from O_3 to O_4 with the change from O_4 to O_5). Of course, to accomplish this, waiting-list control group subjects must be reassessed after they finally receive treatment.

The waiting-list control group does not completely ameliorate the ethical problems of withholding treatment but may help a little. Now the issue is not withholding treatment from some of the clients. Rather, all clients receive treatment and differ only according to when they receive it. Ethical problems arise if clients request or require immediate treatment and delaying treatment may have serious consequences. Obviously, a waiting-list control group is not ethically defensible with acutely suicidal patients. Apart from such situations and as an alternative to the no-treatment control group, a waiting-list group offers a distinct advantage because clients eventually receive treatment.

No-Contact Control Group

Description and Rationale.   The effects of participating in a study, even if only in the capacity of a no-treatment or waiting-list control subject, may have impact on the subjects because participation can be reactive. In the context of treatment research, participating in a control group may exert some therapeutic change. Indeed, it has been known for some time that clients who receive only the initial assessment battery on separate occasions before any treatment is given show marked improvements (Frank et al., 1963). Although regression alone might account for improvement upon repeated testing, the anticipation of relief from participating in a treatment project may be responsible as well.

Occasionally, it is possible to evaluate the impact of participation by using as a control group individuals who have no contact with the project. These individuals constitute a *no-contact control group*. The requirements for a no-contact group are difficult to meet because the *subjects do not receive treatment and do not realize that they are serving in this capacity*. To obtain such a group of subjects, pretest information usually is needed for a large pool of subjects who are part of a larger assessment project. Some of these subjects, determined randomly, are selected for the no-contact group. To obtain the initial pretest information requires that assessment devices are administered under some other guise (e.g., part of routine class activities in an undergraduate course). Also, obtaining subsequent test information must be conveyed as part of a routine activity so it is not associated with a treatment project.

It is worth illustrating this group briefly even though it is used infrequently. A classic example is a study in which college students were treated for speech anxiety (Paul, 1966). Several students who qualified for treatment were used as no-contact control subjects. Measures were administered under the guise of requirements for and a follow-up to ordinary college speech classes. No-treatment subjects, also a separate group in the study, received several assessment devices as part of the study, telephone contact and interviews, and other procedures related to the treatment project. A no-contact group received none of these and had no basis to infer that they were in the study. Because the assessment before and after treatment was related to participation in the course, data were available without revealing use of the information as part of a treatment study. At the end, comparisons could be made assessing the effect of receiving contact with the program versus no contact. Among subjects who did not receive treatment, those who had no explicit contact with the study (no-contact controls) performed less well on various measures of anxiety and personality at the end of the study and at follow-up than those subjects who did (no-treatment controls who knew they were part of the study). Thus, serving as a no-treatment subject explicitly connected with the study was associated with some improvements that did not occur for no-contact subjects.

Special Considerations.   In outpatient research a captive group of subjects analogous to college students is not usually available. In addition, administering measures under a guise other than treatment is likely to violate both the letter and spirit of current informed consent requirements for subjects who participate in research. Studies in institutional settings—such as clinics, psychiatric hospitals, prisons, and schools—might permit no-contact control groups. Assessment devices could be administered routinely on separate occasions and be used to provide data for comparisons with subsamples that serve in the study. However, use of data as part of research requires informing subjects and obtaining consent. Thus, subjects would know they are serving in a study.

The main issue is not in whether a no-contact group could be formed but rather the requirements of the research question. In most studies the investigator is not likely to be concerned with separating the effects of contact with the treatment or research project from no-contact; a no-treatment or waiting-list control group is likely to serve as the appropriate measure of improvement against which the effects of treatment can be evaluated. On the other hand, it might be important for conceptual reasons to evaluate whether serving in a project, even as a no-treatment subject, influences a particular set of measures or clinical problem.

An investigator may also wish to use no-contact procedures for all conditions and subjects to avoid the influences associated with knowing that one is participating in an experiment. For example, in one program, over 500 7th graders from 10 different schools were included in a study to control classroom discipline (Matthews, 1986). Children within each school were assigned randomly to experimental or control conditions. Teachers in the experimental condition were trained to conduct relaxation exercises in their classes, which they did on a daily basis for approximately 7 months. The objective was to calm the children and to develop a means for coping with tension. Control children did not receive the special program. Neither teachers nor students were aware that they were participating in a study; the intervention was provided as part of the curriculum for some students in their homerooms. The dependent measure consisted of discipline infractions at the school (fighting, cutting class), which were collected routinely and not associated specifically with this study. The results indicated that experimental youth, when compared with controls, showed significantly fewer discipline infractions. The fact that persons in experimental and control group(s) were uninformed about their participation minimizes the impact of potential threats to validity (e.g., special treatment or reactions of the control group, reactivity of the experimental arrangements, reactivity of assessment). In this study the no-contact feature applied to both intervention and control conditions. In general, no-contact procedures or control groups may be useful to address the impact of serving in a study or to eliminate the potential reactivity of such an arrangement. Counsel is required to ensure that subject rights are protected and that the study meets ethical requirements of informed consent (elaborated upon in Chapter 17).

Nonspecific-Treatment or "Attention-Placebo" Control Group

Description and Rationale.   No-treatment and waiting-list control groups are employed primarily to address threats to internal validity (history, maturation, repeated testing). In the context of treatment research a *nonspecific-treatment control group* addresses these threats but focuses as well on threats to construct validity. In any treatment many seeming accouterments may contribute to or be responsible for therapeutic change. Such factors as attending treatment sessions, having personal contact with a therapist, hearing a logical rationale that describes the genesis of one's problem, and undergoing a procedure directed toward ameliorating the problem may exert influence on client performance and generate their own therapeutic effects. These factors are referred to as *common or nonspecific factors of psychotherapy* because they are ingredients in most treatments. Moreover, when we consider specific therapy techniques (cognitive behavioral treatment, structural family therapy), we do not consider the mechanisms of action or processes through which change is achieved to be due merely or solely to the common factors. Rather, additional processes are proposed to explain both the problem and way in which the problem will be resolved or addressed.

Common factors may be critical to therapy because of the processes they mobilize within the individuals and the changes they produce. When clients participate in treatment, they are likely to believe in the procedures and have faith that some therapeutic change will result (Frank & Frank, 1991). We have learned from many years of medical research that the belief in treatment is important. Placebos, inert substances (e.g., sugar tablets) given under the guise of treatment, can alter a variety of disorders ranging in severity from the common cold to cancer (Shapiro & Shapiro, 1998; Spiro, 1998). Placebo effects, by definition, result from factors other than active ingredients in the substance itself. Hence, the belief of the patient in treatment and perhaps the belief in the physician who administers treatment and similar factors appear to be responsible for change.

Effects analogous to placebo reactions influence individuals who come to psychotherapy. Indeed, the history of psychological treatments can be traced by drawing attention to procedures and therapists (Franz Anton Mesmer [1734–1815] and Emile Coué [1857–1926]) whose effects we recognize to have been largely due to suggestion. Consequently, in an empirical investigation of psychotherapy, a simple comparison of treatment and no-treatment control groups does not establish what facet of "the intervention" led to change, that is, construct validity. To identify if the specific intervention or the unique properties of a treatment are important in producing change in the clients, a nonspecific-treatment group can be included in the design.

A nonspecific-treatment control may include procedures in which clients meet with a therapist, hear a rationale that explains how their problem may have developed, and discuss something about their lives in sessions that are similar in number and duration to those in the treatment group. From the standpoint of the investigation, these subjects are considered to be receiving a psychological placebo, as it were. This is why a nonspecific treatment control group is also referred to as an *attention-placebo control group*. Either term is used to refer to any procedure that might be credible to the clients and appear to be effective but is not based on theoretical or empirical findings about therapeutic change.

In developing a nonspecific control condition, a goal is to provide some form of pseudointervention that involves clients in an experience of some sort. The goal is to control for factors common to coming to treatment but without the putatively critical ingredient. Special care is needed to decide in advance what the investigators wish to control. As an illustration, one study evaluated an intervention to resolve unfinished emotional business, that is, unresolved issues related to a significant other (Paivio & Greenberg, 1995). The treatment consisted of the Gestalt empty-chair dialogue, in which a client engages in a dialogue with an imaginary significant other as if that other person were in the empty chair. The intervention is part of experiential therapy and is designed to access important feelings and to allow the feelings to come to some sort of resolution in the context of a structured and safe therapy environment. Adults were recruited and screened for unfinished business and assigned to the empty-chair treatment or to an attention-placebo control condition. The control condition included group sessions that discussed unfinished business but did not provide opportunities to experience and to access these feelings in the way of the empty-chair technique. The control condition is very good insofar as the themes and topics were very similar to those in the treatment condition. This would make this condition more than just coming to treatment and seeing a therapist because in the end we might be able to say that merely raising the topic of unfinished business is not enough (because the control group did this).

As for the findings, at posttreatment the experimental (empty-chair) group showed greater reduction in stress and resolution of unfinished business than did controls. Because this was a pretty good attention control group, we would want to be able to say that focus on the empty chair, rather than just talking about unfinished business, was the reason for group differences. Unfortunately, the treatment and control groups differed in three ways (individual versus group treatment, 12 versus 3 sessions, approximately 10 versus 6 hours of treatment, respectively) that raise a plausible rival interpretation of the results, namely, multiple characteristics favored the treatment condition, apart from the manipulation of interest. Also, a critical issue for nonspecific-treatment control groups is to control for level of expectations that are mobilized in the subjects. It is likely that the treatment group was much more credible than the control condition, and these different expectations could account for the outcome differences. The issues raised here convey some of the difficulties in providing an attention-placebo group that is similar in some ways but dissimilar in crucial ways (just the putative active ingredients the investigator wishes to study) from the treatment group.

A nonspecific-treatment control group is designed to control for common factors that are associated with participation in treatment. There is sufficient evidence that merely coming to sessions and meeting with a mental health professional can lead to significant therapeutic change. Consequently, if the investigator wishes to discuss why treatment led to change or whether a particular approach (e.g., cognitive therapy) really was shown to be important in a given study, some version of an attention-placebo group or another treatment is essential.

If a treatment group is shown to be more effective than an attention-placebo group, this does not necessarily mean that the processes proposed by the investigator to characterize the treatment group (changes in cognitions, resolving conflict) are necessarily supported. Nonspecific-treatment control groups rule out or make implausible some common factors as an explanation of the results, but they do not necessarily point to the construct in the treatment group that is responsible for change. If the investigator wishes to argue for the basis for change in the treatment group, some evaluation of the processes considered to be central to change (cognitions, alliance) ought to be assessed directly and tested in relation to the amount of therapeutic change.

Special Considerations.   Several issues emerge in developing a nonspecific-treatment control condition. To begin, the conceptual problems are not minor. What is an "inert" intervention that could serve as a control? A placebo in medicine is known in advance, because of its pharmacological properties (salt or sugar in a tablet), to be inert, that is, not to produce effects through its chemical properties in relation to the clinical problem. In psychological treatment one usually does not know in advance that the properties of the nonspecific-treatment group are inert. Merely chatting with a therapist or engaging in some activities vaguely related to one's problem might be cast in theoretical language to make them seem plausible as genuine treatments. This is why in the therapy research business, one investigator's treatment group is another investigator's control group. It is difficult to devise an intervention that is credible to the clients and yet one that could not also be construed by someone as a theoretically plausible treatment.

Another issue that emerges pertains to the credibility of the procedure. One ingredient in therapy is the client's beliefs or expectancies that treatment will work. Presumably a plausible nonspecific-treatment control group would have this ingredient as well so that client expectations for improvement could not explain outcome differences between treatment and control conditions. However, devising a credible control condition requires a rationale about why this "treatment" is likely to be effective and why procedures in or outside of the treatment sessions look like credible means toward therapeutic change. Highly credible control conditions are often just as effective (when compared to no treatment) as treatment conditions (see Lambert & Bergin, 1994). This has implications for conducting experiments (larger sample sizes are needed to detect small group differences) and for their interpretation (isolating the construct that accounts for change). Also, measures can be used at the beginning of treatment to assess treatment credibility and client expectancies for improvement. For example, clients can be asked questions about how credible treatment is, how logical it appears, and how likely treatment is to be successful. Responses to such items can be evaluated in relation to treatment outcome (e.g., is therapeutic change a function of initial credibility of the treatment?). Whether treatment and control conditions vary in credibility can also be evaluated (see Borkovec & Nau, 1972 for a measure). The data can be brought to bear on the likelihood that expectancies or differential expectancies play a role in treatment outcome.

Ethical issues also emerge in providing nonspecific-treatment conditions, beginning with the problem of providing a treatment that is not well based on theory or empirical findings. In addition, if clients are in need of clinical care, this type of group may not be defensible. The ethical issues have become even more salient in light of current developments in the ethics of medical research. Although we take up ethical issues in greater depth later, a key point is pertinent now.

Research guidelines include many professional codes, but one is worth mentioning in the context of the present discussion. The 1964 Declaration of Helsinki was devised to provide guidelines for research. The guidelines were prompted by gruesome medical experiments of the Nazi era and designed to protect subjects. Recent revisions of the Declaration by the World Medical Association provide a guideline that notes placebo control groups should not be used in medical research. Rather, the comparison ought to be the best current treatment method available (see Enserink, 2000b). This particular recommendation, which has now been approved, grew out of recent medical research on such serious conditions as HIV, in which efforts were made in Africa and Asia to evaluate new medications (e.g., to prevent pregnant HIV positive mothers from passing HIV to their newborns). The use of placebos in such trials has been controversial, to say the least. Citizens have lobbied against use of placebos when there is a reasonable basis for providing the drug or another treatment. Whether or not the research focus is life threatening, patients ought not to be subjected to placebo control conditions if any reasonable alternative conditions could be provided. There is no justification for unnecessary suffering. Arguments on the other side have focused on the need to establish the effects of treatment to ensure the greatest benefit. Obviously, these brief comments do not reflect the different arguments or the range of protections provided by the guidelines. The net effect is that as of late 2000, the New Declaration of Helsinki specifies international guidelines that disapprove of placebo controls. It is too early to judge the impact on medical research. The Declaration is not legally binding but represents an international group whose views are significant.

The leap from placebos in medical research for any clinical disorder to attention-placebo conditions in psychological research is not that great. Whether or not guidelines confine the investigator, the broader point is weighty. Ought one ever to use a nonspecific-treatment control condition, and if so, under what circumstances? From the standpoint of the scientific underpinnings of therapy, the control for common factors is rather important. Indeed, claims are made that the specific effects of therapy (over and above client expectancies or common factors) are responsible for the benefits of therapy (Eisner, 2000). However, there are reasons to be skeptical. Therapy may work in part because of "placebo-like" effects.

Use of a nonspecific-treatment control condition can have deleterious effects on the clients, apart from the absence of immediate benefit for the clinical problem leading them to treatment. Assume for a moment that one is able to devise a nonspecific-treatment control group and provide this to clients. Perhaps the client is not likely to get better, although the rate of improvement will vary as a function of client problem and quality/credibility of the attention-placebo group. Participation in the nonspecific-treatment control condition might influence beliefs about therapy in general and have impact on the client's subsequent use of treatment. The client who receives a "fake treatment" might be turned away from therapy in the future when a veridical treatment might help with the stresses and strains of life. The nonspecific-treatment group may not be very credible or does not help the client, and hence leads the client away from a potentially useful resource. Conceivably, ordinary therapy might teach a given client such lessons; using a control condition without a veridical treatment merely increases the likelihood of such an effect.

Research to date tends to support the view that psychotherapy is more effective than nonspecific-treatment control conditions and that nonspecific-treatment control conditions are more effective than no treatment (Lambert & Bergin, 1994). At the same time, this has been a difficult area of research because of the obstacles of designing and implementing attention-placebo conditions that generate as much expectancies for change as the treatment conditions to which they are compared. In developing or evaluating a new treatment, it is critical to show that treatment effects surpass those achieved with the common factors that arise from merely participating in treatment. This can be accomplished by using a nonspecific-treatment control group or another treatment that has already been shown to be effective. Routine treatment is a viable comparison group, too, and is discussed next.

Routine or Standard Treatment

Description and Rationale. In clinical research, assigning individuals to no-treatment, waiting-list, and nonspecific-treatment control conditions may not be ethically defensible or feasible in light of presenting problems of the clients and the context in which treatment is provided. In such circumstances the investigator may still wish to test whether a new treatment is effective. One alternative is to compare the new treatment with the standard one that is provided in the setting. For example, multisystemic therapy is an intervention that has been used to treat adolescent sexual offenders and juvenile offenders (Henggeler, Schoenwald, Borduin, Rowland, & Cunningham, 1998). The treatment combines multiple interventions (parent training, cognitive therapy) to address peer, school, adolescent, parent, and family problems. The youths have multiple offenses and obviously cannot be assigned to no-treatment or nonspecific-treatment conditions. Consequently, the treatment studies evaluated the extent to which multisystemic therapy surpasses routine or standard care (individual therapy or as-usual procedures, such as being placed on probation). The random assignment of cases to these different conditions is feasible and addresses the question of interest without other control groups. In several studies multisystemic therapy has been much more effective than routine treatments, as reflected on measures of emotional and behavioral problems and arrest and criminal behavior.

At least four advantages accrue to the use of standard treatment or routine care as a comparison condition. First, demands for service and ethical issues associated with many other control conditions are met. All persons in the study can receive an active treatment. No one receives a condition that is not designed to work (such as a nonspecific-treatment control condition). Second, because everyone receives a veridical treatment, attrition is likely to be less than if various control conditions were used (no-treatment, waiting-list). Third, routine treatment is likely to control for many of the common or nonspecific factors of therapy (contact with a therapist, participation in sessions). Thus, receipt of an or any intervention is not a viable rival interpretation of the results in most studies, although "new and improved" therapies, when compared to standard treatments, tend to have more enthusiasm, investigator hype, and therapist expectations, than business as usual. Finally, clinicians who might serve as therapists in the study as well as clinicians who might be consumers of the research results are likely to be much more satisfied with the study that uses standard treatment as a comparison condition. The question is one that is clinically relevant (is the new treatment really better?), and the study more closely resembles clinical work by including a standard treatment.

Special Considerations.   Standard and routine treatments or programs raise their own dilemmas. It is often difficult to know what these entail at a clinic, hospital, or school, no matter what the descriptions and brochures actually say. The investigator ought to monitor and assess carefully what is done as part of routine treatment. If possible, it is better from the standpoint of the design for the investigator to administer the condition so that integrity of the procedure and assessment before, during, and after treatment can be closely monitored. Stated less diplomatically, standard and routine treatment at many clinics is administered sloppily, inconsistently, and with great therapist discretion as to what to include. (All of this is understandable due to the varied training experiences of the clinicians and their attempts to individualize treatment to the clients, which we do not quite know how to do at this point.) In addition, ethical dilemmas often arise after a study is completed and treatment is shown to be better than routine care. In such studies (e.g., as cited above with multisystemic therapy), routine care may quickly become ethically indefensible because it is shown to be inferior to a new treatment.

The investigator may wish to compare the treatment of interest to another active treatment other than a standard or as-usual intervention that is routinely used. In a simple version of such a study, two active or viable treatments are compared, and there is no "control" group in the usual sense. Assuming random assignment, the comparison group addresses the usual threats to internal validity (history, maturation). The only danger is that improvements in both groups and no outcome differences between groups could be explained completely by threats to internal validity. This is not a minor issue and has limited the conclusions that can be drawn in many studies, as I have mentioned and illustrated previously. Even so, the use of a standard care intervention group is likely to circumvent many of the ethical and practical issues of nonspecific-treatment control conditions and to enhance the conclusions that can be drawn about treatment.

The control and comparison groups discussed here are those more commonly used in research to address many threats to internal or construct validity. The range of suitable or appropriate comparison groups that can be used in a study extends beyond the groups noted here. A study may focus on theory or analyze quite specific constructs that may underlie a particular treatment. Comparison groups become specially crafted to the goals of the study. The range of comparison conditions is illustrated later in the chapter by examining the progression of questions addressed in psychotherapy research.

Yoked Control Group

Description and Rationale. Differences in procedures or events to which the subjects are exposed may arise during the investigation as a function of executing the study or implementing a particular intervention. The problem with these differences is that they are not random but may vary systematically between groups. If the effect of the intervention is to be distinguished from these differences that inadvertently arise across groups, the latter influences must be controlled.

One procedure to rule out or assess factors that may arise as a function of implementing a particular intervention is called the *yoked control group*. The purpose of the yoked control group is to ensure that groups are equal with respect to potentially important but conceptually and procedurally irrelevant factors that might account for group differences (Church, 1964). Yoking may require a special control group of its own. More likely in clinical research, yoking can be incorporated into another control group. In this case yoking refers to equalizing the groups on a particular variable that might systematically vary across conditions.

Consider a hypothetical study designed to evaluate a specific therapy technique for the treatment of acrophobia (fear of heights). Three groups are used, including (1) the "new and improved" treatment, (2) a nonspecific-treatment control group that meets with a therapist but engages in a task not likely to be therapeutic (e.g., discussing the development of fears among people they know), and (3) no treatment. Suppose that clients in the treatment group are allowed to attend as many sessions as needed to master a set of tasks designated as therapeutic. For example, clients might have to complete a standard set of anxiety-provoking tasks in therapy to help them overcome anxiety. The number of sessions that clients attend treatment could vary markedly, given individual differences in the rate of completing the tasks. A nonspecific-treatment control group might receive a bogus treatment in which group members merely come in and discuss fears of their friends and relatives. One might raise the question, how many sessions should the control group subjects receive? It would be important to design the study so that any differences in effects of treatment cannot be due to the different number of sessions that the groups received. Yet the control subjects should not simply be given a fixed number of sessions since that would not guarantee equality of sessions across groups.

A solution is to yoke (match) subjects across groups by pairing subjects. The pairs might be formed arbitrarily unless matching was used to assign subjects to groups. A subject in the experimental group would receive a certain number of therapy sessions on the basis of his or her progress. Whatever that number turned out to be would be the number of sessions that would be given to the control subject to whom the subject was yoked. That is, the number of sessions for each control subject would be determined by the subject to whom he or she was paired or matched in the experimental group. Obviously, the yoking procedure requires running the experimental subject first so that the number of sessions or other variable on which yoking was done is known in advance and can be administered to the control subject. The behavior of the experimental subject determines what happens to the control subject. At the end of treatment, the number of treatment sessions will be identical across groups. Hence, any group differences could not be attributable to the number of sessions to which clients were exposed. Yoking would have ensured that the number of sessions did not vary. The yoking would hold constant the number of sessions between the treatment and nonspecific control groups.

The yoking might be extended to address the other group in the design, namely, the no-treatment control group. If pre- and posttreatment assessments are provided, how long should the interval between these assessments be for the group that does not receive any treatment? Subjects in the no-treatment group could also be yoked to persons in the treatment group in terms of the number of weeks between pretreatment and posttreatment assessment. Thus, at the end of the study, yoking would yield the following result. Both treatment and nonspecific control groups would have received the same number of sessions and the time elapsed in weeks or days between pretreatment and posttreatment assessment would be the same for all treatment and control conditions. The means and standard deviations would not differ for the number of sessions (for the two treatment groups) or the number of days or weeks between pre- and posttreatment among groups. As evident from this example, the yoked control procedure may not necessarily constitute a "new" control group. Yoking often can be added to such a group as a nonspecific-treatment control group.

Special Considerations.   Conceivably, an experimental and a control group can be yoked on all sorts of variables that may differ between groups. Whether yoking is used as a control technique needs to be determined by considering whether the variables that may differ across these groups might plausibly account for the results. For example, in a given therapy study it might make sense to yoke on the number of treatment sessions because the amount of contact with a therapist and treatment may contribute to the differences between a treatment and nonspecific-treatment control group, particularly if therapy subjects receive many more sessions. Stated differently, it may be plausible that the *number* of sessions, rather than the *content* of the sessions, is viewed as a threat to construct validity. "The intervention" confounds content and amount of treatment and hence raises ambiguities about why the intervention was more effective. On the other hand, it may be unimportant to yoke subjects in such a way that the time of the day that therapy sessions are held or the attire of the therapists is perfectly matched across groups. The variables that serve as the basis of yoking are often based on considerations of construct validity, that is, what the investigator wishes to say about the treatment and what facets of treatment, if allowed to vary systematically, might plausibly account for the results. By yoking, the investigator controls those variables that potentially can confound the results.

Nonrandomly Assigned or Nonequivalent Control Group

Description and Rationale.   Many groups might be added to an experiment that utilizes subjects who were not part of the original subject pool and not randomly assigned to treatment. These groups, referred to as *nonequivalent control groups* or *patched-up control groups*, help rule out specific rival hypotheses and decrease the plausibility of specific threats to internal validity. One use of nonrandomly assigned subjects is to help rule out such threats to validity as history, maturation, testing, and instrumentation. Such a group may be used when a no-treatment control group cannot be formed through random assignment. Although the purpose of this group is exactly that of the randomly assigned no-treatment group mentioned earlier, there may be special interpretive problems that arise because of the way in which the group is formed. These groups are useful in helping to rule out threats to internal validity, but they may be weak for comparative purposes, depending upon how they were formed.

As an example, a nonequivalent control group was used in a classic study that evaluated the effects of client-centered psychotherapy (Rogers & Dymond, 1954). Clients who applied for treatment at a university counseling center were assigned either to treatment (individual client-centered therapy) or waiting-list control conditions. Waiting-list control subjects waited for 60 days before they were reassessed and given treatment. This group, though similar to the treatment subjects in motivation for treatment and various personality factors, did not completely control for such threats to internal validity as history, maturation, and testing. The reason for this is that the interval between being assessed during the waiting period was only 60 days, a period shorter than the average interval that it took for therapy subjects to complete treatment. Technically, differences between these two groups might result from changes occurring over the different testing periods that elapsed, independently of treatment.

To help examine the plausibility of such threats to validity as history, maturation, and testing, the authors used a nonequivalent control. Specifically, volunteers were solicited for an experiment on personality. These subjects had not applied for treatment and hence were different from treatment and waiting-list subjects in that regard. Yet, these controls were matched to subjects who applied for treatment in terms of sex, student–nonstudent status, approximate age, and socioeconomic status. One half of the control subjects were yoked to treatment subjects and the other half to control subjects in terms of the time that was allowed to elapse between testing periods. In other words, the nonequivalent control group, while very different in subject composition, helped evaluate the effects of history, maturation, and testing on changes in the dependent measures. Moreover, this group assessed the influence of such threats over treatment and follow-up periods (6 to 12 months after treatment), by which time waiting-list subjects had long completed treatment. The nonequivalent control group was not composed through random assignment among all subjects in the study and hence not ideally comparable to the other groups. Yet, the general failure of this group to show systematic improvements over the treatment period helped diminish the plausibility of various threats (history, maturation, retesting) in accounting for the changes that occurred in the therapy group.

Special Considerations.   Nonequivalent control groups can vary widely and have to be evaluated on their individual merit. Their purpose is to reduce the plausibility that other influences (internal validity or construct validity) could explain the results. Because the group is not composed randomly, the data may not be as persuasive as parallel data resulting from a randomly composed control or comparison group. Yet, in any given case the absence of randomness may not be a fatal limitation. The question is whether some specific threat (e.g., selection × history or maturation) is as plausible as the interpretation the investigator wishes to place on the data. Although nonequivalent controls are less-than-perfect control groups, they can serve to tip the balance of plausibility among alternative interpretations of the data.

Not all of the nonequivalent control or nonrandomly assigned groups in clinical research address threats to internal validity. Groups might be added to provide useful information and to expand the conclusions that can be reached about the outcome. In treatment research a valuable use of nonrandomly selected subjects is to compare the extent to which clients in the study are distinguished from their peers who have not been referred for treatment. By comparing individuals who have been identified as a treatment population with their peers who apparently are functioning with little or no problem, one can assess whether treatment has brought the clients within a "normal" range of behavior. The use of normative data to evaluate treatment is part of a larger area of evaluating the clinical importance of changes made in treatment (see Chapter 15).

KEY CONSIDERATIONS IN GROUP SELECTION

The previous discussion describes control and comparison groups that are likely to be of use in experimental research, that is, studies in clinical psychology in which the investigator controls the manipulation through assignment of subjects to conditions. It is tempting to provide rules or guidelines for selecting a particular group in certain kinds of situations but not in others. Yet, the precise groups that should be used in clinical research depend upon at least three considerations: the interests of the investigator, previous research findings, and practical and ethical constraints.

The interests of the investigator refer to the claims that one would like to make at the end of the experiment. The interests embrace internal and construct validity. The investigator wishes to rule out the usual threats and at the same time to say something about why the effect was obtained. Addressing internal validity is relatively straightforward; addressing construct validity is more intricate because it depends on the investigator's view of what is critical to the intervention and the specificity of the desired conclusions.

The same collection of treatment groups would require different controls, depending upon what the investigator wishes to conclude when the study is completed. For example, consider a study that compared client-centered and cognitive therapy. If the investigator were interested only in discussing which of two treatments is better for a particular disorder, this design without any of the familiar groups mentioned earlier would be adequate. On the other hand, another investigator may be interested in asking whether either one of these treatments exerts therapeutic effects beyond those that can be accounted for by nonspecific-treatment effects. In this case a control group that provided a nonspecific-treatment "experience" would be critical. Thus, if these client-centered and cognitive treatments were equally effective, one could compare these groups to a nonspecific-treatment condition to determine whether the treatment effects were likely to be the result of attending treatment per se. The latter design, with its addition of a nonspecific-treatment control group, is not necessarily superior to the previous one in which only the two treatment groups were included. The issue of superiority of one design over another is not measured by how many control groups there are but whether the question of interest to the investigator is adequately addressed. Both of the above experiments appear to address their respective questions adequately. One could take a broader view of experimentation and note that the reader or consumer of research may wish to draw more inferences from an experiment than did the investigator, in which case an extra control group here and there might be useful. However, the main purpose of a given study should be to deploy resources to provide the best test of a limited question, rather than to try to control for or anticipate all of the questions that might be asked, even though they were not of direct interest.

There are no rules for deciding specifically what control groups to include, and investigators probably proceed in different ways to reach the final decisions. In my own research, it has been useful to ponder the anticipated patterns of results to decide some of the groups that might be included. Specifically, this procedure involves plotting possible variations of results (differences between or among groups) that might come from the study while the study is still in the design stage. Initially, the "ideal" or expected results with respect to a particular hypothesis and prediction, if they can be specified, might be diagrammed; then more likely data patterns are considered. As variations of possible results are considered, the following question can be asked: "What other interpretations can account for this pattern of results?" The answer to that question is likely to lead to changes in the experimental groups or addition of control groups to narrow the alternative interpretations that can be provided. Permutations of likely patterns or results and critical evaluation of rival interpretations of the findings are useful in generating additional comparison groups that are needed in a given study or bolstering the design by increasing the sample, to ensure a strong test of the major comparisons of interest.

Previous research also may dictate the essential control groups for a given investigation. For example, in the study of a particular treatment, it is not always necessary to use a no-treatment or waiting-list control group. If there are consistent data that the absence of treatment has no effect, at least on the dependent measures of interest, these groups might be omitted. Of course, to justify exclusion of a no-treatment group, one would want convincing data about the likely changes over time without treatment. Relying on data from studies completed by other investigators at different research facilities might not provide an adequate basis to exclude a no-treatment group unless there is consensus that the problem is immutable without treatment. For example, "depressed clients" in one investigator's research may vary markedly from the "same" sample at another facility because of the different measures used in screening and the different locales. This is true even if depressed clients all meet criteria for major depression. They could still differ on severity and duration of their depression and the presence of other disorders. On the other hand, within a research program, continued studies may reveal that no-treatment or nonspecific-treatment groups lead to no change in the clients. In such a case omitting these groups after several studies have been completed is somewhat more justifiable and also permits the investigator to move on to more sophisticated questions about the effects of treatment.

There is another way to view the elimination of particular groups, such as no-treatment groups, as a program of research progresses. As investigations build upon one another, the research questions become increasingly refined, and there may be no need for some of the control groups used early in the research. Again, it is difficult to be specific about when various groups can be abandoned; however, as noted earlier, experimental demonstrations vary in their persuasiveness to the scientific community, depending upon a host of factors. In advance of the study, consider the pattern of possible or probable results. Then one can decide whether the addition of one or more groups will aid in the interpretation of the results (internal and construct validity). One might say, "Just in case add another control group here and there." However, from a statistical standpoint (power of the test), it is better to have more subjects in each of the groups or conditions, than more conditions with fewer subjects in each group.

As a final consideration, the selection of control groups is limited greatly by practical and ethical constraints. Practical issues such as procuring enough subjects with similar treatment problems, losing subjects assigned to control conditions for a protracted period, and related obstacles mentioned earlier may dictate the types of groups that can be used. Ethical constraints—such as withholding treatment, delivering treatments that might not help or might even exacerbate the client's problem, deception about ineffective treatments, and similar issues—also limit what can be done clinically. In the context of clinical samples both practical and ethical issues may make it impossible to perform the comparisons that might be of greatest interest on theoretical grounds.

PROGRESSION OF CONTROL AND COMPARISON GROUPS: EVALUATING PSYCHOTHERAPY

The use of various control and comparison groups isolated from an area of research is somewhat abstract. Also, the discussion does not convey the progression of research, which can be measured in the level of sophistication of the questions that are asked and the complexity of the conditions to which an experimental group is compared. Psychotherapy research usefully illustrates the progression of research and the role of various control and comparison groups.

The goals of psychotherapy research are to identify effective treatments, to understand the underlying bases of therapeutic change, and to elaborate the client, therapist, and other factors on which treatment effects depend. Over the course of therapy research, the goals have been cast as questions, and these questions have changed over time. Initially the question, "Does psychotherapy work?" guided reviews of research (Eysenck, 1952). Recognized early was the likelihood that therapy would vary as a function of the clinical problem, type of treatment, and potentially all sorts of other moderators (Kiesler, 1966, 1971). The question to guide research changed too, namely, "What treatment, by whom, is most effective for this individual with that specific problem, under which set of circumstances?" (Paul, 1967, p. 111). This question has continued to dominate the research agenda (Roth & Fonagy, 1996). Actually, we want to know much more than what is embedded in this question (Kazdin, 2000). Many more questions better reflect the agenda. Table 7.1 presents major strategies for evaluating treatment, the questions they are designed to address, and types of control and comparison groups that are likely to be required.

Treatment-Package Strategy

Perhaps the most basic question is to ask whether a particular treatment or treatment package is effective for a particular clinical problem. This question is asked by the *treatment-package strategy,* which evaluates the effects of a particular treatment as that treatment is ordinarily used. The notion of a "package" emphasizes that treatment may be multifaceted and include several different components that could be delineated conceptually and operationally. The question addressed by this strategy is whether treatment produces therapeutic change. To rule out threats to internal validity, a no-treatment or waiting-list control condition is usually included in the design.

TABLE 7.1.   Treatment Evaluation Strategies to Develop and to Identify Effective Interventions

Treatment Strategy	Question Asked	Basic Requirements
Treatment package	Does treatment produce therapeutic change?	Treatment versus no-treatment or waiting-list control
Dismantling strategy	What components are necessary, sufficient, and facilitative of therapeutic change?	Two or more treatment groups that vary in the components of treatment provided
Constructive strategy	What components or other treatments can be added to enhance therapeutic change?	Two or more treatment groups that vary in components
Parametric strategy	What changes can be made in the specific treatment to increase its effectiveness?	Two or more treatment groups that differ in one or more facets of the treatment
Comparative-treatment strategy	Which treatment is more or most effective for a particular problem and population?	Two or more different treatments for a given clinical problem
Treatment-moderator strategy	What patient, family, or therapist characteristics does treatment depend on to be effective?	Treatment as applied separately to different types of cases, therapists, etc.
Treatment-mediator strategy	What processes occur in treatment that affect within-session performance and that may contribute to treatment outcome?	Treatment groups in which patient and therapist interactions are evaluated within the sessions

As an example, a treatment-package study examined an intervention to alleviate marital distress among couples with chronically ill children (Walker, Johnson, Manion, & Cloutier, 1996). Chronic illness in children can place special burdens (financial, interpersonal) on the family and has been associated with increases in marital stress, conflict, poor communication, lack of intimacy, and ultimately marital break-up. In this study, couples whose child was receiving care for a chronic condition (cancer, diabetes, epilepsy, kidney disease, muscular dystrophy, and others) agreed to participate and were assigned to treatment or a waiting list. Treated couples, seen individually rather than in a larger group, attended 10 sessions that focused on identifying sources of conflict, needs, experiences, and efforts to promote acceptance and new interaction patterns and relationship issues in relation to the child's issues. Waiting-list cases were not treated during the study, but were offered treatment when the study was completed. The results indicated that treated couples improved significantly on measures of marital adjustment at the end of treatment and at a 5-month follow-up. Control cases tended to decrease in marital adjustment over time. The treatment was effective compared to no treatment in improving marital adjustment among families with a chronically ill child.

Strictly speaking, evaluation of a treatment package requires only two groups, as in the example noted above. Random assignment of cases to groups and testing each group before and after treatment controls the usual threats to internal validity. However, there has been considerable debate about the impact of nonspecific-treatment factors and the effects they can exert on clinical dysfunction (Lambert & Bergin, 1994). Consequently, treatment-package research is likely to include a group that serves as a nonspecific-treatment control condition that requires clients to come to the treatment and receive some "control" type of active experience.

Dismantling-Treatment Strategy

The dismantling-treatment strategy consists of analyzing the components of a given treatment package. After a particular package has been shown to produce therapeutic change, research can begin to analyze the basis for change. To dismantle a treatment, individual components are eliminated or isolated from the treatment. Some clients may receive the entire treatment package while other clients receive the package minus one or more components. Dismantling research can help identify the necessary and sufficient components of treatment.

As an illustration, in one treatment study, social problem-solving therapy was evaluated for the treatment of depressed adults (Nezu & Perri, 1989). Problem-solving treatment included separate components: (1) a problem-solving orientation process, which pertains to how individuals respond when presented with a problem or stressful situation, and (2) a set of skills or goal-directed tasks that enables people to solve a potential problem successfully. The investigators evaluated whether the full package of training was superior to an abbreviated version in which only the skills component was provided. Clients were assigned to one of two groups to receive either the full treatment or the skills component only. A waiting-list control group was included in the design. At posttreatment and a 6-month follow-up, clients who received the full package (orientation and skills training) were less depressed than those who received the abbreviated treatment (skills training). The authors suggest that the orientation component provides a critical feature of the treatment. The findings suggest that the package offers more than orientation training alone. Of course, the effect of skills training alone in relation to the overall package was not studied. For present purposes, it is important to note that the specific question about treatment led to a comparison group that itself was a veridical treatment.

Constructive-Treatment Strategy

The constructive-treatment strategy refers to developing a treatment package by adding components to enhance outcome. In this sense, the constructive-treatment approach is the opposite of the dismantling strategy. A constructive-treatment study begins with a treatment, which may consist of one or a few ingredients or a larger package. To that are added various ingredients to determine whether the effects can be enhanced. The strategy asks the question, "What can be added to treatment to make it more effective?" A special feature of this strategy is the combination of individual treatments. Thus, studies may combine conceptually quite different treatments, such as verbal psychotherapy and pharmacotherapy.

There is a keen interest in testing treatment combinations because the scope of impairment of many clinical problems (depression, antisocial personality) affects many different domains of functioning (symptoms, social and work relations). Also, many contextual influences on the individual (parents, spouses) may need to be integrated into treatment to help promote change or to reduce influences that may contribute to or sustain dysfunction in the client. For example, some families of patients diagnosed with schizophrenia are highly critical, hostile, and overinvolved, a set of characteristics that is referred to as *expressed emotion*. Schizophrenic patients who leave the hospital after treatment and return home to families who are high in expressed emotion have a much higher relapse rate than patients who return home to families low in expressed emotion (Tarrier & Barrowclough, 1990). A single treatment (such as medication) that focuses on symptoms of schizophrenia (hallucinations, delusions) without attention to family interaction is limited. Several studies have shown that medication combined with a family-based component designed to address interpersonal communication significantly reduces relapse rates, compared to treatment without the family communication component (Klerman et al., 1994; Lam, 1991).

Treatment combinations are often used in both clinical practice and research (Kazdin, 1996a). The obvious view is that combining treatments may overcome the limits of any individual treatment and, at the very worst, would not hurt. Occasionally, a combined treatment is worse (less effective) than one of the constituent treatments presented by itself—that is, the whole is less than the sum of its parts. For example, in the treatment of antisocial behavior among adolescents, treatment that combined a parent program and teen-focused group *increased* behavioral problems and substance use in comparison to the parent group alone (Dishion & Andrews, 1995). Bringing problem youths together may introduce deleterious influences that compete with treatment effects. In any case one cannot assume that combined treatments will automatically be neutral or better than their constituent treatments.

There is an obvious way in which combined treatments may be better. If the combined treatment addresses more facets of a problem (a broader range of symptoms or range of factors that maintain the problem), or if the treatments act in concert (produce some interactive effect), then they are likely to be more effective than the individual components. Combinations of some medications (e.g., HIV) operate in this way and can be shown to be more effective than the constituent medications given by themselves. It is not always better or even likely to be better to provide combined treatments, counter to common assumptions. Combined treatments come at a price. If treatment is medication, then the number of side effects or problems of adherence (take two or more medications) raise obstacles. If treatment is psychotherapy and the duration of treatment is fixed (only a certain number of therapy sessions), then squeezing two (or more) treatments into this period may dilute the individual components and their effects. Clients will not remain in therapy forever, of course, while the therapist provides her or his special brand of combined treatments. In any case, in studies that combine treatments it is obviously important to include as a comparison condition a group in which the most powerful constituent treatment or each of the treatments that comprise the package is evaluated alone.

Parametric-Treatment Strategy

The parametric-treatment strategy refers to altering specific aspects of treatment to determine how to maximize therapeutic change. Dimensions or parameters are altered to find the optimal manner of administering the treatment. These dimensions are not new ingredients added to the treatment (as in the constructive strategy) but variations within the technique to maximize change. Increases in duration of treatment or variations in how material is presented are samples of the parametric strategy.

A basic parameter of treatment is duration. More treatment tends to produce greater change. Also, some domains (e.g., interpersonal and more enduring characteristics) require more time to change in therapy than others (e.g., acute symptoms) (see Kopta, Howard, Lowry, & Beutler, 1994). Duration has not been tested directly in many studies. A rather interesting study was completed to evaluate the effects of 8 versus 16 sessions of psychotherapy with clinically depressed adults (Barkham et al., 1996). Cases were randomly assigned to either cognitive behavioral treatment or psychodynamically oriented therapy and to one of the two durations. The different durations reflect evaluation of parameters of treatment; the use of two different therapies is an example of comparative treatment evaluation, as highlighted later. The two treatments were not different in their effects, but duration effects proved to be interesting. In general, the longer duration was associated with greater changes and greater changes across those characteristics of treatment that are likely to require more time (interpersonal spheres, views of oneself). Interestingly, by session 8, those clients assigned to the shorter treatment showed greater changes than did those who were at the same session but were at their halfway point. That is, 8 sessions had different effects if clients were assigned to receive 8, as opposed to 16, sessions. Somehow being involved in the shorter treatment accelerated the rate of change. In any case the results indicated that duration of treatment was an important parameter that contributed to outcome. The duration question was addressed without the need for special control groups, because active treatment groups addressed the threats to internal and construct validity.

An interesting parametric variation of treatment pertains to the continuation of treatment or use of maintenance therapy. Maintenance therapy refers to the intervention that is provided after the initial (acute) treatment phase. Continuation of treatment has been evaluated in the context of adult depression because many patients may show a relapse or recurrence of depression after treatment (see Frank, Johnson, & Kupfer, 1992). Outcome studies evaluating the use of continued, albeit tapered or reduced, therapy has shown that continuation of medication (imipramine) for a period of three years after the initial two-year treatment course has had a significant prophylactic effect on the recurrence of depression (Frank et al., 1993; Kupfer et al., 1992). Continuation of full-dose medication (imipramine) was more protective than continuation of half-dose medication and placebo. Interpersonal psychotherapy and cognitive therapy have also been effective in reducing relapse when continued as maintenance strategies after the initial treatment phase (see Frank et al., 1992). As a general conclusion from multiple studies, adults with recurrent depression are very likely to profit from maintenance therapy and to experience much higher rates of relapse without such therapy. Evidence with adolescence also suggests that maintenance therapy (cognitive-behavioral treatment) following an acute-treatment phase decreased relapse (Kroll et al., 1996). Maintenance therapy or continued therapy might be conceived as either a parametric variation of treatment—because it is more of the original treatment—or as a constructive-treatment approach because a slightly different variation of treatment is added.

Comparative-Treatment Strategy

The comparative-treatment strategy contrasts two (or more) treatments and addresses the question of which treatment is better (best) for a particular clinical problem. Comparative studies attract wide attention not only because they address an important clinical issue but also because they often contrast conceptually competing interventions. Classic battle lines that served as the basis of comparative outcome studies included psychoanalysis versus behavior therapy, cognitive therapy versus medication, family therapy versus individual therapy, and many others. Such studies seem to draw much more attention, interest, and predictable controversy because they are cast as a contest for a gold medal. The yield (in my opinion) of such studies has been minor, except for mobilizing and sometimes clarifying particular positions. Clinical psychology has moved away from narrow camps and approaches, and hence comparative studies are less of a battleground now than they were in the past 25 years. Movement in the field toward integrative conceptual positions (e.g., integrationism in psychotherapy), emphasis on approaches with outcome evidence (e.g., evidence-based treatments), managed-care pressures, and increased accountability in general have mobilized and unified factions and changed the nature of competing views of treatment.

Comparative studies are still important but often serve different purposes. One such purpose is to evaluate the varied effects of different treatments. For example, structured family therapy and psychodynamic therapy were compared for the treatment of Hispanic boys (6–12 years old) referred for a variety of different problems (conduct disorder, anxiety disorder, adjustment disorders) (Szapocznik et al., 1989). In the family therapy condition, families were seen. Treatment emphasized modifying maladaptive interaction patterns among family members. Psychodynamic therapy consisted of individual therapy with the child. Treatment focused on play, expression of feelings, transference interpretations, and insight. Diverse outcome measures were included to reflect changes unique to the individual treatments.

The results indicated that both groups attained equivalent reductions in behavioral and emotional problems at posttreatment, and both groups were better at posttreatment than a nonspecific-treatment control condition in which recreational activities were provided. Family therapy was superior to psychodynamic therapy on a measure of family functioning at a one-year follow-up. The main contribution of the study was in showing differential impact of the two treatments on family functioning. In passing, it is useful to mention that the control group in this study was very important. If the two treatment groups were equally effective without this control, it is possible that the improvements for both groups could be attributed to history, maturation, retesting, and other threats to internal validity or to nonspecific treatment influences, which serve as a threat to construct validity. Evidence that the treatment conditions led to greater change than the control condition addressed these concerns.

Treatment-Moderator Strategy

The previous strategies emphasize the technique as a major source of influence in treatment outcome and searches for main effects of treatment, that is, that treatment is better or worse for all of the individuals as a group. Yet, it is much more likely that the effectiveness of treatments varies as a function of characteristics of the patients, the therapists, and contexts in which the patient functions (type of family, support system available). For example, we know that most individuals coming to treatment, who meet diagnostic criteria for one psychiatric disorder, are likely as well to meet criteria for at least one other disorder (Brown et al., 1995; Kazdin, 1995; Wetzler & Sanderson, 1997). The effects of a given treatment may vary, depending on comorbidity, that is, whether patients meet criteria for more than one disorder. Comorbidity is one client characteristic that would be a reasonable focus for the client-and-therapist-variation-treatment evaluation strategy.

The overall goal of this evaluation strategy is to examine factors that may *moderate* treatment effects, that is, whether attributes of the client, therapist, or context contribute to outcome. As noted previously, moderators refer to the variables that influence the effects of some other condition or variable (in this case, treatment). In the usual conceptualization of this strategy in relation to treatment, characteristics of the clients or therapists are the primary moderators that are discussed. The strategy would be implemented by selecting clients and/or therapists on the basis of specific characteristics. When clients or therapists are classified according to a particular selection variable, the question is whether treatment is more or less effective with certain kinds of participants. For example, questions of this strategy might ask if treatment is more effective with younger versus older clients, or with certain subtypes of problems (e.g., of depression) rather than with other subtypes.

An example of a treatment-moderator study was reported in the treatment of alcoholic patients (Kadden, Cooney, Getter, & Litt, 1989). The investigators evaluated two treatments: coping-skills training and interaction group therapy. Three subject variables were investigated, including sociopathy, overall psychopathology, and neuropsychological impairment, each of which has prognostic significance in relation to alcoholism. The authors reasoned that higher-functioning patients (low on the three subject variables) would benefit from interaction experiences. Patients with greater impairment and relatively poorer prognosis would profit more on coping-skills training that emphasized relapse prevention. The findings indicated that patient characteristics interacted with type of treatment in outcome results, as reflected in days of drinking during the 6 months of treatment. Interaction-based treatment was more effective with higher-functioning patients; coping-skills training was more effective for patients higher in sociopathy and psychopathology. This pattern of results was maintained at a two-year follow-up assessment (Cooney, Kadden, Litt, & Getter, 1991).

The type of research illustrated by this example is more sophisticated in the sense of the type of predictions that are made. Rather than main effects of treatment (for all individuals in the experimental or treatment group), the question focuses on interactions (whether some individuals respond better to treatment than others or whether some individuals respond to one form of treatment whereas other individuals respond better to another form of treatment). Different types of variables (treatment, subject) are combined. Although the usual control conditions might be used, the question focuses on comparison groups that are comprised of combinations of treatment and subject characteristics.

The main focus of the *treatment-moderator strategy* is to identify characteristics that influence the effectiveness of treatment, that is, what works for whom (Roth & Fonagy, 1996). Occasionally, a single variable (e.g., a particular characteristic of the client) is studied as a potential moderator. Finer-grained questions can be asked that incorporate multiple characteristics of the client (ethnicity, range or type of symptoms), therapist, and context (family factors of the client). Indeed, it is likely that multiple moderators affect treatment outcome (Kazdin & Crowley, 1997). However, it is difficult to develop conceptual models to provide focused hypotheses and predictions about what combinations might be effective, with whom, and why. Nevertheless, the search for moderators represents a more sophisticated approach to treatment evaluation than the search for main effects alone.

Treatment-Mediator Strategy

The previously noted strategies emphasize outcome questions or the impact of variations of the intervention on clients at the end of, or subsequent to, treatment. The *treatment-mediator strategy* addresses questions pertaining to the mechanisms of change of therapy, that is, through what processes does therapy lead to, or cause, change? What processes unfold that are responsible for improvement? The most common focus in adult therapy has focused on what transpires between the delivery of an intervention and the ultimate impact on the client. Topics may focus on the transactions between therapist and client and the impact of intervening events on the moment-to-moment or interim changes during treatment. Many issues address questions of process, including the sequence, stages, and progression of client or therapist affect, behavior, and cognition over the course of treatment or within individual sessions.

An example is provided in a study that examined the relation of therapy processes and outcome in the treatment of depression (Rounsaville et al., 1986). Patients ($N = 35$) received interpersonal psychotherapy for depression. Therapists ($N = 11$) who provided treatment were evaluated by their supervisors after observing tapes of several therapy sessions. Processes rated by the supervisors included therapist factors (exploration, warmth and friendliness, and negative attitude) and patient factors (participation, exploration, hostility, psychic distress). Treatment outcome was assessed with measures of psychiatric symptoms, social functioning, and patient-evaluated change.

The results indicated that only one patient factor (hostility) was related to outcome on a measure of change completed by the patients. In contrast, therapist factors were much more strongly related to outcome. Therapist exploration was significantly and positively related to reductions in clinician evaluations of depression and patient-rated improvements. Therapist warmth and friendliness correlated significantly with improved social functioning and patient-rated improvements. These results convey the importance of specific therapist relationship characteristics in relation to treatment outcome. In this study no control or comparison was used. The purpose was to correlate specific processes with specific outcomes within a particular technique. Here, too, this level of question is based on prior studies demonstrating that the treatment is effective when compared to various control conditions. After such demonstrations it becomes meaningful to ask about the factors that contribute to change.

Treatment processes can be evaluated in the context of a larger-scale study that has multiple other purposes (e.g., with other treatment evaluation strategies). For example, in a large-scale, multisite study for the treatment of depression, four different treatment and control conditions were compared (interpersonal psychotherapy, cognitive-behavior therapy, imipramine with clinical management, and placebo with clinical management) (Krupnick et al., 1996). Clinical management consisted of meeting briefly with the patient to review medication or placebo. The therapeutic alliance was evaluated during the course of treatment and assessed by raters who viewed videotapes of selected sessions. The alliance reflects the quality of the bond between the therapist and the client. The results indicated that ratings of alliance during treatment significantly predicted treatment outcome, that alliance accounted for more outcome variance (magnitude of effect) than did treatment technique, and that alliance did not vary among the treatment and control conditions. This study suggests a critical role of alliance in treatment outcome. Further research is needed to explain what alliance is, its correlates and predictors, and whether alliance or factors with which it is correlated account for the effect. Among the strengths of this study—the largest study of alliance—is the integration of multiple treatment evaluation strategies within the same study.

General Comments

The strategies noted previously reflect questions frequently addressed in current treatment research. The questions posed by the strategies reflect a range of issues required to understand fully how a technique operates and can be applied to achieve optimal effects. The treatment package strategy is an initial approach followed by the various analytic strategies based on dismantling, constructive, and parametric research. The comparative strategy probably warrants attention after prior work has been conducted that not only indicates the efficacy of individual techniques but also shows how the techniques can be administered to increase their efficacy. Frequently, comparative studies are conducted early in the development of a treatment and possibly before the individual techniques have been well developed to warrant such a test. A high degree of operationalization is needed to investigate dismantling, constructive, and parametric questions. In each case, specific components or ingredients of therapy have to be sufficiently well specified to be withdrawn, added, or varied in an overall treatment package.

The progression requires a broad range of control and comparison groups that vary critical facets of treatment. The usual control conditions (no-treatment, nonspecific-treatment control) may continue to play a role. However, the interest in evaluating change over time without treatment or factors common to treatment gives way to more pointed questions about specific facets of treatment that account for or contribute to change. Comparison groups are aimed to provide increasingly specific statements related to construct validity, that is, what aspects of the intervention account for the findings.

SUMMARY AND CONCLUSIONS

Control groups rule out or weaken rival hypotheses or alternative explanations of the results. The control group appropriate for an experiment depends upon precisely what the investigator is interested in concluding at the end of the investigation. Hence all, or even most, of the available control groups cannot be specified in an abstract discussion of methodology. Nevertheless, treatment research often includes several specific control procedures that address questions of widespread interest.

The no-treatment control group includes subjects who do not receive treatment. This group controls for such effects as history, maturation, testing, regression, and similar threats, at least if the group is formed through random assignment. The waiting-list control group is a variation of the no-treatment group. While the experimental subjects receive treatment, waiting-list control subjects do not. After treatment of the experimental subjects is complete, waiting-list control subjects are reassessed and then receive treatment. A no-contact control group may be included in the design to evaluate the effects of participating in or having "contact" with a treatment program. Individuals selected for this group usually do not know that they are participating in a treatment investigation. Hence, their functioning must be assessed under the guise of some other purpose than a treatment investigation.

A nonspecific-treatment control group consists of a group that engages in all of the accouterments of treatments, such as receiving a rationale about their problem, meeting with a therapist, attending treatment sessions, and engaging in procedures alleged to be therapeutic. Actually, the purpose is to provide the generic ingredients of the treatment to the nonspecific-treatment control group and to address the question of whether the effects of veridical treatment were due merely to its nonspecific-treatment components.

Routine or standard care consists of the usual treatment that is provided for a problem and can be quite useful as a comparison group. Clients assigned to this treatment receive a veridical intervention (unlike a nonspecific-treatment control condition), and many of the factors common to most treatments are controlled. Few objections arise from therapists and clients regarding the use of routine care as a comparison condition. From a methodological standpoint a difficulty with routine or standard care is that these are often unstructured and unspecified treatments and vary considerably from therapist to therapist.

A yoked control group controls for variations across groups that may arise over the course of the experiment. Implementing treatment procedures may involve factors inherent in, but not relevant to, the independent variables of interest to the investigator. Yoking refers to a procedure that equalizes the extraneous variables across groups by matching or pairing subjects in the control groups (or one of the control groups) with subjects in an experimental group and using information obtained from the experimental subject to decide the conditions to which the control subject will be exposed.

Nonequivalent control groups refer to a category of groups that is characterized by selection of subjects that are not part of random assignment. These groups are added to the design to address specific threats to validity (usually internal validity such as history or maturation) that are not handled in the usual way (random assignment to experimental and no-treatment control groups). A nonequivalent control group, by virtue of its selection, imperfectly controls these threats but still strengthens the plausibility of the conclusions that can be drawn.

The addition of control and comparison groups to experimental designs usually addresses threats to internal and construct validity and hence adds precision to the conclusions that can be reached. The progression of research and the different control and comparisons groups that are used were illustrated in the context of psychotherapy research. Several different treatment evaluation strategies were discussed to convey various control and comparison groups and questions that do not require control conditions in the usual sense.

KEY CONCEPTS AND TERMS

Nonequivalent Control Group

Nonspecific or Common
   Factors of Psychotherapy

Treatment-Mediator Strategy

Treatment-Moderator Strategy

Treatment-Package Strategy

Waiting-List Control Group

Yoked Control Group

FOR FURTHER READING

Bergin, A.E., & Garfield, S.L. (Eds.) (1994). *Handbook of psychotherapy and behavior change* (4th ed.). New York: Wiley & Sons.

Castonguay, L.G. (1993). "Common factors" and "nonspecific variables": Clarification of the two concepts and recommendations for research. *Journal of Psychotherapy Integration, 3,* 267–286.

Dehue, T. (2000). From deception trials to control reagents: The introduction of the control group about a century ago. *American Psychologist, 55,* 264–268.

Ilardi, S.S., & Craighead, W.E. (1994). The role of nonspecific factors in cognitive-behavior therapy for depression. *Clinical Psychology: Science and Practice, 1,* 138–156.

Klein, D.F. (1998). Groups in pharmacotherapy and psychotherapy evaluations. *Prevention and Treatment, 1,* no pages. (Electronic journal—see http://journals.apa.org and select *Prevention and Treatment;* see also three commentaries following this article.)

Parloff, M.B. (1986). Placebo controls in psychotherapy research: A sine qua non or a placebo for research problems? *Journal of Consulting and Clinical Psychology, 54,* 79–87.

Stevens, S., Hynan, M.T., & Allen, M. (2000). A meta-analysis of common factor and specific treatment effects across the outcome domains of the phase model of psychotherapy. *Clinical Psychology: Science and Practice, 7,* 273–290.

Chapter 8

Assessing the Impact of the Experimental Manipulation

In an experiment the independent variable is manipulated by providing a particular condition to one group and omitting it from another group, providing varying degrees of a given condition to different groups, or presenting entirely distinct conditions to groups. Great care is required to ensure that the manipulation is a strong test of the hypothesis, that the variable or condition is manipulated as intended, and that the manipulation is consistent across cases within a group (all subjects intended to receive the manipulation, in fact, do). Careful control and administration of the manipulation are required for interpretation of the findings (construct validity) and for a sensitive evaluation of the manipulation (statistical conclusion validity). This chapter discusses the adequacy with which the independent variable is manipulated, the different ways in which the manipulation can be assessed, and the implications for interpreting the results of an experiment. The primary focus is on experimental research wherein the independent variable is controlled or manipulated by the investigator.

CHECKING ON THE EXPERIMENTAL MANIPULATION

The hypothesis of interest in the investigation is based upon the assumption that the independent variable was effectively implemented. When the study is planned, the investigator has an experimental manipulation in mind as administered in a particular way. When the study is actually implemented, will the procedures be carried out as intended by those responsible for manipulation or execution of that manipulation (experimenters, therapists, parents, teachers)? It is extremely useful in clinical research to check whether the independent variable, experimental manipulation, or intervention was implemented as intended. Providing a check on the manipulation refers to independently assessing the independent variable and its effects on the subjects. The assessment is designed to determine whether the subject is exposed to conditions as intended.

Assessment of the independent variable or a manipulation check is distinguished both procedurally and conceptually from dependent variables included in the study. The check on the independent variable assesses whether the conditions of interest to the investigator were altered or provided to the subjects. This may mean merely that the stimulus was presented as intended or that the intervention was received or perceived by the subject. For example, in a treatment study a check on the independent variable would be achieved by ensuring that participants actually received the treatment, that the number of sessions was provided as intended, and that subjects in one group did not receive conditions appropriate for another group. These are checks on the independent variable or interventions and are quite separate from the dependent measures (therapeutic change, symptom reduction, improved adjustment). Manipulation checks are critical in all studies in which it is possible that the experimental condition was not faithfully rendered or presented.

In one sense the best check on the effects of an independent variable is the dependent measure because the change in the independent variable is intended to alter the dependent measure. If the predicted results of an experiment are obtained, assessment of the independent variable to ensure that it has had the intended effect on the subject may not seem to be essential. Presumably, the independent variable accounted for the results, barring obvious confounds. Even so, it is possible that the intervention produced the change by affecting a host of intervening processes in the individual, and the construct of interest to the investigator was not the "crucial" one in the sense of being directly responsible for change. Checking the extent to which the independent variable is effectively manipulated provides information that can greatly illuminate the findings. In some cases one can evaluate the extent to which a particular intervention was administered or received and changes on the dependent measure. This, too, can provide greater confidence that the experimental manipulation was responsible for the outcome.

Types of Manipulations

Variations of Information.   The way in which the success of the experimental manipulation can be assessed varies as a function of the type of manipulation or independent variable. In many experiments the manipulation refers to different information given to subjects across experimental conditions. The initial question to be answered for the check on the success of the manipulation is whether the information was, in fact, delivered. Assume that the experimenter provided the information. The check on the manipulation is whether subjects received, attended to, and believed the information. Typically, a manipulation check consists of providing subjects with a questionnaire immediately after hearing the rationale or after exposure to the information. For example, the independent variable might consist of telling subjects about some aspect in the news, or some personality characteristics of a hypothetical individual who is later evaluated as part of the study, or arguments designed to change beliefs about some healthful or unhealthful practice. Presumably different groups in the study will vary in the information that is presented. A questionnaire might be administered after the instructions were administered or later in the experiment to assess whether the subject heard or grasped the information. Presumably, if subjects respond to alternatives that reflect what they were told in their respective experimental conditions, the investigator could have more confidence that the independent variable was manipulated as intended. Whether the independent variable has impact on the dependent measures is another matter, but at least the investigator would know that the manipulation was implemented as intended and registered with the subjects.

When the experimental manipulation relies upon information, self-report questionnaires are frequently used to assess the success of the manipulation. A few questions might be all that are needed. These questions might be in true–false, multiple-choice, or open-ended (essay question) format. It is useful to include a true–false or multiple-choice format in most cases so that each question can be easily scored and answered. Open-ended questions might be used, such as "What information did you learn from the experimenter?" or "What did the experimenter say when you began the experiment?" These questions seem useful and maybe even clever because they do not reveal the purpose of the experiment or give away the correct answers as readily as true–false or multiple-choice questions. Yet, it is very difficult to score the subjects' responses to open-ended questions. Many subjects do not answer them, reply with only one or two words, or elaborate extended discussions that miss the point of interest to the investigator.

In general, when the independent variable involves variation of information to the subject, the manipulation check is relatively straightforward. There usually is a check to ensure that the experimenter delivered the information, that it was received or perceived by the subjects, and that experimental groups are distinguishable on a measure that assesses that information. Self-report measures are commonly used because they are readily adaptable to the experiment by merely constructing examination-type questions.

Variations in Subject Behavior and Experience. Many manipulations consist of having subjects do something, engage in a particular task, actually carry out the instructions, or experience a particular state. The research question of interest is likely to be whether a certain task facilitates or hinders some outcome. For example, many forms of psychotherapy use homework assignments, exercises, or tasks that individuals are supposed to do outside of the therapy sessions. This would qualify as a task. Groups might differ in whether or not they are assigned homework or the kind and amount of homework as part of an investigation. Checking on the manipulation would consist of evaluating whether the homework was assigned (by the therapist) and completed (by the subject) and, as relevant, was carried out as specified (one kind of assignment rather than another).

Assessment of the success of the manipulation can take many forms, depending upon what it is that subjects are supposed to do. An interesting manipulation was reported in a study of encounter groups (Dies & Greenberg, 1976). Years ago, encounter groups were part of a cultural movement whereby individuals could become in touch with themselves and others, sometimes for self-enhancement and occasionally for treatment. In such groups, physical contact was considered important, and this investigation set out to evaluate whether such contact among participants in encounter groups contributed to various measures of affect and experience. The manipulation consisted of having three different levels of physical contact in encounter groups that performed similar activities. One group made no physical contact during the sessions; another engaged in moderate physical contact; and a final group engaged in a high amount of physical contact (hand holding, embracing, sitting together with knees or shoulders touching). The groups engaged in similar encounter group exercises but were instructed to maintain differences in the amount of physical contact. The investigators checked the manipulation to determine whether the groups really differed in the amount of contact. Several observers recorded the actual amount of physical contact they witnessed during the sessions. The conditions differed in the amount of physical contact and could be distinguished statistically. Incidentally, the results indicated that greater contact was associated with greater feeling of closeness, willingness to engage in risk-taking behaviors, and more positive attitudes toward oneself and others.

Not all tasks subjects perform are as readily observable as physical contact. Subjects may be asked to engage in various activities in their everyday lives (think specific thoughts, perform various activities in the privacy of their own homes). If the tasks are not observable by a researcher or someone in the setting (relative, friend), self-report can assess whether they adhered to the task requirements. Of course, self-report, if not corroborated by some other measure (reports of others such as roommates, partners, spouses), may not reflect actual adherence. The manipulation check for task variables assesses what subjects do rather than what they know or even say they did (self-report). Even so, answering questions (self-report) about specific tasks and activities that were performed is better than not assessing the manipulation at all.

The manipulation may consist of more than a task. For example, instructions, activities, or tasks may be designed to induce a particular mood or emotional state in the subject. Exposure to the experimental manipulation or task alone is insufficient as a manipulation check. The investigator wishes the subjects to experience something in a particular way, and the experimental test depends on achieving this state. For example, the purpose of an experiment may be to induce high levels of euphoria or similar states in some of the subjects and moderate or low levels in other subjects. If a self-report measure were used to assess the experimental manipulation, items would be included to allow participants to report the extent to which they experience euphoria. Items might have participants rate on a 5-point scale how euphoric they feel (1 = not at all euphoric, 3 = moderately euphoric, 5 = very euphoric). The investigator could infer with some degree of confidence that the independent variable was successfully manipulated if groups differed in the extent of euphoria on their ratings according to the respective conditions to which they were assigned.

Variation of Intervention Conditions.   Many interventions in clinical research consist of varying the conditions to which subjects are exposed. Actually, variation of information or experiences could be categorized here, but the present category is better as a way of covering a range of procedures provided to the subject. Primary examples of this type of manipulation would be exposing subjects to different therapy, prevention, counseling, educational, or remedial interventions. In these cases the manipulation is implemented or carried out by the therapists or trainers.

In the simplest case one group receives the intervention and the other group does not (treatment versus no treatment or a waiting-list control). Specification of the experimental manipulation consists of how well treatment was delivered. Obviously, the implied hypothesis is that treatment, when conducted appropriately and as intended, is likely to produce greater change than no treatment. Of primary interest is an evaluation of the extent to which treatment was conducted as intended, a concept referred to as *treatment integrity* or *treatment fidelity*.

The importance of treatment integrity in relation to interpretation of the results can be conveyed by considering a well-designed study that evaluated various treatments for antisocial youth (ages 8–17) who attended a community activities setting where the interventions were conducted (Feldman et al., 1983). Three treatments were evaluated, including group social work (focus on group processes, social organization, and norms within the group), behavior modification (use of reinforcement contingencies in the group, focus on prosocial behavior), and minimal treatment controls (sessions involving spontaneous interactions of group members, no explicit application of a structured treatment plan). The treatments were provided to different groups of subjects and conducted over a period of a year, in which the youths attended sessions and engaged in a broad range of activities and discussions (sports, arts and crafts, fund raising).

Few differences emerged as a function of treatment technique. Interestingly, checks on how treatment was carried out by direct observations of selected sessions revealed a breakdown in treatment integrity. Specifically, observations of treatment sessions indicated that only 25 percent of the observed sessions for the group social work condition and 65 percent of the sessions for the behavior modification condition were correctly implemented, that is, with procedures appropriate to their treatment. These percentages convey that for a substantial portion of time within a given treatment, the appropriate conditions were not administered. The minimal treatment condition, which served as a control, yielded interesting results as well. For approximately 44 percent of observed sessions, systematic interventions (i.e., treatment) were provided, even though this was not intended to occur at all. This alone would lead one to expect a diffusion of treatment effects, a bias operating to reduce any treatment differences. Based on the treatment integrity data, it is difficult to draw conclusions about the relative impact of different treatments. It is still possible that there would be sharp outcome differences among the treatments and substantially different conclusions when the treatments are implemented as intended. It is to the original authors' credit to have assessed integrity, which greatly enhances interpretation of the findings.

Treatment integrity is important to assess and remains relevant whether or not treatment outcome differences are evident. A study comparing two or more treatments, for example, may show that both treatments "worked" but were no different in their outcomes. A pattern of no difference might result from a failure to implement one or both of the treatments faithfully. Large variation in how individual treatments are carried out across patients within a given condition (within-group variability or error in the statistical analysis), and blending or mixing of treatment conditions that ought to be distinct (diffusion of treatment and reduction of between-group variability needed for statistical significance) could also lead to no differences. Ensuring treatment integrity can help avoid these pitfalls. Even when two treatments differ, it is important to rule out the possibility that the differences are due to variations of integrity with which each was conducted. One treatment, perhaps because of its complexity or novelty, may be more subject to procedural degradation and appear less effective because it was less faithfully rendered. Thus, integrity of treatment is relevant in any outcome study, independently of the specific pattern of results (see Waltz, Addis, Koerner, & Jacobson, 1993).

The breakdown of treatment integrity is one of the greatest dangers in intervention research. Occasionally, dramatic examples can be found in which treatment integrity was sacrificed in the most extreme fashion, namely, the sessions were not actually held with the clients (see Sechrest, White, & Brown, 1979). The difficulty is that until relatively recently, most intervention research did not include efforts to ensure or to assess the fidelity of treatment. This has left as a lingering question, whether the weakness or absence of treatment effects or the absence of differences between two treatments could be the result of how they were implemented (or not implemented). Current intervention research is more likely to include integrity checks and hence reflects an important methodological improvement.

Several steps can be performed to address treatment integrity. First, the criteria, procedures, tasks, and therapist and patient characteristics that define the treatment ought to be specified as well as possible. Many investigators have described treatment in manual form, which includes written materials to guide the therapist in the procedures, techniques, topics, themes, therapeutic maneuvers, and activities (see Addis, 1997; Wilson, 1996). When treatment is explicitly described, it is easier to develop guidelines to decide when a session or treatment was or was not delivered as intended and what level or type of departures are considered tolerable within the study.

Second, therapists can be trained carefully to carry out the techniques. It is useful to specify the requisite skills for delivering treatment and to provide training experiences to develop these skills (role-play, practice cases with sessions that are videotaped for feedback and further training). For many treatments many of the components may not be specifiable as discrete behavioral acts and hence not trained as initially learning a motor skill or musical instrument (e.g., Henggeler et al., 1998). Yet, some of the fuzzy concepts and processes of therapy might be trained explicitly. Videotapes of "good" or prototypical sessions can be used to convey the style and to provide guidelines regarding how that style is likely to be achieved. Years of experience in providing a treatment, often a criterion espoused in clinical work, is not an adequate criterion for stating or assuming that therapy was administered well or with integrity. Experience alone does not ensure proficiency in adhering to a specific technique or set of techniques. Providing special and uniform training experiences for the therapists (experimenters, trainers) is useful and can have important implications for how faithfully treatment is likely to be rendered.

Third and related, when treatment has begun, it is valuable to provide continued case supervision. Listening to or viewing tapes of selected sessions, meeting regularly with therapists to provide feedback, and similar monitoring procedures may reduce therapist drift (departure) from the desired practices. If there are multiple therapists, group feedback and supervision sessions are especially valuable to help retain homogeneity in how treatment is implemented across a heterogeneous group of people.

Whether treatment has been carried out as intended can be evaluated definitively only after the treatment has been completed. This evaluation requires measuring the implementation of treatment. Audio or videotapes of selected treatment sessions from each condition can be examined. Codes for therapist and/or patient behaviors or other specific facets of the sessions can operationalize important features of treatment and help decide whether treatment was conducted as intended. Checklists can be used to assess whether specific discrete tasks were performed; ratings can be used to assess more qualitative and stylistic features, if these too are relevant to integrity.

Treatment integrity is not an all-or-none matter. Hence, it is useful to identify what a faithful rendition of each treatment is and what departures fall within an acceptable range. For some variables decision rules may be arbitrary, but making them explicit facilitates interpretation of the results. For example, to consider a relatively simple characteristic, treatment may consist of 20 sessions of individual psychotherapy. The investigator may specify that "receiving treatment" or an "adequate test of treatment" would be any instance in which the client received 75 percent or more or so many weeks of the sessions. For other variables, particularly those within-session procedures that distinguish different treatments, specification of criteria that define an acceptable range may be more difficult. In some cases the presence of select processes (discarding irrational beliefs, improving one's self-concept) might be sufficient; in other cases a particular level of various processes (anxiety or arousal) might be required to denote that treatment has been adequately provided.

Utility of Checking the Manipulation

Data showing that the independent variable was manipulated as intended increase the confidence that can be placed on the basis for the results. Two situations are worth highlighting because manipulation checks provide particularly useful information, namely, where the experiment produced no significant differences between groups and where experimental conditions particularly need to be kept distinct.

No Differences between Groups. If the predicted results of an experiment are not obtained and, in fact, no significant group differences are evident, assessment of the independent variable may prove to be remarkably helpful in interpreting the results. As an example, consider an experiment that provides treatment to two groups that differ only in what the subjects are told about treatment. The goal is to vary expectancies that are generated about treatment and to see whether such expectancies influence therapeutic changes. Both groups receive the same treatment. However, one group is told that the treatment is a very effective therapeutic procedure and alleviates a wide range of clinical problems; the other group is told that the procedure is experimental and is not yet known to work in improving adjustment. At the end of a treatment period, suppose there are no differences between groups on outcome measures. What can be said about the impact of the instruction/expectancy manipulation on treatment outcome?

It is very important to ask whether the independent variable was manipulated adequately so that the different instructional sets were salient to the subjects. Certainly, we would want to know whether subjects heard, knew, or believed the instructions about treatment. If the subjects did not hear or attend to the crucial instructions, then the results of the study would be viewed differently from the situation in which the subjects fully heard and believed the instructions. If the subjects had not perceived the instructions, then the hypothesis under study was not really tested. An additional experiment would be required to test the hypothesis under conditions wherein the instructions were much more salient.

On the other hand, if the subjects had perceived the instructions, and the dependent measures reflected no group differences, this would suggest that the intervention was, in fact, manipulated and did not affect treatment outcome. In such a case the investigator would be more justified in noting that the original hypothesis at least was tested. The adequacy of the test was partially demonstrated by showing that the subjects could distinguish the conditions to which they were assigned. There might well be better tests and stronger manipulations of expectancies that could be provided. But that is another matter.

Keeping Conditions Distinct.   Another way in which checking on the manipulation is useful is to ensure that the experimental conditions are, in fact, distinct. The investigator may intend to administer different conditions, instruct experimenters to do so, and provide guidelines and specific protocols of the procedures to ensure that this occurs. Yet, the normal processes associated with the intervention may override some of the procedural distinctions envisioned by the investigator.

One place wherein conditions may not remain distinct is the evaluation of different therapy techniques. Part of the problem may be inherent in the subject matter and the way in which it is studied. In therapy investigations the different techniques often are insufficiently specified, and thus the defining conditions and ingredients supposedly responsible for change are not distinguished among groups. Without sufficient specificity, nondistinct global procedures or loosely defined conditions ("supportive psychotherapy," "insight," or "behavior therapy") are implemented. Such treatments are likely to overlap with any other treatment that has some of the components of social interaction and interpersonal relationships. Indeed, in some "classic" therapy studies, general guidelines for applying different treatments led to considerable overlap (diffusion of treatment) among the procedures and could readily explain the absence of outcome differences among the treatments (Sloane et al., 1975; Wallerstein, 1986). Overlap per se may not be detrimental as long as the areas that distinguish treatments are specified and corroborated by a manipulation check. Were the treatments implemented correctly and did they remain distinct along the supposedly crucial dimensions specified by their conceptual and procedural guidelines?

Treatment differentiation refers to showing that treatments in a study of two or more treatments were distinct along predicted dimensions. Ensuring that the treatments are distinct (different on key characteristics) is somewhat different from ensuring that the treatments were administered as intended (treatment integrity). For example, in comparing interpersonal psychotherapy and cognitive-behavior therapy, measures (ratings of audio or videotapes of selected sessions, coding of therapist verbal statements) of how much the therapist focused on interpersonal roles and relationships versus cognitions may show that the treatments were, in fact, different in what the therapist did. That is, interpersonal therapy sessions may have had significantly more discussion, time, and therapist verbalizations of role-related topics than the cognitive-behavioral treatment; and the reverse pattern may also be evident, showing that for time spent on cognitions, the cognitive-behavioral treatment was higher. This is important, but it is still possible that one or both treatments were not administered as intended. It may be that one or more of the therapies suffered a significant departure from the treatment manual, there was a diffusion of treatment, or sessions were omitted for some of the clients, even though the treatments were distinct.

Therapy studies have reported difficulty in keeping techniques distinct. Therapists who administer different treatment conditions may include similar elements in both conditions despite efforts to keep treatments distinct. Comparisons of different treatments can be illuminated greatly by gathering information to ensure that the treatments are conducted correctly (integrity) and did not overlap (differentiation) more than might be expected from any common elements associated with therapy or interventions in general.

INTERPRETIVE PROBLEMS IN CHECKING THE MANIPULATION

Checking the effects of the manipulation not only can provide important information that aids interpretation of the findings but also may provide important guidelines for further research. The increase in information obtained by *checking on the manipulation* and its effects is not without risk. Discrepancies between what is revealed by the check on the manipulation and the dependent measures may introduce ambiguities into the experiment rather than eliminate them. To convey the interpretive problems that may arise, it is useful to distinguish various simple patterns of results possible in a hypothetical experiment.

Varied Data Patterns

Consider a hypothetical experiment that checks whether the independent variable was, in fact, implemented as intended. After this manipulation check, subjects may complete the dependent measures. When the results are analyzed, it is possible to infer whether the intervention was implemented effectively from two sources of information, namely, the assessment of the independent variable manipulation check and the dependent measures. These two sources of information may agree (e.g., both suggest that the intervention had an effect) or disagree (where one shows that the intervention had an effect and the other does not). Actually, there are four possible combinations, which are illustrated as different cells in Figure 8.1. For each cell, a different interpretation can be made about the experiment and its effects.

Effects on Manipulation Check and Dependent Measure.   Cell A is the easiest to interpret. In this cell the intervention had the intended effect on the measure that checked the manipulation (subjects believed the instructions or performed the tasks as intended, or the treatment was delivered as appropriate to the treatment condition). Moreover, the independent variable led to performance differences on the dependent measures (subjects improved). For present purposes it is not important to consider whether the predicted relation was obtained but only that the independent variable was shown to have some effect on the dependent variable. In Cell A the check on the manipulation is quite useful in showing that the procedures were executed properly but certainly is not essential to the demonstration. The positive results on the dependent measures, particularly if they are in the predicted direction, attest to the effects of the independent variable. Because of the consistencies of the data for both the manipulation check and the dependent measure, no special interpretive problems arise.

No Effect on Manipulation Check and Dependent Measure.   In Cell D there also is little ambiguity in interpreting the results. However, the check on the manipulation greatly enhances interpretation of the investigation. In this cell the check on the

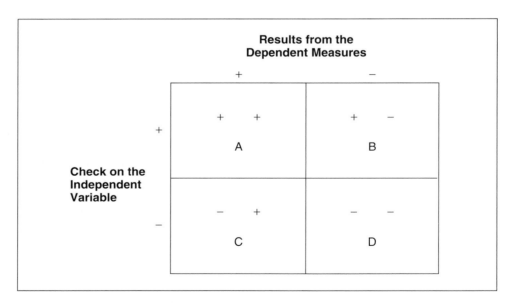

FIGURE 8.1.   Possible agreement or disagreement between the manipulation check and dependent measures. A "+" signifies that the measure shows the effect of the manipulation or that experimental conditions differ on the dependent measures. A "−" signifies that the measure does not show the effect of the manipulation or that experimental conditions do not differ on the dependent measures.

manipulation shows that the independent variable did *not* have the desired impact. The experimental manipulation or intervention was somehow missed by the subjects or was too weak to show on the manipulation check. Consequently, the lack of changes on the dependent measures might be expected. The investigator predicted changes on the dependent measures on the presumption that the intervention was effectively manipulated. This pattern of results is instructive because it suggests that additional work is needed to perfect the experimental manipulation. The hypothesis of interest really was not tested. The manipulation check clarified the results by showing that the absence of the predicted effects of the independent variable might have resulted from providing a very weak manipulation.

Effect on Manipulation Check but No Effect on the Dependent Measure.   In Cell B the manipulation check revealed that subjects were influenced by the intervention, but the dependent variable did *not* reflect any effect. This is equivalent to the medical cliché that "the operation was a success, but the patient died." This means that the intervention was done well or correctly, but it did not work—not something we as patients are thrilled to hear. (As patients we want Cells A or C, where the outcome is fine no matter how we get there.) The conclusion that would seem to be warranted was that the intervention was well manipulated but that the original hypothesis was not supported. In fact, there may be no relation between the independent variable and the dependent measure, and perhaps this experiment accurately reflected this situation.

Failure to demonstrate an effect on the dependent measures despite the fact that the manipulation check reveals that the independent variable was successfully implemented does not prove the absence of a relation between the independent and dependent variables. It is possible that the manipulation was strong enough to alter responses on the measure of the manipulation but not strong enough to alter performance on the dependent measures. Some measures may be extremely sensitive to even weak interventions and others only to very strong interventions. For example, in social psychology, we have learned that prejudice is more readily reflected on verbal self-report measures than on measures of overt behavior (Kutner, Wilkins & Harrow, 1952; La Piere, 1934). When individuals are asked whether they will discriminate against or not interact with others, they may readily express such negative intentions. Yet, when these same individuals are placed in a real situation in which they have to exhibit an overt act to discriminate against others, they are much less likely to show prejudicial behavior. In other words, prejudice of a given individual or several individuals may vary as a function of how it is assessed. Alternatively, the strength of prejudice might be defined in part by the extent to which it is evident across different situations and measures. Weak prejudice might be shown across only a few situations and strong prejudice across diverse situations and measures.

In research one might view the strength of a given experimental manipulation or intervention in much the same way. For example, a therapeutic technique that is relatively ineffective may change only the way an anxious individual talks about situations that arouse anxiety. After treatment the clients may say they are less bothered on self-report inventories yet continue to show physiological arousal and avoidance behaviors when placed in the actual anxiety-provoking situation. As a general statement more potent interventions would be expected to effect broader and more consistent changes across a range of measures of anxiety and perhaps across other areas of functioning.

The pattern of results in Cell B may indicate that there is no relation between the independent and dependent variable. On the one hand, it may indicate that the manipulation was not sufficiently strong or not implemented in a particularly potent way. If the investigator has reason to believe that the manipulation could be strengthened, it might be worth testing the original hypothesis again. On the other hand, there must eventually be some point at which the investigator is willing to admit that the hypothesis was well tested but not supported.

No Effect on the Manipulation Check but an Effect on the Dependent Measure.
In Cell C the check on the manipulation reveals that the independent variable was not well manipulated, but the dependent measures do reflect the effect of the intervention. In this situation the experiment demonstrated the effects of the independent variable, but ambiguity is introduced by checking the manipulation. If this were to happen, the investigator would probably regret to have checked the effects of the manipulation at all (and understandably would tear out this chapter of this book).

The task of the investigator is to explain how the manipulation had an effect on the dependent measures but not on the check of the manipulation. The dependent measures, of course, are the more important measures and have priority in terms of scientific importance over the measure that checked the manipulation. Yet, the haunting interpretation may be that the dependent measures changed for reasons other than the manipulation of the independent variable. There is no easy way to avoid the interpretation.

One reason that the dependent variable(s) may have reflected change when the available evidence suggests that the independent variable was not manipulated effectively pertains to the nature of statistical analysis. It is possible that the differences obtained on the dependent variable were the results of "chance." The results may have been one of the instances in which the subjects' responses between groups were different, even though there is no real relation between the independent and dependent variables in the population of subjects who might be exposed to the conditions of the experiment. In short, the null hypothesis of the original experiment—that is, that groups exposed to the different conditions do not differ—may have been rejected incorrectly (a Type I error). The probability of this error occurring, of course, is given by the level of significance used for the statistical tests (α).

Another reason that the manipulation check failed to show group differences may be that there were inadequacies with the measure itself. The most obvious question that arises is whether the measure assesses the construct reflected in the independent variable. Usually, manipulation check assessment devices are based upon "face validity," that is, whether the items seem to reflect the investigator's interest. (*Face validity* is the psychologist's term to justify the basis for using specific items on a measure or a measure itself when, in fact, no good validation evidence has been obtained. Presumably, the reason this is called "face" validity is to emphasize how difficult it is for us to face our colleagues after having established the validity of an assessment device in such a shoddy fashion, especially when we know better.) It is quite possible for the manipulation check to reflect some other construct than the independent variable. It is of little consolation to raise this as a possibility after an investigation is completed. The manipulation check is part of the methodology for which the investigator can rightly be held responsible. Hence, prior to the experiment it is important for the investigator to have some assurance that the manipulation check will reflect actual differences across conditions. Reflecting change on the measure should be accomplished prior to the full experiment as a minimal validation criterion of the assessment device.

Other assessment problems with manipulation checks may explain why differences were not found across experimental conditions. For example, the items to assess the manipulation may have been too obscure or unclear. The subjects may have heard the information about the intervention but not have realized its relevance for the assessment device. Alternatively, the variability of the responses to the measure may have been great, leading to the absence of statistically significant group differences. Moreover, the information might not be recalled for manipulation check (e.g., if fill-in items or essay questions were asked) but yet be easily recognized if questions were asked in another way (e.g., multiple-choice questions). Whatever the reason, the failure of the manipulation check to agree with the changes in the dependent measure will interfere with interpretation of most results.

General Comments.   Pointing out the ambiguities that can result from checking how successful the independent variable was manipulated could discourage use of such checking devices. This would be unfortunate because much can be gained from knowing how effectively the independent variable was manipulated. Such checks, as a supplement to information on the dependent measures, provide feedback about how well the hypothesis was tested. A failure to achieve statistically significant group differences on the dependent measures is instructive but does not convey specific details about the experimental manipulation. Changes in dependent measures reflect many events all working together, including whether the intervention was implemented effectively, whether the measures were appropriate for the intervention, and whether procedural errors were sufficiently small to minimize variability. The absence of effects on dependent measures could be attributed to many factors, only one of which is the failure to implement the independent variable effectively. On the other hand, a manipulation check helps provide more specific information and hence can be very useful in interpreting a given study and guiding subsequent studies.

SPECIAL ISSUES AND CONSIDERATIONS

Assessment Issues

Many issues emerge in deciding how and when to use manipulation checks. One assessment issue relevant for deciding whether to check on the manipulation is the possible reactivity of assessment and the importance of reactivity for the particular experiment. By checking on the manipulation, an experimenter may arouse subjects' suspicions about the experiment and raise questions that ordinarily might not arise. The manipulation check may even sensitize subjects to the manipulation. For example, a self-report questionnaire to check on the manipulation may make the manipulation that just occurred more salient to the subject. As an extreme case the experimental manipulation might consist of altering the content of a subject's conversation during a standard interview as a function of events that happen to the subject in the waiting room prior to the interview. *Confederates*, persons who work for the investigator, may pose as waiting subjects but, in fact, engage in prearranged discussions in the waiting room that might influence the subject. The prearranged discussions would vary across subjects, depending upon the exact experimental conditions. To check on this manipulation, the investigator could ask subjects at the beginning of the interview such questions as what they talked about in the waiting room or what their current mood is. The questions might suggest to the subjects that their previous interaction in the waiting room was part of the experiment and arouse suspicions and reactions that would not otherwise be evident if no manipulation check were used.

As a general point, reactivity of the manipulation check per se might not be important depending upon how the investigator conceives the manipulation and the process through which it affects the subject. For interventions involving subtle manipulations, the experimenter might not want to risk the possible influence of the manipulation check. Or, if the check is important, the investigator may wish to design unobtrusive measures that are less likely to arouse suspicions than are direct self-report measures (see Chapter 13). For example, the experimenter might leave the subjects alone with another subject (actually a confederate) who asks, "Say, what is this experiment about anyway?" or "What did the experimenter say about what's going to happen?" Responses to a few such questions could be scored (from audio tapes, through a one-way mirror, or by the confederate) to address the question whether the subjects perceived the purpose of the study or to assess other specific aspects of the manipulation.

Alternatively, the investigator may administer the manipulation check after the dependent measures are assessed. Even if the manipulation check is reactive, this could not influence the results because the dependent measures have already been completed. The disadvantage with this alternative is that the longer the delay between the manipulation and assessment of the manipulation's impact, the greater the chances that the check will not discriminate groups. During the delay, subjects may forget precisely what they heard in the instructions or original rationale. Also, it may be possible that the dependent measures, if completed first, could influence the results on the manipulation check. To avoid reactivity of the manipulation check, the investigator might simply assess the manipulation and its effects in pilot work prior to the investigation. In pilot work, self-report questionnaires to assess the manipulation can be used without even administering the dependent measures. In addition, the investigator will have a good basis for knowing in advance that the independent variable was effectively manipulated.

The decision whether to check on the effects of the manipulation also pertains to whether subject awareness of the independent variable is at all relevant. Effective manipulations do not necessarily operate through a subject's awareness. For some manipulations it may be entirely irrelevant whether subjects know or could recognize what has happened to them in the experiment. For example, in cases in which the manipulation involves administering different treatments to subjects, the check on the manipulation is likely to entail assessment of therapist behavior. Here, assessing subject involvement in the procedure per se is not of primary interest. Whether or not subjects perceive themselves as receiving supportive therapy, as opposed to role-playing, may not be important as long as the manipulation check shows that the defining conditions of these treatments were followed. As discussed earlier, the type of manipulation determines the manner and focus of the manipulation check. This means that in some cases subject perceptions are relevant and in others of ancillary importance.

The Influence of Nonmanipulated Variables

In addition to checking on the independent variable, many occasions arise in which it also may be important to determine whether there are extraneous variables that have changed over the course of the experiment. It is quite possible that the independent variable might change other features of subject behavior or of the situation that would serve as plausible rival hypotheses for the results. For example, if different treatments are to be compared, there might be several variables that could covary with treatment—including warmth, congeniality, or competence of the therapist; the credibility of the treatment rationale; and the confidence that the subjects have in treatment. The number of such dimensions that could be assessed in any one study is vast. However, there is no need of, and little value in, including a large number of dimensions along with the check on the manipulation. Rather, dimensions should be included only if they are of direct interest or could account for, or elaborate, the results.

In treatment evaluation it is often difficult to decide in advance what nonmanipulated variables should be observed. The objective is to assess variables that might enhance interpretation of the results. The variables are determined by substantive findings of the content area itself. If certain variables covaried with the manipulation and could explain the results (alliance of the therapist and patient, amount of advice by the therapist), it would be profitable to make some attempt to assess them.

Excluding Subjects in the Data Analyses

The discussion has presented the notion that an intervention is or is not effectively manipulated as determined by a check on the manipulation. It is unlikely that effectively manipulating an independent variable is an all-or-none matter. The manipulation will usually not succeed or fail completely but will probably affect subjects within a given condition differently. A given proportion of subjects may be affected by the intervention. This proportion could be defined by answers to particular questions. For example, subjects who answer most (> 80 percent) or all questions about the experimental manipulation correctly may be considered those for whom the condition was successfully implemented. Whatever the criteria, usually there will be some people for whom the experimental condition was effectively manipulated and others for whom it was not.

An important methodological and practical question is how to treat subjects in the data analyses who are differentially affected by the manipulation. On the one hand, it seems reasonable to include in the analyses only those subjects who were truly affected by the manipulation. After all, only those subjects provide a "real" test of the hypothesis. On the other hand, merely using subjects who show the effects of the intervention on the manipulation check may lead to select groups of subjects that vary on several characteristics from the original groups that were formed through random assignment. Thus, using only those subjects across different groups who reflect the effects of the intervention on the manipulation check might lead to systematic subject variable differences across groups. Loss of subjects, in this case caused by the investigator excluding subjects from the analyses, can lead to subject-selection bias. Hence, eliminating subjects who do not show the effect of manipulation usually is inappropriate.

As an illustration of this problem, intervention studies are often conducted in the schools to prevent such problems as child maladjustment, cigarette smoking, drug abuse, teen pregnancy, and suicide. Schools represent an opportune setting for such interventions because students are available for extended periods (months), school attendance is required, teachers can integrate interventions in the classroom, and interventions can be administered on a large scale (several classes or schools). In large-scale applications, treatment integrity is difficult to achieve and sustain. Consequently, at the end of prevention trials in schools, large differences can be evident in the fidelity with which classroom teachers implement the interventions. Invariably, some teachers carry out the procedures extremely well, others less well, and still others not at all (Botvin, Baker, Filazzola, & Botvin, 1990; Hawkins & Lam, 1987).

At the end of such a study, investigators occasionally exclude classrooms (teachers and subjects) where the intervention was not carried out or not carried out well. Again, it may seem reasonable to exclude teachers (and their classes) in the intervention group. After all, these teachers did not conduct the intervention or did not meet minimal criteria for delivery of the intervention. The investigator is interested in evaluating the effect of the intervention when implemented or implemented well relative to no intervention. Thus, the investigator selects only those intervention classes where the program was well delivered. These teachers and classes are compared to nonintervention classrooms that, of course, did not receive the program.

Unfortunately, selecting a subgroup of teachers who carried out the intervention with fidelity violates the original random composition of intervention and nonintervention groups or conditions in the study. Data analyses of the selected intervention group and nonintervention group now raise threats to internal validity (namely, selection × history, selection × maturation, and other selection variables that apply to one of the groups) as a plausible explanation of the results. Group differences might simply be due to the special subset of teachers who were retained in the intervention group—these teachers are special. Alternatively, it may be that the teachers who adhered better to the intervention had classes and students that were more amenable to change or in some way more cooperative. That is, adherence may have been easier because of the students in the specific classes. In short, when one omits classes and subjects, it may not be the integrity of the intervention that is being evaluated as much as it is the specialness of the teachers or students who adhered to the procedures.

The most appropriate analysis of results is to include all subjects who were run in the various experimental conditions, ignoring the fact that only some of them may have shown the effect of the intervention on the manipulation check. An analysis that includes all subjects provides a more conservative test of the intervention effects. The inclusion of all subjects in this way is often referred to as *intent-to-treat analysis* or evaluation of the results (a topic discussed further in Chapter 15). Intent to treat is usually used in the context of subjects who drop out of a study (before posttreatment or follow-up assessment) (Mazumdar, Liu, Houck, & Reynolds, 1999). One includes subjects in the data analyses and uses the last data that the subjects have provided (e.g., pretreatment data) for any subsequent analyses (e.g., posttreatment). Thus, if subjects dropped out of treatment, the pretreatment data would be used as both pre- and posttreatment scores. Intent-to-treat analysis has two virtues. First, it allows inclusion of all subjects, even those who did not complete the study. This preserves the random assignment and hence makes any selection biases unlikely. Second, the analysis provides a conservative test of the hypotheses. If pretreatment is used to estimate pre- and posttreatment, the data for that subject will show no change. Any effect will have to come from strong intervention effects from other subjects.

Although intent-to-treat analyses are mostly discussed in the context of subjects who drop out, the central points pertain to considerations related to manipulation checks. The hypothesis of a study is that administration of different conditions will lead to differences in performance. This is best evaluated by looking at all subjects who received the different conditions. To include only those subjects who were exposed to the condition and who meet requirements on the manipulation check is to test a different hypothesis, namely, that individuals who are the most responsive to their respective conditions will show changes on the dependent measures.

Another reason for not discarding subjects in the analyses is that the manipulation may have accomplished the intended results without showing any effect on the manipulation check (see Cell C of Figure 8.1). It is important to stress that the dependent measures are the major measures of the effect of treatment. Also, validity of dependent measures is more likely to be established, and one can place more confidence in what the measure actually assesses than is true of the manipulation check. The check on treatment integrity may have missed critical issues or may be a poor measure of anything (low internal consistency, no validity as a measure of implementation of the intervention). In other words, the manipulation check, while useful, may not provide a great estimate of treatment integrity. Hence, data on the dependent measures should not be excluded on the sole basis that the manipulation check has not demonstrated an effect.

There is value in post hoc, unplanned, and explanatory analyses of the segments of data as a supplement to the major analysis of all of the data. First, the intent-to-treat analyses would include all subjects. Second, additional analyses could include only those subjects who showed the appropriate intervention effects on the manipulation check to see whether the scores on the dependent measures were suggestive of a more potent effect. It may not necessarily be the case that subjects who score in a particular way on the manipulation check do better or worse on the dependent measures with respect to the investigator's hypotheses. Third, other analyses might be completed by separating subjects who showed a predicted directional change in behavior (if pre- and posttest assessment data are available) and comparing the scores of these individuals on the manipulation check. Similarly, correlations might be computed within groups (within the intervention group) between the dose of treatment (amount, quality) and treatment outcome (degree of change). All of the analyses must be interpreted cautiously because "receiving a high or good dose of the intervention" is not a randomly distributed variable. The factors that accounted for who received the good dose (a great therapist, teacher, trainer) could explain the dose effect, but these could be tested (is dose related to other confounding variables such as IQ, social class, or plausible variables that were assessed?). Still, such analyses can be very instructive for the investigator and a guide for further work.

In large-scale investigations (school- or districtwide preventive programs) and for small-scale interventions in which the manipulation is complex or vulnerable to poor execution (e.g., therapy in a clinical setting), special means may be needed to assess and monitor implementation. It is the investigator's responsibility to ensure in advance of the investigation that the intervention is manipulated in a potent fashion. Thus, it is useful to begin an investigation armed with information (pilot work, a few cases) that have established an effective or likely-to-be-effective and potent intervention as well as procedures that can be used to monitor and ensure treatment integrity.

ESTABLISHING POTENT MANIPULATIONS

Establishing the efficacy of an experimental manipulation probably is best accomplished in preliminary (or pilot) work before an investigation, especially if an investigator is embarking in an area of research in which he or she has not had direct experience. *Pilot work* is a test or preliminary effort to test aspects of the procedures to see if they work (equipment, recruitment methods), are feasible, and are having an effect (on the manipulation check or even dependent measures) before the full study is run. The actual study itself should be based on preliminary information that the manipulation can be implemented and implemented effectively. Preliminary or pilot work to learn how to manipulate the independent variable successfully can be invaluable for the subsequent results of a research program.

Pilot work usually consists of exploring the intended manipulations by running a set of subjects who may or may not receive all the conditions and measures that will be used in the subsequent experiment itself. In pilot work the subjects can contribute directly to the investigator's conception and implementation of the manipulation. For example, the subject can receive the manipulation and complete the manipulation check. At this point the subject can be fully informed about the purpose of the investigation and provide recommendations about aspects of the procedure that appeared to the subject to facilitate or detract from the investigator's overall objective. Detailed questions can be asked, and the ensuing discussion can reveal ways in which the manipulations can be bolstered. An increasingly common practice is the use of focus groups—that is, meetings with individuals who are knowledgeable in light of their special role (consumers, parents, teachers, adolescents)—to identify what is likely to have impact in a particular area. Focus groups are a way to obtain opinions, often informally, about a question of interest. Meeting with groups of individuals before designing a manipulation (e.g., remedial program) or after running a program can be useful for generating concrete ideas to improve the intervention as well as ways to assess the manipulation.

Another reason for developing the manipulation in pilot work is that some of the problems of checking the manipulation can be eliminated. As discussed earlier, checking on the manipulation in an experiment may sensitize subjects to the manipulation and presumably influence performance on the dependent measures. Pilot work can check the success of the manipulation with, for example, self-report questionnaires. There is no need to obtain measures of performance on the dependent variable if preliminary work is to be used merely to establish that the experimental conditions are administered effectively. If the manipulation has been shown to be effectively manipulated in pilot work, the investigator may wish to omit the manipulation check in the experiment to avoid the possibility of sensitization effects. Of course, a pilot demonstration does not guarantee that the experiment will achieve the same success in manipulating the independent variable, because subjects differ in each application. However, a pilot demonstration can greatly increase the confidence that one has about the adequacy of the experimental test.

Pilot work can be very useful in advance of an investigation to develop distinct experimental conditions consistent with the desired manipulation. An investigation usually reflects a considerable amount of effort and resources, so it is important to ensure that the independent variable is successfully manipulated and the experimental conditions are as distinct as possible. If the manipulation is weakly implemented and doubt can be cast on the effectiveness with which the hypothesis is being tested, the interpretation of the final results may leave much to be desired.

SUMMARY AND CONCLUSIONS

The adequacy with which an independent variable is manipulated is a matter of degree. If the independent variable has its intended or predicted effects on the dependent measure, this is usually sufficient evidence that the intervention was adequately manipulated. It is desirable to have additional information to assess whether the independent variable was adequately manipulated. A check on the manipulation can be obtained by determining whether the subjects were affected by the particular changes in conditions or whether the procedures to which they were exposed were executed properly. This check, distinct from performance on the dependent variables, provides some assurance about the adequacy of the experimental test.

The manner in which this check is accomplished depends upon the type of manipulation. When the manipulation consists of different kinds of information or instructions provided to the subjects, self-report questionnaires often are used to assess whether subjects noticed, heard, believed, or remembered the information presented. When the manipulation consists of varying the type of tasks subjects perform, self-report questionnaires or direct observation of subject performance may be used. When the manipulation consists of different treatment conditions to which the subjects are exposed, it may be checked by examining the behavior of the experimenters or therapists directly. Providing checks on the adequacy with which the independent variable was manipulated is particularly useful in situations where there are no differences between groups on the dependent measures, in clinical treatment where there is no therapeutic change or the amount of change is insufficient, and where there may be a problem in keeping experimental conditions distinct. Treatment integrity (were the treatments rendered the way they should be?) and treatment differentiation (were the treatments different from each other along expected dimensions?) were two concepts used to evaluate how well interventions are administered.

Occasionally, interpretive problems may arise if there are discrepancies between the information provided by check on the manipulation and the dependent variables. However, as a general rule, assessing the adequacy with which the independent variable is manipulated can be extremely useful both for interpreting the results of a particular experiment and for proceeding to subsequent experiments. Interpretive problems that can arise in experiments can be attenuated in advance by conducting pilot work to explore different ways to manipulate the conditions of interest. Assessment of the experimental manipulation can ensure that the independent variable receives the most potent empirical test.

In passing, it is important to reiterate that checking on the manipulation was discussed in this chapter in relation to experimental, as opposed to observational, studies. As described in the next chapter, in observational studies (e.g., a case-control study), checking on the manipulation is rather different and is based on how the sample is selected. In both experimental and observational studies, the general task of the investigator is similar, namely, ensuring that there was an intervention (or manipulation), that the intervention differentiates groups, and that the intervention was provided in ways consistent with the investigator's hypotheses.

KEY CONCEPTS AND TERMS

Checking on the Manipulation   Treatment Integrity

Intent-to-Treat Analysis

FOR FURTHER READING

Hoffart, A. (1994). Use of treatment manuals in comparative outcome research: A schema-based model. *Journal of Cognitive Psychotherapy, 8,* 41–54.

Mazumdar, S., Liu, K.S., Houck, P.R., & Reynolds, C.F., III (1999). Intent-to-treat analysis for longitudinal clinical trials: Coping with the challenge of missing values. *Journal of Psychiatric Research, 33,* 87–95.

Waltz, J., Addis, M., Koerner, K., & Jacobson, J.S. (1993). Testing the integrity of a psychotherapy protocol: Assessment of adherence and competence. *Journal of Consulting and Clinical Psychology, 61,* 620–630.

Wilson, G.T. (1996). Manual-based treatments: The clinical application of research findings. *Behaviour Research and Therapy, 34,* 295–314.

Yeaton, W.H., & Sechrest, L. (1981). Critical dimensions in the choice and maintenance of successful treatments: Strength, integrity, and effectiveness. *Journal of Consulting and Clinical Psychology, 49,* 156–167.

Chapter 9

Observational Research

Case-Control and Cohort Designs

The prior chapters focused primarily on designs in which some condition is manipulated experimentally by the investigator and on the control and comparison groups that these designs often include. In much of clinical research, subject characteristics and other variables are not manipulated directly by the investigator. Rather, the variables are "manipulated by nature," and the investigator evaluates the impact of these variables through selecting persons for study who have the characteristic of interest. Such studies are sometimes referred to as *observational research*, and distinguished from *experimental research*, to convey that the role of the investigator is to observe (assess) different characteristics and their associations, rather than to intervene experimentally. Although observational research can identify many patterns of association (correlates) and can describe the nature of various characteristics (e.g., disorders), the goal is to understand causal relations in much the same way as experimental research.

Designs in which intact groups are studied concurrently or over time are not presented very often in teaching research design in psychology. There is a strong experimental tradition (manipulation of conditions) within the field in which "correlational" research has secondary status. This has changed considerably for a number of reasons. First, key questions of interest for many domains within clinical psychology and indeed many disciplines (astronomy, economics, anthropology) do not permit experimental manipulation. For example, in clinical psychology, we are interested in understanding the effects of being exposed to special conditions or experiences (trauma, war, parents who are depressed) and having special status or characteristics (individuals who are first-born among siblings, criminals, octogenarians, Nobel laureates). Within the mental health professions, a great deal of research focuses on studying persons with various types of clinical disorders (individuals with a diagnosis of depression, anxiety, schizophrenia), and these, of course, are not manipulated by the investigator. In each of these areas research is designed to address a host of questions, such as "What are the past, present, and future characteristics of such individuals? What factors predict who will show the outcome of interest? What are the causes of the outcome?" and even, "What may be done to prevent the outcome?" Obviously, one cannot assign individuals to experience one condition versus another (receiving harsh versus mellower child rearing; receiving versus not receiving a Nobel Prize). However, individuals with these varying characteristics can be identified and studied.

Second, the influence of other disciplines on clinical research has expanded the design strategies that are used within psychology. In particular, epidemiology and public health have had tremendous impact on clinical psychology, psychiatry, and related disciplines (health psychology, psychiatric epidemiology).[1] Within epidemiology studying special groups of interest (e.g., cigarette smokers versus nonsmokers) represents the primary research strategy, and design variations and special data-analytic strategies have been well developed (Hulley & Cummings, 1988; Schlesselman, 1982). Strong inferences can be drawn from such designs, including causal inferences, even though conditions are not manipulated experimentally. For example, the vast majority of studies on the factors leading to diseases (AIDS, heart disease, and various forms of cancer) have come from observational, rather than experimental, studies. From the research, we have learned about multiple influences on diseases (morbidity) and death (mortality), the relative weight of various influences, and whether some influences are likely to play a causal role. The designs can be very powerful indeed.

Third, models in science have evolved in ways that also accord greater value to observational designs. Experimental research, as powerful as it is, is often restricted to the manipulation of one or two variables at a time. Isolation of variables is a key ad-

---

[1]Epidemiology refers to the study and the distribution of diseases and related conditions and the factors that influence the distribution. Research focuses on associations between characteristics and diseases and the nature of these associations (risk factors, causes). The study of clinical disorders from an epidemiological perspective, an area sometimes referred to as psychiatric epidemiology, is directly relevant to many topics of interest in clinical psychology (Verhulst & Koot, 1992).

vantage of experimentation to understand how variables operate. However, in many areas of science (physiology, meteorology, economics), including psychology, we know that multiple variables may influence a phenomenon of interest, and these variables may be related in dynamic, interactive, and reciprocal ways. Observational studies can take into account multiple variables, study them over time, and examine the influences of variables on each other. Fourth and related, data-analytic techniques have advanced over the past decades; these can strengthen the inferences drawn from observational research. Diverse methods of analysis (path analysis, structural equation modeling) have emerged and developed; other methods widely used in other disciplines (logistic analysis, survival analysis) are used increasingly in clinical, counseling, and educational psychology. The net effect is to provide better means of drawing inferences from longitudinal data and the direction and type of influence that one variable exerts on another. The findings have provided information that could not be obtained from experimental research. This is nicely illustrated in observational studies of the relations among depression, heart disease, and death. Depression is a risk factor for subsequent heart attack, especially among men. This influence cannot be explained by the more commonly known risk factors (high blood pressure, low physical activity, family history of heart disease) (Wulsin, Vaillant, & Wells, 1999). Moreover, among individuals who have a heart attack, those who are depressed have a greatly increased risk (up to 2 to 4 times greater) of dying within 6 months of the attack (Frasure-Smith et al., 1993; Murberg et al., 1999). A great deal remains to be learned, particularly about whether reducing depression among patients with heart disease can increase survival. Nevertheless, the relations of depression, heart disease, and death have emerged from observational studies, longitudinal research, and careful analyses of possible confounds and moderators that might influence the connections.

There are many options for observational research. This chapter considers major design strategies, with an emphasis on those that are more commonly used in psychological research. In each design strategy the central characteristics are the study of intact groups (no random assignment) and examination of variables and influences that the investigator usually cannot manipulate directly.

CASE-CONTROL DESIGNS

Case-control designs refer to strategies in which the investigator studies the characteristic of interest by forming groups of individuals who vary on that characteristic and studying current or past features of the groups. The key characteristic is in identifying groups who vary in the outcome (criterion) of interest, that is, have the "problem" or characteristic that the investigator wishes to elaborate. Case-control design is used extensively in epidemiology and public health, where "case" typically means someone who has the disease or condition (heart disease, high blood pressure) that is to be studied.

In the most basic, two-group version the investigator compares subjects who show the characteristic (cases) with individuals who do not (controls). The independent variable is the characteristic or criterion that served as the basis for selection and may reflect a particular experience (being abused, exposure to a particular parenting style) or status (being first-born, widowed, divorced). The investigator compares the two groups on the measures of interest and then interprets the differences to reflect a critical facet of the problem. Two major variations of the designs are worth distinguishing, based on the time perspective in which the groups are studied.

Cross-Sectional Design

In a *cross-sectional case-control design*—the most commonly used version in psychology—subjects (cases and controls) are selected and assessed in relation to current characteristics. This is distinguished from studies that are designed to evaluate events or experiences that happened in the past (*retrospective studies*) or that will happen in the future (*prospective studies*). The goal of a cross-sectional case-control study is to examine factors that are associated with a particular characteristic of interest. The study can describe and explore characteristics of interest (e.g., what are peer and family relations like of young women who have poor versus good body image?) or test theoretical propositions or conceptual models (first- and second-born children might be compared to test a hypothesis about different patterns of attachment in their current adult relations).

In the usual case the investigator begins with hypotheses about how various groups will differ, perhaps based on a theoretical perspective. The subjects are identified and assessed on multiple characteristics beyond those used to delineate their status as cases or controls. Because all of the measures are obtained at the same time, the results are correlational; that is, one cannot know from the study whether the outcome preceded or was caused by a particular characteristic. (There are some exceptions where a characteristic such as sex or race may be assumed to antedate an outcome of interest such as onset of a disorder.)

Cross-sectional designs are useful for identifying correlates and associated features, and these findings may be quite informative and significant. For example, the investigator may wish to test whether depressed mothers interact differently with their children (infants, toddlers) when compared to nondepressed mothers. Mothers are identified and assessed on a measure of depression and classified as depressed (cases) or not (controls); they are then brought into the laboratory or observed at home to assess how they interact with their children. Several studies with this focus have shown that depressed mothers, compared with nondepressed controls, display decreased attention, affection, and vocal behavior, are less expressive (flatter affect), and show more anger, negativism, and hostility in their interactions (see Hammen, 1991). This work has very important implications regarding early child development, patterns of emotional attachment of parents to children, and the likely risk that children may have for later dysfunction.

Cross-sectional designs are commonly used and have generated provocative findings, theories, and further research. For example, from such studies we have learned that (1) individuals who are depressed are likely to show a set of negative cognitions (helplessness, hopelessness) compared to nondepressed controls; (2) that children whose parents survived the holocaust experience significantly greater psychological dysfunction than matched controls whose parents have no such experience; (3) that children who are depressed, compared to those who are not, have significant impairment in peer relations and school functioning; and (4) that girls who mature early (in relation to their peers) are more likely to have low self-esteem than those who mature later, to mention a random (well not entirely random) list of fascinating findings. Many examples mentioned in previous chapters—related to the health benefits of drinking wine, participating in religion, and not being depressed after a heart attack—were based on case-control studies. Findings that compare intact groups are very useful in generating theory and concrete hypotheses to analyze further the reasons for these relations and the conditions under which they do and do not operate. Indeed, many case-control studies lead to experimental research (studies with animals) to test directly some characteristic expected to play a causal role that may be suggested by a case-control study.

Retrospective Design

In a *retrospective case-control design*, the goal is to draw inferences about some antecedent condition that has resulted in, or is associated with, the outcome. This design represents an explicit effort to identify the time line between possible causes or antecedents (risk factors) and a subsequent outcome of interest. Subjects are identified who already show the outcome of interest (cases) and compared with those who do not show the outcome (controls). So far this is just like the cross-sectional case-control design. The retrospective design includes measures that are designed to elaborate the past of the individuals in each of the groups.

As an example, a retrospective case-control design was used to examine the relation of attachment patterns to suicidal behavior among adolescents (Adam, Sheldon-Keller, & West, 1996). Attachment refers to a system in which the infant maintains close proximity to the caregiver, particularly under conditions in which there may be danger or distress (Bowlby, 1969). Several different patterns of attachment have been delineated. The most adaptive of these is considered to be a secure attachment in which the infant is confident that the caregiver will respond to the threat, and the infant may adapt quickly after the threat has passed. In contrast, insecurely attached infants are uncertain of caregiver availability and adopt strategies to maintain proximity to caregivers.

In this study, maladaptive early attachment patterns were hypothesized to characterize suicidal adolescents. Adolescents (13–19 years old) from multiple inpatient and outpatient treatment services were identified and completed several measures within a two-week period. The measures included an interview that evaluated whether they had significant suicidal ideation in their past (none, moderate, or greater-than-moderate suicidality, based on assessment of frequency, intensity, or duration). From the interview, case (suicidal) and control (nonsuicidal patient) groups were formed. Among many other measures was an interview to assess early attachment relationships, that is, how individuals represented (conceived) of their relations with their parents. The main results indicated that suicidal patients, compared with controls, showed disturbed early attachment patterns (lack of resolution of attachment-related trauma such as parent death or abuse and greater preoccupation with the parents in an angry or passive fashion). The study is important in raising the prospect that attachment patterns early in life play a role in delineating suicidal and nonsuicidal patients. Subsequent work can now test additional hypotheses about paths, mechanisms, and moderators that might explain or elaborate the connection between attachment and suicidality.

The retrospective nature of the study raises cautions as well, of which the authors were aware. Attachment (A), suicidality (B), or other variables (C) have relations whose temporal ordering is not resolved by the design. The authors propose that a type attachment pattern is an antecedent to suicidality (A → B), but from the standpoint of the design, it is possible that the results could be explained another way (B → A). Maybe suicidal and nonsuicidal adolescents had identical attachment patterns when they were young. Yet, when youths become suicidal, perhaps they view all of their relations quite differently and recast their parents somewhat differently. Stated more colloquially, perhaps becoming suicidal removes one's rose colored glasses about one's past and one becomes more critical or alert to more negative features of one's childhood, parents, and attachment. In short, the direction of A to B or B to A is not entirely clear.

In addition, other variables not included in the study (C) may well lead both to suicidality and reevaluation of relations with significant others (C → A & B). The point is that one cannot know the relation of these influences from the design of the study. With all of these interpretations, is there any value to the findings? Absolutely! Knowing that attachment is related, knowing that there are specific identifiable patterns (not just "attachment problems" generically), and knowing that these patterns could not be accounted for by other subject and demographic variables (age, socioeconomic status) advances an area of research considerably.

Obviously, a key issue in retrospective designs pertains to the assessment. As a general rule, retrospective reports permit the investigator to identify correlates. One of the correlates may be recall of a past event. Significant problems usually preclude establishing the recalled event as a risk factor (antecedent) for the outcome of interest. First, selective recall, inaccurate recall, and recall biased by the outcome (e.g., dysfunction) all interfere with drawing valid conclusions about the past event, its occurrence, or differential occurrence for groups that vary in a later outcome. Memory is a matter of *recoding* rather than *recording* events and experiences that happened previously (Roediger & McDermott, 2000). Thus, recall has some inherent limitations. In some cases, historical records (school truancy, participation in high school activities) are used as the data. With such records the quality, reliability, and completeness of the data also raise potential interpretive problems.

Not all retrospective measures are necessarily flawed. There are different methods of retrospective assessment (self-report, archival records), types of events that are assessed (parenting practices, death of a relative), time frames (recall of events or experiences within the past week versus the past 25 years), and means of soliciting or prompting the recalled material (see Brewin, Andrews, & Gotlib, 1993; Kessler, Mroczek, & Belli, 1999). These are not all subject to the same sorts or degrees of bias. As a general rule, retrospective reports of psychological states (family conflict, mental health, difficulties of childhood) and duration, level, and dates of particular events are rather poor; recall of discrete events (e.g., changes in residences) and more stable characteristics (e.g., reading skills) tends to be more reliable but still not great. For example, longitudinal studies have asked people to evaluate some characteristic at a concurrent time; years later, retrospective data are obtained on the same characteristic. The results indicate little relationship between the concurrent and retrospective data when the same person evaluates the same events (Henry, Moffitt, Caspi, Langley, & Silva, 1994).

Considerations in Using Case-Control Designs

Strengths and weaknesses of case-control designs are summarized in Table 9.1. Among the strengths, the designs are well suited to studying conditions that are relatively infrequent. In clinical psychology, groups with particular disorders, personality characteristics, or exposure to particular experiences would be difficult or impossible to obtain from sampling a population randomly or from following a community population over time until individuals showed the characteristic of interest. For example, there is keen interest in understanding characteristics of individuals (1) with a diagnosis of depression, schizophrenia, and, of course, other disorders; (2) who have engaged in or been victimized by abuse; or (3) who are altruistic, heroic, model parents, spouses, gifted, and so on. A case-control study identifies individuals with and without the characteristic and asks, "How are the individuals alike and different from controls, and what are some of the reasons they may have reached this particular outcome?"

Second, the designs are feasible and efficient in terms of costs and resources. The investigator selects the sample and makes the comparisons between cases and controls at a single point in time (now). The designs do not involve following samples prospectively, so there is not a long delay in answering questions from the research. Longitudinal research, while methodologically advantageous for all sorts of reasons, as noted in the next section, is costly in time and personnel. Third and related, loss of subjects, a constant concern in longitudinal studies, is not a problem in the usual

---

TABLE 9.1.   Major Strengths and Weaknesses of Case-Control Designs

Strengths

- Well suited to studying conditions or characteristics that are relatively infrequent in the population
- Efficient in terms of resources and time because of the cross-sectional assessment
- No attrition because of assessment at one point in time
- Can study magnitude and type of relations among variables (direct influence, moderating influence)
- Allows the investigator to match (equalize) subjects on one of the variables assessed at pretest (e.g., level of anxiety) that may influence the results
- Can rule out or make implausible the role of influences that might be confounded with the characteristic of interest
- Can generate hypotheses about causal relations or sequence of characteristics and how they unfold to produce a problem

Weaknesses

- No time line is shown among the variables of interest (depressed [A] individuals have a certain type of cognitive style [B]), so one cannot usually establish whether one characteristic (A or B) preceded the other or emerged together
- Causal relations cannot be directly demonstrated, even though various analyses (e.g., dose–response relations) can provide a strong basis for hypotheses about these relations
- Sampling biases are possible, depending on how the cases (e.g., depressed clients) were identified and whether some special additional characteristic (e.g., coming to a clinic) was required

case-control design. Subjects are assessed at a single time, usually in one assessment period.

Fourth, case-control studies can go well beyond merely showing that two (or more) variables are correlated. The magnitude and type of relations (direct and indirect relations) can be studied, and different patterns of relations within a sample can be delineated. Identifying subtypes within a sample, for example, occurs when the variables of interest correlate differently for one type of case (e.g., males versus females) rather than another. These differences are considered as moderator variables and can lead to hypotheses about different types of onset and clinical course.

There are weaknesses of the designs as well. First, the designs demonstrate correlations, and the direction of the relation between one characteristic and another may not be clear at all. For example, it may be true that individuals who are happy in their marriages had a happy childhood, as demonstrated in a retrospective case-control design. Yet, it is always possible that childhood was recalled in a special way *because* of marital happiness or because of some factor correlated with marital happiness. In a case-control study there is inherent ambiguity in how the characteristics of interest relate to each other (which came first, whether they were caused by some other variable). The retrospective study, too, is usually limited, unless there can be some certainty that the antecedent occurred prior to the outcome.

Second and related, a causal relation between one characteristic (cognitions) and another (depression) cannot be demonstrated. Even though case-control designs are not well suited to demonstrating causal relations, they are often very good at generating hypotheses about them. The hypotheses can be bolstered by various analyses within the study that help to rule out other influences (socioeconomic status, physical health) that might be plausible explanations for the finding. Also, dose–response relations (showing that the variables are related in a way consistent with a causal hypothesis) can be helpful.

Third, sampling biases may influence the relation between the characteristics of interest. Selection of cases and controls may inadvertently draw on samples in which the relation is quite different from the relation in the general population. For example, if one is interested in studying women who are abused by their spouses, one can identify cases at a women's shelter and compare them to a control group (in the community, or from another clinic but who have not been abused). The goal may be to identify whether abused women, compared to controls, have fewer social supports (friends and relatives on whom they can rely). Although the women in the case group may, in fact, be abused, they may not represent the larger population of abused women who do not go to shelters. Indeed, most abused women do not go to women's shelters; many of these women do not even consider themselves to be victims of abuse. In addition, the absence of a support system (and other characteristics such as level of stress) may influence who comes to shelters so that this is a unique group. That is, the lack of social support may actually relate to who comes to shelters to begin with. Consequently, the correlation between abuse and social support may be spurious because support influences the referral process, that is, who comes to a shelter. Stated more generally, how cases are identified can greatly influence the relations that are demonstrated within the data. If a special sample is identified because they have self-selected by volunteering to come to a clinic facility or have been directed to do so (e.g., court ordered), the relations that are demonstrated may have little generality to the larger population of interest. It is for this reason that epidemiological research, where these designs are commonly used, relies heavily on random sampling from the general population to identify cases and controls.

On balance, the design strategy is quite valuable. Apart from elaborating concurrent and past characteristics associated with a given problem, characteristic, or facet of functioning, the designs can identify relations among multiple influences. Related, among multiple variables that might be studied, the magnitude of the relations and variation in the relations as a function of other variables such as sex, age, or race may be very important.

COHORT DESIGNS

Cohort designs refer to strategies in which the investigator studies an intact group or groups over time, that is, prospectively. *Cohort* is the term that means a group of individuals who are followed over time. The design is also referred to as a *prospective, longitudinal study*. Two key differences help distinguish case-control and cohort designs. First, cohort designs follow samples over time to identify factors leading to (antedating) an outcome of interest. Second, the group is assessed before the outcome (e.g., depression) has occurred. In contrast, in case-control designs, the groups (cases and controls) are selected based on an outcome that has already occurred.

The special strength of cohort designs lies in establishing the relations between antecedent events and outcomes. Because cases are followed over time, one can be assured of the time line between events, that is, that the antecedent occurred before the outcome of interest. The time frame of a prospective study may be a matter of weeks, months, or years, depending on the goals of the study. In such a study the antecedent condition (birth defects, early attachment, sibling relations) is assessed and one is assured that the outcome has not occurred (school competence, anxiety disorder). That is, the temporal order of antecedent and outcome is clear. Hence, a necessary condition for demonstrating a causal relation is met within the design. Of course, demonstrating that an antecedent condition preceded an outcome, by itself, does not establish a causal relation but provides a critical prerequisite. The design has many variations; three are considered here.

Single-Group Cohort Design

Typically, a cohort design begins by identifying a group of subjects and following the group over time. This is referred to as a *single-group, cohort design* to note that all subjects who meet a particular criterion are selected (all cases born in a given year, all cases in a particular community or hospital). The group is selected to study the emergence of a later outcome (a disorder, successful employment, drug addiction). The basic requirements include assessment at two (at least) different times and a substantial sample that, during that span of time, changes status on the outcome of interest. For example, all cases referred to a clinic may be identified and assessed. They are then followed prospectively (e.g., over the next 3 years) to identify who shows a relapse (return of symptoms) and who does not. Although the subjects were identified and selected as a single group, following cases over time has as its goal identification of those who have different outcomes, that is, delineation of subgroups at the point of outcome assessment.

When one considers a longitudinal, prospective study, this immediately conjures up an image of a study of several years or decades. In fact, most uses of this design have a much shorter time frame (one or two years). The characteristics and strength of the design still apply. For example, a cohort design was used to study the impact of a hurricane (Hurricane Andrew in Florida in 1992) on children (La Greca, Silverman, Vernberg, & Prinstein, 1996). This hurricane was one of the worst national disasters in the United States, leaving 175,000 families homeless and without adequate food or supplies and exceeding costs of any other national disaster (over $15.5 billion). The investigators examined the extent to which the hurricane led to persistent symptoms of posttraumatic stress over the ensuing months. These symptoms include reexperiencing the disaster (intrusive thoughts and dreams), difficulty sleeping and concentrating, and detachment and avoidance of disaster-related activities. In current psychiatric classification these symptoms characterize posttraumatic stress disorder (PTSD), impairment that results from the experience of trauma or disaster (exposure to war, rape, or other extremely stressful events).

School children (grades 3–5, $N = 442$) exposed to the hurricane were identified and assessed over time on three occasions: 3, 7, and 10 months after the hurricane. Among the goals was to predict which children showed PTSD symptoms at the final assessment and what factors predicted this from the earlier assessments. The results indicated that PTSD symptoms decreased for the sample over time. At the final (10-month) assessment, 12 percent of the children continued to show severe symptom levels. The most salient predictors of who showed severe PTSD symptoms were the extent to which the initial disaster was perceived by the youths to be life threatening and the severity of loss and disruption during and after the disaster (loss of property; disruption of housing, routines). Greater threat and disruption were associated with more severe PTSD symptoms. Less social support from family and friends, the occurrence of other life events, and high efforts to cope with the trauma (e.g., blame and anger) also predicted persistence of symptoms. These results help investigators to understand factors that lead to persistence of symptoms of trauma and also provide clues of what might be addressed to intervene early (stabilize the disruption as soon as possible and help restore normal routines) among youths at greatest risk. The design nicely illustrates selecting a single group, following the group over time, delineating different outcomes (e.g., remission versus continuation of symptoms), and identifying antecedent factors that are associated with varied outcomes.

Several prospective, longitudinal studies have contributed to our understanding the emergence of clinical dysfunction and antecedent–outcome relations. Especially noteworthy are *birth-cohort studies* in which a group of subjects is identified at birth and followed for an extended period, often spanning up to 10, 20, and 30 years (Esser, Schmidt, & Woerner, 1990; Farrington, 1991; Silva, 1990; Werner & Smith, 1982). Multiple measures are administered at several points over the course of childhood, adolescence, and adulthood. Antecedent events at different points in development can be used to predict outcomes of interest (criminality, psychopathology).

For example, a birth-cohort study has been ongoing for some time in New Zealand to understand the development of psychopathology and adjustment (Silva,

1990). The study began by sampling all children that could be identified ($N = 1037$) who were born in the city of Dunedin (approximate population of 120,000) within a 1-year period (1972–1973). From the ages of 3 to 15, subjects were assessed every two years, and then again at ages 18 and 21. At each assessment period participants came to the research setting (within two months of their birthday) and completed a full day of assessments (physical exam, mental health interview, and so on) with measures, of course, changing with age of the subjects. Many findings have emanated from this project. For example, one report evaluated whether temperamental style of the children at age 3 predicted psychiatric disorders at age 21 (Caspi, Moffitt, Newman, & Silva, 1996). Based on observations of the children at age 3, behavioral characteristics were rated by examiners who classified children as inhibited, undercontrolled, well adjusted, confident, and reserved.

Consider only two groups for the moment, inhibited (very socially inhibited and reticent) and undercontrolled (irritable, impulsive, difficulty in sitting still, uncontrolled in their behavior). At age 21, 92 percent of the subjects were interviewed to obtain information about their mental health. Official crime records and informant reports were also obtained. Among the many findings, inhibited and undercontrolled children were the most likely groups to show psychiatric disorders at age 21. Inhibited children were at increased risk for mood disorders in particular. Undercontrolled children were more likely to show antisocial personality disorder and to have more violent offenses in adulthood. Both inhibited and undercontrolled children were more likely than other groups to attempt suicide and (for boys) to report alcohol-related problems. Overall, the study shows that early child behavior predicted psychopathology in adulthood. Although the richness of the findings cannot be fully represented here, the few results mentioned convey the benefits of a birth-cohort study. Apart from looking at antecedents and later outcomes, interim assessments along the way can help elaborate the steps from one age to another as a particular outcome unfolds. In the process one can generate theory regarding how disorders emerge (causes, risk factors), what factors decrease the likelihood that the outcome will emerge (protective factors), and what might be done to intervene early before the outcome emerges (prevention).

The effort, cost, and obstacles (retaining investigators, cases, and grant support) make birth-cohort studies relatively rare. From the standpoint of this chapter the critical point to note is that cohort studies do not necessarily mean *birth*-cohort studies. The defining advantage of the cohort study is being able to identify the time line between antecedents and outcomes, and one to a few years is the usual time frame for such studies within psychological research.

Multigroup Cohort Design

The multigroup cohort design is a prospective study in which two (or more) groups are identified at the initial assessment (Time 1) and followed over time to examine outcomes of interest. One group is identified because they have an experience, condition, or characteristic of interest; the other group who is identified does not. So far, this description is exactly like a case-control design. A case-control design and two-group cohort designs are distinguished in the following way. A case-control design selects two groups, one of which shows the *outcome* of interest (e.g., is depressed), and the other group, which does not (e.g., not depressed). A two-cohort design begins by selecting two groups that vary in exposure to some condition of interest or risk factor (e.g., prisoners of war) or not and follows them to see what the outcomes will be. As noted before, the distinguishing feature of a cohort design is that cases are *followed prospectively* to see what happens, that is, the outcomes that emerge.

As an example, two-cohort design was used to determine whether a head injury in childhood increases the chances of later psychiatric disorder (Rutter, 1981; Rutter, Chadwick, & Shaffer, 1983). The hypothesis was that brain damage is one factor that can lead to psychiatric disorders later. Youths who received head injury (e.g., accident) were identified and assessed over time for a 2-year period. The obvious control group would be a sample of youths without a head injury, matched on various subject (e.g., sex, age, ethnicity) and demographic (e.g., social class) variables that are known to influence patterns of psychiatric disorders. However, a noninjury group may not provide the best comparison or test of the hypothesis. The hypothesis focused on *head* injury. Maybe the experience of *any* injury would increase later psychiatric impairment. Perhaps any injury (whether to the head or toes) that leads to hospitalization for a child (or anyone) is traumatic, and perhaps that trauma and entry into a hospital alone could increase later impairment. Thus, even if a head injury group showed greater subsequent psychiatric impairment, that would not be a strong test of the hypothesis. In this study the second group consisted of youths who were hospitalized for orthopedic injury (broken bones from accidents). Thus, both groups experienced injury, but head injury was the unique feature of the index group expected to predict later psychiatric disorder. Both groups were followed for 2 years after the injury and evaluated at that time.

As predicted, the results indicated that youths with head injury had a much higher rate of psychiatric disorder at the follow-up 2 years later when compared to orthopedic injury youths. The study might end here and still be considered to support the original hypothesis. However, more was accomplished to strengthen the inferences that could be drawn. First, one interpretation of the results is that children who get head injuries are not a random sample of youths in the population. Perhaps they already have more psychological and psychiatric problems to begin with (before the head injury). In fact, emotional and behavioral problems among children are correlated with more risky and impulsive behavior, which could increase the risk of head injury. Showing that a head injury group, when compared to another group, has a higher rate of psychiatric disorder would not establish the temporal order of head injury and later psychiatric disorder. The goal of this study was not only to show that injury was related to later psychiatric impairment but also to establish that it preceded such impairment. Collection of retrospective data during the study helped address this. Immediately after the injury, families of both head and orthopedic injury group children completed assessments that evaluated pre-injury emotional and behavioral problems of the children in both groups. Pre-injury problems did not differ between groups nor predict later child psychiatric impairment. Thus, it is unlikely that preexisting psychological problems could explain the relation of head injury and later psychiatric disorder.

Second, if brain damage were the key factor, one hypothesis would be that severity of the injury and subsequent incidence of psychiatric disorder would be related. As mentioned previously, observational studies often look for a dose–response relation within the index or case group to see if there is a gradient in the association between the amount of one variable and the rate of the outcome. The presence of a dose–response relation is one more bit of evidence suggesting that the construct of interest is key in explaining the outcome. In this study, severity of brain injury was considered to provide a further test of the hypothesis. As a measure of severity of brain injury, the authors used number of days of postinjury amnesia (not remembering the incident). Youths with more days of amnesia (≥ 8 days), compared with those of few days of amnesia (≤ 7 days), showed much higher rates of later psychiatric impairment. This further suggests that the construct, head injury, is likely to explain the relation. Overall, noteworthy features of this study are the use of a comparison group that helped evaluate the specific role of head injury, the use of assessment (albeit retrospective) to address one threat to construct validity (that group differences were due to preinjury emotional and behavioral problems), and data analyses (dose–response relation) to suggest further that head injury was the likely variable accounting for the follow-up results.

Does this study establish that head injury is a *cause* of psychiatric disorder? The study did establish that head injury preceded psychiatric disorder, and hence one condition of a causal relation was established, namely, a time line wherein the proposed event (cause) comes before the outcome. Further analyses also established that head injury (rather than just injury) was the likely influence. At the same time we cannot be absolutely certain that there is a causal relation. It could be that some other construct not assessed in this study is the factor and head injury, is not the main variable. For example, children vary in the extent to which they are clumsy early in life, as defined by motor movement and coordination. Clumsiness in early childhood is a predictor of later psychiatric impairment (Sudgen & Wright, 1998). It is possible and plausible that the head injury group varied on clumsiness. Perhaps head injury was merely a correlate of this clumsiness, and clumsiness is the key factor. An alternative explanation stems from a study that demonstrated the impact of head injury of a child on the family. Specifically, head injury to a child leads to more stress and depression among the parents than other (e.g., orthopedic) injuries (Wade, Taylor, Drotar, Stancin, & Yeates, 1998). Perhaps parent dysfunction is involved somehow in later psychiatric disorder of the child with head injury, and the injury itself plays a little role. These latter interpretations of the original study are a matter of surmise. The study cannot rule out all other causes. Yet, the careful selection of controls, assessment, and data analyses act in concert to reduce the plausibility that other factors than head injury were responsible for the findings. The original study went very far to establish that head injury plays a role. Additional research might unravel whether the effect is a direct influence (injury harms brain functioning that disrupts social, emotional, and behavioral processes) and/or indirect influence (head injury leads to other processes, perhaps in the family, leading to disorder).

A two-group cohort design was used to understand wife assault among men who engaged in violence against their wives (Aldarondo & Sugarman, 1996). Men who were identified as engaging in violence against their wives were interviewed annually for a 3-year period. The goal was to identify factors that predicted who continued to assault their wives versus those who ceased assaultive behaviors. A control group of nonviolent men who never engaged in violence was also included. Key factors that differentiated groups pertained to reported childhood experiences of the violent men.

Violent men, whether they continued or ceased their violence, reported more exposure to violence when they were teenagers, both in terms of witnessing their fathers assault their mothers and in receiving abuse themselves, when compared to nonviolent men. Among the violent men, those who persisted rather than desisted, experienced greater marital discord during the course of the study, were younger, and had greater exposure to violence (especially witnessing violence) when they were young, compared to those who discontinued their violence. This is an interesting example of a cohort design because individuals with an identified problem were evaluated to see what factors predicted continuation and discontinuation.

Accelerated, Multicohort Longitudinal Design

An *accelerated, multicohort longitudinal design* is a prospective, longitudinal study in which multiple groups (two or more cohorts) are studied in a special way. The key feature of the design is the inclusion of cohorts who vary in age when they enter the study. The design is referred to as *accelerated* because the period of interest (e.g., development over the course of 10 years) is studied in a way that requires less time than if a single group were followed over time. This is accomplished by including several groups, each of which covers only a portion of the total time frame of interest. The groups overlap in ways that permit the investigator to discuss the entire development period (see Stanger & Verhulst, 1995).

Consider an example to convey how this is accomplished. Suppose one were interested in studying how patterns of cognitions, emotions, and behavior emerge over the course of childhood, say from ages 5–14, a period which might be of keen interest in light of school entry, school transitions, and entry into adolescence. An obvious study would be to identify one group (a cohort) and to follow them from first assessment (age 5) until the final assessment when they become 14. That would be a single-group cohort design, as discussed previously. Another way would be to study the question with an accelerated, multicohort longitudinal design. The study could begin with three groups that vary in age. For this example, let us say that a group of 5-, 8-, and 11-year-olds are identified. Each group is assessed at the point of entry and then followed and assessed for the next three years. Assume that assessments are conducted annually during the month of each child's birthday.

Figure 9.1 diagrams the study with three groups to show that each group is assessed for a period of 4 years beginning at the point of entering the study. There is a *cross-sectional component* of this design that consists of comparing all youths at the time they first enter the study and are at different ages. Also, we are interested in comparing the 5-year-old group when they become 8 years old with the data from the 8-year-olds when they entered the study to see if the two groups are similar on the measures. That is, there are two 8-year-old groups at some point in the design, and one can see if the data are similar from different cohorts when they are the same age. The *longitudinal component* of the design examines development over the period of 5–14 years of age. By seeing how each cohort develops and the relations over time within a group, one hopes to be able to chart development across the entire period from ages 5 through 14, even though no one group was studied for the entire duration. The example conveys only one way of selecting groups. The number of groups,

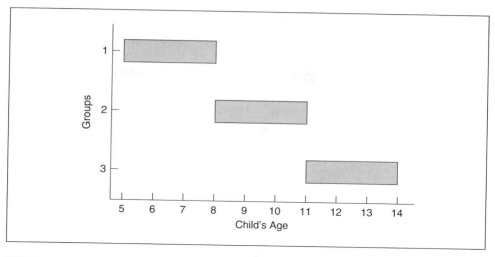

FIGURE 9.1.   An accelerated, multicohort longitudinal design in which separate groups are selected and assessed. The groups are selected so that their ages span the entire period time frame of interest (ages 5–14 in this hypothetical example) but no one group is followed for the entire duration. Time 1 (first assessment) is when the youths are 5, 8, and 11 years of age, respectively.

the assessment intervals, and the overlap among the groups over the course of development can all vary.

An accelerated longitudinal design is intended to address two salient issues. First, the design can identify if the characteristics of a particular cohort are due to historical influences or special features of the period in history in which the cohort is assessed. Consider this potential artifact. In a single-group cohort design a group is followed over an extended period. It is quite possible that the information generated by the group is special in light of the period in time in which the study was completed. For example, if one is interested in studying the relation of factors that occur during the course of adolescence to outcomes in young adulthood, obviously a longitudinal design can begin by identifying adolescents and assessing them repeatedly at various intervals until they become adults. The data may reveal patterns among the measures (correlations among key characteristics), changes over time, and factors that predict particular outcomes that are unique. There is the possibility that the results might be attributable in part to the *period* in which the individuals have been studied; that is, this cohort may show special results because of being youths who grew up during a period with or without the availability of some factors that might influence the variables that are studied. For example, changes in the availability of television, computers, cell phones, cigarettes, birth control, illicit drugs, and two parents in the home (low rate of divorce), or unemployment rates in the country (which affects individual families), are influences that could affect a given cohort and many outcomes of interest (violence, addictions, marital happiness of that cohort).

The results of some studies raise the likelihood of cohort effects due to the historical period in which the cohort was studied. As an example, adolescents in the 1980s who used small amounts of alcohol appear to show *better* psychological and social adjustment than their peers who are abstinent (Newcomb & Bentler, 1989). Some alcohol use had become normative, and those who engaged in that use were not an extreme group. It is likely that the finding has to do in part with the historical period that was sampled. When grandparents and parents of these teenagers were young, alcohol was not so readily available (prohibition) and, even if available, was probably more restricted to a very special group of teenagers. In other words, alcohol use and its correlates probably vary at the time in which the sample is studied. More generally, culture is always changing (unemployment and crime rates, wars, values), and these historical events can influence the pattern that any particular cohort shows. Thus, in a single-group cohort design, it is possible that the group shows a pattern that is influenced in critical ways by events occurring during this period (i.e., history as a threat to *external* validity). The results (relations among variables, developmental paths) may differ if another cohort were studied at a different period or time.

An accelerated, multicohort design allows one to better separate any historical period effects from developmental change. Each cohort within the study has a slightly different history, and one can make comparisons to address whether there are period influences. In the example (Figure 9.1), the investigator can compare the data of the 5-year-olds when they turn 8 years of age with the data of 8-year-olds. These groups ought to provide similar information, namely, how 8-year-olds are on the measures of interest. Major differences at this point raise the prospect of some other broad historical influence that is at work. In any case, one advantage of an accelerated longitudinal design is the ability to evaluate whether the findings for the cohort are restricted to possible historical influences that are unique to that group.

Second and more obvious, the accelerated longitudinal design addresses the most difficult part of longitudinal designs, namely, they take an extended period to complete. The period can be reduced by using multiple cohorts to represent different and overlapping periods of that time frame. In the example in Figure 9.1, the goal was to study development covering a period of 10 years. Using an accelerated design, each of the three groups in the example was assessed over a 4-year period, although the 10 years of interest was examined. In making the study shorter, some of the problems of longitudinal research (attrition, expense of following and finding cases) are likely to be reduced.

Considerations in Using Cohort Designs

Cohort designs have their strengths and weaknesses and these are highlighted in Table 9.2. As to the strengths, the first and foremost is the fact that the time line between proposed antecedents (risk factors, causes) and the outcome of interest can be firmly established. This is not a minor point and serves as the primary basis for distinguishing the variations of observational designs (case control versus cohort designs) we have discussed. Second, careful assessments can be made of the independent variables (antecedents, predictors) of interest. Because the outcome of interest has not yet occurred, one can be assured that the outcome did not bias the measures. Measurements at Time 1 (and other occasions) will not be influenced by the outcome, which will not be determined until much later at Time 2. Third and related, because the designs are prospective and assessments are made on multiple occasions, the in-

TABLE 9.2.   Major Strengths and Weaknesses of Cohort Designs

Strengths

- Can firmly establish the time line (antecedent comes before some outcome of interest)
- Measurement of the antecedents could not be biased by the outcome (being depressed now could not influence past recall of events early in life—those events were assessed before being depressed)
- Multiple methods and assessments at different points in time can be used to assess the predictors to chart the course or progression from the antecedent to the outcome.
- All of the permutations can be studied in relation to the antecedent (occurred or did not occur at Time 1) and outcome (subjects did show or did not show the outcome at Time 2).
- Good for generating and testing theory about risk, protective, and causal factors and mediators and moderators

Weaknesses

- Prospective studies can take considerable time to complete, and answers to critical questions (effect of asbestos and smoking on health, effect of physical or emotional abuse on youths) may be delayed.
- Studies conducted over time can be costly in terms of personnel and resources. Retaining cases in a longitudinal study often requires full-time efforts of researchers in the study.
- Attrition or loss of subjects over time can bias the sample.
- Cohort effects may serve as a moderator; that is, it is possible that the findings are due to the sample assessed at a particular point in time.
- The outcome of interest (who becomes depressed, engages in later criminal behavior, becomes a priest or rabbi or a professional musician) may have a relatively low base rate. Statistical power and sample sizes become issues to evaluate the outcome.

vestigator can plan and administer measures that will thoroughly assess the predictors (multiple measures, multiple methods of assessment) at the different points in time. A given influence may be assessed on more than one occasion, and the accumulation of different influences over time can be examined as predictors of an outcome.

Fourth, among the many strengths of a prospective, longitudinal study is the ability to examine the full set of possibilities among those who do and do not experience the antecedent condition and those who do and do not show the outcome. For example, consider the hypothesis that watching aggression on television in early childhood is associated with aggressive behavior in adolescence. Assume for a moment that we will conduct this study with a two-group cohort design and assess all children in the community who are 5–7 years old. We follow these children for 10 years and evaluate their aggressive behavior (fighting at school). For simplicity's sake, let us classify exposure to aggression on TV and later aggressive behavior in a dichotomous fashion, even though we know that each of these is a matter of degree (dimensional). So let us say, at Time 1 (childhood) we can identify children who are exposed to high levels of TV aggression or not exposed to high levels (2 groups). This makes the study a two-group, cohort design. At Time 2 (adolescence), let us identify the outcome as high in aggression at school or not (2 outcomes). We can divide the cohort into 4 subgroups based on these combinations. The subgroups (Cells A, B, C, and D) are diagramed in Figure 9.2 and described here:

A. Those who *experienced the antecedent* in childhood (exposed to high levels of TV aggression) and *the outcome* (they are high in aggression in adolescence);

B. Those who *experienced the antecedent* (exposed to high levels of TV exposure), but *did not show the outcome*;

C. Those who *did not experience the antecedent*, but *did show the outcome*; and

D. Those who *did not experience the antecedent* and *did not show the outcome*.

The four cells in Figure 9.2 convey one of the strengths of a prospective design. The design allows one to evaluate whether exposure to TV aggression, in fact, has higher rates of later aggression; but it has many other interesting possibilities. For example, in Cells A and B, we have all of the children exposed to aggressive TV. Some of these children became aggressive later (Cell A) but others did not (Cell B). Comparing these individuals on a host of antecedent conditions may suggest why individuals who are exposed do not develop aggression later. This can be very useful in generating hypotheses about why individuals did not become aggressive in adolescence. Also, we can look at those children who were not exposed to TV violence at all. Some of these children became aggressive anyway (Cell C) but others did not (Cell D). What factors are involved in developing aggression in adolescence among youth who have not been exposed to TV violence? Measures obtained before the outcome that are available in the study may shed light on these questions. I have not elaborated all of the comparisons of interest. Yet, the larger point can be made, namely, that an

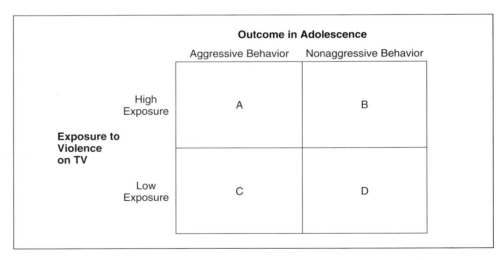

FIGURE 9.2. A hypothetical two-group cohort design in which youths are identified during childhood and assessed on a number of factors. Based on this initial assessment, youths are classified as exposed to aggressive television or not exposed to aggressive television. They are then followed prospectively. Typically, in such research, assessment continues on multiple occasions (every year or few years), but in this example we are considering only Time 2 assessment at some later point in adolescence. In adolescence we assess all cases and classify them at that point on whether they are exhibiting aggressive behavior. The four groups resulting from the design are delineated in the cells.

advantage of a prospective study is evaluation of the rates of onset of some outcome in the cohort of interest and exploration of factors that increase or decrease the likelihood of the outcome, based on comparisons of subgroups who vary on the presence (or degree) of the antecedent condition and the presence (or degree) of the outcome.

As an example, over 800 children born on the island of Kauai in Hawaii in 1955 were included in a single-group cohort study (Werner & Smith, 1982, 1992). Many domains were assessed in infancy (prenatal events, temperament), childhood (social development, school and educational achievement, stress), adolescence (stress, academic performance, criminal behavior), and adulthood (mental health problems, military records, criminal behavior). By their early thirties, 505 cases remained in the sample. Consider a small portion of the findings. One set of findings focused on all youth who were exposed early in life to factors that were associated with later delinquency. These factors included parental conflict, alcohol abuse of a parent, and below normal intellectual functioning. If one considers all such youth at risk, two groups could be delineated at the outcome, namely, those who, in fact, became delinquent and those who did not. This would be equivalent to Cells A and B in Figure 9.2, that is, individuals who were exposed to the risk factors, but who varied in their outcome. A comparison of these groups was completed to identify other factors that might differentiate them. The at-risk group that did *not* become delinquent showed a number of characteristics that seemed to protect them from deleterious influences. They were more likely to be first-born, to be perceived by their mothers as affectionate, to show higher self-esteem and locus of control, and to have alternative caretakers in the family (other than the parents) and a supportive same-sex model who played an important role in their development. (*Protective factor* is the term commonly used to refer to characteristics, events, or experiences that decrease the likelihood of an undesirable outcome among a high-risk group.) The prospective nature of the design, the multiple assessments over an extended period, and the different outcomes for subgroups within the design permit very interesting and important analyses.

A final strength of the cohort designs is that they are good for testing theories about risk, protective, and causal factors. The time line permits evaluation of the different ways in which one variable can influence another. Generating and testing theories of mechanisms in particular are possible in light of the time line of possible mediators that may lead to a later outcome.

With all of the wonderful benefits of prospective cohort designs, why are they not dominant in clinical research? There are weaknesses of prospective longitudinal designs as well (see Table 9.2). First, and foremost, the design can take a considerable time to complete. Depending on the time frame (5 or more years), the designs may not be well suited for addressing questions for which immediate or, indeed, urgent answers are needed (questions related to health, social policy, and welfare). Second, longitudinal studies can be quite costly. The usual costs of personnel are evident in any project, but longitudinal work may require additional costs of special personnel to remain in close contact with the subjects to retain them in the study and multiple payments to subjects and all participants (parents, teachers, children) who provide data or allow the project to go on. Third, if the study is conducted over an extended period (two or more years), many cases can be lost over time (attrition). The potential for selection biases in the remaining sample and obstacles in estimating rates of the outcome are two of the problems that can emerge. The threat and likelihood of attrition are why very special attention is provided to the subjects, and project staff often are needed that are committed just to the retention of subjects. The special attention may include routine phone calls and letters, birthday and holiday cards, newsletters, and reminders about the project throughout the year just to keep the subjects interested or involved. Fourth, it is possible there will be cohort effects. That is something special about when the study was begun and completed that may make the results specific to the group (cohort) that was studied. This is not usually a major detriment in initiating a study but is something to be aware of when discussing the findings.

Finally, the outcome of interest that one wishes to examine (onset of depression, criminal behavior) may have a low base rate in the population. Thus, if one is looking for the onset of criminal behavior, perhaps only 10 percent would be expected to show this in the cohort selected. A sample of 100 cases (e.g., adolescents who seem at risk for criminal behavior) would not be sufficient for the data analyses because of the weak statistical power in detecting 10 cases in the at-risk group. If the 100 cases were divided into at-risk and not-at-risk groups, there might be no difference in the outcome (criminal versus no criminal) because of weak statistical power. A larger sample size is needed, or cases need to be selected that are likely to have a higher base rate of the outcome of interest. (Power is discussed further in Chapter 15.)

CRITICAL ISSUES IN DESIGNING AND INTERPRETING OBSERVATIONAL STUDIES

I have not exhausted all of the variations of case-control and cohort designs (see Hulley & Cummings, 1988). The variations that I have discussed are those most frequently used within psychology. More importantly, the designs convey the scope of questions that can be addressed. The challenge of the designs is isolating the construct of interest and the direction of influence among predictors and outcomes.

Case-control and cohort studies raise special issues to which the investigator ought to be particularly sensitive at the design stage. The issues pertain primarily to the construct validity of the findings, that is, the extent to which the results can be attributed to the construct that the investigator wishes to study. Table 9.3 outlines several interrelated issues pertaining to construct validity.

Specifying the Construct

Level of Specificity of the Construct.   The first issue for the investigator is to specify the construct to study. As basic as this sounds, this can have tremendous implications for interpretation of the findings. Constructs that serve as the impetus for observational studies can vary in their level of specificity. Broad and global variables such as age, sex, social class, and race are less preferred as the basis of an investigation than more specific variables with which these may be associated (patterns of interacting with friends, child-rearing practices, social support patterns). The more specific construct helps move from description of a relation (e.g., that males and females differ) toward explanation (those processes that may explain the differences).

TABLE 9.3.   Critical Issues in Designing and Evaluating Case-Control and Cohort Studies

Specifying the Construct

What is the construct of interest?

What are the operational criteria to separate or delineate groups (the specific measures or selection criteria)?

To what extent is the assessment procedure (criteria, measure) known to reliably separate or select persons with and without the characteristic?

Selecting Groups

From what population, setting, or context (community, clinic) will the index sample be drawn?

If one group is to be compared to another that is selected at the outset of the study, why is this particular control or comparison group the one most suitable for the study? For what influences or constructs is that group intended to control?

Are the groups with and without the characteristic of interest similar on subject and demographic variables (age, sex, race, socioeconomic status)?

Does the comparison group (without the characteristic) share all the characteristics but the one of interest? If not, how are these other characteristics to be evaluated, partialled out, or addressed in the design (additional control group[s] or data analyses)?

Could the construct as described (e.g., depression) be interpreted to reflect a broader construct (having a disturbance, being a patient)?

Direction and Type Influences

Do the results permit conclusions about the time line, that is, that one characteristic of the sample (exposure to an event, some experience) antedates the other?

Do the results permit conclusions about the role that one or more variables play in the outcome (risk factor, causal factor, mediator)?

To illustrate the point, consider for a moment that we are interested in studying the impact of socioeconomic status (SES) on health. SES is a broad variable that encompasses (is related to) a plethora of other variables. SES has been studied extensively, and from this research we have learned that low SES (as measured by income, educational and occupational status) predicts a very large number of untoward mental and physical health outcomes (higher rates of physical and mental illness, earlier death) (Adler et al., 1994; Luthar, 1999). This research has been extremely important. A limitation of the work is that we know very little about the reasons why these effects occur. The construct is very broad and encompasses so many other variables that we now need more specific studies to identify possible bases for the findings.

Some work of this kind has been completed. For example, cohort studies have shown that low SES relates to later psychopathology in children (Dodge, Pettit, & Bates, 1994; Lipman, Offord, & Boyle, 1994). Several factors correlated with SES have been evaluated, including low parent educational attainment, family dysfunction, harsh child-rearing practices, limited parental warmth, single-parent families, peer group instability (e.g., moving to different child-care facilities), lack of cognitive stimulation, and exposure to aggressive behavior (in the home). Each predicts later psychiatric dysfunction in children and partially accounts for the relation between low SES and clinical dysfunction. Even after these factors are taken into account, SES still contributes to the prediction indicating that other factors are operative. Fine-grained analyses have indicated that some of the previously mentioned factors are more highly related to the outcomes than others. For example, harsh-discipline practices on the part of the parents is one of the stronger contributors to later aggressive child behavior (Patterson, Reid, & Dishion, 1992; Dodge et al., 1994). Armed with this finding, we can better theorize about how discipline might be involved in developing aggressive behavior.

As a general guideline, broad constructs—such as socioeconomic status, sex, and minority group status—often serve as a useful point of departure at the beginning of research. However, understanding is likely to be greatly enhanced by moving toward more specific constructs that might explain the processes through which the outcome might occur. On a continuum of description to explanation, research that can move toward the explanation side is usually more informative. In brief, specify the construct of interest and, when possible, hypothesize and test why the differences would occur.

Operationalizing the Construct.   In a study wherein two or more groups are compared (e.g., depressed versus not depressed), operationalizing the criteria to delineate groups raises important issues. What will be the specific criteria to delineate cases from controls? There are many separate issues. In the earlier discussion of single- and multiple-operationism, I noted that different measures may yield different groups. Thus, a self-report measure or clinical rating scale may be used to define individuals as cases in a case-control study. Among the questions, to what extent are the procedures, methods, and measures used to delineate groups valid and in keeping with prior findings? If possible within the design, it is desirable to have more than one operational definition that can be used to delineate groups.

In some areas of research there have been single methods or measures that have been used to classify individuals. As examples, there are standard, single, and frequently used measures to assess marital satisfaction (Dyadic Adjustment Scale), adult psychopathology (Hopkins Symptom Checklist), child abuse (Child Abuse Potential Inventory), conflict and violence between marital partners (Conflict Tactics Scale), and many others (from various subscales of the Minnesota Multiphasic Personality Inventory). In these cases a research tradition and literature have emerged in which one measure has become standard as a way of defining who is a case and who is a control. On the one hand, the fact that one measure has been used in an area so extensively allows the findings to accumulate in a way that permits comparison and accretion of studies. On the other hand, one measure bears some risk, even when the measure is well investigated. The use of a single method of assessing the characteristic or problem (self-report, special format of the measure) may restrict generality of the conclusions across other modalities. For example, self-report of prejudice, alcohol consumption, or marital satisfaction may yield different results from other report or direct observation in the lab.

Regardless of what measure or operational criterion is invoked to classify subjects as cases or controls, we want to be sure that the measure is consistent and accurate in how individuals are classified. If the measure or criterion used to delineate the groups is unreliable, it could be that some of the individuals counted as "depressed" really ended up in the control group, and some of the individuals not identified as depressed ended up in the case or index group. There would be a *diffusion* of the variable (internal validity threat) because both "cases" (individuals with the characteristic) and "controls" (individuals without the characteristic) were inadvertently in both groups instead of being restricted to their respective groups. The unreliability of measures is often surprising. Among the dramatic examples, there is keen interest in research in identifying racial and ethnic differences. One of the dilemmas for research is that there is tremendous unreliability in classifying races (European American, African American, Hispanic American) because there are no standard criteria and no firm biological classification system. When investigators or subjects themselves identify race, the classification can be very unreliable (Betancourt & López, 1993; Beutler et al., 1996). In considering the major or broad classifications of racial differences, obviously the unreliability within a study and across multiple studies will yield very inconsistent findings.

For many variables, reliability of classification does not seem to be a problem because groupings are obvious ("obvious" usually precipitates a severe anxiety reaction among methodologists—I have taken heavy medication just to write these next paragraphs). For example, sex differences are a frequent source of research in biological and social sciences. Sex (being male or female) could be the most obvious classification variable before us (just took some more medication). Sex is not so easily or perfectly classified because by any or most measures there are some males who will be classified as female and females who are classified as males. Visually looking at individuals to make the classification would not work perfectly. Hard-core biological indices (chromosome composition and hormone levels) would not work either (see Blackless et al., 2000).

A brief digression conveys the point in an interesting way. In the Olympic games there has been keen interest in classifying athletes as males or females, in large part to stop male competitors from entering women-only events. Sex testing was introduced into competitive sports in the 1960s after some interesting instances of athletes who competed in such events (e.g., one male who bound his genitals, entered as a woman named Dora [not the same Dora that Freud talked about], and competed in the 1936 Olympics, entering the women's high jump—he placed fourth). Methodologically speaking, assessment is the issue—how to measure sex differences? (Socially, interpersonally, and politically a bunch of other issues emerge.) To redress such instances, and there are others, in the mid and late 1960s women were required to undress before a panel of doctors for international competitions. Other methods were used, such as directly examining an athlete's genital region (so much for self-report measures). At the 1968 Olympics genetic testing was introduced as a less demeaning method (by analyzing for a sex chromatin; this was further modified in a later Olympics that allowed detection of a Y chromosome gene). While such methods were less demeaning, they were hardly flawless. For example, for chromosome testing, some women (approximately 1 in 500 or 600) would show an abnormal result and could be disqualified. There are a number of disorders of sexual differentiation that could lead to aberrant (although quite reliable) results on a measure designed to differentiate sexes. For a few reasons, accuracy being one, the Olympic committee no longer screens for sex differences. The larger methodological point rises above the interest of this example. Although boys and girls and men and women can be distinguished, the classification is not perfect, and merely looking at an individual (visual inspection) is not quite accurate. This discussion also merely refers to gross biological differentiation. When one adds to this, gender identity—or how one conceives of one-self, that is, as more male or female—this becomes a bit more complex.

In cases where there may be unreliability of the measure, sometimes a large sample is assessed and only the extremes of the distribution are considered. For example, on some personality trait, one might assess a large group and for purposes of the study select those who are high ($\geq$ 67th percentile) and compare them to those who are low ($\leq$ 33rd percentile). The rationale is that it is the middle group that is likely to be more unreliably identified because a few points in one direction or the other could move them above or below the median. Selecting extreme groups can be very useful, depending on the goals of the study, but deleting a large segment of the sample (in our example, the middle third) can greatly distort the relations among the measures. The statistics that result (correlations, multiple correlations, beta weights, odds ratios) will be quite different from what would come from using the entire sample. The desirable practice here depends on the question. Sometimes one is interested in talking about and studying only a very special subgroup (e.g., extremely inhibited children), and focusing on a very special group is quite fine.

Selecting Groups

Special Features of the Sample.   Identifying the construct and the means through which it will be assessed usually dictates the sample. Yet, it is useful to distinguish issues related specifically to the sample to draw attention to concerns that can undermine the inferences the investigator wishes to draw. The key question is to ask, "What is the population from which the cases will be drawn?" Among the options are samples from the community, clinic, or other social agency. Cases who are drawn from a clinic or social agency may have special characteristics that make them unrepresentative of the larger community sample. As mentioned previously, these special characteristics may distort the direction or magnitude of the relation between the variables of interest from what it would be like in the community sample. This is a particularly important point to underscore in psychology studies using case-control designs. In epidemiology, where case-control designs flourish, large-scale investigations often are completed that focus on representative and randomly selected cases. For example, representative cases might be identified by sampling from multiple sites to represent the population of interest. Drawing from different geographical areas (of the country) and rural and urban settings, or sampling across different countries, would be examples. Once the areas are selected, random selection may be used by sampling randomly on the basis of streets, neighborhoods, or phone numbers. Invariably, such sampling (like the census) is not perfect (not everyone is home, has a telephone), but the sample is clearly representative of the population within sampling error to the best that research can accomplish.

In psychology's use of case-control and cohort designs, samples are often selected from special settings (clinics, agencies, schools) where some feature about the recruitment process may influence the associations that are studied. For example, if one is interested, say, in studying agoraphobia (fear of open places) and in comparing cases versus controls, the population from which one samples may be critical. Agoraphobics who come to a clinic for treatment may be very special insofar as they have come to a clinic, by whatever means, and that variable alone may contribute to or interact with the results. Agoraphobics referred for treatment may be more severely impaired (or less severely impaired because they could leave their homes to begin with) or more (or less) likely to have additional (comorbid) disorders than agoraphobics in the community who never sought treatment. It is not necessarily the case that one sample is better than another—it depends on the question of the investigator. However, it is important to think about the population in a case-control or cohort study because features of that population may limit the external validity of the results and the construct validity, that is, the basis for group differences between cases and controls.

Selecting Suitable Controls.   In case-control and two-group cohort studies emphasis is given to defining the "case" group, that is, those who have the characteristic or problem of interest. The control or comparison group warrants very careful consideration because it is often this group that limits the study and the kinds of statements the investigator can make. Typically, the investigator is interested in evaluating a special group (depressed patients, children with a specific disease, persons exposed to a special experience, people with interest in methodology) and wishes to make specific statements about this group on a set of dependent measures. The difficulty arises when that special group is compared to a "normal" (community sample) control group. This latter group includes persons who are identified because they do not have the disorder, dysfunction, or special experience. The results invariably show that the special group is different from the "normal" group. Although the interpretation may focus on the special group, the "normal" comparison group is often insufficient to permit specific inferences to be drawn about the special group and the construct of interest.[2]

For example, in a cross-sectional case-control study, the investigators proposed that antisocial youths would show a particular type of personality organization according to object–relations theory (Matthys, Walterbos, Njio, & van Engeland, 1989). Children diagnosed as having conduct disorder, the psychiatric diagnosis for child antisocial and aggressive behavior, were compared with control children from an elementary school. The children wrote various descriptions about other children, adults, and themselves. These descriptions were scored to evaluate personality traits, organization of writing, affective statements, and other characteristics. The results indicated several differences in object–self relations between conduct disorder and control children.

The construct of interest from the independent variable side was conduct disorder and how children with this disorder respond on important measures of personality style. However, the comparison group of "normals" raises interpretive ambiguity. Perhaps any patient group (with any social, emotional, or behavioral problem) would

---

[2]In case-control studies, one usually considers the cases as those individuals showing the problem or characteristic of interest and the controls as not showing that characteristic of interest. The term *normal* is not too meaningful or helpful in this context. Apart from the methodological issue, there is the politically correct and insensitive issue. Use of the term *normal* to describe the control group implies that the group of cases (with the characteristic of interest) is not normal. It is likely that the case group is normal, whatever that is, in all sorts of ways and hence ought not to be characterized by the feature that led to their selection in a particular study.

show the demonstrated pattern. By design, the study does not speak specifically to conduct disorder. Case and control group differences on several variables (child age, proportion of cases living in single-parent homes) might plausibly explain the results. Also, conduct disorder youth were residents of an inpatient setting, whereas controls lived in their own homes. These latter group differences can be ignored for the moment to convey a more subtle point. The selection of a patient sample versus a community sample does not necessarily permit conclusions about the specific dysfunction of the patient sample. The primary conclusion one might draw is that patients and nonpatients differ. To draw more specific statements would require an additional group. A patient group without conduct disorder, added to the design, would permit evaluation of whether object–relations and personality–organization patterns found in the study are specific to conduct disorder. Children with anxiety disorder or attention deficit disorder (but no conduct disorder) would be a great addition to the design and permit a discussion at the end of the study about the hypotheses and constructs of interest to the investigators.

In general, case-control studies require special efforts to isolate the construct of interest. Special attention is required in assessing the construct by making implausible other interpretations that might explain group differences. The selection of groups that vary in the construct of interest, and to the extent possible *only* in the construct of interest, is a critical beginning. Emphasis in developing a study is on identifying the case group, when as much more attention must be given to deciding and finally selecting controls to which cases will be compared.

An excellent example of careful consideration of control conditions is in a study that evaluated characteristics of homeless adults (Toro et al., 1995). Many studies have reported that homeless adults suffer greater impairment and dysfunction than non-homeless adults. Specifically, homeless adults show high levels of psychopathology, substance abuse, criminal behavior, and health problems. A difficulty is that most studies have focused on comparing the homeless to the general population (very much like the comparison in the study noted previously regarding conduct problem children). However, if one is interested in characterizing homelessness and its special contribution to psychopathology, it is important to control for other influences that are likely to be part of, related to, but distinguishable from homelessness. For example, level of poverty ought to be controlled because it would represent a rival interpretation of many prior findings; that is, being poor, whether homeless or not, is likely to be associated with a variety of untoward mental health outcomes (Adler et al., 1994).

In this study homeless adults were compared with individuals who were equally poor but not homeless (and, less relevant to the present point, a third group of individuals who had been, but were not currently, homeless) (Toro et al., 1995). The results indicated that homeless persons showed higher levels of stress, more substance abuse, and victimization from domestic violence, and were more likely to have a history of child abuse, when compared to poor nonhomeless controls. However, differences did not emerge in relation to severe mental illness, physical health symptoms, social support, and social networks. The findings are important in suggesting that when poverty is controlled, a number of differences previously considered to be associated with homelessness may not emerge. The use of a control group permitted conclusions that were more precise (about homelessness) and informative (about poverty). While the homeless need special resources, many of the problems they experience are related to poverty. Any efforts to remediate the problems of the homeless may have much broader relevance to the poor in general. The methodological point is more narrow than these important other implications; the careful attention to the control or comparison group is very important in relation to the inferences that the investigator can draw about the construct.

In many instances the use of community ("normals") controls is the appropriate comparison, depending on the questions the investigator is asking and the specificity of the conclusions he or she wishes to reach about the case sample. Even so, other considerations emerge in relation to the use of "normal" controls in case-control studies. In a study of a particular disorder, cases may be readily identified through an interview or standard questionnaire. Controls may be identified from a community sample and defined as individuals who do not meet criteria for the diagnosis of interest or indeed for any diagnosis. Excluding individuals from the group of controls based on diagnostic information is fine; however, it is important to bear in mind that "normals" have a significant amount of clinical dysfunction. Individuals sampled from the community—whether children, adolescents, or adults—show relatively high rates (approximately 20 percent) of psychopathology (Robins et al., 1984; US Congress, 1991). Thus, sampling individuals from the community to serve as a control will inevitably include some individuals with clinical dysfunction. This may or may not be important to consider in the screening criteria used for controls. Again, it is important for the investigator to consider quite precisely what purpose the control group is to serve and to make sure, to the extent possible, the selection criteria that are invoked address the specific issues the investigator has in mind.

Possible Confounds.   A critical issue is that there may be variables that are possibly confounded with the selection criterion for delineating groups. Some effort has to be made within the study to address these other variables and their role in differentiating groups. If confounding variables are not evaluated, conclusions will be reached that the primary variable was the basis of the findings.

Confounds can be addressed in several ways—some from the design of the experiment and some from the data analyses. From the standpoint of the design, groups (e.g., in a case-control study) can be matched on variables that could confound the group differences. For example, one might compare teen mothers and female teenagers who do not have children. Any group differences on a set of dependent measures might be due to the differences in being a mother. Obviously, other characteristics may differ between the groups. Prominent examples would be SES and educational achievement, which are known to be related to early teen pregnancy. How can one rule out SES and educational achievement rather than motherhood as an explanation of the results?

One can match mothers and nonmothers on potentially confounding influences. A dilemma is that if groups are equalized or matched on such variables, the investigator cannot evaluate the impact of these variables in differentiating groups. Matching on a set of variables has to be decided on the basis of the purpose of the study, that is, whether one wishes to hold one variable constant so that others can be evaluated, or whether one wishes to identify the range of predictors that delineate groups. From the standpoint of the design it is often useful to make the comparison with the confounds present (compare all the mothers and nonmothers) to see what the differences are. Then it is useful to compare the mothers with a matched subsample (within the study) of nonmothers where the confounding differences (SES, education) are controlled. Thus, a comparison might be mothers with just those other nonmothers in the sample who are matched for SES and education. The logic of this is very much like the prior example in the investigation of homeless adults. A great deal of research has shown how homeless and nonhomeless individuals differ. But most of these studies did not control for a huge confounding influence, namely, poverty. Additional comparison of homeless with nonhomeless individuals who are equally poor led to more precise findings. Similarly, in a single study one might wish to make the gross comparison—in our example, teen mothers and nonmothers. This can be followed by evaluation of subgroups wherein the confounds are controlled by selecting a subset of nonmothers matched in the characteristics one wishes to control.

Data-analytic strategies play a major role in evaluating potential confounds. The goal of data analyses usually is to identify whether the variable of interest makes a contribution to the outcome independently of the confounding variable(s). Analysis of the role of the confounding variable may be of interest as well to assess whether it contributes to the outcome on its own or only because of its association with the primary variable of interest. For example, if one is interested in comparing parents who physically abuse their children with parents who do not, it is possible that other variables (education, SES) will also distinguish the groups. At the end of the study, the investigator wishes to talk about abuse, when in fact powerful confounding variables may be the basis for the differences. Statistical adjustments for possible confounding variables can be made (partial correlations, analyses of covariance) to consider confounding variables individually or as a group. Also, regression analyses can be completed (hierarchical regression, logistic regression) to test individual predictors (primary variable, confounding) in relation to the outcome.

Statistical analyses (path analyses, structural equation modeling) are tools to evaluate the relations. It is useful to precede statistical analyses with a conceptual model of the relation among variables that are being assessed. Conceptual models can specify the relations of constructs to each other (education, SES, abuse practices) and in relation to the outcome. For example, in the hypothetical example of teen mothers versus females of the same age who are not mothers, the models can test whether education and SES make separate contributions to the outcome, whether their influence is direct or indirect (through some other variable), and the relative contribution (strength of the relations among different variables). Testing a model to evaluate multiple variables is an excellent way to handle potentially confounding variables. The reason is that "confound" is a relative concept—that is, the main variable and potential confound in *my* study (e.g., SES and diet, respectively) may be the confound and main variable, respectively, in *your* study. If the issue is to understand multiple influences on an outcome and how they work together, use of models to explain the interrelations among influences is an excellent design strategy.

Time Line and Causal Inferences

A critical issue in case-control research pertains to the time line and type of inferences that are drawn. One of the hazards the investigator must consider is to keep the conclusions in line with what the design can demonstrate. The most common problem is to imply a causal relation when the design does not permit comments about the time line. Consider as an example a cross-sectional case-control study. The outcome of interest (grouping variable) may be an anxiety disorder in children (present or not), and the other characteristic (hypothesized antecedent) may be family stress. Children and their parents are assessed on a single occasion and complete various measures of child anxiety and family stress. The results may indicate that children who show the outcome (anxiety disorder cases), compared to those who do not (no-disorder controls), come from families that are more highly stressed. Clearly, the study demonstrates a correlation between two variables. The theory underlying the study may pose a directional relation in which family stress occurs before child dysfunction and through some process makes the child vulnerable, so that new stressors manifest themselves in anxiety. Actually, the results are consistent with hypotheses in either direction: stress as an antecedent to anxiety or anxiety as an antecedent to stress. In the absence of other evidence, this study does not establish stress as a risk factor for anxiety.

Statistical analyses commonly used in this type of research (discriminant analysis, logistic regression, structural equation modeling) may inadvertently contribute to the view that one variable precedes the other. The language of many data-analytic strategies identifies some variables as *predictors* or independent variables (e.g., family stress) and others as *outcomes* or dependent variables (e.g., presence or absence of anxiety disorder). Also, computer printouts may have fancy lines and arrows to imply that one construct leads to another. The data analyses make no assumption of a time line for the variables that are entered; the distinction between antecedent (independent) and outcome (dependent), from the standpoint of the steps (discriminant function) of the analyses, is arbitrary. Clearly, the statistics are not at fault, but it is easy to misinterpret the results. The language used in reporting results often exacerbates the misunderstanding. In our example, a typical conclusion might be worded that, "Family stress *predicted* child anxiety disorder" [discriminant function], or "Family stress *increased the risk of* child anxiety disorder" [logistic regression]. Such communications could be mistaken to suggest that family stress came first in the family stress–child anxiety sequence and even perhaps had a causal role in anxiety.

Although the example is hypothetical, the problem is not. There are many instances within clinical psychology wherein concurrent correlates from cross-sectional case control studies are taken to imply that one condition is an antecedent to another. For example, one interpretation of unipolar depression is that the disorder emerges as a result of negative cognitions about oneself, the world, and the future (negative triad) (Beck, Rush, Shaw, & Emery, 1979). When studied in cross-sectional designs, the results show that, in fact, the cognitions and depression often go together. These findings are taken as support for the conceptual model of a temporal ordering of cognitions preceding—and, indeed, leading to—depression. Yet, prospective, longitudinal studies suggest that the negative triad may emerge with, rather than precede, depression (see Barnett & Gotlib, 1988; Lewinsohn, Steinmetz, Larson, & Franklin, 1981). This does not detract from the findings relating cognitions to depression, but it does show that it is important to note that by just changing one letter in the word, we can move from *casual* thinking to *causal* thinking.

Misleading inferences about the time line are often drawn from retrospective studies. For example, several studies have focused on the extent to which the experience of sexual abuse in childhood places individuals at risk for untoward mental health outcomes in adulthood (see Wyatt & Powell, 1988). Retrospective, case-control designs are used by identifying adults who have been abused and comparing them to controls who have not. Retrospective assessment (interviews, questionnaires) is used to identify the onset, nature, type, duration, and other characteristics of sexual abuse (the antecedents), by asking adults to recall earlier experiences. Findings have been fairly consistent in showing that adults who report early sexual abuse, compared to matched clinic or community controls who do not, have higher rates or greater degrees of depression, sleep disorder, sexual dysfunction, and substance use and abuse (Briere & Runtz, 1988; Stein, Golding, Siegel, Burnam, & Sorenson, 1988). The conclusion explicitly drawn in such studies is that early sexual abuse is a risk factor for many untoward consequences.

Although the conclusions might be correct (child abuse may lead to or is associated with later problems), consider plausible rival interpretations. First, it is possible that clinical dysfunction *preceded* sexual abuse. Individuals with dysfunction very early in life might have a higher base rate of being abused. However, persons may not recall the time sequence in that way. Second, persons with greater current dysfunction may be more likely to report abuse when it did not happen or to attribute their problems to the experience of abuse when it did. People with little or no dysfunction may be less likely to report the same type of events that people with more dysfunction would recall as abusive. Third, perhaps those who have been abused but who *cannot recall* the experience (due to forgetting, dissociation, repression) are less likely to show symptoms. These persons would not be selected for inclusion as index cases because they have little or no dysfunction and/or have abuse in their past but do not recall that abuse. These are only some of many possibilities that must be considered in interpreting the results of retrospective studies based on self- or other report. This is a good example where the retrospective study is extremely valuable in generating causal hypotheses, but where a prospective study is likely to be needed to provide the critical test.

General Comments

Case-control designs and their variations permit evaluation of many variations of human characteristics and experiences that cannot be readily studied experimentally. The designs are not inherently weak because they are observational, rather than experimental. Indeed, major advances in medicine, health, and nutrition, as just a few exemplary areas (risk factors for heart disease, various forms of cancer, impact of fats in one's diet) have emerged from such studies. The thinking and methodological sophistication of the investigator must be particularly acute with observational designs. Ingenuity of the investigator in selecting cases and controls and in data-analytic strategies that might be used to partial out influences are particularly important. Most courses in methodology and research design in psychology do not include observational designs and their many options. This is unfortunate because the designs are often used in published research within clinical, counseling, and educational psychology. Of course, the main task of the investigator in observational or experimental research is essentially the same, namely, to decide in advance of the study precisely what he or she wishes to conclude. The precision of the statements one wishes to make determines key features of sampling, group formation, the design, and data analyses. In observational research some threats to validity, such as subject selection (internal and external validity) and interpretation of the relation between the independent and dependent variables (construct validity), emerge in ways that differ from their equivalent in experimental studies.

This chapter has focused on observational designs because of their frequent use in clinical research. The designs were treated at length to give attention to the many issues that can emerge in their execution and interpretation. It is important to note, in passing, that observational and experimental research can be combined in a single study. One might hypothesize that two groups of individuals (new criminal offenders versus career criminals; or new methodologists versus career methodologists) will respond differently to an experimental manipulation (e.g., a task that is designed to induce empathy). The study is both observational (cases, controls) and experimental (manipulation provided to one-half of the cases and one-half of the controls), and forms a 2 × 2 factorial design. Factorial designs are a convenient way to combine different types of variables and now, in this context, a way of combining different types of designs. I mention the designs again only to avoid the impression that research is *either* experimental or observational.

SUMMARY AND CONCLUSIONS

In observational studies the investigator evaluates the variables of interest by selecting groups rather than experimentally manipulating the variable of interest. The goals of the research are to demonstrate associations among variables, but these associations may move beyond correlations to causal relations. The studies can be descriptive and exploratory, by trying to assess the scope of characteristics that may be associated with a particular problem, or theoretically driven, by trying to test models that explain the characteristics and how different influences relate to each other and to the outcome.

Case-control studies were identified and include those investigations in which groups that vary in the outcome or characteristic of interest are delineated. Typically, two groups are compared (e.g., depressed and nondepressed patients) to evaluate a range of characteristics that may be evident currently (cross-sectional case-control study) or may have occurred in the past (retrospective case-control study). These designs are extremely valuable in understanding characteristics associated with a particular outcome, in unraveling the patterns of multiple influences and their relations, and in delineating subtypes by showing distinctions among individuals who have experienced the outcome (e.g., types of depression among the depressed group). A limitation of these designs is that they do not permit strong influences to be drawn about what led to the outcome of interest.

Cohort studies are quite useful in delineating the time line, that is, that some conditions are antecedent to and, in fact, predict occurrence of the outcome. In a single-group cohort design, a group that has not yet experienced the outcome of interest is assessed on multiple occasions and followed over time. At a later assessment, subgroups are delineated as those who do or do not show the outcome of interest. Analyses can then identify what antecedents predicted the outcome. Although a cohort study may begin with a single group, sometimes two or more groups are studied (multigroup cohort design) to evaluate their outcomes. In this case individuals may be selected because they show a characteristic but will be followed to examine yet another outcome. In some cases multiple cohorts of different ages may begin the study and be followed over time (accelerated, multicohort longitudinal design). The goal is to chart a particular developmental course over an extended period by drawing on different groups to sample portions of that period.

Case-control and cohort designs provide very powerful research strategies. The designs address a range of questions pertaining to how variables operate to produce an outcome (mediators, mechanisms) and the characteristics (moderators) that influence whether and for whom a particular outcome occurs. The designs have been developed in other disciplines (epidemiology and public health) but are used increasingly in clinical psychology and related disciplines. The designs require special attention to ensure construct validity of the results, that is, that the conclusions can be attributed to the constructs the investigator has in mind, rather than to other influences. Critical issues in designing and interpreting observational studies were discussed, including the importance of specifying the construct that will guide the study, selecting case and control groups, addressing possible confounds in the design and data analyses, and drawing causal inferences.

KEY CONCEPTS AND TERMS

Birth-Cohort Study	Cohort Design
Case-Control Design	Prospective Study
Cohort	Retrospective Study

FOR FURTHER READING

Hulley, S.B., & Cummings, S.R. (Eds.) (1988). *Designing clinical research: An epidemiologic approach*. Baltimore, MD: Williams & Wilkins.

Magnusson, D., Bergman, L.R., Gudinger, G., & Torestad, B. (1991). *Problems and methods in longitudinal research*. New York: Cambridge University Press.

Schlesselman, J.J. (1982). *Case-control studies: Design, conduct, and analysis*. New York: Oxford University Press.

Tohen, M., Bromet, E., Murphy, J.M., & Tsuang, M.T. (2000). Psychiatric epidemiology. *Harvard Review of Psychiatry, 8*, 111–125.

Verhulst, F.C., & Koot, H.M. (1992). *Child psychiatric epidemiology: Concepts, methods, and findings*. Newbury Park, CA: Sage.

Chapter 10

The Case Study and Single-Case Research Designs

Traditionally, psychology has focused upon experimentation with groups of individuals and has reached conclusions about important variables on the basis of group differences. Laws based upon group analyses provide general statements that apply to many individuals on average. Yet, research design refers broadly to an approach toward evaluating phenomena and establishing valid inferences, and there is nothing inherent in the approach that requires groups. Perhaps even more cogent, findings obtained with groups are not necessarily more generalizable than those obtained with the individual case, a strong claim to which I will return. Evaluation and valid inferences can be readily accomplished with the individual subject or single case. Illustrations can be provided from virtually every branch of psychology where the individual subject has provided important information, as reflected in such diverse topics as memory, animal behavior, cognitive development in children, language, and psychopathology, among others (Bolgar, 1965; Dukes, 1965). A long tradition within clinical and experimental research advocates the use of systematic research methods to study the individual (Chassan, 1967; Shapiro, 1966; Skinner, 1957). Beyond psychology, other disciplines (psychiatry, education, rehabilitation, anthropology, and business) have used the study of cases to advance knowledge (see Yin, 1994).

The case study is a generic term that indicates a focus on the individual, and depending on the discipline, that can be an individual person, group, culture, and so on. Within clinical and counseling psychology the term has been used mostly to refer to an uncontrolled and *anecdotal case study* from which valid inferences cannot be drawn. The case study can be much more than these somewhat loose descriptions of the individual and can serve as the basis for drawing causal inferences (Sechrest, Stewart, Stickle, & Sidani, 1996). The uncontrolled case study serves as an important backdrop for experimental methods with the single case. Also, the case study is interesting from the standpoint of empirical knowledge. It is easy to identify instances in which a case study does not permit any rigorous inferences at all; and, indeed, the history of clinical psychology and psychiatry is strewn with extremely fascinating cases from which few inferences can really be drawn about what happened, why, and how. The contribution of fascinating but otherwise weak cases has been to generate theory and hypotheses rather than to provide strong empirical tests. However, case studies can contribute to knowledge and can be more rigorous than the descriptions of fascinating stories that have emerged in the history of psychotherapy.

At the other extreme from loose descriptions are single-case experimental designs.[1] The unique feature of these designs is the capacity to conduct true experiments with the single case, that is, one subject. The designs can evaluate—and often have evaluated—the effects of interventions with large groups. As we shall see, the logic of the designs pertains to how data are collected and how the intervention is presented, rather than the number of cases that are studied. In this chapter and the next, methodologies of studying the individual and the criteria for drawing inferences are elaborated. The focus will be on methodologies for experimental and quasi-experimental research.

---

[1]In psychological research the designs have been referred to by different terms, such as intra-subject–replication designs, $N = 1$ research, and intensive designs, to mention a few. Each of the terms to describe the designs is partially misleading. For example, the terms single-case and $N = 1$ designs imply that only one subject is included. Yet, a number of subjects and entire communities and cities have been included in some single-case designs (Kazdin, 2001a). The term intrasubject is a useful term because it implies that the methodology focuses on performance of the same person over time. Yet, this term, too, is partially misleading because some of the designs depend on looking at the effects of interventions across (i.e., between) subjects. The term intensive design has not grown out of the tradition of single-case research and is used infrequently. Also, the term intensive has the unfortunate connotation that the investigator is working intensively to study the subject, which probably is true but is beside the point. The term single-case designs has been adopted here to draw attention to the unique feature of the designs, that is, the capacity to conduct empirical research with individual subjects, and because this term enjoys the widest use. (Of course, in emphasizing *single* cases, it is important to bear in mind that these designs can be used for *married* cases as well.)

THE CASE STUDY

The case study encompasses quite diverse practices and foci, when one considers the application across diverse disciplines (see Sechrest et al., 1996). There are some general commonalities or characteristics that define what a case study is, and these are highlighted in Table 10.1. As noted there, the case study refers to the intensive study of the individual. However, this could be an individual person, group, institution (e.g., political body), or society. That these are "cases" pertains to the intensive focus on one or a few instances. Obviously, in clinical psychology the focus is on individual clients. The intensive focus reflects the concept that detailed description is provided to convey multiple levels and contextual influences that might be operative. One thinks of research as efforts to simplify the situation by isolating variables to avoid confounding influences and by operationalizing key constructs so their definitions are clear, restricted, and easily understood. Indeed, in research there is always the risk of defining something so carefully and narrowly (e.g., an operational definition of self-esteem based on a questionnaire) that one can distort the larger phenomenon one wishes to discuss at the end of the study. Case studies focus on the complexity and usually make an effort to illustrate the details fully and richly. Consequently, narratives, lengthy descriptions, and prose, rather than scores on measures, usually constitute the main method of evaluation.

In clinical psychology and other mental health professions, the focus usually is on the individual client, often in the context of therapy. Information is reported about the case that is based on anecdotal information, that is, unsystematic measurement that is difficult to replicate or verify. A clinician or client recounts experiences and places the information together in a cohesive narrative that explains how a clinical problem developed, why the individual is like he or she is, why and how treatment worked, and similar issues.

Many things are a matter of degree, and case studies fit this well. It is quite possible to have a case study that is methodologically rotten but utterly persuasive and even replicable. It is also possible to have a well-controlled group experiment that is "methodologically wonderful but utterly rotten" (quoting again from my dissertation

TABLE 10.1.   Major Characteristics of Case Studies

- The intensive study of the individual. However, this could be an individual person, family, group, institution, state, country, or other level that can be conceived as a unit
- The information is richly detailed, usually in narrative form rather than as scores on dependent measures
- Efforts are made to convey the complexity and nuances of the case (contexts, influence of other people, special or unique features that may apply just to this case)
- Information is often retrospective; past influences are used to account for some current situation, but one begins with the current situation

Note: Among diverse sciences, case studies have taken many different forms, so that exceptions to the above characteristics can be readily found. The focus of this chapter is on case studies as they have been commonly used in psychology, psychiatry, social work, criminology, and related areas. For a broad and comprehensive view of case studies, see Sechrest et al. (1996).

committee) in its contribution. Consequently, I shall make but also blur distinctions about the case study and research to help convey the conditions under which inferences can be drawn from studying the individual. It is possible to be able to infer little or nothing from the study of the individual or to draw very strong causal statements.

The Value of the Case Study

The lack of controlled conditions and failure to use measures that are objective (replicable, reliable, valid) have limited the traditional case study as a research tool. Yet, the naturalistic and uncontrolled characteristics also have made the case a unique source of information that complements and contributes to theory, research, and practice. Case studies, even without serving as formal research, have made important contributions. First, case study has served as a *source of ideas and hypotheses* about human performance and development. For example, case studies from quite different conceptual views, such as psychoanalysis and behavior therapy (e.g., case of Little Hans [Freud, 1933]; case of Little Albert [Watson & Rayner, 1920]), were remarkably influential in suggesting how fears might develop and in advancing theories of human behavior that would support these views.

Second, case studies have frequently served as the *source for developing therapy techniques*. Here, too, remarkably influential cases within psychoanalysis and behavior therapy might be cited. In the 1880s the treatment of a young woman (Anna O.) with several hysterical symptoms (Breuer & Freud, 1957) marked the inception of the "talking cure" and cathartic method in psychotherapy. Within behavior therapy, development of treatment for a fearful boy (Peter), followed by evaluation of a large number of different treatments to eliminate fears among children (Jones, 1924a, 1924b), exerted great influence in suggesting several different interventions, many of which remain in use in some form in clinical practice.

Third, case studies permit the *study of rare phenomena*. Many problems seen in treatment or of interest may be so infrequent as to make evaluation in group research impossible. The individual client with a unique problem or situation can be studied intensively with the hope of uncovering material that may shed light on the development of the problem as well as effective treatment. For example, the study of multiple personality—in which an individual manifests two or more different patterns of personality, emotions, thoughts, and behaviors—has been elaborated greatly by the case study. A prominent illustration is the well-publicized report of the "three faces of Eve" (Thigpen & Cleckley, 1954, 1957). The intensive study of Eve revealed quite different personalities, mannerisms, gait, psychological test performance, and other characteristics of general demeanor. The analysis at the level of the case provided unique information not accessible from large-scale group studies. The fact that the investigators were systematic in collecting a range of objective measures made this novel and quite informative.

Fourth, the case is valuable in *providing a counterinstance* for notions that are considered to be universally applicable. For example, in such traditional forms of treatment as psychoanalysis, treatment of overt symptoms was discouraged, based on the notion that neglect of motivational and intrapsychic processes presumed to underlie dysfunction would be ill-advised if not ineffective. Without treating the supposed (but never demonstrated) "underlying cause," there might be other symptoms that emerge. This was referred to as *symptom substitution*. Yet, repeated case demonstrations that overt symptoms could be effectively treated without the emergence of substitute symptoms cast doubt on the original caveat (see Kazdin, 1982b). Although a case can cast doubt upon a general proposition, it does not itself allow affirmative claims of a very general nature to be made. By showing a counterinstance, the case study does provide a qualifier about the generality of the statement. With repeated cases, each showing a similar pattern, the applicability of the original general proposition is increasingly challenged.

Finally, case studies have *persuasive and motivational value*. From a methodological standpoint, uncontrolled case studies generally provide a weak basis for drawing inferences. However, this point is often academic. Even though cases may not provide strong causal knowledge on methodological grounds, a case study often provides a dramatic and persuasive demonstration and makes concrete and poignant what might otherwise serve as an abstract principle. Seeing is believing even though philosophy and psychology teach us that perception is a shaky basis of knowledge and that believing influences seeing. Cases may be especially convincing because of the way anecdotal information is compiled to convey a particular point. The absence of objective measures or details that might be inconsistent often convey unqualified support for a particular belief.

Another reason that cases are often so dramatic is that they are usually selected systematically to illustrate a particular point. Presumably, cases selected randomly from all those available would not illustrate the dramatic type of change that typically is evident in the particular case provided by an author. This point can be readily illustrated by merely referring to advertisements for fad diets or exercise devices. Typically, such advertisements show "before and after" photographs of someone who has completed the recommended program. The case is used to illustrate the "miraculous" effects of the program and may show someone who has lost 50 pounds, supposedly after being on the program for only 10 minutes. Even if the illustrated case were accurately presented, it is likely to be so highly selected as not to represent the reaction of most individuals to the program. Nevertheless, the selection of extreme cases does not merely illustrate a point, but rather often compels us to believe in causal relations that reason and data would refute.

The example of obesity conveys well what might be the four main functions that case studies often serve, namely, to inform, intrigue, inspire, and incite (Sechrest et al., 1996). Seen in this context, there is nothing like a case to convey the points, to provoke thought, to motivate others, and to move to action. It is not that the case will invariably accomplish any of these, but they often do so better than a wonderful finding from a study with a large *N* and excellent controls. Large studies may not accomplish what a well-placed case can do. Indeed, a possible failing of science is to take findings and translate them in such a way that they might have broader influence (e.g., on health), and case studies might be a more systematic part of that translation effort.

As noted earlier, case studies often have been the basis for developing specific therapeutic techniques as well as hypotheses about the nature of clinical disorders. Successful applications of a treatment technique at the case level can be very persuasive to the therapist–investigator, but the persuasive appeal here is a mixed blessing. Often a case is so convincing that writers frequently fail to maintain scientific restraint as they evaluate the specific findings. On the other hand, rigorous endorsement of a position usually stimulates research by others who test and critically evaluate the claims based previously on only anecdotal information. Thus, the very persuasiveness of a case study may lend it heuristic value. Because cases often provide dramatic and concrete examples, they often stimulate investigation of a phenomenon. Empirical research can put to the test the claims made previously on the basis of case studies alone.

Illustrations

Case studies can be quite useful. Indeed, even the single aspect of generating hypotheses for research would make the case study quite valuable. In clinical psychology a few dominant anecdotal case studies (e.g., some of the key cases of Freud) have become classics in the mental health professions. These and others of their ilk are not strong demonstrations of the case because of the anecdotal assessment, likelihood of selective reporting, and optimal bias that these foster. The cases make wonderful sense and are cohesive. In many instances in-depth analyses refute or undermine the very basis for presenting the case.

For example, recall the case from the 1880s in which Joseph Breuer (1842–1925), a Viennese physician and collaborator of Sigmund Freud (1856–1939), treated Anna O. (Breuer & Freud, 1957). Anna was 21 years old at the time and had several symptoms, including paralysis and loss of sensitivity of the limbs, lapses in awareness, distortions of sight and speech, headaches, and a persistent nervous cough. These symptoms were considered to be due to anxiety rather than to medical or physical problems. As Breuer talked with Anna and used a little hypnosis, she recalled early events in her past and discussed the circumstances associated with the onset of each symptom. As these recollections were made, the symptoms disappeared. This case has had enormous effect and is credited with marking the beginning of the "talking cure" and cathartic method of psychotherapy. We have no really systematic information about the case, what happened, and whether and when the symptoms changed. Also, the case provides an odd basis for the development or effectiveness of talk therapy. For one, talk therapy was combined with hypnosis and rather heavy doses of medication (chloral hydrate, a sleep-inducing agent), which was used on several occasions and when talk did not seem to work (see Dawes, 1994). Thus, the therapy was hardly just talk and, indeed, whether talk had any impact cannot really be discerned. Also, the outcome of Anna O.—including her subsequent hospitalization—raises clear questions about the effectiveness of the combined talk-hypnosis-medication treatment. Cases such as these, while powerful, engaging, and persuasive, do not permit inferences about what happened and why.

There are more compelling instances that show what a case can do under better circumstances than the literary pen of a clinician. The well-known case of Phineas Gage is a better example of what an uncontrolled case study can show (Macmillan, 2000). Mr. Gage was a 25-year-old man working on the railroad (in Vermont) and was going to use an explosive to fracture a rock. An accident occurred and caused a large metal bar (tamping iron, 3 ft, 7 in. long) to blast entirely through his skull and to land some 20 meters away (for photos and further details of the story, see www.hbs. deakin.edu.au/gagepage). A physician who treated Mr. Gage within 90 minutes of the accident recorded that he spoke rationally and described what had happened. Follow-up of the case indicated that his personality had changed. Prior to the accident, he was regarded as capable, well balanced, and very efficient as a foreman. After the accident, he was impatient, obstinate, grossly profane, and showed little deference to others. Also, he seemed to lose his ability to plan for the future. His friends noted he was no longer like the person they knew.

This was a tragic experiment in nature that has become a classic case within neuropsychology. The case is used to reflect the impact of an intervention on cognitive and personality functioning. The case is compelling because of the abruptness and scope of the accident, so that the causal agent is fairly clear. Also, permanent changes seemed to be induced by the accident, so that other influences were not likely. Later we shall discuss the role of the latency between an intervention and change as a way of drawing inferences about cause in case studies and in clinical work. The conditions of Mr. Gage made drawing inferences from the case the clearest one can expect without formal investigation.

Case studies have played a strong role in elaborating the relation of brain and behavior. The reason is that a variety of special injuries, diseases, and interventions occur that cannot be induced experimentally. As these are carefully documented, one can see affect, cognitive, and behavioral functioning over time, and whether and what consequences result. For example, in one case a young boy had one half of his brain (one hemisphere) removed as part of treatment to control epilepsy. Tracking his development over the course of childhood revealed that several functions thought to be specific to the lost hemisphere were developed. The boy was functioning well in several spheres (academic, language learning), all of which were reasonably well documented (Battro, 2001). This suggests the brain's ability to compensate and how training can overcome significant deficits.

The careful assessment of a case can make the results quite persuasive. For example, a recent report of a 25-year-old man with a stroke revealed that he had damage to specific areas of the brain (insula and putamen) suspected to be responsible for the emotion of disgust (Calder, Keane, Manes, Antoun, & Young, 2000). The damage could be carefully documented (by fMRI [functional magnetic resonance imaging]) and hence shows an advance in specification of the assault in comparison to the Phineas Gage example noted previously. His damage could be located to these areas. The man was systematically tested, during which he observed photos of people experiencing different emotions (happiness, fear, anger, sadness, and surprise). He had no difficulty identifying these emotions. However, he could not identify the photos of disgust. Disgusting photos or ideas presented to him (such as friends who change underwear once a week or feces-shaped chocolate [remember, I am just the messenger here; I am not making this up]) were also difficult to identify as disgusting. This is an interesting example because the case was systematically evaluated, and hence the strengths of the inferences are commensurately increased. Also, the investigators compared this case to male and female control subjects without brain injury to provide a baseline on each of the tasks. The demonstration becomes even more interesting by falling somewhere between a case study and a case-control design.

Limitations of the Case Study

The purpose of highlighting a few case studies outside of clinical psychology is to convey that what one learns as the typical anecdotal and uncontrolled case study is not the only option. Rigor can be introduced in varying degrees and, indeed, the case can yield quite useful and powerful information. The conditions and methodological features that would accomplish this have been very nicely described elsewhere (Sechrest et al., 1996).

In clinical work the usual way in which cases are described leads to their many limitations. First, case reports rely heavily on anecdotal information in which clinical judgment and interpretation play a major role. Many inferences are based upon reports of the clients; these reports are the "data" upon which interpretations are made. The client's reconstructions of the past (remembered events from one's past, particularly those laden with emotion) are likely to be distorted and highly selective. To this is added interpretation and judgment of the therapist in which unwitting (but normal human) biases operate to weave a coherent picture of the client's predicament and the change of events leading to the current situation. The reports may have little bearing upon what actually happened to the client in the past. Unless subjective accounts are independently corroborated, they could be completely unreliable. Many case reports give the appearance of literary descriptions of stories rather than scientific investigations, not merely because of the style of writing but also because of the type of information made available.

Second, many alternative explanations usually are available to account for the current status of the individual other than those provided by the clinician. Indeed, virtually all of the basic threats to internal validity can be applied to the anecdotal case. The basic information provided in case studies often can be seriously challenged. Postdictive or retrospective accounts try to reconstruct early events and show how they invariably led to contemporary functioning. Although such accounts frequently are persuasive, they are scientifically indefensible. Many events in the individual's past might have accounted for contemporary functioning other than those highlighted by the clinician or client. More important, there is no way to test a hypothesis with the usual case report to assess the causal events in the past.

Third, a major concern about the information derived from a case study is the generalizability to other individuals or situations. Scientific research attempts to establish general "laws" of behavior that hold without respect to the identity of any individual. It is possible that the individual case will reflect marked or unique characteristics and not provide widely generalizable findings. The absence of standardized or replicable procedures to evaluate the case makes replication of the study often difficult. Hence, knowledge about several potentially similar cases is difficult to achieve.

Sometimes several cases may be studied as a basis for drawing general conclusions beyond the individual. Although each case is studied individually, the information may be aggregated in an attempt to reveal relations that have broad generality. For example, the development of psychiatric diagnosis, which is concerned with the identification of psychological disorders, was greatly advanced by Kraepelin (1855–1926), a German psychiatrist. He identified specific "disease" entities or psychological disorders by systematically collecting thousands of case studies on hospitalized psychiatric patients. He described the history of each patient, the onset of the disorder, and its outcome. From this extensive clinical material he elaborated various types of "mental illness" and provided a general model for contemporary approaches to psychiatric diagnosis (Zilboorg & Henry, 1941).

When individual cases are aggregated, the resulting information may be more convincing than information obtained from a single case. Conclusions drawn from several individuals seem to rule out the possibility of idiosyncratic findings characteristic of one case. Yet, the extent to which information from many combined cases can be informative depends upon several factors, such as the manner in which the observations were made (anecdotal reports versus standardized measures), the number of cases, the clarity of the relationship, and the possibility that the individuals studied were selected in a biased fashion. Generally the accumulation of cases provides a better basis for drawing inferences than an individual case. However, the number of subjects is not the critical dimension. Rather, assessment and design of the demonstration determine the extent to which valid inferences can be drawn.

In clinical psychology and other mental health-related disciplines, the accumulation of multiple cases is common among persons involved in clinical practice. The absence of objective measurement has made difficult the codification and utilization of this experience as part of the knowledge base. Even so, aggregated experience among professionals involved in practice occasionally reveals consistencies in beliefs about factors that contribute to treatment and therapeutic change (Kazdin, Siegel, & Bass, 1990). Consensus based on experience does not substitute for demonstrated findings. However, the information provides important leads to be pursued in research.

The case study serves an important function in clinical and counseling psychology and has provided leads for theory, research, and practice. Yet, from a methodological standpoint, the traditional, anecdotal case study raises several problems because of the lack of experimental control techniques to determine what actually accounted for the client's performance or functioning. Single cases can be studied rigorously in true and quasi-experiments to address and make implausible the various threats to validity. The next section elaborates true experiments to convey the logic and practices they entail. The next chapter elaborates approximations of these that are especially useful for clinical work.

SINGLE-CASE EXPERIMENTAL DESIGNS: KEY CHARACTERISTICS

Single-case experiments are at the opposite end of a dimension of rigor when contrasted with the anecdotal case study. As true experiments, single-case designs can demonstrate causal relations and can rule out or make implausible threats to validity with the same elegance of group research. The underlying rationale of single-case experimental designs is similar to that of the more familiar group designs. All experiments compare the effects of different conditions (independent variables) on performance. In traditional group experimentation the comparison is made between groups of subjects who are treated differently. Based on random assignment to conditions, some subjects are designated to receive a particular intervention and others are not. The effect of the intervention is evaluated by comparing the performance of the different groups. In single-case research, inferences are usually made about the effects of the intervention by comparing different conditions presented to the same subject over time. Key characteristics of single-case experiments permit one to draw inferences about the effects of intervention. These are highlighted in Table 10.2 and elaborated here.

Continuous Assessment

The most fundamental design requirement of single-case experimentation is the reliance on repeated observations of performance over time. The client's performance is observed on several occasions, usually before the intervention is applied and continuously over the period while the intervention is in effect. Typically, observations are conducted on a daily basis or at least on multiple occasions each week. These observations allow the investigator to examine the pattern and stability of performance. The pretreatment information over an extended period provides a picture of what performance is like without the intervention. When the intervention eventually is implemented, the observations are continued, and the investigator can examine whether changes in the dependent measures coincide with the intervention.

The role of *continuous assessment* in single-case research can be illustrated by examining a basic difference of group and single-case research. In between-group

TABLE 10.2. Key Characteristics of Single-Case Experimental Designs

Characteristic	Definition	Purpose
Continuous assessment	Observations on multiple occasions over time prior to and during the period in which the intervention is administered	To provide the basic information on which data evaluation and intervention phases depend; decisions are made (e.g., when an intervention is effective or not, when to change phases in the designs), based on data derived from continuous assessment
Baseline assessment	Assessment for a period of time prior to implementation of the intervention	To describe current performance and to predict what performance is likely to be like in the immediate future
Stability of performance	Stable performance is one in which there is relatively little variability over time	To permit projections of performance to the immediate future and to evaluate the impact of a subsequent intervention. Highly variable performance (large fluctuations) and a trend (slope) during baseline that is in the same direction as one hopes for with the intervention can interfere with the evaluation
Use of different phases	Phases are periods of time (several days, weeks) in which a particular condition (baseline or intervention) is implemented and data are collected	To test whether performance continued in the predicted pattern from a prior phase or changed as the intervention or other conditions were altered. Inferences about the effects are drawn from the pattern of the data across phases

research, treatment is evaluated by giving the intervention to some persons (treatment group) but not to others (no-treatment group). One or two observations (pre- and posttreatment assessment) are obtained for several different persons. In single-case research, the effects of the intervention are examined by observing the influence of treatment and no treatment on the performance of the same person(s). Several observations are obtained for one or a few persons. Continuous assessment provides the several observations over time to allow the comparisons of interest within the individual subject. In short, many subjects and few assessments (group research) stand in contrast to few subjects and many assessments (single-case research), although there are exceptions and combinations that make this useful way to remember the differences not flawless.

Baseline Assessment

Each of the single-case experimental designs usually begins with observing performance for several days before the intervention is implemented. This initial period of observation, referred to as the *baseline phase*, provides information about the level of functioning on the dependent measures before the intervention begins. The baseline phase serves two functions. First, data collected during the baseline phase describe the existing level of performance. The *descriptive function* of baseline provides information about the extent of the client's problem. Second, the data serve as the basis for predicting the level of performance for the immediate future if the intervention is not provided. Even though the descriptive function of the baseline phase is important for indicating the extent of the client's problem, from the standpoint of single-case designs, the *predictive function* is central.

To evaluate the impact of an intervention in single-case research, it is important to have an idea of what performance would be like in the future without the intervention. Of course, a description of present performance does not necessarily provide a statement of what performance would be like in the future. Performance might change even without treatment. The only way to be certain of future performance without the intervention would be to continue baseline observations forever without implementing the intervention. However, the purpose is to implement and evaluate the intervention and to see if the client improves in some way. Baseline data are gathered to help predict performance in the immediate future before treatment is implemented. Baseline performance is observed for several days to provide a sufficient basis for making a prediction of future performance. The prediction is achieved by projecting or extrapolating into the future a continuation of baseline performance.

A hypothetical example can illustrate how observations during the baseline phase are used to predict future performance and how this prediction is pivotal to drawing inferences about the effects of the intervention. Figure 10.1 illustrates a hypothetical case in which observations were collected on a hypochondriacal patient's frequency of complaining. As evident in the figure, observations during the baseline (pretreatment) phase were obtained for 10 days. The hypothetical baseline data suggest a reasonably consistent pattern of complaints each day in the hospital. The baseline level predicts the likely level of performance in the immediate future if conditions continue as they are. The projected (dashed) line suggests the approximate level of future

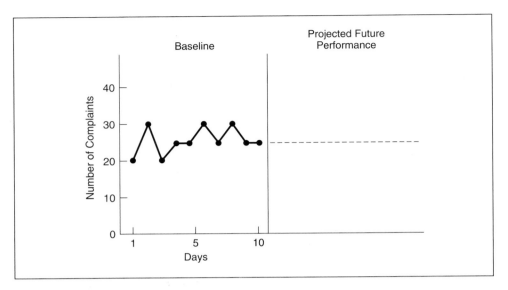

FIGURE 10.1.   Hypothetical example of baseline observations of frequency of complaining. Data in baseline (solid line) are used to predict the likely rate of performance in the future (dashed line).

performance and helps to evaluate whether the intervention leads to change. Presumably, if treatment is effective, performance will differ or depart from the projected level of baseline. For example, if a program is designed to reduce a hypochondriac's complaints, and is successful in doing so, the level of complaints should decrease well below the projected level of baseline. In any case, continuous assessment in the beginning of single-case experimental designs consists of observation of baseline or pretreatment performance. As the individual single-case designs are described later, the importance of initial *baseline assessment* will become especially clear.

Stability of Performance

Because baseline performance is used to predict how the client will behave in the future, it is important that the data are stable. A *stable rate* of performance is characterized by relatively little variability in performance and the absence of a slope (or trend) in the data. The notions of variability and slope raise separate issues, even though they both relate to stability.

Variability in the Data.   Stability of the data refers to the fluctuation or variability in the subject's performance over time. Excessive variability in the data during baseline or other phases can interfere with drawing conclusions about treatment. As a general rule, the greater the variability in the data, the more difficult it is to draw conclusions about the effects of the intervention. Excessive variability is relative; whether the variability is excessive and interferes with drawing conclusions about the intervention depends on many factors, such as the initial level of behavior during the

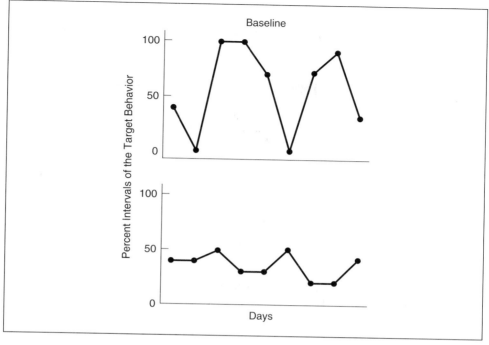

FIGURE 10.2.   Baseline data showing relatively large variability (upper panel) and relatively small variability (lower panel). Intervention effects are more readily evaluated with little variability in the data.

baseline phase and the magnitude of behavior change when the intervention is implemented. In the extreme case, baseline performance may fluctuate daily from extremely high to extremely low levels (0 to 100 percent). Such a pattern of performance is illustrated in Figure 10.2 (upper panel), in which hypothetical baseline data are provided. With such extreme fluctuations in performance, it is difficult to predict any particular level of future performance.

Alternatively, baseline data may show relatively little variability. A typical example is represented in the hypothetical data in the lower panel of Figure 10.2. Performance fluctuates, but the extent of the fluctuation is small compared with the upper panel. With relatively slight fluctuations, the projected pattern of future performance is relatively clear, and hence intervention effects will be less difficult to evaluate. Ideally, baseline data will show little variability.

Slope in the Data.   A slope (or trend) refers to the tendency for performance to decrease or increase systematically or consistently over time. Slope is a better term to use for the concept than trend because it entails the mathematical and statistical description, that is, "What is the line that best represents the data?" (Also, trend in psychological research tends to be used weirdly in the Results section when an investigator did not obtain the findings he or she wanted, and the results are not statistically significant, but the investigator still wants to hold onto the hypothesis. When reading descriptions of data analyses, slope often is evaluated statistically, and trends often seem to be in the eyes of the beholder. The terms will be used interchangeably, but the distinction is worth noting.)

A slope in the data may or may not compete with drawing inferences about the effects of an intervention, depending on the pattern of the data. One of three simple data patterns might be evident during baseline observations. First, baseline data may show no accelerating or decelerating slope. In this case a horizontal line indicating that it is not increasing or decreasing over time best represents performance. As a hypothetical example, observations may be obtained on the disruptive and inappropriate classroom behaviors of a hyperactive child. The upper panel of Figure 10.3 shows baseline performance with no trend. The absence of an accelerating or decelerating slope in baseline provides a relatively clear basis for evaluating subsequent intervention effects. Improvements in performance are likely to be reflected in a slope that departs from the horizontal line of baseline performance.

If behavior does show a trend during baseline, behavior would be increasing or decreasing over time. The slope during baseline may or may not present problems for evaluating intervention effects, depending on the direction of the slope in relation to the desired change in behavior. Performance may be changing in the direction *opposite* from that which treatment is designed to achieve. For example, a hyperactive child may show an *increase* in disruptive and inappropriate behavior during baseline observations. The middle panel of Figure 10.3 shows how baseline data might appear; over the period of observations the client's behavior is becoming worse, that is, more disruptive. Because the intervention will attempt to alter behavior in the opposite direction, this initial slope is not likely to interfere with evaluating intervention effects.

In contrast, the baseline slope may be in the *same direction* that the intervention is likely to produce. Essentially, the baseline phase may show improvement in behavior. For example, the behavior of a hyperactive child may improve over the course of baseline as disruptive and inappropriate behavior decrease, as shown in the lower panel of Figure 10.3. Because the intervention will attempt to improve performance, it may be difficult to evaluate the effect of the subsequent intervention. The projected level of performance for baseline is toward improvement. A very strong intervention effect of treatment would be needed to show clearly that treatment surpassed this projected level from baseline.

If improvement occurs during the baseline phase, one might raise the question of why an intervention should be provided at all. Yet, even when behavior is improving during baseline, it may not be improving quickly enough. For example, an autistic child may show a gradual decrease in head banging during baseline observations. The reduction may be so gradual that serious self-injury might be inflicted unless the behavior is treated quickly. Hence, even though behavior is changing in the desired direction, additional changes may be needed.

Occasionally, a trend may exist in the data and still not interfere with evaluating treatments. Also, when accelerating or decelerating slopes exist, several design options and data evaluation procedures can help clarify the effects of the intervention. For present purposes it is important to convey that the one feature of a stable base-

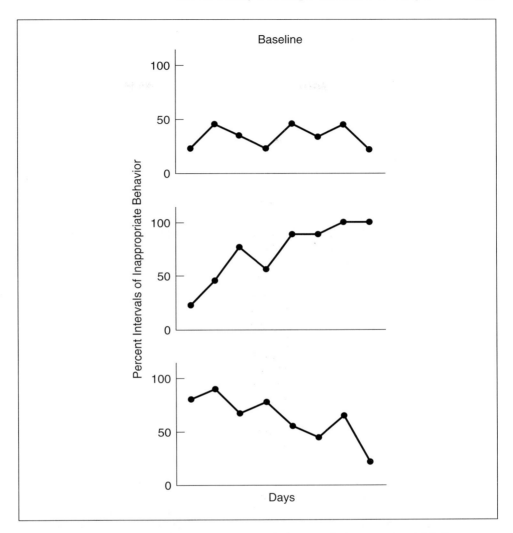

FIGURE 10.3. Hypothetical data for disruptive behavior of a hyperactive child. Upper panel shows a stable rate of performance with no systematic trend over time. Middle panel shows a systematic trend with behavior becoming worse over time. Lower panel shows a systematic trend with behavior becoming better over time. This pattern of data (lower panel) is the most likely one to interfere with evaluation of interventions, because the change is in the same direction of change anticipated with treatment.

line is little or no trend, and that the absence of trend provides a clear basis for evaluating intervention effects. Presumably, when the intervention is implemented, a trend toward improvement in behavior will be evident. This is readily detected with an initial baseline that does not already show a slope in this direction to begin with.

MAJOR EXPERIMENTAL DESIGN STRATEGIES

A key characteristic of single-case designs is the way the intervention is presented and evaluated over time. The different ways reflect varied experimental designs. Major designs are presented and illustrated here. (See Further Readings at the end of the chapter for sources with additional design options.) It is worth noting in advance that illustrations of the designs will be made with behavior modification applications. Although the designs are not restricted to a particular type of treatment, behavioral interventions have commonly been evaluated with these designs and provide a rich pool of examples.

ABAB Designs

Description.   *ABAB designs* consist of a family of experimental arrangements in which continuous observations of performance are made over time for a given client (or group of clients). Over the course of the investigation, changes are made in the experimental conditions to which the client is exposed. Specifically, two separate phases are alternated over time, including the baseline condition (A phase), when no intervention is in effect, and the intervention condition (B phase). The A and B phases are repeated again to complete the four phases. The effects of the intervention are clear if performance improves during the first intervention phase, reverts to or approaches original baseline levels of performance when treatment is withdrawn, and improves when treatment is reinstated in the second intervention phase.

The design begins by observing behavior under baseline (no-treatment) conditions. When a stable rate of behavior is evident and is not accelerating or decelerating, treatment is implemented. Treatment may consist of a particular intervention conducted by a therapist, parent, spouse, or any other person and carried out in individual outpatient therapy sessions and at home. Assume that the intervention is associated with some change in the observed behavior. When this change is stable, the intervention is temporarily withdrawn. The baseline condition or absence of treatment is reinstated. The return-to-baseline condition sometimes is referred to as a *reversal phase* because the behavior is expected to "reverse," that is, return to, or close to, the level of the original baseline. After behavior reverts to baseline levels, the intervention is reinstated. Because this is a family of designs, one need not be rigid about four phases. Sometimes ABA designs (baseline, intervention, return-to-baseline phases) are used; in other instances many additional phases are added, as discussed below. In all cases, the intervention effects are clear if performance improves during the intervention phase(s) and reverts to or approaches original baseline levels of performance when the intervention is withdrawn.

Figure 10.4 provides a hypothetical example of observations of some desirable behavior plotted over several days. The data suggest that there are rather clear differences in the phases. Each phase shows performance that departs from what would be expected (projected and predicted) from extrapolating the pattern from the prior phase, as described previously in discussing the logic of single-case designs. A dashed line has been added to show an extrapolation of baseline or the predicted level of performance if baseline conditions were to continue. The changes whenever the in-

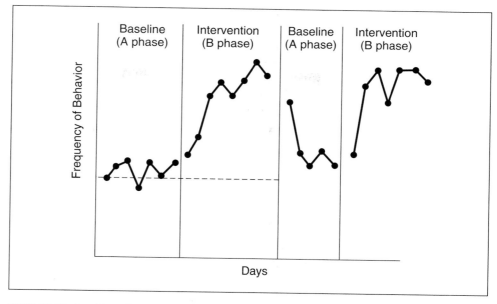

FIGURE 10.4. Hypothetical rate of some behavior plotted over baseline (A) and intervention (B) phases.

tervention is introduced and return to baseline levels when the intervention is withdrawn strongly suggest that the intervention was responsible for change. Other factors than the intervention (the various threats to internal validity) would be difficult to propose to plausibly account for this pattern.

The design is referred to as an ABAB design because A and B phases are alternated. The design is also referred to as a reversal design because phases in the design are reversed to demonstrate the effect of the program. If performance changes in the experimental phase relative to baseline, reverts to baseline or near baseline levels during the second baseline phase, and again changes in the final experimental phase, this provides a clear demonstration of the effectiveness of the experimental condition.

The ABAB design and its use can be illustrated with a relatively simple treatment application to eliminate thumbsucking in a 9-year-old boy (Ross, 1975). The thumbsucking was associated with malocclusion of the front teeth, which could not be treated until sucking was eliminated. Thumbsucking was altered at home by the boy's mother. The parents recorded sucking at predetermined times during the day (while the boy watched television) and at night and early morning (while asleep). Treatment consisted of simply turning off the television set for five minutes if he was caught sucking his thumb during the day. His siblings also were told to help keep him from thumbsucking so that their TV time would not be lost also. This program was implemented and withdrawn in accord with requirements of the ABAB design.

The effects of the program are extremely clear (see Figure 10.5). When treatment was in effect, thumbsucking was almost eliminated. Sucking returned and approached baseline levels when treatment was withdrawn and again was virtually eliminated

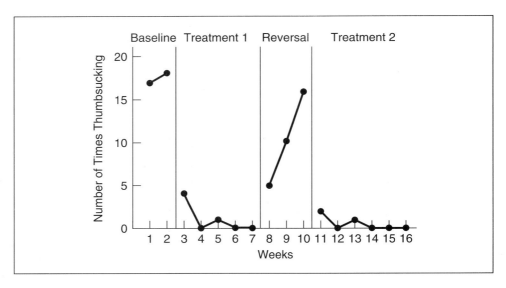

FIGURE 10.5.   Thumbsucking frequency during television viewing (21 observations per week).

Source: Ross, J.A., (1975). Parents modify thumbsucking: A case study, *Journal of Behavior Therapy and Psychiatric and Experimental Psychiatry, 6,* 248–249. Copyright © 1975 by Elsevier Science. Reprinted with permission.

when treatment was reinstated. Interestingly, observations at night and in the early morning while the boy had been asleep showed a similar pattern even though the program was not introduced from nighttime thumbsucking. The daytime program was continued for six months beyond the sixteenth week as shown in the figure, with reportedly similar effects.

Considerations.   The most commonly used version of the ABAB design has been discussed here as a four-phase design that alternates a single treatment with baseline phases. However, designs are available that include more than one treatment and more than four phases. For example, suppose that the treatment (B_1) does not change behavior after the baseline phase. The therapist–investigator would not continue the phase but would try another treatment (B_2). This latter treatment would constitute a new phase and would probably be implemented later in the design. The design could be represented as an $AB_1 B_2 AB_2$ design. The ability to improvise treatment as part of the design is a key feature that makes variations compatible with and quite useful for clinical application.

The central requirement of the design is having stable levels of behavior. Evaluating data in an ABAB design and drawing a conclusion about the causal role of treatment are difficult when treatment effects seem merely to continue a pattern of behavior or slope in the data already evident in the baseline phase. Hence, most investigators recommend waiting until behavior is stable (is relatively consistent over time and or shows no trend or a trend only in the direction opposite of the change anticipated with treatment). Statistical techniques have been developed to take into account baseline trends that might interfere with drawing conclusions about interventions (see Kazdin, 1984; Krishef, 1991).

Another key feature of the design is demonstration of a causal relation by showing that behavior reverts to or approaches the original baseline level after the intervention is withdrawn or altered (during the second A phase). This requirement introduces problems that restrict use of the design in clinical work. One problem is that withdrawing treatment does not always show a change in behavior. Indeed, it is the prime hope of therapists and clients alike that once treatment is terminated, its therapeutic effects will continue. Clinically, continued performance of the appropriate behavior is important; yet, from the standpoint of an ABAB design, it could be disappointing. If behavior is not made to revert to baseline levels after showing an initial change, a causal relation cannot be drawn between the intervention and behavior. Some events other than treatment might account for change since behavior is not under the control of the administration or termination of treatment.

Even if behavior did revert to baseline levels when treatment was suspended temporarily, such a change would be clinically undesirable. Essentially, returning the client to baseline levels of performance amounts to making behavior worse. Of course, treatment can be withdrawn for only a brief period, such as one or a few days. In most circumstances the idea of making a client worse just when treatment may be having an effect is ethically unacceptable. There may be important exceptions if, for example, the required treatment has undesirable side effects, and suspension of treatments tests whether the intervention is still needed. Aside from ethical problems, there are practical problems as well. It is often difficult to ensure that the client, therapist, or relatives responsible for conducting treatment will actually stop once some success has been achieved.

As a general rule, problems related to reversing behavior make the ABAB design and its variations undesirable in clinical situations. If a reversal does occur, that may be problematic if the behavior is important for the clients or for those in contact with them. If a reversal does not occur, this raises obstacles in concluding that the intervention led to the change. Yet, the power of the design in demonstrating control of an intervention over behavior is very compelling. If behavior can, in effect, be "turned on and off" as a function of the intervention, this is a potent demonstration of a causal relation. Other designs can also demonstrate a causal relation without using a reversal of conditions.

Multiple-Baseline Designs

Description.   The *multiple-baseline designs* demonstrate the effect of an intervention by showing that behavior change accompanies introduction of the intervention at different points in time. Once the intervention is presented, it need not be withdrawn or altered to reverse behavior to or near baseline levels. Thus, the clinical utility of the design is not limited by the problems of reverting behavior to pretreatment levels.

The key feature of the designs is evaluation of change across different baselines. The intervention is introduced to the different baselines at different points in time. Ideally, change occurs when the intervention is introduced in sequence to each of the baselines. The different baselines might, for example, consist of two separate behaviors of a person in his or her home. Each behavior is observed and graphed separately. After baseline observations, the intervention is introduced to *one* of the behaviors. Both behaviors continue to be observed. Later the intervention is introduced to the other behavior as well so that both behaviors now are receiving the intervention. The effect of the intervention is demonstrated by showing a pattern of change as the intervention is introduced. That is, each behavior changes when and only when the intervention was introduced.

There are different versions of the multiple-baseline design. In each version, data are collected continuously and concurrently across two or more baselines. The intervention is applied to the different baselines at different points in time. Mentioned already was the version in which the baselines represent *different behaviors* (studying, working, reading) for a given individual. Other design options include instances in which the baselines are the same response across *different individuals* or the same response for an individual across *different situations*. For example, in the multiple-baseline design across responses, a single individual or group of individuals is observed. Data are collected on two or more behaviors, each of which eventually is to be altered. The behaviors are observed daily or at least on several occasions each week. After each of the baselines shows a stable pattern, the intervention is applied to only one of the responses. Baseline conditions remain in effect for the other responses. The initial response to which treatment is applied is expected to change while other responses remain at pretreatment levels. When the treated behavior stabilizes, the intervention is applied to the second response. Treatment continues for the first two responses while baseline continues for all other responses. Eventually, each response is exposed to treatment but at different points in time. A causal relation between the intervention and behavior is clearly demonstrated if each response changes only when the intervention is introduced and not before.

As an example, an imagery-based flooding procedure was used to treat a 6 1/2-year-old boy, named Joseph, who suffered a posttraumatic stress disorder (Saigh, 1986). This disorder is a reaction to a highly stressful event or experience and has a number of symptoms, such as persistently re-experiencing the event (thoughts, dreams), avoidance of stimuli associated with the trauma, numbing of responsiveness, outbursts of anger, difficulty in sleeping, and exaggerated startle responses. Joseph experienced the disorder after exposure to a bomb blast in a war zone where he lived. His reaction included trauma-related nightmares, recollections of the trauma, depression, and avoidance behavior. To treat Joseph, five scenes were developed that evoked anxiety (e.g., seeing injured people and debris, approaching specific shopping areas). To measure discomfort to the scenes, he rated his level of anxiety as each scene was described to him. During the sessions he was trained to relax, after which scenes were presented for extended periods (over 20 minutes). During this exposure period, he was asked to imagine the exact details of the scenes. The five scenes were incorporated into treatment in a multiple-baseline design, so that exposure to scenes occurred in sequence or at different points in time. In each of the sessions, discomfort was rated in response to all of the scenes.

The results, presented in Figure 10.6, showed that Joseph's discomfort consistently decreased after only 10 sessions (1 session of baseline assessment, 10 sessions of treat-

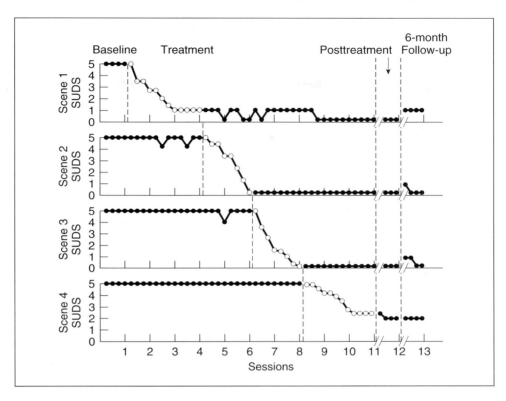

FIGURE 10.6. Joseph's ratings of discomfort referred to as Subjective Units of Disturbance (SUDS) where 5 = maximum discomfort and 0 = no discomfort. Assessment was conducted to measure discomfort for each scene during treatment session. Treatment (graphed as open circles) reflects the period in which imagery-based exposure (flooding) focused on the specific scene.

Source: Saigh, P.A. (1986). In vitro flooding in the treatment of a 6 year old boy's posttraumatic stress disorder. *Behaviour Research and Therapy, 24,* 685–688. Copyright © 1986 from Elsevier Science. Reprinted with permission.

ment). The reduction of anxiety for each scene was associated with implementation of the intervention. Assessment immediately after treatment and 6 months later indicated that he was no longer discomforted by the situations. The results from other measures also reflected change. Before and after treatment Joseph was assessed in the market place where the bomb blast had occurred. His performance had improved after treatment as reflected by remaining in the area longer and thereby showing less avoidance. Other measures—including assessment of anxiety, depression, and classroom performance at school—indicated improvements after treatment as well. Thus, the effects of treatment appeared to affect several important areas of functioning.

The multiple-baseline design can be extended across individuals. Baseline data can be collected for a behavior across different individuals (siblings in a family, children in a classroom, patients on a ward), introducing the intervention at different points in time to each individual. Similarly, baseline data can be collected across different situations (at home, at work) for a given individual, with the intervention implemented at different points in time for each situation. In each version, the impact of the intervention is demonstrated if behavior changes when and only when the intervention is introduced.

Considerations.   The multiple-baseline design demonstrates the effect of the intervention without a return-to-baseline conditions and a temporary loss of some of the gains achieved. Two major considerations that affect the clarity of the demonstration are the number and the independence of the baselines. The number of baselines adequate for a clear demonstration is difficult to specify. Two baselines are a minimum, but one or two more can really strengthen the demonstration. The clarity of the demonstration across a given set of baselines is a function of such factors as the duration of baseline, the presence of extensive variability of behavior and slopes in the direction of improvement during the baselines phase, the rapidity of behavior change after treatment is implemented, and the magnitude of behavior change. Depending upon these factors, even a few baselines may provide a sufficiently convincing demonstration.

The number of baselines needed to demonstrate clear effects may depend upon the problem of interdependence of the baselines. The design depends upon showing that the behavior changes when and only when the treatment is implemented. Ideally, behaviors still exposed to the baseline condition do not change until the intervention is applied. If they do, it suggests that the intervention may not have been responsible for change. Rather, extraneous factors (history, testing) may have led to the change. Occasionally, the effects produced by an intervention may be general rather than specific, so that a change in one behavior is associated with changes in other behaviors, but generalized effects across different baselines appear to be exceptions rather than the rule. When generalized effects are present, features from other single-case designs (e.g., a brief reversal phase) can be added in separate experimental phases to demonstrate a causal relation between treatment and behavior change.

Multiple-baseline designs are often user friendly in clinical applications because the intervention is applied in a gradual or sequential fashion across different responses of the individual (or different individuals, or different situations). If the intervention is effective, then it can be extended to all of the other responses for which change is desired. As importantly, if the intervention is not effective or not effective enough to achieve important changes, it can be altered or improved before it is extended.

Changing-Criterion Designs

Description.   The *changing-criterion design* demonstrates the effect of an intervention by showing that behavior changes in increments to match a performance criterion. A causal relation between an intervention and behavior is demonstrated if behavior matches a constantly changing criterion for performance over the course of treatment. The design begins with a baseline phase after which the intervention is introduced. When the intervention is introduced, a specific level of performance is chosen as a criterion for the client. The daily criterion may be used as a basis for providing response consequences or an incentive of some sort. The criterion can be negotiated with the client. When the performance meets or surpasses the criterion level on a given day (certain number of cigarettes smoked, number of calories consumed), the response consequence (e.g., monetary reward) is provided.

A specific criterion usually is invoked continuously for at least a few days. When performance consistently meets the criterion, the criterion is made more stringent (fewer cigarettes or calories consumed daily). Consequences are provided only for meeting the new criterion on a given day, and the criterion again is changed if the performance meets the criterion consistently. The criterion is repeatedly changed throughout the intervention phase until the terminal goal of the program is achieved. The effect of the intervention is demonstrated if behavior matches a criterion as the criterion is changed. If behavior changes with the criterion, it is likely that the intervention and criterion change rather than extraneous influences accounted for behavior change. By implementing a given criterion for at least a few days (or even longer), the behavior shows a step-like effect that is not likely to result from a general incremental change occurring as a function of extraneous events.

One program used a changing-criterion design to evaluate a program to decrease caffeine consumption in three adults (Foxx & Rubinoff, 1979). Caffeine consumed in large quantities has been associated with a variety of symptoms ranging in severity from general irritability and gastrointestinal disturbances to cardiovascular disorders and cancer. The intervention consisted of having participants, at the beginning of the program, deposit money ($20), which was returned in small portions if caffeine consumption fell below the criterion set for a given day. Participants signed a contract that specified how they would earn back or lose the money. Each person recorded daily caffeine consumption on the basis of a list of beverages that provided their caffeine equivalence (in milligrams).

The effects of the program for one subject, a female schoolteacher, are illustrated in Figure 10.7. During baseline, her daily average caffeine consumption was 1000 mg (equal to approximately eight cups of brewed coffee). When the intervention began, she was required to reduce her daily consumption by about 100 mg less than baseline. When performance was consistently below the criterion (solid line), the criterion was reduced further by approximately 100 mg. This change in the criterion continued over separate subphases. In each subphase, money was earned back only if caffeine consumption fell at or below the criterion. The figure shows that performance consistently fell below the criterion. Assessment 10 months after the program had ended indicated that she maintained her low rate of caffeine consumption.

Considerations.   The design depends upon repeatedly changing the performance criterion and examining behavior relative to the new criterion. The design is especially well suited to those terminal responses that are arrived at or approximated gradually. For most therapeutic problems, individuals usually must acquire the skills, overcome problematic situations, or gain comfort gradually so that this requirement may be met. If behavior change occurs in large steps and does not follow the criterion, the specific effect of the intervention in altering behavior will not be clear. Thus, the design tends to be limited to demonstrating gradual rather than rapid changes because of the requirement of the changing criterion.

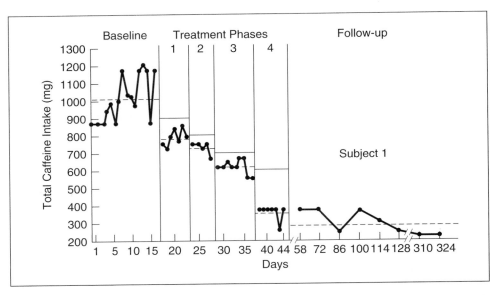

FIGURE 10.7.   Subject's daily caffeine intake in milligrams during baseline, treatment, and follow-up. The criterion level for each treatment phase was 102 milligrams of caffeine less than that of the previous treatment phase. Solid horizontal lines indicate the criterion level for each phase. Broken horizontal lines indicate the mean for each condition.

Source: Foxx, R.M. & Rubinoff, A. (1979). Behavioral treatment of caffeinism: Reducing excessive coffee drinking. *Journal of Applied Behavior Analysis, 12*, 335–344. Copyright © 1979. Reprinted with permission.

In general, the changing-criterion design is less powerful than other single-case designs because the effects of extraneous events could account for a general increase or decrease in behavior. The design depends upon showing a unidirectional change in behavior (increase or decrease) over time. However, extraneous events rather than the intervention could result in unidirectional changes. The demonstration is unambiguous only if performance matches the criterion very closely and the criterion is changed several times. Making bi-directional changes in the criterion during the intervention phase strengthens the design. Rather than simply making the criterion increasingly stringent, it can be made more stringent at some points and less stringent at others to weaken the plausibility that extraneous events account for the results. Of course, reversing behavior, even if only to a small degree and for a brief period, may be countertherapeutic.

As with the multiple-baseline design, the changing-criterion design can be quite compatible with demands of the clinical situation. Many therapeutic regimens focus on gradual development of behavior or skills (improving marital communication, participation in activities) or reduction of problematic function (e.g., overcoming anxiety). Shaping these behaviors or gradually exposing individuals to anxiety-provoking situations may proceed in ways that can reflect increasing the performance criteria as changes are evident. Thus, progress can be monitored and evaluated in a changing-criterion design.

General Comments

Single-case research encompasses many different designs, only a few of which could be illustrated in this chapter. The designs are true experiments in the sense that causal relations can be demonstrated and threats to validity, particularly internal validity, can be ruled out. The designs offer a distinct advantage for treatment research. To begin with, single-case methodology provides the means to investigate treatments empirically with individual clients. Traditionally, study of the individual client has been restricted to anecdotal reports about the course of change. Therapist impressions and uncontrolled implementation of treatment eliminate the possibility of drawing unchallenged causal inferences. In contrast, single-case designs allow careful evaluation of treatment by addressing threats to internal validity, which serve as the basis for drawing causal inferences. Actually, several different questions can be addressed. The methodology permits evaluating the effects of an overall treatment package, withdrawing components of treatment over time to determine an essential treatment ingredient, adding components of treatment to enhance behavior change, and comparing different treatments.

Another advantage of single-case designs is that they permit investigation of problems that are not likely to be studied in between-group research. Many clinical problems are relatively rare, so that it would be extraordinarily difficult to recruit subjects for a large-scale treatment evaluation project. Yet, single-case designs allow careful investigation of an individual client. Thus, information can be obtained from experimentation with a single case that otherwise might not be available.

For example, psychological treatment of transsexual behavior is relatively rare, and careful evaluation of such treatment is not likely to emerge from randomized controlled treatment trials with groups of cases. A very interesting case was reported and evaluated using a single-case design (Barlow, Reynolds, & Agras, 1973). The case was a 17-year-old male who desired to be a female. His behaviors and attitudes reflected his transsexual interest as evident in attraction to other males; a history of cross-dressing; interest in traditionally feminine role behaviors such as knitting, crocheting, and embroidering; sexual fantasies in which he imagined himself as a woman; and effeminate mannerisms in sitting, standing, and walking. Extensive treatment based upon modeling, rehearsal, and feedback was used to alter a variety of effeminate mannerisms, speaking patterns, social skills, sexual fantasies, and sexual arousal. The effects of training were demonstrated in a combined ABAB and multiple-baseline design. This report is unique in experimentally demonstrating successful psychotherapeutic treatment of a transsexual. It is unlikely that this demonstration could have been accomplished with several transsexuals in a between-group design if for no other reason than the difficulty in recruiting such clients in sufficient numbers who would be interested in treatment other than direct physical change through surgery.

While single-case designs provide an important contribution to treatment evaluation, they have distinct limitations. For example, the designs are weak in revealing subject characteristics that may interact with (moderate) the effects of treatment. It may be that the intervention would be effective with males versus females or younger versus older people. If this were the case, we could say that treatment is moderated by subject sex or age. Focusing on one or a few subjects, of course, does not allow systematically comparing treatments across multiple subjects who differ in various characteristics, at least within the same experiment. Examination of subject variables is more readily accomplished by group research, specifically factorial designs, where multiple subjects necessarily are required.

Related to the study of subject variables, the results of single-case investigation provide no hint of the generality of findings (external validity) to other subjects. Quite possibly, the effects of treatment demonstrated with the individual case will not generalize to other individuals. Within the single-case investigation, the investigator cannot determine how many clients would reveal the same pattern of change. However, it is important to note that the lack of generality of findings has not been a limitation of current research. Findings obtained in single-case experiments have had no less generality, and possibly greater generality, than findings from between-group research. Part of the reason for the generality of findings from single-case research is that treatment applications with the single case have sought extremely potent effects. Consequently, it has been argued that interventions with such effects for the single case are likely to generalize more broadly than are interventions that may meet the relatively weaker criterion of statistical significance (see Baer, 1977). Within a group study (e.g., treatment versus no treatment), a statistical difference does not really say anything about the range of persons to whom the effects apply. Not everyone, in fact, is likely to have responded in the same way, and it is untrue to say that the statistical difference means the finding applies even to most individuals within the study, leaving aside within the population at large (Mohr, 1985).

DATA EVALUATION IN SINGLE-CASE RESEARCH

For most readers trained in traditional group methodology, the idea of single-case experiments is at least mildly discomforting. There is a skepticism if not total disbelief that one can really demonstrate causal relations and rule out the various threats to validity with one single subject. This has to do more with our training as psychologists than with the point. I make this comment because if you were skeptical about the designs, please brace yourself for the discussion of methods of data evaluation.

In areas of clinical research where single-case designs are used, data typically are evaluated without relying upon statistical tests. Statistical tests are available for single-case designs, even though they involve techniques that are somewhat less familiar (time-series analyses, randomization tests) than the usual methods taught in graduate training (see Kazdin, 1984). It is not the *availability* of statistical tests for the single case that is the issue. Investigators working with single-case designs as a matter of choice often *prefer* nonstatistical evaluation of the data. Given the training of most students and professionals in psychology, nonstatistical evaluation seems sacrilegious. An obvious concern is that by not using statistical techniques, subjective judgment may enter into deciding which findings are significant or veridical and which are not. The concern is reasonable because however arbitrary statistical evaluation or decision making seems, the criteria appear quite explicit (e.g., $p < .05$) and consistent across investigators.[2] Before entering into objections and concerns, it is useful to consider the rationale and use of nonstatistical evaluation. At the very least, the approach sensitizes us to critical properties of the data we collect; at best, it provides another viable approach for determining the reliability, significance, and importance of a particular result.

Nonstatistical evaluation usually refers to examining the data and determining whether the intervention had an effect by *visual inspection*. Visual inspection is commonly used in single-case research where continuous data are available for one or several subjects. With single-case designs the investigator has the advantage of seeing the data for a single subject for consecutive periods without the intervention, followed by similar data with the intervention in effect. If the intervention abruptly changes the pattern of data, an inference about the effect of the intervention is clearer than by simply looking at pre- and postintervention differences across two observations. Assessment of the individual's performance on several occasions makes examination of the data through visual inspection less arbitrary than the method might appear at first glance.

Criteria for Visual Inspection

Evaluation of data nonstatistically has the same goal as statistical analysis, namely, to identify if the effects are consistent, reliable, and unlikely to have resulted from chance fluctuations between conditions. Although visual inspection is based on subjective judgment, this is not tantamount to noting that decisions are by fiat or vary with each person making the judgment. In many uses of single-case designs where visual inspection is invoked, the applied or clinical goals are to achieve marked intervention effects. In cases where intervention effects are very strong, one need not carefully scrutinize or enumerate the criteria that underlie the judgment that the effects are veridical.

Several situations arise in applied research in which intervention effects are likely to be so dramatic that visual inspection is easily invoked. For example, whenever the behavior of interest is not present in the client's behavior during the baseline phase (social interaction, exercise, reading) and increases during the intervention phase, a

[2]Statistical evaluation and statistical tests are laced with subjectivity and not as straightforward as the comments here imply. Hence, one has to be rather careful in invoking the subjectivity argument in relation to use of nonstatistical evaluation methods. Many statistical tests (factor analysis, regression, cluster analyses, time-series analysis, path analyses) include a number of decision points about various solutions, parameter estimates, and levels or criteria to continue or include variables in the analysis or model. These decisions are rarely made explicit in the data analyses. In many instances "default" criteria in the data-analytic programs do not convey that a critical choice has been made and that the basis of this choice can be readily challenged because there is no necessary objective reason that one choice is better than another. One can site more concrete examples that show the vagaries of statistical evaluation. For example, meta-analyses of psychotherapy are extremely popular, and those less familiar with the methods of conducting meta-analyses may view these as straightforward. As it turns out, conclusions about the effectiveness of psychotherapy can vary widely, depending precisely on how the statistics for meta-analyses (e.g., effect size) are computed (Matt, 1989; Matt & Navarro, 1997; Weisz et al., 1995). Concerns related to statistical evaluation will be addressed in a later chapter.

judgment about the effects of the intervention is easily made. If the behavior never occurs during baseline, there is unparalleled stability in the data. Both the mean and standard deviation equal zero. Even a minor increase in the target behavior during the intervention phase would be easily detected. Similarly, when the behavior of interest occurs frequently during the baseline phase (reports of hallucinations, aggressive acts, cigarette smoking) and stops completely during the intervention phase, the magnitude of change usually permits clear judgments based on visual inspection. In cases in which behavior is at the opposite extremes of the assessment range before and during treatment, the ease of invoking visual inspection can be readily understood. Of course, in most situations, the data do not show a change from one extreme of the assessment scale to the other, and the guidelines for making judgments by visual inspection need to be considered more deliberately.

Visual inspection depends on many characteristics of the data, but especially those that pertain to the magnitude of the changes across phases and the rate of these changes. The two characteristics related to magnitude are changes in *mean* and *level*. The two characteristics related to rate are changes in *slope* and *latency of the change*. These are defined in Table 10.3 and elaborated here.

Changes in means across phases refer to shifts in the average rate of performance. Consistent changes in means across phases can serve as a basis for deciding whether the data pattern meets the requirements of the design. A hypothetical example showing changes in means across phases is illustrated in an ABAB design in Figure 10.8. As evident in the figure, performance on the average (horizontal dashed line in each phase) changed in response to the different baseline and intervention phases. Visual inspection of this pattern suggests that the intervention led to consistent changes.

Changes in level refer to the shift or discontinuity of performance from the end of one phase to the beginning of the next phase. A change in level is independent of the change in mean. When one asks about what happened immediately after the intervention was implemented or withdrawn, the implicit concern is over the level of performance. Figure 10.9 shows change in level across phases in ABAB design. The figure shows that whenever the phase was altered, behavior assumed a new rate, that

TABLE 10.3.   Criteria for Data Evaluation in Single-Case Designs

Characteristic	*Definition*
Changes in means (averages)	The mean rate of the behavior shows a change from phase to phase in the expected direction
Change in level	When one phase changes to another, a level refers to the change in behavior from the last day of one phase (baseline) and the first day of the next phase (intervention). An abrupt shift facilitates data interpretation
Change in slope (trend)	The direction of the slope changes from phase to phase, such as, for example, showing no slope (horizontal line) in baseline and an accelerating slope during the intervention phase
Latency of change	The speed with which change occurs once the conditions are changed (baseline to intervention, intervention back to baseline)

Note: These criteria are invoked by examining the graphical display of the data.

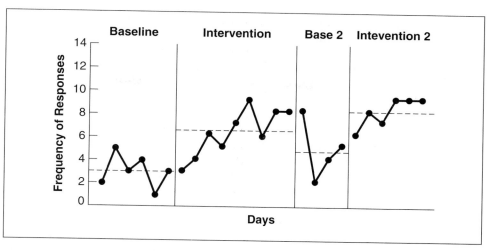

FIGURE 10.8.   Hypothetical example of performance in an ABAB design with means in each phase represented by dashed lines.

is, it shifted up or down rather quickly. It so happens that a change in level in this latter example would also be accompanied by a change in mean across the phases. However, level and mean changes do not necessarily go together. It is possible that a rapid change in level occurs but that the mean remains the same across phases or that the mean changes but no abrupt shift in level has occurred.

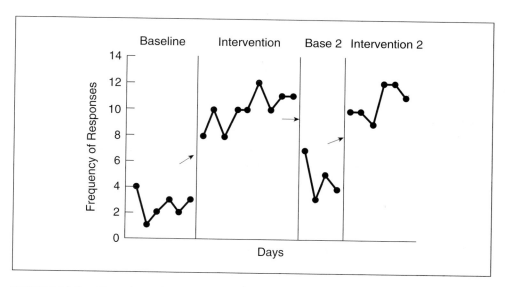

FIGURE 10.9.   Hypothetical example of performance in an ABAB design. The arrows point to the changes in level or discontinuities associated with a change from one phase to another.

Changes in slope or trend are of obvious importance in applying visual inspection. Trend refers to the tendency for the data to show systematic increases or decreases over time. The alteration of phases within the design may show that the direction of behavior changes as the intervention is applied or withdrawn. Figure 10.10 illustrates a hypothetical example in which slopes have changed over the course of the phase in an ABAB design. The initial baseline trend is reversed by the intervention, reinstated when the intervention is withdrawn, and again reversed in the final phase. A change in slope would still be an important criterion even if there were no accelerating or decelerating slope in baseline. A change from no slope (horizontal line) during baseline to a slope (increase or decrease in behavior) during the intervention phase constitutes a change in slope.

Finally, the *latency of the change* that occurs when phases are altered is an important characteristic of the data for invoking visual inspection. Latency refers to the period between the onset or termination of one condition (intervention, return to baseline) and changes in performance. The more closely in time that the change occurs after the experimental conditions have been altered, the clearer the intervention effect. A hypothetical example is provided in Figure 10.11, showing only the first two phases of separate ABAB designs. In the top panel, implementation of the intervention after baseline was associated with a rapid change in performance. The change would also be evident from changes in mean and trend. In the bottom panel, the intervention did not immediately lead to change. The time between the onset of the

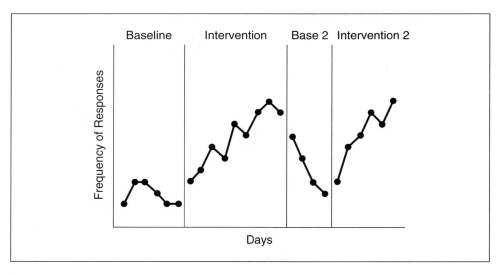

FIGURE 10.10. Hypothetical example of performance in an ABAB design with changes in trend across phases. Baseline shows a relatively stable or possibly decreasing trend. When the intervention is introduced, an accelerating trend is evident. This trend is reversed when the intervention is withdrawn (Base 2) and is reinstated when the intervention is reintroduced.

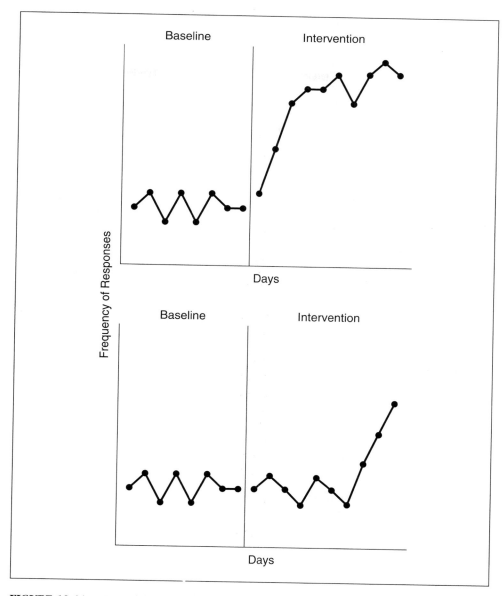

FIGURE 10.11.   Hypothetical examples of first AB phases as part of larger ABAB designs. Upper panel shows that when the intervention was introduced, behavior changed rapidly. Lower panel shows that when the intervention was introduced, behavior change was delayed. The changes in both upper and lower panels are reasonably clear. Yet as a general rule, as the latency between the onset of the intervention and behavior change increases, questions are more likely to arise about whether the intervention or extraneous factors accounted for change.

intervention and behavior change was longer than in the top panel, and it is slightly less clear that the intervention may have led to the change.

As a general rule, the shorter the period between the onset of the intervention and behavior change, the easier it is to infer that the intervention led to change. The rationale is that as the time between the intervention and behavior increases, the more likely that intervening influences may have accounted for behavior change. Of course, the importance of the latency of the change after the onset of the intervention depends on the type of intervention and behavior studied. For example, one would not expect rapid changes in applying diet and exercise to treat obesity. Weight reduction usually reflects gradual changes after treatment begins. Similarly, some medications do not produce rapid effects. Change depends on the buildup of therapeutic doses.

Changes in means, levels, and slopes, and variations in the latency of change across phases frequently accompany each other. Yet, they are separate characteristics of the data and can occur alone or in combination. Visual inspection is conducted by judging the extent to which changes in these characteristics are evident across phases and whether the changes are consistent with the requirements of the particular design. When changes in mean, level, and slope go together with latency of change, visual inspection is relatively easy to invoke. In such cases the data across phases may not overlap. *Nonoverlapping data* refer to the pattern in which the values of the data points during the baseline phase do not approach any of the values of the data points attained during the intervention phase.

Invoking the criteria for visual inspection requires judgments about the pattern of data in the entire design and not merely changes across one or two phases. Unambiguous effects require that the criteria be met throughout the design. To the extent that the criteria are not consistently met, conclusions about the reliability of intervention effects become tentative. For example, changes in an ABAB design may show nonoverlapping data points for the first AB phases but no clear differences across the second AB phases. The absence of a consistent pattern of data that meets the criteria mentioned above limits the conclusions that can be drawn.

Problems and Considerations

Visual inspection has been quite useful in identifying reliable intervention effects in both experimental and clinical research. When intervention effects are potent, the need for statistical analysis is obviated. Intervention effects can be extremely clear from graphic displays of the data in which persons can judge for themselves whether the criteria have been met; many methods of displaying the data graphically can facilitate the evaluation (Kazdin, 1982a; Krishef, 1991).

The use of visual inspection as the primary basis for evaluating data in single-case designs has raised concerns. The major issue pertains to the lack of concrete decision rules for determining whether a particular demonstration shows or fails to show a reliable effect. The process of visual inspection would seem to permit, if not actively encourage, subjectivity and inconsistency in the evaluation of intervention effects. Studies of how individuals invoke the criteria for visual inspection have shown that judges, even when experts in the field, often disagree about particular data patterns and whether the effects were reliable (DeProspero & Cohen, 1979; Gottman & Glass,

1978). The disagreement among judges using visual inspection has been as an argument to favor statistical analysis of the data as a supplement to or replacement of visual inspection. The attractive feature of statistical analysis is that once the statistic is decided, the result that is achieved is usually consistent across investigators. Presumably, the final result of any statistical evaluation and determination of the highly hallowed statistical significance are not altered by the judgment of the investigator in the way they could be with visual inspection.

Another criticism levied against visual inspection is that it regards as significant only those effects that are very marked. Many interventions might prove to be consistent in the effects they produce but are relatively weak. Such effects might not be detected by visual inspection and would be overlooked. Overlooking weak but reliable effects can have unfortunate consequences. First, weak but reliable effects may have theoretical significance in relation to understanding personality, dysfunction, or treatment. Second, the possibility exists that interventions when first developed may have weak effects. It would be unfortunate if these interventions were prematurely discarded before they could be developed further. Interventions with reliable but weak effects might eventually achieve potent effects if investigators developed them further. On the other hand, the stringent criteria may encourage investigators to develop interventions to the point that they do produce marked changes before making claims about their demonstrated efficacy.

A final problem with visual inspection is that it requires a particular pattern of data in baseline and subsequent phases so that the results can be interpreted. Visual inspection criteria are more readily invoked when data obtained during baseline show little or no slope, or slope in direction opposite from the trend expected in the following phase, and slight variability. However, trends and variability in the data may not always meet the idealized data requirements. In such cases visual inspection may be difficult to invoke. Other criteria, such as statistical analyses, may be of use in these situations.

General Comments

The data evaluation procedures highlighted here and single-case designs with which they are associated are infrequently taught in undergraduate or graduate training. These methods are of special relevance in clinical psychology and other areas where research findings are applied and where clinically significant (important) change is a goal. The degree of change required by visual inspection criteria is usually much greater to infer a reliable (veridical) effect than the degree demonstrated by statistical significance testing.

Objections to nonstatistical data evaluation methods are strong because the methods, by their very nature, appear not merely to permit subjectivity but to court it directly. Yet, visual inspection can be reliably invoked and has generated a body of research with outcomes that are at least as reliable and replicable as those obtained through statistical evaluation. Whether the criteria are adopted or not in a given study, the criteria of visual inspection are worth noting. Changes in mean, level, slope, and latency of change sensitize us to critical properties of the data. In the evaluation of continuous data and in clinical and research situations where performance is scrutinized over time, these properties can greatly influence decision making, treatment planning, and evaluation.

SUMMARY AND CONCLUSIONS

The study of the individual can take many different forms. The case study is the most generic term to describe the intensive investigation of the individual. In clinical psychology and other mental health professions, the case study has been largely restricted to uncontrolled and anecdotal reports. Even so, the case can contribute enormously as a source of ideas and hypotheses, as a basis for developing therapy techniques, as a way of studying rare phenomena, as a demonstration of a counterinstance, and because of the persuasive and motivational value. As a basis for developing scientific knowledge, the case has been restricted. Yet, even this claim is a matter of degree. It is possible to structure the case and to collect information in a way that greatly increases the yield, but this is rarely accomplished in clinical work. Indeed, the limitation of the case study, as traditionally presented, is not so much in the focus on one individual but rather the unsystematic and rather subjective assessment (e.g., therapist views).

At one extreme one can identify anecdotal case studies in which well-based and valid conclusions are difficult to reach (problems with virtually all threats to validity). At the other extreme are single-case experiments that rule out threats to validity and that can be used as a basis for identifying causal relations. Single-case designs allow experimentation with the individual subject or client. The methodology is different from the usual group research and relies on continuous assessment over time, assessment of baseline, and the use of multiple phases in which performance is altered. The designs allow examination of several questions traditionally of interest in treatment evaluation: evaluating an overall treatment package, analyzing the components of treatment, building more effective treatments by adding components, and comparing different treatments. Three major design strategies—ABAB, multiple-baseline, and changing-criterion designs—were highlighted. The designs vary in the questions that can be addressed, the way in which treatment effects are demonstrated, and the requirements for experimental evaluation. Also, the designs vary in their suitability in light of practical or clinical considerations.

Single-case designs help draw inferences through nonstatistical evaluation or visual inspection of the data. This is greatly facilitated by the collection of continuous data over time and across phases of the designs. Nonstatistical criteria for judging whether independent variables have produced reliable effects include changes in mean, level, and slope and in the latency of changes across phases. Judgments are required to invoke these criteria in situations that are not always clear.

This chapter has outlined the extremes of methodologies that can be used with the individual case from anecdotal uncontrolled case studies to single-case experimental designs. Single-case designs are rigorous and meet the stringent demands for drawing causal relations as that term is used in science. The next chapter focuses on variations of single-case designs that fall into the middle between case studies and experiments. The middle is important to elaborate because several methodological features of single-case designs permit one to conduct rigorous research and to evaluate the impact of treatment in clinical work.

KEY CONCEPTS AND TERMS

ABAB Designs

Anecdotal Case Study

Baseline Phase

Continuous Assessment

Multiple-Baseline Designs

Single-Case Experiment

Visual Inspection

FOR FURTHER READINGS

Kazdin, A.E. (1982). *Single-case research designs: Methods for clinical and applied settings.* New York: Oxford University Press.

Krishef, C.H. (1991). *Fundamental approaches to single subject design and analysis.* Malabar, FL: Kreiger Publishing Company.

Sechrest, L., Stewart, M., Stickle, T. R., & Sidani, S. (1996). *Effective and persuasive case studies.* Cambridge, MA: Human Services Research Institute.

Stake, R. (1995). *The art of case study research.* Thousand Oaks, CA: Sage.

Yin, R.K. (1994). *Case study research: Design and methods* (2nd ed.). Thousand Oaks, CA: Sage.

Chapter 11

Evaluation of the Single Case in Clinical Work

CHAPTER OUTLINE

Quasi-Experiments with the Single Case
> What to Do to Improve the Quality of Inferences
> Design Variations
> Case Illustrations

Methods for Assessment and Evaluation in Clinical Practice
> Steps for Evaluation in Clinical Work
> Case Illustration
> Issues and Limitations

Summary and Conclusions

The previous chapter covered two methodological extremes, namely, the uncontrolled anecdotal case study on the one hand and single-case experimental designs on the other. The single-case experimental designs are true experiments, that is, they make implausible the various threats to internal validity and permit causal conclusions about the effects of various interventions. Between the extremes of the uncontrolled case study and true single-case experiments are many evaluation options, and these are the topic of this chapter.

Although methodology and research design are considered to be uniquely relevant for researchers, this is not quite true. I have noted before that methodology is not a set of research practices and strategies (random assignment, statistical evaluation), but rather a way of thinking about phenomena and obtaining information and knowledge. This way of thinking is as relevant to clinical work as it is to laboratory research. Both research and clinical work are interested in drawing inferences, in knowing, and in understanding and hence share some of the thought processes as well as methodological strategies. Of course, clinical work has significant additional obligations and ethical responsibilities to the individual client. In the history of clinical psychology and psychiatry, the priority of the client and concerns for his or her well being have been used as an argument for not evaluating therapy or treatment progress. This is a wonderful example of a nonsequitur. Assessment, evaluation, and drawing informed inferences are especially important when an effort is made to help someone.

This chapter focuses on valuation in clinical practice for the individual client. In such applications the clinical investigator brings to bear critical information, assessment and data evaluation to draw inferences about whether change has occurred and the nature and bases of the change. Approximations of single-case designs that can be used for clinical work and a broader evaluation strategy are elaborated here. The purpose of this chapter is to convey evaluation of the single case that can be used to obtain knowledge in relation to patient care.

QUASI-EXPERIMENTS WITH THE SINGLE CASE

In the discussion of group experiments, true experiments were mentioned as those designs in which all of the conditions of experimentation can be met (random assignment of subjects to conditions, careful control over the situation). Quasi-experiments were approximations that were not quite as good. Although true experiments are wonderful as a basis of drawing inferences, there is no need to be too righteous, exclusive, or elitist about their role. The fact is that most studies in the biological, physical, and social sciences are *not* on true experiments, if for no other reason than the investigator cannot manipulate many of the conditions of interest. Strong inferences can be drawn from quasi-experiments in which there is systematic assessment, evaluation, and analytic thinking (about threats to validity, possible confounds, sources of bias and artifact).

In clinical work the investigator wishes to demonstrate that there is a treatment effect and that treatment is likely to be responsible for change. The fact that this is a case study (single case) does not mean that this has to be a loose and anecdotal case study. The question is, "What can be done on the part of the investigator to improve the quality of the inferences that can be drawn?" Stated another way, "What can the investigator do to help make implausible competing interpretations of the results?"

What to Do to Improve the Quality of Inferences

The essential features of true single-case experiments are control of the intervention (withdrawing and presenting intervention and/or baseline conditions), assessing performance continuously over time and under different conditions, and looking for stable patterns to make and test predictions about performance. Case studies can be arranged to deploy various combinations of these to greatly increase the extent to which threats to validity are ruled out or made implausible (Kazdin, 1981; Sechrest et al., 1996). The challenge is adding and utilizing available information to improve the information and quality of inferences that can be drawn.

Collect Systematic Data.   Case studies vary in the type of data or information that serves as a basis for claiming that change has occurred. At one extreme, anecdotal information may be used, which includes reports by the client or therapist that therapeutic change has been achieved. At the other extreme, case studies can include systematic assessment information, such as self-report inventories, ratings by other persons, and direct measures of overt behavior. Various scales and measurement devices have their own problems (reactivity, response biases) but still provide a stronger basis for determining whether change has occurred. If more standardized information is available, at least the therapist has a better basis for claiming that change has been achieved. The data do not allow one to infer the basis for the change. Objective assessment and the resulting data serve as a prerequisite because they provide information that change has, in fact, occurred.

Assess on Multiple Occasions.

Another dimension that can distinguish case studies is the number and timing of the assessment occasions. Major options consist of collecting information on a one- or two-shot basis (posttreatment only or pre- and posttreatment) or continuously over time (every day, a few times per week, or right before each therapy session). When information is collected on one or two occasions (pre, post), threats to internal validity associated with assessment (testing, instrumentation, statistical regression) can be especially difficult to rule out. With continuous assessment over time, these threats are much less plausible, especially if continuous assessment begins before treatment and continues over the course of treatment. Continuous assessment allows one to examine the pattern of the data and whether the pattern appears to have been altered at the point in which the intervention was introduced. If a case study includes continuous assessment on several occasions over time, some of the threats to internal validity related to assessment can be ruled out.

Consider Past and Future Projections of Performance.

The extent to which claims can be made about performance in the past and likely performance in the future can distinguish cases. Past and future projections refer to the course of a particular behavior or problem. For some behaviors or problems an extended history indicating no change may be evident. If performance changes when treatment is applied, the likelihood that treatment caused the change is increased. Problems that have a short history or that tend to occur for brief periods or in episodes may change anyway without the treatment. Problems with an extended history of stable performance are likely to continue unless some special event (e.g., treatment) alters its course. Thus, the history of the problem may influence the plausibility that extraneous events or processes (history, maturation), other than treatment, could plausibly account for the change.

Projections of what performance would be like in the future might be obtained from knowledge of the nature of the problem. For example, the problem may be one that would not improve without intervention (e.g., terminal illness). Knowing the likely outcome increases the inferences that can be drawn about the impact of an intervention that alters this course. The patient's improvement attests to the efficacy of the treatment as the critical variable because change in the problem controverts the expected prediction.

Projections of future performance may derive from continuous assessment over time exactly in the way elaborated in the previous chapter and the discussion of single-case experiments. If a particular problem is very stable, as indicated by continuous assessment before treatment, the likely prediction is that it will remain at that level in the future. If an intervention is applied and performance departs from the predicted level, this suggests that the intervention rather than other factors (history and maturation, repeated testing) may have been responsible for the change. This was the logic of ABAB designs.

Consider the Type of Effect Associated with Treatment.

Cases also differ in terms of the type of effects or changes that are evident as treatment is applied. The immediacy and magnitude of change contribute to the inferences that can be drawn about the role of treatment. Usually, the more immediate the therapeutic change after the onset of treatment, the stronger a case can be made that the treatment was responsible for change. An immediate change with the onset of treatment may make it more plausible that the treatment, rather than other events, led to change. On the other hand, gradual changes or changes that begin well after treatment has been applied are more difficult to interpret because of the intervening experiences between the onset of treatment and therapeutic change.

Aside from the immediacy of change, the magnitude of the change is important as well. When marked changes in performance are achieved, this suggests that only a special event, probably the treatment, could be responsible. Of course, the magnitude and immediacy of change, when combined, increase the confidence one can place in according treatment a causal role. Rapid and dramatic changes provide a strong basis for attributing the effects to treatment. Gradual and relatively small changes might more easily be discounted by random fluctuations of performance, normal cycles of behavior, or developmental changes.

Use Multiple and Heterogeneous Subjects.

The number of subjects included in a case report can influence the confidence that can be placed in any inferences drawn about treatment. Demonstrations with several cases, rather than with one case, provide a stronger basis for inferring the effects of treatment. Essentially, each case can be viewed as a replication of the original effect that seemed to result from treatment. The more cases that improve with treatment, the more unlikely that any particular extraneous event was responsible for change. Extraneous events probably varied among the cases, and the common experience, namely, treatment, may be the most plausible reason for the therapeutic changes.

The heterogeneity of the cases or diversity of the types of persons may also contribute to inferences about the cause of therapeutic change. If change is demonstrated among several clients who differ in subject and demographic variables (age, gender, race, social class, clinical problems), the inferences that can be made about treatment are stronger than if this diversity does not exist. With a heterogeneous set of clients the likelihood that a particular threat to internal validity (history, maturation) could explain the results is reduced.

Design Variations

The previously mentioned characteristics, when applied to clinical work, can greatly increase the strength of inferences that can be drawn relative to uncontrolled case studies. Depending on how the different characteristics are addressed within a particular demonstration, it is quite possible that the inferences closely approximate those that could be obtained from a true single-case experiment. Not all of the dimensions are under the control of the clinician/investigator (e.g., immediacy and strength of treatment effects). On the other hand, critical features upon which conclusions depend—such as the use of replicable measures and assessment on multiple occasions—can be controlled in the clinical situation and greatly enhance the demonstration.

It is useful to consider a few of the examples of quasi-experiments with the single case that vary on the characteristics mentioned previously. These convey how the quality of the inferences that are drawn can vary and what the investigator can do in clinical applications or research to strengthen the demonstration. Table 11.1 illustrates a few types of case studies that differ on some of the dimensions mentioned previously. Also, the extent to which each type of case rules out the specific threats to internal validity is presented. For each type of case the collection of data was included because, as noted earlier, the absence of objective or quantifiable data usually precludes drawing conclusions about whether change occurred.

Case Study 1: With Pre- and Postassessment.   Use of pre- and posttreatment assessment for the individual increases the informational yield; systematic assessment, more than unsystematic anecdotal reports, improve clinical information greatly. Table 11.1 illustrates a case with pre- and postassessment but without other charac-

TABLE 11.1.   Selected Types of Hypothetical Cases and the Threats to Internal Validity They Address

Type of case study	Case Study 1 (Pre- and postassessment)	Case Study 2 (Repeated assessment and marked changes)	Case Study 3 (Multiple cases, continuous assessment, stable performance)
Characteristics of case present (yes) or absent/not specified (no)			
Objective data	yes	yes	yes
Continuous assessment	no	yes	yes
Stability of problem	no	no	yes
Immediate and marked effects	no	yes	no
Multiple cases	no	no	yes
Major threats to internal validity ruled out (+) or not ruled out (−)			
History	−	?	+
Maturation	−	?	+
Testing	−	+	+
Instrumentation	−	+	+
Statistical regression	−	+	+

Note: In the table a "+" indicates that the threat to internal validity is probably controlled, a "−" indicates that the threat remains a problem, and a "?" indicates that the threat may remain uncontrolled. In preparation of the table, selected threats were omitted because they arise primarily in the comparison of different groups in experiments. They are not usually a problem for a case study, which, of course, does not rely on group comparisons.

teristics that would help rule out threats to internal validity. Improved assessment permits comments about whether change has occurred. This is not trivial. The goal of most therapy is to effect some change (in affect, behavior, and/or cognition). The failure to systematically assess change routinely in treatment goes beyond methodological issues and, indeed, raises questions about the entire enterprise of treatment, professional accountability, ethical issues, and high moral ground beyond the purpose of this chapter.

Assessment alone is valuable for identifying change, but determining the basis of the change is another matter. Ruling out various threats to internal validity and concluding that treatment led to change depends on other dimensions (listed in the table) than the assessment procedures alone. It is quite possible that events occurring in time (history), processes of change within the individual (maturation), repeated exposure to assessment (testing), changes in the scoring criteria (instrumentation), or reversion of the score to the mean (regression)—rather than treatment—led to change. In short, threats to internal validity are not ruled out in this situation, so the basis for change remains a matter of surmise.

Case Study 2: With Repeated Assessment and Marked Changes.   If the case study includes assessment on multiple occasions before and after treatment and the changes associated with the intervention are relatively marked, the inferences that can be drawn about treatment are vastly improved. Table 11.1 illustrates the characteristics of such a case, along with the extent to which specific threats to internal validity are addressed. The fact that continuous assessment is included is important in ruling out the specific threats to internal validity related to assessment. Also, therapeutic changes coincide with the onset of treatment. This pattern of change is not likely to result from exposure to repeated testing or changes in the instrument. When continuous assessment is used, any changes due to testing or instrumentation would be evident before treatment began. Similarly, regression to the mean from one data point to another, a special problem with assessment conducted at only two points in time, is eliminated. Repeated observation over time shows a pattern in the data. Extreme scores may be a problem for any particular assessment occasion in relation to the immediately prior occasion. However, these changes cannot account for the pattern of performance for an extended period.

Aside from continuous assessment, this illustration includes relatively marked treatment effects, that is, changes that are relatively immediate and large. These types of changes produced in treatment help reduce the possibility that history and maturation explain the results. Maturation in particular may be relatively implausible because maturational changes are not likely to be abrupt and large. Nevertheless, a "?" was placed in the table because maturation cannot be ruled out completely. In this case example, information on the stability of the problem in the past and future was not included. Hence, it is not known whether the clinical problem might ordinarily change on its own and whether maturational influences are plausible. Some problems that are episodic in nature (e.g., depression) conceivably could show marked changes that have little to do with treatment. With immediate and large changes in behavior, history and maturation may be ruled out, too, although these are likely to depend on other dimensions in the table that specifically were omitted from this case.

Case Study 3: With Multiple Cases, Continuous Assessment, and Stability Information.   Several cases rather than only one may be studied. The cases may be treated one at a time and accumulated into a final summary statement of treatment effects or treated as a single group at the same time. In this illustration, assessment information is available on repeated occasions before and during treatment. Also, the stability of the problem is known in this example. Stability refers to the dimension of past–future projections and denotes that other research suggests that the problem does not usually change over time. When the problem is known to be highly stable or to follow a particular course without treatment, the investigator has an implicit prediction of the effects of no treatment. The results can be compared with this predicted level of performance.

As is evident in Table 11.1, several threats to internal validity are addressed by a case report meeting the specified characteristics. History and maturation are not likely to interfere with drawing conclusions about the causal role of treatment because several different cases are included. Not all cases are likely to have a single historical event or maturational process in common that could account for the results. Knowledge about the stability of the problem in the future also helps to rule out the influence of history and maturation. If the problem is known to be stable over time, this means that ordinary historical events and maturational processes do not provide a strong enough influence in their own right. Because of the use of multiple subjects and the knowledge about the stability of the problem, history and maturation probably are implausible explanations of therapeutic change.

The threats to internal validity related to testing are handled largely by continuous assessment over time. Repeated testing, changes in the instrument, and reversion of scores toward the mean may influence performance from one occasion to another. Yet, problems associated with testing are not likely to influence the pattern of data over a large number of occasions. Also, information about the stability of the problem helps further to make implausible any changes due to testing. The fact that the problem is known to be stable means that it probably would not change merely as a function of repeated assessment.

In general, the case study of the type illustrated in this example provides a strong basis for drawing valid inferences about the impact of treatment. The manner in which the multiple-case report is designed does not constitute an experiment, as usually conceived, because each case represents an uncontrolled demonstration. However, characteristics of the type of case study can rule out specific threats to internal validity in a manner approaching that of true experiments.

Case Illustrations

A few illustrations convey more concretely the continuum of confidence one might place in the notion that the intervention was responsible for change. Each illustration qualifies as a quasi-experiment because it captures features of true experiments and varies in the extent to which specific threats can be made implausible. In the first illustration, treatment was applied to decrease the weight of an obese 55-year-old woman (180 lb., 5′5″) (Martin & Sachs, 1973). The woman had been advised to lose weight, a recommendation of some urgency in light of her recent heart attack. The woman was treated as an outpatient. The treatment consisted of developing a contract or agreement with the therapist based on adherence to a variety of rules and recommendations that would alter her eating habits. Several rules were developed pertaining to rewarding herself for resisting tempting foods, self-recording what was eaten after meals and snacks, weighing herself frequently each day, chewing foods slowly, and others. The patient had been weighed before treatment, and therapy began with weekly assessment for a four-and-one-half-week period.

The results of the program, which appear in Figure 11.1, indicate that the woman's initial weight of 180 was followed by a gradual decline in weight over the next few weeks before treatment was terminated. For present purposes what can be said about the impact of treatment? Actually, statements about the effects of the treatment in accounting for the changes would be tentative at best. The stability of her pretreatment weight is unclear. The first data point indicated that the woman was 180 lb. before treatment. Perhaps this weight would have declined over the next few weeks even without a special weight-reduction program. The absence of clear information regarding the stability of the woman's weight before treatment makes evaluation of her subsequent loss rather difficult. The fact that the decline is gradual and modest, albeit understandable given the expected course of weight reduction, introduces further ambiguity. The weight loss is clear, but it would be difficult to argue strongly that the intervention—rather than historical events, maturational processes, or repeated assessment—led to these results.

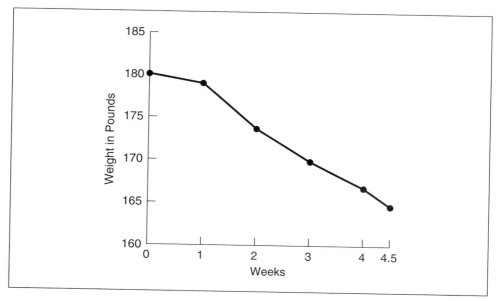

FIGURE 11.1.   Weight in pounds per week. The line represents the connecting of the weights, respectively, on the days 0, 7, 14, 21, 28, and 31 of the weight loss program.

Source: Martin, J.E., & Sachs, D.A. (1973). The effects of a self-control weight loss program on an obese woman. *Journal of Behavior Therapy and Experimental Psychiatry, 24,* 155–159. Copyright © 1973 by Elsevier Science. Reprinted with permission.

The next illustration provides a slightly more persuasive demonstration that treatment may have led to the results. This case included a 49-year-old woman with a long-standing history of obsessional thoughts related to shame and worry about toilet odors and flatulence (Ladouceur et al., 1993). The woman had a history of intestinal problems and anxiety disorders. The goal of treatment was to reduce intrusive thoughts, which usually took the form of internal statements (I'm going to fart, and I'm going to have diarrhea) that occurred several (12–21) times a day. A program was designed to decrease these thoughts by repeatedly exposing her to these thoughts via a tape recording she made. The tape simply repeated these statements. She listened to the tape through a cassette recorder she used in everyday life. She listened to the tape over the course of the day and was instructed *not* to engage in distracting thoughts. These thoughts were considered to maintain these intrusive thoughts inadvertently by not letting obsessions extinguish their anxiety-evoking properties. Before treatment her initial rate of intrusive thoughts was self-monitored. After several days the program was introduced, and thoughts continued to be self-monitored. The results of the program appear in Figure 11.2, which shows her daily rate of intrusive thoughts across baseline and intervention phases.

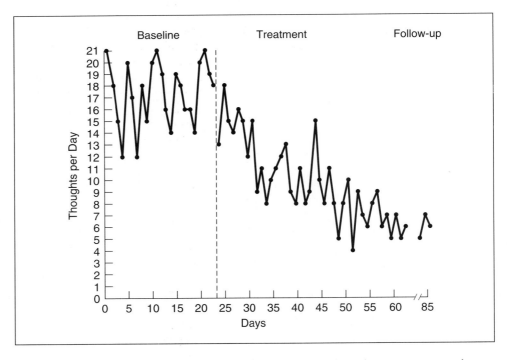

FIGURE 11.2.   Intrusive thoughts per day over the course of baseline, treatment, and follow-up (3 weeks after treatment ended).

Source: Ladouceur, R., Freeston, M.H., Gagnon, F., Thibodeau, N., & Dumont, J. Idiographic considerations in the behavioral treatment of obsessional thoughts. *Journal of Behavior Therapy and Experimental Psychiatry, 24,* 301–310. Copyright © 1986 by Elsevier Science. Reprinted with permission.

The results suggest that the intervention may have been responsible for change. The inference is aided by continuous assessment over time before and during the intervention phase. The number of intrusive thoughts fluctuated during baseline, but still was relatively stable (no clear slope). The baseline pattern suggests that no change was likely to occur with continued observations alone. When the intervention was introduced, intrusive thoughts declined and continued to show a decline, which was maintained at a follow-up assessment three weeks after treatment ended. The data pattern suggests that intervening was probably responsible for the change.

A few features of the demonstration may detract from the confidence one might place in according treatment a causal role. The gradual decline evident in the figure might also have resulted from other influences than the treatment, such as increased attention to the problem (historical event) or boredom with continuing the assessment procedure (maturation). Also, the fact that the patient was responsible for collecting the observations raises concerns about whether accuracy of scoring changed over time (instrumentation), rather than the actual rate of intrusive thoughts. Yet, the data can be taken as presented without undue methodological skepticism. As such, the intervention appears to have led to change, but the quasi-experimental nature of the design and the pattern of results make it difficult to rule out threats to internal validity with great confidence.

In the next illustration the effects of the intervention appeared even clearer than in the previous example. In this report a female adult with agoraphobia and panic attacks participated in outpatient treatment to overcome her fear of leaving home and her self-imposed restriction to her home (O'Donohue, Plaud, & Hecker, 1992). The patient kept a record of all activities in which she engaged and the time devoted to them. At the beginning of treatment, activities that might be reinforcing were also identified. The intervention consisted of instructing the case to engage in rewarding activities (time with her pet, reading, entertaining visitors) only when outside of the home. Examples included walking down the street, socializing with neighbors, and watching TV at a neighbor's home.

The effects of the procedure in increasing time out of the home are illustrated in Figure 11.3. The baseline period indicated a consistent pattern of no time spent outside of the home. When the intervention began, time outside the home sharply increased and remained high at a 2-month and an 18-month follow-up. Acquaintances and relatives, who reported on specific activities in which the patient had engaged, corroborated these changes. The stable and very clear baseline and the marked changes with onset of the intervention suggest that history, maturation, or other threats could not readily account for the results. Within the limits of quasi-experimental designs, the results are relatively clear.

Among the previous examples, the likelihood that the intervention accounted for change was increasingly plausible in light of characteristics of the report. In this final illustration, the effects of the intervention are extremely clear. The purpose of this report was to investigate a novel method of treating bedwetting (enuresis) among children (Azrin, Hontos, & Besalel-Azrin, 1979). Forty-four children, ranging in age from 3–15 years, were included. Their families collected data on the number of nighttime bedwetting accidents for seven days before treatment. After baseline, the training procedure was implemented: The child was required to practice getting up from bed at

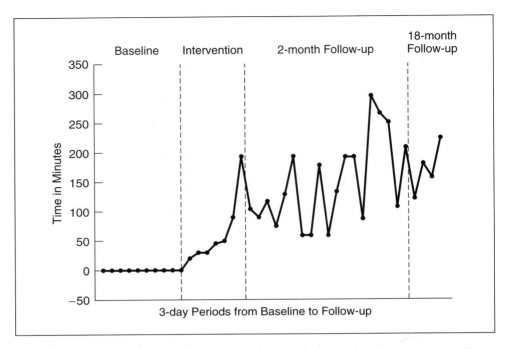

FIGURE 11.3.   Total time an adult patient with agoraphobia and panic spent in activities outside of the home over baseline, intervention, and two follow-up assessment periods.

Source: O'Donohue, W., Plaud, J.J., & Hecker, J.E. The possible function of positive reinforcement in home-bound agoraphobia: A case study. *Journal of Behavior Therapy and Experimental Psychiatry, 23,* 303–312. Copyright © 1992 by Elsevier Science. Reprinted with permission.

night, remaking the bed after he or she wet, and changing clothes. Other procedures were included as well, such as waking the child early at night in the beginning of training and developing increased bladder capacity by reinforcing increases in urine volume. The parents and children practiced some of the procedures in the training session, but the intervention was essentially carried out at home when the child wet his or her bed.

The effects of training are illustrated in Figure 11.4, which shows bedwetting during the pretraining (baseline) and training periods. The demonstration is a quasi-experimental design, because several of the conditions discussed previously were included to help rule out threats to internal validity. The data suggest that the problem was relatively stable for the group as a whole during the baseline period. Also, the changes in performance at the onset of treatment were immediate and marked. Finally, several subjects were included who probably were not very homogeneous because the subjects' ages encompassed young children through teenagers. In light of these characteristics of the demonstration, it is not very plausible that the changes could be accounted for by history, maturation, repeated assessment, changes in the assessment procedures, or statistical regression.

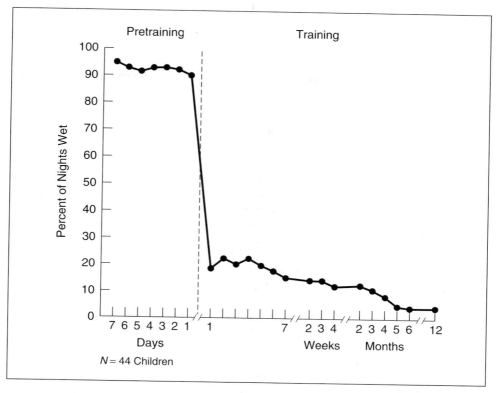

FIGURE 11.4.   Bedwetting by 44 enuretic children after office instruction in an operant learning method. Each data point designates the percentage of nights on which bedwetting occurred. The data prior to the dotted line are for a seven-day period prior to training. The data are presented daily for the first week, weekly for the first month, and monthly for the first six months and for the twelfth month.

Source: Azrin, N.H., Hontos, P.T., & Besalel-Azrin, V. (1979). Elimination of enuresis without a conditioning apparatus: An extension by office instruction of the child and parents. *Behavior Therapy, 10*, 14–19. Copyright © 1979 by the Association for Advancement of Behavior Therapy. Reprinted by permission of the publisher.

The use of features of single-case designs as aids in clinical situations addresses a broader point. Threats to internal validity in any given research and clinical situation warrant close scrutiny. Plausible threats when recognized in advance can be circumvented or addressed in many ways. In clinical work, adopting many of the features of true single-case experimental designs can greatly strengthen the conclusions that can be drawn. In any given case the arrangement of approximations or quasi-experiments can reduce the plausibility of threats to validity in ways that are as clear as true experiments. Design features from single-case experiments are not mere methodological niceties. When integrated with clinical work, they can greatly improve the quality of patient care and evaluation of treatment progress (Kazdin, 1993). Such work no doubt entails complexities not addressed here, such as developing measures to assess special characteristics, using standard measures in novel ways they have not been used, (continuous assessment of psychopathology, depression, with standardized scales). However imperfect quasi-experimental evaluations may prove, they offer distinct advantages over and above anecdotal cases, with which they often compete.

METHODS FOR ASSESSMENT AND EVALUATION IN CLINICAL PRACTICE

It may be that the quasi-experimental designs already highlighted still represent too stringent requirements to introduce into clinical practice or are not sufficiently concrete to guide outpatient therapy. It is useful to convey more concretely how systematic assessment and evaluation can be used in clinical practice to enhance evaluation. It is important to clarify a basic point about clinical work, namely, assessment and evaluation are routinely going on in all clinical work. We do not consider it that way because it is so unsystematic (no measures, no objective way of measuring progress). As the quasi-single-case designs illustrate, the key to all evaluation is careful assessment. A model of clinical evaluation is highlighted here to draw on elements from single-case designs but to do so in ways that are sensitive to the demands of clinical practice.

An important point of departure for developing a methodology for clinical practice is to identify the central requirements. Clearly, the first requirement of a methodology for clinical practice is recognition of the priority of clinical care. Unequivocally, methodological practices are to be used toward the benefit of the individual patient. Second, assessment and evaluation practices and other methodological requirements must be in harmony with exigencies of the clinical situation. The assessment methods must be able to accommodate a wide range of clinical problems and situations. We must begin with clinical situations and develop systematic assessment and evaluation with these characteristics in mind.

Although one can emphasize practices of assessment, design, and evaluation, methodology is also a way of thinking about phenomena and systematizing the information we obtain to draw inferences. The thought processes reflect concerns about ways of operationalizing critical constructs, posing hypotheses about interventions and processes leading to change, and testing assumptions about interventions and their impact. Assessment, design, and evaluation are not alien to clinical practice. Invariably, practitioners are always drawing inferences, actively or passively making decisions on what they perceive, and so on. A methodology for clinical practice does not introduce assessment, design, and evaluation. Rather, it brings these practices into harmony with tenets of science (testing hypotheses, operationalizing critical concepts, fostering replication). The special feature is to utilize evaluation concepts and practices to advance therapeutic progress of individual clients. To that end, the primary goal of a methodology for clinical practice is to assess, evaluate, and demonstrate change. Single-case research designs provide useful leads and, as an approach, are more relevant and useful to clinical work than group methods. Assessment and evaluation, more than experimental design, are key features of single-case research that might be applicable.

Steps for Evaluation in Clinical Work

Systematic assessment and evaluation of the effects of treatment in clinical practice have as their goals fostering the high-quality patient care and contributing to the knowledge base on the effects of therapy. High-quality care must come first, given the priorities of treatment in clinical work. Contribution to the knowledge base refers to addressing important questions about the effects of treatment, as elaborated in the range of questions we wish to answer about treatment. Introducing systematic assessment to clinical practice is not merely the addition of a few measures to supplement clinical judgment. Several steps are essential to evaluation in clinical work. The steps are summarized in Table 11.2 and elaborated here.

Specifying and Assessing Treatment Goals.   Identifying treatment goals is a prerequisite to the selection of measures for assessment and evaluation. The goals refer initially to the objectives for the client (reduction of symptoms, improved functioning at home and at work) that treatment is designed to address. Identifying the goals is a prerequisite to the selection of measures. Therapy can have many different goals, and, indeed, in clinical work these are tailored to individual clients. Consequently, prioritizing the goals is important as well. There may well be several interrelated areas to which the treatment is directed. They ought to be prioritized in a way that permits

TABLE 11.2.   Key Steps for Systematic Evaluation in Clinical Practice

---

1. Specifying and Assessing Treatment Goals

Explicitly identifying the initial focus of treatment and the goals or changes that are desired. Selecting or developing a measure that reflects the current status of the individual on these characteristics (symptoms, functioning).

2. Specifying and Assessing Procedures and Processes

Explicitly identifying the means or processes (procedures, tasks, activities, and experiences) that are expected to lead to therapeutic change. Measuring the extent to which these means or their performance, execution, or implementation are achieved during treatment.

3. Selecting Measures

Identifying or developing the instruments, scales, or measures that will be used to assess progress over the course of treatment. This may require developing or individualizing a measure for the child, adolescent, and family. Identifying the measure of process or procedures depends heavily on whether the procedures are straightforward (execution of tasks in the session) or emergent processes (alliance, bonding) that require separate measures.

4. Assessment Occasions

Measuring performance on the domains or goals toward which treatment is directed before treatment begins and then on a regular, ongoing basis over the course of treatment. Ongoing assessment may be every session, every other session, or some other regimen that allows one to see any patterns or trends over time.

5. Design and Data Evaluation

Displaying the information obtained from the assessment to permit one to examine changes, patterns, or other features of progress that can directly inform treatment decisions (changing or ending treatment, shifting the focus of treatment). Graphical displays are especially useful.

---

initial assessment as well as treatment decisions. It is unlikely that treatment will affect all areas equally well or even in the same way or direction (e.g., improvement). Assessment of treatment outcome often shows that different measures can yield different conclusions (Kazdin, 2000; Lambert, 1983). Hence, it is useful to identify the initial salient goals and to select measures to assess progress toward them.

The selection of one or a few initial goals does not mean that this is the only focus of treatment. Rather, it means that assessment will sample critically relevant facets of client functioning on which to examine progress and treatment impact. The goals may vary over time, based on changing priorities and progress in treatment. For example, excessive dieting and maladaptive food consumption may serve as the initial treatment focus for a young adult referred for an eating disorder. The focus may shift toward less immediate but no less important domains such as body image, management of stress, and relations with peers. The critical point is that specifying goals does not mean that these goals become a destination toward which the course of treatment is irrevocably plotted. The goals of therapy are often multiple, and making them explicit is an initial as well as ongoing step. For our purposes specification and operationalization of treatment goals are central.

Specifying and Assessing Procedures and Processes.   We must also specify the means of achieving the goals. This usually refers to one of two possibilities. First, the means of achieving therapeutic change may refer to the procedures used in treatment, that is, what the therapist does and what the client is asked to do in or outside of the sessions. Second, the means of achieving change may refer to emergent processes or relationship issues (experiencing emotions, developing a therapeutic alliance). Specifying procedures or processes is not an end in itself. The primary goal is to utilize the information to benefit the client based on how well treatment was implemented and the ends that were achieved.

Treatment integrity, mentioned previously, is relevant to evaluation of the treatment in clinical work. Ongoing assessment of client progress (change on the measures related to the goals) may reveal that there is no therapeutic change. Assessment of procedures or processes that the therapist believes are important may provide useful information regarding how to proceed. The information may reveal that treatment procedures (addressing certain topics, experiencing special types of insight, engaging in role play during the sessions) were not implemented very well, or processes within sessions (developing an alliance, dealing with a particular conflict) were not achieved. Hence, it is reasonable to try different strategies to alter these processes.

On the other hand, assessment of treatment processes or means may reveal that the processes have been evoked fairly well, but no therapeutic changes are evident. Here a different treatment approach might be reasonable to try. In general, assurances are needed that the procedures were tried or that the processes identified by the therapist were achieved. Making the procedures or means explicit in relation to the goals is an initial step toward this end. As with the goal of treatment, specification of the means to obtain them is an initial step for developing assessment procedures.

Selecting Measures.   Specification of the goals of treatment identifies the constructs of interest to the therapist and client. The next step is to operationalize the constructs by noting the specific measure(s) that will be used. Selecting the measure requires decisions about the source of information (self-, other-, clinician report) and assessment method (objective measures of personality or psychopathology [various standard questionnaires and inventories], client diaries, card sorts, projective methods, interviews, direct observation, and others). In principle the available measures include the full range of psychological instruments that have been developed. As noted further below, a significant problem is that very few measures have been developed for repeated assessment and clinical work. This is no reason to revert to clinical judgment a la the anecdotal case study. Judgment can be codified and completed in a systematic and reliable way. Systematic assessment is almost always preferred even if the measure is not yet validated. Indeed, the process of validation and test development is all about collecting systematic data on measures not yet well developed.

Measures can be devised and individualized by selecting items from a large symptom list, a standardized instrument, or an open-ended clinical interview. For examples, subscales from the Minnesota Multiphasic Personality Inventory (MMPI) for adults or MMPI-A (for adolescents) (Williams, Butcher, Ben-Porath, & Graham, 1992) or the Child Behavior Checklist (Achenbach, 1991) for children and adolescents might be useful to generate items for clinical use. Several items can be selected from a larger pool to provide an individualized measure specific to the problems of the client (see Clement, 1999; Kiresuk & Garwick, 1979; Shapiro, 1964).

In clinical work, measures will need to be developed that can be individually tailored to the client and treatment. Familiarity with scale development and available instruments will be useful. Measures useful in clinical work, drawing on a variety of different assessment methods, have been identified elsewhere (Alter & Evens, 1990; Epstein, Kutash, & Duchnowski, 1998; Faulkner & Gray, 1997). Rating scales represent a particularly useful format and present an endless array of options that can be developed and evaluated (see Aiken, 1996). Such measures have been described and formatted to facilitate their use in clinical settings (Clement, 1999; Wiger, 1999).

In addition to measurement of client functioning, measurement of the treatment means or processes are important as well. The specific type of treatment and putative processes or features leading to change dictate the assessment focus. The therapist proposes (hypothesizes) that specific means are central to therapeutic change. If these (e.g., quality of the relationship with the client) can vary with treatment administration, their assessment is likely to be useful. The reason is that, as part of decision making, we wish to know whether the components or processes of treatment were reasonably delivered and tested. Also, the therapist may want to try different interventions to alter the processes, that is, to improve parent participation. The assessment priority is evaluating clinical outcome and systematically collecting information on whether the client is changing over the course of treatment. Other assessments may be luxury items for practical reasons. At the same time, there ought to be documentation of the means of achieving change and sufficient description that the procedures (what treatment, number of sessions, content of the sessions) could be replicated.

Assessment Occasions. Before treatment begins, clinics often administer measures to obtain basic subject and demographic information, to evaluate broad domains of functioning, to attain information for diagnostic purposes, and to rule out conditions that might require other interventions or attention (e.g., medical diagnosis). Initial assessment is critical to identify characteristics of persons who are treated. Descriptive variables are not a major burden on the delivery of services in treatment; indeed, many of the descriptors are required for administrative purposes (e.g., insurance). Presumably, a significant portion of the information obtained at pretreatment also determines the goals and foci of treatment. In addition, the information can be useful for developing the knowledge base. As cases accumulate in clinical practice, treatment outcomes (dropping out, therapeutic change) can be evaluated in relation to moderators and predictor variables.

Central to evaluation in clinical practice and the major change that is needed is ongoing, continuous assessment before and during the course of treatment. This is a critical component of single-case designs and can be adopted for clinical work. Ongoing assessment can be used to chart where the client is at the beginning of treatment and to see if changes are made over time. Several data points are needed, not merely to assess the mean level of functioning over time but also to have an idea regarding variability and trends on the measure. There are many opportunities for flexible application of continuous assessment. For example, pretreatment assessment for as little as two or three assessment occasions (although more occasions generally are better) provides a baseline to help evaluate subsequent progress. At least two or three assessment occasions are needed prior to treatment. It is quite possible that the level of performance on the measure is at an extreme due to stress or crisis, and that marked changes from the first to second assessment occasion would be expected due to statistical regression, passing of the crisis, and repeated testing on the instrument (see Kazdin, 1998b). Assessment on three occasions can help rule out such artifacts. The assessment during baseline may even show improvement and hence has implications for redefining the goals of treatment, the means to obtain them, and the selection of measures to evaluate treatment.

As highlighted in the context of single-case designs, the initial assessment provides descriptive information (baseline) about the level of performance and its variation. It is possible that only one assessment occasion will be feasible or, indeed, that no assessment is feasible due to the urgent nature of the treatment. In most psychotherapy cases it is not clear at the first contact that intervention is absolutely essential. Usually, assessment can begin while there is some effort to manage the situation. In cases wherein treatment begins immediately, there may also be the prospect of retrospective baseline, in which the client and others in his or her life provide an estimate of recent performance. Apart from baseline assessment, evaluation during the treatment phase is pivotal to evaluate change during this period.

Typically, therapy does not involve systematic assessment in an ongoing way. Consequently, an initial step is to integrate assessment and treatment as part of service delivery. Several practical decisions and options for implementing the assessments can serve the goals of empirical evaluation. Many of the options may be dictated by individual characteristics, problems, and circumstances of the patient, the nature and type of treatment service, and characteristics and preferences of the therapist. For example, among assessment options, therapists might conduct a brief assessment (10–15 min) with the client at the beginning or end of each treatment session. Or the client or a relative can complete measures and bring them to the sessions, or call and leave recorded messages on a clinic answering machine if a log is kept or to be reported. It would not be difficult for clients to submit coded information (responses to questionnaire items from an individualized symptom checklist) from home on their computer that is automatically recorded on a clinic web site. Perhaps more readily available, secretarial staff or assistants can conduct a brief telephone interview covering critical items or direct the client to a room immediately before a session so the client can complete the measure(s). Similarly, a staff member or volunteer can sum scores or enter the information or data on an office computer software program to summarize or to graph the information. A number of options are possible for administering or assisting with assessment or summarizing the data. Ethical protections for office information apply to all such information in the usual way.

Whatever the assessment method, implementation requires discussion with the client. Use of the measures during clinical treatment is introduced in a way that conveys the interconnectedness of treatment and evaluation so the client understands that assessment is an important part of the care and service that is provided. The rationale for assessment can be provided at the outset when treatment is explained. Salient points include the importance of an initial evaluation and goal selection. Goals, and hence measures, may change during treatment. Thus, the focus on initial presenting complaints and their assessment would not preclude a subsequent shift.

Even if goals do not change, evaluation of the assessment procedure is important. Before or early in treatment it would be important to assess whether the level of client functioning is dysfunctional. It is possible that the measure would show that the client is functioning well. For example, if depression was assessed in an adolescent and a low Beck Depression Inventory score (0–3) was evident in pretreatment, reconsideration of the construct or measure would be important. If further discussion and interview revealed that depressive symptoms are manifest, another measure or an individualized measure might be needed.

Design and Data Evaluation.   Research design and data evaluation could easily be those components that undermine adoption of systematic methods of evaluation in clinical practice. Yet, each can be crafted to address the critical priorities and practical exigencies of clinical work. In clinical practice the central design issue is whether therapeutic change has occurred and whether it is likely to be due to treatment. As noted earlier in the chapter, the pattern of data over the course of therapy can help to decide whether change has occurred and the likely basis for change. The assessment of therapeutic procedures or processes also can assist in determining the likelihood that influences intended to achieve change contributed to outcome.

Data evaluation refers to identifying whether change has occurred, is reliable, and departs from the fluctuations one would expect without the intervention. Ongoing assessment provides data before and during the course of treatment that serve as the basis for this evaluation. Several methods are available to evaluate single-case information. Of all methods, graphical display (e.g., a simple line graph) is particularly useful for seeing the pattern in the data obtained over time (see Kazdin, 1982a; Parsonson & Baer, 1978). Nonstatistical data evaluation methods (changes in means, levels, and slope, and latency of change across phases), drawn from single-case experimental research, can be used for clinical evaluation. These criteria do not require computations, but follow directly from graphical presentation of the data. Also, if the data are entered regularly on a database, then graphical presentation and simple slope or trend lines (e.g., regression lines) can be plotted automatically or with a couple of mouse clicks.

Graphical displays and nonstatistical data evaluation are examples and by no means exhaust methods of evaluating change. A variety of other available evaluative aids vary in degrees of sophistication and complexity. For example, several methods of graphing (stem-and-leaf plots, box plots) data points for multiple subjects from group research might also be considered to plot multiple data points for individual subjects as a means to describe and to evaluate progress (see Rosenthal & Rosnow, 1991). Also, descriptive and inferential statistical techniques are available for continuous data obtained from the single case, as noted in the previous chapter. Nonstatistical and statistical evaluation methods examine whether improvements have been achieved, and say nothing about whether the changes are important or make a genuine difference in the everyday life of the client. Clinical significance of change addresses these latter concerns and will be covered in a later chapter.

Case Illustration

A methodology for clinical practice begins with development of assessment for the individual case. Selection and identification of initial goals and ongoing assessment of progress are central. A case description highlights these initial steps to show use in practice by focusing on assessment, leaving aside other features including design and data evaluation methods.

Brief Background. Gloria is a 39-year-old European-American woman who referred herself for outpatient treatment. She is married, with two children (ages 16 and 17). She and her husband are both college educated. Based on education, income, and husband's occupation, they are from a middle socioeconomic class. Gloria is not employed outside of the home; her husband is a manager of a computer software firm. She and her husband have been married for 18 years.

Gloria scheduled an appointment because she said she was depressed and needed to talk to someone. During the initial interview at the clinic, Gloria saw a male therapist, who asked, with open-ended questioning, about the reasons she sought treatment, sources of satisfaction and dissatisfaction in her life, relationships with significant others, symptoms, and related matters. Toward the end of this discussion, the therapist queried Gloria about what she expected and wished to obtain from treatment.

At the interview Gloria indicated that she had been treated for depression on separate occasions in her life, once during college and once after the birth of her first child. On each occasion she was placed on medication. She reported some relief but also complained about side effects and did not feel really helped overall with her problems. Currently, she said she was depressed again. She reported feeling "empty and lost" about her life and marriage. She said that she lacked meaning and direction in her life. She felt her life was "wasted" because she was not engaged in anything productive. She felt alienated from her husband and her children. In the case of her husband she felt great emotional distance due to years of reduced intimacy, joint activity, and time together. Her children were very important to her but she felt they did not need her very much now that they were teenagers. Gloria identified as her own goals for treatment simply feeling better about her life and not being depressed. She wished to feel some direction and to improve relations with her spouse and others. The therapist explained that he felt that a cognitive-behavioral treatment would be appropriate for these goals and explained how the treatment worked.

Assessment. In the initial interview the therapist introduced systematic assessment after the open-ended discussion provided an initial formulation of the focus. The assessment procedures were used to help make goals and directions of treatment more explicit and to quantify the domains that were to be the foci. The therapist used three measures. The first measure was designed to reflect the domains Gloria identified as important. At the end of about one hour of the interview, the therapist identified four major concerns, themes, or areas as a beginning for them to work on: (1) depressive thoughts and feelings, (2) little involvement in meaningful and fulfilling activities for herself, (3) disengagement from her family, and (4) few supportive contacts outside of the home. These four areas were identified by the therapist based on the interview and were discussed to see if they captured Gloria's experience, since they did not follow exactly from Gloria's formulation of the problems.

For each theme Gloria was asked to help construct statements that were graded to indicate different levels of functioning. The goal was to comprise a 4-point scale for each theme in which the 1 = worsening of the problem, 2 = current functioning/feelings, 3 = some improvement, and 4 = her goal of how she wanted to be/feel on this domain. The therapist referred to this as the Gloria Scale (G Scale) to help guide them during treatment. The therapist conveyed the concept of the 4-point scale, but Gloria provided the content of each of the statements. He asked her to describe a way to characterize her current functioning or where she was now, what it would be like if she became worse, what some improvement might look like, and how things would be if she really made the kind of change she wanted. Table 11.3 presents the four themes and the graded statements Gloria and the therapist constructed. For the assessment on the G Scale she was instructed to select the statement under each theme area that characterized how she felt during the previous week. After the scale was developed in the initial session, Gloria was asked specifically if the second statement of each theme area really captured her current feelings; she reported it did.

Two other measures were described and given to her to complete. She also completed the Beck Depression Inventory (BDI; Beck et al., 1961) to reflect severity of depressive symptoms. The measure includes 21 items; for each item, 1 of 5 (but scored 1–3) statements is selected. The statements differ in severity of the depressive symptoms. Gloria also completed the Quality of Life Inventory (QOLI; Frisch, 1998). The measure is a self-report scale that assesses overall quality of, and satisfaction with, life. Seventeen domains of life (love relationship, home, learning, recreation, friendships, philosophy of life, work, health, neighborhood) are covered. The weighted score is used for each domain based on the client's rating of the importance of that domain in his or her life (0 = not at all important, 2 = very important), then multiplied by the satisfaction derived from that domain (-3 = very dissatisfied to +3 = very satisfied). The BDI and QOLI took approximately 20 minutes total to complete.

TABLE 11.3.   Four Themes and Items for Gloria

I. Depressive Thoughts and Feelings

1. I feel more depressed and dejected than I did before I started treatment.
2. I feel about the same level of depression and dejection as I did when I started.
3. I feel a little better about my mood, and things are not as bad as before.
4. I feel a lot better; I do not think about my feelings as negative, and I have more energy to get out and do things.

II. Involvement in Meaningful and Fulfilling Activities

1. I really feel paralyzed about doing anything any more.
2. I am not doing anything differently now or anything special I like compared to when I started treatment.
3. I feel better that I have some direction and focus in what to do.
4. I am totally involved in some things as a career that give me good feelings about life.

III. Disengagement from the Family

1. I do less with my husband and children than before and don't seem to care about doing things with them.
2. Things really have not changed about my feelings. Everyone at home does his or her own thing, and my husband and I mostly just eat meals together.
3. My husband and I are a little better. We go out once in a while and are a couple again.
4. My husband and I are really "together." We are intimate in many ways and I can feel that he cares for me.

IV. Supportive Contacts Outside the Home

1. I am isolated from people in general, including my relatives who live in town.
2. Once in a while I see someone when I shop or at a school event with my children. We chat a bit but nothing beyond the superficial.
3. I meet someone to have coffee with or to go to an event or shopping with during the day.
4. I meet a few people by myself or some couples that my husband and I can get together with, and we do this on a regular basis.

Note: The theme areas were derived from an open-ended interview with Gloria. The specific statements were generated by her to reflect what it would be like to become worse, to remain the same, to improve a little, and to achieve her goal for that theme. These alternative outcomes reflect numbers 1 through 4, respectively, under each theme. Each time this particular measure was completed, Gloria selected the alternative statement under each theme that was closest to how she felt during the previous week.

The initial contact with Gloria lasted approximately 2 hours. Approximately 1.5 hours was spent with the therapist for the interview and development of the G Scale. After this, Gloria completed the BDI and QOLI and was scheduled to return the following week. She was asked to come 20 minutes before the session. When she returned for the second session, she completed the BDI and QOLI before the session began. After these were completed, she brought them to the therapist.

The therapist began the session by asking her to select one statement from each of the four theme areas that they had discussed. The material had now been typed (similar to Table 11.3). They briefly discussed whether the areas were still important to her and whether she felt that their last interview missed critical material. The therapist conveyed that the initial goals were a place to begin and that the information within the sessions and from the assessments would be important to make any mid-course corrections as needed.

At this point the therapist described and began treatment. The treatment employed by the therapist consisted of cognitive therapy combined with features of interpersonal psychotherapy. Cognitive therapy focused on maladaptive cognitions about herself related to her depressive affect, poor self-esteem, feelings that life was not worthwhile, and internal attributions regarding her views of herself (see Beck, Rush, Shaw, & Emery, 1979). Interpersonal psychotherapy focused on her interpersonal relations, roles, and the sources of satisfaction and emotion associated with each, and many of her feelings about herself as a spouse and parent (see Klerman, Weissman, Rounsaville, & Chevron, 1984). Therapy was an integration of these treatments (cognitions about her relations, emotions associated with them, her own attributions and those of others). She was also given specific tasks at the end of each session that were designed to increase mutually shared activities with her husband and to expand her activities and roles outside of the home. These activities were part of "assignments" developed with Gloria at the end of the sessions based on work within the session, any prior progress on other activities, and so on. Treatment was conducted weekly. Highlighted here is the assessment information and its use rather than the details of the treatment.

Each week Gloria was asked to arrive about 20 minutes before the session and to complete the G Scale, BDI, and QOLI. At the first and second sessions, the full scales were administered. However, there were symptoms and domains within the two standardized scales that problematic or not seemingly relevant to Gloria. Abbreviated versions of the BDI (15 items) and the QOLI (13 domains) were constructed and used throughout treatment, based on elimination of selected items.

The assessment information included scores from the G Scale, BDI, and QOLI. From each scale, performance was quantified with a summary total score for that measure to examine whether any systematic pattern or change might be evident as treatment progressed. The assessment information is graphed in Figure 11.5. The two assessment occasions prior to treatment were delineated as baseline (weeks B1, B2 in the Figure). Added to each graph is a linear regression line to characterize the slope that best fits the data. Overall, the individual data points and regression line suggest a trend toward improvement over time.

Although the overall scores are useful in summary form, the mean for all of the items of a given measure (e.g., BDI) with an individual case can suffer the same liability of using means in group research, to wit, they can obscure information that would be important to identify. In Gloria's case the G Scale and the QOLI indicated that she had made little progress in her relationship with her husband. The relationship issues emerged more fully in the treatment session of week 14. At the beginning of the session the therapist indicated that he thought this would be good time to discuss at length the original goals of treatment and how she had been doing, based on the assessment information and Gloria's appraisal of treatment.

Gloria indicated that she had felt much better about herself and her life. Her thoughts about her life, what is important, and her direction were much better. Over the course of treatment she had initiated a number of activities. She began a class at a local university and now planned to seek a degree in nursing. She had developed more interaction with a neighbor whom she met almost daily to engage in routine activities. Also, from her class she met a few people whom she enjoyed. Time with her

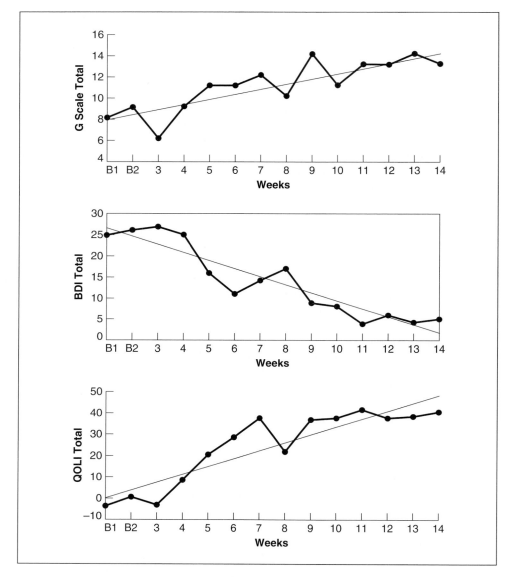

FIGURE 11.5. Session-by-session scores for Gloria on three measures including the "Gloria Scale" (G Scale, upper panel), the modified Beck Depression Inventory (BDI, middle panel), and the modified Quality of Life Inventory (QOLI, lower panel). The scores for each measure represent those items (BDI, QOLI) that were selected as relevant to the client and do not reflect the complete scales. Data are presented for 14 sessions (weeks). The first week was devoted entirely to interview and assessment. The second week began with completion of assessments followed by the initiation of treatment. The first two weeks (B1, B2) refer to baseline or pretreatment assessment. Given the direction of scoring of the measures, improvement would be reflected in increases for the G Scale and QOLI and a decrease in the BDI. Fitted to each graph is a linear regression line over the course of all data points.

children was more enjoyable. In general, she felt much better about her overall well being. At the same time she felt her relationship with her husband was not helped at all by treatment. Although she and her husband went out on a couple of "dates," she felt this turned out merely to be time together with no connection or closeness. She said she loved her husband and could not imagine being without him but that there seemed to be no closeness or contact like there used to be. The therapist suggested that they focus more on this for a few sessions but that the immediate goal would be for her and her husband to consider joint steps toward improving her marriage. The method highlighted previously for developing the G Scale was used again to identify theme areas within her marriage that were significant and the anchor points. The measure was added at this time to the assessment.

Treatment was continued for five more weeks. Gloria no longer completed the BDI and QOLI weekly. These were now completed every other week. Weekly assessment continued for the original G Scale and for added thematic areas related specifically to her marital relation. After five weeks Gloria and her husband agreed to begin marital counseling, and Gloria was no longer seen individually.

Discussion.   Some useful features of this case illustrate an approximation toward a methodology of clinical practice. First, efforts were made to make initial goals of treatment explicit and to quantify these. Second, systematic, clinically relevant, and user-friendly assessments were introduced. The assessment procedures included a highly individualized scale (the Gloria Scale). The two standardized measures (BDI, QOLI) were altered to address the specific domains that seemed relevant to the client. Finally, the information was charted to evaluate progress and this information was used both to alter treatment as well as suggest the need for further assessment.

One can identify many limitations as well, although some may be unfair because not all of the details of the case can be presented. First, the three measures are reasonable, in part because of the domains they assess and the clinical feasibility of their administration and completion. Yet, each is a self-report scale. The argument could be made that self-report is pivotal, given self-referral as the basis for initiating treatment. Yet, the common method variance (all self-report) and likely overlap of foci (G Scale depression theme and BDI) might have made these measures highly correlated. Assessment with one other method would have augmented the evaluation of progress. Examples might be engaging her husband (with Gloria's active consent, of course) in periodic assessment (telephone call to rate an adjective checklist or Gloria's depression or activities, or his own feelings about their relationship). Related, all of the assessments were completed in the treatment setting, even though they were designed to reflect feelings during the prior week. If all self-report measures were to be used, it may have been useful to diversify the formats and observation setting. For example, Gloria could have kept a daily log of cognitions or pleasant activities engaged in between the sessions.

Second, the issue about marital dissatisfaction might have been identified earlier and taken a more central role early in treatment. From the brevity of the description, we do not have a sense of the range of clinical problems and their priorities. Consequently, we cannot tell if marital functioning was central early in treatment or appropriately deferred until other issues were addressed. The therapeutic strategies and assessment procedures might have been different. Alternatively, the marital issues may have become more salient as treatment progressed precisely because the client felt progress in other domains. The lack of progress on her relationship with her husband may have been clarified by assessment. The information suggests that the assessment and focus of treatment warranted change. The case reveals a more general problem, namely, how decisions are reached in treatment. The case shows the collection of systematic assessment information. How this information is to be used and the criteria for shifting treatment foci are not automatic. These matters are not raised by collection of systematic data but rather brought to light more clearly because of assessment.

Third, the data presented to us to evaluate ongoing treatment are helpful to be sure. At the same time, the means from each measure include multiple items. For the therapy process, it might be important for the therapist to consider areas (items) within a measure that may not have changed, even though psychometrically we are aware of the limits of individual items. Some evidence for use of individual items comes from evaluation of the G Scale items that focus on Gloria's relationship with her husband. The lack of progress here was used as a basis for further discussion of this theme, a reasonable use of the information.

Fourth, the use of regression lines to describe the data is helpful in charting overall trends. Also, computer programs that permit data entry can calculate these automatically, so the computational tasks are not onerous. The interpretation of the regression lines in the present case must be made cautiously. The lines suggest an overall improvement and hence are very useful in conveying a pattern. Presumably, the absence of improvement in a given area would have led to differences in treatment. At the same time, the changes over time cannot be interpreted as being the result of treatment. Denoting change is, of course, different from understanding the basis of the change. In this case, clinically, we might be satisfied in having systematically charted progress.

Finally, we do not have an idea of how treatment was executed, that is, how Gloria adhered to the tasks in the session as well as the homework assignments. The improvement suggests she profited from treatment in the domains that were assessed. Yet, we would like to have an idea of whether she adhered to assignments and whether the therapist felt that cognitive issues and interpersonal functioning were suitably addressed within each session. Such information over the course of treatment would help a bit to identify relations between treatment and outcome.

Overall, the case highlights the use of systematic assessment and evaluation. The assessment was individualized but also included standardized measures pertinent to the treatment focus. Also, the data obtained during treatment were useful not only to evaluate progress but also to make decisions about treatment and its focus over time.

Issues and Limitations

Methodological Issues.   Systematic assessment and evaluation can be readily implemented in clinical work to improve the inferences that can be drawn about whether change occurs and the likelihood that treatment is responsible for the change. Yet, there remain some obstacles beginning with the assessment tools available for clinical practice. Several nonstandardized measures have been recommended for ongoing evaluation of treatment, particularly in the context of adult therapy (Clement, 1999; Sederer & Dickey, 1996). These measures have not been well validated in the usual ways, and such validation would be very helpful to ensure that they measure the intended constructs and reflect functioning in everyday life. Standardized measures (Beck Depression Inventory, Minnesota Multiphasic Personality Inventory, Child Behavior Checklist) might be used on repeated occasions (as was the case with Gloria). These measures have been well validated on the basis of administering the instrument on one or two occasions (test–retest reliability or part of longitudinal studies) to large groups. Clinical evaluation will require repeated administration of the measure to the individual over the course of treatment. The basic questions are whether the measure can reflect change and will the correlates of the measure (i.e., evidence for validity) be the same on repeated use of the measures? Existing measures will be useful to provide relevant items of key constructs (anxiety, aggression, depression), but basic research will be needed to validate assessment strategies for ongoing assessment in clinical work.

Similarly, data evaluation methods are available but not well described or standardized for clinical use. Nonstatistical data evaluation in treatment research is generally unfamiliar beyond the cadre of researchers who use single-case designs, as highlighted in the previous chapter. Descriptive statistics of the sort mentioned previously (changes in means, slope) can be used for inferential purposes. However, the methods need to be developed for general use. It is likely that computerized data management programs could be used to enter data and to provide graphical displays with little effort. Various computerized programs are available for use in therapy and provide documentation of progress in user-friendly ways (OPTAIO, 1997; www.quicdoc.com).

Clinical Issues and Concerns. Several concerns and objections may emerge from individuals in clinical practice about the utility of systematic assessment and evaluation. First, therapists are often concerned that assessment may interfere with the therapeutic relationship. The therapist is responsible for treatment; adding to that the role of the assessor or evaluator may, on conceptual grounds, mix roles and be viewed as anti-therapeutic. Yet, the presumption that evaluation harms is arguable; indeed, alternative assumptions are plausible as well (not evaluating the patient can permit harm to occur, evaluation may have no impact, evaluation may help). How clients perceive systematic evaluation has to do with the therapists' views of evaluation and how the evaluation objectives and methods are presented. If evaluation is presented as a matter of course, as central to treatment, and purposeful, then the clients' views are likely to be positive. Ongoing assessment can be conceived as central to treatment and presented similarly.

Second, another concern is that measures of a clinical problem may oversimplify the problem. Yet, for a measure to be useful, it need not capture all there is about the construct. A measure provides a key sign, correlate, or sample of the problem, that is, an operational definition. We are usually not interested in measures but rather in constructs, that is, the characteristics the measures are designed to assess. We use measures even though they are not the entire scope of the problem.

Third and related, assessment seemingly may ignore the individuality or uniqueness of the client. Yet, systematic assessment can be quite individualized (see Clement,

1999; Kiresuk & Garwick, 1979; Shapiro, 1957, 1964). The clinician can decide with the patient those domains of functioning that are most relevant and build the assessment devices to reflect that. Clinical practice, unlike the usual research context, permits individualization of both assessment and treatment. The methods can be tailored to the patient's priorities, resources, and characteristics. Standardized assessment does have a critically important role in therapy and complements individualized assessment in critical ways. The profile of a client on a standardized measure and his or her standing relative to a normative group of peers of the same age, sex, and ethnicity, for example, can provide meaningful data that may also guide treatment. This point will be illustrated in measures of clinical significance in a later chapter. The standardized nature is not a threat to patient individuality, but rather an opportunity to examine that individuality against a broader backdrop (Lambert & Brown, 1996).

Fourth, an objection against evaluation in clinical work is based on the dynamic nature of treatment. Specifically, in most psychotherapy there is not a not a single, simple patient problem that remains constant. Problems change and foci are redefined over the course of treatment. Indeed, over half of clients seen in therapy add new target complaints over the course of treatment (Sorenson, Gorsuch, & Mintz, 1985). The changing focus of treatment and the multifaceted nature of the foci are not arguments against assessment. Rather, they make systematic assessment all the more important. It is critical to identify changes in problem domains and priorities of the foci from the standpoint of the patient and therapist. An excellent feature of clinical work and clinical evaluation, unlike most clinical research trials, is that the assessment and treatment are not fixed. Therapists and clients can set new goals and present or withdraw assessments to reflect these changes. The changes in treatment and treatment foci are not in conflict with assessment. In fact, the changes are likely to be very important. We would want more than impressionistic information to chart these changes and to make informed decisions about treatment.

If the goal of clinical work is to help patients and to address the concerns of this individual here and now, then the case for systematic evaluation is easily made. In fact, the case does not need to be made for systematic assessment and evaluation. Just the opposite—in clinical work, where the individual is so important and direct benefits are a goal, unsystematic evaluation is hard to advocate. There are clearly urgent circumstances wherein intervention must proceed immediately (disasters, suicide attempts in progress). The important exceptions certainly preclude collecting baseline data; they do not preclude evaluating impact after the crises have abated.

SUMMARY AND CONCLUSIONS

In clinical settings the conditions for using true single-case experiments cannot always be met. Nevertheless selected features of the designs can be used to form *quasi-single-case experiments*. The use of key features, such as assessment over time and consideration of some of the criteria for data evaluation, can strengthen the inferences that can be drawn about intervention effects. In this chapter several types of case studies were presented that included critical components of single-case experiments and information about the nature of change, the abruptness of change, the likely course without treatment that can be used to make threats to internal validity implausible.

A methodology of clinical practice that encompasses assessment and evaluation of progress and that can be used in clinical practice is needed. Several steps for systematic evaluation were discussed, including (1) specifying and assessing treatment goals, (2) specifying and assessing procedures and processes, (3) selecting measures, (4) assessment occasions, and (5) design and data evaluation. The methodology was illustrated with a case to convey the use of systematic evaluation in clinical work. Methodology and evaluation are not just for empirical research; they are for instances in which one wants to know whether there is a change, difference, or effect and to isolate possible reasons.

KEY CONCEPTS AND TERMS

Characteristics of a case that can help draw influence about the impact of treatment

Role of assessment in drawing inferences about the basis of change

Role of assessment in therapeutic change

Steps for systematic evaluation in clinical practice

Systematic versus anecdotal assessment

FOR FURTHER READINGS

Clement, P.W. (1999). *Outcomes and incomes: How to evaluate, improve, and market your practice by measuring outcomes in psychotherapy.* New York: Guilford.

Cone, J.D. (2000). *Evaluating outcomes: Empirical tools for effective practice.* Washington, DC: American Psychological Association.

Kazdin, A.E. (1993). Evaluation in clinical practice: Clinically sensitive and systematic methods of treatment delivery. *Behavior Therapy, 24,* 11–45.

Sechrest, L., Stewart, M., Stickle, T. R., & Sidani, S. (1996). *Effective and persuasive case studies.* Cambridge, MA: Human Services Research Institute.

Chapter 12

Qualitative Research Methods

An Overview

When we discuss or consider empirical research, we have a specific methodological paradigm in mind. That paradigm or approach is within the positivist tradition and includes the whole package of concepts and practices (theory, hypothesis testing, operational definitions, careful control of the subject matter, isolation of the variables of interest, quantification of constructs, and statistical analyses). Such is the approach of this book, an approach wherein one tries to devise investigations to rule out threats to validity, to test specific hypotheses, to identify the impact of variables on some outcome of interest, and to analyze the data statistically. Even the single-case designs of the previous chapters fall into this tradition because of the nature of assessment, specification and careful control of key variables of interest, and methods of data evaluation. For present purposes it is useful to refer to the dominant research paradigm in the field with the above characteristics as *quantitative research*. When people speak of scientific or empirical research, they are usually referring to quantitative research. Among most scientists the term itself is not even used, because this is viewed as *the* approach or the *only* approach. Indeed, with only rare exceptions, research in the premier and not-so-premier journals (or the level one notch below these, where my articles often end up) are entirely based on studies in the quantitative tradition.

Another approach to research is referred to as *qualitative research*. This is an empirical approach to the subject matter. The tradition of qualitative research is by no means new. The 1970s to 1990s was characterized as a "quiet methodological revolution" (Denzin & Lincoln, 2000, p. ix). Qualitative research is a broad term that encompasses multiple approaches, disciplines, and definitions. This chapter provides an overview of qualitative research methods, conveys key commonalities and similarities of qualitative and quantitative research, and illustrates the approach through detailed examples.

Qualitative research has its own methodology, including strategies for assessment, design, and data evaluation. Actually, in part because the research approach encompasses many different disciplines—including psychology, sociology, anthropology, communications, education, ethnography, and nursing, as a partial list—there are multiple methods and approaches within qualitative research. Understandably, these approaches are detailed in various handbooks and research methods books. A chapter cannot provide just due to the different approaches, which is why qualitative research can only be highlighted here.

It is important to present qualitative research, even if only an overview, for several reasons. First, the research is a legitimate methodological approach in its own right and, as already noted, is receiving increased attention. Qualitative research seeks knowledge in ways that are systematic, replicable, and cumulative. The approach is very relevant to many of the topics within psychology because of the frequent focus on individuals with special experiences, conditions, or status. Hence, researchers trained in the current quantitative tradition ought to be familiar with key tenets of the approach, its goals, uses, and relation to quantitative research.

Second, as a different approach toward obtaining knowledge, qualitative research yields data and information not likely to emerge from quantitative studies. Qualitative research looks at phenomena in ways that are intended to reveal many of those facets of human experience that the quantitative tradition has been designed to circumvent—the human experience, subjective views, and how people represent (perceive, feel), and hence react to, their situations in context. For example, quantitative research has elaborated many of the factors that contribute to or are associated with homelessness. A qualitative study is likely to focus on the experience of being homeless, the details of the frustrations, and conflicts and demands the experience raises (Lindsey, 1998) in ways that are not captured by quantitative studies.

Third, qualitative research provides detailed (sometimes referred to as "thick") descriptions and the details of individual experiences. Thick refers to multilayered and rich details. Qualitative research embraces the complexity of the experience by encouraging participants to convey the depth and scope of their perceptions, feelings, and thoughts. These descriptions can serve as an unusually good basis for developing theory about the many variables involved in a phenomenon and for hypotheses. Early in the book I discussed sources of ideas for research. Qualitative studies are an excellent way to begin to understand a phenomenon of interest (peer relations, martial happiness or discord, clinical depression) and to develop hypotheses. Qualitative researchers often speak of *grounded theory,* a term used to reflect the development of theory from careful and intensive observation and analysis of the phenomenon of interest. Through close contact with the details of the phenomenon, analytic interpretations are developed; these are refined through rechecking and further confirmation. Essentially, the distinction between research and theory is purposely blurred by building theory from close and detailed analysis of the data (see Charmaz, 2000). Interpretations and analyses of the data generate hypotheses that can be pursued in further research, whether qualitative or quantitative.

Fourth, delineating the unique features of qualitative research will also help one understand the strengths, contributions, and limitations of quantitative research. By way of analogy, the purposes of requiring undergraduates to learn a foreign language is to expose them to many facets of another culture but also to bring to light and to provide perspective on their own language and culture. Learning another language brings to light features of one's native tongue, by making the tacit explicit and by seeing how similar goals (conjugating verbs, using gender-based pronouns) can be achieved in different ways. Discussion of qualitative research has parallel benefits. We take as a given that quantitative research methods (hypothesis testing, statistics) is the only way to obtain empirical knowledge—and if not the only way, then certainly the best way. There is no need to take either of these positions. Qualitative research is different, but it is research and empirical and can be evaluated on its own grounds. Highlighting qualitative research can bring into sharp focus critical issues of quantitative research that serve as the central basis of this book.

Finally, the term *qualitative research* can mean many things, but more often than not it is misused in clinical and counseling psychology, as well as other disciplines (psychiatry, sociology). Qualitative is sometimes used to refer to descriptive, anecdotal, and case-study material. That is, the term has been inappropriately adopted to refer to any nonquantitative evaluation. This is a misuse—qualitative is not a synonym for loose, unsystematic, or "my opinions." Indeed, it is an antonym for these characteristics. Qualitative research is rigorous, scientific, disciplined, and replicable. In terms I have used in prior chapters, experimental validity (internal validity, construct validity) are central concerns in qualitative research, and methodological practices are designed to address the quality of inferences that are drawn. Anecdotal case studies are not qualitative research.

KEY CHARACTERISTICS

Background

Many influences and traditions within philosophy and various scientific disciplines underlie qualitative research (Vidich & Lyman, 2000). A few key influences place qualitative research in context so it does not in any way appear as a recent fringe movement by scientists who like case studies. Three broad influences place into context the emergence of qualitative research. First, a tradition within philosophy focuses on description, meaning, intentions, purpose, and context (see Schwandt, 2000). Approaches within phenomenology in particular (as, for example, reflected in the works of Husserl and Merleau-Ponti) provide an important starting point in light of the emphasis on description of the human experience, the role of the perceiver in understanding (constructing) the world, and such constructs as intentionality, purpose, and meaning.

The development of science and practices that we refer to as part of the scientific method (experimental controls, operational definitions) has been marked by explicit efforts to shy away from facets of subjectivity and related internal processes and states (how one perceives, thinks, and experiences the world). These processes and states are studied ("cognitive processes"), but an effort is made to move these away from the individual and out of the contexts in which they are experienced. For example, within the quantitative tradition, efforts to operationalize facets of experience (stress, fear, loneliness, love, altruism) are reflected in various inventories, scales, and questionnaires. So much has been gained by being able to measure and quantify experience in the quantitative tradition. At the same time, facets of experience are not captured by inventories and questionnaires. This is not necessarily a function of poor inventories and questionnaires, but rather the very nature of assessment within the quantitative tradition.

For example, at a clinic where I work, we measure parent stress among children referred for treatment and use a measure or two that are valid, well based, and useful. The measures have subscales to assess types of stress (related to sources generated largely by the child, and those related to the parent's own life). The measures include all the wonderful psychometric properties mentioned in the next chapter. That said, the measures leave a lot out that qualitative research would capture. At our clinic we have mothers who are waiting for their husbands or significant others to return home after a prison term. While the partner has been in prison, sometimes for relatively brief periods (3 months to a year), the mother may have begun a new relationship with a live-in significant other and/or has become pregnant with someone else's child. The mother may live in great fear of her life as the date for release from prison approaches. Now that we have seen this on a number of occasions, it is really difficult to imagine any psychological measure of stress to even approximate the stress, dread, and terror these mothers experience, as they have voiced to us. Yes, of course, this stressor could be operationalized and measured and one could imagine developing a scale with a bunch of questions (each on a five-point scale) such as, "To what extent do you fear your life is threatened by the release of your husband from jail?" This level of quantification misses so much of the stress the mothers experience in the circumstances I have highlighted. Most of us have not experienced this type of relationship and stress. Something closer—such as the death of a parent, sibling, or close relative—is a better illustration. What measure of pain, loss, emotion, could capture the experience, and how we are changed by it? To be sure, there are objective measures and quantitative indices. Yet, qualitative research is designed specifically to reflect the richness, depth, meaning, and complex situations in which they emerge and would be an approach to better capture the experience of stress of the mothers I mentioned and of the loss of a significant other that death reflects. (Pretty intense chapter so far!)

Second, within the social sciences, particularly sociology and anthropology, there has been a tradition of research in which the investigator participates in and elaborates the subject matter in great detail as a way of bringing to light key facets. Familiar examples within these disciplines can be seen from many descriptions of indigenous (once called "primitive") societies, gangs, and life in the slums (Vidich & Lyman, 2000). This work is qualitative in the sense that it encompasses in-depth knowledge of the people in context, participation with these cultures, rich description and narration of activities, and interpretation to place the belief, culture, and practices in context. This work is usually regarded as informative, even by quantitative researchers, and perhaps useful for generating ideas, but not usually considered as science. As we shall see, much of the above descriptive work is in the tradition of qualitative research, but perhaps would not meet many standards of rigor that characterize current qualitative studies.

Third, there has been a dissatisfaction with and reaction to quantitative research, as currently conceived and practiced. The focus on groups of individuals (e.g., mean differences between groups), the view of participants as objects of study and the investigator as an objective observer, simplification of the research situation to isolate variables, and reducing experience to quantitative results are central points of concern. As I mentioned, in quantitative research there has been an effort to relabel "subjects" as "participants" in journal articles and research proposals (APA, 2001b), in part, as a way of trying to soften the effort to objectify people. To a qualitative researcher, such efforts might be mildly entertaining because the way "subjects" are conceived and evaluated in research has not changed and still attempts to treat them like—well, objects of study. That is, in quantitative research we are concerned primarily with how many objects we have (sample size and power), what their responses are (means, standard deviations), and whether objects we treated in one way (treatment subjects) give different output from those treated in another way (control subjects). This is stated somewhat extremely to convey the point. To the qualitative researcher, the goal of understanding requires elaborating rather than simplifying the phenomena of interest; rather than control contexts (in the laboratory) and key variables, the goal is to investigate phenomena in context and as experienced by the individual. The emphasis is on the participants and how they perceive and experience the world. That is, the research really is participant focused. The experimenter is not a distant observer of subjects, but jumps in to learn close hand what is going on and must learn and get to know the subjects in a way that is more intimate than one usually considers in research. To understand behavior, key concepts such as meaning and purpose, usually avoided in quantitative studies of human functioning, are central topics within qualitative research. The broad variables including context in which "variables" operate, perceptions, goals, and interactions are the central foci of qualitative research.

Definition and Core Features

Qualitative research is an approach to the subject matter of human experience and focuses on narrative accounts, description, interpretation, context, and meaning. The goal is to describe, interpret, and understand the phenomena of interest. Through description and interpretation, our understanding of the phenomena can be deepened. The process of achieving this goal is to study in depth the experience of the participants—that is, those who are studied—and to convey how that experience is felt and perceived, and the meaning it has for those whose experience is being presented.

Table 12.1 lists general characteristics of qualitative research, although there are several variations of the approach. As a general rule, qualitative research relies heavily on description and interpretation of the experience or action that is studied. The purpose is to describe the experience (thoughts, feelings, and actions of a person in a particular context; interactions in which people engage) but to do so in a way that captures the richness of the experience and the meaning it has for the participants. We say that qualitative analysis increases our understanding because the level of analysis is detailed and in-depth and ideally brings to light new ways of speaking about the phenomena that the investigator, reader, and, indeed, participants, may have not fully understood prior to the analysis. As a way of describing this more colloquially, we know *about* many of life's experiences (being infatuated, being in love, breaking up of relationship, experiencing stress). A qualitative analysis is designed to bring these experiences to light and to make the tacit explicit in ways that provide a deeper and more empathic understanding.

All of the above may appear too fuzzy, so permit a brief time out and quasi-digression. Any reader who has been trained in the scientific method (the quantitative tradition) ought to experience a little discomfort (or a panic attack) at this point in the discussion. Perhaps qualitative research sounds loose, laced with subjectivity, and riddled with precisely those problems (e.g., subjective interpretation of the investigator) that current scientific methods were designed to redress. Moreover, qualitative research may sound like writing or reading a good book or hearing a good case study, each of which may be a richly detailed account of some facet of human experience. Qualitative research very much relies on the traditions captured by literature,

TABLE 12.1. Key Characteristics of Qualitative Research

- Qualitative research is conducted through an intense and/or prolonged contact with a "field" or life situation. These situations are typically "banal" or normal ones, reflective of the everyday life of individuals, groups, societies, and organizations.
- The researcher's role is to gain a "holistic" (systemic, encompassing, integrated) overview of the context under study: its logic, its arrangements, and its explicit and implicit rules.
- The researcher attempts to capture data on the perceptions of local actors "from the inside," through a process of deep attentiveness, of empathetic understanding and of suspending preconceptions about the topics under discussion.
- Reading through these materials, the researcher may isolate certain themes and expressions that can be reviewed with informants, but that should be maintained in their original forms throughout the study.
- A main task is to explicate the ways people in particular settings come to understand, account for, take action, and otherwise manage their day-to-day situations.
- Many interpretations of this material are possible, but some are more compelling for theoretical reasons or on grounds of internal consistency.
- Relatively little standardized instrumentation is used at the outset. The researcher is essentially the main "measurement device" in the study.
- Most analyses are done with words. The words can be assembled, subclustered, broken into semiotic segments. They can be organized to permit the researcher to contrast, compare, analyze, and bestow patterns upon them.

Source: Miles and Huberman (1994). Key Characteristics of Qualitative Research. *Qualitative data analysis: An expanded source book. (2nd ed.)* (pp. 6–7), Thousand Oaks, CA: Sage.

namely, descriptive accounts that elaborate experience. Yet, qualitative research provides a systematic approach to description and understanding and provides replicable, reliable, and valid accounts, although these terms have somewhat different meanings. That is, there is an effort to be systematic in qualitative research that moves applications out of the realm of pure literature per se. Mind you, there is nothing wrong with literature, and some of my best friends even read books once in a while. Yet, qualitative analysis goes beyond this by providing systematic (but not usually quantitative) methods of data collection, analyses, replications, and efforts to address biases that can influence the data (Maxwell, 1996; Miles & Huberman, 1994; Ryan & Bernard, 2000). This makes qualitative research a systematic method for obtaining knowledge and hence different from other efforts (e.g., within the arts) that also may capture experience.

Contrast of Qualitative and Quantitative Research

Qualitative and quantitative research both seek to understand natural phenomena, to provide new knowledge, to permit the experience to be replicated by others, and to do so in systematic ways. Several key differences in how the subject matter is approached help to convey those special characteristics of qualitative research. Table 12.2 provides salient dimensions of how one approaches research and the differences in quantitative and qualitative approaches.

Clearly, the key difference is in the major goals of quantitative and qualitative research because from these goals the different methods and foci naturally result. Qualitative research seeks to understand action and experience and hence must view broad sweeps of functioning (affect, cognition, behavior) in context. Apart from studying the complexity of experience in its full bloom (as it happens in uncontrolled everyday situations), the qualitative approach views the investigator quite differently from how he or she is viewed in the quantitative approach. The model in quantitative research is that of an objective scientist, looking through a telescope; the goal is to have the investigator serve as an objective instrument, and, indeed, it is even better if the material observed through the telescope can be recorded in ways that minimize the influence or active role of the investigator. Quantitative research methods in psychology, and social sciences more generally, have been very much modeled

TABLE 12.2.   Select Characteristics that Distinguish Quantitative and Qualitative Research

Characteristic	Quantitative Research	Qualitative Research
Goals	Test theory and hypotheses; identify causal relations, seek group differences or patterns	Describe and interpret experience; provide new insights, describe and explain with few or no initial hypotheses; generate theory
How to study	Isolate variables, control potential artifacts and extraneous influences; rule out rival hypotheses	Consider variables as they appear in context with all of the natural influences; complexity is embraced to elaborate the gestalt as well as any key influences in context

TABLE 12.2.   (*continued*)

Characteristic	Quantitative Research	Qualitative Research
Subjects	Study (or try to study) a large number of subjects for statistical power	Study one or a small number of cases (individual, culture, organization) intensively
Use of control conditions	Usually, control or comparison groups are included to address threats to validity (internal, construct)	No control group. The goal is to elaborate the richness of a particular group and the commonalities and differences that may emerge within that group
Role of the subject	The subjects are the object of study, the people who provide the data; the subjects do not reflect on the data or help the experimenter make sense out of the results	The participants are not objects; the experimenter and subjects become one in the sense that the experience described and understood cannot be removed from the one who describes (experimenter); the subjects are often consulted to ask whether the description and interpretation capture the experience
Role of investigator	Minimize the investigator's role; the perspective, views, and feelings of the investigator are reflected in the hypotheses or focus of the study, but not in the methods, presentation of the findings, nor interpretation of the data; the investigator is detached to the extent possible	The investigator is part of the interpretation in light of his or her perspective; the perspective is made explicit, but it can never be removed; empathy of the investigator is encouraged as a key to deeper understanding; the investigator is *engaged* rather than *detached* and can understand better to the extent that meaning of the situation is experienced
The data	Scores on measures that operationalize the constructs; standardized measures are used whenever possible; the data refer to information that has been reduced to numbers	Narrative descriptions, full text, lengthy interviews, accounts, examples; the "story" details the subject matter in the context of how it unfolds, happens, and is experienced; the "words" are the data and are not reduced to numbers
Data evaluation	Statistical analyses to find patterns, averages, to control influences further, to identify the impact of variables on each other and on an outcome	Literary, verbal, nonreductionist, go from description to interpretation to identify themes to bring new qualities to light. Systematically identify themes and ways of categorizing experiences for purposes of presentation
Criteria for knowledge	Procedures and findings can be replicated	Descriptions are coherent and viewed by others (colleagues, participants) as internally consistent, capturing the experience; procedures and findings can be replicated
A major contribution	A new theory, hypothesis, or relation is brought to light that will increase our understanding of the phenomenon	Our understanding of the experience is elaborated and brought to light in depth as well as in ways that extend our understanding

Note: As a general rule, I strongly personally object to tables that contrast approaches with two columns because the structure implies qualitative (i.e., categorical) differences, emphasizes extremes, and fails to consider the inevitable fuzziness of many of the distinctions. The value of the table is to draw sharp lines to introduce the approach, but it is not difficult to identify a study in one tradition (quantitative or qualitative) and show how many of its features are captured by the column of the table designed to characterize the other tradition.

after the "hard" sciences (biology, physics, astronomy), and keeping the investigator separate from the subject matter is axiomatic.

In qualitative research the investigator is not someone who "collects data," but rather someone who integrates the information in a way that affects the data, that is, gives it meaning and substance. Elimination of a frame of reference or perspective of the investigator may not be possible, and if possible, not necessarily desirable. In fact, to really understand the phenomenon, many qualitative investigators become deeply involved in the subject matter; understanding is optimal when one experiences the phenomenon directly. Thus, studies of other cultures that have provided the greatest insights often stem from those who enter and live in the culture for an extended period.

METHODS AND ANALYSES

The Data for Qualitative Analysis

The basic information (data) used for a qualitative study can be obtained in many different ways. Among the salient methods and sources are interviews, direct observations, statements of personal experience, documents (personal journals, letters, biographical materials, stories passed across generations), photographs, audio or video recordings, and films. Each of these methods has its own recommended approaches and options for data collection (see Denzin & Lincoln, 2000). At first blush, these methods do not look all that different from many measures and ways of collecting data in quantitative research. For example, direct observation and interviewing are also used in quantitative clinical research. In qualitative research direct observation is more naturalistic, that is, it occurs in naturalistic contexts as the subjects would normally participate and interact. The investigator is drawn into the world of the subjects (the family, playground, school), and predetermined categories (to code behavior) are not usually used. In contrast, within the quantitative approach, much of the direct observation consists of standardized assessments in which the world of the subjects is brought into the lab (observe marital interaction on standardized tasks) or the world of the investigator is brought to natural settings (observations conducted in the home with efforts to standardize the situations that govern family interactions). In both instances the investigator knows the codes to operationalize constructs of interest. Beginning a study with codes to assess functioning and the constructs of interest is typical of (and essential to) quantitative research. It is usually the case that the qualitative researcher wishes to take the phenomena as presented and to derive the constructs and codes from them.

Information obtained from these sources is initially taken as descriptive material and serves as the basis for analysis. The analysis takes many different forms because there are multiple orientations and approaches to the information. A key approach is to interpret the meaning and to better understand the subject matter (an individual, group, culture) in context. However, this can be accomplished by looking for recurring themes or key concepts that emerge in peoples' descriptions of their experiences, identifying processes or a progression that seems to show the flow of experience, linking variables that emerge concurrently or over time, and, in general, looking for consistencies and patterns in the material. Computer software is available that is designed to facilitate making these connections and interpretation from qualitative data by displaying the information and pointing to possible patterns (see Miles & Weitzman, 1994). Occasionally, the approach to cull meaning and to examine connections among variables utilizes methods of quantitative analyses. For example, in some qualitative studies the descriptive material is coded into categories and analyzed statistically to examine the occurrence of themes and their interrelations, although these are exceptions. In other cases a goal of the interpretation is to develop theory from the material. Indeed, one of the advantages of the approach is to discover and to generate new conceptualizations of phenomena in the process of bringing special features to light.

Drawing Valid Inferences

As in quantitative research, central to qualitative research is the validity of the data, that is, that the analyses yield findings that are plausible, trustworthy, and confirmable. Five types of validity convey the nature of qualitative research methods (see Johnson, 1997; Maxwell, 1996). These are summarized in Table 12.3. The types of validity convey the issues to be addressed in qualitative research, and even listing these as types of validity illustrates that qualitative research is not mere description and extended narratives. The research begins with validity concerns and then utilizes specific strategies to address them to strengthen the inferences that can be drawn.

I have used the term *experimental validity* to draw connections between qualitative and quantitative research. Also, the use of the terms helps to sharpen the distinc-

TABLE 12.3.   Unique Types of Validity that Convey Features of Qualitative Research

Descriptive Validity

The extent to which the account reported by the investigator is factually accurate. The account may reflect descriptions of events, objects, behaviors, people, settings, times, and places.

Interpretive Validity

The extent to which the meaning of what has been described is accurately represented. Is the descriptive material understood adequately? Are the views, intentions, feelings, or other data interpreted in a way that represents or understands the experiences?

Theoretical Validity

If explanations are designed to address how and why a phenomenon or experience has occurred, how well does the explanation fit the data? The theory is more abstract and at a higher level of inference than interpretive validity and conveys the possible reasons or underpinnings of the phenomenon.

Internal Validity

Similar to the notion in quantitative research, are there other sources of influence that could explain the results apart from the influence the investigator identifies?

External Validity

Also, similar to the notion in quantitative research, are the findings generalizable across people, time situations, and settings?

Note: Further information can be obtained from Johnson (1997) and Maxwell (1996).

tion between empirical and scientific research (both qualitative and quantitative studies) and richly interesting literary descriptions (literature, anecdotal case studies, my dissertation), which do not permit strong and valid inferences to be drawn. All of that said, qualitative researchers have their own terms that capture the meaning of validity. The terms are important because they convey additional and different meaning.

A key concept on which validity depends is triangulation. *Triangulation* refers to using multiple procedures, sources, or perspectives to converge to support the conclusions. Triangulation may rely on separate bits of data, different methods of qualitative analyses or qualitative and quantitative analyses of the same data, use of different theoretical frameworks, and different investigators. When different ways of examining the problem or phenomenon converge in the information they yield, this is triangulation and strengthens (better establishes) the validity of the finding.

Triangulation can be achieved in different ways. The investigator can use multiple sources of data (interviews and questionnaires to combine qualitative and quantitative methods). Also, multiple sources can be used to examine the descriptions and interpretations. Often the participants themselves are asked to reflect on the data and interpretations of the investigator to see if they concur or have information to add or alter. Peers (other colleagues) might be involved to challenge the interpretations and conclusions. Often investigators of the study will independently develop or evaluate the interpretations as a check, but peers not involved in the study may participate in this role as well. Finally, considering cases that seem to disconfirm the researcher's conclusions is a check. Counterinstances may not refute the explanation but may provide other explanations that ought to be considered, that might apply to others, or raise themes about the experience that were not previously considered.

Triangulation is used to bolster the conclusions and affects each type of validity noted in Table 12.3. Essentially, in more familiar terms, triangulation reflects a multimethod approach to qualitative methods. However, the methods are designed to cover more than multiple assessment methods, but multiplicity or generality across many different aspects of the study, including the range of participants (investigators, subjects) used to derive conclusions. In general, as with quantitative research, methods within qualitative research address alternative interpretations, bias and artifact, and replicability of the results.

The notion of *confirmability* is often used to evaluate the validity of the study and refers to the extent to which an independent reviewer could conduct a formal audit and re-evaluation of the procedures and generate the same findings. The extent to which results are confirmable by others depends on the care with which the original investigator conducts the study to begin with and the methods of triangulation used for the demonstration. Confirmability, of course, reflects replicability of findings and is central to all scientific research.

In qualitative research, coherence of the interpretation, agreement among others about that interpretation (including, when possible, the participants themselves), and consensus that our understanding of the experience or phenomenon is enhanced as a result of the analysis are salient among the criteria to evaluate the findings. Does the analysis capture the experience and extend our understanding (of the experience of living with AIDS, of growing older, of being a child, of living in a particular culture, of serving as a prisoner of war)? This is sometimes referred to as *credibility* or believability of the results. As a measure of this, would the descriptions provided by the investigator be viewed as credible by the participants and by others who have also had that experience but were not included in the study? In everyday life, credibility in this way is occasionally experienced when a friend mentions something and we recognize this immediately as exactly the feeling or experience we had.

The perspective and approach of the qualitative investigator necessarily influences and shades the interpretations that are generated. The perspective of the investigator is likely to influence quantitative research as well. We know, for example, that in psychotherapy outcome research, the theoretical allegiance of the investigator seems to influence the results of the study in some way. Investigators tend to find results that are in keeping with their conceptual view (see Luborsky et al., 1999), a finding in need of much further attention. The "objectivity" of quantitative research is not entirely accurate for other reasons. Many components of quantitative research—such as the formulation of the research question, what is viewed as "noise" versus the variable of interest, the entire business of what is "statistically significant" (e.g., the criterion of $p < .05$), and other facets of statistical analyses (e.g., linear models)—are part of the subjectivity, even though these are rarely made explicit or discussed in that way. Yet, plainly, qualitative research raises even greater issues of subjectivity on the part of the investigator.

Understandably, in qualitative research there is the concern that the views of the investigator may play a particularly significant and unchecked role in the interpretation. Although the perspective of the investigator is important, as consumers of research we do not accumulate findings that are pertinent to or generalizable to only the particular investigator. Procedures are included to check on the extent to which this case or focus may be representative, whether the researcher's views, made explicit at the outset, are likely to account for a particular slant in the interpretation, and whether others who view the data or similar cases converge on a common understanding and interpretation.

Multiple strategies are used to help ensure that the data are not mere reflections of the investigator's perspective. First, investigators are encouraged to make explicit their own views, including how their expectations may have been met or not, what was consistent and discrepant from any preconceived views, and what orientation or approach they may be taking to the subject matter (observing it from a particular perspective or even theoretical orientation, discipline, or frame of reference). Noting this perspective, orientation, and expectation permits others in the scientific community to evaluate the interpretations in light of potentially important influences.

Second, there is an iterative process in which investigators are encouraged to consult other investigators to identify the extent to which the raw material (lengthy narratives, audio or videotaped materials) are likely to reflect key tenets the investigator has identified. Are the interpretations cohesive, and do they capture the experience? These are questions posed to others who evaluate the qualitative material. The participants are also part of this verification process, when possible. During the process of collecting the information or after the information is collected, participants are encouraged to review the categories, broader concepts, and sequence of experiences that have been proposed, and to make comments. These comments themselves are brought into the process to elaborate, refine, or alter what has been proposed by the investigator. Thus, the fact that the investigators are people and have their own perspectives, experiences, and shaded glasses does not doom in any way the resulting data to an idiosyncratic perspective. The consensual process involves other investigators as well as participants.

Other investigators evaluate the process of reaching the interpretation by examining the procedures, raw data, and analytic strategies as well as the conclusions themselves (see Miles & Huberman, 1994). The investigator is encouraged to make raw data available to others during the investigation to permit a check on how the information (e.g., transcripts) reflects themes that have been identified. Thus, there is an internal replicability that is part of the evaluation, that is, scrutiny by others. All of this is facilitated by procedures and computer software alluded to earlier that help to display, code, systematize, and retrieve the data and to test the emergence of broader constructs and categories that form the basis of the investigator's interpretation.

As evident in this discussion, concepts underlying qualitative research are similar to those of quantitative research, namely, "Are the findings reliable and valid?" Reliability pertains both to the methods of studying the data (how themes and categories are identified, how interpretations are made) and to coherence or internal consistency of the interpretations. Validity refers to the extent to which there is a finding that makes sense, captures experience, and is confirmed and confirmable by others. Many additional terms than those I have used mentioned help capture both reliability and validity (see Miles & Huberman, 1994). Two that are commonly mentioned are trustworthiness and transferability. *Trustworthiness* of the data is often used to reflect the extent to which the data have transferability, dependability, and confirmability (Lincoln & Guba, 1985). *Transferability* pertains to whether the data are limited to a particular context (are context bound) and is evaluated by looking at any special characteristics (unrepresentativeness) of the sample. Transferability is similar to generality of findings and hence external validity, as discussed in quantitative research, but warrants separate consideration.

Generality of the Results

External validity or generality of the results is different in qualitative and quantitative research. In qualitative research, if the findings are dependent on the special context and experience of the participants and the investigator, how can any finding be replicable or provide any general understanding? In the terms of a quantitative tradition, can there be external validity to any qualitative finding in light of the tenet that person–context–investigator form a very special gestalt? There are separate answers. In one way, experiences are always different because people (participants, experimenters) bring to bear unique histories and perspectives. In another way, there are thematic similarities. For example, falling in love, getting married, experiencing the death of a child or parent, recovering from trauma, and living with a disability are never identical for two individuals. Yet, understanding and elaborating the experiences of one or a small group of individuals may bring to light intricacies and nuances, but also common reactions. Although the qualitative researcher seeks to elaborate experience of the particular (this individual, group, culture), the interpretive facet moves to broader themes with greater universality. We know that intense appreciation of the individual experience rings with great universality. Individuals who experience trauma (diagnosis of a terminal illness, disaster) often join and profit from support groups with others who have shared this experience. The constant emergence of these support groups and their documented benefits, such as increased longevity among terminally ill patients (Spiegel, Bloom, Kraemer, & Gottheil, 1989), suggests that the individual and unique experience also has universal features that can be elaborated and appreciated by others. Similarly, appreciation of literature may derive from the very special experiences of the protagonist, but also from appreciation of experiences that are rather universal (love, impulsiveness, grief, despair, ambition).

Although many experiences that are elaborated are likely to have facets that are universal, many qualitative researchers would say that universality and generalization to all people are not the criteria for evaluating the contribution of qualitative research. If a particular account is restricted to a context (individual in a situation), that is not a flaw or limitation. The goal of the approach is to elaborate meaning, understanding, and experience, and many facets will be specific to particular contexts. This, too, is much like quantitative research in which general findings are sought, but we have developed many laboratory paradigms for studying something that is not likely to have very much generality beyond that particular paradigm. We do not value findings only in terms of their generality.

The value and contribution of qualitative research can be highlighted informally by showing the relation of the general to the specific in a qualitative-like description. There are, for example, lessons to be learned from the biblical rendition of Job. From the perspective of the description, it is unlikely that another person would experience the set of "life events" that Job experienced nor would have the special background, beliefs, and perceptions of these events as experienced. The specificity of the case does not in any way detract from its contribution. The value of the description stems from deepening our understanding of faith, and that has considerable generality beyond the specific case. The description of Job is not qualitative research in psychology, but merely is noted here to convey that placing a microscope on experience has value in deepening our understanding.

Qualitative researchers vary in their views of the generality and importance of the results. Qualitative analysis is influenced by the investigator, participants, and context, each of which can further be divided into multiple influences. Consequently, it is possible—and, in principle, likely—that analyses of similar cases will not be the same, in any future replication attempt, as the key influences change. However, analyses are assumed to have some generality as well as specificity in the sense that the experience—while unique, special, and nonreplicable—may resonate with the experiences of others. Also, some qualitative studies include multiple cases, so the issue of common themes in understanding experience is evaluated directly. Although general themes may emerge, it is important to reiterate that qualitative research is not intended to derive or discover *the* experience that characterizes all people.

ILLUSTRATIONS

Although qualitative studies are available in psychological research journals, they are relatively rare. For example, consider the collection of journals published under the aegis of major psychological associations (American Psychological Association, American Psychological Society). It would be difficult to peruse a journal issue in any of the areas of psychology these journals reflect and find a qualitative study.[1] Consequently, a few illustrations are provided here in detail to convey the approach, methods, and nature of findings from qualitative research.

Inner-City Youth Who Cease to Commit Crimes

Overview. Delinquent and criminal behaviors have been studied extensively to identify factors that predict such behaviors, interventions that might be used to prevent or alter such behavior, and factors that influence changes in the trajectories among those who engage in criminal behavior, to mention a few of the domains of research. In this example (Hughes, 1998), the goal was to identify inner-city youth who had engaged in criminal behavior (violence, illegal drug marketing), but who ceased engaging in such acts. The purpose was to elaborate some of the personal and environmental influences that may contribute to change, as perceived by the individuals themselves.

Twenty young men (ages 18–27, African-American and Hispanic-American) were drawn from several cities. Criteria for selection included a history of criminal behavior, evidence of positive life changes (obtaining employment, participating in positive community programs, volunteering, helping youth, speaking against crime in various school programs), and a statement that they no longer participated in crime. Subjects were identified by community leaders, directors of intervention programs, and contacts of the investigator. Each participant was interviewed in offices or the participant's home. The interview (approximately 90 min) focused on verifying the selection criteria, various subject and demographic variables, and then the primary focus of the study.

The primary focus was to identify factors that may have influenced how individuals moved from a life of crime to their current situation. The interview was open-ended, with questions focusing on experiences with family, school, law enforcement, significant people, intervention programs, and life events. Also, participants were asked to detail periods and events related to their decisions to make positive changes. Several subjects were interviewed a second time to validate interpretations and information. This involved the participants as a check on the findings, a characteristic often used in qualitative studies.

Each tape was transcribed, and computer software was used to help analyze the interview, by coding and categorizing statements of experiences from the data. A priori codes were included that focused on influential agents in the participants lives (family, school, church, peers, employers), developmental periods (childhood, ado-

---

[1] A number of scientific journals are devoted to qualitative research. Examples include *Qualitative Health Research, Qualitative Studies in Education,* and *Culture, Medicine, and Psychiatry.*

lescence), factors associated with onset of crime and with stopping crime, and others. Four themes were identified: (1) respect and concern for children, (2) fear of physical harm or incarceration, (3) time away from their chaotic environments to contemplate their lives, and (4) support and modeling from others. For example, regarding the concern for children, several participants noted they left the life of crime over concern for children, in part due to their own untoward child experiences (e.g., absent father) or the danger their own children witnessed (e.g., when the participant was dealing with drugs). Regarding contemplation time, several participants mentioned being in a residential program or prison that allowed time away from their lives and how this helped them break away from their influences. The time away and relocation helped them decide to make changes. The most common experience was related to support and caring from others. These persons included significant others (wives, girlfriends) who they felt they could trust and who cared for them.

The very nature of qualitative research means that summaries such as the type I have attempted cannot represent the richness of the data. The themes and points emerged from systematic evaluation of the interview material, but qualitative studies often include extended narratives and direct quotes to illustrate the themes so that the reader can see in the words of participants the richness of the comments.

Comment.   So what have we learned from this and why is a qualitative study helpful or of use? We have learned a lot of information that deserves to be followed further in qualitative and quantitative studies. Intensive analysis of persons who desist from crime conveys perceptions about possible influences. For example, intervention or retention programs were perceived as helpful to allow individuals to reflect on their lives. Does this mean that the interventions included in these programs were helpful, that the time away was the critical component, or some combination? Perceptions of influence and actual influence can be quite different (see General Comments at the end of all of the illustrations). Yet, this is rather interesting and raises prospects for intervening. Perhaps residential programs ought to foster opportunities to reflect on one's life to exert influence on career criminals. Similarly, connections with one's own children also were felt by the participants as contributing to leaving a life of crime. Is there a way to harness the critical components to influence criminals? Perhaps fostering such connections further (having some individuals serve as a Big Brother when they do not have their own children) could have a positive influence.

The research is provocative in raising themes that are not commonly discussed in quantitative research and also elaborating others that are discussed. For example, it has been known for some time that a positive relationship with someone can decrease the risk for delinquency and criminal behavior. This research elaborates this by conveying in some detail how, among young male adults, involvement with a partner whom they felt genuinely loved them was perceived to make a difference. Does this mean it really did make a difference? We would need more research to address that question. For example, it could easily be the case that males who are brighter, more engaging and endearing, and on the "good path" already, will be more likely than hardcore criminals to develop such relations.

The research identifies many areas that ought to be pursued. For example, it is always a leap to go from describing possible influences on a problem (e.g., criminal behavior) or trajectory (e.g., no longer engaging in criminal behavior) to developing interventions. At the same time, this study raises interesting issues and themes. For example, relationships (with children and a partner) emerge as quite positive influences among the men who were interviewed. Would it be worthwhile in interventions to move away from the usual psychosocial therapies and rehabilitation programs, and to do something more to foster relationships in the world for individuals who might break away from crime? Although one might not provide spouses or mates for everyone, one could foster positive and caring relationships (by Big Brother opportunities, volunteering to work with others on a regular basis). This is a leap, but efforts for getting individuals to stop from lives of crime are not rich with wonderful interventions or ideas, so a leap like this is worth pursuing. For present purposes the example is useful to convey the yield from qualitative studies. The detailed interviews suggest new themes and different ways of considering themes studied in quantitative research.

Gender, Power, and Who Gets the Remote Control During TV Time

There is no easy transition from criminal behavior to this next example, except to note perhaps that not all injustices in the world involve crime. In this study, watching television was investigated as a way to examine social structure of relationships, power, status, and gender-typed behavior among couples (Walker, 1996). TV viewing, as it turns out, is the dominant recreational activity in the United States. A goal of the study was to examine whether power is exerted in the domain of leisure activity, as reflected in TV viewing. Specifically, the author examined whether in couples, one person exerted power over the other in controlling what was watched on TV and specifically how the remote control was used to do so.

Heterosexual ($N = 62$) and lesbian or gay ($N = 10$) couples were included. The requirements for inclusion were that all couples be in a romantic relationship, be living together for at least one year, and have a television with a remote control. European-American, African-American, and Hispanic-American couples were included. Within each relationship, each partner was interviewed (order determined by a coin toss).

The interview was open-ended and raised multiple questions regarding TV viewing, processes for decision making, expectations in relation to viewing, how conflict was addressed and resolved, and several other experiences related to this interaction (characteristics, use of the remote control, partner behavior, expectations, frustrations, decision making, and changes in viewing patterns over time). Additional questions were included that allowed quantitative summaries of specific responses (how happy individuals felt with the way things were regarding TV viewing, how much the person enjoyed time they spent together).

The interviews were audiotaped and transcribed. The quantitative data were examined in the usual way (means, standard deviations, comparison tests). The quantitative information will be omitted here, but for descriptive purposes it is interesting to mention that couples watched a mean of approximately 3 hours per day, that couples watched TV together about 5 days per week, and that partners often differed considerably in the frustration they experienced in watching TV. (For example, in the heterosexual couples, 42% of the women but only 10% of the men expressed frustration in use of the remote control).

The qualitative results indicated clearly that use of the remote control was a source of conflict, that men (in the heterosexual relationships) dominate use of the remote control and program selection, that women have to engage in special ploys (advance warning, repetition) to "get to watch" their preferred shows, and are much less successful than men in having access to a preferred show, that women believe they are less able than their male partner in changing the other person's TV watching behavior, and that the whole experience is a source of frustration. In lesbian and gay couples one person was more likely to be the heavier user of the remote control, but the interviews suggested a stronger interest in resolving the conflict over TV and establishing a more egalitarian role in TV use. Seeming solutions (have 2 TVs, videotape shows the other person wants to watch) reduce time together or only convey the problem further (the woman is likely to have to wait to view her show).

Comment.   This study conveys how social status and gender role affirmation are expressed and developed in relationships, as evident by TV viewing. The issue of who controls TV is in keeping with other areas of functioning in the home (child care, responsibility for housework). In many instances women yield to pressure to engage in activities that are discussed within the relationship as equal or close to equal, when in fact they are not. Many of these issues contribute to unhappiness and frustration as women yield to pressures and explicit efforts of their partners to exert their will.

The qualitative data provided interview material regarding the nature and scope of the frustration, how women handle the problem, and another way in which activities within the relationship can reflect power and role behavior. TV viewing might be viewed as trivial in the large scheme of relationship issues. Apparently not, if TV viewing is the most frequent source of leisure activity and so much joint time among couples is spent in TV viewing.

The contribution of qualitative information is especially useful to convey the level of resentment that can emerge and the power that is invoked. (One male partner noted, "If I don't care what's on [TV], I let her have it [the remote control].") Also, the detail conveys a sequence that would not otherwise be easily captured by a quantitative study, assessments, or a simple self-report survey. For example, the study revealed the following sequence of TV viewing: A couple watches sports together (male partner selection), and if a sports event is not on, then he selects something else, but if nothing else is on, then the female partner gets to choose. However, during the female's preferred show, the male is likely to continue to search for a sports program. The richness of this detail is not only interesting in its own right, but suggests ways of approaching, handling, and negotiating situations that may extend well beyond TV viewing. Of course, for those who insist that science must have immediate practical implications, perhaps consider the following. Before you move in or marry your partner, watch a few TV shows together with one remote control and see how it goes. Research suggests your observations and reactions may be a preview of coming attractions.

Single Women and Their Experience

Overview.   The meaning and experience of being single has changed remarkably over a period of a few generations, pertaining to the role of women in society. For example, in the 1950s being a single for a woman was viewed (by women) as negative (a result of feeling ugly, not liking men). Later decades each had a slightly different emphasis. In the 1990s, research suggested single women were pleased with their situation and leading contented, full lives. Single women might like to have a partner, but the absence was not viewed as something as negative as it had been in prior years. The purpose of this study, wherein the issues about the nature of being single were reviewed, was to understand the experience of being a single woman in midlife in contemporary society (Lewis & Moon, 1997). Qualitative methods were viewed as especially relevant because little information is available, and a detailed examination of perceptions would be useful to explore issues, themes, and experience.

The study included two phases encompassing 66 women (ages 30–65). They were recruited and asked if they were willing to participate in a study on the experience of being a single woman. In the initial phase single women ($N = 37$) were interviewed in small focus groups. The groups were composed on the basis of the primary reason the women were single (never married, divorced, widowed).

A brief but important digression is warranted. Focus groups are used in many ways in research, business, and industry. Such groups meet informally with an investigator or leader. For example and outside the context of this study, focus groups might be conducted with a group of teenagers to see what they think about a product or line of advertising, with children who might use a line of toys, and with school teachers to get reactions about a new teaching method. Such groups are often viewed by quantitative researchers as an informal way to seek input from the group of interest (e.g., therapists, potential subjects). Within qualitative research, focus groups can occupy a more formal role as part of a methodology to systematically solicit material for qualitative analysis. They can be conducted in a research setting or where the participants ordinarily live and function (classrooms, homes, churches) (see Madriz, 2000; Morgan, 1998).

To return to the example, each focus group was interviewed for 3–4 hours, based on open-ended questions ("What does it mean to you to be single?"). All of this material was transcribed. The material was searched for themes, and these themes were used to develop a questionnaire that was used in the second stage. In this latter stage a second sample ($N = 39$) was studied. The questionnaire consisted primarily of open-ended questions (essay format) that allowed comments along several domains and hence was not the questionnaire (rating scale) one might see in the typical quantitative study. The two samples and the two methods of collecting information (open-ended interview, questionnaire) are examples of triangulation, that is, seeing if different methods and sources of information would produce converging findings. Themes were searched from the transcripts to identify commonalities across both samples. Coding techniques were used to identify themes. Developing the themes and then rechecking them against the narrative process were an iterative process to refine the results.

Among the findings was an overriding theme that emerged, namely, single women in this sample had unresolved or unrecognized ambivalences about being single. They were aware of both the advantages and drawbacks of being single, they were ambivalent about their own status, and although content with being single, many women also expressed feelings of loss and grief. In describing the reasons for being single, examples fell into four categories: physical characteristics (e.g., overweight), personality (shyness, independence or dependence), psychological issues (selfishness, low self-esteem), and cognitive characteristics (too much or too little intelligence, learning disability). As I mentioned before, merely stating the themes cannot represent the richness of the information. The report includes examples of the language used by many of the women.

Much of the richness of the data raises provocative issues that would be unlikely to emerge from responses sought in a different format. For example, most women said they would not do anything different with their lives if they knew for sure they would never marry or remarry. They also noted that there would be relief in knowing that they would not marry. Although they would be sad, at least they would know for sure. Their lives might be more productive and focused more constructively if this issue (procuring a mate) were not in the back of their minds.

Comment. The study provides an in-depth evaluation of the perceptions about being single and raises dimensions that would be difficult to capture by a set of standardized or homemade questionnaires with the usual response formats. Many perceptions were identified, and similar perceptions often were associated with different cognitions. For example, some women said they were single by choice whereas others said they were not single by choice. However, in both types of responses, women gave the same reason, namely, they had not met anyone they would want to marry. Other perceptions emerged—such as most men do not marry someone who is intelligent, has a job, and has money. The richness of such material is that it identifies areas that might be addressed to prepare women for being single, to help those who, in fact, are bothered by being single after being married. Yet, we do not need these implications to appreciate the value of the study. One has a much better idea about single women and perhaps about development more generally as adults negotiate life.

Worth noting is the representation of different views on a given dimension. That is, the authors describe subgroups by noting that most or some women said this or that and others did not for a given dimension. This gives a richness to the material and conveys that there might be meaningful subtypes or groups that could be identified. Clearly, the material provides multiple opportunities for additional qualitative and quantitative research.

A comment about the methodology of this study warrants mention. The interviews were extensive (lasting hours) and yielded a vast amount of data. This is typical of qualitative research. Although many subjects might be studied, the more critical issue is the detailed and intensive evaluation of the experience of the individual subjects. The sample size of some qualitative research is sometimes influenced by the data and the yield. As subjects accumulate, the increment of new information or new themes may reach an asymptote and the recruitment may stop.

Parents' Experience in Treatment for Their Children

Overview.   Parent management training is a psychosocial treatment that is used to treat children who engage in disruptive, aggressive, oppositional, and antisocial behavior. Among therapies for children, this is probably the most well investigated and established (e.g., Brestan & Eyberg, 1998; Kazdin, 1997). In parent training, parents are trained to interact with their children differently, primarily based on techniques such as reinforcement, shaping, and the use of prompts. Many randomized controlled trials have been conducted in the tradition of quantitative research and have attested to the effects of treatment. Qualitative studies have been completed and are especially interesting because they have emerged from an exemplary program of research that has contributed so remarkably to the quantitative research literature (Webster-Stratton, 1996).

To better understand the experience of therapy, parents' perceptions, and reactions to the training program, separate qualitative studies have been completed (Spitzer, Webster-Stratton, & Hollinsworth, 1991; Webster-Stratton & Spitzer, 1996). From a sample of 77 families (children ages 3–8 years), random selection was made of taped material from participants in treatment. The materials included intake assessment interviews for all families, videotaped sessions among parents who received group treatment, and audiotaped material from those who received self-administrated treatment but then consulted individually with a therapist. Material was transcribed, and each family was studied separately over time. The transcripts were examined in small units to try to identify concepts raised by the parents, using their own words as the parents described their responses to the program. Tentative codes were identified and used to reflect broader categories, akin to a conceptually based factor analysis wherein one looks for groupings of codes (items) into larger constructs (factors).

From analyses of the transcripts the investigators identified experiences of the families and cognitive, social, and behavioral changes from intake, through the end of the treatment program, up to approximately one year later. The experience of the parents was represented by five phases that seemed to emerge over time: (1) acknowledging the family's problem, (2) alternating between despair and hope in achieving change, (3) recognizing that hopes and expectations for the child needed to be tempered, (4) tailoring the concepts and procedures of treatment to the needs of their child, and (5) coping effectively. Within each of these, subcategories and subthemes were identified. For example, the final phase of coping effectively included such themes as parents' recognition that the child had chronic problems or would require ongoing special attention at home, improved acceptance and understanding of the child's perspective and acceptance of their own limitations as parents, the need for the parents to take time for themselves to gain a more positive perspective, and the benefits of a support group for the parents.

Several checks were made within the approach of qualitative analysis to ensure some validity to the results and show that we can have confidence both in how the investigators reached the conclusions and in the conclusions themselves. The criteria related to trustworthiness of the data (credibility, transferability, dependability, and confirmability), defined earlier, were examined. The credibility was established by focusing on the sample of interest for the inquiry. Is the sample really the group of relevant persons to study? Yes, this study focused on the parents of problem children who are candidates for and, in fact, received treatment, so this criterion is satisfied. Transferability or whether the project was limited to a highly specific context was addressed. Was the sample special in some way that would make the findings unrelated to any other sample? The investigators noted that the sample represented different socioeconomic strata and the children had diverse behavioral problems, so a very narrow context was not evident in the sample. Dependability or reliability of the conclusions was also examined. Can one trust the data procedures, consistency of invoking definitions, and related matters? Yes, coding and recoding the data and evaluating actual agreement (reliability) among coders helped address these questions (using quantitative methods of checking agreement). Finally, confirmability, or an effort to independently check on the conclusions was examined. One of the investigators reviewed and audited the procedures in a step-by-step fashion to provide a check on the other.

Comment.   What do we know from this qualitative analysis that we did not already know from scores of quantitative controlled trials? A great deal. The transcripts describe individual experience of the families and some common themes that emerge during treatment. Among the benefits of the analyses is that there are phases that can be meaningfully described to capture the experience; that there is a waxing and waning of expectations, enthusiasm, despair, and realistic appraisals of child-rearing processes and likely outcomes; that parental morale is likely to play a pivotal role in treatment; and that there are points in treatment where certain types of obstacles are likely to emerge.

Quantitative research on parenting practices among children with oppositional and aggressive behavior has emphasized how inept the parents are in disciplining their children and how they unwittingly exacerbate their children's problems as a result. Qualitative analyses have revealed another side, namely, that parents with such children often feel they are "held hostage." They inadvertently are sacrificing their relations with their partner as the problem child dominates the focus of the family and the spouses become more distant and alienated (Webster-Stratton & Spitzer, 1996). Parents in this position often come to feel helpless. The qualitative analyses revealed the progression from efforts to cope, to intense feelings of inadequacy, and finally to helplessness. The authors related the qualitative results to learned helplessness and self-efficacy as a way of conceptualizing parenting experiences. Drawing these connections can help understand parenting experiences, facets of the home environment that may contribute to family relations and interactions more generally, and what feelings, expectations, and sources of hope and despair are likely to emerge during the course of treatment. This information raises many prospects for conceptualizing and understanding the clinical problem as well as for intervening to address the panoply of parent and child issues. In addition, the results suggest that many parent feelings and experiences (despair, helplessness) might be worthwhile outcomes to examine when children are treated.

General Comments

The prior examples illustrate qualitative research, but there is an inherent paradox in summarizing the results from the studies. Qualitative studies focus on thick descriptions and details and eschew glossing over richness of the material. I have highly abbreviated methods and findings to illustrate the work and yield. (See For Further Reading for additional examples in their full bloom.)

A few issues are worthy of note. No doubt the reader has noted that qualitative research generally does not use a control group. The task of research is to elaborate how a particular group of interest experiences some facet of life, and a control group does not have the same role as it would in quantitative studies. There might be use for a control group. For example, in the study of single women, several characteristics focused specifically on how these women felt about being single. It would make no sense to ask a control group (e.g., married individuals) how they felt about that. What would one want to control for? A possible reply to this might be that some of the responses indicated ambivalence, self-blame, and concerns about their life focus. Maybe these themes and issues would emerge in an age cohort that was married. Even though one could not ask about being single, the ambivalence and self-blame may not be unique to singleness. This would be useful to know. Still, my comments are a stretch; the goal of the research was to elaborate the experience of one group.

Another comment warrants mention about the findings from qualitative research and with reference to the above illustrations. In some of the studies there is a blurring of the distinction between assessing the phenomenology (or experience of the participants) and demonstrating relationships about variables in the world. For example, in the study on possible factors that influence criminals into changing their ways, participants were interviewed to identify factors that contributed to their decisions to leave a life of crime. The detailed interviews were quite informative as already noted and convey how individuals perceived or experienced their transition from a life of crime to life of non-crime. That is important, interesting, provocative, and five or six other such adjectives. Yet, self-report has inherent limitations whether in a qualitative or quantitative study.

I would argue that people are not necessarily in a position to comment on what changed their lives to move in one direction or another. We all have stories and firm views about what influenced us here or there, but there is no evidence that the factors we report as influential really account for the paths we have chosen. There may be multiple influences, many of which we cannot verbalize, and these influences vary in their weight (strength of impact they exert). We are not in a position to identify, in fact, the scope of influences and their weight, by the virtue of human limitations (cognitive heuristics, implicit attitudes, impact of learning experiences at different stages, temperamental influences). This is more easily seen in a different context. People who live to be 100 years old invariably are asked by the media and others, "What is the secret of your longevity?" The answers are interesting, suggest hypotheses, and so on. However, the reasons provided cannot be taken seriously. Longevity is multiply determined, and any particular practice identified by the person may have little or no role. In fact, the person might well have lived much longer by dropping the habit, person, or philosophy to which he or she ascribes the longevity. In general, it would be a mistake to conclude that his (or anyone else's) rendition reflects the actual sequence of influences. Self-report is interesting and important, but asking someone why he or she did something does not necessarily reveal the causal influences or sequence. This is a limitation of self-report and not qualitative research. I mention it here because qualitative analyses with humans often rely on self-report.

CONTRIBUTIONS OF QUALITATIVE RESEARCH

The contribution of qualitative research is its systematic approach to the subject matter. There are formal procedures and guidelines for

- Collecting information;
- Guarding against or minimizing bias and artifact;
- Making interpretations;
- Checking on these interpretations and on the investigator;
- Ensuring the internal consistency and confirmability of the findings;
- Seeking triangulation of methods and approaches to see if conclusions are similar when the methods of study are varied; and
- Encouraging replication, both within a particular data set (by other investigators) and with additional data (e.g., multiple cases).

The purpose of qualitative research is to understand, to elaborate meaning, and to uncover the experience of the participants. The concerns with experimental validity, as elaborated previously, and specific methods in which these concerns are addressed are unique to empirical research, both quantitative and qualitative research. There is not much more we can ask of an empirical approach to psychological phenomena than formal procedures and explicit guidelines on data collection and evaluation.

Qualitative research can make a special contribution to clinical psychology and to dominant research methods in general. First, qualitative research makes a *unique contribution to knowledge and understanding* by elaborating the nature of experience and its meaning. The information and level of analysis does not replace, compete with, or address the yield from quantitative research on such factors, for example, as incidence, prevalence, risk factors associated with a problem, or differences between groups (e.g., depressed versus not depressed) on a variety of other measures (family history, cognitive processes, and so on). Yet, the information from quantitative studies, however important, omits the richness of individual experience and what it is like to be depressed or to live with someone who is. Also, the quantitative research tradition by necessity has to omit many variables to study some. The qualitative approach emphasizes many variables in their multiplicity and context and brings to bear another level of analysis by elaboration and consideration of the details.

A major initial contribution of qualitative research, stated another way, is the ability to bring phenomena to life and to do so in a systematic way. Many investigators who conduct programmatic quantitative research have sought avenues to accomplish this, that is, to convey the qualitative details of the subject matter well beyond the confines of the usual journal publications. As examples, one investigator who has studied adolescents and families, provided in a separate source of detailed narrative material focusing on individual cases in contexts and how adolescents and parents interact on a daily basis over key issues (Hauser, Powers, & Noam, 1991). Another researcher provided a film of autistic children who participated in a special treatment program (Lovaas, 1988). The treatment had been evaluated in the usual quantitative tradition, which could not convey the impact of the intervention on the daily lives of children and their families in context for each family (Lovaas, 1987). Yet, another researcher provided a detailed personal account about the experience, treatment, and recovery of depression (Endler, 1990). The account provides the rich details about how depression affects, and is affected by, life. These accounts convey keen interest in providing the rich details of experience. The contribution of qualitative research is in providing guidelines and options for systematically developing, presenting, and interpreting such data.

Second, qualitative research can have enormous impact by bringing experience into sharp focus. A qualitative analysis can make a phenomenon vivid and include the complexity of experience that can move others to action. For example, quantitative research can convey the worldwide epidemic of HIV and AIDS. Qualitative research can describe in detail what life is like on a daily and, indeed, moment-to-moment basis to learn of one's diagnosis, to interact with one's partner and relatives, to worry about taking medication, and to face death. These details make the experience of HIV and AIDS vivid and poignant. This latter analysis can very much move others and have remarkable impact.

Third, qualitative research can elaborate causal relations and paths over the course of development. Quantitative approaches have made enormous gains in identifying multiple factors and their contribution to a particular outcome. The findings are valid at the level of group analyses. It is important to know the general variables that are likely to yield a particular outcome, but also to view these in the contexts in which they may or may not operate. The causal sequence and path leading to an outcome for *individuals* is not really addressed in quantitative research. Literature can provide intriguing accounts and generate many hypotheses about the individual, but a more systematic approach to elaborating the richness of individual experience is needed. Qualitative analyses provide a systematic way of looking at potential causal paths, unfolding of events, and dynamic and reciprocal influences of events for individuals (see Miles & Huberman, 1994).

Finally, qualitative research can contribute directly to quantitative research. Much of qualitative research is discovery oriented; by detailing human action and experience in ways that can generate theory and hypotheses. We already know that in-depth study of individuals (e.g., Kraeplin's work on diagnosis, as noted in the previous chapter) has had a major contribution on topics within clinical psychology. Knowing a phenomenon in-depth permits one to generate hypotheses about what the key constructs are for understanding that phenomenon and what the likely causal paths and influences are. Becoming deeply involved with the subject matter without restricting oneself to a very small set of constructs as measured in a narrow way is an excellent strategy for beginning quantitative research. Apart from its own contributions to knowledge, qualitative research can also influence quantitative research directly by suggesting what to study, what the key influences are, and how they may interact to influence a particular outcome.

Although qualitative and quantitative research derive from and pursue somewhat separate traditions, they can be combined in various ways. For example, one can use the rich detail and extensive records of the qualitative analysis for testing as well as for generating hypotheses. Coding the content, looking for themes and sequences, not only describe interactions but also pose and test the extent to which some events or explanations are plausible. The constructs and categories that emerge from qualitative analyses can be used to develop new measures, that is, new ways of operationalizing concepts for empirical quantitative research. Indeed, measures would probably be much better in capturing constructs of interest if they began from in-depth appreciation of the construct and how individuals experience life. When we develop a measure, there is often a concern with the psychometric properties, that is, reliability and validity. Qualitative analysis in this context alerts us to other issues, namely, the extent to which experience is suitably captured by the items. As a case in point, in treatment evaluation, researchers examine whether the changes clients have made are clinically significant, that is, a change that has genuinely affected their lives (see Chapter 14). Sophisticated and fancy measures, blessed with many psychometric properties, have been devised (see Kendall, 1999). The difficulty is that no matter how a client scores on the measures, we still have no idea about whether the change affects the daily life of the client or whether he or she is better in a palpable way (Kazdin, 1999, 2001c). Developing the measures through qualitative studies would be one strategy to identify relevant outcome assessment. That is, measurement of an important and clinically significant change could begin with an intensive evaluation of client experience after treatment among those who feel they have changed or among those who are so identified by their relatives.

In developing measures, occasionally the term "face validity" is used and reflects an informal way of saying whether the items of a scale seem to be relevant. Qualitative methods provide ways of codifying experience, generating items (from themes and emergent content), and checking to see if others (e.g., participants) view the items as relevant and as reflective of the experience. Clearly, the approach could help develop better measures of constructs related to experience in everyday life. These measures then could be subjected to the usual methods of scale development and evaluation, but would begin with content well grounded in experiences and contexts to which the investigator may wish to generalize.

SUMMARY AND CONCLUSIONS

Qualitative research is designed to describe, interpret, and understand human experience and to elaborate the meaning that this experience has to the participants. The data are primarily words and are derived from in-depth analysis of cases. The cases can be one or a few individuals or a group, but also a culture, tribe, organization, and other unit of in-depth analysis, depending on the discipline (sociology, anthropology, education). A key feature of the approach is a detailed description without presupposing specific measures, categories, or a narrow range of constructs to begin with.

The approach differs in many ways from the dominant research paradigm, referred to as quantitative research, in how the study is completed, the roles of the participants and investigator, what the data are, how they are examined, and the conclusions. Although extensive data (narratives, case descriptions, video or audio records) are collected, they are not reduced in a quantitative way. Rather, from the data, interpretations, overarching constructs, and theory are generated to better explain and understand how the participants experience the phenomenon of interest. Although there are major differences in qualitative and quantitative research, there are also fundamental similarities that make them both empirical research. Among the key similarities are interest in reliability and validity of the methods of procuring the data, efforts to address sources of bias that can impede the conclusions that are drawn, replication of both how the study was done and the conclusions that are reached, and the accumulation of knowledge verifiable by others. Qualitative research can contribute to psychology by elaborating the nature of experience and its meaning, by bringing everyday experiences into sharp focus, by elaborating causal relations and paths over the course of development, and by guiding directly the focus of quantitative studies.

KEY CONCEPTS AND TERMS

Confirmability   Triangulation

Grounded Theory   Trustworthiness

Qualitative Research

FOR FURTHER READING

Berg, B.L. (2001). *Qualitative research methods for the social sciences* (4th ed.). Needham Heights, MA: Allyn & Bacon.

Denzin, N.H, & Lincoln, Y.S. (Eds.) (2000). *Handbook of qualitative research* (2nd ed.). Thousand Oaks, CA: Sage.

Glesne, C. (1999). *Becoming qualitative researchers: An introduction* (2nd ed.). New York: Addison Wesley Longman.

Krahn, G.L., Hohn, M.F., & Kime, C. (1995). Incorporating qualitative approaches into clinical child psychology research. *Journal of Clinical Child Psychology, 24*, 204–213.

Maxwell, J.A. (1996). *Qualitative research design*. Newbury Park, CA: Sage.

Miles, M.B., & Huberman, A.M. (1994). *Qualitative data analysis: An expanded sourcebook* (2nd ed.). Thousand Oaks, CA: Sage.

Milinki, A.K. (Ed.) (1999). *Cases in qualitative research: Research reports for discussion and evaluation*. Los Angeles: Pyrczak.

Stiles, W.B. (1993). Quality control in qualitative research. *Clinical Psychology Review, 13*, 593–618.

Strauss, A.L., & Corbin, J.M. (1998). *Basics of qualitative research: Techniques and procedures for developing grounded theory*. Thousand Oaks, CA: Sage.

Assessment Methods and Strategies

Assessment is a fundamental element in scientific research and can play multiple roles. The usual role one considers is the selection of measures to test a particular hypothesis or conceptual view. This is certainly an important role of assessment and one this chapter will emphasize. At the same time, assessment can contribute directly to theory and application in other ways. For example, advances in assessment often lead to new theory and new lines of research. Improved assessments via telescopes (e.g., Hubble), neuroimaging (fMRI, PET), genetic mapping (e.g., genome project), and identification of subatomic particles have changed fundamental views about many areas within the disciplines in which these assessments are used. Fine-grained, improved, and more precise measurement can reveal phenomena and empirical relations that otherwise would not be evident. For example, fundamental advances in the psychology of learning, as reflected in the work of Ivan Pavlov (1849–1936) and B.F. Skinner (1904–1990), derived from novel and creative conceptualizations of the subject matter. In addition, novel assessment methods used in the research (e.g., drops of saliva, rate of response) contributed greatly to the advances.

When we consider identifying measures for research, attention usually is drawn to the dependent measures or outcomes that will serve to evaluate the hypotheses. Yet, assessment can encompass three facets of the study, namely, assessment of the independent variables (as used to delineate and compare groups of depressed versus nondepressed persons), mediators and intervening processes (alliance in therapy, cognitions or motivational states), and dependent variables (treatment outcome). Indeed, as a general but not infallible rule, studies that assess all three of these facets are more inspired and informative than those that do not. (My dissertation omitted all three, and this was a sore spot among my committee.) The fundamental issues of assessment pertain to all assessment aspects of the study. Specifically, interpretation of a study depends heavily on the precise measures that are used and the confidence one can place on precisely what these measures mean. This chapter addresses fundamental issues of assessment, key criteria that ought to be considered in selecting measures, and strategies for assessing the construct(s) of interest. The emphasis will be on the dependent measures used for a study, but the key points pertain to assessment and selection of measures more generally.

SELECTING MEASURES FOR RESEARCH: KEY CONSIDERATIONS

The selection of measures for research is based on several considerations related to the construct validity of the measure, psychometric properties, and sensitivity of the measure to the changes or differences predicted by the hypotheses.

Construct Validity

As a general rule, in our research we are not really interested in measures. An exception, of course, is when we are developing or evaluating a measure or making a career out of a particular measure. In the usual case, we are interested in constructs or the concepts that these measures reflect. As obvious as this sounds, it is critical to bear in mind, because measures are often selected without sufficient attention to the extent to which they actually measure the construct or facet of the construct of interest to us. For example, there are many measures of stress or social support, two constructs often studied in clinical, counseling, and health research. But the measures are not interchangeable, do not invariably examine the same aspects of stress or social support, and may be quite different in their utility and relevance based on the facets of the constructs they emphasize. This point could be supported with really good research, but let me use my own work instead! At a clinic where I work, parents of aggressive and antisocial children complete a measure of social support that includes three scales: how often they have received support from someone (in the past two months), how many supportive relatives are in their lives, and how many supportive friends are in their lives (Aneshensel & Stone, 1982). All of these measure social support, but the interrcorrelation of the scales (N = 300) ranges from r = .22 to .36—all significant (p < .001) but all rather small. Which really measures social support? Not the right question. Which ought I to use for my study? This is the better question, and this chapter is intended to address the considerations to make an informed answer.

As a beginning, the initial criterion for selecting a measure is evidence that the measure assesses the construct of interest. In assessment the term *construct validity* is used to refer generally to the extent to which the measure assesses the domain, trait, or characteristic of interest (Cronbach & Meehl, 1955). Construct validity has been used throughout this text to refer to a type of experimental validity that relates to the interpretation of the basis for the effect of the experimental manipulation. In the context of assessment, the interpretation of the measure is at issue, namely, "To what extent does the construct underlying the measure serve as the basis for interpretation of the measure?" In assessment, *construct validity refers to the link between the concept behind the measure and research that attests to the utility of the construct in explaining the findings.* Construct validity does not reduce to a correlation between measures or the measure and some other criterion. Rather, it refers more broadly to the pattern of findings and to many other types of validity, as presented later. In a given study the investigator may be interested in measuring "adjustment" or "emotional distress." There should be some initial assurance that the measure actually reflects the construct. The assurance comes from accumulated evidence that findings are consistent with this construct and findings that another construct that might be related is not very plausible.

It is easy to be enticed by many available measures into the assumption that they assess a particular construct. Measures usually have names that reflect the construct the investigator *intended* the scale to measure (and, of course, often the name of the investigator as well). Unfamiliar (and fictitious) examples readily convey the sorts of measures that are available such as the Lipshitz Depression Inventory, Stop-Following-Me Scale of Paranoia, or the You-Bet-Your-Life Measure of Risk-Taking. The names of various measures may be based on supporting evidence that a particular characteristic or construct, in fact, is assessed (construct validity) or merely reflect what the originator of the measure had in mind without the requisite evidence. As investigators, we are often very careful to get our name right in the measure, but a little less careful to be sure we have the construct right.

Related, many questionnaires and inventories have been evaluated through factor analysis, a statistical procedure designed to identify sets of correlated items that cluster together. Names of the factors also suggest what is "really" measured. Essentially, the factors may be presented as "minimeasures," that is, scales to assess different constructs or different facets of a single construct. Here too, one must be cautious because the connection between the name of the factor and what the items have been shown to measure (construct validity) is not always clear. Also, whether a scale, factor, or subscale with a given name is what the investigator means by the construct underlying the investigation is not automatic. For example, one might develop a measure of love, but there are different types of love and different relations in which they are manifest. Is this measure of love the type the investigator has in mind, is it distinguished from other types of love, or from liking a lot, from loyalty, from positive affect in general (technically known as "warm fuzzies") that is not necessarily love? (As a construct validity exercise, ask each of these questions the next time someone says, "I love you" to you.) These are construct validity questions and are not trivial. Needless to say, there should be some evidence that the measure selected for research, in fact, assesses the construct of interest. If no evidence is available, some steps within the study should be taken to provide information on validity and other psychometric properties.

Psychometric Characteristics

There are many steps for establishing or deciding whether a measure adequately assesses the construct of interest. These steps, broadly conceived, refer to how the measure behaves in relation to a variety of circumstances. These can be discussed as the characteristics, or rather psychometric characteristics, of the scale or measure. *Psychometric characteristics* refer here to reliability and validity evidence in behalf of a measure. Reliability and validity have diverse definitions. *Reliability* generally refers to consistency of the measure. This encompasses consistency within the measure (i.e., how the items relate to each other), consistency between different parts or alternate forms of the same measure, and consistency in performance on the measure over time (test-retest for a given group of subjects). *Validity* refers to the content and whether the measure assesses the domain of interest. This encompasses the relation of performance on the measure to performance on other measures at the same time or in the future and to other criteria (school achievement, occupational status, psychiatric diagnosis). Any single definition of reliability or validity is hazardous because both are broad concepts and each has several subtypes. Also, over the years the different types of reliability and validity and their meanings have varied (see Angoff, 1988; DeVellis, 1991). The net effect is that there has been remarkable unreliability in use of the terms reliability and validity. Table 13.1 presents major types of reliability and validity that are commonly referred to and of clear relevance in evaluating measures for possible use in research.

The concepts of reliability and validity sensitize the investigator to a range of considerations. In any given situation a specific type of reliability and validity may or may not be relevant. For example, high test–retest reliability over a period of a few months might be expected for a measure designed to assess a stable characteristic (a trait such as extroversion) but not for a more transient characteristic (a state such as irritated mood or perhaps anger). Apart from characteristics of the construct, evaluation of the

TABLE 13.1.   Commonly Referred to Types of Reliability and Validity

Type	Definition and/or Concept
Reliability	
Test–retest reliability	The stability of test scores over time; the correlation of scores from one administration of the test with scores on the same instrument after a particular time interval has elapsed.
Alternate-form reliability	The correlation between different forms of the same measure when the items of the two forms are considered to represent the same population of items.
Internal consistency	The degree of consistency or homogeneity of the items within a scale. Different reliability measures are used toward this end, such as split-half reliability, Kuder-Richardson 20 Formula, and coefficient alpha.
Interrater (interscorer) reliability	The extent to which different assessors, raters, or observers agree on the scores they provide when assessing, coding, or classifying subjects' performance. Different measures are used to evaluate agreement, such as percent agreement, Pearson product–moment correlations, and kappa.
Validity	
Construct validity	A broad concept that refers to the extent to which the measure reflects the construct (concept, domain) of interest. Other types of validity and other evidence that elaborates the correlates of the measure are relevant to construct validity. Construct validity focuses on the relation of a measure to other measures and domains of functioning, of which the concept underlying the measure may be a part.
Content validity	Evidence that the content of the items reflect the construct or domain of interest; the relation of the items to the concept underlying the measure.
Concurrent validity	The correlation of a measure with performance on another measure or criterion at the same point in time.
Predictive validity	The correlation of a measure at one point in time with performance on another measure or criterion at some point in the future.
Criterion validity	Correlation of a measure with some other criterion. This can encompass concurrent or predictive validity. In addition, the notion is occasionally used in relation to a specific and often dichotomous criterion when performance on the measure is evaluated in relation to disorders (e.g., depressed vs. nondepressed patients) or status (e.g., prisoners vs. nonprisoners).
Face validity	The extent to which a measure appears to assess the construct of interest. This is not a formal type of validation or part of the psychometric development or evaluation of a measure.
Convergent validity	The extent to which two measures assess similar or related constructs. The validity of a given measure is suggested if the measures correlate with other measures with which it is expected to correlate. The correlation between the measures is expected based on the overlap of relation of the constructs. A form of concurrent validity that takes on special meaning in relation to discriminant validity.
Discriminant validity	The correlation between measures that are expected *not* to relate to each other or to assess dissimilar and unrelated constructs. The validity of a given measure is suggested if the measures show little or no correlation with measures with which they are not expected to correlate. The absence of correlation is expected, based on separate and conceptually distinct constructs.

Note: The types of reliability and validity presented here refer to commonly used terms in test construction and validation measure depends on its demonstrated psychometric characteristics. Measures known to reflect the construct of interest and to do so in a reliable and valid fashion bolster the confidence to which the investigator is entitled when interpreting the results of the study. In selecting a measure, it is important for the investigator to examine the available literature to identify the extent to which the measure has in its behalf relevant data on reliability and validity in ways that approximate the use in the present study. Many resources are available to help obtain this information (Murphy, Conoley, & Impara, 1994; Schutte & Malouff, 1995). Much of this is facilitated by available resources on the Web (www.unl.edu/buros; ericae.net/testcol.htm).

Sensitivity of the Measure

The measure ought to be sensitive enough to reflect the type and magnitude of change or group differences that the investigator is expecting. *Measurement sensitivity* in this context refers to the capacity of a measure to reflect systematic variation, change, or differences in response to an intervention, experimental manipulation, or difference group composition (as in a case-control study). The sensitivity required to reflect differences or change depends upon the manner in which the independent variable is manipulated and, of course, precisely what the variable is. For example, if a study compared the effects of relaxation training versus no training to reduce anxiety among persons visiting a dentist, a relatively large difference (effect size) might be expected between these two conditions. But, if the comparison were between two treatments (brief versus extended relaxation training), the differences might be more subtle. Whether an effect is obtained in either case might well be a function of the sensitivity of the dependent measure. Of course, a less sensitive measure would be needed to reflect change in the first comparison (relaxation versus no relaxation) than in the case of the second comparison (very brief versus more extended relaxation training).

Whether and how sensitive a dependent measure is to change are difficult to specify in advance of a study. A few general desirable characteristics of the dependent measure can be identified. First, the dependent measure should permit a relatively large range of responses so that varying increments and decrements in performance can be detected. If a scale has a narrow range (scores can span only from 0 to 10), the ability of the measure to delineate different groups or conditions may be a problem. Second, if subjects score at the extremes of the distribution at pretest, this, of course, will allow the investigator to detect varying degrees of change in only the opposite direction at postassessment. If it is necessary to be able to detect change in only one direction, as might be the case in studies designed to compare two treatments both known to be effective, then the measure need not allow for bidirectional changes. Yet, as a general rule, allow for bidirectional changes. The intervention or experimental manipulation often has the opposite of the intended effects, at least for some of the subjects, and assessing and evaluating these changes can be very important. In general, there should be some assurance in advance of the intervention that ceiling or floor effects will not be a limitation that could interfere with detecting differences among various experimental and control conditions.

Psychometric data for the measure and the possibility of a wide range for scores to vary are important, but it is also useful for the investigator to ponder the items a bit. Often scales are used without really looking at the items carefully to see if it is reasonable to expect scores on the items to reflect change for a given group or differences between groups. Also, scrutiny of the items may lead to hypotheses about some portions of the scale (subscales, factors) that might be more sensitive to group differences than others and that may provide a more direct or specific test of the hypotheses. As the investigator ponders the contents of a scale, he or she may begin to think of alternative or additional measures to better test or elaborate the construct.

Overall, the sensitivity of a measure in an investigation should be ensured prior to conducting the study. If a body of literature already shows the sensitivity of the measure to the intervention, manipulation, or group comparisons of interest, then preliminary work in this issue can be avoided. If such evidence is not available, preliminary work before the full investigation might evaluate whether different manipulations reflect change on the measure. A small pilot study (e.g., 10–20 cases, 5–10 in each of two groups) can provide preliminary information about whether the measure yields differences. It is important to know whether the measure could reflect the predicted relation between independent and dependent variables. If no relation were demonstrated between the independent and dependent variables at the end of the investigation, it would be reassuring to know that the reason for this was not the insensitivity of the dependent measure. An alternative to pilot work is to include the measure with several others on an exploratory basis and explicitly acknowledge in the investigation that one purpose is to explore the relation of a new measure with those already available in the literature. This latter alternative is a full-scale investigation rather than just pilot work.

General Comments

Selecting measures for a study is often relegated to looking at the existing literature and seeing what other investigators have used. Measures that have been used frequently and appear to show the effects of interventions or group comparisons by other investigators continue to be used frequently as new investigations are designed. On the one hand, using a common or consistent set of measures drawn from the literature has the advantage of permitting comparison of results across studies. One can tell if subjects were similar (e.g., in degree of depression) and whether the independent variable affects the dependent variable in roughly the same way (direction, magnitude). Common assessment methods across studies greatly facilitate such comparisons. On the other hand, much research is conducted in a tradition of weak or narrow assessment with little innovation to push or elaborate the limits of a construct. Precedence is a de facto criterion for measurement selection, but not one of the stronger criteria. As a quick guideline ask a fellow researcher (or yourself), "Why are you using *that* measure?" If the answer begins with a comment that others have used the measure, this conveys the potential problem. There are important considerations in selecting measures, and prior use of the measure by someone else may or may not be a very good reason. But it should not be the first reason. The reasons ought to be based on construct validity, psychometric characteristics, and sensitivity of the measure.

The measures that are used are critically important and influence the conclusions that are drawn. For example, if the measure is not very reliable (includes a great deal of error variability), the statistical tests that compare groups or conditions may show no differences that are present and would be obtained with a more reliable measure. The error or variability may reduce the power to detect differences because of the impact on effect sizes. Also, occasionally, limitations in the range of scores permitted in a measure (ceiling or floor effects) may restrict obtaining group differences that would exist if the measure were not restricted in this way. When effects are obtained, it is still critically important to know precisely how the dependent variable was measured. Indeed, when hearing the results of a study, it is almost always meaningful, cogent, and important to ask, "But how was x (e.g., dependent variable) measured?" (It is important to name the dependent variable—my experience is that people look quizzical if you actually say "x.") The reason is that there may be little generality of the findings from one measure of a construct to another measure of the same construct, as I illustrate later.

USING AVAILABLE MEASURES OR DEVISING NEW MEASURES

Using a Standardized Measure

In most cases the investigator will use available measures whose psychometric characteristics are known. Many measures are available in an area of research, and there is usually tacit agreement that certain types of measures, modalities of assessment, and specific instruments are important or central. For example, in studying adult depression, an investigator is likely to include a self-report measure (Beck Depression Inventory) and clinician rating scale (Hamilton Rating Scale for Depression). These modalities and these specific instruments have enjoyed widespread use, a feature that does not necessarily mean that the measures are flawless or free from ambiguity. These scales are considered to be the most well researched within this area, and performance on the scales (scores that relate to degree of depressive symptoms and correlates among these different levels of symptoms) is quite meaningful among investigators. The frequent use of the measures has fostered continued use, and researchers embarking on a new study (e.g., evaluating treatment for depression) usually include one or both of these in the broader assessment battery.

Another reason for using standardized measures, of course, is because of the amount of work that may have gone into the measures by other researchers. That work facilitates interpretation of the measure. For example, to assess intellectual functioning or psychopathology among adults, one might rely on the Wechsler Intelligence Tests and the Minnesota Multiphasic Personality Inventory (MMPI-2), respectively. Extensive research on these measures facilitates their interpretation. Also, use of such well-studied measures lends credence that the study assessed the construct of interest. The investigator need not worry about defending the measure or providing support for the construct validity in light of the prior work that has been completed. Yet, there can be a tradeoff. Does the standardized measure assess the precise construct or aspect of the construct of interest? If yes, that is wonderful. If no, this means one might have a wonderful measure of the wrong construct. The following discussions favor selecting a less-than-wonderful measure of the right construct.

Varying the Use or Contents of an Existing Measure

A standardized measure of functioning, personality, behavior, or some other domain may be available, although some facet of the investigator's interest may make that measure not quite appropriate. The measure may have been developed, established, and validated in a context different from that of the proposed study. For example, one might wish to assess a geriatric sample, but the measure of interest has been developed, evaluated, or standardized with young adults. Alternatively, the investigator may wish to assess a particular ethnic group whose language, culture, and experiences differ from those samples with whom the measure was developed. The reason for selecting the measure is that the method or content seems highly suitable for the investigator's purposes. Yet, the measure has not been used in this new way or validated in the new context.

In such cases, the investigator may elect to use the measure. In so doing, it is essential to include within the study some effort to evaluate psychometric properties. The task is to provide evidence that the measure behaves in a way that parallels the standard use of the measure. Evidence regarding reliability is very useful, but greater concerns are likely to be voiced in relation to validity of the measure in its new use. Evidence might include correlating scores on the measure in its new use with scores on other measures in the study, or using the measure to delineate subgroups and showing that the findings resemble those obtained in studies when the original measure has been used as intended. It may not be sufficient to show that the new use of the measure leads to predictable differences on the dependent measure, although this may vary as a function of the complexity of the predicted relations and the plausibility of alternative interpretations of the results on the measure. In the general case, it is advisable within the study or as part of pilot work to provide additional evidence that the construct of interest is still measured in the new use of the measure and that the measure still enjoys adequate psychometric properties relevant to the study.

Use of existing measures in novel ways is often preferable to creating entirely new measures because the available research on the existing measure (original factor structure, correlations with other measures, and psychometric characteristics) is still relevant for interpretation of the measure. If an entirely new measure were created instead, none of this background information would be available. On the other hand, use of standardized measures in novel ways may be viewed and labeled by colleagues who review the research as inappropriate or beyond the intention of the founding fathers and mothers who devised the measure. There becomes a point at which applicability of the measure to new samples, populations, and circumstances is strained and the challenge is appropriate. For many colleagues that point consists of any extension beyond the specific purposes for which the measure has been developed and standardized. Reasonable people differ on this point; but reasonable investigators provide some validity data to allay the cogent concern that the novel use is inappropriate or difficult to interpret.

Investigators often make slight variations in a standardized measure, such as deleting a few items, rewording items, or adding new items. The purpose is to make the measure better suited to the new population or application. For example, questions asking about suicide attempts or violent acts may be omitted in a study of a community sample because the base rates of these behaviors might be low, and the items would be potentially upsetting and provocative in that context. The same measure in a clinic setting would include the items, given the goal of identifying the full range of symptoms and the expectation that such items may be required. Omission of one or two items is a minimal alteration of the scale, and the items usually can be interpreted as if the scale were the original, by making changes in subscale or total scores (by prorating missing items).

Little data are available on the extent to which investigators make minor alterations in measures and the impact of these changes on the findings. An evaluation of research using the Hamilton Rating Scale for Depression, already mentioned, found at least 10 distinct versions of the scale in use, based on variations in wording and number of the items (Grundy et al., 1994). Moreover, each variation of the measure did not have suitable reliability or validity in its behalf or the strength of data that characterized the original version of the scale. It is likely that many researchers have lost track of the original scale, because as Grundy and colleagues noted, citations to the scale in a given study often are mistaken, that is, they refer to a different version from the one used in the study. In short, standardized tests are likely to be altered; it is important to provide data that the altered version is as meaningful and valid as the original version. As a more general rule, when one tinkers with the content or format of a measure, the requirements are similar. As a minimum, some evidence is needed within the study to show the measure continues to assess the construct of interest and behaves psychometrically in a defensible fashion. To the extent that the measure is altered and that the new use departs from the one for which the measure was standardized, stronger and more extensive validity data are likely to be demanded by the research community.

As an illustration, in the work of our research group we have been interested in measuring hopelessness in children. Among the issues that make hopelessness interesting is the relation to depression and to suicidal attempt and ideation in adults. Hopelessness, or negative expectations toward the future, has been reliably assessed in adults with a scale devised for that purpose (Beck, Weissman, Lester, & Trexler, 1974). In developing the scale for children, the items from the adult scale were altered to simplify the content and to be more relevant to children's lives. Clearly such changes are not minor modifications of a scale but lead to qualitative differences in focus and content. Hence it is not very reasonable to assume that the original validity evidence would apply. Initial studies were conducted to provide reliability and validity data. Internal consistency data and analyses of items paralleled the results obtained with the adults scale. In addition, the construct of hopelessness in children generated results similar to those obtained with adults. For example, hopelessness correlates positively with suicide ideation and attempt and depression and negatively with self-esteem (Kazdin, Rodgers, & Colbus, 1986; Kazdin, French, Unis, Esveldt-Dawson, & Sherick, 1983; Marciano & Kazdin, 1994).

The initial findings on the Hopelessness Scale for Children are promising insofar that they support the construct validity of the measure and are similar to findings with adults. Even so, the results are quite preliminary. In developing a new measure or revising an existing one, one or a few studies are limited, perhaps especially so if they emanate from one research program. In the case of our research, the children were within a restricted age range (6–13) and were all inpatients from a psychiatric hospital. Also, a limited range of constructs and other measures were examined to evaluate validity of the scale. In short, the studies provide some, albeit very incomplete, evidence regarding the new scale and how it behaves. The task in developing a measure is not necessarily to complete the full set of validational steps. Once an investigator provides preliminary evidence and places the measure within the public domain, others may complete further studies that greatly extend research on construct validity and psychometric issues, as is the case for the measure of hopelessness in children (Donaldson, Spirito, & Farnett, 2000; Wehmeyer & Palmer, 1998; Spirito et al., 1988b).

Developing a New Measure

Sometimes measures of the construct of interest are simply not available. The investigator may wish to develop a new measure to address the questions that guide the study. Instrument development can serve as a program of research in itself and occupy a career. In most cases investigators are not interested in developing or evaluating a measure with that in mind. Rather, the goal is to address a set of substantive questions and to conduct studies that measure the construct in a new way.

Developing a new measure is a weighty topic in its own right in light of advances in measurement theory and scale construction (DeVellis, 1991; Reckase, 1996). In developing a new measure, some evidence is required, either in pilot work reported in the write-up of the study or as part of the study itself, which attests to the validity of the measure. The steps extend beyond face validity, that is, that the content of the items is reasonable or obvious. Various types of reliability and validity, as presented previously in Table 13.1, might be relevant. Particularly crucial would be evidence that supports the assertion that the measure assesses the construct of interest. Such evidence might be reflected in one or more of the following:

1. Differences between groups on the measure (older versus younger, clinically referred versus nonreferred cases) in ways that are consistent with the construct (criterion validity);
2. A pattern of correlations showing that the new measure behaves as predicted, that is, evidence that the direction and magnitude of these correlations are consistent (low, moderate, high) with what would be predicted from the relation of the constructs encompassed by the new and more established measures (concurrent, predictive, or concurrent validity);
3. Evidence that the new measure is not highly correlated with standardized measure of some other, more established construct, which might suggest that the new construct is fairly well encompassed by or redundant with the other (more established) construct (discriminant validity); and
4. Evidence that over time, performance on the measure does or does not change depending on the nature of the construct (e.g., mood versus character trait) (test–retest reliability).

With the use of a new measure, evidence on one or more types of validity is a minimum required to argue that the construct of interest is encompassed by the measure. As noted in the discussion of altering a standardized measure, it is usually insufficient to add the measure to the study and to show that it reflects changes that are predicted. Within the study separate and independent types of evidence are needed about the measure apart from, or in addition to, how the measure reflects change as a dependent measure. However, the persuasiveness of any particular demonstration on behalf of a new measure depends on a host of factors (e.g., complexity of any predictions and clarity of the findings).

As an example from our own work, we have been interested in why families drop out of therapy prematurely, that is, early and against advice of the therapist (Kazdin, 1996b). Actually, I was not very much interested in this, but the topic was forced on me in doing treatment outcome research with aggressive and antisocial children. Rates of attrition in child therapy are high in general (40–60 percent), but are particularly high among children with aggressive and antisocial behavior. Some of the factors that predict dropping out are well studied (low socioeconomic status of the family, parent stress, single-parent families). Variables such as these are helpful in predicting *who* drops out but not very informative because they do not shed light on *why* someone drops out and hence what might be done to reduce dropping out.

We felt that for many families treatment itself raises barriers or obstacles that influence who drops out. We developed a scale, called the Barriers to Participation in Treatment Scale, based on our experiences with parents and obstacles they report in coming to treatment (Kazdin, Holland, & Crowley, 1997; Kazdin, Holland, Crowley, & Breton, 1997). The scale consists of 44 items that reflect stressors and obstacles that compete with treatment, treatment demands, perceived relevance of treatment, and relationship of the parent and therapist. The parent or therapist completes the scale; both versions are designed to capture parents' experience in coming to treatment. The results of initial studies showed that scores on the measures predicted dropping out of treatment and other measures of participation in treatment (canceling appointments, not showing up) and that scores on the measure were not explained by other more easily assessed variables that also contribute to dropping out (lower socioeconomic status, stress, and others). What do we know from these initial studies? Probably only that the measure is worth pursuing further. The results are consistent with the construct and provide preliminary support. All sorts of questions remain about the scale, content, and correlates, and we have only begun to examine some of them (e.g., Kazdin & Wassell, 1999, 2000). Developing a new scale begins the path of validation completely anew, and initial studies are only a very first step.

General Comments

The strength, specificity, and very likely the value or utility of the conclusions from a study depend on interpretation of what was measured and the meaning of performance on the measures. If extensive evidence is available for the construct validity of the measure, which is usually the case for standardized measures, the burden of interpretation is reduced. The burden is never eliminated even here because psychological measures by their very nature raise manifold issues about construct validity, external validity, and potential bias. Intelligence tests, for example, tend to be the most well-studied psychological instruments. At the same time the tests are surrounded in controversy related to their interpretation and use. If extensive evidence is not available for the measure, if a standardized measure is altered in some way, either through application to novel circumstances or by item tinkering, or if a new measure is developed, validity data are essential to include within the study.

MODALITIES AND METHODS OF ASSESSMENT

The diverse measures available in clinical research and the range of characteristics they assess would be difficult to enumerate, let alone elaborate, here. Measures used in clinical psychology vary along a number of dimensions. Table 13.2 presents salient characteristics that vary among measures and that have implications for selecting measures. In a given study it is usually important to select more than one measure of the construct of interest and to select measures that vary in their methodological characteristics. In this way the investigator can be assured that the finding is not restricted to the construct as measured in a particular way. Characteristics in Table 13.2 help to identify different types of measures that may be selected and major selection options.

The characteristic that may distinguish measures most sharply (and not encompassed by Table 13.2) is the modality or type of measure. Although the different types of measures and the requirements for devising useful measures within each modality

TABLE 13.2.   Dimensions/Characteristics of Psychological Measures

Characteristic	*Definition and/or Concept*
Global–Specific	Measures vary in the extent to which they assess narrowly defined versus broad characteristics of functioning. Measures of overall feelings, stress, and quality of life are more toward the global side; measures of narrowly defined domains and experience are more specific.
Publicly Observable Information–Private Event	Measures may examine characteristics or actions that can be observed by others (cigarette smoking, social interaction) or assess private experience (headaches, thoughts, urges, and obsessions).
Stable–Transient Characteristics	Measures may assess traitlike characteristics or long-standing aspects of functioning or short-lived or episodic characteristics (mood immediately after being subjected to a frustrating experience in an experiment).
Direct–Indirect	Direct measures are those whose purpose can be seen by the client. Indirect measures are those that obscure from the client exactly what is being measured.
Breadth of Domains Sampled	Measures vary whether they assess a single characteristic (introversion, anxiety, risk-taking ability, or need for social approval), or reveal many different characteristics of personality or psychopathology (several personality traits or different types of symptoms within a single measure).
Format	Measures vary in the methods through which subjects can provide their replies, such as true–false, multiple-choice, forced-choice, fill-in, and rating scale formats of self-report scales and inventories and extended narrative reports subsequently coded as in projective techniques.

are beyond the scope of the present chapter, much can be gained by highlighting major modalities of assessment and the kinds of uses and problems they raise for clinical research.

Global Ratings

Characteristics.   *Global ratings* refer to efforts to quantify impressions of somewhat general characteristics. They are referred to as "global" because they reflect overall impressions or summary statements of the construct of interest. Typically, ratings are made by the therapist or by significant others who are in contact with the clients. A major justification for use of these ratings is that select individuals other than the client may be in a position by virtue of expertise (therapist, ward staff member of a psychiatric hospital) or familiarity with the client (spouse, parent) to provide a well-based appraisal. However, there are global self-ratings as well. Who completes the ratings is not critical in defining global ratings.

The judgments may vary in complexity in terms of precisely what is rated. Very often global ratings are made in such areas as overall adjustment, improvement in therapy, social adequacy, ability to handle stress, and similar broad concepts. These ratings are usually made by having raters complete one or a few items rated on a multiple-point continuum where the degree of the rated dimension can be assessed. For example, a typical item might be one of these:

To what extent has the client improved in therapy? (check one)

_____	_____	_____	_____	_____	_____	_____
1	2	3	4	5	6	7

no improvement   moderate improvement   very large improvement

or

How much do the client's symptoms interfere with everyday functioning?

_____	_____	_____	_____	_____	_____	_____
1	2	3	4	5	6	7

not at all   moderately   very much

The preceding samples illustrate not only a commonly used format for global ratings but also the generality of the dimension frequently rated. Usually, ratings ask for an appraisal of a multifaceted or complex area of functioning.

Global ratings provide a very flexible assessment format and can include virtually any construct of interest (symptoms, overall functioning, comfort in social situations). The flexibility also means that a general characteristic can be used to rate individuals who may differ greatly in their individual problems. By rating clients on a global dimension that encompasses diverse problems (degree of improvement, extent to which symptoms interfere with ordinary functioning), a similar measure can be used for persons whose characteristics at a more molecular level vary greatly. Another reason that global ratings have been popular is that they provide a summary evaluation of a client's status. The problems clients experience may include many facets. It is important to determine with specificity how these different facets have changed, but also useful to have an overall statement that distills the effects of treatment into a relatively simple statement ("Are you better off now than you were when you came for treatment?").

Global ratings also provide a convenient format for soliciting judgments of experts, peers, or other informants. Presumably, an expert in the nature of clinical dysfunction is uniquely skilled to evaluate the status of the client, the severity of the client's disorder, and the degree to which change, deterioration, or improvement has occurred. Similarly, individuals in everyday life who interact with the client (peers, spouses, employers) also are in a unique position to evaluate performance. In this context, global ratings of client change often have been incorporated into treatment evaluation. For example, the Global Assessment of Functioning Scale, used to assess overall functioning on a mental health–illness continuum, consists of a single item from 1–100 (American Psychiatric Association, 1994). Broad descriptive guides are provided at 10-point increments (e.g., 1–10—some danger of hurting self or others; 51–60—moderate symptoms or moderate difficulty in social, occupational, or school functioning; 91–100—superior functioning in a wide range of activities). Multiple constructs and domains are interspersed on the continuum (symptoms, interpersonal relations, work and school functioning). The rating scale is global in the sense that one summary item is designed to represent how one is doing in life.

Issues and Limitations.   One of the major problems with global ratings is evaluating precisely what they measure. The phrasing of global ratings *suggests* what the item is designed to measure (e.g., symptoms). However, there is no assurance that this, in fact, is what is actually measured. Few or, more often, no concrete criteria are specified to the assessor who completes the ratings. By definition, the ratings are rather general, and all sorts of variables may enter into the rater's criteria for evaluating the client.

Because the criteria are not well specified, it is possible that the global ratings may change over time independently of whether the client has changed, as reflected on some other, more specific measure. For example, therapists may view clients as improving over time simply because of changes in the criteria used in making their overall ratings of improvement. Thus, a client's greater ease, candor, or warmth within the therapy session may influence a therapist's rating of client improvement at the end of therapy whether or not clinical change in the problem area (e.g., obsessions or compulsive rituals) has occurred. Changes in the measurement procedures or criteria over time were referred to previously as instrumentation, a threat to the internal validity. Instrumentation can account for changes over time as a function of assessment (procedures, definitions, or criteria) rather than change in client behavior. Global ratings are especially vulnerable to the instrumentation threat because the criteria that go into making ratings are general, and varying definitions are fostered by the generality of the items or questions.

Another problem with global ratings, certainly related to the problem of what they measure, is their potential lack of sensitivity. Essentially, global ratings ask the general question for a given dimension, such as: "How severe are the client's symptoms?" "How much improvement has there been?" and "How anxious is the client?" By posing general questions, the measures lose some of the sensitivity that could be obtained from assessing very specific characteristics of the relevant dimensions of interest. Global ratings greatly oversimplify the nature of functioning and therapeutic change. By utilizing a global measure, the richness of detail is lost. The loss of detail may or may not be important, depending on other measures.

The strengths and limitations of global ratings can be illustrated by a survey completed by *Consumer Reports* (1995) that asked adults to report on the extent to which they were satisfied with psychotherapy. Approximately 3000 individuals, who had seen a mental-health professional, completed questions about their treatment. Global questions asked about how much they were helped, whether the problem for which they sought treatment improved, and the degree to which they were satisfied with their treatment. The results showed that people were generally very satisfied with their treatment and that they were helped. Different treatments did not make a difference in the results. Overall, the results could be interpreted as a glowing report of psychotherapy for a host of problems that people bring to treatment. Indeed, some have interpreted the data to be a very strong endorsement of treatment effectiveness (Seligman, 1995), but this is by no means a majority view (Jacobson & Christensen, 1996). It would be very difficult to make the case that the ratings reflect effectiveness in light of the absence of validity data. This is not mere skepticism for its own sake. We have developed the steps for validating measures precisely to protect against drawing simple conclusions without basis. For example, the global items in the *Consumer Reports* survey might, when validated, reduce to measures of a completely different construct (how much one liked one's therapist, whether symptoms improved spontaneously). Global ratings, as any other measure, are meaningful, but that meaning requires evidence.

Global ratings raise significant problems, two of which are particularly salient. First, the generality of the items fosters conclusions that are also likely to be general. That is, there is little precision in what is being asked. The format of a global rating usually does not permit sufficient variation (a wide range of scores from multiple items known to measure the construct) to identify differences (e.g., treatments) if they exist. Consider as an alternative for a large-scale evaluation of therapy, use of a well-developed self-report scale (e.g., MMPI-2) with multiple scales and subscales that have been thoroughly validated. If all of the treatments showed no differences on such a measure that would be more interpretable than the same results demonstrated with global ratings because we know that the scale *can* differentiate populations, clinical problems, and status of individuals who vary in their psychological conditions.

Second and related, global ratings, like the one in *Consumer Reports*, often are homemade. There are no data that attest to the construct validity of the individual scales. Indeed, a frequent problem with surveys is that they rely on face validity—that is, they seem reasonable to the persons who invent them, to those who answer them, and to those who read the results about them. Yet, there are rarely data that show the measures are valid, that is, actually reflect the constructs of interest, or, indeed, reliable (would show high test–retest reliability).

Surveys and self-report data more generally are readily influenced by assessment conditions (e.g., reactivity), artifact (socially desirable responding, fabrication), and contextual conditions (the setting in which items are completed, and how the items are presented and ordered). Indeed, as researchers we may insufficiently appreciate the extent to which self-report responses are vulnerable to minor changes in how the items are worded, the format of the question, and the context in which any particular item is embedded. Consider a few of the many findings to convey the point (see Schwarz, 1999 for a review). The extent to which people

- view themselves as successful in life varies as a function of whether they rate this on a scale from 1 – 10 or from – 5 to + 5 (people rate themselves as more successful with the – 5 to +5 scale);
- view marital satisfaction as a contributor to their overall life satisfaction varies as a function of the order of presenting questions about each type of satisfaction; and
- say they experience a variety of physical symptoms depends on the wording of the response alternatives, so that the frequency endorsed depends on other alternatives along the continuum for providing answers; 62 percent say they experience symptoms when the scale goes from "twice a month or less" to "several times a day," whereas only 39 percent respond in this way when the scale goes from "never" to "more than twice a month."

These findings only sample many similar results that convey that response can vary markedly with format changes. Subtle changes in item wording, and the placement of a particular item in the context of other items, greatly alter the responses. Placement of the items can also influence key psychometric properties of the measure. For example, items toward the end of a questionnaire correlate more highly with the total score (minus that item) than items at the beginning of the test, holding constant the specific items. Also, if items that are similar are grouped together (e.g., items that measure anxiety, stress) rather than interspersed, the items that go together are more highly intercorrelated than they are when they are interspersed (mixed) throughout the measure. Thus, the structure of the scale (factor analysis) is clearer when the items are grouped (Knowles & Condon, 2000). It appears that early items, serial position of various items, organization (grouping) of the items, and response formats help subjects discern meaning of what is and is not being measured. Fundamental interpretative, memory, and perceptual processes that shape the answers are involved (Knowles & Condon, 2000; Schwarz, 1999).

The implications of this research on how responses can be changed so easily as a function of the structure of the questionnaire are rather significant. We often recognize that any method of measurement (self-report, other report) may have some systematic error in it (apart from random) in that a different measure might yield slightly different information. That is, a measure is getting at the construct, but there may be a little fluff (error) here and there. The work highlighted here shows that with regard to self-report measures, including global scales but other measures (discussed next), several seemingly minor facets of the questions, their format, and order of presentation can have a huge impact on the responses. That is, much of the question determines the answers. This is one of the reasons that multiple measures that draw on multiple methods ought to be used to define a construct.

In a larger battery wherein specific constructs are assessed, one may want to include a global rating scale. After all is said and done and after one has addressed changes or group differences on the main constructs of interests, we may want to know answers to such questions as, "Do the clients feel better, see life differently, and relate better to significant others?" These are global questions, but the global questions of life are not trivial. In using measures to address them, it is important to ensure that other measures are also included to better evaluate the critical constructs that the investigator may wish to talk about in explaining the findings. Also, it is useful to evaluate the global ratings within the study (to correlate them with other measures and to regress other variables onto them) to facilitate interpretation of what they measure and mean.

Self-Report Inventories, Questionnaires, and Scales

Characteristics.   Self-report inventories, questionnaires, and scales are the most commonly used types of measures within clinical, counseling, and educational psychology. These measures require clients to report on aspects of their own personality, emotions, cognitions, or behavior. Unlike global ratings, such measures typically include multiple items that are designed to sample specific domains of functioning (depression, quality of life, social support) and often have extensive supportive data on the construct validity of these domains.

The widespread use of self-report measures can be traced to several factors. First, many states, feelings, and psychological problems are defined by what clients say or feel. People often feel helpless, self-critical, or generally unhappy, or have a low self-esteem, and self-report is a direct assessment of these feelings, thoughts, and perceptions. Second and related, self-report measures permit assessment of several domains of functioning that are not readily available with other assessment techniques. The client is in a unique position to report upon his or her own thoughts, feelings, wishes, dreams, and overt acts and can report on his or her states and behaviors across a wide range of different situations and hence can provide a comprehensive portrait of everyday performance. Third, the ease of administration has made such measures especially useful for purposes of screening. Screening refers to the initial assessment phase wherein the investigator must select a small sample of cases from a larger population. Often a simple assessment device (self-report scale) is used as a means to divide the sample. Individuals who meet particular criterion levels on the self-report measures or questionnaires can be selected and studied more intensively through other techniques.

There are many different types of self-report measures—so many that it is difficult to consider them as part of a single category. For many self-report measures, extensive research exists. For example, one of the most widely investigated measures in clinical psychology is the Minnesota Multiphasic Personality Inventory, an objective self-report test that has been the topic of over 12,000 books and articles and has now spanned research for a period of almost 6 decades. The revised version (MMPI-2) includes 567 true–false items and multiple scales that assess different facets of personality and psychopathology (Butcher, Graham, Williams, & Ben-Porath, 1990; Graham, 1990). The measure is often used in its entirety, but several of its subscales have been used and validated separately (to measure alcoholism, depression, anxiety). The over-all scale has been used with diverse populations (psychiatric patients, prisoners) and for multiple purposes (screening of prospective employees, treatment planning, evaluation of therapy outcome, and even graduate student admissions). Apart from any single measure, an extraordinarily large range of measures are designed to assess an overwhelming number of characteristics, traits, states, moods, feelings, impulses, strivings, and trepidations. Self-report measures can assess diverse aspects of a given characteristic or multiple characteristics merely by having the client respond to many different items. The number of measures available and the number of personality characteristics that can be assessed make self-report measures very convenient and widely used.

Issues and Limitations. Two general categories of problems characterize many self-report measures. First, as mentioned in the discussion of global ratings, responses to items can be greatly influenced by the wording, format, and order of appearance of the items. These influences have been well studied in some contexts (Schwarz, 1999), but rarely in relation to measures used in clinical research. There are exceptions. For example, interviews used to obtain psychiatric diagnoses of individuals cover multiple symptoms so that a psychiatric diagnosis can be derived. One does not think about this very much because the order in which the sets of items that cover symptoms of a particular disorder are presented to the subject is a bit arbitrary. Consequently, the impact of this order is rarely studied. Yet, when self- or other-report diagnostic measures are administered, the order in which the disorders are presented influences significantly the number of symptoms the patient shows, whether they meet diagnostic criteria for particular disorders, and how impaired they appear to be (Franke, 1999; Jensen, Watanabe, & Richters, 1999). In general, it is good that our standardized measures are used in a consistent way across investigators so that the order of the items, subscales, and other domains (e.g., disorders) is constant. At the same time, it is instructive to note that the results are dictated in part by the structure of the measure.

Second, there is the possibility of bias and distortion on the part of the subjects. Distortion refers to the alteration of participants' responses in some way in light of their own motives or self-interest. At the extreme, participants can dissimulate to such a degree that the answers they report are simply untrue. Occasionally, inventories have special scales (lie scales) to assess the extent to which the subject is not telling the truth, is being inconsistent, or is endorsing response alternatives that are extremely unlikely. Blatant dissimulation aside, subjects are likely to alter slightly the image of themselves that they present and to interpret very loosely the meaning of the items so that they appear to place themselves in the best possible light. The tendency to do this is referred to as *social desirability* and has been shown to be extremely pervasive on self-report measures. Long ago we have learned that inventories designed to measure psychiatric symptoms and personality traits often correlate very highly with measures of social desirability (Edwards, 1957). Thus, individuals who complete self-report items are likely to endorse the socially condoned behaviors rather than the socially inappropriate behaviors. The pervasiveness of social desirability as a response style has led investigators to posit a specific personality trait referred to as the *need for social approval* (Crowne & Marlowe, 1964). Individuals who are high in their need for social approval on a self-report measure behave in experimental situations in a way that maximizes approval from others. Thus, the bias on self-report inventories has behavioral correlates beyond the testing situation.

Other biases may operate, depending on the format of the self-report measure. Showing a tendency to acquiesce or agree with items (e.g., in true–false format) regardless of their content, to check extreme values on rating scales, to give cautious or qualified answers, and to be inconsistent across items are primary examples. In treatment evaluation another source of bias that has been discussed, but not well studied, pertains to changes in severity of symptoms that have little to do with genuine improvements. Before therapy, clients may exaggerate their complaints because these exaggerations may ensure that they receive treatment or increase the speed with which treatment is provided. After therapy, clients may respond to the same measures in a more socially desirable fashion in the sense that they provide the therapist and clinic with evidence of improvement, presumably the reward of providing treatment. The changes in self-report responses before and after therapy due to exaggeration and underplaying of problems has been referred to as the *hello-good-bye effect* (see Meltzoff & Kornreich, 1970). Of course, this effect is difficult to estimate because of the actual changes in treatment or because of influences such as statistical regression, that is, improvements that may result simply from having extreme scores at the initial assessment.

The biases that may result from distortion are perhaps especially likely in many of the contexts in which clinical research is conducted, that is, the topics and foci of the research. For example, at the clinic where I work, parents (usually mothers) complete the Conflicts Tactics Scale (CTS; Strauss, 1979) to measure domestic violence (abuse between spouses). The CTS is a well-validated and heavily used measure, and my comments do not challenge or impugn the measure. In the context of the present discussion, a problem with the measure is that there is not a strong incentive for parents to report violence and good reasons to deny or underestimate how much abuse there is (saving face, avoiding consequences of being reported for exposure of the child to violence). Unlike an assessment study that may consist of a single session in which subjects complete the measures, work at a clinic provides ongoing treatment. Consequently, we see parents and children weekly for several months and have considerable telephone contact between the sessions. We often learn of spouse abuse over the course of treatment (a parent comes into a session with several bruises that are visible on the face and arms). Parents often remove the need to infer abuse; they state exactly what has happened because we have come to know them rather well over time. In many cases the CTS scores suggested marital tranquility. Most studies of marital violence compare those who have versus those who have not engaged in a particular type or level of aggression. Because of the incentive to underreport violence, there can readily be a diffusion of groups (some with marital violence in the no-violence groups because they did not report the violence).

The problems of distorting answers on self-report inventories (socially desirable responding) stem from the fact that the subjects are aware that they are being assessed and may act differently than they ordinarily would respond without this awareness. Participants bring to bear their own motives and self-interest in responding. The extent to which distortion may occur is a function of many factors, including whether subjects can detect the purpose of the measure and whether their motives are consistent with those of the investigator. Presumably, the conditions for responding on self-report measures can be arranged in such a fashion as to minimize distortion, although how low the minimal level will be is open to question. Having clients complete tests under conditions of anonymity, ensuring confidentiality, providing incentives for candor, or conveying to the client that his or her best interests are served by honest self-evaluation—these conditions are designed expressly for this purpose. Even so, it is naive to assume that the investigator's motivations for obtaining candor will override the subject's motives for self-protection and self-enhancement or concern about consequences of specific responses.

The pervasive use of self-report inventories and questionnaires, in part, derives from their ease of use. However, the use of such measures would have ended or diminished greatly if they provided meaningless information. In fact, self-report inventories have been extensively validated and shown in many instances to relate to nonself-report criteria. Even in cases where we might expect maximum bias or distortion, meaningful validation data are provided. For example, if we ask parents to complete a measure that assesses the likelihood that they physically abuse their children (Milner, 1989) or ask adolescents to report the extent to which they engage in delinquent behavior (Elliott, Dunford, & Huizinga, 1987), we would expect socially desirable responding and denial as a rule. Yet, quite reliable and valid data have been generated that relate specifically to other criteria (measures of behavior, archival records of crime). Thus, the use of self-report is not merely a matter of convenience in selecting measures. The primary concern is the pervasive use of self-report measures and, in any given study, the sole reliance on self-report as a method of assessing the construct or domain of interest.

Projective Techniques

Characteristics. *Projective techniques* refer to a specific class of measures that attempt to reveal underlying intrapsychic characteristics, motives, processes, styles, themes, and sources of personality conflict. These characteristics are measured indirectly. Clients are provided with an ambiguous task where they are free to respond with minimal situational cues or constraints. The ambiguity of the cues and minimization of stimulus material allow the client to freely project onto the situation important processes within his or her own personality.

Many projective techniques differ according to the responses required of the subject, the type of stimuli presented, the manner in which content or style of responding is interpreted, the purposes of the test, and other factors. Among the most commonly used are the Rorschach and Thematic Apperception Test, which serve as a useful frame of reference (Groth-Marnat, 1997). These tests present stimuli to the subject that consist of inkblot designs or ambiguous drawings, respectively. The participant is required to interpret what he or she sees. The stimuli are ambiguous so that they can be interpreted in an indefinite number of ways. The purpose of making the stimuli ambiguous is to examine the material or content the subject produces. Given the ambiguous stimuli, this material is considered to be a product of the individual's personality and to reflect unconscious processes, underlying themes and motives, and conflicts.

Responses to projective techniques are considered to be traceable to content themes and perceptual processes that unify and organize personality. Content domains—such as how the individual handles sexual or aggressive impulses, relates to authority, or expresses need for achievement—as well as stylistic or coping methods, such as expressing affect and managing needs, are inferred. The many different interpretations provided by the subject usually are condensed to reflect a small number of themes or processes. Performance on projective tests has been viewed as a way to provide insights on the inner workings and organization of personality. Indeed, in conveying this point, some projective techniques (e.g., Rorschach) are considered to reflect a method to evaluate perceptual and associative processes rather than a test per se (Weiner, 1995). The measures provide broad themes, styles of coping, attitudes, and other general facets of personality. The level of analyses has contributed to the widespread use of the measures in clinical settings (see Watkins et al., 1995). Among the advantages considered to accrue to projective techniques such as the Rorschach is the reduced vulnerability to response sets and biases that might be evident on self-report inventories. Although subjects may adopt particular strategies as they make their responses, the specific areas that are to be measures and the scoring of answers are clearly less transparent to the subject than would be the case in self-report inventories.

Issues and Limitations.   Projective techniques have received considerable attention in personality assessment. Their use and popularity have waxed and waned over the last 50 years due, in part, to their association with a particular theoretical approach toward the nature of personality. Several projective techniques have adhered to intrapsychic models, primarily psychoanalytic models, that explain human functioning in terms of underlying personality characteristics and psychodynamic processes.

Developments and current topics of central interest in psychoanalytic theory (e.g., object relations) and methods of scoring diverse scales have been reflected in accelerated research on projective techniques (Erdberg, 1990; Stricker & Healey, 1990). Nevertheless, use of the measures is generally restricted within clinical psychology. The measures are not routinely incorporated into studies related to such topics as the diagnosis, assessment, and treatment of clinical dysfunction, treatment process research, and studies of special populations. Studies utilizing projective techniques do address these diverse topics. However, when compared to other types of measures, such as self-report inventories or direct observations, projective techniques are less frequently employed.

Many projective techniques traditionally have relied heavily upon interpretations and inferences of the examining psychologist. Scoring methods of many projective techniques are somewhat cumbersome and complex (Groth-Marnat, 1997) and major scoring methods have been subject to criticism (Exner, 1995; Nezworski & Wood, 1995). These interpretations often have been shown to be inconsistent across examiners, which has led researchers to question the basis for making judgments about personality. The scientific evidences in support of many of the scoring methods have been challenged (see Lilienfeld, Wood, & Garb, 2000).

Many changes within the field of clinical psychology have reduced the attention accorded projective techniques in research as well as in graduate training. Some of these changes include the emergence of areas and assessments that relate, even if only tangentially, to the thrust of projective techniques. For example, cognitive psychology and assessment of cognitive processes (beliefs, attributions, expectations) address perceptual process within the individual (other than intrapsychic) that influence adaptive and maladaptive functioning. Also, personality research and personality assessment (e.g., Big Five personality characteristics) address enduring characteristics within the individual and how these influence, and are influenced by, interactions with the environment. Both these advances have siphoned off some of the focus on intrapsychic processes as assessed via projective techniques. In addition, psychiatric diagnosis has moved away from intrapsychic explanations in delineating the various disorders in favor of more descriptive psychopathology (American Psychiatric Association, 1994). Projective techniques are still actively researched, but they are less mainstream (as reflected in core clinical psychology journals and as part of course work in clinical training programs) than once was the case.

In light of the complexity of scoring, many projective measures are not likely to be adopted casually to expand an assessment battery. Thus, if the investigator would like to assess aggression, symptoms, or stress and wishes to choose multiple methods to operationalize the construct, projective tests are not the usual choice. Investigators are more likely to select measures that are more convenient to administer and score. Notwithstanding these considerations, projective techniques have occupied a very special place in clinical assessment. The full range of clinical topics including "normal" functioning of personality, characteristics of different diagnostic groups, personality and human performance, and other areas can be evaluated from the standpoint of intrapsychic processes. Elaboration of the content areas of the field as well as development of new tests and scoring methods have made projective assessment an area of work in its own right.

Direct Observations of Behavior

Characteristics. Several measures assess behavior of interest by looking at what the client actually does. The overt behaviors may be sampled from how the client performs in everyday situations or in situations that are designed explicitly to reveal specific responses. Thus, the resulting responses provide direct samples of the relevant behaviors rather than more indirect indices such as global ratings, self-reports, and projective tests.

The potential utility of direct assessment of overt behavior can be illustrated in the context of therapy. Many problems that arise in therapy consist of overt behavioral problems. Examples include such problems as interpersonal (e.g., marital) communication, sexual dysfunction, inadequate social or dating skills, enuresis, tics, stuttering, insomnia, and verbalizations of hallucinations and delusions. The fact that these problems include behavioral components does not in any way deny that other modalities of assessment are important or relevant. A key tenet of this chapter is that rarely is one measure or assessment modality sufficient to evaluate a construct. Yet, as a modality of assessment, direct observations operationalize problems in terms of ordinary types of performance.

Direct observations occasionally are conducted in the client's natural environment (at home, at school, in the community). Sampling behavior under conditions of the natural environment or conditions resembling these is designed to assess the behavior of interest directly to diminish concerns about external validity of the findings, that is, whether the results generalize to everyday life. For example, parent and child interaction patterns have been observed directly in the home to understand the factors that contribute to and maintain aggressive behavior (Patterson, 1982). Observations of parent–child interaction included multiple behaviors that are coded in brief time intervals (e.g., 30 seconds) over a time span of an hour and for a period of several days. Prosocial and deviant child behaviors (complying with requests, attacking someone, yelling) and parent behaviors (providing approval, playing with the child, humiliating the child) are included. Observations are conducted in the home when family members are together and under conditions that are standardized to the extent possible (no TV watching, no outgoing phone calls). The observational system has led to significant advances in understanding parent–child interaction and the development of aggressive behavior (Patterson et al., 1992).

Observation in the natural environment is not always feasible because many behaviors are private, have low base rates, or raise logistical nightmares (e.g., getting observers into the situations where the behaviors are likely to occur). Thus, although directly observing sexual activity, firesetting, gambling, and binge eating at midnight could make the research assistant's task more interesting than usual, the investigator is not likely to obtain the data of interest. Observations are often more convenient when they are conducted in the laboratory under contrived or simulated conditions (see Haynes, 2001). Also, laboratory conditions often permit more detailed and in-depth evaluation because the assessments can be readily recorded (e.g., videotaped) or evaluated by multiple observers (e.g., behind a one-way mirror). Of even greater significance from the standpoint of assessment, laboratory arrangements can hold constant some factors that could vary enormously in the natural environment.

For example, an interaction pattern referred to as expressed emotion (EE), consists of how family members feel about and interact with each other. EE encompasses a pattern in which members tend to be critical of and hostile toward each other. EE is rather important in relation to treatment because it predicts the likelihood of relapse among patients treated for affective disorder and schizophrenia (Butzlaff & Hooley, 1998). The extent to which family members tend to be critical of, and hostile toward, each other could be studied in the home. The home conditions might be standardized in some way (no children in the room, no incoming or outgoing phone calls, no use of weapons while observers are conducting their observations). Yet, EE is more readily assessed under standardized conditions in the laboratory where an interview of family members is provided and taped and later evaluated for comments that define EE. Also, in the laboratory, one can evaluate interpreter agreement to ensure that the responses were reliably assessed. Laboratory assessment of behavior has other advantages. Additional measures can be integrated with direct assessment. For example, one could observe stressful marital communication in the lab and also have subjects connected to physiological monitoring devices to provide another way of assessing stress. All of this is possible in the natural environment, but not as feasible.

Role-play tasks are often used to provide data for observations in the laboratory. For example, in a study to treat social phobia in young children, several role-play situations were given to children (starting a conversation with another child, giving a compliment, and reading aloud in front of a small group) (Beidel, Turner, & Morris, 2000). The tasks would be expected to be difficult for the children who were referred to treatment. The anxiety levels of the children were rated on a few dimensions (e.g., a 4-point scale from very relaxed to very nervous) by observers. Such measures nicely supplement the usual ratings, self-, and other-report measures.

Issues and Limitations.   Because the behaviors of interest are observed directly, the measures seemingly are straightforward indexes of the problems. Yet, even direct samples of behavior are not necessarily representative samples of what behaviors are like during periods when samples are not obtained. It is possible that the sampled behaviors or period of time when assessment is conducted do not accurately portray the client's performance at other times. If the periods of observation samples (e.g., one hour of observation per day) are to represent all of the potentially available observation periods (all waking hours), assessment methods need to ensure that no differences occur across the available periods of assessment. This can be accomplished by randomly selecting periods throughout the day for observation. Although this is not feasible for most behaviors from practical considerations, it would seem to resolve the problem of obtaining a direct and representative sample of behavior. More important, perhaps, than randomness of the period in which behavior is assessed are the conditions in which assessments are conducted. Individuals are aware of assessment and, indeed, in the usual situation must be aware as a matter of ethical obligations of the investigator. Performance may change when individuals are aware they are being studied.

As noted earlier, many direct observations are made in contrived situations in the laboratory. Yet, performance in contrived situations may differ considerably from what would be reflected in everyday life. Marital interaction and communication in a laboratory may reflect dysfunction but still not resemble very closely the nature of the interactions in everyday life in the privacy of one's own home. Participants may be aware of the special assessment arrangement and respond differently as a result (show less intense conflict and no physical abuse). Simulated situations are not inherently limited. However, direct observations cannot be assumed to be valid, that is, to relate to performance in other settings any more than other types of measures (e.g., self-report inventories). Validational evidence is needed to draw conclusions about the generality of the measures to the extent that the conditions of measurement differ from those of behaviors in everyday life.

On balance, direct observations provide a unique focus that extends the method of evaluation beyond the more familiar and commonly used self-report scales and inventories. Also, for many facets of functioning studied in clinical psychology (attachment patterns, agoraphobia, panic attacks, child-rearing practices), overt behavior plays a major role. Evaluation of samples of behaviors can provide central information.

Psychobiological Measures

Characteristics.   Psychobiological measures refer to assessment techniques designed to examine biological substrates of affect, cognition, and behavior or the links between biological processes and psychological constructs. There have been enormous advances in the available measures and the scope of domains within psychology to which they are applied. The measures encompass many different types of functions (e.g., arousal of the autonomic system), systems (cardiovascular, gastrointestinal, neurological), and level of analysis (microelectrode physiology that permits analysis of the response of individual neurons in the brain, perceptual stimuli in animal research, images of brain regions in response to tasks in animal and human research). Measures are obtained in many different ways: connecting subjects to noninvasive apparatus to assess respiration, heart rate, and blood pressure; connecting subjects to apparatus that are a little more invasive (e.g., to assess sexual arousal, mentioned later in the chapter); and sampling saliva or drawing blood to assay a range of biological metabolites, just to mention a few. The purpose of mentioning psychobiological measures as a general category here is merely to make the case for use of multiple measures and methods whenever possible. However, measures within this domain are sufficiently different as to involve many different methods insofar as they raise different issues, sources of bias, and artifact.

Advances in neuroimaging are particularly noteworthy in behavioral neuroscience as reflected in such techniques as magnetic resonance imaging (MRI) and positron emission tomography (PET). For example, functional magnetic resonance imaging (fMRI) permits one to identify areas of the brain that are activated when individuals are given a task to perform. The nature of the task can call on different psychological abilities (memory, problem solving). From activity that is evident from the imaging techniques one can hypothesize neurological processes involved. Although imaging techniques are used routinely among psychologists in behavioral neuroscience and cognitive psychology, they are used increasingly in clinical psychology as well. For example, imagery techniques provide new opportunities to identify and distinguish different psychiatric disorders (depression, schizophrenia), subtypes of disorders, and changes over time and how these relate to symptom change (de Groot et al., 2000; Mathalon, Sullivan, Lim, & Pfefferbaum, 2001). Such work can begin to describe and then to theorize about neurological underpinnings and correlates of clinical dysfunction. Obviously, imaging techniques require quite special equipment, facilities, and training and hence are not standard fare in assessment batteries in most programs of clinical research.

Much more common are measures of physiological arousal and reactivity, in part because these relate to areas of research studied extensively in clinical work (anxiety, stress, pain) and because technological advances have facilitated assessment (portable and noninvasive measures that do not require high-level technical maintenance) and data collection (automated scoring and conversion to a database). For example, studies of response to stress may use self-report measures, but also are likely to use such measures as heart rate to convey through more direct measures the extent to which stress has been induced (Connor-Smith et al., 2000). Measures such as heart rate, skin conductance, respiration, blood pressure, and many other such measures can be obtained by connecting subjects to apparatus while they are engaging in experimental tasks. Outside of the context of anxiety, other commonly used measures focus on muscle tension (electromyographic [EMG] responses) and brain wave activity (electroencephalographic [EEG] responses). Technological advances have made such assessments easier to complete and less intricate from the standpoint of the subjects (portable, small equipment, as opposed to ominous-looking wires connected to several places in one's body).

Biochemical measures also are frequently used. Cortisol level is a good example and worth mentioning because of its frequent use in research and because of the non-invasiveness of the measure. Cortisol levels and changes reflect critical neuroendocrine functioning (the limbic-hypothalamic-pituitary-adrenal axis). Cortisol is often used to assess degree of stress and stress reduction in response to intervention. Levels can be assessed directly from samples of saliva, although occasionally blood samples are used. Cortisol has been measured extensively to assess the extent to which individuals are stressed in an experimental arrangement, or to delineate subtypes of individuals (high versus low reactivity), and to evaluate possible mechanisms in response to various activities. For example, changes in neuroendocrine functioning, as assessed by cortisol, have been implicated in child abuse and maltreatment, gambling, and clinical depression, to mention a few of the areas encompassed by clinical research.

Psychobiological measures are not mere add-ons to an assessment battery but clearly are the primary measure in many areas of clinical research. For example, much clinical research focuses on the onset, course, treatment, and prevention of the use of drugs (e.g., marijuana), alcohol, or tobacco. One could readily use a self-report measure to assess substance use (by asking subjects in a drug-treatment study or world-class athletes about to compete in Olympic events whether they have used any illicit substance). Reliance on self-report might be limited if not simply humorous. (There might be a group self-report measure used where a psychologist shouts out to all the Olympic weight lifters, "would all of those who use steroids step forward.") Psychobiological measures are obviously essential. Some assay techniques (e.g., from urine) are not too difficult to obtain, provide validated (even if not perfect or foolproof) measures of substance use, and give finer-grained information (how much or how recent the use) (Budney, Higgins, Radonovich, & Novy, 2000).

Depending upon the target focus, physiological functioning may be viewed as a direct, or as the most direct, measure of the problem of interest. For example, in the area of sexual arousal, sexual stimuli can be presented in the actual situation, on slides, or on audiotape to determine whether they arouse the clients. Arousal to the stimuli can be assessed directly by looking at blood volume changes in the penis (penile plethysmography) or lining of the vagina (vaginal photoplethysmography). Such assessment does not replace or obviate the need for a self-report assessment of arousal, but rather points to the possibility of direct assessment of the physiological aspects of arousal.

Psychobiological measures have obvious benefits in assessment and have figured prominently in many areas of clinical research (e.g., measures of anxiety and stress). The modality of psychobiological measures is highlighted briefly here for methodological reasons. Such measures are important to incorporate when relevant and possible because they are less subject to some of the common artifacts that seem to plague many other measures. For example, response patterns such as socially desirable responding and acquiescence do not seem relevant when monitoring such measures as heart rate, blood pressure, and respiration. Also, voluntary alteration of responses to psychobiological measures in light of demands of the experiment situation are likely to be less than the alteration likely on self-report or behavioral test measures. For these reasons, psychobiological measures often have been regarded as direct measures to circumvent many sources of artifact and bias present in other modalities of assessment. Of course, psychobiological measures have their own sources of problems, artifact, and bias, but the issue in assessment is not usually eliminating bias but rather being able to draw inferences in which bias may be estimated, minimized, or controlled. Studies in which only self-report measures are used—quite common in clinical research—have as a potential bias that the findings hold only for this type of measure.

Issues and Limitations.   A view traditionally adhered to in psychophysiology, but long since challenged, was that many psychological states can be identified with specific and straightforward physiological measures. There was a hoped-for simplicity in which the measure could relate directly and simply to some underlying state. As measures become more fine-grained and more complex and dynamic biological processes can be assessed, there may be greater movement in this direction. However, the view tended to oversimplify the nature of psychobiological responses. Response systems can be measured physiologically, but they are not isomorphic with psychological states, and there are remarkable individual differences in the patterns of responding among subjects. For a set of measures within a given system (heart rate, blood pressure, and blood volume as measures of the cardiovascular system) and across systems (measures of cardiovascular functioning, respiration, skin resistance), responses to specific events may not be interrelated in a consistent fashion for different subjects. This state of affairs has led to much less emphasis on measuring general constructs, such as anxiety or emotional states, and more emphasis on viewing assessment alternatives as reflecting more specific psychobiological functions. Specific research is needed to validate measures of physiological measurement to ensure that they are, in fact, related to the construct of interest. Indeed, interpretation of many psychobiological measures—that is, what processes they *really* reflect—is a significant issue for many measures (Tomarken, 1995). The ambiguity in many cases stems from the fact that multiple systems and processes can affect performance on the measure, and inferring one specific type of process as mediated by a specific system alone is not always clear.

Some considerations in using psychobiological measures are much more mundane than concerns about precisely what is being measured. Psychobiological recording often requires rather expensive equipment, particularly if multiple response systems are monitored simultaneously. Also, someone in the lab usually is needed to maintain, repair, and calibrate the equipment. The expense is prohibitive for many research programs. For some other measures that are not so difficult to obtain (blood samples, salivary cortisol), procedures to maintain the samples and to ensure their proper analyses are obviously critical.

Artifacts unique to particular assessment methods can influence responsiveness on measures. Movements of the subject, changes in respiration, electrical interference from adjacent equipment, and demands of the situation may enter into the responses of subjects who are connected to various devices. Whether the potential sources of artifact occur is, in part, a function of the particular measures used and the nature of the recording system. For example, inadvertent or intentional changes in respiration on the part of the participant can affect heart rate data and can introduce artifacts. Such influences can be readily controlled or addressed by monitoring systems that might mediate changes in the response of interest or by ruling out the possibility of involvement in a specific system by removing its influence (as in the case of animals given curare so that skeletal responses cannot alter heart rate).

Psychobiological measures provide unique information and levels of analysis in relation to the available assessment modalities. The measures continue to develop in two directions. First, higher resolution and finer-grained methods of assessing brain processes and functions no doubt will continue to emerge, and these require continued advances in hardware and software. The advances have permitted and will continue to elaborate mechanisms, processes, and substrates of more complex and dynamic biological functions. Second, more physiological measures are likely to be available that permit wider use beyond well-equipped laboratories. More portable, less expensive, and user-friendly measures also have increased (caps that can be worn to assess EEG activity or sleep patterns, automated blood pressure cuffs). Thus, many measures have become more practical and less expensive and can be more easily integrated into assessment batteries.

Computerized Assessment

Characteristics. Computerized assessment reflects a different dimension from modalities of assessment highlighted to this point. Use of computers can span different modalities, including self-report and psychobiological measures as prime examples. However, the main purpose of highlighting the different types of assessment is to underscore two key points related to methodology and research design. First, conclusions in any study may be restricted to the specific measure and modality of assessment (e.g., self-report) and to the specific measure within that modality (e.g., Beck Depression Inventory). Second, therefore, it is quite important to include multiple modalities or methods of assessment to assess the construct of interest whenever possible. In the context of these points, computerized assessment represents a novel method.

Computerized assessment has come to refer to the use of computers and automated collection of information as well as scoring and evaluating that information. The topic goes well beyond the present discussion and encompasses many alternative test formats, the use of computers for different facets of testing (administration, interpretation), client reactions to computers, ethical issues (e.g., privacy of Web-based assessment), and others (see For Further Readings). The focus here is on administration of measures via computer and encompasses the Internet and Web-based assessments as well.

With computerized assessment an individual is presented with a task on a computer or merely as part of a usual experimental arrangement, and responds to the computer (touch-screen monitor, keyboard) to convey responses. As an example, the presence of psychiatric disorders is frequently assessed in clinical psychology, psychiatry, social work, epidemiology, and other fields. Computerized psychiatric diagnosis is available wherein the individual answers questions presented directly on screen. One method is referred to as the Quick Diagnostic Interview Schedule (Q-DIS; Marcus, Robins, & Bucholz, 1991; Bucholz, Marion, Shayka, Marcus, & Robins, 1996). The computerized interview achieves its brevity based on the patient's answers. As soon as criteria are met for a diagnosis, the remaining pertinent questions are asked, or the measure moves to the next set of symptoms. The measure is particularly useful when a large number of interviews need to be administered and personnel costs would be high. For example, in one study over 1000 medical and surgical hospitalized patients (males in various veterans' medical centers) were studied to examine the extent to which medical disorders are associated with psychiatric disorders (Booth, Blow, & Cook, 1998). Use of computerized diagnostic assessment made this feasible. Incidentally, the results showed that almost half (47 percent) of patients met criteria for at least one psychiatric disorder over the course of their lives. This is in keeping with other research that has shown that individuals with chronic medical conditions have high rates of psychiatric disorders.

Computerized assessment, including clinical interviews, has been well studied. Often there are advantages to computerized assessment, including more reliable administration of the measure (e.g., not skipping questions), elicitation of more information, and incurring lower costs (personnel costs of test administrators or interviewers) (see Newman, Consoli, & Taylor, 1997). Also, often computerized assessment is preferable to the subjects than are clinician-administered interviews. With various palm-held computer devices, wireless phones, and Internet technological advances, the potential of computerized assessment has yet to be exploited. As with other modalities, computerized assessment is noted here as a modality to incorporate to expand an assessment battery.

Issues and Limitations.   A key issue is whether computerized assessment is valid and yields results that are comparable to those obtained with the usual assessment. No statement can be made that applies to all measures, constructs, and samples. However, many studies have been completed in the context of social, emotional, and behavioral problems; academic functioning; screening and diagnosis; and across multiple disciplines and applications and have shown that results usually are comparable to noncomputerized assessment. That is, correlations are high between the standard way of administering the measure (live interviewer) and computerized administration (Gottschalk et al., 2000; Halfors et al., 2000; Vispoel, 2000). Evaluation and use of some measures are particularly well developed (e.g., MMPI-2; see Butcher, 2000), with many studies on administration, scale analyses, and interpretation.

There are a number of advantages of computerized assessment. The measures often permit large-scale administration (e.g., as available on the Web), in which case subjects may be able to complete the measures from their homes. Accuracy of administration is often improved, especially with complex measures such as diagnostic instruments, in which case decisions are made regarding which items to skip, based on answers provided by the subject. Computerized assessment has the advantage of immediately having the data on a database. Intervening steps of scoring, editing, and then entering data for analyses are skipped. Consequently, there are often cost savings. These savings may also result from the reduced need to train assessors to the same level as would be the case if live interviews were obtained. Clients often prefer computerized assessment and may reveal information that they would not otherwise reveal in the presence of a live examiner. Perhaps the greatest advantage is the flexibility of computerized assessment. A given measure can "branch" into specific items or subscales based on the subject's responses and provide greater in-depth analysis and, indeed, go to other measures as needed to elaborate a particular disorder or symptoms. For example, depression can be assessed by computerized administration. It would be easy for the computer to go automatically to a measure of suicide risk or to screen for other disorders (comorbidity), based on responses to the initial measure.

The benefits of computerized assessment have yet to be fully developed. One benefit not yet realized is in the context of clinical work. Routine, computerized assessment would provide low-cost information that could easily improve the data (opinions, judgment) on which clinicians rely for decision making about patient care, progress, and when to alter or end therapy. The goal is not necessarily to replace judgment but rather to provide better data than what is currently available. There are many products for such use in clinical work (OPTAIO, 1997; *www.quicdoc.com*), but these are still infrequently used in clinical settings or in settings affiliated with academic training programs (universities, internships) that might be most amenable to their use.

Another benefit of computerized assessment yet to be exploited pertains to advances in technology. Current methods are low-grade technology, merely presenting many of the same old measures by computers. But computers can process vast sets of data. It is readily conceivable (and technologically feasible) to have an individual sit in front of a computer and simultaneously measure voice, several psychobiological modalities, responses to specific items, and facial expression, and to integrate these. Also, with a palm-held device, one could measure reactions (anxiety, elation) in diverse situations in which clients can take their devices. Instead of pulling out a cell phone and making calls annoying to others in a public place, one can take out a palm-held device that has beeped (at preset intervals) to evaluate one's mood, anxiety, or meaning of life. In the coming years, no doubt computerized assessment will provide its own battery of measures and will sample multiple modalities by itself.

From the standpoint of the present chapter computerized assessment provides another modality of assessment. Computerization does not reduce or alter method factors (variance attributed to any particular assessment modality). The strength of assessment in a given study comes from using multiple measures of a construct and varying the methods of assessment. Computerized assessment provides an alternative with several practical and cost advantages.

General Comments

This overview of major modalities of assessment is not intended to be complete in terms of either the number of modalities available or the variations within each modality. Major options were highlighted that may be differentially relevant for an investigation, depending upon the purpose and constructs of interest on the part of the investigator. Selection of a given modality of assessment might be dictated by theoretical predictions, the nature of the client's complaint, and interpretation of the therapist as to the primary modality of the problem. Practical decisions as well might dictate the methods of assessment finally selected.

The discussion has focused on assessment modalities free from the content areas of clinical, counseling, and related areas of psychology. Often the measures are dictated by the content area and the interests they inherently reflect. For example, within clinical psychology a great deal of research focuses on neuropsychological assessment. The area considers the diagnosis and evaluation of functioning and damage to the brain as, for example, associated with injury, psychological dysfunction, medical illness, and aging. A variety of specific measures and tasks are routinely included to assess intellectual skills, sensation, memory, speech perception, tactile discrimination, and other domains (see Lezak, 1995). Many measures are regarded as standard to address the range of questions that neuropsychological assessment requires. For other areas of research in clinical psychology as well, one might identify measures and modalities in frequent use. The issue for our discussion was options for selecting dependent variables more generally.

In most studies it may be difficult to discern precisely why one modality of assessment was selected rather than another. Yet the description of the purpose of the research should directly state why a particular modality has been selected. Within that modality it is desirable to justify further why a particular measure was selected. In most cases where such a justification is not explicit, there may be extensive evidence attesting to the utility, reliability, and validity of the assessment technique. In other cases many options might be available, and the decision appears arbitrary. Specific hypotheses about the constructs that constitute the dependent measures may dictate not only the modality of assessment (e.g., psychobiological measures) but also the particular measure within the modality (e.g., heart rate rather than skin conductance). For a given research or clinical purpose one modality may be more well suited than another because it reflects the construct and level of analysis of interest (projective techniques for unconscious processes; behavioral measures for samples of everyday interactions). However, one type of measure is not inherently superior to another. The investigator's purpose or concern over a particular source of bias or artifact may dictate which modality of assessment and which measurement devices within a given modality will be appropriate.

The use of different assessment modalities in light of purposes of the study is nicely illustrated in an investigation of adult heterosexual males who varied in their attitudes toward gay individuals (Adams, Wright, & Lohr, 1996). The study compared homophobic and nonhomophobic males and the extent to which they were sexually aroused by various stimuli. Homophobia was defined as negative emotional responses (fear, anger, anxiety, discomfort, and aversion) in the context of interacting with gay individuals. Males who identified themselves as exclusively heterosexual were divided (median split) into two groups (homophobic and nonhomophobic), based on a measure used to operationalize homophobia. All subjects were then exposed individually to videotaped segments of erotic material depicting "explicit" heterosexual activity, female homosexual activity, and male homosexual activity (presented in counterbalanced order across subjects). Sexual arousal in response to these videos was measured with two modalities. Self-report ratings of arousal included subjects' reports of their arousal (how "turned on" they were) and ratings of the degree of penile erection (1–10-point scale). The psychobiological measure was a penile plethysmograph, a strain gauge (mercury in rubber ring) that assessed penile circumference. This is a frequently used and validated measure of degree of male sexual arousal.

Among the findings, homophobic and nonhomophobic males did not differ in subjective ratings—both groups reported arousal to heterosexual and female homosexual videos, and these ratings were higher than those given for the male homosexual videos. On the psychobiological measure, both groups were aroused by, and did *not* differ from each other in their arousal to, heterosexual and female homosexual videos. However, homophobic males were significantly more aroused to male homosexual videos than were the nonhomophobic males. In light of the different patterns across measures, the authors concluded that homophobic males are sexually aroused by homosexual stimuli, although they may not recognize this. The different patterns of responding across modalities raise intriguing hypotheses about potential discrepancies between response systems and aspects of homophobia.

In the previous study, separate assessment modalities were central to the goals of the study, namely, to see if awareness of arousal (self-report) and physiological arousal might show a different pattern. Multimeasures and measures from different modalities are valuable as a general strategy in research, whether or not one is making predictions about discrepancies among measures. Each modality of assessment includes different sources of bias and potential limitations. No single measure overcomes all of the problems that arise in assessment. Indeed, the measures are complementary. Selecting several different measures, each with different sorts of problems, increases confidence that the response dimension of interest, in fact, is being assessed. Using separate measures can help distinguish those responses that may be due to methodological idiosyncrasies of a given assessment device from systematic changes in the construct or domain of interest.

UNOBTRUSIVENESS AND REACTIVITY OF PSYCHOLOGICAL MEASURES

Nature of the Problem

Measures most frequently used in research are presented to participants who are well aware that their performance is being assessed. Such measures are said to be *obtrusive* to denote that participants are aware of the assessment procedures. Obviously, participants know some facet of their personality or behavior is being assessed when they complete a self-report questionnaire or projective test, or are placed into a somewhat contrived situation in which their behavior is observed. Yet, in almost all of the modalities mentioned previously, participants are aware that their performance is being assessed, whether or not they know the specific purposes or foci of the measures.

Awareness raises the prospect that performance on the measure is altered or influenced by this awareness. If performance is altered by awareness of the measure, the assessment is said to be *reactive*. It is not necessarily the case that subjects' awareness (obtrusiveness) influences their performance (*reactivity*). Knowledge of the purposes of the measures, motivation of the subjects, and subject roles, among other influences, contribute to reactivity.

Several interrelated problems are likely to result from reliance on obtrusive measures. First, reactivity is a *method factor*, that is, a characteristic that may contribute to the results or scores on a measure. When two measures are administered, their correlation may be due, in part, because they were both obtrusive and reactive. Essentially, subjects may respond in a similar way across the two measures. For example, participants may show a general set of responding, such as placing themselves in a socially desirable light. To the extent that this response set influences each of the measures because they are reactive, the correlation between different measures may be high. The correlation between the measures might be lower if one measure were reactive and the other were not. In general, interpretation of psychological measures can be greatly enhanced by using multiple measures that vary in reactivity (one reactive, another not). If similar results are obtained across such measures, the investigator has greater assurance that conclusions are not restricted to some aspect of the assessment method.

Second, the use of obtrusive and reactive measures may *limit generality* of research findings. The problem of reactivity of assessment can be elaborated by discussing external validity more directly. Because almost all psychological research with humans relies on subjects who know that their performance is being assessed, one can legitimately question whether the results would be evident if subjects did not know their performance was being assessed. We know that the subject brings meaning to the assessment situation and responds accordingly (Orne, 1962; Schwarz, 1999). We take for granted that how subjects respond to our questionnaires about stress, social support, and other key constructs really identify performance, perceptions, or feelings outside of our experiment. It is reasonable to assume that obtrusive measurements (e.g., questionnaires in the lab) are *correlated* with real-life (unobtrusive) indices of the constructs. Yet, we have little idea of whether the correlation is very high. The generalization question in relation to assessment is, "How does the subject respond when there is no special assessment situation (e.g., my study)?" Any time this question is examined, it invariably improves the quality of the study.

Whether results of an experiment extend to *unobtrusive measures* is especially important in therapy research and related areas (prevention, education) in which the goal is to change ordinary behavior of the clients in everyday life, under conditions where they do not believe they are being specially monitored. Obtrusive and reactive assessment in a laboratory or clinic setting does not really provide the vital information needed about performance in everyday life, unless evidence is available that the laboratory or clinic-based measures, in fact, correlate highly with everyday experience assessed unobtrusively.

Third, obtrusive and reactive measures may *evoke response styles* that greatly influence performance. If participants are aware that their behavior is being assessed, they can often alter their responses accordingly to achieve their own purposes. Participants may respond to present a certain kind of image (place themselves in a socially desirable light). Although we tend to think of self-report questionnaires as vulnerable to such biases, projective techniques and direct samples of behavior can show such effects as well (Crowne & Marlowe, 1964).

Fourth, obtrusive and reactive assessment may increase the *likelihood that the assessor influences the results.* The responses of participants in an experiment can be influenced by various characteristics of the individuals who administer the assessment devices (assessors). For example, results obtained from questionnaires or interviews may be influenced by such variables as age, sex, race, social class, and even religion of the assessor or interviewer (e.g. Masling, 1960; Rosenthal, 1969). The assessor may be a source of influence primarily because the subject is aware that assessment is conducted and is exposed to someone in the role of an assessor. Assessor characteristics could not as readily exert their direct influence if assessment did not expose the subject to someone in the position of an assessor. That is, this source of bias can be reduced or eliminated through unobtrusive assessment.

Potential Solutions with Traditional (Obtrusive) Measures

Several solutions can minimize or even eliminate entirely the influence of subject awareness on performance. These solutions vary as a function of the specific method of assessment. With self-report questionnaires and rating scales, the instructions given to the participants often are designed to increase their candor and to decrease the influence of reactivity. One tactic is to tell the participants that their answers to the test items are anonymous and that their individual performance cannot be identified. Of course, in most investigations these claims are accurate, although the participants may not believe them. In other situations, instructions may be provided to minimize the likelihood that participants will answer the items in a particular way. Subjects are more likely to respond candidly and less likely to place themselves in a socially desirable light if they believe they cannot be identified.

Another strategy to minimize the influence of subject awareness on performance is to add *filler* or *buffer items* on a given measure. The filler items are provided to alter the appearance of the focus or to make the measure appear less provocative or intrusive. In the process the true purpose of the measure, that is, the construct of interest, is obscured. For example, a self-report measure of various psychiatric symptoms, criminal activity, or sexual practices might be infused with items about interests, hobbies, and physical health. The participants are aware of the assessment procedures, but the filler items may obscure or diffuse the focus that would heighten reactive responding. The filler items may soften the impact of the measure and the reactions that might otherwise be prompted. Of course, the success of such items to obscure or attenuate the emphasis is a matter of degree; adding a few buffer items ("Do you get colds frequently?" "Have you ever collected coins?") to a newly developed the Jack-the-Ripper Tendency Scale may not help very much.

Another solution is to vary what participants are told about the task and how it should be performed. For example, the purpose of the test may be hidden, or participants may be told that their test responses have no real bearing on their future and will not be used for or against them. Extremely bright or suspicious subjects recognize that statements like this reflect that, in fact, this information will be used for or against them. (This is sort of like a doctor saying to a child that, "This will not hurt!" One learns only through development that such a statement often is a clear signal that something will be painful.) Alternatively, participants may be told to respond to the items very quickly. The purpose of "speed instructions" is to have subjects give little attention to what actually is measured and hence not deliberate about the content or purpose of the items. These instructional ploys may or may not be plausible to the subjects, depending upon the circumstances of testing and the exact facets of personality or behavior that are assessed.

The use of computers in psychological assessment may have implications for reducing the reactivity of assessment. Computers permit participants to answer questions directly by responding to items presented on a monitor or screen. The questions are presented and answers are recorded automatically without a human examiner. As mentioned previously, computerized assessment, when compared with the measure administered by an examiner, often yields more information about sensitive topics such as alcohol consumption and sexual problems. In addition, respondents often report favorable attitudes toward computerized test administration. In short, although computerized assessment is obtrusive, it may be less reactive.

When reactive procedures are used because of the unavailability of alternative assessment devices, one of the strategies that might be adopted is to encourage participants to respond as honestly as possible. Although this may be naive when participants have a particular interest in their performance in light of some goal (job procurement, discharge from a hospital), the overall approach may be sound. In many cases, such as evaluation of progress in therapy, it is usually in the best interests of the client to respond as candidly and accurately as possible. In such cases this message may be worth elaborating to the respondents to obtain samples of performance during assessment that are as representative of daily performance as the measures allow.

Assessment occasionally consists of direct observation of behavior over an extended period. With such measures, different solutions have been sought to decrease the influence of reactivity. For example, when behavior is directly observed in a naturalistic situation such as the home or at school, there may be a novelty effect, and the early data may not represent performance. Usually, the first few days are needed for individuals to habituate to the observers. It is assumed that after a period of time, obtrusive assessment will become less reactive and exert little or no influence. Whether performance under obtrusive and unobtrusive assessment conditions is similar requires empirical evaluation. Even under ideal conditions of administration, the fact that participants are aware that their behavior is to be assessed might affect generality of the results. Possibly the results of an experiment have little bearing on behavior outside of the reactive assessment procedures.

UNOBTRUSIVE MEASURES

Several measurement strategies can be used that are unobtrusive. Their use can bolster the conclusions drawn from a study by showing that the results are similar across obtrusive and unobtrusive measures. The measures that are used are not discussed very often even in books (e.g., various handbooks) that are devoted to psychological assessment. It is useful to mention the major types of unobtrusive measures and il-

TABLE 13.3.   Major Methods of Unobtrusive Measurement

Type of Measure	Definition	Examples
Simple observation	Observing behavior in a naturalistic situation in which the assessor does not intervene or intrude. The assessor is passive and does nothing to alter the normal behavior or to convey that behavior is being observed.	Observing nonverbal gestures or body distance as in a study of social behavior; recording the clothing individuals wear to reflect mood states.
Observations in contrived situations	Simple observation of behavior in naturalistic situations in which the experimenter or assessor intervenes or does something to prompt certain kinds of performance. The assessor plays an active role without violating the reactivity of the situation.	Using confederates who seem to be in need of assistance to test for altruism; testing for honesty in a situation that allows cheating.
Archival records	Records kept for reasons other than psychological research, such as institutional, demographic, social, or personal records.	Records of birth, marriage; institutional data such as discharge records or patient history; documents.
Physical traces	Physical evidence, changes, or remnants in the environment that may stem from accumulation or wear resulting from performance.	Wear on pages to discover magazine or book passages read; deposits of trash to study littering; graffiti to study sexual themes.

lustrate their relevance for psychological research (see Webb et al., 1981). The major techniques of unobtrusive measurement are listed in Table 13.3. The techniques include simple observation, observation in contrived situations, archival records, and physical traces.

Simple Observation

Directly observing behavior as it occurs in naturalistic settings, unbeknownst to the subject, is the most obvious unobtrusive measure. Simple observations in naturalistic settings sample behavior unaffected or less affected by the situational constraints of the laboratory and methodological characteristics of the more commonly used assessment procedures. The fact that the observations are outside of awareness of the subjects eliminates reactivity. The actual behaviors that are observed, too, may be relatively subtle and ones that subjects would not suspect reflect the construct of interest.

   An interesting example of simple observation derived from the study of people touching each other. One function of touching other individuals (having a hand on another person's back, putting an arm around someone's shoulder, holding someone's arm while talking to them) is to convey status or power (Henley, 1977). Higher-status or more powerful individuals may be more likely to touch others than to be touched by others. If touching is a sign of power or unwitting efforts to display power, then individuals with higher status or who wish to convey that status (persons who have higher socioeconomic status, are older, male) would be expected to touch others (their respective counterparts) more than to be touched. In fact, unobtrusive observations of touching in public situations supported the prediction. Individuals who were male, older, and rated as higher in socioeconomic status more frequently touched others (females, younger individuals, persons of lower socioeconomic status, respectively) than were touched by them. The findings do not establish that touching necessarily assesses status or power. Yet, the observational data have supplemented questionnaire research that has related touching others to dominance, status, and being placed in a position of power (see Henley, 1977). Thus, direct observation adds credence to other assessment methods for evaluating social behavior.

Simple observation is very useful because of the almost unlimited situations in everyday life that are open to scrutiny and direct tests of hypotheses. Of course, the method has potential problems. One problem that may arise that would defeat the value of unobtrusive observation in naturalistic situations is detecting the presence of the observer qua observer. As an unobtrusive measure, the observer must not influence the situation. Usually, this amounts to disguising the role of the observer, if an observer actually is required in the situation. If performance can be sampled without observers, perhaps by hidden cameras, even less opportunity might be present to alter the nonreactivity of the situation.

Another problem with simple observation is ensuring that the behaviors of interest occur with sufficient frequency to be useful for research purposes (e.g., differentiation of groups, data analyses). Merely watching participants in the situations of interest does not guarantee that the responses will occur. This assessment problem is very familiar for various television shows that capture the predatory behavior of tigers and lions as they hunt and devour an animal. The behavior is filmed for later editing and television viewing and is clearly much better than giving animals a self-report questionnaire. Yet, to get the footage of the behavior requires many hours because the base rate of the "desired" behaviors (hunting, killing, devouring) is low in relation to hours in the day. Moreover, on many occasions in which the behavior does occur, it cannot be easily assessed for practical reasons (the photographer could not keep up with the animal; a huge rock, bush, canyon blocked the camera). Simple observation in naturalistic situations for research has similar obstacles. The response of interest may be so infrequent as to make assessment prohibitively expensive, inefficient, or of little use.

A final problem with simple observation pertains to the standardization of the assessment situation. The environmental conditions in which the response occurs may change markedly over time. Extraneous factors (e.g., presence of other individuals) may influence behavior and introduce response variability into the measure. The net effect of this variability might be to obscure the effects of the independent variable. Simple and naturalistic observation can be influenced by uncontrolled factors that make it difficult to assess performance in a relatively uniform fashion.

Observation in Contrived Situations

Observations in contrived situations resolve some of the problems of simple observation. Contrived situations maximize the likelihood that the response of interest will occur. Hence, the problem of infrequent responses or conditions that do not precipitate the response is resolved. Also, arranging the naturalistic situation allows for standardizing extraneous factors, and hence the data are less subject to uncontrolled influences. The important requirement of observations in contrived situations, of course, is to control the situation while maintaining the unobtrusive conditions of assessment. This may be accomplished by utilizing an observer, experimenter, or confederate working with the observer, to help stage the conditions that are designed to evoke certain kinds of behaviors.

A prime example of contrived situations for the purposes of assessment are television programs (*Candid Camera, Totally Hidden Video*) that place people into situations varying in degrees of frustration. The situations are well planned so that as each new unwitting subject enters into the situation (e.g., a cafeteria), the stimulus conditions presented to him or her are held relatively constant (e.g., someone sitting next to the subject wearing a feathered hat that keeps hitting the subject in the face while he or she is eating at the counter). The subject's behavior is recorded on film, which serves as the basis for the television program. The reactions of the participants when they are informed that they are really being filmed for the show often reveal the success in hiding the contrived nature of the situation. Of course, even though the conditions are relatively natural, subjects may occasionally see through them. Even so, seeing how individuals actually do respond in such situations is likely to be quite different from what they would say on a self-report questionnaire about how they would respond.

Archival Records

Institutional records in schools, medical facilities, government (e.g., census data), work history, use of various social services, credit history, and the Internet (what sites we visit, for how long) provide a wealth of information about people. Such measures occasionally have been sampled in psychology to test specific hypotheses. The unique feature of such records is that they usually can be examined without fear that the experimenter's hypothesis or actions of the observers may influence the raw data themselves, although there are exceptions. For example, people are now aware that their behavior is being monitored and recorded as they search Web sites.

A classic study in clinical psychology that used archival records examined whether schizophrenic patients had a history of social isolation prior to their hospitalization (Barthel & Holmes, 1968). One characteristic of schizophrenic patients is social withdrawal and isolation. This study examined the history of hospitalized patients through an archival record, namely, high-school yearbooks. The number of social activities in which each patient participated was counted from the yearbooks from each patient's senior year. Social activities included participation in clubs, organizations, special-interest groups, student government, and others. As predicted, schizophrenic patients engaged in significantly fewer activities than did control subjects (who were drawn from individuals in the yearbooks who were pictured next to them). The results supported the notion that schizophrenic patients are socially isolated prior to hospitalization. The study reflects a creative use of archival records.

Archival records have their own sources of measurement problems. One problem is the possible changes in criteria for recording certain kinds of information. For example, records of crime rate may vary over time as a function of changes in the definition of crime, sociological variables that may alter the incidence of reporting certain crimes (e.g., rape), and mundane issues such as whether there are budget cuts in an agency that affect whether or how carefully the data are gathered. The changes in the criteria for recording information (an example of instrumentation) may lead to interpretive problems regarding the "true" rates of the problem and changes over time.

A related problem is the selectivity in the information that becomes archival. For example, historical records of births are likely to omit many individuals. Before more extensive methods of recording births and population statistics came into use, many births were likely to have gone unrecorded. Those births unlikely to be recorded may have varied as a function of socioeconomic status, age, and marital status of the mother, geographical location, and race. Thus, there may be a selective deposit of the information that becomes archival for subsequent research.

Physical Traces

Physical traces consist of selective wear (erosion) or the deposit (accretion) of materials. Either the wear or deposit of materials may be considered to reflect specific forms of behavior. An excellent example of a physical trace measure was used to evaluate the long-term impact of lead exposure in school-age children. Lead is a heavy metal to which individuals can be exposed through multiple sources, including water, air (from leaded automobile fuel exhaust), paint, and other sources. Lead leaves a physical trace by accumulating in one's bones and teeth. Ethics and research review committees tend to be a little testy when an investigator proposes removal of bones from children as part of research. A creative alternative was to collect baby teeth that were normally extruded (Needleman & Bellinger, 1984). Teeth were collected from thousands of children to assess lead deposits. High- and low-lead-exposure children were formed from this assessment and compared in their academic and classroom performance over a period of several years. The results indicated that relatively low doses of lead exposure are associated with hyperactivity, distractibility, lower IQ, and overall reduced school functioning in children (Needleman et al., 1990). Moreover, follow-up 11 years later showed that these impairments are maintained. This work has led to other studies (replicating the deleterious effects of lead on child behavior, animal research locating specific sites in the brain that are deleteriously affected) and to changes in government policies regarding the control of lead levels.

A potential problem with physical trace measures is that changes over time may occur as a function of the ability of certain traces to be left. For example, research on wall inscriptions (graffiti) in public bathrooms has shown differences in the frequency of inscriptions between males and females and cross-cultural differences in erotic themes (see Webb et al., 1981). If one wished to study graffiti over time, as a physical trace, this might be difficult. Many institutions have "seen the writing on the wall" and have used surface materials that are less readily inscribed or have covered marks before they accumulate. Thus, the material upon which traces are made may change over time.

The selective deposit of physical traces is another potential problem. Physical trace measures may be subject to some of the same limitations of archival data. It is possible for the traces to be selective and not represent the behavior of all the participants of interest. Also, physical traces may be influenced by a number of variables that determine what marks are left to evaluate and hence what data will be seen. For example, fingerprints are the example par excellence of a physical trace measure. However, they are not always available as signs of someone's presence at the scene of a crime. Individuals not interested in leaving such traces are well aware of the necessary procedures to ensure that their presence and fingerprints go unrecorded. Yet, criminals are more likely to leave samples of DNA (from hair, blood; in the case of sexual crimes, semen). Physical traces have gone way beyond mere fingerprints.

A final problem with physical traces is that they may become reactive. Once the trace becomes known as a measure of interest, potential subjects may become aware of this and respond accordingly. For example, social scientists and news reporters occasionally have a keen interest in the trash of celebrities and politicians to measure their private affairs (correspondence) and potential vices (weekly consumption of alcohol). Publicity about these practices probably has limited the types of items that are publicly discarded for trash pickup. Secretive, cautious, and perhaps wise celebrities alike may use other means of disposal (paper shredder, trash compactor, dumpster behind the supermarket).

General Comments

One advantage of unobtrusive measures is that they can supplement more commonly used techniques and thereby add strength to the external validity of experimental findings. For example, unobtrusive measures of therapy outcome (hospital visits, days of work missed) would provide tremendously important information about treatment efficacy and would uniquely supplement the data obtained from the more frequently relied upon self-report questionnaires and inventories. If findings are obtained across diverse measures with different methodological features (obtrusive and unobtrusive measures), this suggests the robustness of the relation between the independent and the dependent variables.

Another advantage of unobtrusive measures is their persuasive appeal. Such measures are often drawn from everyday life (arrest rates, doctors visits, truancy). Research that reports such measures often are much more persuasive to consumers of research (e.g., policy makers) because the measure (rather than the construct) is of interest in its own right. For example, evidence that psychotherapy reduces scores on a self-report inventory is not likely to be viewed by consumers of research as nearly as important as evidence that psychotherapy reduces the number of visits people make to medical doctors, days of missed work, and calls to a suicide hot line. Thus, adoption and dissemination of findings may be improved by supplementing more commonly used psychological measures with unobtrusive measures in which society has interest.

Unobtrusive measures have their own problems. Apart from the issues mentioned already, each of the measures must be interpreted with some caution. Unlike more commonly used measures, unobtrusive measures usually undergo little validation research, so there are few assurances that they measure what the investigator wishes to measure. In addition, whether the unobtrusive measure will be sufficiently sensitive to reflect the relation of interest is difficult to determine in advance. In general, there is less collective experience with a given unobtrusive measure than with standardized measures such as questionnaires and inventories. The diverse types of reliability and validity are not readily known for most unobtrusive measures.

Unobtrusive measures need to be corroborated with other measures in the usual way that assessment devices are validated. This can be done both by empirical research that examines the relation among different measures and by theoretical formulations that place a particular measure into a context that makes testable predictions. Increasingly greater confidence can be placed in the measure as additional predictions are corroborated. This logic, of course, applies to any psychological measure, whether or not it is unobtrusive.

Unobtrusive measures can raise very special ethical issues. Research obligations to participants require that they provide informed consent regarding assessment and intervention facets of the experiment. Unobtrusively observing performance in everyday life and using information to which subjects have not consented violate the letter and spirit of consent (see Chapter 17). On the other hand, unobtrusive measures may vary widely in the ethical issues they raise. For example, archival measures and physical traces may not raise concern because they address past performance and could not threaten or jeopardize in any way the identity of the individual participants. Yet, even here one has to be cautious. It is possible that the measures will place a particular group (e.g., ethnic) or locale (geographical) that unwittingly casts a sample or population in a poor light. The identity of specific individuals is not the only concern in research, a point discussed in the chapter on ethical issues. The very nature of unobtrusive assessment (perhaps no informed consent, no immediate option to withdraw from the study) means that the investigator must be quite sensitive to possible ethical concerns when these measures are contemplated.

MEASUREMENT STRATEGIES AND ISSUES

Use of Multiple Measures

As a general rule, multiple measures ought to be used in a given study to assess the (or each) construct of interest. It is rare that a single measure captures the construct completely or well. There are important exceptions where one measure is viewed as *the* critical index of the construct of interest and there is relatively little or no ambiguity about the measure and the construct it reflects. For example, death is often used as a dependent measure in research on diseases and their treatment (e.g., treatment of heart disease and cancer). Single measures (heart rate, respiration) often work just fine. The measure (mortality) usually does not raise epistemological questions ("How do you know they were really dead?") or methodological challenges ("Does 'not breathing' *really* get at the central features of the construct?" "What was the test–retest reliability of the measure?"). Of course, definitional questions arise when discussing life and death in the context of personal, social, and ethical issues (abortion, termination of life support systems) but not usually in the context of assessment for research purposes.

Multiple measures of a construct usually are advisable in research. Use of multiple measures may make the study more complex in many ways (more measures for the subject to complete, more data scoring and analyses, potential inconsistencies in the results). Even so, the recommendation is based on three considerations.

Nature of Clinical Problems.   Most constructs of interest (personality characteristics, clinical problems) are multifaceted, that is, they have several different components. No single measure is likely to capture these different components adequately. Consider the construct of depression. Some components of depression are based on self-report. Individuals *report* that they feel sad, worthless, and no longer are interested in activities that were previously pleasurable. In addition, there are *overt behavioral components*, such as reduced activity and social interaction and changes in eating (more or less eating). Similarly, *psychobiological components* include changes in sleep electroencephalogram activity. *Unconscious processes* may reflect sad affect and negatively valenced interpretations of ambiguous stimuli as assessed by projective techniques. These different facets of depression may overlap, but they are not likely to be so highly related as to be redundant. Any evaluation of depression in, say, a test of treatment would be incomplete if change were demonstrated merely in one modality. Single measures might well be fine if the problem or focus is highly circumscribed (enuresis, isolated fears, and specific habit disorders), if the measure is one that the world views as rather definitive (death, DNA profile), or if the goal is to address a single facet of a problem (blood pressure as an outcome among hypertensive patients). However, in most research, multiple methods ought to be used whenever possible, at least for the core constructs of interest or that reflect the primary hypotheses.

Specificity of Performance.   The prior rationale for using multiple measures focused on the *response* or behavior, that is, that many different components may be of interest. Another side also argues for multiple measures. Performance may vary greatly as a function of changes in the *stimulus conditions* or *situations* in which the behavior is assessed or observed. Multiple measures assess how an individual responds under different stimulus conditions. The measures (format, items, domains or context in which the construct is presented) consist of different stimulus configurations in which the construct is assessed, and performance is likely to vary across these configurations.

Traditionally, personality has often been characterized as a set of traits. These traits reflect dispositions to respond in ways that are consistent over time and across situations. Trait views emphasize characteristics of performance within the individual. Broad dispositions (extroversion, kindness, altruism) might lead one to expect performance consistently over time and across diverse situations. Indeed, there are remarkable consistencies in performance over time. At the same time, performance also varies markedly across situations for a given individual. In other words, there is a specificity of performance so that individuals high in a particular trait may behave quite differently as the situation or stimulus conditions change.

Recall the classic studies of Hartshorne and May (1928; Hartshorne, May, & Shuttleworth, 1930), who examined the moral conduct of children in a variety of different settings. Children were given the opportunity to be dishonest about their performance and to steal on various tasks at home, at school, and in athletic contests. Unbeknownst to them, cheating could be readily detected. One might expect to find rather high correlations among the measures of dishonesty, suggesting that individuals have general dispositions to be honest or dishonest and are consistent across diverse situations. In fact, there were small positive correlations across situations, indicating consistency to some degree. Yet, the correlations were lower than expected and raised the question about the existence of a general trait of honesty. The major finding was that honesty varied considerably across situations. Thus, how children performed tended to be situation-specific. The greater the differences among the situations, the lower the relation between cheating across these situations.

Understanding and predicting performance are greatly enhanced by knowing both the disposition and trait within an individual as well as the stimulus conditions and situational determinants in which the individual is placed. From the standpoint of assessment, this means that a person's performance is likely to vary across different measures (stimulus conditions, situations) of a given construct. Thus, the investigator should be prepared for the possibility that changes in dependent measures may be confined to peculiar aspects of a given problem or a particular aspect only in certain situations. Placing faith on demonstrating behavior change in any one situation or for any single facet of performance may be unwise. Also, multiple measures provide a broader picture of the facets of performance of the construct (e.g., anxiety) to which the results might apply.

Trait and Method Variance.   Multiple measures of a construct are needed to ensure that the results are not restricted to the construct as assessed by a particular method and measure. Performance on a given measure (score, level of the characteristic) is a function of both one's standing on that characteristic (e.g., level of self-esteem) and the precise method in which assessment is conducted (self-report questionnaire, one questionnaire versus another). In other words, the measure itself contributes to the findings and conclusions. Indeed, even minor aspects of a particular measure, such as the format and ordering of the items, as mentioned previously, can greatly influence a person's standing on a particular characteristic (Schwarz, 1999).

The contribution of the method of assessment to the score for a given dependent measure can be seen by looking at some of the characteristics of measurement devices in general. When a new measure is developed, it is important to establish that the measure correlates with other measures of the same construct (assuming some other measures or criteria are available) and that the measure does not correlate with measures of seemingly unrelated constructs (Campbell & Fiske, 1959). *Convergent validity,* mentioned earlier, was used to denote that independent methods of assessing a given construct agree with each other, that is, correlate positively and perhaps in the moderate-to-high range. For example, if two measures that supposedly assess empathy correlate highly, this would be evidence of convergent validity. The fact that the measures converge suggests that they assess the same construct.

Discriminant validity was introduced to denote that a newly proposed measure should be distinguished from measures of other constructs—that is, show little or no correlation. We ought to expect a measure not to be related to other measures of entirely different constructs. Evidence that is consistent with this expectation supports discriminant validity. For example, a newly proposed measure of empathy probably would not be expected to be highly correlated with such other constructs as intelligence, social desirability, or anxiety. Evidence that all of these were not very highly related to empathy would support the discriminant validity of our measure. Of course, if high correlations were found between the newly proposed measure and a more established measure of another construct, this would suggest that the measures really were assessing similar characteristics, no matter what the two assessment devices were called. The new measure would be suspect to the extent that the results can be explained by a more well-validated measure whose construct validity (for some other construct) has been established.

The way in which convergent and discriminant validity can be examined is to conduct a study designed to evaluate the interrelations among various measures. Whether one measure *converges* with other measures of the same construct, of course, can be assessed by administering two or more measures designed to assess the *same construct* and seeing whether they correlate highly. The way to see whether a measure *diverges* from others with which it should not correlate is achieved by including measures of *different* or *unrelated constructs* and seeing whether they do not correlate or correlate only to a very small degree. To obtain this set of correlations requires administering a number of measures to the same individuals. Some of the measures would be designed to assess the same construct or personality dimensions; some would assess different constructs or dimensions.

The correlations obtained to determine convergent and discriminant validity cannot be viewed uncritically. It is quite possible that correlations between two measures will be influenced not only by the *construct* that is being assessed but also by the *method of assessment*. For example, if two paper-and-pencil measures of empathy were administered, they might correlate rather highly. Is this evidence of convergent validity? Actually, it may be that the high correlation is due to the similarity in the method of assessment (two self-report scales) rather than, or in addition to, the construct being assessed. In addition, it is possible that a high correlation will be obtained between measures because of a common source of bias or artifact. For example, participants may respond in a socially desirable fashion across both measures, and this will be misinterpreted as convergent validity for the construct that the investigator originally had in mind.

To evaluate the contribution to the assessment method, it is important to include with the assessment of multiple constructs or dimensions some measures that rely upon different modalities or methods. A *multitrait–multimethod matrix* refers to the set of correlations obtained from administering several measures to the same participants when these measures include more than one trait (construct) and method (Campbell & Fiske, 1959). The purpose of the matrix (a set of several correlations) is to evaluate convergent and discriminant validity and to examine the extent to which the correlations between measures is due to the similarities in the way the responses are assessed (method variance) rather than in what constructs supposedly are measured (trait variance).

Consider as an example, a study that assessed depression and aggression (two constructs) among inpatient children ($N = 120$, ages 5–13; Kazdin, Esveldt-Dawson, Unis, & Rancurello, 1983). Children, mothers, and fathers completed a questionnaire and an interview designed to assess depression and then a parallel questionnaire and interview designed to assess aggression. Consider this a study with two constructs (depression, aggression) and three methods of assessment (raters). All measures focused on the depression and aggression of the child. Table 13.4 presents the correlation matrix in the form that permits examination of convergent and discriminant validity and the role of the rater (method variance) in the correlations. First, several numbers are

TABLE 13.4. Correlations of Children and Their Parents for Measures of Depression (Children's Depression Inventory [CDI] and Bellevue Index of Depression [BID]) and Aggression (Hostility Guilt Inventory [HGI] and Interview for Aggression [IA]).

| | | Children (N = 120) | | | | Mothers (N = 120) | | | | Fathers (N = 57) | | | |
| | | Depression | | Aggression | | Depression | | Aggression | | Depression | | Aggression | |
		CDI	BID	HGI	IA	CDI	BID	HGI	IA	CDI	BID	HGI	IA
Children[a]													
Depression	CDI												
	BID	0.62[c]											
Aggression	HGI	0.38[c]	0.42[c]										
	IA	0.41[c]	0.49[c]	0.26[b]									
Mothers													
Depression	CDI	0.10	0.24[b]	0.14	0.29[b]								
	BID	0.16[a]	0.27[c]	0.10	0.20[a]	0.71[c]							
Aggression	HGI	0.13	0.17	0.24[a]	0.24[a]	0.46[c]	0.56[c]						
	IA	0.03	−0.04	0.10	0.23[a]	0.26[b]	0.54[c]	0.60[c]					
Fathers													
Depression	CDI	0.40[c]	0.33[b]	0.36[b]	0.27[a]	0.74[c]	0.37[b]	0.36[b]	−0.11				
	BID	0.33[b]	0.41[b]	0.24[a]	0.27[a]	0.65[c]	0.69[c]	0.32[a]	0.25[a]	0.54[c]			
Aggression	HGI	0.28[a]	0.28[a]	0.37[b]	0.20	0.55[c]	0.56[c]	0.79[c]	0.46[c]	0.60[c]	0.57[c]		
	IA	0.14	0.01	0.22	0.37[b]	0.27[a]	0.54[c]	0.54[c]	0.68[c]	0.12	0.55[c]	0.53[c]	

[a]The *solid-line triangles* include correlations of measures completed by the same rater. The *dashed-line triangles* include correlations of measures completed by different raters. The *diagonal rows* of numbers between the dashed-line triangles are validity correlations (completion of the same measures by different raters).
[a]$p < 0.05$; [b]$p < 0.01$; [c]$p < 0.001$.

Source: Kazdin, A.E., Esveldt-Dawson, K., Unis, A.S., & Rancurello, M.D. (1983). Child and parent evaluations of depression and aggression in psychiatric inpatient children. *Journal of Abnormal Child Psychology, 11*, 401–413.

in diagonals (and not enclosed within a triangle). These are correlations when the rater is different but the construct and measure are the same. These are used to support convergent validity. For example, child and mother score for the Children's Depression Inventory was $r = .10$. Child and father score for this measure was $r = .40$. These correlations and others in the diagonals indicate that child and parent ratings correlate in the low-to-moderate range both for depression and aggression. These are not especially high correlations considering that the constructs were the same but the raters differed.

Of greater interest are the correlations enclosed in the triangles. The *solid triangles* include measures completed by the same rater. In general, the correlations within a given solid triangle correlate relatively highly. This means that measures completed by the same rater or informant share an important source of variance even if the constructs they rate are quite different. Indeed, correlations by the same rater who rates different constructs (depression, aggression) tend to be higher than correlations of the same construct (depression) by different raters. For example, child ratings of depression and aggression on two interviews (BID, IA in the table) were correlated at $r = .49$ (same rater and measures but different constructs). This is higher than ratings of depression between mother and child which were correlated at $rs = .10$ and $.27$ (same construct, different raters).

The example permits separation of construct (*trait variance*) from rater (*method variance*). The study and many others like it show the strong contribution of rater variance. That is, measures of different traits within raters often are more likely to correspond than measures of the same traits between different raters. This finding has been consistent across different informants, including children, parents, teachers, peers, and hospital staff as sources of information. Stated more succinctly, there is a strong method (rater) component that often pervades the ratings, even though children can be reliably distinguished in terms of their depression and aggression (Kazdin, 1994).[1]

Assessment in experiments can profit from knowledge that both substantive and methodological characteristics of assessment devices contribute to a subject's score. If information is desired about a construct, it is important to use more than a single measure. Any single measure includes unique components of assessment that can be attributed to methodological factors. Evidence for a particular hypothesis obtained on more than one measure increases the confidence that the construct of interest has been assessed. The confidence is bolstered further to the extent that the methods of assessing the construct differ.

Interrelations of Different Measures

Although the use of multiple measures is advocated as a general strategy for evaluating a construct, this strategy has a price. The main issue stemming from use of multiple measures is that the results may be inconsistent across measures (see Meyer et al.,

---

[1]There are many ways to analyze the results of multitrait–multimethod matrices to identify the extent to which trait and method variance contribute to the results (Kenny & Kashy, 1992; Schmitt, Coyle, & Saari, 1977).

2001). Some dependent measures may reflect changes or differences in the predicted direction, and others may not. Indeed, some measures may even show changes or differences in the opposite direction. When results vary across measures designed to assess the same construct, this makes interpretation difficult or at least more complex.

As an example, the longitudinal study of physical abuse, sexual abuse, and neglect has shown that youths who experience abuse in childhood (≤ 11 years old), compared to nonabused children, show greater violence and criminal behavior 20 years later (Widom & Shepard, 1996). Interestingly, the results varied by how the key predictors and outcomes were assessed. Early physical abuse in children was identified in two ways (official records, self-report in adulthood), and violence was also assessed in two ways (records of arrest and reports of violent activity). Early physical abuse, as measured by official records, predicted later arrest for violence in young adulthood. However, self-reported physical abuse did not predict later arrests. Interestingly, self-report measures of early abuse predicted self-report of violent activity. The results suggest that common method components (predictors and outcome measures that share the same methods) are related. Measures predicted less well or not at all when methods varied. A strength of the study is assessing predictors and outcomes using multiple measures and methods.

The failure of multiple measures to agree in a study is a "problem" only because of some traditional assumptions about the nature of personality and human behavior and the manner in which independent variables operate. Actually, there are many reasons to expect multiple measures not to agree. Four explanations of lack of correspondence among measures pertain to the contribution of method variance in assessing behavior, the multifaceted nature of behavior, the magnitude of a client's standing on the characteristic, and the course of changes across different facets of behavior.

Contribution of Method Variance.   An overriding assumption of traditional assessment has been that there are different measures of a given construct and that these should correlate highly. The notions of convergent and discriminant validity, described earlier, embody this assumption. The notion of convergent validity fosters the view that measures of a given personality or behavioral characteristic have a common component that is highly correlated. The view encourages researchers to conceptualize constructs as unidimensional, that is, they are single and relatively simple constructs that measure roughly the same thing but in many different ways. Hence, investigators should search for correlations among measures of a given trait.

The view that measures of the same construct invariably go together no doubt holds in many situations. Yet, more often than not measures of the same characteristic or trait should not necessarily go together or correlate highly in a given investigation. If the methods of assessment differ (true–false versus multiple-choice self-report measures, or self-report versus behavioral measures), the modest-to-very-low correlations between the measures might be due to the contribution of method variance. With this explanation, method variance becomes the culprit that interferes with interpretation of experimental results. Indeed, different methods of assessment (method variance) may account for the correlations or lack of correlations between measures. The potential problem with this interpretation is that it implies that lack of correspondence between measures is merely a methodological artifact stemming from the assessment devices. Systematic error variance associated with the measurement devices is used to explain lack of correspondence between measures that seemingly would otherwise be related. However, we have come to learn that performance may well differ as a function of different stimulus, situational, and assessment conditions. The imperfect agreement among measures is not an artifact or limitation of the measure but an expected feature. Different methods of assessment present different conditions to the subjects, and these yield, generate, and promote genuinely different responses.

Multifaceted Nature of Personality and Behavior.   The view that characteristics of personality or behavior are multifaceted has challenged the notions of convergent validation to some extent. As discussed earlier, if one views a given characteristic as multidimensional, the insistence on or expectation of correspondence between dependent measures of that characteristic is reduced. Personality characteristics may have several different components that overlap but are not interchangeable, redundant, or isomorphic. For example, several measures are available to assess depression. However, depression is not a unidimensional characteristic or simply sadness. Manifold characteristics can be identified involving affect (e.g., sadness), cognition (e.g., beliefs that things are hopeless), and behavior (e.g., diminished activity). Within a given domain several finer distinctions can be made. Thus, within the cognitive domain of depression, measures are available to assess negative beliefs about oneself, hopelessness, helplessness, disinterest, apathy, and other features. Given the multidimensional nature of personality, behavior, and clinical dysfunction, as illustrated by depression, the lack of correspondence between measures is to be expected. Different measures of the same construct might simply emphasize or give different weight to different components, and little correspondence is quite understandable.

For convenience and parsimony, psychologists have adhered to general construct labels such as anxiety, personality, and extroversion. Although proposing such constructs helps simplify findings across different areas of research or different measurement devices, it does not follow that all components of any one of these constructs occur together in a given individual (co-occur) or change together even if they are present (co-vary). There may be largely independent components that individuals refer to under a general construct label. Lack of correspondence among dependent measures related to a particular construct or target problem may not be a problem at all from the standpoint of interpreting research. While some of the lack of correspondence could well be attributable to different methods of assessment, measuring different aspects of the problem could account for the low correlations as well.

Consider an example of lack of correspondence among measures and the potential significance of this. Sexual arousal obviously can be measured by self-report. In studies this is usually assessed in response to presentation of stimulus material (e.g., slides, photos). As mentioned previously, psychobiological assessment of sexual arousal can be assessed in men by a strain gauge on the penis that measures penile circumference (penile plethysmography) and in women by a clear acrylic tampon-shaped device that assesses blood flow of the capillary bed of the vagina (vaginal photoplethysmography). Interestingly, in men, but not in women, there is a high correspondence between self-report and plethysmographic measures of sexual arousal (Meston & Frohlich, 2000). This raises intriguing questions beyond assessment, such as the experience of arousal and cues used to report arousal. In any case the lack of correspondence of measures, here moderated by sex of the subject, may be important for theoretical reasons.

Magnitude of the Characteristic.   Another way to interpret the lack of correspondence among dependent measures relates to the magnitude of the characteristic, trait, disposition, or clinical problem. It may well be that different measures designed to assess the same characteristic of personality or behavior will co-vary as a function of the client's standing on the characteristic. For example, in the case of anxiety, clients may be measured on self-report, overt behavioral, and psychobiological measures. The different measures may or may not correspond, depending on the magnitude of the client's anxiety. Perhaps clients who are overwhelmed by anxiety would score at a very high level on each of the measures. At the other extreme might be individuals who show absolutely no anxiety and score the equivalent of zero or "none" on each measure. These extreme groups (very high versus no anxiety) may show a consistent or a more consistent pattern across measures.

Most people are not at the extreme and hence are likely to show quite varied patterns on measures of the construct across several measures. For example, individuals in the group with only slight or moderate anxiety might report anxiety on self-report measures. Such mild levels of reported anxiety may not be associated with any specific overt behaviors or autonomic arousal. Verbal reports may be more capable of reflecting gradations of reactions relative to measures of overt behavior or psychobiological states. Thus, some anxiety is evident on portions of the assessment battery.

Lack of correspondence among measures might be expected, based upon varying levels of intensity of the characteristic for which clients are selected. Consistency may be expected and found for extreme groups (low or high) on the construct when different measures are used, but most individuals in the middle may show greater variability among measures. In this formulation, seeming inconsistencies among measures is based on characteristics of the sample and the organization of behavior for individuals with different levels of the characteristic of interest.

Course of Behavior Change.   The lack of correspondence between measures can be explained by considering how different facets of affect, behavior, and cognition may change over time. Quite possibly, different facets of behavior change at different rates or at different points in time. Hence, studies showing a lack of correspondence between measures from, say, pretreatment to posttreatment assessment, may only reflect the fact that different aspects of performance change at different rates.

Changes over time among multiple measures of a given client characteristic, state, or behavior might or might not go together. When changes across measures do correspond, this is referred to as *synchrony* (Rachman & Hodgson 1974). When changes do not go together, this is referred to as *desynchrony*. In the case of desynchrony, different measures of change might vary independently or even inversely. For example, in the context of adult psychotherapy, evidence suggests that the changes clients make traverse phases—that is, not all domains that are to change occur at the same time. Clients first change in their subjective well-being, followed by changes in symptoms, and, finally, followed by changes in life functioning and more enduring characteristics (Howard et al., 1993). If measures of these three domains were administered at a given point in time to reflect improvements, the measures would not correspond. This does not reflect inconsistencies or have to do with method variance among measures; it has to do with how different systems (feelings, behavior) and different domains change.

Overall, the lack of correspondence between measures of change, or desynchrony, may occur because some aspects of personality or behavior change before others. The lack of correspondence may be a function of looking at the measures at one point only (e.g., immediately after treatment). The different facets of behavior may become synchronous as time progresses and separate response systems come into line with each other. Essentially, therapy may more readily alter some systems than others and alter some systems more rapidly than others. Indeed, analyses of behavioral and self-report measures in outcome studies have shown increases in the correspondence among measures over time (see Hodgson & Rachman, 1974). In general, the notions of synchrony and desynchrony allow for the correspondence or lack of correspondence among diverse measures and highlight the importance of evaluating the relations among measures over time.

SUMMARY AND CONCLUSIONS

Selection of measures for research is based on several considerations, including construct validity, psychometric properties, and sensitivity of the measures to reflect change or differences. Standard or currently available measures are usually used in a given study because these considerations have evidence in their behalf. Occasionally, investigators alter standardized measures to apply them to populations or in contexts in which the measures have not been used or intended. The measure may be used as is or modified slightly by rewording or omitting items. Investigators may develop an entirely new measure because a standard measure is not available or alteration of an existing measure would, on prima facie grounds, render this of limited value. If a measure is used in a novel way, altered in any way, or if a new measure is developed, it is essential to include validity data within the study or as pilot work to that study to support construct validity.

Several modalities were highlighted as a means of encompassing the broad range of measurement strategies used in clinical research. Commonly used measures fall within several modalities: global ratings; self-report inventories, questionnaires, and scales; projective techniques; direct observations; psychobiological measures, and computerized assessment. In most psychological assessment, subjects are aware that some facet of their performance is assessed (obtrusiveness of assessment) and hence there is the possibility that their performance may be altered in some way as a result (reactivity of assessment). Unobtrusive measures can be used to provide data free from reactive influences. Several unobtrusive measures were discussed, including simple observation, observation in contrived situations, archival records, and physical traces.

In general, it is useful to rely upon multiple measures rather than a single measure because (1) constructs of interest (clinical problems, personality, social functioning) tend to be multifaceted and no single measure can be expected to address all of the components; (2) performance may vary as a function of the assessment modalities and devices used; and (3) an individual's standing on a particular dimension or construct is partially determined by the method of assessment. It is useful to demonstrate that changes in the construct of interest (e.g., anxiety) are not restricted to only one method of assessment. Essentially, demonstrations relying upon multiple assessment techniques strengthen the confidence that can be placed in the relationship between independent and dependent variables.

The agreement (correspondence, convergence) and lack of agreement among measures of the same construct raises many methodological issues. The evaluation of trait and method variance was discussed in the context of a multitrait–multimethod matrix. The purpose of the matrix was to evaluate the convergent and discriminant validity of a measure and also the contribution of method variance. It is possible that two measures are related (highly correlated) to each other, in part because they share similarities in the method of assessment (e.g., two self-report inventories). The use of multiple measures to assess a construct and the use of measures that involve different methods of assessment are recommended.

An important issue in using multiple measures pertains to the lack of correspondence among measures. Thus, an investigation using multiple measures may demonstrate that the independent variable affects some measures in one way and has no effect or an opposite effect on others. Hence, what might have been a clear conclusion with a single measure seems to be obfuscated by the use of several different measures. Yet, the relation between different measures itself is an important aspect of understanding human functioning and the way in which it is affected by independent variables.

KEY CONCEPTS AND TERMS

Construct Validity	Reactivity
Convergent Validity	Reliability
Discriminant Validity	Unobtrusive Measures
Multitrait–Multimethod Matrix	Validity

FOR FURTHER READING

Butcher, J.N. (Ed.) (1995). Special Issue: Methodological issues in psychological assessment research. *Psychological Assessment, 7,* Whole Issue Number 3.

Drasgow, F., & Olson-Buchanan, J.B. (Eds.) (1999) *Innovations in computerized assessment*: Mahwah, NJ: Lawrence Erlbaum.

Groth-Marnat, G. (Ed.) (1997). *Handbook of psychological assessment* (3rd ed.). New York: Wiley.

Haynes, S.N. (2001). Special section: Clinical applications of analogue behavioral observation. *Psychological Assessment, 13,* 3–98.

Lilienfeld, S., Wood, J.M., & Garb, H.N. (2000). The scientific status of projective techniques. *Psychological Science in the Public Interest, 1,* 27–66.

Lowman, R.L. (Ed.) (1996). Special section: What every psychologist should know about assessment. *Psychological Assessment, 8,* 339–368.

Meier, S.T., & Wick, M.T. (1991). Computer-based unobtrusive measurement: Potential supplements to reactive self-reports. *Professional Psychology: Research and Practice, 22,* 410–412.

Meyer, G.J., Finn, S.E., Eyde, L.D., Kay, G.G., Moreland, K.L., Dies, R.R., Eisman, E.J., Kubiszyn, T.W. & Reed, G.M. (2001). Psychological testing and psychological assessment. A review of evidence and issues. *American Psychologist, 56,* 128–165.

Murphy, L.L., Conoley, J.C., & Impara, J.C. (Eds.) (1994). *Tests in print. IV* (Vols. 1 & 2). Lincoln, NE: Buros Institute of the University of Nebraska. Buros Institute of Mental Measurements: University of Nebraska Press.

Nelson, L.D. (Ed). (2000).Special section: Methods and implications of revising assessment instruments. *Psychological Assessment, 12,* 235–303.

Schwarz, N. (1999). Self-reports: How the questions shape the answers. *American Psychologist, 54,* 93–105.

Suzuki, L.A., Ponterotto, J.G., & Meller, P.J. (Eds.) (2000). *The handbook of multicultural assessment: Clinical, psychological, and educational applications* (2nd. ed.). New York: Wiley.

Chapter 14

Assessment and Evaluation of Interventions

A major area of assessment in clinical psychology pertains to the evaluation of interventions, as reflected in treatment, prevention, education, and enrichment programs. Evaluating interventions raises special issues and opportunities for assessment. Intervention studies are usually randomized controlled clinical trials, as discussed previously. When they are conducted with clinical or other special populations, such studies are often costly in time and money. It may take years to recruit cases, provide treatment, and assess follow-up. For example, I conduct treatment trials with clinical samples of aggressive and antisocial children (inpatient and outpatient). It takes me at least 5 years to complete a mediocre study, and that includes the time required to enroll cases, provide the treatment, complete pre, post, and one-year follow-up assessment, and analyze the results. (Other investigators add such steps as planning the study carefully, deeply thinking about the findings, and writing up the results in a way that others can understand. I avoid all of these because, no doubt, they would make the process even longer.) Because of the duration, replication of such studies is less likely than it is in other areas of research that might be completed more quickly (e.g., laboratory studies with college students that are completed in a session or two) and might not have some of the difficulties of clinical research (recruiting subjects who meet special criteria, subject dropping out or failing to complete follow-up). Consequently, one wishes to maximize the yield from clinical studies because they are less likely to be replicated. This has direct implications on the scope of assessments that are used to evaluate intervention effects in any individual study.

This chapter considers assessment and evaluation issues of outcome research. The topics include those facets of the study that can be included to maximize the information about the impact of the intervention. Much of intervention research is methodologically stilted with tacit agreement of what to assess and how to assess it. Expansion and creativity in the evaluation of interventions are encouraged in this chapter. Assessment and design do not merely reveal relationships in nature; they also partially determine directly what relationships are evident. That is, methodology at once actively contributes to and limits our knowledge. Expansion of design and assessment can expand what we know, and this will be illustrated here in the discussion of assessment of processes during therapy, evaluation of patient change, and evaluation of treatment. All intervention studies by definition evaluate outcome, that is, what happened by or at the end of treatment, so we shall begin with outcome assessment and later move to process assessment.

ASSESSING CLINICAL SIGNIFICANCE OF THE CHANGES

Treatment research evaluates the effects of interventions by showing statistically significant changes from pre- to posttreatment (e.g., reduction in symptoms of depression) and statistically significant differences (e.g., one treatment is better than another). Statistical significance does not address the question of the applied importance of the outcome or effect. That is, did the intervention make a difference that has impact on the client? Clinical significance is designed to address this question. *Clinical significance* refers to the practical value or importance of the effect of an intervention, that is, whether it makes any "real" difference to the clients or to others in their functioning and everyday life.

Before moving to the criteria that are assessed to evaluate clinical significance, it is important to convey the meaning with a few examples. Treatment of anxiety (e.g., fear of open spaces or debilitating anxiety in social situations) might improve patients (statistically) on some measures, but outside of the sessions has treatment had any impact on adaptive functioning? Now that the clients have been treated, can they go out of the house, participate in social situations, or enjoy life in ways that were somehow precluded by their anxiety? Changes on the usual psychological measures (self-report, interviews) do not directly provide answers to these questions; it is possible to see change in various inventories and questionnaires without any of these other benefits. Clinical significance raises the concern about changes in these other areas.

The prior example suggests that clinical significance includes different measures from those usually used in outcome studies. The issue is whether the change makes a difference, and this need not raise new measures. Sometimes the magnitude of change on the regular outcome measures is the issue. For example, consider a study on the treatment of obesity in which there are two groups, one that receives a "new and improved" treatment and the other no treatment. Suppose further that subjects in the treatment group lost an average of 25 lb. (11.4 kg.). This is a fairly large change. The question of clinical significance is whether this change makes a difference of any practical value, that is, would it affect health and everyday functioning? One may not be able to answer this question without other information. For example, the impact on health and daily functioning may depend on the initial weight of the subjects who participated (mean weight 500 or 600 lb. [227 or 272 kg.] versus mean weight of 175 lb. [79.6 kg]).

Sometimes a clinically significant change can be inferred when a problem is reduced to zero or no longer occurs at the end of treatment. For example, at the beginning of treatment the clients may show high rates of panic attacks, tics, illicit substance use, and criminal behavior. Reducing these to zero by the end of treatment would clearly be an important change. Changes in most problems of therapy (depression, anxiety, social withdrawal) are a matter of degree, and hence decisions need to be made about whether the change is one that really makes a difference in the lives of the clients. Several methods of evaluating the clinical significance of treatment effects have been elaborated (see Kendall, 1999; Ogles, Lunnen, & Bonesteel, 2001). Each method is based on quantitative evaluation to make the decision about the importance of the change. Three broad strategies can be delineated, including comparison methods, subjective evaluation, and social impact; they are highlighted in Table 14.1.

TABLE 14.1.   Primary Means of Evaluating Clinical Significance of Change in Intervention Studies

Type of Measure	Defined	Criteria
Comparison method	Subject's performance is evaluated in relation to the performance of others (normative sample, patient sample)	Similar to normative samples at the end of treatment, or Departure from dysfunctional sample, or No longer meeting criteria for a psychiatric diagnosis
Subjective evaluation	Impressions of the client or those who interact with the client that detect changes or changes that make a difference	Ratings of current functioning and whether the original problem continues to be evident or affect functioning
Social impact	Change on a measure that is recognized or considered to be critically important in everyday life; usually, not a psychological scale or measure devised for the purposes of research	Change reflected on such measures as arrest, truancy, hospitalization, disease, and death

Comparison Methods

At the end of treatment the client can be compared to some other standard to determine whether the change is clinically significant. Different methods have been used, based on normative or ipsative comparisons. *Normative comparisons* refer to comparing the person's performance with the performance of others; *ipsative comparisons* refer to comparing the individual with himself or herself. Consider the most commonly used methods for comparison.

Normative Samples.   The question addressed by this method is, "To what extent do patients or clients, after completing treatment (or some other intervention), fall within the normative range of performance?" Prior to treatment the clients presumably would depart considerably from their well-functioning peers on the measures and in the domain that led to their selection (anxiety, depression, social withdrawal). Demonstrating that after treatment, these same persons were indistinguishable from or within the range of a normative, well-functioning sample on the measures of interest would be a reasonable definition of a clinically important change (Kazdin, 1977; Kendall & Grove, 1988). To invoke this criterion, a comparison is made between treated patients and peers who are functioning well or without significant problems in everyday life. This requires that the measures used in the study have normative data available from community (nonpatient) samples.

As a rather typical example, one of our own studies evaluated treatments for aggressive and antisocial children ages 7–13 (Kazdin et al., 1992). The effectiveness of three conditions was examined, including problem-solving skills training (PSST), parent management training (PMT), and PSST+PMT combined. Two outcome measures are plotted for the three groups at pretreatment, posttreatment, and a one-year follow-up (see Figure 14.1). The measures were the parent- and teacher-completed versions of the Child Behavior Checklist (Achenbach, 1991), which assess a wide range of emotional and behavioral problems. Extensive normative data (of nonreferred, community children) are available for boys and girls within the age group; these have indicated that the 90th percentile score on overall (total) symptoms is the score that best distinguishes clinic from community (normative) samples of children. In the treatment results plotted in Figure 14.1, scores at this percentile from community youths were used to define the upper limit of the "normal range" of emotional and behavioral problems. Clinically significant change was defined as whether children's scores fell below this cutoff, that is, within the normative range. The figure shows that children's scores were well above this range before treatment on the parent (left panel) and teacher (right panel) measures. Each group approached or fell within the "normal" range at posttreatment, although the combined treatment was superior in this regard.

The results in the figure provide group means (average performance of each group). One also can compute how many individuals fall within the normative range at the end of treatment. In the present example, for the parent-based measure referred to in the figure, results at posttreatment indicated that 33 percent, 39 percent, and 64 percent of youths from PSST, PMT, and combined treatment, respectively, achieved scores that fell within the normal range. These percentages are different (statistically significant) and suggest the superiority of the combined treatment on the percentage

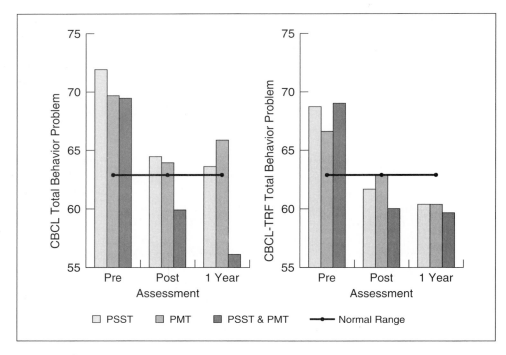

FIGURE 14.1.   Mean scores (T scores) for Problem-Solving Skills Training (PSST), Parent Management Training (PMT), and both combined (PSST + PMT) for the total behavior problem scales of the parent-completed Child Behavior Checklist (CBCL, left panel) and the teacher-completed Child Behavior Checklist—Teacher Report Form (TRF-CBCL right panel). The horizontal line reflects the upper limit of the nonclinical ("normal") range of children of the same age and sex. Scores below this line fall within the normal range

Source: Kazdin, A.E., Siegel, T., & Bass, D. (1992). Cognitive problem-solving skills training and parent management training in the treatment of antisocial behavior in children. *Journal of Consulting and Clinical Psychology, 60,* 733–747.

of youths returned to "normative" levels of functioning. The results underscore the importance of evaluating clinical significance. In this study, even with statistically significant changes within groups and differences between groups, most youths who received treatment continued to fall outside of the normative range of their nonclinically referred peers.

Dysfunctional Samples.   Another method to define clinical significance uses a dysfunctional sample for comparison. Presumably, in a treatment study, all subjects might be considered to reflect a dysfunctional sample (assuming that recruitment and screening were intended to identify such a sample). At the end of treatment, if a clinically important change is made, scores of the clients ought to depart markedly from the original scores of the dysfunctional cases. The departure, of course, ought to be in the direction of improvement (e.g., lower symptoms). There is no logical justification for deciding how much of a change or reduction in symptoms is needed, and different criteria have been suggested and used (Jacobson & Revenstorf, 1988; Jacobson, Roberts, Berns, & McGlinchey, 1999). One variant denotes as clinically significant, a departure of two standard deviations from the mean of the dysfunctional sample. Thus, at posttreatment, individuals whose scores depart at least two standard deviations from the mean of the dysfunctional group (untreated cases from a no-treatment control group) would be regarded as having changed in an important way.

At first blush, this criterion seems similar to the one used for ordinary statistical significance, namely, a comparison of two groups with the same problem; one group is treated, the other is not. However, the criterion for clinical significance is invoked in relation to the performance of individual clients. Clinically significant change is evaluated in relation to whether a given client has improved by at least two standard deviations and the percent of individuals who do so within a given experimental condition. Why a criterion of two standard deviations? First, if the individual is two standard deviations away from the mean of the original group, this suggests that he or she is not represented by that mean and distribution from which that sample was drawn; indeed, two standard deviations above (or below) the mean reflects the 98th (or 2nd) percentile. Second and related, two standard deviations approximates the criterion used for statistical significance when groups are compared (1.96 standard deviations for a two-tailed t test that compares groups for the $p < .05$ level of significance).

As an illustration, a study for the treatment of depression among adults compared two variations of problem-solving strategies (Nezu & Perri, 1989). To evaluate the clinical significance of change, the investigators examined the proportion of cases in each group whose score on measures of depression fell 2 or more standard deviations below (i.e., less depressed) the mean of the untreated sample. For example, on one measure (the Beck Depression Inventory), 85.7 percent of the cases that received the full problem-solving condition achieved this level of change. In contrast, 50 percent of the cases that received the abbreviated problem-solving condition achieved this level of change. The more effective treatment led to a clinically significant change for the large majority of the cases and clearly one treatment was better than the other in this regard. The comparisons add important information about the impact of treatment.

For many measures used to evaluate treatment or other interventions, normative data that could serve as a criterion for evaluating clinical significance are not available. That is, we cannot tell whether at the end of treatment cases fall within a normative range. However, one can still evaluate how much change the individual made and whether that change is so large as to reflect a score that is quite different from the mean of a dysfunctional level (pretreatment) or sample (no-treatment group). Of course, if normative data are available, one can evaluate the clinical significance of change by assessing whether the client's behavior returns to normative levels and also departs from dysfunctional levels.

No Longer Meeting Diagnostic Criteria. Clinical significance is also assessed by evaluating whether the diagnostic status of the individual has changed with treatment. In many treatment studies, individuals are recruited and screened on the basis of whether they meet criteria for a psychiatric diagnosis (major depression, posttraumatic stress disorder). Those with a diagnosis are included in the study and assigned to various treatment and control conditions. A measure of clinical significance is to determine whether the individual, at the end of treatment, continues to meet criteria for the original (or other) diagnoses. Presumably, if treatment has achieved a sufficient change, the individual no longer meets criteria for the diagnosis. Sometimes this is referred to as showing that the individual has recovered. For example, in one study, adolescents who met standard psychiatric diagnostic criteria for clinical depression were assigned to one of three groups: adolescent treatment, adolescent and parent treatment, or a wait-list condition (Lewinsohn, Clarke, Hops, & Andrews, 1990). At the end of treatment, 57 percent and 52 percent of the cases in the two treatment groups, respectively, and 95 percent of the cases in the control group continued to meet diagnostic criteria for depression. Clearly, treatment was effective in an important way. A smaller proportion of cases in the treatment groups continued to meet diagnostic criteria for the disorder.

There is something appealing about showing that after treatment the individual no longer meets diagnostic criteria for the disorder that was treated. It suggests that the condition (problem, disorder) is gone or "cured." For many physical conditions and diseases (strep throat, "the flu," rabies,), no longer meeting the diagnostic criteria can mean that the disorder is completely gone. That is, presence or absence of these disorders is categorical. Yet, in psychiatry and psychology not meeting criteria for the diagnosis of a disorder (e.g., depression) can be achieved by showing a change in only one or two symptoms. Also, we know that with some diagnoses (depression, conduct disorder), falling below the threshold for meeting the diagnostic criteria does not mean the individual is problem free or no longer has features of the disorder. Individuals who do not quite meet the criteria for the diagnosis but are close can still have current and enduring social, emotional, and behavioral problems (Gotlib, Lewinsohn, & Seeley, 1995; Lewinsohn, Solomon, Seeley, & Zeiss, 2000: Offord et al., 1992). Above and below the precise cutoff point for defining disorder is not the point at which clinical dysfunction, impairment, or a poor prognosis begins and ends. Showing that an individual no longer meets criteria for a diagnosis still is informative insofar as the diagnostic criteria have become a meaningful way to communicate about dysfunction and rates of dysfunction. However, no longer meeting diagnostic criteria does not necessarily mean the patient is appreciably better.

Problems and Considerations.   The comparison methods raise several issues that beg for empirical investigation. An initial question is who should serve as the normative group when that is used as the basis for deciding clinical significance? For example, to whom should mentally retarded persons, chronic psychiatric patients, or prisoners be compared in evaluating treatment or rehabilitation programs? Developing normative levels of performance might be an unrealistic ideal in treatment, if that level is based on individuals functioning well in the community. Defining and identifying a normative population raises additional problems. Rates of dysfunction and symptom patterns vary as a function of social class, ethnicity, and culture. Presumably, forming a normative group ought to take such moderators into account.

Second, even if a normative group can be identified, exactly what range of their behaviors would be defined as within the normative level? Among individuals whose behaviors are not identified as problematic there will be a range of acceptable behaviors. Defining the upper and lower limits of that range (e.g., + one standard deviation) is somewhat arbitrary unless data show that scores above or below a particular cutoff have different short- or long-term consequences on other measures of interest (hospitalization, showing another disorder).

Third, using symptoms (depression, anxiety) as a criterion can be challenged. Presumably, one has many symptoms or relatively severe symptoms before treatment, and by the end of treatment, one has fewer and/or they are less severe. However, symptoms (characteristics associated with impairment) among community and "normative" samples are not rare at all. Among children, adolescents, and adults, approximately 20 percent of community samples meet criteria for at least one psychiatric disorder (Burke, Burke, Regier, & Rae, 1990; US Congress, 1991), that is, show multiple symptoms (a syndrome) that form currently recognized disorders. This rate is an underestimate because many more individuals have subsyndromal disorders, that is, too few symptoms to meet criteria for the formal diagnosis, but still have current impairment and prognoses that approximate those who meet criteria for the syndrome. Anecdotal evidence (my last Thanksgiving dinner with a large assortment of relatives) suggests that the 20 percent rate of frank psychiatric disorder is a huge underestimate and that adding subsyndromes could easily bring the figure to well over 100 percent. In any case, many people with symptoms are not in treatment and a proportion of these, no doubt, are functioning adequately. Bringing symptom level to within the normative range raises interesting interpretive challenges, given that normative samples have their own problems and psychopathology. Perhaps domains other than symptoms (impairment, quality of life) may be as important as, or more important than, symptoms in defining clinical significance.

Fourth, for many measures of interest, bringing individuals into the normative range is a questionable goal. Consider for example, reading skills of elementary school children. A clinically significant change might well be to move children with reading dysfunction so that they fall within the normal range. However, perhaps the normal range itself should not be viewed as an unquestioned goal. The reading of most children might be accelerated from current normative levels. Thus, a normative criterion itself needs to be considered. More extreme would be bringing youth who abuse drugs and alcohol to the level of their peers. For some groups, the peer group itself might be engaging in a level of deviant behavior that is potentially maladaptive.

Finally, it is quite possible that performance falls within the normative range or departs markedly from a deviant group but does not reflect how the individual is functioning in everyday life. Paper-and-pencil measures, questionnaires, interviews, and other frequently used measures may not reflect adaptive functioning for a given individual. Even for measures with high levels of established validity, performance of a given individual does not mean that he or she is happy, doing well, or adjusting in different spheres of life. I shall return to this point further because it applies broadly to the validity of measures of clinical significance.

Subjective Evaluation

The subjective evaluation method refers to determining the importance of behavior change in the client by assessing the opinions of individuals who are likely to have contact with the client or in a position of expertise (Wolf, 1978). The question addressed by this method of evaluation is whether changes have led to differences in how clients and other people see the change. The views of others are relevant because people in everyday life often have a critical role in identifying, defining, and responding to persons they regard as dysfunctional or deviant. Subjective evaluations permit assessment of the extent to which the effects of an intervention are apparent to the clients or to others.

Consider the case of Steven, a college student who wished treatment to eliminate two muscle tics (uncontrolled movements) (Wright & Miltenberger, 1987). The tics involved head movements and excessive eyebrow raising. Individual treatment sessions were conducted in which he was trained to monitor and identify when the tics occurred and in general to be more aware of their occurrence. In addition, he self-monitored tics throughout the day. Assessment sessions were conducted in which Steven read at the clinic or college library and observers recorded the tics. Self-monitoring and awareness training procedures were evaluated in a multiple-baseline design in which each tic declined in frequency as treatment was applied.

A central question is whether the reduction was very important or made a difference either to Steven or to others. At the end of treatment Steven's responses to a questionnaire indicated that he no longer was distressed by the tics and that he felt they were no longer very noticeable to others. In addition, four observers rated randomly selected videotapes of Steven without knowing which tapes came from before or after treatment. Observers rated the tics from the posttreatment tapes as not at all distracting, normal to very normal in appearance, and small to very small in magnitude. In contrast, they had rated tics on the pretreatment tapes as much more severe on these dimensions. Observers were then informed which were the posttreatment tapes and asked to report how satisfied they would be if they had achieved the same results as Steven had. All observers reported they would have been satisfied with the treatment results. The subjective evaluations from Steven and independent observers help attest to the importance of the changes, that is, they made a difference to the client and to others.

Subjective evaluation is obviously important. If treatment is working and has an important impact, the effects ought to make a perceptible difference to clients themselves and to those with whom they interact. The opinions of others in contact with the client are important as a criterion in their own right because they often serve as a basis for seeking treatment in the first place and also reflect the evaluations the client will encounter after leaving treatment. Subjective evaluation is relevant as a criterion.

Problems and Considerations.   A few salient concerns emerge in the use of subjective evaluations. First, global rating scales usually serve as the basis for obtaining subjective evaluations. Such scales are regarded with suspicion because, as discussed in the previous chapter, they are more readily susceptible to biases on the part of raters than are questionnaires and interviews or direct observations, in which the items are more concrete and anchored to clearer descriptors. Because the evaluations are global rather than concrete, they are likely to be highly variable (have different meanings and interpretations) among those who respond. Also, subjective evaluations, whether completed by the clients or others in contact with the clients, are likely to be fairly nonspecific in their ability to differentiate among different treatments.

Second, the fact that the client or persons associated with a client notice a difference in behavior as a function of the client's treatment does not mean that the client in fact has changed or has changed very much. Persons in contact with the client may perceive a small change and report this in their ratings. But this does not necessarily mean that treatment has alleviated the problem for which treatment was sought or has brought the client within normative levels of functioning.

In general, one must treat subjective evaluations cautiously; it is possible that subjective evaluations will reflect change when other measures of change do not. Subjective evaluations would be extremely limited and of unclear value as the sole or primary outcome measure for most clinical dysfunctions. For example, clients might really believe they are doing much better (subjective evaluation) but continue to have the dependence or addiction (e.g., alcohol) or impairment that they experienced at the beginning of treatment. It is quite possible that one feels better about something without having changed at all. This concern raises caution about interpretation but does not condemn subjective evaluation.

Subjective ratings provide important information. It really does make a difference how people feel and think (about themselves, their lives, their marriages, their partners). When all is said and done, whether treatment makes people experience life as better is no less central as an outcome criterion than performance on the best available psychological measure. Subjective evaluation is designed to supplement other measures and to address these broader issues.

Social Impact Measures

Another type of measure that helps to evaluate the clinical or applied importance of treatment outcomes is to see if measures of social impact are altered. *Social impact measures* refer to outcomes assessed in everyday life that are important to society at large. For example, rates of arrest, truancy, driving while intoxicated, illness, hospitalization, and suicide are prime examples of social impact measures. Such measures are often regarded by consumers of treatment (clients who seek treatment, insurance companies or employers who pay for treatment) as the bottom line. To the public at large and those who influence policy, the measures are often more meaningful and interpretable than the usual psychological measures. At the end of treatment, psychologists may become excited to show that changes were reflected in highly significant effects on the usual psychological measures (Hopkins Symptom Checklist, Beck Depression Inventory). However, what does this "really" mean? To the public, the effects are clearer if we can say that the effects of treatment are reflected in reduced absenteeism from work, fewer visits to the doctor for health problems, or fewer suicides. As for a real example, research with terminally ill cancer patients has shown that supportive psychotherapy increases the months of survival (Spiegel, Bloom, Kraemer, & Gottheil, 1989). This is a measure of clear impact and one the public would be concerned with.

Social impact measures have often been used in clinical and applied studies. For example, prevention programs often focus on infants or young children from socio-economically disadvantaged homes who are at risk for later mental and physical health problems (Mrazek & Haggerty, 1994). Occasionally, follow-up data are obtained 10–20 years later. Social impact measures—such as higher rates of school attendance, high school graduation and subsequent employment, and lower rates of arrest and reliance on welfare—are evident among those who received an early intervention, compared to nonintervention controls. These measures and outcomes are clearly significant to society.

Problems and Considerations.   Measures of social impact are by definition very important and provide a bridge from our research to consumers and society at large. In much of our research, we are speaking to ourselves and do not connect in outcome assessment to measures to which the public (consumers of treatment, policy makers) can relate. This problem is not raised here as a public relations issue but rather as a methodological one. Without use of such measures, it is not clear that treatment effects extend to everyday life (beyond standardized measures) and reflect a palpable change in patient behavior or functioning. Consequently, as a measure of intervention effects, the addition of social impact measures to the assessment battery is to be encouraged.

Social impact measures have a number of liabilities that prompt interpretive caution. First, they are gross measures and subject to a variety of influences other than those associated with the intervention. Indeed, one of the reasons we have developed psychological measures of various constructs has been to provide a more valid and comprehensive measure than is ordinarily available. For example, individuals with alcohol dependence miss more work than those who do not have this dependence. A social impact outcome measure to reflect the effects of treatment might be number of days of work missed. This would be fine and is encouraged here as a supplementary measure. At the same time, we know that employees miss days of work for all sorts of reasons, and many people with problems of alcohol addiction make it to work but have dysfunction in other areas of life (marital relations, contact with the law). In short, social measures are very relevant to society and researchers but often raise test validity issues.

Second, many social impact measures are not assessed or recorded very reliably, and hence error in the measures can be relatively high. Consider our example of recording missed days from work for the hypothetical treatment study of individuals with alcohol dependence. Not all "work" situations (university professors, freelance consultants, business executives) record "missed days," and not all jobs or businesses would record this consistently, unless wages are based on time at work. Leaving aside our example, error may come from variations in how consistently the measures are recorded, as in the case of many archival records (attendance in school, records in city hall). We take for granted that most psychological measures have a standardized method of administration. Social impact measures are more likely to be recorded and scored somewhat haphazardly over time, which introduces noise (error variability) into the results. For archival records, changes in funding (usually budget cuts at the local, state, or federal level), policy, procedures, and persons responsible for recording all may operate in a systematic way to influence the reliability and validity of the data. Also, error may be introduced by systematic changes in how the measure is scored (instrumentation) over time.

Third and related, social impact measures often do not mean what we may think. Consider crime rate as an example because it is of interest for psychological as well as social interventions. What does "crime rate" really mean, as evaluated in official reports (Uniform Crime Reports)? Crime is usually recorded in a hierarchical fashion, which means that any time there is a given crime incident, only the worst crime is counted (see DiLulio, 1997). For example, on a given day a criminal may rape someone, steal a getaway car, and assault the person from whom the car was taken. This is also counted as one crime; the worst crime is counted (rape, in this case). Similarly, if two cars are stolen on the same night and two people are beaten up in the process, but the same criminal completed these incidents, this is counted as one crime. In general, the most serious crime is counted, only that crime is counted in a given episode, and counted only once. Therefore, crime rate does not necessarily reflect the number of crimes completed or number of victims. Showing a change in crime rate might be important, but the meaning of the measure is not obvious to most of us.

Fourth, instrumentation (changes in the measure) is often a problem for social impact measures. Continuing with crime rate as an example, most crimes (approximately 65 percent) are not reported. Annual household surveys are conducted (by the Bureau of Justice Statistics) to assess crimes, whether or not they have been reported to the police. The difficulty is that the survey (begun in 1973) has changed over time and hence there are major changes (increases) in crime rates as a function of changes in the instrument (DiLulio, 1997). Changes in rates again may reflect intervention effects, social changes, or instrumentation in varying degrees and combinations. Apart from any misleading statistics in actual rate of crime, changes in criteria for recording crimes add variability over time. Showing an intervention effect superimposed on that variability may be difficult, even when there is a veridical effect. The overall point is that social impact measures, in this case crime rate, can harbor all sorts of problems that make their interpretation ambiguous.

Social impact measures are often seized on by the public, the media, and policy makers as reflecting the bottom line to evaluate the value and effectiveness of an intervention or social program. There is good reason for this; a danger of research is to develop interventions that have remarkable results in the lab but do not help anyone in everyday life. On the other hand, if intervention effects are not evident on social impact measures, this is often considered by the media or by consumers of research as evidence that the intervention makes no difference, is not important, and perhaps has failed. Yet, social impact measures need to be thoughtfully evaluated and interpreted. The absence of change on such a measure, given the very nature of many of these measures, may not be an adequate, reasonable, or interpretable index of the program's effect. The dilemma of social impact measures comes from their two most salient characteristics, namely, their high believability and their often poor psychometric properties (alternative types of reliability and validity).

Notwithstanding these caveats, social impact data can be quite useful to see if the improvements identified on specific psychological measures are reflected directly on measures of primary interest to consumers of treatment and to society at large. The use of these measures is particularly important in areas such as clinical, counseling, and educational psychology, and other areas of research in which science extends to practice. When such measures show a change, they convey important evidence that the impact of the intervention was socially important. In general, it is reasonable of the public to ask that our dependent variables include constructs and measures that are socially relevant. Armed with knowledge of the importance of reliability and validity, one has to be cautious about what measures to use and how to use them.

General Comments

There is no single way to measure clinical or applied significance of intervention effects. In a given project, measures such as truancy, crime, or school dropout rates may be included as a matter of course because they were the impetus for designing and evaluating the intervention. Measures other than those highlighted previously might also be devised to evaluate clinical significance. It is not difficult to conceive of other ways to operationalize clinical significance. For example, in therapy research, measures of symptoms are usually used to evaluate clinical significance. Yet, one might assess other constructs such as quality of life, impairment, or participation in life (activities, relationships). The investigator involved in intervention research ought to attend to the question, "Did the treatment make a genuine difference to the lives of the recipients?" and select one or more measures to provide an answer.

One need not slavishly adhere to currently used measures of clinical significance, highlighted here. Indeed, some words of caution are in order for the commonly used measures. Measures of clinical significance are defined largely by researchers, with the exception of social impact measures. That is, the measures are operational definitions of what we consider reasonable bases for saying that there was a clinically important impact. As paradoxical as it may sound, there is little or no evidence (depending on the measure) that what we as researchers call clinically significant makes any real difference in the lives of the persons who receive treatment (see Kazdin, 1999). Even obvious examples are at best murky. For example, returning to normative levels of functioning on a psychological measure does not necessarily mean the client has improved in some palpable way in everyday life or that someone who changed but did not meet the criterion of within normative range is doing worse. Measures of clinical significance have not been validated against each other or other indices of functioning (work performance, relationships). Consequently, we have no way of calibrating their meaning (see Sechrest, McKnight, & McKnight, 1996).

A related issue, also not well studied, is that small effects of therapy—or making a little difference—might not meet criteria for clinical significance but still make a big difference in people's lives. If treatment makes people a little better (a little less depressed or anxious, a little more confident, they drink or smoke less), this may be enough to have them enter parts of life (social events, relationships, work, new hobbies) that they would not otherwise do. It is easy to conceive of instances in which a small effect of therapy could have just enough impact to affect people's lives in important and palpable ways. As an example, making a dysfunctional marriage a little better may have important impact on the couple and the individual spouses (e.g., deciding to remain married), even though on a measure of marital bliss, the couple still falls outside the normative range or has not changed two or so standard deviations.

Notwithstanding these considerations, the researcher is encouraged to include one or more measures of clinical significance in any intervention study. The purpose of the addition is to move beyond mere statistical significance and also to help foster dissemination of the findings. The results are likely to have impact on society at large to the extent they are interpretable by nonresearchers. Consequently, use of measures of clinical significance advances clinical work by suggesting that patients are helped to an important extent and also addresses a broader research agenda by encouraging dissemination of findings.

SCOPE AND BREADTH OF THE CHANGES

The outcome measures in intervention research often are narrowly focused. For example, in the context of treatment, the focus usually is on symptoms of the disorder or problem that is being treated (anxiety, depression). Indeed, clinical significance of therapeutic change often reflects the magnitude of change on measures of deviance or symptoms (to see if symptoms have been reduced sufficiently to bring people to within the normative range). Symptom changes are quite important. At the same time, there is no need to restrict outcome to this focus, particularly since there is no compelling evidence that symptom change rather than some other measure (impairment, social competence) are the best predictors of long-term adjustment, subsequent clinical dysfunction, and return to treatment. Many other outcomes are critically important because of their significance to the client and in many cases to society at large.

It is difficult to enumerate all the criteria that might be relevant because this could vary as a function of the clinical problem and features associated with the symptom and age of the client. A few domains can be identified that convey the value of expanding outcome assessment beyond symptoms. For the treatment of adult patients with anxiety or depression, for example, one would want to see treatment reduce key symptoms and to do so in clinically significant ways. In addition, other domains of functioning could be very relevant, including impairment, marital or family interaction, work adjustment, and participation in "life" (social activities, hobbies, interests). It is likely that many of these domains are relevant most of the time and that the conclusions about what techniques are effective will vary somewhat by the outcome criteria.

Among the many criteria, perhaps special emphasis ought to be given to impairment, that is, the extent to which the individual's functioning in everyday life is impeded. Meeting role demands at home, work, or school; interacting prosocially and adaptively with others; and being restricted in the settings, situations, and experiences in which one can function—all can vary considerably among clients with a given disorder or problem. Impairment is related to, but distinguishable from, symptoms or meeting criteria for a disorder (Sanford et al., 1992) and contributes significantly to the likelihood of being referred for mental health services (Bird et al., 1990). A significant issue from the standpoint of treatment is the extent to which functioning is impaired initially and improved by treatment. Assessing impairment and moving individuals toward reduced impairment may be a considerable accomplishment of treatment.

By singling out impairment, I do not intend to imply that one criterion (impairment) ought to replace another (symptoms). Just the opposite, multiple criteria might be relevant in identifying effective treatments. Also, a critical feature that distinguishes treatment may not be changes in symptoms, but rather ancillary changes. For example, in developing medications, the superior medicine is often one that has fewer side effects or is easier to take (fewer doses during the day). The superiority may not derive from the ability to reduce symptoms in comparison to another treatment. Stated more generally, the benefit of one treatment over another may derive from criteria other than change in the target symptoms.

Psychotherapy has had rather broad effects on human functioning. In addition to the standard fare (improvements in symptoms of various disorders), therapy also has been shown to reduce physical symptoms, increase survival among terminally ill patients, and improve fertility among couples, to mention some of the dramatic effects (see Kazdin, 2000). For example, treatment of clinically disturbed children is associated not only with changes in their symptoms and prosocial functioning, but also with improvements in the parents (reduced depression, symptoms more generally, and stress) and the family (improved relationships) (Kazdin & Wassell, 2000). Broad changes suggest that therapy is not a surgical intervention that has a narrow or specific focus and effect. (Actually, even surgical interventions [heart bypass, liposuction] can have broad effects on health, socialization, affect, and quality of life.)

Researchers ought to expand outcome assessment to encompass domains that are of importance to client functioning, and these extend beyond symptom change. In the context of evaluating treatment, it would be quite important to know if two interventions, equally effective in reducing symptoms, varied greatly in other domains that are important and relevant. One treatment that is broad in its effects may even be preferred to one that is narrow in its effects but slightly more effective in symptom reduction.

CHARACTERISTICS OF THE TREATMENT

The prior comments pertain to the evaluation of therapeutic effects or impact of treatment on the client. A rather neglected area is evaluation of characteristics of treatment, particularly those features that may be related to adoption, use, or dissemination of treatment. That is, apart from patient change, are there characteristics of the treatment that we wish to know about? Obviously, evaluating characteristics of treatment becomes irrelevant if the treatment has not been shown to produce therapeutic change. However, can the treatments that have been shown to produce change be distinguished in important ways? Table 14.2 provides three criteria to evaluate treatment that are somewhat separate from the therapeutic changes produced in the clients. Consider these criteria briefly and their relevance to establishing treatments as effective.

Disseminability of Treatment

Treatments vary in the ease with which they may be extended beyond the confines of the research study. *Dissemination* refers primarily to extending treatment to new settings, clients, and services beyond those in which treatment effects were demonstrated. This may include extending treatment to those individuals who select treatments for their clientele (social service agencies, insurance providers, health care systems), who provide treatment in direct services (therapists), and who seek treatment (clients). The ease of dissemination can refer to a variety of treatment charac-

TABLE 14.2.   Criteria for Evaluating Treatment Procedures

Disseminability

The extent or ease of extending the treatment widely to other clinicians and clients. This criterion may be related to complexity of the procedures, type and amount of training needed to implement the procedures, likelihood of adherence to those who implement the procedures, and degree to which departure from the prescribed procedures is associated with loss of effectiveness.

Cost

The monetary costs of providing treatment and delivering services are pertinent measures of treatment. Cost is not usually a question of scientific interest in treatment evaluation, but provides data that can influence dissemination, adoption, and policy. There are many ways to evaluate cost, such as expenses in relation to obtained benefits or outcomes (cost–benefit analyses).

Acceptability of Treatment

The extent to which those who participate in treatment (clients, persons in close contact with them, and mental health professionals) view the treatment as reasonable, justified, fair, and palatable. Among treatments that are equally effective, those viewed as more acceptable are probably more likely to be sought, adhered to, and executed correctly than those that are less acceptable.

teristics, including the complexity of the procedures; the type and amount of training needed to implement the procedures; the likelihood that clients will initiate, participate in, and adhere to the treatment; and the likelihood that those who deliver treatment can carry out the procedure faithfully. Also, disseminability encompasses the efficiency of treatment, as reflected in how many persons in need can be served. For example, if treatment can be delivered in a group rather than individually, this is more efficient, assuming both versions were equally effective.

Some techniques may be widely disseminated because they can be implemented by clients themselves or because they might be able to be presented through mass media (books, a CD ROM disk, videotape, television, Internet). For example, many self-help manuals, also referred to as bibliotherapy, are designed to treat diverse problems, including overeating, cigarette smoking, depression, stress, anger, sexual dysfunction, anxiety, social skills deficits, and conduct problems (Rosen, 1993; Santrock et al., 1994). Often extravagant claims are made about the effectiveness of "do-it-yourself" treatments where empirical evidence is absent. Yet, many treatments have evidence in their behalf. Indeed, a meta-analysis concluded that self- and therapist-administered treatments were equally effective, when compared to controls, and retained their benefits at follow-up (Marrs, 1995). Even if bibliotherapy were less effective, the self-administered treatment may be preferred because it is more easily disseminated to the public on a larger scale than therapist-administered outpatient treatment. It is likely that extremely severe cases (e.g., of depression, substance abuse) may not respond to self-help manuals, but many less severe cases may respond well.

Under some circumstances, writing about one's problems (e.g., feelings about traumatic experiences) can have quite significant therapeutic impact, at least in adults (Smyth, 1998). Controlled studies have shown that briefly writing about one's thoughts and feelings can alter psychological and physiological functioning and overall well being, measured at least one month after the writing task. In principle, structured writing tasks could be readily disseminated on a large scale, but this has yet to be tested.

Media and information technology, such as the Internet and personal computerized devices (Palm Pilot, cell phones) to provide information, to help monitor behavior, and to deliver therapeutic regimens (directives, practice assignments) may help to devise highly disseminable interventions. Even though many people do not have such devices, many do, and the reach of therapy can be extended widely. Access to the Internet through personal computers, television, cell phones, and yet-to-be-invented devices could reach a large number of individuals for a host of concerns (e.g., child-rearing, coping with stress), problems of living (divorce, bereavement), and clinical dysfunction (anxiety disorders, depression). Computerized psychotherapy has been available in some form for decades and continues to develop in treatment outcome studies (Marks et al., 1998; Newman et al., 1997). Applications are increasing among these treatments, and disseminability takes on increased importance as a criterion for evaluating therapy (Newman, 2000).

In discussing the ease of disseminating treatment, it is important to mention medication. An advantage of medication is that treatments often can be widely disseminated. For example, when a new drug for depression emerges from clinical trials and is approved for use, it is widely prescribed and quickly reaches millions of clients. An effective psychotherapy, if equally effective or, indeed, even more effective, is clearly less readily disseminated to others. Of course, *disseminability of treatment* is only one criterion for evaluating an intervention. The difficulty is that medication, although widely disseminable, raises such other issues as problems of adhering to treatment, side effects associated with use, and restrictions in other behaviors (no driving, use of alcohol while taking the medication, or use of other medications that might be needed for other condition. The ease of dissemination may be counterbalanced by other issues related to use and effects.

There are no simple measures to assess the ease of disseminating a treatment. Several variables may determine disseminability, such as the cost of professional training, complexity of the procedures, need for ancillary equipment or apparatus, and likelihood that the procedures will retain their effects when disseminated. Some of these criteria should be assessed carefully when evaluating treatment. Disseminability is not an esoteric or incidental criterion and perhaps ought to be an initial consideration rather than an afterthought when developing treatment.

Cost

Disseminability of treatment is related to cost; in general, less costly treatments are more widely disseminable. However, cost is important to consider on its own as a criterion for evaluating treatment. Obviously, a less costly treatment is preferred to a more costly treatment, given evidence that both are effective. Yet, there are more subtle but no less important cost questions. It may be possible for a given treatment to cost x dollars to effectively treat 60 percent of the people, but $x + y$ dollars if additional treatment is provided that effectively treats 80 percent of the people (Simon et al., 2001). Increments in cost for additional benefits provide important data for policy makers who often make critical decisions that affect who receives treatment and what those treatments are likely to be.

One cost question for evaluating both large-scale social interventions as well as individual treatment is the benefits that derive from the costs. Cost–benefit analysis is designed to evaluate the monetary costs of an intervention with the benefits that are obtained. The benefits must be measured in monetary terms also. Evidence that clients return to work, miss fewer days of work, have fewer car accidents, or stay out of hospitals or prisons are examples of benefits that can be translated into monetary terms. Of course, many important outcomes (personal happiness, family harmony) might not be readily translated to monetary gains (Yates, 1995).

Cost-effectiveness analysis does not require placing a monetary value on the benefits and can be more readily used for evaluating treatment. Cost-effectiveness analysis examines the costs of treatment relative to a particular outcome. The value for therapy evaluation is that cost-effectiveness permits comparison of different treatment techniques if the treatment benefits are designed to be the same (reduction of drinking, increase in family harmony). For example, one study compared two variations of parent training for parents of kindergarten children with behavior problems (Cunningham et al., 1995). One variation consisted of individual treatment provided at a clinical service; the other consisted of group-based treatment conducted in the community (at community centers or schools). Both treatments were better than a wait-list control condition. On several measures, the community-based treatment was more effective. Even if the treatments were equally effective, the monetary costs (start-up costs, travel time of families, costs of the therapist/trainer in providing treatment) of individual treatment were approximately six times greater per family than the group costs of treatment. Also, the community-based treatment is much more likely to have impact on individuals—because more are likely to subscribe to it—and to society at large, because it can be disseminated more broadly than individual therapy.

Within psychotherapy research, costs, cost–benefit, and cost-effectiveness measures are infrequently used, with notable exceptions (Cunningham et al., 1995; Simon et al., 2001). Cost is deceptively simple as a measure, which is one of the reasons why the measure is not used very often in intervention studies of psychology. The complexities include the fact that cost is not merely the price of a few items on a list. In a treatment study, for example, the cost of delivering the treatment includes some portion of the overhead of the clinic and some of the salary of the therapists as part of that, but even more. How much does the treatment cost insurance companies or employees, and how much does it cost to have a therapist trained to deliver this treatment? What is included in cost estimates, how to place a price on them, and how to evaluate the costs of not providing treatment hint at a few of the issues.

Because any intervention costs something, the simple measure of cost—and this is an oxymoron—is not of interest or perhaps even important by itself. The interest in cost stems primarily from evaluating cost of this treatment in relation to the alternatives. So, for example, one could or could not treat alcoholism among workers at a major company. Both of these have costs. Treating alcoholism has the costs of the sort mentioned previously. Yet, not treating alcoholism has costs as well, because alcoholism leads to many missed days at work, reduced worker productivity, and increased illness and injury (associated with alcoholism). Hence, the cost of treatment is not the issue but rather the cost of treatment versus no treatment, both of which may be expensive. A common statement that better reflects this is the notion that the cost of education in society is very high, but not that high when compared to the cost of ignorance. Similarly, the costs of not treating some problems (depression, substance use, conduct disorder) are enormous but must be weighed against the cost of not providing treatment. For example, the annual cost of anxiety disorders in the United States is estimated at $42.3 billion dollars (or $1,542 per sufferer) (Greenberg et al., 1999). These costs include lost productivity at work, psychiatric and nonpsychiatric treatment, and other costs. Clearly, mental health problems can have exorbitant costs. Studies have shown that the benefits of psychotherapy are reflected in reduced costs of subsequent treatment and reduced work impairment (see Gabbard, Lazar, Hornberger, & Spiegel, 1997), but cost outcomes are infrequently measured.

I mentioned the cost–benefit analysis, that is, considering benefits of treatment in relation to costs. But evaluating the benefits makes cost measures a bit more complex. For example, one or a few sessions of therapy by telephone or computer (Web) is very inexpensive relative to 10–20 sessions of individual psychotherapy. The benefits may be less for the one session of treatment, but the costs relative to benefits favor the brief treatment. This example is not dramatic enough to convey the point. Consider the following health example. In the United States colorectal cancer is a significant health problem that accounts for approximately 11 percent of all cancer deaths. Each year in the United States 150,000 individuals will die of this disease. A new treatment has been developed that improves the outcome of individuals with the disease. The standard treatment consists of 2 medications (5-fluorouracil and leucovorin). Clinical trials have shown that standard treatment is not as effective as it is when combined with a third medication (irinotecan] (Saltz et al., 2000). The medication is delivered intravenously as part of a chemotherapy regimen for cancer (for details, see http://www.meds.com/colon/camptosar/fullrx.html). The US Food and Drug Administration (FDA) has provided approval for the treatment in light of these results. So far, so good.

It turns out that the estimated costs of treatment (actual costs not available at the time of this writing) are $15,000 for 6 months. This is the cost for one patient to have the added medication that improves standard treatment. Already, this raises alarms—this is not a treatment for everyone merely because of the cost. As to the benefits or outcomes, the median survival of patients is improved compared to the standard treatment. There are now many trials (see Web site noted above as one of many sources). In some of the trials, survival with standard treatment is in the range of 12–14 months. With the improved treatment, the median survival time is 15–17 months). Is the added cost ($15,000) worth the added benefits (about 3 months of life)?[1] To any of us individually, for our families, and ourselves, this is not even debatable. To society at large and taxpayers who ultimately cover such costs, the question can be debated. The example is not mentioned here to take any other position than costs are very rel-

---

[1]The actual numbers provided here (cost of a treatment regimen and months of survival) are provided from sources, as opposed to invented here, but ought not to be taken as fixed or accurate. Cost of treatment can be reduced as treatments are in wider use or delivery methods change (dose, duration of treatment). Also, as a new treatment becomes standard, the cost to the individual is often reimbursed or covered. Finally, survival time varies with many characteristics of the sample, including stage of the disease. The more general point holds, namely, that cost requires evaluation in relation to benefits and alternatives.

evant and pertain to clinical significance along a dimension that has impact on the individual and society at large. For most researchers, use of cost may require collaboration with a health economist for guidance on some of the standard practices and obstacles for cost assessment (see Yates, 1995).

Acceptability of Treatment

Different treatments for a given problem may not be equally acceptable to prospective clients. Efficiency and cost considerations may contribute to the *acceptability of a treatment,* but there are other factors as well. Procedures may be more or less objectionable in their own right independent of their efficacy. This is evident from everyday life. There are a number of procedures that clients find quite acceptable, even though they have little or no demonstrated efficacy. Examples include commonly advertised procedures to control diet or to reduce the circumference of one's thighs or waist. Many of these are very acceptable because they are quick, easy, inexpensive, and promise great gains. The examples convey that acceptability of the treatment can be distinguished from the effectiveness of treatment. For this discussion the presumption is made that the investigator is to assess the acceptability of a treatment that has been shown to be effective. (There already exist a large number of treatments that clients apparently find acceptable but for which no evidence exists [see Kazdin, 2000].)

Clients can readily distinguish the degree to which effective treatments for a given clinical problem are acceptable (Kazdin, 1986; Kazdin, French, & Sherick, 1981; Tarnowski & Simonian, 1992). For example, various psychotherapies and medication are viable options with supportive data for the treatment of depression. Some evidence suggests that forms of psychotherapy (cognitive therapy, behavior therapy) are viewed as more acceptable than medication for depression (Banken & Wilson, 1992).

The extent to which treatment is acceptable can influence several facets of the treatment process. For example, professionals who refer children to psychological treatment (e.g., pediatricians) are likely to recommend those procedures they consider to be more acceptable (Arndorfer, Allen, & Alijazireh, 1999). Also, how well and carefully professionals carry out treatment is a function of the extent to which they view the intervention as acceptable (Allinder & Oats, 1997). Among clients, treatments that are acceptable are more likely to be sought—and adhered to once clients have entered into treatment (Reimers, Wacker, Cooper, & DeRaad, 1992). It is likely that acceptability also influences the decision to remain in treatment. Seeing treatment as demanding or irrelevant contributes directly to dropping out of therapy (Kazdin, Holland, & Crowley, 1997). Clearly, professional and client views of the acceptability of treatment contribute to multiple aspects of treatment utilization and adherence. Acceptability may be an important dependent variable for developing effective treatments. It will be useful to understand what can be done in the delivery of treatments to make them more acceptable (Foxx et al., 1996).

ASSESSMENT DURING THE COURSE OF TREATMENT

Assessment during treatment is logically and temporally prior to outcome assessment. Yet, outcome assessment was first because it is less esoteric. Outcome studies invariably assess treatment outcome (posttreatment performance), and the prior discussion focuses on expansion of that. Not many investigators assess clients during or over the course of treatment. There are two main reasons to conduct assessments during the course of a treatment outcome study. These include assessing change in the client and evaluating the mechanisms or factors that explain why change comes about.

Pre–Post and Continuous Assessment

A central feature of therapy research is assessment of the participants before and after treatment (pre–post treatment assessment). From the standpoint of research design, there are many statistical and clinical advantages to assessing individuals before and after treatment, as mentioned previously. However, there are a few difficulties with the focus on pre- and posttreatment assessment. First and foremost, the entire practice is a bit odd because this does not provide the information needed to understand treatment effects and to develop treatments for clinical practice. What can we say from pre–post assessment? At the end of the postassessment, we can make such statements as this client improved, did not change much, or became worse. We do not want our evaluation of therapy to be restricted to when treatment is over. We need to know what is happening during treatment, that is, how the patient is functioning while treatment is in process. From the standpoint of understanding treatment we want to see the pattern of data (function) and see how change is occurring. From the standpoint of clinical work we want to see that change is occurring either on the outcomes of interest or on putative processes that will lead to the outcomes of interest.

Second, the vast majority of therapy studies provide a fixed regimen of treatment with minor opportunities for flexibility (e.g., adding one or a few sessions). Presumably, some patients would require more and others less than the fixed regimen the investigator selects somewhat arbitrarily. Because the regimen needed for therapeutic change is not known, it makes sense to evaluate treatment in an ongoing way rather than just at the end of some predetermined time period. Data on client change during the course of treatment may help determine when to end treatment.

The discussion of continuous assessment in the chapter on single-case design conveyed the advantages of ongoing assessment. In group designs it would be helpful to integrate additional assessments over the course of treatment. For example, at the beginning of each treatment session, a few minutes (in the waiting room or treatment session) might be used to have the client complete a brief measure to evaluate if there are any changes in key domains of interest. Data obtained every other session or on some days during the week between sessions are other options to achieve the same goal, namely, to monitor progress in therapy.

In clinical work the treatment cannot be evaluated at the end in the way that posttreatment assessment is conducted in research. There usually is no formal end point because regimens of treatment are not fixed as they are in research. Rather, an effort is made to treat until progress is made. Also, in clinical work one wants systematic information to make decisions of when to end treatment or to provide different treatment if little or no progress is made. If the results of research are to be applicable to clinical practice, some interim assessments to assess progress would be very important to integrate into treatment research.

Evaluating the Mechanisms of Change

A major reason to administer measures during the course of treatment is to understand the course of therapy and to study the processes involved in change. Understanding the course of change can reflect what aspects of the client change (symptoms, subjective feelings) and the course of these changes over time. For example, do symptoms improve steadily over the course of treatment, do some symptoms change sooner, are changes linear or do they occur early and reach an asymptote? Work of this kind is relatively rare, but there are good examples (Howard et al., 1993). The work is descriptive insofar as it charts the course of changes in therapy.

The study of mechanisms of change in therapy, or the reasons why therapy produces effects, requires assessment during the course of treatment. Virtually all therapies have a conceptual view about why people get better in treatment, although rarely is there any supportive evidence for that interpretation. A study might propose that changes in cognitions are the reason patients get better. At the end of treatment the investigator may show that symptoms changed and, as hypothesized, cognitions changed too. If both symptoms and cognitions have changed at the end of treatment, it is not possible to state that change in one caused a change in another. As noted previously, among the many requirements of a causal role, establishing the time line is essential.

As an illustration, a great deal of research has focused on the therapeutic alliance, that is, the extent to which the client and the therapist bond, work collaboratively, and have a positive relationship. There are many measures and views of alliance, and their differences need not detain us. One view has been that alliance leads to therapeutic change. That is, during the course of treatment an alliance develops, and if this is a good alliance, this predicts improvement in symptoms. To study this requires that one looks at alliance during treatment. Assessment is usually based on videotaping one or a few sessions early and midtreatment, coding alliance from the tapes, and showing that alliance predicts later therapeutic change. To conduct this research requires that there are assessments during the course of treatment rather than just pre- and post-treatment assessment. There are scores of studies showing the therapeutic alliance predicts therapeutic change (Henry, Strupp, Schacht, & Gaston, 1994).

To show a causal relation requires that the putative cause, in this case alliance, comes before the outcome, in this case therapeutic change. It is possible that alliance and symptoms both changed in the middle of treatment, and showing that alliance predicts later symptom change by itself does not show that alliance plays a causal role. To show the temporal relation, one must show that alliance has changed and symptoms have not but eventually change later. Just because symptoms are not assessed by the middle of treatment, this does not mean they have not already changed. Indeed, it is conceivable that very early in treatment, clients get a little better (some symptom improvement) and that they form a better alliance with the therapist as a result. Actually, the pertinent research to sort this out has been completed. A recent study of psychodynamically oriented supportive therapy showed that symptom changes early in treatment predict alliance and that alliance also predicts further symptom change (Barber, Connolly, Crits-Christoph, Gladis, & Siqueland, 2000). This suggests that symptom change and alliance mutually influence each other. Assessment of both symptom change and alliance were completed at multiple points during the course of treatment to identify these interesting relations.

As a more general point, relatively little work is completed that attempts to understand why therapy works and then to design studies so processes or mechanisms can be studied to provide support. Interim assessment of the sort discussed here addresses a key methodological requirement. Precisely what assessments are used, when they are administered, and so on depend on the substantive view about what process is involved.

FOLLOW-UP ASSESSMENT

Assessment immediately after treatment or other intervention is referred to as post-treatment assessment; any point beyond that, ranging from weeks to years, is referred to as *follow-up assessment*. Ideally, intervention research provides long-term follow-up data (i.e., several years after the intervention), although this is quite difficult and hence rare. Follow-up raises important substantive questions for intervention research, such as whether the gains are maintained and whether any gains surpass those achieved without formal intervention (no-treatment groups sometimes "catch up" to the treatment groups by the time follow-up assessment is conducted). There are significant methodological and assessment questions as well. The most dramatic of these is whether conclusions can be reached at all, given attrition that may ensue during the follow-up interval.

Attrition

Certainly the main problem in assessing follow-up status of the clients is attrition. As has been well demonstrated across many settings and samples, the longer the follow-up period, the greater the loss of subjects (Phillips, 1985). Obviously, over time it is increasingly difficult to locate participants or to induce them to respond. Subjects change addresses, change their names (usually through marriage), enter institutions, die, and do other things that show that the original treatment investigation in which they participated is not the most important event in their lives. Even if subjects can be located, they do not always wish to comply with requests for follow-up data.

Loss of subjects is a problem because the follow-up data may not represent the "true" level of functioning if the complete sample of subjects were reassessed. The subjects who could be located and included in follow-up may represent a highly select sample and vary from other subjects within the same treatment group in ways that are directly related to the treatment outcome. For example, subjects who are located one year after treatment, compared to those not located at follow-up, may vary in subject and demographic variables, mobility (moving from city to city), severity of the target problem or related problems, and other factors that could relate to their degree of symptoms or functioning that are measured at follow-up. As significantly, loss of subjects destroys the random composition (random assignment) of the groups. Treatment groups or treatment and control groups are no longer comparable, and hence group differences at follow-up and the absence of group differences could be a function of group characteristics rather than treatment. Investigators often are reassured (falsely) by the fact that the number of subjects who dropped out is few or equal across groups. (Data-analytic options to address the matter are discussed in Chapter 15.) As a general rule, it is difficult to interpret the follow-up data when attrition takes a significant toll.

Loss of subjects is always an issue in studies that last more than one session. Follow-up assessment in intervention studies raises special issues. Participants may vary in their cooperativeness with attempts to obtain follow-up data as a function of their impressions of treatment (e.g., acceptability), their relationship with the therapist or clinic staff, and benefits they obtained from—or perceived they received from—treatment. Hence, there may be a differential responsiveness to solicitations for follow-up among groups partially caused by the intervention and control conditions of the study.

Practical Assessment Decisions and Options

Several assessment decisions need to be made about the nature of follow-up, including modalities of assessment, setting or location of the assessment, informant, and method of contacting the clients. These decisions are the same as those required for pretreatment and posttreatment assessment. Yet, it is worth delineating follow-up assessment because different obstacles are involved. Subjects are not captive at that point, that is, they are not routinely coming to the treatment setting and do not want something from treatment (e.g., the intervention). Hence, their incentive or propensity to complete measures is reduced.

Assessment of pretreatment and posttreatment are often identical in terms of the measures, procedures, and locale. Of course, the identical assessment conditions at pre and post optimize the comparability of the results. Yet, there is no need to make follow-up the same as posttreatment assessment. In light of the difficulty in obtaining follow-up data, the investigator may want to use quite different assessments (e.g., an abbreviated assessment battery) or different ways of contacting subjects (e.g., have subjects complete a questionnaire from a secure Internet Web site). Table 14.3 highlights key decisions and options for the researcher contemplating follow-up assessment.

Where the assessment will be conducted may have relevance for the likelihood of obtaining the data. There are many advantages to having the clients return to the clinic or laboratory if this is where the original assessments were completed. If the follow-up assessments are conducted in the laboratory or clinic, the clients can be seen and evaluated by trained assessors or can be observed directly for their behavior in the interview situation. Many assessment options (videotaping, physiological measurement) and better standardization of assessment procedures characterize the laboratory setting. Of course, any advantages of having clients come in for an assessment may be offset by a greater loss of subjects. Asking participants to come in makes follow-up more difficult and costly for the subjects. Subjects are likely to be more willing to chat on the phone for a few minutes at their convenience or perhaps complete questions from home that can be called up and answered from their home computer. Of course, multiple options can be given to persons so they have a choice of how to complete measures. This sounds wonderful, but providing subjects with multiple options in the ways assessments are completed and obtained gives methodologists

TABLE 14.3.   Key Decisions and Options for Follow-Up Assessment

Decision	Main Options	Comment
What measures will be used?	Same as pre- and postassessment; Fewer, different, or novel measures	Consider breaking away to use measures that might increase the likelihood that subjects will complete the measures and hence be included
Where will assessment be conducted?	At the clinic or laboratory, in the home (visit the clients), from home (via phone, mail, Internet connection)	Some of these options (e.g., assessment over the phone) can greatly increase the likelihood of obtaining compliance
Who will provide the data or serve as informant(s)?	Original informants used for pre- and posttreatment assessment; others, archival records (or other unobtrusive measures) such as attendance, arrests, rehospitalization	Some combination of options may be pertinent, but again some of these may be easier to obtain than others
What can be done to increase the likelihood subjects will participate in/complete follow-up?	Remaining in close contact with subjects before follow-up data are obtained, providing monetary inducements, making few demands in precisely what is asked of subjects	Investigator creativity and resources can make a huge difference. Who contacts subjects for follow-up, what they say, and how they say it are pivotal. Common sense and warmth in interpersonal interactions with people have no substitutes

panic attacks.[2] The reason is that different ways of completing the same measures are not likely to yield identical results. At the very least, using many different ways at follow-up (some by phone, some by direct interview, some by Internet) can lead to increased variability (error) in the data and hence reduce statistical power. Follow-up assessment, like other parts of life, is a matter of tradeoffs, so obtaining high compliance may require providing options for clients.

Decisions need to be made about the informants to be used at follow-up, that is, the persons who will provide information about the status of the client. Obviously, the client is in a unique position to provide information about the benefits of treatment. For many clinical dysfunctions, clients are the primary, or occasionally the sole, source of information, especially when private events and subjective states (headaches, obsessive thoughts, feelings of despair, urges) are evaluated. Concomitant behaviors might well be assessed by observers, but self-report is viewed as the most direct assessment of such states. Even outside of the context of private events,

---

[2]In my spare time, I run an S & M Outpatient Treatment Clinic. We treat only statisticians and methodologists (ergo S & M), and the main problems are anxiety disorders (raised when colleagues hand them data after a study is completed), especially panic attacks (precipitated by nonrandom assignment or missing data), and delusions of power (statistical power, of course, as in running studies with very large sample sizes). I never write up data from the clinic because the clients constantly complain about the quality of the measures, threats to validity, my informed consent form, and absence of follow-up data. These complaints are common when working with statisticians and methodologists.

the perspective of the client is usually central. Consequently, most follow-up assessment utilizes the clients themselves as the source of information.

Someone in contact with the client—such as peers, spouse, roommates, teachers, employers, friends, and colleagues—may be able to serve as informants. Sometimes clients are asked to identify a relative or close friend who could be contacted by mail for information about how the client is doing. There are obvious ethical issues and practical problems in soliciting and utilizing informants. It is important to ensure that the informant not jeopardize the status or standing of the client (e.g., having an employer rate problems of the client's substance abuse, of which the employer was unaware). Informed consent with the client is obviously a requisite for any use of informants. In addition, the investigator ought to have confidence that the informants have access to the relevant information.

An overarching question that encompasses all of the decisions about follow-up is, "What can be done to increase the likelihood that the researcher will have subjects complete the follow-up assessment?" In many longitudinal studies (birth cohort studies, studies of child and adolescent development) outside of the context of treatment, extensive efforts are made to remain in close contact with subjects over an extended period. Several phone calls and mailings (birthday cards, holiday cards, newsletters, periodic phone calls just to schmooze) are conducted to remain in close contact and to keep participants involved in, and aware of, the study. These activities also keep close enough contact to maintain correct addresses. Also, monetary inducements (e.g., few hundred dollars) may be provided for completing repeated assessments on a regular basis (every 6 months or few years). In contrast, in treatment studies, investigators usually want to assess clients on one follow-up occasion after treatment. Although monetary inducements may be provided, as a rule, researchers do not devote very much time or resources (research staff, money) to remaining in close contact with clients. Also, it may be more difficult to keep in contact with subjects in a "treatment" study than in a more neutral or stigma-free project such as charting shoe size, cognition, and altruism over time. Subjects often want to hide their history of participation in treatment in slight fear of what might happen if the information became known to others.

For all types of studies, follow-up may simply be an inconvenience to the subjects. Sometimes mailing completed assessments or completing assessments over the phone is more convenient for clients than the usual face-to-face assessment. With advances in technology and the likelihood that more clients will have access to computers (from their homes, public libraries), wireless communication (cell phones, hand-held computers) and contact through the Internet, assessments might be more easily obtained than has been the case in the past.

Compliance with follow-up might be greatly enhanced by making assessment as user-friendly and as brief as possible. The investigator might contemplate use of a very brief assessment battery or set of items for follow-up as well as very convenient ways of completing the measure. The method that is to be used for follow-up could be part of the pre- and posttreatment assessment battery as well. That way, the researcher can show the relation of the abbreviated measures to the overall battery at pre and post and hence have evidence to support the use of abbreviated measure(s) at follow-up. For example, if a brief self-report questionnaire is contemplated for follow-up, this could be used at pre- and posttreatment assessment as well. The correlations of this measure with other measures in the battery could aid the interpretation of the follow-up data, which may use only this one measure.

General Comments

Too little follow-up data are collected in intervention studies. The options discussed vary in convenience, cost, and likely success in procuring the data. A number of options can be combined, and at least one option ought to be feasible to obtain follow-up. A very small follow-up assessment battery can be selected from the data obtained at pre- and posttreatment assessment. Usually, pre- and posttreatment assessment batteries are quite comprehensive and cover multiple domains, methods of assessment, and measures. From the data obtained at these assessment periods, one can identify statistically which few measures, subscales, or items provide the best estimate of other, more extensive measures in the battery. The follow-up assessment can be more abbreviated if the full battery is not possible. The specific measures that are used can be dictated by the data as well as by convenience so the burden to the subject and cost to the project are minimal.

SUMMARY AND CONCLUSIONS

Intervention research is a main focus within clinical, counseling, and related areas and raises many assessment issues. Among these are how to assess outcomes of the intervention. A range of criteria and assessment strategies were discussed, beginning with evaluation of the clinical significance of change. Three general strategies to assess clinical significance include comparison methods, subjective evaluation, and social impact measures. In addition, recommendations were made to expand the scope of outcome assessment, beyond the usual restricted and exclusive focus on symptoms. There are many clinically relevant effects of therapy (outcomes that relate to adjustment, mental, and physical health). Measures to evaluate characteristics of treatment were also discussed and included disseminability, cost, and acceptability of treatment. These features are likely to affect use of treatments that are developed in research.

Follow-up assessment is a key facet of intervention research. Loss of subjects is the main obstacle in conducting follow-up. Loss of subjects raises significant substantive and methodological issues for research. Several issues and recommendations were made to increase the likelihood of obtaining data from the subjects after they have left treatment. Options and decision points to increase subject compliance pertain to what measures are used, where the assessments will be conducted, and who provides the information or data. All sorts of strategies can be used to increase the likelihood that subjects will participate in follow-up, and these are important to consider at the outset of the study.

KEY CONCEPTS AND TERMS

Acceptability of a Treatment

Normative Comparisons

Clinical Significance

Social Impact Measures

Disseminability of Treatment

FOR FURTHER READING

Kazdin, A.E. (2001). Almost clinically significant ($p < .10$): Current measures may only approach clinical significance. *Clinical Psychology: Science and Practice, 8,* 455–462.

Kendall, P.C. (Ed.) (1999). Special section: Clinical significance. *Journal of Consulting and Clinical Psychology, 67,* 283–339.

Lyons, J.S., Howard, K.I., Mahoney, M.T., & Lish, J.D. (1997). *The measurement and management of clinical outcomes in mental health.* New York: Wiley.

Ogles, B.M., Lunnen, K.M., & Bonesteel, K. (2001). Clinical significance: History, application, and current practice. *Clinical Psychology Review, 21,* 421–446.

Sechrest, L., McKnight, P., & McKnight, K. (1996). Calibration of measures for psychotherapy outcome studies. *American Psychologist, 51,* 1065–1071.

Sperry, L., Brill, P., Howard, K.I., & Grissom, G. (1996). *Treatment outcomes in psychotherapy and psychiatric interventions.* New York: Brunner/Mazel.

Yates, B.T. (1995). Cost-effectiveness analysis, cost–benefit analysis, and beyond: Evolving models for the scientist–manager–practitioner. *Clinical Psychology: Science and Practice, 2,* 385–398.

Chapter 15

Statistical Methods of Data Evaluation

Assume that we have designed and run the study, gathered data on multiple measures, executed all elegant controls possible, and now are ready, in the privacy of our own labs, to find out what the effects were. At last, we are ready to examine the data statistically. Statistical evaluation refers to the use of quantitative techniques to describe the data or to draw inferences about the effects, that is, whether they are likely to be due to "chance" or to a veridical effect. As referred to previously, those facets of the statistical evaluation that influence the conclusions that can be drawn pertain to statistical conclusion validity. The quantitative evaluation of the study depends on more than merely running a few statistical tests. Current research in psychology and other sciences is based primarily on null hypothesis testing using statistical tests. The vast majority of articles utilize this approach, as reflected in familiar phrases in Results sections noting that the findings are or are not "statistically significant." Mastering research methodology requires understanding central features of statistical evaluation insofar as they influence designing experiments and drawing valid inferences. This chapter conveys key issues and practices of conventional statistical evaluation, problems with testing for statistical significance, and strategies to supplement or replace conventional tests of the null hypothesis.

SIGNIFICANCE TESTS AND THE NULL HYPOTHESIS

Overview

Once upon a time there was no statistical testing and no statistical evaluation. Actually, this statement probably reflects my poor scholarship. No doubt one of the first uses of statistical tests, like so many other firsts, can be traced to the ancient Greeks and specifically most likely to Aristotle. The first statistical evaluation emerged when Aristotle's mother played the money game with him when he was 4 years old. His mother held out two closed hands (fists) and said in a playful way, "Ari, which hand holds *more* drachma? If you guess correctly, you can keep the money in that hand." Ari replied, "Trick question, Mom, although one hand has three coins and the other has one coin, the two numbers are not really different statistically speaking. Aristotle's mom, no slouch herself (after all, she spoke ancient Greek fluently), quickly replied, "If they are not different, then let me give you what is in this hand!" at which point she handed him the one coin. (Aristotle learned early that one can accept the *null hypothesis*—no difference—when it is really not wise to do so.) In any case, invoking statistical significance as a criterion for decision making was a major contribution to science, for which we thank Aristotle; showing that even when there is no statistical difference, there may be a real and important difference is also a major contribution, for which we thank his mother.

Moving forward a bit in time and to nonfictional history, it is useful to stop in the 1920s and 1930s. During this period, statisticians devised practices that dominate current statistical methods of evaluation in psychology, and indeed in the sciences in general (Fisher, 1925; Neyman & Pearson, 1928). The practices include posing a null hypothesis (an assumption that there are no differences between groups in our study) and using tests of significance to determine whether the difference obtained in the sample is of a sufficient magnitude to reject this hypothesis. Of course, we "really" believe and want group differences, but we begin with the assumption that unless there is compelling evidence, we shall take the stand that there are no differences.

A goal of statistical evaluation is to provide an objective, or at least agreed-upon, criterion (e.g., significance levels) to decide whether the results we obtained are sufficiently compelling to reject this no-difference hypothesis. After all, there are likely to be some differences between groups (a treatment and control group) on whatever measures we used to evaluate the results. Means would rarely be identical for any two (or more) groups on any measure. Statistical tests are used to decide whether the results obtained in a particular study are likely to reflect a "real" difference, that is, one that goes beyond normal fluctuation and variation that groups would show. From null hypothesis testing and statistical evaluation, all sorts of worries emanate, as reflected in the concepts of statistical power, effect size, chance, and other problems that are presumably so horrible that we have to disguise their real names (Type I and Type II errors).

The characteristics of significance testing are sufficiently clear to most individuals that they need not be elaborated. Essentially, in most research, *statistical evaluation* examines whether groups differing on a particular independent variable (e.g., different conditions) can be distinguished statistically on the dependent measure(s). Statistical evaluation consists of applying a test to assess whether the difference obtained on the dependent measure is likely to have occurred by "chance." Typically, a level of confidence (such as .05 or .01) is selected as the criterion for determining whether the results are *statistically significant*.[1] A statistically significant difference indicates that the probability level is equal to or below the level of confidence selected, for example, $p \leq .05$. This means that if the experiment were completed 100 times, a difference of that magnitude found on the dependent variable would be likely to occur only five times on a purely chance basis. If the probability obtained in the study is lower than .05, most researchers would reject the null hypothesis and concede that group differences reflect a genuine relation between the independent and dependent variables.

To state that a relation in an experiment is statistically significant does not mean that there is necessarily a genuine effect, that is, a relationship really exists between the variables studied. Even a statistically significant difference could be the result of a chance event because of sampling of subjects and other factors. In any particular study, chance can never be completely ruled out as a rival explanation of the results. Nevertheless, by tradition, researchers have agreed that when the probability yielded by a statistical test is as low as .05 or .01, it is reasonable to conclude that a relation between the independent and dependent variables exists.

Essentially, statistical evaluation provides a criterion to separate *probably veridical* from *possibly chance* effects. Although subjectivity and bias can enter into the process of statistical evaluation—for example, in terms of the tests that are applied and the criteria for statistical significance—the goal of statistics is to provide a relatively bias-free and consistent method of interpreting results. The prevalent use of statistics does not imply that agreement on their value is universal. Diverse facets of statistical evaluation have been challenged and these are covered later in the chapter. It is first important to address key concepts and practices that will be needed for the researcher because hypothesis testing and statistical evaluation to detect relations among variables continue to dominate research.

Statistical evaluation provides consistent criteria for determining whether an effect is to be considered veridical. This advantage is critically important. We lose sight of this

---

[1]As mentioned previously, many statistical tests (factor analysis, regression, cluster analyses, time-series analysis, path analyses) include a number of decision points about various solutions, parameter estimates, cutoffs for including or deleting variables in the analysis or model, and so on. These decisions often are not made by the investigator but are accepted by the "default" criteria in the data-analytic programs. Independently of who makes the decision, there are assumptions and sources of subjectivity in the decision that can greatly influence the yield from statistical tests.

advantage as researchers because we are sequestered from nonresearch-based influences and advocacy where the cannons of research are largely neglected. Claims for effective treatment—for example, for losing weight or reducing cigarette smoking, as advocated in trade books and magazine articles—and new exercise devices (e.g., to tighten one's stomach muscles ["abs"]) are rarely based upon experimental methods and statistical evaluation. Testimonials by proponents of the techniques or those who have participated in the programs serve as the basis for evaluation. It would be valuable in these cases to apply experimental methods and to evaluate the results statistically.

There is another side. Statistical significance is required in part because it is not otherwise clear in many, or indeed most, situations whether effects are beyond the differences or variations that would be evident by chance or without an intervention. Yet, clearly, in some situations statistical evaluation is not needed. I mentioned marked changes in the chapter on single-case experimental designs where nonstatistical data evaluation criteria are invoked. Indeed, the visual inspection criteria often used with these designs are intended to serve as a gross filter that allows only strong effects to be considered as veridical. In any type of research, whether single-case or group, very dramatic changes might be so stark that there is no question that something important, reliable, and veridical took place, the type of changes referred to as "slam bang" effects (Gilbert, Light, & Mosteller, 1975). Clarity of the finding may have to do with both the extent of impact and the confidence one can place in the outcome measures. For example, most of us would be persuaded if three individuals who were terminally ill continued to live after a special treatment, whereas three others who did not receive the treatment died. The characteristics of this demonstration, including our trust in the reliability and importance of the dependent measure (death), the predicted outcome without treatment, and the vast differences in the outcomes make this persuasive, even though as always we want replication of the demonstration. Most situations from which we wish to draw inferences do not show such "slam bang" effects, and hence it is important to use some criterion to decide whether the results, differences, or changes within or between groups are likely to be due to chance or random fluctuations. Statistical significance is designed to serve this purpose.

Endorsement of statistical evaluation does not mean that statistics provide "the answer" or "real truth." Statistical evaluation is subject to all sorts of abuses, ambiguities, misinterpretation, and subjectivity. Different methods of analyzing the same data can lead to different conclusions, even with seemingly minor variations in decision points and default criteria in the analyses.[2] Yet, an advantage is that these ambiguities can often be made explicit, studied, and understood. The explicitness of statistical procedures helps us raise questions and understand the limits of the conclusions.

---

[2] An interesting and very readable discussion of how these p levels came to be adopted—and hence why they ought to be viewed quite tentatively—is available elsewhere (Cowles & Davis, 1982). That article conveys that conventional levels of .05 and .01 are rather arbitrary. Early in my career—actually when analyzing the results of my dissertation—I began to abandon $p < .05$ and adopted $p < .33$ as *the* level for significance. Through a rather amazing coincidence, most of the hypotheses of my dissertation were supported at $p < .33$. The bulk of my dissertation orals was spent by my committee quibbling with my attorney about my right to adopt this level for alpha (the US Constitution is rather hazy on individual, state, and federal rights in selecting alpha) and whether I could be charged with impersonating a scientist.

Statistical evaluation is strongly emphasized in psychology; indeed, statistical significance often is regarded as the definitive test of whether the variables under investigation are important or worth pursuing. Yet, statistical significance is a function of many different features of an experiment, only one of which is whether there is a relation between the independent and dependent variables. Testing for statistical significance depends on multiple, interrelated concepts. The researcher ought to know the concepts, how they interrelate, and how to "control" them. In this section I consider key concepts, what they mean, and what the investigator can do to maximize the likelihood of demonstrating an effect when, in fact, there is a difference.

Significance Level (alpha)

Significance level or *alpha* (α)is well known as a criterion for decision making in statistical data evaluation. Tradition has led us to use alphas of $p < .05$ and $.01$ for decision making.[3] Will the results of my experiment be statistically significant? Among the determinants of the answer is the number of subjects per group in the study. It can be assumed that groups will never (well, hardly ever) have identical means on the outcome measures, due simply to normal fluctuations and sampling differences. Even if the observed difference is not statistically significant, the investigator can be assured that the same magnitude of difference between groups might be statistically significant or much closer to statistical significance if two or three times as many subjects were used.

Statistical significance is a direct function of sample size. That is, the larger the sample size, the smaller the group differences needed for statistical significance for a given level of confidence. Stated another way, a given difference between two groups will gradually approach statistical significance as the size of the samples within each group increases. Indeed, statistical significance is virtually assured if a large number of subjects is used. For example, correlation coefficient (Pearson product-moment correlation or r) represents the association (relation) between two variables. A correlation can range from -1.00 to $+1.00$, inclusive. A correlation of 0 or anywhere thereabouts means the variables are not linearly related. Yet, $r = .01$ (that is, a correlation of essentially 0) would be statistically significant at the $p < .05$ level with a sample of 40,000. But who ever has a sample this large? There are two answers. Some studies are large scale. As a case in point, when psychological studies began in the military, large-scale testing was completed that encompassed thousands of subjects. Invariably, investigators reported that statistical significance was virtually guaranteed no matter what variables were studied (Bakan, 1966; Nunnally, 1960). Large sample sizes make small, trivial, and chance differences more likely to lead to the conclusion that the results are "statistically significantly." A second answer to the question is more pertinent to the present discussion. Statistical significance depends rather heavily on

---

[3]It is worth complaining for a moment about the poor choice of the word "significant" in statistical evaluation. In everyday parlance "significance" is close to the meanings of "importance," "consequential," and "meaningful." Naturally, we, as investigators, move with regrettable ease in noting that a statistically significant effect is important. In fact, a statistically significant effect may not be important at all in any sense that affects anyone or anything.

sample size. We want to know what variables are related to each other, how, and why. In obtaining this knowledge, we do not want our findings to wander in and out of any zone of statistical significance because some samples are larger than others. Clearly, more information is needed than statistical significance, a point to which I return shortly.

Power

The Problem.   *Power,* or the extent to which an investigation can detect a difference when one exists, was discussed in an earlier chapter. It is important to revisit the issue because weak power is the Achilles' heel of psychological research. That is, if we are going to use tests of statistical significance to evaluate our results, it is critical to ensure that there is a good chance (adequate power) to show a difference when one, in fact, exists.

The level of power that is "adequate" is not derived mathematically. As with the level of confidence (alpha), the decision is based on convention about the margin of protection one should have against accepting the null hypothesis when, in fact, it is false (*beta*). A convention has been proposed and generally accepted—namely, that power in a study ought to be .80 when alpha = .05 (Cohen, 1965). Power of .80 can be explained in statistical terms (beta = .2 and 1 − beta or power = .8), but there is a better way to state all of this. If power is .80 in a study, this means that the investigator's chance of detecting a difference in his or her study is 4 out of 5 (.80), if there is a real difference in the population. (Remember that power is the likelihood of finding a difference, but only the *likelihood* of finding a difference if there really is a difference in the population.) Although power ≥ .80 is used as a criterion here, higher levels (.90, .95) are often encouraged as the acceptable criterion (Freiman et al., 1978; Friedman, Furberg, & DeMets, 1985).

Reviews of research within many different specialty areas of psychology and other fields as well have shown that most studies have insufficient power to detect differences (Cohen, 1992; Sedlmeier & Gigerenzer, 1989). Moreover, repeated exhortations about the problem and consistently clear recommendations to rectify the problem have had little or no impact on research. (The value of the future exhortations in relation to clinical psychology has been in showing that insight and awareness into a problem are not very potent interventions for changing what people do.) Consequently, from the early power analyses over 40 years ago to current analyses (Kazantzis, 2000; Moher et al., 1994), studies as a rule do not have sufficient power to detect small and medium effects.

Weak or insufficient power is not a minor nuisance or merely a worry for misinterpreting a particular study. Broad areas of research can be characterized by weak power, and the conclusions that these areas have generated might well be attributed to this characteristic. For example, noted before was the finding in psychotherapy outcome research that treatments usually do not differ from each other. A conclusion that treatments are no different—that is, support of the null hypothesis—is often interpreted to mean that many treatments are probably equally effective. This may or may not be true. We cannot really tell because, for most psychotherapy research, weak power is a rival interpretation of the absence of differences. The sample sizes of studies that compare two more treatments, as a rule, are very small (10–30 subjects per group) and power is quite weak (see Kazantzis, 2000; Kazdin & Bass, 1989).

Relation to Alpha, Effect Size, and Sample Size.   Four different concepts of statistical inference have been discussed at varying points, including the criteria for statistical significance (alpha), effect size (ES), sample size, and power. These concepts are interrelated in the sense that when three of these are specified, the remaining one can be determined. Their interrelations are critical in that they permit one to consider all sorts of options in an experiment, such as the level of power (given a specific level of alpha, ES, and a fixed *N*), what ES is needed (if alpha, power, and sample size are predetermined), and so on. The most frequent use of this information is to decide how many subjects to include in a study. Thus, to identify our sample size, we need to make decisions to set the other three parameters, alpha, power, and ES. At this point let us adopt alpha of .05 to adhere slavishly to tradition. As for level of power, we also might follow convention and design our study to have power of .80. Now we must estimate ES. How can we possibly do this because the ES formula requires us to know the difference between the groups on the dependent variables of interest and the standard deviation [ES = $(m_1 - m_2)/s$]?

Actually, in many areas of research, ES has been studied. The secondary analysis procedure, referred to as *meta-analysis*, has been used extensively for evaluating research (Cook et al., 1992). Meta-analyses provide estimates of ESs for research in a given area. The ES is used as a common metric to combine studies using different dependent variables. We can consult such analyses to identify likely ESs for the study we propose to undertake. For example, if we are about to conduct a psychotherapy study comparing treatment versus no treatment, we can estimate ES from the many meta-analyses of psychotherapy and summaries of the meta-analyses (see Roth & Fonagy, 1996; Weisz & Weiss, 1993). Effect size for such comparisons tends to be about .70. Alternatively, if we are comparing two or more treatments to each other, we know that ESs are likely to be smaller (in the range of .40–.60). In short, ES estimates can be obtained from published research, including individual studies, or more conveniently from meta-analyses. Effect sizes vary across measures, so there is no *one* ES. Even so, estimating the likely ES for the main dependent measures is wise to do in advance of the study.

If meta-analyses are unavailable, maybe one or more studies can be found in the journals that have compared the conditions (groups) of interest or that used the measures (dependent variables) in a related way. Another study on the topic (or closely related) can be consulted. From the statistical tests or means and standard deviations in the published article, one can often find the likely ES. I shall mention later in this chapter easy ways to derive ES even if the author of the original study never calculated ESs.

When individual studies or meta-analyses are unavailable, ES can be estimated on a priori grounds (guessing in advance of the study). The investigator may believe that there is no precedent for the type of work he or she is to conduct. (Indeed, we often tend to believe this already about our research.) The investigator may have to guess whether the ES is likely to be small, medium, or large. Cohen (1988) has provided us with admittedly arbitrary but quite useful guidelines in this regard by noting small, medium, and large ESs to correspond to .2, .5, and .8, respectively. It is helpful to select a conservative estimate. If the investigator is new to an area of research (first or second study), it is likely that the strength of the experimental manipulation and many sources of variability may be unfamiliar and difficult to control. In such cases it is likely that the investigator is slightly overoptimistic about the ESs he or she expects to achieve and may underestimate the sources of variability that attenuate group differences.

In any case, assume that by one of the above methods we consider the likely ES to be about .50. We have alpha = .05, power = .80, and ES estimated at .50. At this point we can enter tables of various books (Cohen, 1988; Kraemer & Thiemann, 1987). As an illustration, Table 15.1 reprints portions of a power table for comparing two means, using an alpha of .05. The column marked *n* is the number of cases per group; across the top of the table is *d* or ES, with each column representing a different ES. The entries within the body of the table itself reflect power. So let us enter the table in the column with ES = .50 just to get an idea of how the table works. As we go down the column, we are looking for .80, which is the power we would like for our study. The table is marked to show .80 and then the horizontal line moving to the left shows the *n* we need. When alpha = .05, ES = .50, and desired power is .80, we need 64 subjects per group (i.e., *N* = 128 for our two-group study).

Most studies do not have a sample size this large, so maybe we can loosen up a bit. In fact, after seeing the *N* we need, we might say, "Who cares about power anyway?" If we lighten up and reduce power to .50, this means we need a sample size of only 32 per group (or *N* = 64). Relaxing power in this way is very risky. In my own research I care a lot about power. I am not going to do many studies in my lifetime, so I am not too keen on handicapping myself with weak power for those that I do conduct. So, designing a powerful test is quite important to get the most sensitive test feasible. If one adheres to the tradition of statistical significance testing, power and its related concepts are absolutely critical and cannot be neglected.

When we consider power in advance of a study, we are likely to learn that to detect such a reasonable (medium) ES, we need a much larger *N* than we planned or perhaps even than we can obtain. This is excellent to identify in advance of conducting the study. We may then decide to vary alpha (e.g., *p* < .10), reduce power slightly (e.g., power = .75), or to select experimental conditions (or variations of the manipulation) that are likely to yield larger ESs. Such informed deliberations and decisions are praised when they are completed *prior* to an investigation. The use of power tables helps one to experiment intelligently with possible options regarding alpha, power, ES, and *N*.

The frustrations of persons advocating attention to power stem in part from the ease of using power tables. The information is readily available, and estimating power, or sample size, or ES, or alpha when the others are fixed requires little time (2 minutes for the unseasoned researcher, 1 minute for the seasoned researcher). (The 1 minute is divided as follows: 40 seconds for turning to the correct table in one of the books, 10 seconds for getting the correct columns, 10 seconds to react and make such statements as, "You've got to be kidding.") The task has become easier because computer software is readily available that allows one to enter any parameter (*N*, ES, alpha, power) and to see any or all other parameters (see Thomas & Krebs, 1997, for a review

TABLE 15.1.   Sample Power Table: Power, Sample Size, and Effect Size for a *t* test at *p* < .05

Power of t test of m₁ = m₂ at .05

n	.10	.20	.30	.40	.50	.60	.70	.80	1.00	1.20	1.40
10	06	07	10	13	18	24	31	39	56	71	84
15	06	08	12	18	26	35	45	56	75	88	96
20	06	09	15	23	33	45	58	69	87	96	99
25	06	11	18	28	41	55	68	79	93	99	
30	07	12	21	33	47	63	76	86	97		
31	07	12	21	34	49	64	77	87	97		
32	07	12	22	35	50	65	78	88	98		
33	07	13	22	36	51	67	80	89	98		
34	07	13	23	37	53	68	81	90	98		
35	07	13	23	38	54	70	82	91	98		
36	07	13	24	39	55	71	83	92	99		
37	07	14	25	39	56	72	84	92	99		
38	07	14	25	40	57	73	85	93	99		
39	07	14	26	41	58	74	86	94	99		
40	07	14	26	42	60	75	87	94	99		
42	07	15	27	44	62	77	89	95	99		
44	07	15	28	46	64	79	90	96			
46	08	16	30	48	66	81	91	97			
48	08	16	31	49	68	83	92	97			
50	08	17	32	50	70	84	93	98			
52	08	17	34	51	71	86	94	98			
54	08	18	34	53	73	87	95	98			
56	08	18	35	55	74	88	96	99			
58	08	19	36	57	76	89	96	99			
60	08	19	37	58	77	90	97	99			
64	09	20	39	61	80	92	98	99			
68	09	21	41	64	82	93	98				
72	09	22	43	66	85	94	99				
76	09	23	45	69	86	95	99				
80	10	24	47	71	88	96	99				
84	10	25	49	73	90	97	99				
88	10	26	51	75	91	98					
92	10	27	52	77	92	98					
96	11	28	54	79	93	99					
100	11	29	56	80	94	99					
120	12	34	64	87	97						
140	13	38	71	92	99						
160	14	43	76	95	99						
180	16	47	81	97							
200	17	51	85	98							
250	20	61	92	99							
300	23	69	96								
350	26	75	98								
400	29	81	99								
450	32	85	99								
500	35	88									

Note: *p* < .05 The column *n* is the number of subjects needed within each of the two groups; the column across the top marked *d* is effect size; the numbers within the body of the table are power. The example we are discussing in the text is one that asks: What sample size do we need if we have an effect size of .50, alpha = .05, and power of .80? Obviously, the table can be used another way by saying, if I start with a certain number of subjects (e.g., 50), what will be the power for a given effect size, and so on. Only a portion of the table is provided here. (The decimals are omitted from the power figures.)

Source: Adapted from Cohen, J. (1988). *Statistical power analysis in the behavioral sciences* (2nd ed.), pp. 36–37. Hillsdale, NJ: Erlbaum. Reprinted with permission.

of 30 different programs). Indeed, some of the commonly used software for multipurpose statistical packages includes options to estimate power. In addition, on the Web are many resources that calculate power. These can be found by searching for "statistical power" through the various search engines sites. In short, many resources are available. An investigator can readily identify needed sample size with a keyboard click or two. This places a lot of power at the investigator's fingertips.

One further point about sample size and power is worth noting. Power pertains to the statistical comparisons the investigator will make, including subanalyses that may divide groups into various subgroups. For example, the investigator may have N = 100 subjects in two groups. The main comparison of interest may contrast group 1 (n = 50) with group 2 (n = 50). The investigator may plan several analyses that further divide the sample, for example, by sex (males versus females), age (younger versus older), intelligence (median IQ split), or some other variable. Such comparisons divide the groups into smaller units (or subgroups). Instead of groups with n = 50, the subgroups are much smaller, and power is commensurately reduced. The lesson is simple. Ensure adequate power for the comparisons of primary interest.

Variability in the Data.   Power is a function of alpha, N, and ES. However, there is more to power than the formula for its computation. Noted already was the notion that excessive variability within an experiment can threaten statistical conclusion validity. Variability is inherent in the nature of subject performance in any investigation. However, the investigator can inadvertently increase variability in ways that will reduce the obtained ES. Obviously, if the mean difference between groups = 8 on some measure, ES will increase or decrease, depending on the size of the standard deviation by which that difference is divided. The standard deviation can be larger as a function of the heterogeneity of the subjects (in age, background, sex, socioeconomic class, and other variables). The effects of the intervention or experimental manipulation are likely to be less consistent across subjects whose differences (heterogeneity) are relatively great. The heterogeneity of the subjects is reflected in a larger within-group variability. This variability, referred to as error variance, is directly related to ES and statistical significance. For a given difference between groups on the dependent measure, the larger the error variance, the less likely the results will be statistically significant. As discussed in Chapter 3, error variance can be increased by sloppiness and lack of care in how the experiment is conducted, by using heterogeneous and diverse subjects who vary on characteristics related to the outcome, and by using measures that have poor reliability. Procedures and practices that reduce or minimize extraneous variability increase the obtained ES and power.

Ways to Increase Power

There are many ways to increase power. These are highlighted in Table 15.2. Mentioned first, of course, is increasing sample size. This is important because it is the most obvious and the first line of attack. When college student samples can be run and a large subject pool is available, that alternative is quite useful. In clinical settings, increasing sample size is not always that easy and sometimes simply not possible because there are relatively few subjects available with the characteristics of interest

TABLE 15.2.   Ways to Increase Power

1. Increase sample size (N or n/group)

2. Increase expected differences by contrasting conditions that are more likely to vary (stronger manipulations, sharper contrasts)

3. Use pretests/repeated measures, which reduces the error term in the effect size

Effect Size Formula

Without repeated measures	With repeated measures
$$ES = \dfrac{m_1 - m_2}{s}$$	$$ES = \dfrac{m_1 - m_2}{s\sqrt{1 - r^2}}$$

4. Vary alpha (a priori) if the case can be made to do so, if, for example . . .
   A. Classification of groups (e.g., case-control study) is imperfect
   B. Measures are not well established (dubious psychometric properties)
   C. Small effects/differences (ES and significance) are predicted
   D. Consequences of the decision vary markedly as a function of the direction and hence one wishes to detect difference in one direction rather than another (e.g., one-tailed and lenient alpha)

5. Use directional tests for significance testing

6. Decrease variability (error) in the study as possible by . . .
   A. Holding constant versus controlling sources of variability
   B. Analyzing the data to extract systematic sources of variance from the error term

(children with a particular chronic disease, cohabiting adults of the same gender raising children, professors with social skills). Obtaining large numbers of cases might require sampling across a wide geographical area or continuing the study over a protracted period and, in fact, would preclude conducting the research. In short, increasing sample size is not always feasible, especially if an investigator wishes to complete the study in his or her lifetime. Alas, there are many options, and selecting one or more of these can help enormously.

Increasing Expected Differences between Groups.   Assume for a moment that an investigator is comparing two different groups (conditions). These conditions are selected to test a particular hypothesis. In relation to power the investigator can ask, "Is this the strongest test or comparison of the different conditions? Can the hypothesis be tested by making the manipulation stronger or by establishing a sharper contrast between conditions?" For example, instead of comparing a little versus a lot, the contrast would be sharper if one compared none versus a lot or very little versus quite a lot. Another way to illustrate this is to say the investigator is interested in comparing three groups—low, medium, and high levels of depression—on some other measures. A stronger test might be to compare the two groups, low and high. The groups are more extreme and more likely to show a stronger effect, assuming that the characteristic of interest (depression) operates on a linear way so that more is worse on some other measures. Also, for a given number of subjects—say 100 in our hypothetical study—a test of two groups each with 50 subjects is more powerful than a test of three groups, each with 33 subjects.

The overall point is that conditions selected in a study might be made more extreme to provide a test of a hypothesis that is likely to lead to stronger effects. As investigators we ought to ask ourselves at the design stage of the study, "Can the study be designed so that the anticipated ES is large, or at least larger than our first idea?" For a given sample size and alpha, a larger ES is, of course, much easier to detect. That is, power increases if ES is increased. Increasing ES is, in part, a function of the specific conditions selected and tested in a study.

Use of Pretests. Noted previously were experimental designs that used pretests. From a design standpoint advantages of using pretests were manifold and included issues related to the information they provide (about magnitude of change, number of persons who change, and others). The statistical advantages of a pretest are the most universal basis for using such designs. The advantage of the pretest is that with various analyses, the error term in evaluating ES is reduced. With repeated assessment of the subjects (pre- and posttest), the within-group (subject) variance can be taken into account to reduce the error term. Consider the impact on the ES formula.

As noted in Table 15.2, the usual formula for effects is ES = $(m_1 - m_2)/s$. When there is a pretest measure or another measure that is related to performance at post-treatment (e.g., covariate), the ES error term is altered. The formula is represented by ES = $(m_1 - m_2)/ s\sqrt{1 - r^2}$, where r equals the correlation between the pretest (or other variable) and posttest. As the correlation between the pre- and posttest increases, the error term (denominator) is reduced, and hence power of the analysis increases. Several statistical analyses take advantage of the use of a pretest, such as analyses of covariance, repeated measures analyses of variance, and gain scores (see Lipsey, 1990). As feasible, using designs with repeated measures is advantageous because of the benefits to power.

Varying Alpha Levels within an Investigation. Alpha levels are quite related to power, and hence their use and variation warrant attention. Alpha at $p < .05$ or $< .01$ is rather fixed within the field and represents constraints over which the investigator would seemingly have little control. Yet, there are circumstances in which we may wish to reconsider the alpha level. The investigator may decide to relax the alpha level (reduce the probability of Type II error) based on substantive or design issues that are decided in advance of data collection. By reducing the probability of *Type II error* (saying there are no differences when there really are), we increase the likelihood of a *Type I error* (saying there is a difference when there really is none). Yet, in any given circumstance, there may be great reason to tinker with these levels.

Several circumstances may lead the investigator to anticipate specific constraints that will reduce the likely ES and the differences between groups or conditions. First, the criterion for selecting groups in a case-control study might be known to be imperfect or somewhat tenuous. Thus, some persons in one group (e.g., nondepressed controls) might, through imperfect classification, belong in the other group (depressed persons). Comparison of groups will be obscured by variability and imperfect classification. Second and related, the measures in the area of research may not be very well established. The unreliability of the measure may introduce variability into the situation that will affect the sensitivity of the experimental test. The predicted relation may have been evident with more sensitive and reliable measures. Third, the specific comparison of interest may be expected to generate a very small difference between groups. If we expect small differences, the usual advice would be to increase sample size so that power will be high for this small effect.

Fourth, we might alter alpha level based as well on consideration of the consequences of our decisions. Consequences here may refer to patient care (benefit, suffering, adverse side effects), cost, policy issues (ease of dissemination, providing the greatest care to the greatest number), and other considerations where the weight of accepting or rejecting the null hypothesis has greatly different implications and value. For example, if we are studying whether a particular procedure has side effects (e.g., illness, death), we might want to alter alpha to, say, $p < .20$. In such a study we may wish to err (Type II) on the side of stating the side effects exist if there is any reasonable suggestion that they do. Indeed, we would not want to say that more people in the treatment died, but this was not a statistically significant difference (e.g., $p < .08$). In this case we want to ease up on the criterion (alpha) for making that claim.

In a given experiment, alpha is one of many decision points. Even though the acceptable level of alpha is deeply ingrained by tradition, the investigator ought to consider thoughtful departures based on circumstances of the particular experiment. There are circumstances when the investigator may plan on using different levels of alpha within an experiment. For example, suppose we are studying three conditions in a psychotherapy study: (1) treatment A, (2) treatment A with an added ingredient to enhance outcome, and (3) no-treatment control. We sample 75 persons who meet various criteria (diagnosis, age, physical health) and assign them randomly to conditions, with the restriction that an equal number will appear in each group. What shall we use for our alpha level? We could use an alpha of .05 and let the matter rest. Alternatively, we might in advance of the study consider the comparisons of interest and their likely ESs. The difference between treatments versus no treatment is likely to be large. The usual alpha level ($p < .05$) to detect a difference might well be reasonable here. In contrast, the difference between treatment A with and without a special ingredient is likely to be smaller. A sample of 75 subjects with 25 cases per group in our hypothetical study is larger than the samples of most studies in psychotherapy research but is still likely to be too small to show statistically significant differences (Kazdin & Bass, 1989). It might be reasonable to use a more lenient alpha level (e.g., $p < .20$) for comparisons of the two treatments.

In general, in a given instance it may be useful to reconsider alpha level before a study either for the entire study or for some of the tests or comparisons. If on a priori grounds special conditions within the design can be expected to reduce ESs, a more lenient alpha may be justified. Both theoretical and applied concerns might lead to reconsidering alpha. Altering alpha level might be guided by evaluating the nature of the consequences of different decisions, that is, concluding that there is or is not a reliable difference between conditions.

Tinkering with alpha levels has to be considered very carefully. Obviously, relaxing alpha levels after the fact or when the results just miss conventional significance levels is inappropriate and violates the model on which significance testing is based. It is tempting to relax alpha levels in this way because few believe that a finding has been supported at $p < .05$ but is unsupported at a p level above that (e.g., $p < .06$ or $< .10$). However, within the conventional model of significance testing, some generally agreed-upon criterion has to be selected. Whatever that criterion is, there would always be instances that just miss and in which the investigator, but not many others of the scientific community, would say that the effect is close enough to be regarded as reliable.

Use of Directional Tests.   Variation of alpha levels raises a related solution to increase power, namely, the matter of using one- versus two-tailed tests of significance. In significance testing, alpha is used to decide whether a difference between groups is reliable. Consider a two-group study and a t test to evaluate group differences. The null hypothesis is that the groups do not differ, that is, the ES = 0. A two-tailed test evaluates the obtained difference in light of departures from 0 in either direction, that is, whether one group is better or worse than another. The alpha of .05 refers to both "tails" or ends of the normal distribution, which are used as the critical region for rejection.

In much research the investigator may have a view about the direction of the differences. He or she may not wish to test if the ES is different from zero but rather whether the treatment is better than the control condition or whether treatment A is better than treatment B. The hypothesis to reject is not bidirectional (better or worse) but unidirectional (better). As such, the investigator may wish to use a one-tailed test. A lower t value is required for the rejection of the null hypothesis if a one-tailed directional test is provided.

Most hypotheses in research are directional in the sense that investigators have an idea and interest in differences in a particular direction. For this reason some authors have suggested that most significance testing should be based on one-tailed tests (Mohr, 1990). However, there is resistance to this to which the reader should be alerted. There is often an implicit assumption that investigators who use one-tailed tests may have done so because the results would otherwise not be statistically significant. Often it is unclear to the reader of the research report that the use of one-tailed tests was decided in advance of seeing the results. The implicit assumption does not give the benefit of doubt to the investigator. At the same time relatively few studies in clinical psychology and related areas utilize one-tailed tests. One rarely sees such tests or sees them in situations where the results would be significant whether the tests were completed as one- or two-tailed tests.

In general, investigators are encouraged to be conservative in their analyses of the data and in drawing conclusions about relations that are reliable or statistically significant. The discussion of multiple comparisons (in the next section) conveys this tradition rather well. Yet, directional hypotheses and use of one-tailed tests warrant consideration. We are not necessarily better off as a science because of conservatism in using two-tailed tests almost all of the time. Indeed, the higher priority is providing good tests of informed predictions. A directional test of a directional prediction is probably the best match.

When using one-tailed tests, clarify the basis of this use (why is the prediction directional?) so that consumers of research can identify whether the tests are reasonable. Also, because one-tailed tests are occasionally viewed suspiciously, the investigator might wish to note in passing those tests that would or would not have been significant with two-tailed tests. Comments on both types of tests within a study do not reflect concerns of the statistician who might lobby for a rational evaluation of using one or the other form of tests (but not both). Yet, comments about the conclusions drawn from statistical tests raise broader issues. Among these is the importance of informing colleagues about the dependence of conclusions on assumptions and methods of analyses.

Decreasing Variability (Error) in the Study.   The final method of increasing power, mentioned in Table 15.2, is decreasing variability in the study. This topic has been discussed previously, and I can be brief as a result. Noted previously has been the fact that increasing variability (e.g., differences between subjects) can stem from many sources, including how heterogeneous the samples are (e.g., children and adults versus just adults) and how carefully the experiment is executed and conducted (monitoring of treatment integrity). Careful control of variability can be achieved by monitoring many facets of the study; many sources of variability can be held constant, as discussed in an earlier chapter. The silent rewards of careful work are reflected in minimal variation that would be counted as error. This translates to a stronger ES in the study than would have been obtained if less care were taken.

Error variability includes all sorts of influences in a study. In fact, somewhat loosely, consider that an investigator is studying a disorder (e.g., anxiety) and compares two groups on several measures expected to relate to the disorder (attachment patterns, cognitions, response to stress). In this study we could say that the investigator is studying the variation (differences) that is a function of one variable, namely, the disorder. There are, of course, many other variables that the investigator is purposely ignoring. For example, not everyone in the study is of the same sex, social class, and so on across a large number of variables. The influences of all of these virtually infinite other variables form part of the error term (standard deviation, variance) of the study. One can reduce the error variance of a study by analyzing the data by one or more of the variables embedded in the error variance. Of course, one selects variables that are worth evaluating because they are used to test, explore, or generate hypotheses of interest. So, for example, one might analyze sex differences if the case could be made that this is worth testing or exploring. The analyses would not include just those with and without the disorder (a *t* test comparing two groups), but also rather disorder × sex analyses (an *F* test with separate effects for anxiety, sex, and anxiety × sex). Sex and the interaction of sex with anxiety disorder now become variables that are evaluated separately and reduce sources of variation that otherwise would be in the error term. In short, either holding constant variables that may increase error variation in the study or analyzing variables that might be included in an error term can be used to decrease error variation. One cannot just analyze all sources of error (all variables that can be imagined), because the case could not be easily made that they are interesting (anxiety, sex, shoe size, height, and so on) as independent variables.

Data Analyses and Designing the Study

Significance testing is the mainstay of contemporary research. Issues related to alpha, power, anticipated ESs, and error rates stemming from multiple tests, to mention a few, are critical to ponder as the study is being planned. These are not esoteric issues nor merely quantitative nuances. Rather, they will squarely affect the conclusions the investigator wishes to draw and the strength and quality of the design. More concretely, as the purpose of the study and design are being formulated, it is useful to write each of the hypotheses and next to each one to outline the tentative data-analytic strategies that will be used. In light of the specific tests and analyses, one can ask

- Do I have sufficient power, given the likely effect size?
- Can I vary alpha or sample size, or reduce variability in some ways (e.g., homogeneity of the sample, how the study is run) to augment power?
- Can I increase the strength or potency of the independent variable or magnify the effect that will occur by using different groups in the design or by contrasting conditions (experimental and control) that are likely to produce stronger effect sizes?
- Do I need each of the groups in this study, or can I deploy all of the subjects to fewer groups (thereby increasing power)?
- Will there be other tests related to this hypothesis that will divide the groups further (e.g., contrasting males versus females) and thereby reduce power?

Addressing, and to the extent possible, resolving these questions at the design stage are very helpful. After the experiment is completed, no doubt other questions and data-analytic issues will emerge, and hence not all of the results and plans for their evaluation can be anticipated. At the same time the plan for the major analyses ought to be worked out at the design stage so that changes can be made in the design to enhance the facets of statistical conclusion validity.

SPECIAL TOPICS IN DATA ANALYSIS

Intent-to-Treat Analysis

Intervention research (treatment, prevention) requires that subjects complete measures usually before and after the intervention, that is, as characteristic of pretest–posttest design that was reviewed previously. After the intervention, assessments include posttreatment measures and follow-up. In any study in which the subject is evaluated over time, there is the likelihood that some subjects will drop out of the study before all the data are collected. Attrition or dropping out can threaten all types of validity, as discussed in previous chapters.

From the standpoint of the present discussion, loss of subjects raises special challenges for data evaluation. Designs begin by randomly assigning subjects to groups, and this is critically important to make implausible that selection biases could account for any group differences at the end of the study. If individuals drop out, the groups are no longer randomly composed. Stated somewhat differently, loss of subjects changes the study from a true experiment to a quasi-experiment. In a true experiment

I noted that subjects are assigned randomly. That is the usual definition. But I did not mention the assumption that is inherent in true experiments, namely, once assigned, subjects remain in their groups. Letting some people drop out of one or more groups changes that. When anyone drops out, there is some unknown and difficult-to-document selection factor at work that leads people to say, "I am not in this group (study) anymore." Even if there are only a few dropouts, there is a problem.

Occasionally, investigators are falsely comforted by the fact that an equal or approximately equal number of subjects dropped out of each of the groups. Even if an equal number of individuals drop out from each group, this still "ruins" the random assignment of subjects to groups and can create selection biases. That an equal number of subjects dropped out from each group does not mean that the same type of subjects or subjects with identical characteristics dropped out. Who drops out—that is, their characteristics—may vary as a function of the condition to which they were assigned (one form of psychotherapy or medication rather than another, or to a control rather than to a treatment group). I have elaborated these points in a prior chapter. For this discussion the question is how to analyze the data.

Two primary methods are used to analyze the data from intervention trials (see Table 15.3). The first is referred to as *completer analysis* and is the most commonly used method in psychological research. Indeed, the method is so common that the term is rarely used to delineate this as an option or special method. With completer analysis the investigator merely analyzes the data for only those subjects who completed the study and who completed the measures on each occasion (pre, post). Thus, if treatments A and B are being compared, completer data analysis to evaluate the relative effectiveness of the treatments will use all subjects who have pre- and posttreatment measures. The subjects without posttreatment (because they dropped out, died, failed to complete the measures correctly) will not be included.

TABLE 15.3. Data Analyses of Treatment Trials when Some Subjects Drop Out of the Study

Name of Analysis	Who Is Included	Comments
Completer analysis	Only those subjects for whom there are complete data, that is, they completed all of the assessments	The problem is that the random composition of the treatment groups is lost and threats to internal validity in particular emerge. The groups can no longer be presumed to be equivalent.
Intent-to-treat analysis	Include all subjects who begin the study whether or not they complete all the measures. For any missing data, use the previous data they have provided	This method preserves the random composition of both groups. The analysis can be a very conservative estimate of the effects of treatment. The reason is that subjects who dropped out during treatment will be included in the data analysis. The last data point they provided was the pretreatment assessment and so these data will be entered at pre and post. Hopefully, if there is a treatment effect, it will override the impact of cases who dropped out.

Completer analysis makes great sense. After all, the prediction was that individuals who receive one treatment will be different from those who receive the other treatment. The prediction is not that people who are assigned to a group but who do not receive the treatment will be different. Understandably, only those are analyzed who complete treatment. Unfortunately, completer analysis maximizes bias in the data analyses—that is, the groups are not randomly comprised anymore, and differences may reflect who remains in the study or who responds to the specific treatment. There is an internal validity problem (selection × history, selection × maturation) and external validity problem (to whom do the results apply since those who completed treatment omit some set of subjects?).

For a completer analysis, whether groups are or are not different from each other, the results are difficult to interpret. Of course, so much of methodology is a matter of degree, and hence common sense is invariably helpful. If each group consists of 100 subjects and there are two groups ($N = 200$), and a total of 4 subjects drop out, it is unlikely that there will be bias. Yet, this is quite rare; in treatment studies, groups are much smaller (<20 subjects) and dropout rates are greater (e.g., 2–5). The potential for selection biases looms large.

A second way to analyze the data is referred to as *intent-to-treat analysis* and is quite commonly used in other disciplines (medicine, epidemiology) but slightly less so in psychology. Intent-to-treat analysis is designed to preserve randomization of the groups by following this rule: The data for any subject ought to be analyzed according to the group to which he or she was assigned, whether or not the intended treatment was given or received (Davis, 1998; Mazumdar, Liu, Houck, & Reynolds, 1999). Thus, even subjects who dropped out, whether at the end of treatment or in the first few minutes of the first session—or indeed, after they were assigned and never showed up again—are to be included in the data analysis (see Table 15.3).

Of course, if someone has dropped out of the study and does not complete the measures (e.g., at posttreatment or follow-up), how can one include them in the data analysis? The usual method is to use in place of the missing data the last (previous) data that subjects have provided. This is sometimes referred to as carrying the last observation forward and conveys what the investigator does to fill in the missing data. For example, if the study includes pretreatment, posttreatment, and follow-up assessment, we presume that all subjects have completed the pretreatment assessment. By the end (post) of treatment, some subjects have dropped out. An intent-to-treat analysis would include these subjects as if they had completed the treatment or served in the condition to which they were assigned. For those who dropped out during treatment, the pretreatment scores are used for the posttreatment scores as well, that is, they are used in both places. This sounds counterintuitive because these subjects did not complete treatment. Yet, the analysis will decrease any likelihood of selection factors to explain group differences.

Using the last (previous) data that subjects provided is the most commonly used method of intent-to-treat analyses. Another option is conducting an assessment of dropouts at the point that they drop out. That is, the posttreatment assessment battery is intended to be completed when treatment is finished and will be completed in this way for most subjects. For dropouts, sometimes one can obtain measures at the point they drop out. If subjects can be contacted and will complete the measures, the data can be used for their "posttreatment" assessment. Even though they have not completed treatment, they have a midassessment that will be used for their data, when analyses are completed at post. It is usually not feasible to collect data from dropouts, but this can be done (with monetary incentives, telephone rather than in-person assessment interviews, and abbreviated assessment packets). With assessment that is more easily completed by the subject, the investigator hopes that the dropouts will complete the measures. Presumably, assessment completed at the point of dropping out is better than merely reusing the pretreatment data as a measure of pre- and posttreatment.

Completer and intent-to-treat analyses, as any other methodological or statistical practices, have tradeoffs. Completer analysis maximizes biases in the data, perhaps bias in favoring treatment because only those who received the full treatment regimens are included, but also biases in selection by including only those who perhaps liked the treatment, were persistent enough, and so on. There is a little loss of power too because dropouts are not included, but this is usually a minor influence. Intent-to-treat analysis redresses the potential bias by preserving groups as originally constructed, but includes in the analyses subjects who did not receive any, much, or the full treatment. Clearly, intent-to-treat analyses are conservative because including such nontreated subjects is likely to attenuate any group differences. In most clinical trial studies, data are analyzed in one or the other way. It may be useful to evaluate the data both ways because they address slightly different questions. Moreover, if the results are consistent in both types of analyses, this strengthens the conclusions that can be drawn.

Analyses Involving Multiple Comparisons

Controlling Alpha Levels. In an experiment the investigator is likely to include multiple groups and to compare some or all of them with each other. For example, the study may include four groups—three treatment groups (A, B, C) and one control group (D). The investigator may conduct an overall test (analysis of variance) to see if there are group differences. If the differences are statistically significant, several individual comparisons may be made to identify which groups differ from each other. Alternatively, the investigator may forgo the overall test. Several two-group (pairwise) comparisons may be completed as each treatment (A, B, C) is compared to each other treatment and to the control (D) group. Alpha might be set at $p \leq .05$ to protect against the risk of a Type I error. This alpha refers to the risk for a given comparison, sometimes referred to as a *per-comparison error rate*. However, there are multiple comparisons. With multiple tests the overall error rate or risk of a Type I error can be much higher. This increase is sometimes referred to as *probability pyramiding* to note that the accumulation of the actual probability of a Type I error increases with the number of tests. How much higher the p level increases depends directly on the number of different comparisons. In fact, with a number of comparisons, each held at the per-comparison rate of .05, the probability of concluding that some significant effect has been obtained can be very high. In our hypothetical example with four groups, the investigator may make all possible comparisons of the groups (six total pairwise comparisons, A versus B, A versus C, and so on). Although the pairwise error rate is

.05, the risk of a Type I error for the experiment is greater because of the number of tests. This overall rate is referred to as the *experiment-wise error rate*. We must control for the probability of a Type I error for all of the comparisons or for the experiment-wise error rate. That is, the alpha selected must account for the number of pairwise comparisons.

Several multiple-comparison tests are available to address the problem of experiment-wise error rate and to control the increased Type I risk (see Benjamin & Hochberg, 1995; Hochberg & Tamhane, 1987). Many of the more familiar multiple-comparison tests are known by the name of the persons primarily responsible for their development (e.g., various tests by Tukey, Duncan, Scheffé). A relatively simple alternative is referred to as the Bonferroni procedure and consists of a way to adjust alpha in light of the number of comparisons that are made. Consider how the test operates. In a set of comparisons the upper boundary of the probability of rejecting the null hypothesis is the number of comparisons (k) times alpha (α) (e.g., $p = .05$). Obviously, if there are 10 comparisons to be made, then the overall error rate is $k\alpha$ or .50. As a protection against a Type I error, $p = .50$ would clearly be unacceptable. To control the overall error rate, alpha can be adjusted for the number of comparisons.

The *Bonferroni adjustment* is based on dividing alpha ($p = .05$) by the number of comparisons. In our four-group study, there are six possible pairwise comparisons, as mentioned before. If we set alpha at .05, we know our risk is actually much higher, given the number of comparisons. To make an adjustment, we divide alpha by the number of tests. In our example, we divide .05/6 which yields $p = .0083$. For each of the individual pairwise comparisons that we complete (group A versus B, A versus C, A versus D, and so on), we use $p \leq .0083$ as the criterion for significance. If we use this criterion, then our overall experiment-wise error rate is controlled at $p = .05$.

The Bonferroni adjustment controls the overall (experiment-wise) error rate, for example, at $p \leq .05$. The error rates for the individual comparisons (per comparison) need not be equal (e.g., all at $p \leq .0083$ in the prior example). Individual comparisons can vary in their per-comparison alpha level, if the investigator wishes greater power for some tests rather than others, as long as the overall per-comparison alpha levels do not exceed the experiment-wise error rate of .05 when summed for all comparisons.

The adjustment of alpha, as noted here, arises when several pairwise comparisons are made on a given measure. A similar concern, elevated alpha, emerges when there are multiple outcome measures and multiple tests comparing the same groups for each measure. For example, if two groups of patients (anxious versus nonanxious patients) are compared on several different measures, the chance of finding a significant difference, when there is none in the population, is higher than $p = .05$ for a given comparison. Here, too, the Bonferroni adjustment can be used for the number of comparisons where k refers still to the number of comparisons or tests. As before, for each pairwise test, the adjusted level is used to decide whether the effects are statistically significant.

Considerations.   There is general agreement that multiple comparisons require some adjustment to control for Type I error. Failure to consider the multiplicity of the comparisons has direct implications for statistical conclusion validity, in this case, often concluding that there are significant differences when, by the usual criteria for alpha, none exists. That is, when so many comparisons are made without controlling for the experiment-wise error rate, the likelihood of obtaining some significant effects by chance increases. Beyond these general points, and at the point investigators need to make data-analytic decisions, agreement diminishes. For example, which multiple-comparison tests are appropriate and whether a given test is too conservative or stringent are two areas where reasonable statisticians can disagree. Use of such an adjustment as the Bonferroni procedure is fairly common. Although the adjusted alpha is reasonable, the consequence can be sobering in a given study. In practice the number of significant effects decreases when an adjusted level is used. Stated differently, as the alpha for individual pairwise comparisons becomes more stringent, power decreases, and the probability of a Type II error increases.

Within the current practices of significance testing, control of Type I error, rather than Type II error and power, is given the highest priority. Hence, investigators are encouraged (by tradition, research advisors, reviewers, editors) to keep alpha at .05 or .01 almost at all costs. The difficulty for this orientation in research is that we already know that power in most psychological studies is likely to be weak. When adjustments are made to control overall alpha levels, power of a study decreases even further. That is, apart from a relatively small sample size, the investigator is burdened by correcting for the number of statistical tests. Understandably, investigators are reluctant to adjust for the large number of tests they complete.

There are alternatives for the investigator who believes central findings are supported by the statistical comparisons but sees them disappear when alpha is adjusted to control the experiment-wise error rate. First, the investigator can present the results for both adjusted and nonadjusted alpha levels. The results can note the tests that remain significant under both circumstances and those that are significant when left unadjusted. This is not a completely satisfactory solution, but addresses the ambivalence and tension both in the author and field at large, namely, to identify what the effects are, to retain power at a reasonable level, but not to get carried away with an extraordinarily large number of tests, only a few of which are statistically significant.

Second, the investigator can select an experiment-wise alpha that is slightly more lenient than $p < .05$, such as $p < .10$, prior to making the adjustment. The Bonferroni adjustment will divide this alpha by the number of comparisons. The per-comparison alpha is still below .05, depending on the number of comparisons. Adopting an experiment-wise rate of .10 is usually less of a concern to other researchers than adopting this rate for individual comparisons (per-comparison rate).

Third, the investigator may not be interested in all possible comparisons, but rather in only a preplanned subset that relates specifically to one or two primary hypotheses. Adjusting alpha for this smaller number of comparisons means that the per-comparison rate (of alpha) is not as stringent. Indeed, for a few planned comparisons, not adjusting for the number of tests is usually viewed as satisfactory. Here the difference is in conveying at the outset of the study what the hypotheses are and what specific tests will be used to evaluate them. Direct, planned, and a priori comparisons are usually favored. If any additional, supplementary, or exploratory analyses are conducted, these might be more conservatively tested (e.g., with adjusted p levels).

The alternatives do not exhaust the range of possibilities. One commonly used option is that investigators note there will be multiple tests and say they will adopt a more stringent criterion (e.g., $p < .001$ instead of .05) for individual tests before they call the effect statistically significant. This is better than ignoring the fact that there are multiple comparisons, but just selecting a more stringent p level is merely an unsystematic way to do the Bonferroni adjustment. The investigator (and reader) will not know the overall experiment-wise error rate. Another option is to use a less conservative variation of the Bonferroni adjustment (Simes, 1986) or a variety of other procedures to control Type I error (Hochberg & Tamhane, 1987). Finally, one can deemphasize tests of significance altogether in the data analysis. Measures of the strength of the relation, such as ES, can be used and are not subject to the same concerns as statistical tests. This alternative is elaborated later because of the broader implications in relation to current research practices. The central point is not to argue for any one solution but rather to underscore the importance of addressing the issue in the data analyses. Any data-analytic issue that can be anticipated also requires consideration at the design stage. Identifying the major comparisons of interest in the study, the statistical tests that will be used, and the number of tests may have implications for sample size and power. All such matters directly affect the conclusions to which the investigator is entitled and hence are critical to consider before the first subject is run.

Multiple Outcomes: Multivariate and Univariate Analyses

In most clinical research multiple measures are used to evaluate the impact of an intervention. For example, in a therapy outcome study, several measures may be obtained to assess different perspectives (clients, relatives, therapists) about the client's functioning in several domains (depression, self-esteem, adjustment at home and at work) and to rely on different assessment formats (interviews, questionnaires, direct observations). When there are multiple measures, the interrelations of the measures raise issues relevant to the data analyses.

Performance on several outcome measures may be *conceptually* related, because they reflect a domain the investigator views as a unit, or *empirically* related, because the measures correlate highly with each other. For instance, if we have 10 dependent measures, we could analyze these separately with t or F tests. This would entail many tests of significance, and we would have an inflated error rate (beyond $p < .05$). We could address the problem of an inflated Type I error with the adjustment (Bonferroni) noted previously. But another issue is pertinent, namely, the fact that the measures may be interrelated. Univariate tests, that is, separate tests for each measure, do not take into account the possible redundancy of the measures and their relation to each other. It is possible, for example, that two outcome measures show significant effects due to treatment. The investigator may discuss how robust the effects are across two measures when, in fact, the high correlation between the measures argues for one construct rather than two. It is possible as well that neither of the measures shows a significant effect, but when viewed as a conceptual whole there is a significant effect. The measures individually may not provide as robust or, indeed, as reliable an effect as they do when combined.

When there are multiple outcome measures, we can consider the data to be multivariate. It may be desirable to conduct multivariate analyses (such as multivariate analyses of variance). *Multivariate analyses include several measures in a single data analysis, whereas univariate analyses examine one measure at a time.* We do not use multivariate analyses merely because we have several dependent measures. Rather, the primary basis is when the investigator is interested in understanding the relations among the dependent measures. The multivariate analyses consider these relations by providing a linear combination of the measures and evaluating if that combination provides evidence for significant differences. For example, the study may include three measures of anxiety. One multivariate analysis might be completed by combining these measures. If the overall multivariate analysis indicates a significant effect, this suggests that some combination of variables has shown the effect of the intervention or independent variable of interest.

After this finding with the overall effect of the multivariate analysis, one might then conduct univariate tests (individual *F* tests on each measure) to identify the specific differences on each of the dependent variables. As before, the alpha would need to be adjusted to avoid elevated Type I error. However, univariate tests may or may not show significant effects following an overall multivariate analysis. The multivariate analysis takes into account the relation of the measures to each other and evaluates the combination of measures. The univariate analyses ignore this facet of the structure of the data and may not lead to similar conclusions.

Considerations.   It may be quite appropriate to analyze the multiple outcome measures with multivariate analysis or with several univariate tests (see Haase & Ellis, 1987; Huberty & Morris, 1989). Multivariate analyses are particularly appropriate if the investigator views the measures as conceptually interrelated and is interested in various groupings of the measures separate from, or in addition to, the individual measures themselves. For example, there may be several measures of patient adjustment and family functioning. Within the study, the investigator may group all of the measures of patient adjustment and conduct a multivariate analysis to identify a combination for this overall conceptual domain and do the same for the measures of family functioning. Separate analyses may also be conducted for the individual scales within each conceptual domain, if they are of interest as well. For example, drug use has been studied among adolescents to understand its onset and course and relation to later adult adjustment (Newcomb & Bentler, 1988). Drug use was conceived as a latent variable (construct with multiple indices) and included three measures, namely, the use of alcohol (beer, wine, liquor), cannabis (marijuana & hashish), and hard drugs (cocaine, barbiturates, LSD, and others). The data analyses focused on drug use (e.g., all of the measures together) because they were conceived as a general tendency toward substance use. The three individual measures were also evaluated separately because some substances (hard drugs) were expected and shown to have particularly deleterious long-term outcomes. However, both levels of analyses—the combined variable and the individual variables—led to quite meaningful and important findings.

Multivariate analyses evaluate the composite variables, based on their interrelations. This is a unique feature and is not addressed by performing several separate univariate tests. Separate univariate tests might be appropriate under a variety of conditions if the investigator does not view the measures as conceptually related, if the measures in fact are uncorrelated, or if the primary or exclusive interest is in the individual measures themselves, rather than how they combine or relate to each other. Investigators occasionally use the multivariate analysis as an overall test. Once significant, they proceed with several univariate tests. Usually, these latter tests are conducted with a per-comparison alpha of .05, and hence the overall risk of Type I error is greatly increased. Findings of statistical significance here is a problem because the multivariate test was assumed to control for a Type I error at the level of alpha ($p <$ .05). The individual univariate tests, if conducted, still require consideration of the number of tests and the experiment-wise error rate.

OBJECTIONS TO STATISTICAL SIGNIFICANCE TESTING

Because statistical significance testing continues to dominate contemporary research, mastery of the issues and methods discussed previously is critically important for those planning a career in research. At the same time there is another side, namely, the view that statistical significance testing, as currently practiced and interpreted, is misleading, counterproductive, and simply flawed (Krueger, 2001). Recommendations include that we either abandon the practice entirely or supplement significance testing with other information (Howard, Maxwell, & Fleming, 2000; Kirk, 1996; Schmidt, 1996; Shrout, 1997). This view is not new, nor is it a radical minority view held by extremists whose dissertations, like mine, turned them against conventional alpha levels.

A brief historical comment is in order. When statistical tests and null hypothesis testing first emerged (Fisher, 1925; Neyman & Pearson, 1928), objections followed challenging the logic and utility of such an approach (Berkson, 1938). From that time until the present, there has been a continuous "crescendo of challenges" (Kirk, 1996, p. 747). For example, among the stronger statements, Meehl (1978, p. 817) noted that significance testing to evaluate the null hypothesis, "is a terrible mistake, is basically unsound, poor scientific strategy and one of the worst things that ever happened in the history of psychology." (Of course, as a clinical psychologist, I find this statement hard to interpret, but it sounds negative to me.) Meehl has been articulate in stating the case but is by no means alone in the concern. The objections to significance testing pertain to what they do and do not accomplish and how they are misinterpreted. The objections are mentioned briefly as a way of moving toward an alternative recommendation for statistical evaluation of research. Table 15.4 highlights major concerns about the use of statistical tests and misconceptions surrounding their interpretation.

Major Concerns

A key concern among statisticians and methodologists is the entire matter of null hypothesis and statistical significance testing. A difficulty with statistical tests is that in their current use they require us to make a binary decision (accept, reject) for the null hypothesis. We set a level of alpha (e.g., $p < .05$) and decide whether or not to reject the null hypothesis, that is, that there is no difference. The criterion of $p < .05$ is recognized to be arbitrary. Perhaps due to training and use of this criterion, researchers tend to believe that findings at $p < .05$ or lower are genuine effects (i.e., that there are group differences) and reflect a relation, but that above this level ($p > .05$) group

TABLE 15.4.   Statistical Significance: Common Concerns and Misconceptions

Concerns

- Arbitrary criterion that is rigidly invoked
- All-or-none decision making
- H_0 is rarely or never true
- Significance is a function (and measure) of N
- Tests are more subjective than meets the eyes
- Says nothing about strength or importance of the effects

Misconceptions (i.e., It is not true that . . .

- p reflects the likelihood that, or degree to which, the null hypothesis (H_0) is true
- Higher p value ($p < .0001$) is a more potent or stronger effect
- Higher p value is an effect more likely to be replicated
- No difference means that there is no real effect, but a difference means that there is
- There are nonsignificant "trends" or there is a difference that "approached" significance ($p < .10$)

differences do not exist or are just chance (Rosenthal & Gaito, 1963). There is no rational basis for this. In their now classic quote, Rosnow and Rosenthal (1989, p. 1277) noted that, "Surely, God loves the .06 nearly as much as the .05."

Related and as noted previously, a concern with significance testing is that the null hypothesis is always, or almost always, false. That is, the means for two groups will always be different (at some decimal), and asking if groups are different "is foolish" (Tukey, 1991, p. 100). This means that whether or not a difference between groups is significant is largely a matter of sample size. With a very large sample size, any difference will become significant. Psychology experiments have become fixed at 10–50 subjects per group in much of the research. This fixes the science at examining what empirical relationships hold, given this sample size. Making a binary decision with this sample size is likely to detect as significant only large ESs. Power to detect differences is weak for most psychology studies for small-to-medium ESs. Weak power is exacerbated when we perform adjustments on the analyses (e.g., Bonferroni) that make alpha more stringent for individual comparisons. Thus, there will be a large tendency to commit Type II errors (not being able to detect a difference when there really is one).

There is the belief that statistical analyses provide a somewhat objective criterion for decision making, and this is the overriding advantage. That is, at least the rules are clear about what is and is not counted as a "real" effect. This is clearly an advantage of statistical tests. At the same time, noted previously was the point that there is considerable subjectivity in selection and use of statistical tests, and hence the conclusions that reached from these. Underlying applications of many statistical tests (default criteria, rules for decision making) are arbitrary and can be changed by the investigator (e.g., when to make cutoffs for allowing variables to enter into a regression equation), and findings can be significant or not significant as a result.

Perhaps the main concern is that tests of statistical significance do not say anything about the strength (magnitude) or importance of an effect. The degree or magnitude of association is more critical than whether the results are statistically significant, especially because statistical significance is so dependent on sample size. It is not difficult to identify strong effects (large ES) where group differences were not statistically significant and weak effects where group differences were statistically significant. An example is provided below to convey how identical findings and a medium-to-large ES can yield both significant and nonsignifcant effects. In general, when groups are truly different, we care less about the actual p value and more about whether the differences are large, small, or in-between. Also, when we consider multiple independent variables (e.g., prediction studies), we want to know their relative impact in relation to some criterion or outcome. Statistical significance testing alone does not provide such information.

Misinterpretations

Leaving aside objections to null hypothesis and statistical testing, there are a number of concerns about how the tests are interpreted by investigators and by consumers. A set of related misconceptions pertain to the obtained p value in a study. Many investigators believe that the p value reflects the likelihood that the findings are true, the potency or strength of the effect, and the likelihood that a finding will be replicated. Thus, a p of < .002 obtained for a statistical test in a study is often considered to be much better than a p of < .05. It is the case that such a p value may represent a stronger relationship between the independent and dependent variable (depending on the measure used to evaluate strength, such as ES or r). However, the p value is not a measure of any of these. Rather, it refers to the likelihood that the finding would be obtained by chance if a large number of tests were run.

Another misconception, usually applied to someone else's research rather than to our own, is that no difference (statistically) means that there really is no difference in the world. That is, when we accept the no-difference hypothesis, this means that, in fact, the effect of the manipulation is zero or that conditions (treatment versus control) really are not different. This is a misconception because a finding of no difference can depend on many aspects of the study, including sample size, but also the conditions under which the hypothesis was tested (sample, how the manipulation was operationalized). There are many circumstances in which a no-difference finding is quite interpretable (discussed in the next chapter), but as a general rule it is not quite right to assume that no difference on a statistical test means no difference or no impact of one variable on another in fact.

Finally and painfully for many of us as authors, null hypothesis and statistical testing requires regrettable and rigid adherence to p levels that are selected in advance of a study. If the study uses p < .05, then we are somewhat stuck with the binary decision of accepting or rejecting the null hypothesis, as said before. Strictly, the tests are conducted to see whether the criterion of p is met or surpassed. Thus, one ought not to discuss "trends" in the data (a trend is a slope, so that term is not properly used anyway). So, if the statistical test shows that p = .07, one does not say the test approached significance. Rather, the test is not significant! There is not a trend, an almost significant effect, a borderline effect, or other creative terms. (Again, this is precisely why I adopted as alpha p < .33 for all my tests—my advisors hated it, but it solved a lot of problems for me.)

By the rules of science to which we have implicitly agreed, a nonsignificant finding is just that. If one wishes to detect almost-significant findings, then there are all sorts of options, such as those discussed previously to increase power. Other options are available as well, such as emphasizing magnitude of effect rather than statistical significance and null hypothesis testing. However, within the rules of the science and null hypothesis testing game, nonsignificance ought to be adhered to in deciding whether to reject or accept the null hypothesis. "Approached significance"—words authors often use—has no special meaning and translates to approached or almost rejected the null hypothesis. Near misses are not what this is all about. They count as misses.

Mentioned above was the fact that a higher level p value (e.g., $p < .0001$ rather than $p < .05$) does not necessarily mean that the effect is more potent, stronger, or important or more likely to be replicated in a subsequent study. Authors often use terms that convey a misconception about this. One can identify authors referring to "highly significant effect." This usually means that p was much less than the alpha selected. The term is funny because there is an implication that the finding may reflect highly significant in some other way than statistical, and it may not.

Significance Testing and Failures to Replicate

Significance testing may impede replication and the accumulation of knowledge. There are all sorts of contradictory findings and failures to replicate. To be sure, many of these might come from the fact that a given finding may depend on moderating influences (age, sex, social class of the population) and variations in the samples among the different studies. In relation to the present discussion we are confronted with a more dramatic point, namely, that *identical findings can yield contradictory results when statistical significance testing is the basis for drawing inferences.*

Consider for a moment that we have completed a study and obtained an ES of .70. This magnitude of effect is one that is about the level of ES demonstrated when psychotherapy is compared with no treatment. An ES of this magnitude indicates a fairly strong relation and would be considered as a moderate-to-large ES. Would an ES of this magnitude also be reflected in statistically significant group differences? The answer depends on the sample size.

Consider two hypothetical studies, both with an ES of .70. In Study I we have a two-group study with 10 cases in each group ($N = 20$). In Study II suppose we have two groups with 30 cases in each group ($N = 60$). (Although this example is hypothetical, there are scores and scores of studies with sample sizes evident in the example.) We complete each study and are ready to analyze the data. In each study we have two groups, so we decide to evaluate group differences using a t test. The t-test formula can be expressed in many ways. The relation between statistical significance and effect size for our two-group study can be seen in the formula:

$$t = \text{ES} \times \frac{1}{\sqrt{1/n_1 + 1/n_2}}$$

where $\text{ES} = (m_1 - m_2)/s$.

In Study I, when ES = .70 and there are 10 cases in each of the two groups, the above formula yields a t = 1.56 with degrees of freedom (df) of 18 (or $n_1 + n_2 - 2$). If we consult a table for the Student's t distribution, we note that a t of 2.10 is required for p = .05. Our t does *not* meet the $p \leq .05$ level, and we conclude no difference between groups 1 and 2.

In Study II, when ES = .70 and there are 30 cases in each of the two groups, the above formula yields a t = 2.71, with a df of 58. If we consult Student's t distribution, we note that the t we obtained is higher than the t of 2.00 required for this df at p < .05. Thus, we conclude that groups 1 and 2 *are* different. Obviously, we have two studies with identical effects but diametrically opposed conclusions about group differences. This is chaos and not how we want our science to proceed.

In this example identical results yielded different conclusions. The implications on a broad scale are enormous. When we express skepticism in noting that a finding was found in one study but not replicated in another, this is based on the fact that in one study the results were statistically different, and in another study they were not. In the accumulation of knowledge we have not separated those failures to replicate that, in fact, reflect similar results (ESs) from those that represent genuine differences in the findings.

ALTERNATIVES OR SUPPLEMENTS TO TESTS OF SIGNIFICANCE

It is easy to criticize statistical significance testing; the arguments have been well articulated for the past 60 years, and real examples can be cited to show the foolishness of our ways. Generating alternatives has not been a problem, and three common suggestions are summarized in Table 15.5 and elaborated here.

Magnitude and Strength of Effect

In place of (or in addition to) statistical significance testing, it would be helpful to report some measure of the magnitude or strength of the relation between the independent and dependent variable or the magnitude of the differences between groups. In clinical research the notion of the strength of the relation is obviously important. For example, if we wish to compare parents who abuse their children with parents who do not, we do not merely wish to demonstrate statistically significant differences on several measures (parent stress, family functioning). In addition, we wish to know the strength of association and magnitude of the relation between parental abuse status and other variables. If all of the variables we study differentiate abusive from nonabusive parents, we would like to know the strength of these connections and the relative contribution of each.

Magnitude of effect or strength of the relation can be expressed in many different ways, including omega^2 (ω^2), eta (η), epsilon^2 (ε^2), and Pearson product-moment correlation (r, r^2), and in multiple regression (R and R^2) (see Haase, Ellis, & Ladany, 1989; Kirk, 1996; Rosenthal, 1984; Rosenthal & Rosnow, 1991). One measure we have already discussed is ES, which illustrates nicely the informational yield provided beyond

TABLE 15.5.   Alternatives or Supplements to Significance Tests

1. **Magnitude or Strength of Effect**

   Familiar examples include effect size (ES or Cohen's *d*), *r*, *r²*, *R*, *R²*, but there are many others (omega², eta, epsilon²)

2. **Confidence Intervals**

   Provide range of values and the likelihood that the ES in the population falls within a particular range

   $$\text{CI} = m \pm z_\alpha s_m$$

   Where

       m = the mean score

       z_α = the *z* score value (two-tailed) under the normal curve, depending on the confidence level (z = 1.96 and 2.58 for *p* = .05 and *p* = .01)

       s_m = the standard error of measurement, that is, the estimate the standard deviation of a sampling distribution of means or the standard deviation divided by the square root of N ($s_m = s/\sqrt{N}$).*

3. **Meta-Analysis**

   Extends the use of ES across many studies—a way to combine studies, to review a literature, and to identify better estimates of population parameters (ES, CIs)

*The standard error of the mean, noted here as s_m, refers to the estimate of the *standard deviation of a sampling distribution of means*. That is, the mean of a study is an estimate of the mean in the population. If one were to run the study many different times—indeed, an infinite number of times, each drawing a random sample of subjects for the population—each study would yield a mean. These means form a sampling distribution of means, that is, each mean is a data point. The overall mean or the mean of these means would provide the "real" or population mean μ. But not all the means that were sampled would be the same; they would vary a bit. The standard error of the mean is the standard deviation of the sampling distribution of the means and reflects how much sample means may be expected to depart from the population mean. In a single study we conduct, the standard error of the mean helps us to estimate, with some level of confidence, the likelihood that the population mean will fall within the range we present. If the standard error of the mean is small, then when multiplied by ± the *z* score (1.96), the range will be relatively small and we can be reasonably assured that the population mean is within the range.

statistical significance. Effect size permits one to provide a point estimate of what the strength of the relation is between variables. The utility of this estimate is in conveying the relation, not deciding whether the relation is or is not statistically significant. Also, ES is familiar in light of its frequent use in meta-analyses. Moreover, with ES, the magnitude of effect is provided in a common metric that allows comparison (and combination) of different experiments using different outcome measures.

An ES of .2, .5, or .8 can be interpreted in terms of standard deviation units. In a study comparing an intervention and a control group, an ES of .70, is readily interpretable in relation to the differences in the distributions between treatment and no-treatment groups. That is, ES can be translated into more concrete terms. Figure 15.1 shows two distributions, one for the treatment group and one for the control group. The means of the group (vertical lines) reflect an ES of .70, that is, the mean of the intervention group is 7/10 of a standard deviation higher than the control group. One

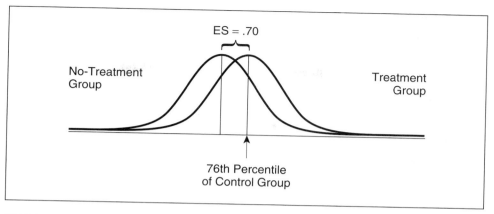

FIGURE 15.1.   Representation of an effect size of .70 between an intervention and a control group. Each group is reflected in its own distribution (normal curve). If the groups, in fact, are not different, the two distributions would be superimposed on one another and look like one distribution (same mean, same standard deviation). With an effect size of .70, the mean of the intervention group is .7 standard deviation units above the mean of the control group. The two distributions are discrepant.

can go to a table of the normal distribution and convert this information into how persons in the intervention group fared relative to control subjects in standard deviation units. Given the ES of .70, the average subject who received treatment is better off than 76 percent of the persons who did not receive treatment. This percentage was obtained by identifying what percentage of the population is below +.70 standard deviation units on the normal distribution.

Another familiar measure for evaluating the strength of the relationship is *r*. The correlation reflects the relation between the independent variable and the dependent variable. The correlation squared is used to reflect shared variance in these variables. Correlation is, in fact, provided in many studies. Studies using multiple regression often report R or R^2 to convey how much variance is accounted for by predictors and outcomes. Both ES and *r* are easily computed from formulae provided in introductory statistics books. Also, these estimates can be computed directly from familiar statistical tests of significance for comparing two groups. Note the easy conversions in Table 15.6. These convey that once one has a *t* or χ^2, one can provide further information on ES and *r*. Thus, in terms of reporting results, one can derive with relative ease more (and perhaps more important) information than statistical significance.

Confidence Intervals

Effect size (or some other measure of magnitude of effect) provides a point estimate, that is, a specific value that estimates the population value. To supplement this estimate, confidence intervals are also recommended (Kirk, 1996; Schmidt, 1996). A *confidence interval* provides a range of values and reflects the likelihood that the ES in the population falls within a particular range. Common values used for confidence

TABLE 15.6.   Some simple conversions to move from tests of statistical significance to magnitude of the relation or effect size

$$ES = \frac{2t}{\sqrt{df}}$$

$$ES = \frac{2r}{\sqrt{1 - r^2}}$$

$$r = \sqrt{\frac{t^2}{t^2 + df}}$$

$$r = \sqrt{\chi^2 (1) / N}$$

intervals are 95 percent or 99 percent, which parallel statistical criteria for alpha of .05 and .01. The formula for computing confidence intervals (CIs) was given in Table 15.5.

Confidence intervals provide a range of values within which the true differences between groups are likely to lie. Even though this is a range, it also includes the information that one obtains from a statistical test of significance, because z values used for significance testing (e.g., z score of 1.96 for $p = .05$) are used to form the upper and lower confidence intervals. Effect size provides a point estimate of the differences between groups in standard deviation units; confidence intervals provide the same metric above and below that mean. In addition, the data can be easily presented in terms of the original measurement unit (total scores, IQ points) so they are more readily interpretable. Thus, the $m_1 - m_2$ portion of the ES formula is the difference in the original measurement unit of the scale (not standard deviation units); confidence intervals can also be presented in this original metric. Thus, one could state, for example, that in a psychotherapy study treatment A was better than treatment B with an ES = .70, with $CI_{95\%}$: .35, 1.05. This means that we can be 95 percent confident that the ES we obtained falls within the range of .35 to 1.05. Alternatively, the same data may be presented as a mean difference (difference scores between groups 1 and 2 on some symptom scale) as 15 points with (for example) a $CI_{95\%}$: 10, 20 points on that symptom measure. Both are equivalent. The ES in standard deviation units is readily interpretable in terms of strength of effect (*a la* Cohen's recommendations for small, medium, and large effects); the mean difference presented on the original metric of scores on a measure, with the confidence intervals, communicates to those familiar with the measure exactly how great the difference is.

Meta-Analysis

For individual studies ES and confidence intervals provide useful statistics that have been proposed to replace, or at the very least to supplement, statistical tests. The advantage extends beyond the individual study. Meta-analysis is an extension of the use of ES for evaluating multiple studies. As mentioned before, meta-analysis is a methodology or secondary analysis in which multiple studies are evaluated and combined.

Meta-analyses have many purposes, one of which is to permit a quantitative evaluation (review) of a literature. In relation to the present discussion meta-analysis is useful to note as a method to contribute to the knowledge base more generally (Howard et al., 2000). The method permits combining several studies but in the process accomplishes much more than merely providing a review of them. We have learned that one has to interpret any single study quite cautiously. Sampling alone might mean that the results are not representative of the true population value (or difference). Also, characteristics of any single study (sample, geography, way in which the intervention was manipulated, specific measures used) raise threats to external validity, that is, the extent to which the results might be generalizable.

Meta-analyses combine many different ESs and many different studies and hence can provide a better estimate of the population parameters. Moreover, questions can be asked of the literature that an individual study cannot easily provide. For example, in meta-analyses of psychotherapy research, investigators have examined whether treatment is more effective (ESs are larger in treatment versus no-treatment comparisons) as a function of experience of the therapist, age of the subjects, types of problems for which subjects are referred for treatment, and methodological quality of the study (Shadish & Ragsdale, 1996; Weisz & Weiss, 1993). The questions are ones that were not asked in the original investigations. However, across many studies, each study can be coded on new variables of interest. Effect sizes become the dependent variable for the new questions that are asked of research. Thus, meta-analysis goes beyond describing a given literature, but also can be used to address questions and test explanations of the literature that were not raised in the original investigations (see Cook et al., 1992).

The use of ES as a part of individual investigations will facilitate the integration of studies in systematic ways through meta-analyses. The meta-analyses, apart from their ability to review a literature in a quantitative way, will permit us to have better estimates of true effects (population ES) and the range within which these lie (confidence intervals of the ESs). This is much more valuable than tests that seek statistical significance. We want to know the impact of our interventions and differences that specific variables yield (e.g., in case-control studies). Estimates of the magnitude of effect or strength of relations through some other measure (ES, r) give us the information we seek. Combining measures across studies, as illustrated by meta-analyses, not only allows us to provide better estimates of ESs but also permits us to use the literature to address new questions.

Statistical Significance, Magnitude of Effect, and Clinical Significance

I have discussed statistical significance and magnitude of effects in this chapter and clinical significance in the context of intervention studies in the previous chapter. Usually, the difference between statistical significance and magnitude of effect (ES, r) is readily understood. More likely to be confused are the differences between magnitude of effect and clinical significance.

Statistical significance has to do with the probability-based criterion for judging whether an effect is reliable and, of course, has little to do with the practical importance of the effect. Strength of effect (ES, *r*) is the magnitude of the experimental effect, the amount of variance shared, and how much the variables are related. A large ES may not have any bearing on whether a finding is clinically significant. One obvious reason is that the dependent variable that shows a large ES may be unrelated to everyday performance (a reaction time, specific cognitive processes). Even if the measure is relevant to a clinical problem, a large ES cannot be translated to clinical significance.

For example, consider the results of a study for the treatment of obesity. Assume that everyone in the intervention group loses 2 pounds (.91 kilogram) and everyone in the control group gains 2 pounds. Yet, at the end of the study all participants may still be very obese. Effect size for this result might be very large, but this does not convey whether the weight and health status have actually improved for anyone. Did treatment help anyone in palpable ways? We do not know from ES, but a 2-pound loss is not very likely to qualify. In other words, statistical significance, effect size (or other magnitude of effect measures), and clinical significance provide different information about the data, even though they are all quantitative methods of evaluating the results.

Evaluation of the clinical or applied importance of the change usually is used as a supplement to statistical methods of determining whether group differences or changes over time are reliable. Once reliable changes are evident, further efforts are made to quantify whether treatment has moved the client appreciably closer to adequate functioning, that is, whether the change is important. Measures of clinical significance are of great importance. Beyond the context of treatment, measures that convey whether a finding makes a difference on a real-world measure are important. Psychology and psychological research is in the public domain and addresses many questions of interest to everyday life and policy. Consequently, beyond the usual research criteria (statistical significance, magnitude of effect), there is often great value in showing that impact of an intervention affects domains and measures that people care about.

General Comments

It is not clear whether statistical significance testing is here to stay. Null hypothesis testing is not the only way in which statistical evaluation of results can be conducted.[4] At this time we know that there has been a continuous literature lamenting the use of significance tests and recommending alternatives. Indeed, R.A. Fisher, who is credited with (or, given fickle history, blamed for) beginning significance testing, recommended that researchers supplement their significance tests with measures of the strength of the association between independent and dependent variables. Indeed, we would like to know more than whether a null hypothesis can be rejected; in fact, we may not really care at all about the null hypothesis, in light of comments noted previously that the null hypothesis is never really true. Also, we want to know about

---

[4]Bayesian analyses represent one alternative that is often advocated. In such analyses the investigator does not test the null hypothesis but rather estimates the likelihood that a particular hypothesis is correct. Bayesian analyses are often advocated for use in psychology (see Howard et al., 2000). Use of these analyses is increasing in many sciences (astrophysics, genomics, medicine) in which null hypothesis testing has been the rule (Malakoff, 1999).

our hypotheses, that is, the size or magnitude of the effects we study and whether they are important (are very strong). Efforts have been made to move away from the exclusive focus on statistical significance testing in favor of methods highlighted here. For example, the American Psychological Association has convened a task force to consider significance evaluation in research and to make recommendations on reporting and interpreting statistical tests (see Wilkinson et al., 1999). Among the recommendations is the call to supplement the usual tests of significance with other indices of the findings (ES, confidence intervals). Statistical significance tests still dominate, and it is important for researchers to be familiar with the key issues (e.g., power) and the benefits of supplementing such tests with additional information.

SUMMARY AND CONCLUSIONS

Statistical significance testing is the dominant method to analyze the results of research. In the vast majority of instances, statistical tests are completed to test the null hypothesis (no difference) and to determine whether the differences between or among groups are statistically significant. Statistical tests use probability levels to make this judgment and are based primarily on the concern for protecting a Type I error, that is, rejecting the null hypothesis when that hypothesis actually is true. Because statistical significance remains the primary criterion in evaluating results of research, it is incumbent on the researcher to understand how to design studies that have a reasonable test of demonstrating differences when they exist.

Issues critical to statistical evaluation were discussed, including significance levels, power, sample size, significance and magnitude of effects, multiple-comparison tests, and multivariate data. Statistical power has received the greatest discussion in research because it shows most clearly the interrelation of alpha, sample size, and ES. Evaluations of research have shown repeatedly that the majority of studies are designed in such a way as to have weak power. The obvious solution to increasing power is to increase sample size, although usually this is not very feasible, in part because adding very many, rather than simply a few, subjects is often required. Additional strategies to increase power include using stronger manipulations or more sharply contrasted experimental conditions (to increase ES), using pretests or repeated measures to reduce the error term, varying alpha (in advance of the data analyses) in selected circumstances outlined previously, using directional tests of significance, and minimizing error variability in all facets of the experiment to the extent possible. There is much an investigator can do, even when sample size cannot be increased.

Several topics related to the use of statistical testing were discussed. Intent-to-treat and completer analyses are two strategies used to handle missing data in intervention research where there are repeated measures and cases that drop out. Also, multiple-comparison tests and the need to control error rates (Type I error) were presented as well. Finally, the uses of multivariate and univariate tests and the relation of these to error rates were highlighted.

Since statistical significance testing emerged, there has been ongoing dissatisfaction about the utility of this approach for research. Among the many concerns is the fact that null hypothesis and statistical significance testing give us arbitrary cutoff points to make binary decisions (accept or reject the null hypothesis), and most importantly does not provide the critical information we would like (direct tests of *our* hypotheses and information about the strengths of our interventions). Moreover, the null hypothesis probably should not be tested; it is never, or almost never, true. Statistical significance is said to be more of a measure of sample size than anything else; with a large sample, a difference between means is more likely to become statistically significant. Among the recommendations there has been some consensus that measures of the strength or magnitude of the relation ought to be provided in presenting the quantitative results. Effect size (ES) and Pearson product-moment correlation (r) were discussed, but there are many such measures. A point estimate of the likely effect (e.g., ES) and a range of values about that effect (confidence intervals) would provide more useful information for interpreting our studies.

KEY CONCEPTS AND TERMS

Bonferroni Adjustment	Experiment-Wise Error Rate
Completer Analysis	Intent-to-Treat Analysis
Confidence Interval	Magnitude of Effect

FOR FURTHER READING

Cohen, J. (1992). A power primer. *Psychological Bulletin, 112,* 155–159.

Howard, G.S., Maxwell, S.E., & Fleming, K.J. (2000). The proof of the pudding: An illustration of the relative strengths of null hypothesis, meta-analysis, and Bayesian analysis. *Psychological Methods, 5,* 315–332.

Hubbard, R., & Ryan, P.A. (2000). The historical growth of statistical significance testing in psychology—And its future prospects. *Educational and Psychological Measurement, 60,* 661–681.

Krueger, J. (2001). Null hypothesis significance testing: On the survival of a flawed method. *American Psychologist, 56,* 16–26.

Mazumdar, S., Liu, K.S., Houck, P.R., & Reynolds, C.F., III (1999). Intent-to-treat analysis for longitudinal clinical trials: Coping with the challenge of missing values. *Journal of Psychiatric Research, 33,* 87–95.

Nickerson, R.S. (2000). Null hypothesis significance testing: A review of an old and continuing controversy. *Psychological Methods, 5,* 241–301.

Shrout, P.E. (Editor). (1997). Special series: Should significance testing be banned? Introduction to a special section exploring the pros and cons. *Psychological Science, 8,* 1–20.

Wilkinson, L. & the Task Force on Statistical Inference, APA Board of Scientific Affairs (1999). Statistical methods in psychology journals: Guidelines and explanations. *American Psychologist, 54,* 594–604.

Interpretation of the Data

In many ways methodology is all about the interpretation of findings in a study. As scientists we engage in special practices so the results can be interpreted in one way rather than another. Thus, we want to interpret the findings by explaining how a particular variable of interest to us, rather than some artifact or bias (threats to validity, preexisting group differences), is the basis for the results. Also, when the data are collected and analyzed, we want to explain what happened and why in ways that are in keeping with what was found. Often an investigator makes a little leap moving from the data analysis to the interpretation of what was found. The study then is revealed to be poorly designed. That is, in reading a report of the study, we say if this is what the investigator wished to conclude, then this was not quite the right way to design the study. Thus, data interpretation issues are squarely within the realm of methodology.

This chapter discusses interpretation of the findings. The focus is on the findings of an investigation and common issues and pitfalls that emerge in moving from the results (and Results section) to the interpretation (Discussion section). Also, the chapter focuses on so-called negative results, that is, the absence of differences. Not finding statistically significant differences in a study is often viewed as noninformative and "negative." There are many exceptions to this, and how and when so-called noneffects are important are elaborated. The final topic of the chapter has to do with interpretation that extends beyond one study and focuses on the critical issue of replication of research findings.

INTERPRETING THE RESULTS OF A STUDY

Overview

Data interpretation has to do with how to talk about and discuss the results. In a later chapter I focus on writing up the results of a study, and the emphasis there is on preparation of the manuscript. Here the focus is on the step from quantitative analysis to description and interpretation of the results in narrative form. The task of interpreting the findings is often considered to be straightforward. For those of us now in psychology, it was in our initial training (preschool class on experimental design) where many of us were told that the first task is to describe what the results showed. The task was to put into words what the findings are without using any of the numbers (ps, rs, t test numbers), and just say what happened.

Data interpretation can be tricky because the meaning of the quantitative results of a study can be easily misinterpreted and overinterpreted. Moreover, mis- and overinterpreted can be in the eyes of the beholder. Of course, it is extremely important to go beyond the quite specific experimental arrangement and the statistical results and to say something more general. For example, we usually do not wish to talk about the measures but rather the constructs they reflect; we do not wish to talk about the way in which we operationalized the independent variable, but rather the concept our operational definition represents and any implications for theory. Consequently, going beyond the data is a matter of degree and pertains to what one is entitled to say based on the design and data analyses. In this section common issues that emerge in moving from the data to data interpretation in clinical psychological research are highlighted.

Common Leaps in Language and Conceptualization of the Findings

The investigator has many opportunities to make leaps from what was shown in the Results section to what is stated in the discussion of the results. By leap I mean a large step from the finding itself to what that finding really is or shows—and a step to which the investigator may not be entitled in light of what actually was found. Let me highlight some common examples we have already covered and move to new ones.

"Highly Significant Effects."   The notions of statistical and clinical significance raise useful opportunities for mis- and overinterpretation. Regarding the former, if a finding is statistically significant and the p level is computed as $p < .0001$, as opposed to the more modest $p < .05$, we as investigators are often thrilled. (Please recall the comments of the previous chapter that the lower the p value is not how null hypothesis testing works.) The results now may be referred to as "highly significant," which has no real statistical meaning or special role in null hypothesis testing. Related, but still distinguishable, in discussing the results, it is very easy to move from the concept and words "statistically significant"—which, of course, has a very restricted meaning—to the word "significant," which has a very general meaning that includes important and noteworthy. In our minds as we interpret the data, we often make this shift. A statistically significant effect can, of course, be important, but it can also be trivial. Similarly, if a clinically significant effect is evident in a treatment outcome study, the investigator is wont to comment on how the lives of the clients have been changed by one treatment more than another. Yet, as also discussed in the prior chapter, we really do not have the data to make this claim when the usual measures of clinical significance are used. That is, clinically significant effects, by and large, have not been shown to really reflect important changes in the repertoire of the clients (Kazdin, 1999). A recommendation from these comments: Be cautious in pairing the words "highly" and "significant." There is no standard meaning to the term, and often it reflects a misunderstanding about hypothesis testing.

One Variable Predicts Another. Another common language/concept leap in a study is one in which several variables are studied at a given point in time (cross-sectional study), and the investigator uses statistical analyses in which the word "prediction" comes up. For example, the investigator may have a conceptual model that notes certain cognitions and personality characteristics underlie depression. A bunch of subjects are assessed, and any one of several analyses (structural equation modeling, multiple regression, discriminant analysis, logistic regression, to mention a few) is used to predict depression. The word prediction may come out of some of the computer printouts of the data analyses. In the context of the data analysis, prediction means only that the measures are correlated. The investigator chose cognitions and personality characteristics as predictors of depression. But all the measures were obtained in the study at the same point in time (time 1), and hence there only is correlation. As the investigator moves to the interpretation of the results, a little leap is often made in the use of the word prediction. That is, the investigator may use the word to imply a time line and to note that some cognitions and personality characteristics come together to produce depression. That is, we have subtly moved from correlate (all that really was shown in the data analysis) to a risk factor (antecedent) for, or even a cause of, depression.

Correlations among variables are important, of course, and may have critical theoretical and applied implications. The only issue here pertains to use of words at the interpretation stage of the study in which there is any implication that one element occurs before another. Any time one sees the word *prediction* in a discussion of the results, it is important to be mindful of whether the design warrants the use in which a time line is implied.

Implications of My Findings. A final illustration in the move from data analysis to discussion and interpretation of the findings has to do with the notion of implications. In a study we discuss the implications of our results. This is critically important, and any comments here are not intended to deter such discussion. Rather, I mention the issue to continue the focus on instances where too much or too far can lead to over-interpretation of the findings. The word "implications" actually is wonderful, and I personally have used the word and concept in occasional articles as I try to make my own research relevant to something that might actually make a difference in the world.

The problem is that "implications" is sometimes used as a ticket to enter any topic one wishes. Indeed, it would be a useful exercise, if not a new measure of intelligence or creativity, to ask students, investigators, and faculty to discuss the implications in relation to . . . (and then draw one random topic from a bowl in which all topics within psychology, social and biological sciences, and social policy more generally are written individually on small pieces of paper). When the investigator uses the word *implications,* he or she is asking for a momentary carte blanche, and we are advised to grant that. The Implications section may stimulate new lines of work and make connections that the reader would not otherwise make.

There are exceptions in which implications seem to be close to the data but are misleading. In clinical psychology and related areas, the one that seems to emerge the most frequently pertains to treatment and prevention. Let us consider a longitudinal study that predicts some outcome (e.g., teen sexual promiscuity and drug exploration) and does so by looking at early risk factors (antecedents). We find that at age 5 poor relations with peers and parents predict early onset of sexual activity and drug exploration. This is hypothetical and please permit the simplifications. We have more than correlates because the antecedents, in fact, occurred before the outcome. The time-line problem is resolved. In the discussion, investigators are often eager to discuss the preventive implications of the findings, and invariably we are told that interventions ought to target (focus on, change, redress) the antecedents. In this case we ought to focus early in childhood on peer and parental relations. No doubt these are good things to do, but the recommendation does not really follow from this study. An antecedent and, indeed, risk factor may not be causally related in onset of the problem, and changing the risk factor may have absolutely no impact on changing the problem. The difficulty stems in part from the many roles that antecedents (risk factors) can play in relation to an outcome (Kraemer et al., 1997). We do not focus on something for purposes of intervention just because it comes before the problem; the something could be a proxy for the variable that really makes a difference. These points have been elaborated better in the prior chapter on case-control designs.

In general, authors often feel compelled to address implications for treatment or prevention in studies of clinical research. In many cases, of course, this may not be a stretch. However, there is an underlying issue to be mindful of. Findings may be important in their own right because they elaborate basic issues about affect, cognition, behavior, disorders, adaptive functioning, and so on. We want implications for theory and understanding as much as for application, and these two former types of implication receive less attention.

Multiple recommendations might be gleaned from the discussion. First, consider carefully the implications, and if there is a stretch, make the connections more clearly. Treatment and preventive implications do not follow from many findings, and the often routine efforts to make these connections are weak conceptually and not well based on the findings. Second, when implications *are* drawn, cover theory, research, and application, to the extent possible.

More Data Analyses Can Enhance Data Interpretation

In most research the investigator is searching for overall group differences. That is, if treatment versus no treatment or two different treatments are compared, the investigator is looking for a main effect (overall effect) of the two (or more) conditions. Although there may be an overall effect, it is unlikely that the overall effect applies to everyone. That is, not all people in treatment A improved, and not all people in the no-treatment condition remained the same or failed to improve. There is variation within a group and condition, even when we have an effective treatment. For example, effective treatments for major depression include a number of medications and forms of psychotherapy (interpersonal psychotherapy, cognitive behavior therapy), but 25 to 50 percent of the clients may not respond to treatment, despite an overall group effect (American Psychiatric Association, 2000). In short, there are varied responses or individual differences in relation to an intervention, and an overall group effect can be readily obtained even though a number of individuals do not show improvement. If the predictions of the study call only for an overall group effect, and some critical theoretical proposition requires only this demonstration, by all means it might be fine to remain at the level of a main effect. Yet, it can be very useful to identify individuals who respond quite differently from the overall pattern of the group. Indeed, major advances in sciences—ours and others'—stem from understanding subgroups.

Exploring Treatment Moderators.   Let us say we are interested in comparing cognitive behavior therapy (CBT) versus an attention-placebo condition. At posttreatment we compare the groups on several measures of anxiety. There are two cells (groups) in the study, as illustrated by Figure 16.1 (top panel). It might be useful and informative as a guide for subsequent research to explore this more fully, even though (dare I say it?) this is post hoc and exploratory. For example, consider that we could classify all CBT participants on the basis of whether they improved (e.g., reduced in their symptom scores by some arbitrary unit (such as ≥.75 of a standard deviation on the key outcome measures) or whether they fell within the normative range (one way to operationalize clinical significance). Let us say, now we have two groups, but they are different groups from before (bottom panel of Figure 16.1). We have omitted the placebo group (but easily could include them as well) and are looking at who improved and who did not within the CBT group. We might analyze responders and nonresponders to see if there are any differences at pretreatment. The purpose of these analyses is to generate hypotheses about what might be pertinent, helpful, or relevant to responsiveness to treatment. Because all of this is post hoc and many analyses may be run, special care is needed in interpreting the findings. That is, mining the data may have greater opportunities for chance effects. This is not a reason to avoid data analyses, but a reason to invoke extra stringent care in data interpretation.

Looking for subgroups in this way can be anywhere from uninspired, to interesting, to provocative, depending on what the investigator does and how he or she makes use of the information in later research. In an example from my own work (perhaps toward the uninspired end of the continuum), we evaluated the impact of

FIGURE 16.1. Hypothetical Example: Analyses of Treatment Effects in a Two-Group Study

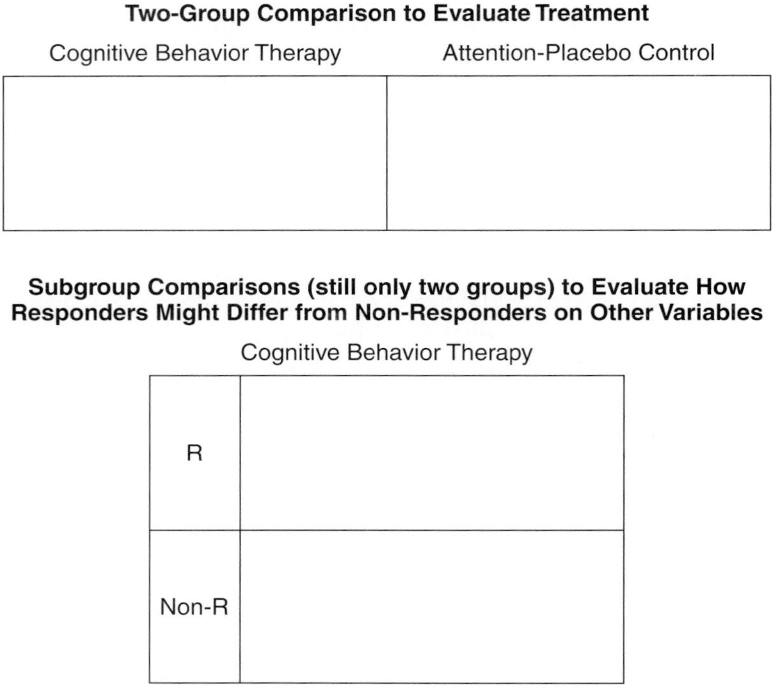

Two-Group Comparison to Evaluate Treatment

Cognitive Behavior Therapy	Attention-Placebo Control

Subgroup Comparisons (still only two groups) to Evaluate How Responders Might Differ from Non-Responders on Other Variables

Cognitive Behavior Therapy

R	
Non-R	

FIGURE 16.1.   A two-group study might be analyzed to make the direct comparison of treatment (upper panel) or to examine influences of possible moderators, that is, factors on which treatment effects may depend (lower panel). In the lower panel the CBT group is divided into two subgroups, based on whether subjects responded well to treatment (R for responders) or did not (non-R for nonresponders). The data can be explored to identify what characteristics differentiate these groups. Likely candidates for analysis in a clinical sample might be severity of clinical dysfunction at pretreatment, presence of comorbid disorders, or, of course, variables that are informed specifically by the theory underlying the therapy or epidemiological findings on the factors that contribute to onset, course, and prognosis of the clinical problem. These are all post hoc analyses rather than predicted, and one must be especially vigilant about limitations (power may be weak, many tests might be done to maximize chance findings). At the same time, not to look at the data has its own drawbacks since multiple clinical studies are difficult to do, and the informational yield for testing and generating hypotheses ought to be maximized.

evidenced-based treatments for children with aggressive and antisocial behavior. In some of the studies we have compared children who completed and therefore received the treatment with those who drop out very early and therefore receive little or no treatment (Kazdin, Mazurick, & Siegel, 1994; Kazdin & Wassell, 1998). We find this rather amazing result—those who complete treatment do much better than those who do not. (How come the Nobel Prize Committee is never around when I report my findings?) Ok. Ok, so this finding is not so special. However, the subgroups become rather interesting—among those who complete treatment, many make large changes and get a lot better, but, of course, some do not get better. Among those who drop out very early (first few sessions), some get much better, but many do not. What distinguishes all of these children, and can this information be used in any way to inform treatment?

It turns out, for very severely disturbed cases (an extreme group in an already clinically referred sample), the outcome differences between completing treatment and dropping out early are not that great. For the rest of the cases, treatment makes a large difference. This is useful to know. Also, further analyses suggest some of the correlates at pretreatment that predict who will improve, whether or not they receive treatment. Some of the factors that predicted who responds to treatment may have "implications" for precisely what is to be done in treatment. For example, if parents perceive barriers to participating in treatment during the treatment course, their children tend to improve less than parents who do not perceive such barriers (Kazdin & Wassell, 1999). Moreover, it appears to be the perception of barriers and not variables that could readily be correlated with such perceptions (socioeconomic disadvantage, stress, degree of parent or child deviance) to account for these results. Post hoc analyses provide useful leads about predicting (i.e., in the next study) who is likely to respond to treatment, to identify more intense or stronger treatments for such individuals, and to test whether one can improve responsiveness of these individuals.

Predicting Treatment Moderators.

Predicting Treatment Moderators.   The search for subgroups or factors that influence who responds to treatment can be described as the search for moderators or for statistical interactions, rather than main effects. The interactions reflect the fact that the impact of one variable is not equal across another condition (sex, severity of dysfunction) but rather varies systematically as a function of that other condition. The search for these other conditions in a post hoc way, as noted previously, is useful, particularly as a guide for subsequent studies.

If at all possible it is especially useful to predict interactions among variables. Predictions about the interactions of independent variables often reflect greater understanding of how the independent variables operate than do predictions about main effects. Interactions begin to delineate the boundary conditions for a particular effect or experimental variable. As the boundary conditions for the effects of a given variable are drawn, a better understanding is available than from the demonstration of a straightforward main effect. For example, an effective treatment for major depression may not be effective for all people with depression or with depression of different types (e.g., resulting from bereavement) or at different ages (e.g., child, adolescent). Post hoc analyses of variables that moderate treatment outcome can be useful, as highlighted previously. Prediction of treatment moderators is usually even better because such research may emanate from a deeper understanding of mechanisms and processes that explain how variables work and why their effects vary under different conditions. Consequently, findings are viewed in the context of how they draw from and contribute to theory and understanding of process. Interactions can provide important leads by identifying what factors are important and by prompting considerations of how these factors might operate.

Aside from the understanding afforded by identifying interactions, these effects often are the most intriguing. Consider an example of an experiment completed many years ago that begs for replication and extension. The goal of the study was to examine factors that contribute to how clients view their therapists (Bloom et al., 1977). In this study the main task of the subject was to rate how qualified, dynamic, and generally believable the therapist was. The investigators proposed that people have stereotypes about therapists based upon many different characteristics of the therapy situation. One of these characteristics may be decor of the therapist's office. So they varied office decor, which was one factor in the design with two different levels: namely, a traditional professional office and a humanistic office.

The traditional professional office was a room with a therapist's chair behind a desk, a file cabinet, and various books. Diplomas were on the wall to help convey the traditional office decor. In the humanistic professional office, using the same room, the desk was placed in a corner so it did not separate the therapist's and client's chair. Indeed, these chairs were placed relatively close together. In lieu of diplomas, posters were displayed around the room with slogans, such as, "Love makes the world go round." Throw pillows and a beanbag chair were also in the room. In short, office decor was varied to create different atmospheres. The authors considered the possibility that the decor might lead to different reactions, depending upon the sex of the subject and the sex of the therapist. Thus, the design included three factors, each with two levels: sex of subject (male, female), sex of therapist (male, female), and office decor (traditional, humanistic). The subjects came to the room individually and read a description of the therapist who supposedly occupied the office. The descriptions were the same for all subjects and for each decor but varied in whether the therapist was said to be a male or female. Subjects never actually met the therapist but filled out a questionnaire about the kind of therapist that was likely to occupy the office.

The major results (in an analysis of variance) yielded an interaction of sex of therapist and office decor. Female therapists were rated as more credible when seen to occupy a traditional professional office than a humanistic office. The opposite was found for males, who were seen as more credible in the humanistic than in the traditional office. One explanation offered for this interesting finding pertains to the stereotypic reactions that individuals might have toward therapists. The investigators suggested that traditional offices might trigger reactions about the occupant being well trained, scientific, and authoritarian. Traditionally, these characteristics might also be stereotypically applied more frequently to males than to females. In contrast, a humanistic office might convey cues that the occupant is sensitive, warm, and caring. These latter characteristics may be more stereotypic of females.

Credibility was the greatest in situations where office cues and gender cues were complementary. Complementary characteristics might convey to subjects the best of both worlds, namely, that the person they are seeing is professional and well trained, but also warm and sensitive. Of course, the precise explanation of the findings remains to be tested further. In addition, there have been so many changes in sexual role identity, activities, and socialization in the past 25 years that one wonders whether the findings are restricted to a specific time period.

The larger point is the one worth underscoring. The interaction of the two variables provides more detail than the search for main effects. Of course, main effects may be all that is needed to support a particular hypothesis or theoretical proposition. Whether one looks for main effects or interactions in her or his research depends largely upon the state of knowledge in a given area of research, the purpose of the research, and one's view of the world.

General Comments

Research would be much simpler if variables operating in the world were restricted to main effects. Results of experiments could be accepted or rejected more easily if a given variable were always shown to have either an effect or no effect. Because variables often do interact with each other, it is difficult to interpret the results of a single experiment. If a variable has no effect, it is always possible that it would have an effect if some other condition of the experiment were altered. That is, the variable may produce no effect for certain subjects, experimenters, or other specific conditions but later produce great effects when any of these other conditions is altered. Often in research we question the external validity (generality) of the findings obtained in a study. Equally, we can question the generality of the findings when an effect is not obtained, that is, whether the variable would have no impact if tested under other conditions.

In one sense, variables studied by psychologists always can be considered to interact with other variables, rather than to operate as individual main effects. Even if no interactions emerge in the analyses of the results, other conditions than those included in the design or data analyses may influence the pattern of results. The conditions of the experiment that are held constant may reflect a narrow set of circumstances under which the variable produces a statistically significant effect. The effect might not be produced as these conditions change. Obviously, the effect of variable X on Y may depend on age of the subjects (infants versus adults) or species (primates versus nonprimates). Few, if any, results obtained by psychologists would be replicated across all possible variations in conditions that could be studied; that is, there are implicit interactions among the conditions studied.

NEGATIVE RESULTS OR NO-DIFFERENCE FINDINGS

In most investigations the presence of an effect is decided on the basis of whether the null hypothesis is rejected. The null hypothesis states that the experimental conditions will not differ, that is, that the independent variable will have no effect. Typically, rejection of this hypothesis is regarded as a "positive" or favorable result, whereas failure to reject this hypothesis is regarded as a "negative" result. Advances in research usually are conceived as a result of rejecting the null hypothesis. As researchers know all too well, many investigations do not yield statistically significant findings or any other evidence that the independent variable influenced the subjects. The term *negative results* has come to mean that there were no statistically significant differences between groups that received different conditions or that the result did not come out the way the investigator had hoped or anticipated. Usually, the term is restricted to the finding that groups did not differ, leading to acceptance of the null hypothesis.

The presence of a statistically significant difference between groups, that is, a "positive result," often is a criterion—indeed, a major criterion—for deciding whether a study has merit and warrants publication. The search for group differences so that the results will be publishable may encourage sacrifice of methodological standards, the possibility of inadvertent bias, or outright dissimulation. Poor methodology and sources of experimental bias are more likely to be overlooked when a predicted or plausible finding of significant differences is obtained. The implicit view is that group differences demonstrate that, whatever failings of the experiment, they were not sufficient to cancel the effects of the independent variable. In contrast, negative results often imply that the independent variable was weak or that the study was poorly designed or conducted.

The value of a study can be assessed as a function of its conceptualization and methodological adequacy, rather than, or at least in addition to, whether differences are found. The conceptualization refers to the importance of the question, the theoretical underpinnings (if applicable), and how well thought out the question is, as described in the report of the study. The methodology refers to all those facts that reflect threats to experimental validity and sources of artifact and bias. Conceptualization and methodology of an investigation bear no necessary relation to the outcome or statistical significance of the findings. A sloppy, ill-conceived, and horribly uncontrolled study can lead to systematic group differences (as my dissertation committee was all too eager to point out in summarizing the main lesson I ought to take from my study). As investigators we wish to proceed with the best or strongest available design and greatest methodological care so that the results of the study, whatever their pattern, will be interpretable. Assuming that the question addressed in the investigation is important to begin with, methodological adequacy of the design, rather than pattern of the results, ought to be the main criterion for evaluating the study. This latter point has been advanced for some time (Greenwald, 1975; Kupfersmid, 1988; Lykken, 1968), although it has yet to be widely adopted. The difficulty in judging the value of any study is that neither the importance of a finding nor methodological adequacy is invariably agreed upon by those who do the judging. Rejection of the null hypothesis and statistical significance are overly relied upon because they present relatively simple bases for evaluating research.

Ambiguity of Negative Results

The absence of group differences in an experiment is not usually met with enthusiasm by the investigator or by the reviewers and editor who may be considering the manuscript for possible publication. This reaction derives from the ambiguity usually associated with negative results. The reason for, or basis of, "no-difference" findings usually cannot be identified in the experiment. (In fact, in most clinical psychological studies the reason for a "difference" finding is not all that clear either in light of construct validity considerations.) The most straightforward reason for accepting the null hypothesis is that there is, in fact, no relation between the independent and dependent variables. There are, however, many other explanations for a "no-difference" finding. Table 16.1 lists some of the main reasons, and they are worth highlighting briefly.

One possibility is that the study had insufficient statistical power to detect a difference that, in fact, was there. Other statistical issues could easily explain the absence of differences, such as whether the assumptions of the data analyses were met, whether adjustments (to control for experiment-wise error rates) were or were not made in the number of tests, and whether outliers (subjects with quite deviant scores) were or were not included in the data analysis, to mention a few. Yet, weak statistical power for detecting small-to-medium effects continues to be the rule in psychological experiments, so this reason alone could explain many of the no-difference findings.

Another possible reason for no differences is that the experimental manipulation was not carried out as intended. No differences between conditions would be expected because of a diffusion of treatment, that is, if not everyone in the treatment group or control group received the planned intervention. Indeed, whether, and the extent to which, therapists adhere to a given treatment manual can influence whether there are effects of that treatment (Frank, Kupfer, Wagner, McEachran, & Cornes, 1991; Huey, Henggeler, Brondino, & Pickrel, 2000). Consequently, diffusion of treatment or variability in delivering a particular treatment may wash out (due to added error variance) any difference that would have been obtained.

We often underestimate the more gross point, namely, can the investigator carry out the intervention at all? For example, assume I invent a new therapy (such as my latest discovery, called *Ear* Movement Desensitization) and show in a controlled trial that it is effective. Now you come along and fail to replicate my results. Ought I to believe this or any other failure to replicate? Only my research group and I are capable

TABLE 16.1.   Some of the Obvious Reasons for No-Difference Findings

- There are no, or very small, differences in the population; that is, the no-difference finding reflects the true state of affairs
- Power was low and probably too weak to detect a difference
- The investigator could not duplicate or carry out the manipulation or intervention, or the intervention was not carried out as intended (diffusion of conditions, poor adherence of experimenters or therapists, groups were not different on a manipulation check)
- Levels of the independent variable (low, medium, high) were not optimal or did not provide a strong test
- Excessive uncontrolled "error" variability (heterogeneity of subjects, loose procedures for implementing the study, weak and unreliable measures)
- Competing influences exerted greater impact on the results than the manipulation (maturation, statistical regression for all groups, or differential impact of these for one group, rather than another) and "washed-out" or overrode any effect of the manipulation

of carrying out the treatment, and your test may not be a good one because you simply do not do the procedure correctly. Negative findings can result when the investigator does not know how to implement the intervention. More seriously, this comes up on other contexts. For example, within psychology Ivan Pavlov is recognized to be an extraordinary scientist, as reflected by his earning a Nobel Prize (in 1904) for his work on digestion. He also devised a technique to isolate a portion of the stomach to assess gastric secretions. The surgical techniques to accomplish this were quite difficult, and several dogs were sacrificed in the process of perfecting the surgery (Cuny, 1965). Of course, Pavlov's work on conditioning has been greatly replicated and extended, but the procedures initially were sufficiently difficult that it would be understandable if many could not even carry out key aspects of the procedures or did so in ways that did not permit the meticulous assessment (individual drops of saliva) that Pavlov achieved. In clinical psychology we worry about treatment integrity, but there are analogues in any area where a task is required of the subject or special talent, skill, or training is required of the experimenter. Poorly implementing a difficult experimental procedure could readily lead to a no-difference finding.

The absence of group differences may also result from the levels of the independent variable selected for the study. Whether or not differences are obtained may be completely determined by what levels were selected. For example, whether, and the extent to which, there is a relation between the amount of psychotherapy (number of sessions) and therapeutic change might be readily influenced by the levels of "amount" evaluated in a given study. The investigator may begin with a reasonable hypothesis that more sessions are associated with greater improvements among the patients. The hypothesis is partially true, but whether this is supported in a given study is another matter. The reason is that the relation between treatment duration and therapeutic change is not linear (Howard et al., 1986).

As shown in Figure 16.2, 50 percent of the patients are markedly improved by session 8 (solid line) and 75 percent markedly improved by session 26. Assume we did not know of this relation and conducted a study to evaluate treatment duration. We may compare a group that receives 20 sessions with another group that receives 30 sessions. The difference between these groups may be too small to produce a statistically significant difference. On the other hand, if the levels of the independent variable were more discrepant and at different stages of treatment (e.g., 10 versus 30 sessions), group differences might be more likely. The example is provided to illustrate the potential problem of not selecting sufficiently discrepant levels of the independent variable to reflect change or inadvertently selecting levels from a range where the discrepancy may not be as relevant to treatment outcome.

In cases where the relation of the independent variable to the dependent variable is not linear, selecting groups that are very discrepant (e.g., very high versus very low) may not lead to sharp differences on the dependent measure. For example, the effects of parental control (e.g., inconsistent discipline) on problem behaviors (aggression, antisocial behavior) of adolescents is curvilinear. High and low levels of control are associated with much greater adolescent problem behaviors than moderate amounts of control (Stice, Barrera, & Chassin, 1993). Not armed with this information, an investigator might design a study in which high and low parent groups were selected. The

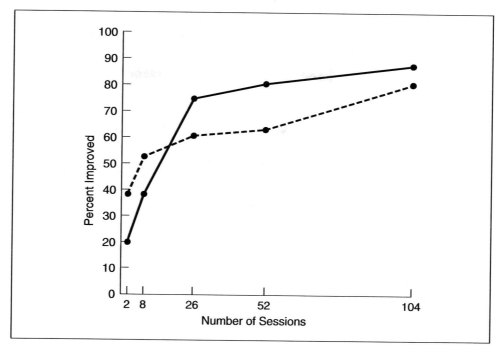

FIGURE 16.2.   The relation between the number of sessions of psychotherapy for adult patients and the percent of patients improved. The solid line reflects ratings at the end of treatment completed by researchers, based on chart review. The broken line reflects patient self-report ratings during the course of treatment.

Source: Howard, K.I., Kopta, S.M., Krause, M.S., & Orlinsky, D.E. (1986). The dose-effect relationship in psychotherapy. *American Psychologist, 41,* 159–164. Copyright © 1986 by the American Psychological Association. Reprinted with permission.

results might not show differences in behavioral problems among adolescents, because high versus low, in this case, are not the most discrepant conditions. An advantage to selecting multiple levels of an independent variable (beyond high versus low) is in part the ability to evaluate whether there is a linear relation or, said another way, whether differences between groups are evident at only some places along the dimension of the independent variable. In any case, a no-difference finding could be due to the levels or points used to represent the independent variable.

Any factor in the experiment that operates to increase within-subject variability also may increase the likelihood of a no-difference finding. As we discussed in relation to statistical conclusion validity and power, the magnitude of an effect can be measured in terms of effect size, or the difference between means divided by the standard deviation. A given difference between means produces a lower effect size as the standard deviation (denominator) increases. The sensitivity of the experiment in detecting a difference can be reduced by allowing uncontrolled sources of variation or "noise" into the experiment. Allowing such factors to vary as the adequacy of training of different experimenters and methods of delivering instructions can increase the variance of within-treatment groups and reduce the likelihood of finding group differences. Indeed, negative results have on occasion been implicitly used to infer that the investigator may be incompetent for not controlling the situation well enough to obtain group differences (Greenwald, 1975; My dissertation committee).

Several facets of an experiment that do not necessarily reflect procedural sloppiness are related to the sensitivity of the experimental test and the likelihood that group differences will be found. The assessment device(s) may show sufficiently variable performance that only the most robust relations would emerge as statistically significant. In addition, the dependent measures may not be the most appropriate for detecting a relation of interest. Measures are often selected because of what they are called rather than what they have been shown to measure empirically, or because they are readily available, inexpensive, and expedient.

When Negative Results Are Interpretable

The absence of group differences is routinely dismissed as ambiguous and is often given much less attention than it should receive. There are numerous situations in which negative results are very informative and interpretable and, of course, many situations in which "positive" results are ambiguous, misinterpreted, and not very informative. Negative effects are interpretable under a number of conditions.

First, in the context of a program of research, negative results can be very informative. A program of research refers to a series of studies conducted by an investigator or group of investigators. The studies usually bear great similarity to each other along such dimensions as the independent variables, subjects, and measures. Presumably, several studies would have produced some group differences (otherwise it would be a masochistic rather than programmatic series of studies). The demonstration of group differences in some of the studies means that the experimental procedures are sensitive to at least some interventions. Thus, one can usually rule out the problem that the experiments are conducted poorly or that the methodology is too insensitive to detect group differences, even though these explanations may be true of one of the experiments. However, if the program of research has established itself in terms of demonstrating group differences across repeated studies, research showing no differences for a related variable can be viewed with greater confidence than would be the case in an isolated study. For example, cognitive-behavior therapy for depression is effective for adolescents, as shown in many controlled clinical trials (e.g., Lewinsohn & Clarke, 1999). In one of the projects a parent component was added; in addition to the group therapy for adolescents, parents received separate sessions and were taught communication and problem-solving skills. The treatments with and without the parent component were equally effective, that is, no difference. In the context of a program of research this finding must be given a bit more weight because we know that many of the reasons for a no-difference finding (listed in Table 16.1) probably were not evident, given the prior findings of this research program. The parent component may be effective in a future study as it is altered, developed, and so on. But the no-difference finding is noteworthy because of the context of many studies where differences have been found.

Second, negative results are also informative when the results are replicated (repeated) across several different investigators. A problem in the psychological literature, and perhaps in other research areas as well, is that once a relation is reported, it is extremely difficult to qualify or refute it with subsequent research. If negative results accumulate across several studies, however, they strongly suggest that the original study resulted either from very special circumstances or possibly through various artifacts. Failures to replicate do not invariably influence how the field interprets or views the status of the original finding. A classic example is the well-known study of Little Albert, an 11-month-old boy, whose story is taught to almost every undergraduate. In this demonstration a loud noise (and a startle reaction) was paired with an object (white rat) that had not previously evoked a reaction from Albert. After several pairings, presentation of the rat alone led to the startle response (Watson & Rayner, 1920). This study has been extremely influential and is cited often in texts (like this one), even though several failures to replicate are well documented (see Kazdin, 1978b). The replication failures did not challenge the finding that fears seemingly could be conditioned.

Third, negative results are informative when the study shows the conditions under which the results are and are not obtained. The way in which this is easily achieved is through a factorial design that permits assessment of an interaction. An interaction between the different factors indicates that the effect of one variable depends upon the level of another variable. An interaction may be reflected in the finding that there are no differences between groups for some levels of the variables but statistically significant differences between groups for a different level of the variables; that is, negative results occur in only some of the experimental conditions. For example, one study examined whether early aggressive behavior (elementary school) predicted later delinquency in adolescence (Tremblay et al., 1992). The results indicated that early aggressive behavior predicted later delinquency for boys but not for girls. A no-difference finding (early aggressive and nonaggressive girls show similar outcomes) was informative because of the demonstration that the presence or absence of one variable (early aggression) depended on another condition (sex). This type of demonstration can advance research considerably by raising hypotheses about different mechanisms involved to explain the development of aggressive behavior in boys and girls.

A related way in which a no-difference finding is informative is in relation to the pattern of results across multiple measures. A no-difference finding may be evident on some measures but not others. For example, another study focused on antecedents of externalizing behavior (aggression, overactivity, delinquency) and internalizing behavior (withdrawal, anxiety, depression) among children (Dodge et al., 1994). Several variables (harsh discipline practices, lack of maternal support, exposure to aggressive behavior in the home, and lack of cognitive stimulation) were shown to predict later externalizing behavior but not internalizing child behavior. That is, the no-effect finding was obtained for one domain of functioning but not another. As a general rule, when an investigator can show within a single study that a particular relation does and does not hold, depending on another variable or set of circumstances (another independent variable), or does not hold across measures (dependent variables), the study is likely to be particularly informative. Such studies often provide a fine-grained analysis of the phenomenon.

When Negative Results Are Important

Noting that negative results are interpretable suggests that a no-difference finding is salvageable. Actually, in a variety of circumstances finding no differences may be extremely important. In clinical and applied research no-difference findings may be especially important in the context of possible harm, side effects, or costs of alternative procedures or interventions. As citizens and consumers of research, perhaps more than in our role as investigators, we care very much about and hope for many "negative effects," that is, no-difference findings across many areas of research. As an example, we would be very interested in a no-difference finding (i.e., no effect) on our safety and health from eating genetically engineered versus nonengineered foods. The move to develop such foods holds promise to overcome worldwide starvation by providing enough food and more nutritious food. (Many who are not starving are still not receiving basic nutrients from the limited diets and have high morbidity and mortality rates as a result.) Will engineered and nonengineered foods be exactly the same (no difference) except for the benefits? Common sense warns otherwise. People fear a difference, and some animal work suggests genetically modified products (e.g., corn) can affect animals in deleterious ways (e.g., caterpillars, see Jesse & Obrycki, 2000). We would all welcome replicated no-difference findings, and such findings would be very important.

Consider the use of cell phones as another example. There is some concern among the public that use of cell phones may increase the risk of cancer, especially brain cancer, leukemia, and lymphoma. This is not a random worry. Cell phones are transmitters that give off and receive radio waves, and these radio waves fall on the same part of the electromagnetic spectrum occupied by more powerful sources, such as microwave ovens and airport radar systems. Does the use or repeated use of cell phones influence (either increase risk or actually cause) cancer? We would like to know that talking on a cell phone versus not talking on a cell phone leads to no differences in rates of brain cancer. That is, we would adore (and perhaps even commit to love) support for the null hypothesis. There is a great deal of research on the topic, and *most* of the findings indicate there is no increased risk (Dreyer, Loughlin, & Rothman, 1999; Morgan et al., 2000). (Actually, there is an increased death rate associated with cell phone use, but this stems from automobile accidents among those who drive and talk on their cell phone.) Despite the weight of the evidence in relation to cancer, there is no certainty. People who are concerned about the cancer risk are encouraged to pursue one of two interventions—cell-ibacy (refraining from excessive use) or use of headsets, which allow speaking on the phone with the phone away from one's head. This is a good example to illustrate the point because it includes a now common practice (cell phone use) and deadly health consequences (cancer mortality).

The example conveys some of the limitations and frustrations of science. Among them, one cannot prove the null hypothesis (that there really is no difference). Research can show in replicated effects using different designs, samples, doses, and types of phones that they do not produce the problem, that is, no difference from noncell phone use. Yet, not all of the conditions, people, and uses can be studied, and certainty that no effect would ever occur is not part of science. Outside of scientific bases of evidence, one case of brain cancer in a cell phone user is enough to induce worry and lead to a lawsuit (which is currently in the courts) claiming a causal relation. Tragically, some people who use cell phones (or who use regular phones) will have brain cancer. The question is whether cell phone use increases the base rate, and this is a statistical question that relies on power and other facets of design covered in this book.

Showing no difference in science has a special meaning and not the exact one the public wants. In science the meaning is that evidence was not sufficient to show that there is a statistically significant difference. No difference means that there *is no evidence of harm* (e.g., for cell phone use). Science can say there is "no evidence of harm," but what the public wishes to know is that there is "evidence of no harm" (Adler, 2000). The distinction is subtle but means only that we cannot provide strong evidence or certainty to prove the null hypothesis. We cannot say that something is without harm, because many situations and circumstances might change this verdict. With increased replication of no difference, the level of confidence we wish as citizens increases, too.

As an example of a valuable no-difference finding, consider the treatment of breast cancer. Research has shown that for many women a radical mastectomy (complete removal of the breast) is no more effective in terms of long-term mortality than a lumpectomy (a more circumscribed operation in which the tumor and a small amount of surrounding tissue is removed) (Fisher et al., 1985, 1996). This no-difference finding in terms of outcome is critically important because the two treatments are very different in their cost (for the surgery, complications, hospitalization, and for subsequent plastic surgery for breast implants) and psychological impact (subsequent depression and body image). The no-difference finding may not be applicable to everyone, but only to those whose cancer has not already metastasized.

A no-difference finding can be very important when the problem or focus is of critical interest. For example, improvements in the treatment of HIV have been enormous. Even with the best current treatment (antiretroviral medication), the chance of the disease progressing to AIDS remains high. New treatments are being actively pursued to enhance current treatments. In a large-scale study involving 77 hospitals and over 2,500 patients with HIV, an effort was made to test a new treatment (Kahn, Cherng, Mayer, Murray, & Lagakos, 2000). Patients received the standard treatment as needed but were randomly assigned to receive an additional new drug or a placebo. It is worth reiterating that all patients received the standard treatment and hence even the placebo group was placebo plus the active treatment. The results indicated that the two conditions produced no differences in progression of the disease or death. The trial was ended early once the data conveyed this was the likely pattern.

Several features of the study warrant mention. This was a multicenter, double-blind, placebo controlled trial. The study appears to be very carefully designed and evaluated. Indeed, because there were many different settings, one can also conceive of the study as having multiple replications across sites and their respective investigators. The no-difference findings are not the results we would like. It would be terrific if the new treatment made even a small difference. Nevertheless, the finding is very important. Unless there is some strong reason, research ought to move on to another treatment or way of bolstering the immune system this treatment was designed to affect. The no-difference finding, demonstrated in a well-designed study, saves intellectual and monetary resources by shifting attention to other avenues. This is not trivial. For important clinical problems we want to achieve the goals (e.g., very effective treatment) as soon as possible. A study that carefully tests a viable alternative can speed the process, even if the results are not "positive."

No-difference findings may also be important because of the potential questions they raise. For example, programs that are extremely costly and mandated for treatment for special populations may be shown to have little or no impact in the outcomes they produce (Weisz et al., 1990). Such findings are critically important to ensure that further resources are not wasted or used in ways that are likely to have minimal impact. In turn, the resources might be better deployed to stimulate innovative and more promising intervention efforts. Indeed, such findings underscore the importance of demonstrating no-difference effects when they are present to ensure that resources are not deployed for ineffective programs.

Selection among alternative interventions also may be influenced by no-difference findings. For example, for many patients with a diverse range of clinical problems (e.g., anxiety, depression) very brief self-administered therapy (computerized therapy, one or two sessions by phone, self-help manuals) is as effective as traditional therapy (one-to-one meetings with a therapist over several sessions). That is, no-difference findings are obtained (see Newman, 2000). This is an enormously important verdict on brief treatments because the disseminability, cost, and acceptability of brief treatments are usually so much more favorable. Of course, the task is to find out for whom such treatment is equally beneficial and then to apply the brief treatment, or perhaps to give the brief treatment to all, except for the most extreme cases, and move to more costly interventions only as needed (see Haaga, 2000).

In the general case, negative results may be important, based on substantive and methodological considerations. The substantive considerations refer to the significance of the experimental or clinical questions that guide the investigation. As in the above examples, the question may be one in which no differences between two groups, conditions, or interventions are actively sought. The methodological considerations refer to the care with which the study is planned, implemented, and evaluated. In particular, given documented weaknesses of research, the power of the study to demonstrate differences if they exist is pivotal. Power analyses, of the type discussed earlier, can be completed before and after a study is conducted to provide the investigator and reader with a statement of the sensitivity of the test in light of actual effect sizes obtained. No-difference findings in a well-conceived and controlled study with adequate power (e.g., > .80) ought to be taken as seriously as any other finding.

REPLICATION

Evaluation of the results of an experiment, whether or not a significant difference is demonstrated, entails more than scrutiny of that one experiment alone. The reliability of a finding across studies greatly enhances evaluation of any particular investigation. Replication is a pivotal topic that relates to evaluation of findings and accumulation of knowledge.

Types of Replication

Replication refers to repetition of an experiment. Many different types of replication have been distinguished, based on the extent to which the replication follows characteristics of the original investigation and the dimensions along which the replication effort may vary (types of subjects, tasks, means of operationalizing independent or dependent variables) (Carlsmith, Ellsworth, & Aronson, 1976; Rosenthal, 1991). The multiple ways in classifying replications are beyond the purposes of this discussion in favor of addressing other key points.

Direct or exact replication and systematic or approximate replication provide a useful way to convey critical points. *Direct replication* refers to an attempt to repeat an experiment exactly as it was conducted originally. Ideally, the conditions and procedures across the replication and original experiment are identical. *Systematic replication* refers to repetition of the experiment by systematically allowing features to vary. The conditions and procedures of the replication are deliberately designed only to approximate those of the original experiment. It is useful to consider direct and systematic replication as on opposite ends of a continuum.

A replication at the direct end of the spectrum would follow the original procedures as closely as possible. This is the easiest to do for the researcher who conducted the original investigation, since he or she has complete access to all of the procedures, the population from which the original sample was drawn, and nuances of the laboratory procedures (tasks for experimenters and subjects, all instructions, data handling procedures) that optimize similarity with the original study. An exact replication is not possible, even by the original investigator, since repetition of the experiment involves new subjects tested at a different point in time and by different experimenters, all of which conceivably could lead to different results. Thus, all replications necessarily allow some factors to vary; the issue is the extent to which the replication study departs from the original investigation.

Direct replication by someone other than the original investigator is often difficult to conduct. Many of the procedures are not sufficiently described in written reports and articles of an investigation. Journals routinely limit the space available in which authors may present their studies. Hence, further materials about how the study was conducted usually must be obtained from the original investigator. Ideally, an individual interested in a close replication of the original experiment would obtain and use as many of the original experimental materials as possible.

A replication at the systematic end of the spectrum would vary the experiment deliberately along one or more dimensions. For example, a systematic replication might assess whether the relation between the independent and dependent variable holds when subjects are older or younger than those in the original experiment, when subject (patient) diagnoses differ, or when the therapists are inexperienced rather than experienced. Of course, a systematic replication tends to vary only one or a few of the dimensions along which the study might differ from the original experiment. If the results of a replication differ from the original experiment, it is desirable to have a limited number of differences between these experiments so the possible reason for the discrepancy of results can be more easily identified. If there are multiple differences between the original and replication experiments, discrepancies in results might be due to a host of factors not easily discerned without extensive further experimentation.

Discussions of replications focus on repeating an experiment. However, there are other contexts in which replication is very important as well. In an individual experiment the results often can be analyzed in many ways. Early in one's statistical education, often one is implicitly taught that the data have to be analyzed after they are collected and that one of several techniques can be used. Perhaps what is not taught sufficiently, is that different data analyses can lead to different conclusions. We saw this in a gross way in comparing the conclusions reached in a replication effort if the results were based on effect size rather than statistical significance. Also, I have mentioned that the conclusions from meta-analysis can vary widely, depending on the precise way in which effect sizes are computed, and that some influences in psychotherapy outcome are not influences at all, depending on the computation method selected.

There are more subtle ways in which the same data can generate different conclusions. A given analysis (e.g., regression) might have different options—all of which are defensible—and these will, or could, lead to quite different conclusions. For example, in regression analyses the criteria (e.g., p levels) or "solutions" (entering variables in a stepwise fashion, all at once, or some other way) can influence whether one variable is a predictor of another or to what extent. Also, in factor analysis the solutions one selects (principal component, varimax rotation, orthogonal factors) greatly influence the conclusions. Often quite different conclusions would be reached with slightly different analyses (e.g., nonorthogonal factors).

One way in which replications occur is a reanalysis of the results from a study. That is, the data originally analyzed by the investigator, may be reanalyzed by a new set of investigators. The goal is to see if new analyses, perhaps controlling for more variables or slightly different assumptions and solutions, would lead to different results. A politically charged example pertains to research on air pollution. There has been disagreement about the level of pollutants in the air, released primarily from motor vehicles and power plants, and their impact on health. A couple of key longitudinal studies spanning several years across many different cities showed that lower-than-expected levels of pollutants increase death rate from heart and lung disease (see Kaiser, 2000). As a result of the findings, the Environmental Protection Agency has proposed lowering the allowable pollutants released from industry. This would be a very expensive enterprise, and industry representatives understandably object. Arguments about the findings have focused on methodology of the original studies (whether factors confounded with air pollution levels were completely ruled out) and also the data analyses. An independent panel was given the data from the studies with the task of reanalyzing the data and looking for possible confounds. The results of the reanalyses supported—that is, replicated—the original findings, and, indeed, bolstered the case because so many additional factors that might confound the relation were considered in the new analyses. Stated another way, the reanalyses replicate and extend the original findings.

Apart from the research context, replication emerges in clinical psychology in a somewhat different way worth mentioning in passing. Considerable research focuses on the efficacy of various forms of psychotherapy. A central question is, once a treatment has been shown to be effective in well-controlled contexts, can it be replicated in clinical work? Many other terms have been used to reflect this concern, such as transporting or generalizing treatment to clinical practice. Replication is useful, if not slightly better, because it conjures up the direct–systematic continuum and reflects the fundamental question, "Can the procedures be repeated in clinical work and will they have the effects they have had previously?" Replication in the context of clinical work is toward the extreme systematic end of the replication continuum. Often many features (who the clients and therapists are, the scope of the clinical problems) vary in clinical application, as compared with research.

Importance of Replication

The importance of replication in scientific research cannot be overemphasized. First, by the nature of null hypothesis testing and statistical evaluation, it is possible that any particular finding may be the result of "chance." As investigators, we invariably assume that when we find statistical significance, this means the finding (relationships among variables) is real, and if the p level is really low ($p < .0001$), then this is very real and clearly beyond chance. Yet, any finding might be due to chance and the special sampling of subjects under the circumstances and time the study was completed. Chance becomes very implausible upon replication of a finding in a new study.

Second, replication is important because many influences might operate in a psychology experiment to lead to the pattern of results, other than the independent variables or conditions we have studied. That is, the findings may reflect a "real" ("nonchance") effect, but some other influence may operate in the study to account for that (threat to construct validity). The influence might be subtle (subject or experimenter effects). A replication of the results does not necessarily rule out such influences but increases the likelihood that the independent variable or experimental condition is the common feature across the two studies that explains the relation. Unfortunately, the importance is not commensurate with the number of replications that seem to be attempted or at least reported.[1] Reviews of journal publications many years ago found that between 0 and 1 percent of studies are replications in some form (Bozarth & Roberts, 1972; Greenwald, 1975)—although, of course, these surveys need to be replicated. One hears of replication in the news, often for critical findings that have significant scientific implications or that controvert something that has been assumed for many years (cloning animals, discovery of new planetary bodies). More is needed.

Within the social sciences there are few professional rewards for replication attempts, particularly direct replication attempts. Direct replications may be met with

---

[1]The sweeping statement about the dearth of replication studies has important exceptions (see Neuliep, 1991). In some areas of experimental and social psychology more than others, for example, replication studies are included in a single publication in which multiple investigations are combined. In laboratory investigations with animals as subjects or with college students who attend a single session, replication tends to be more common, in part as a function of the brevity of the experiment and ease of recruiting subjects. In contrast, research that requires special populations (e.g., those with a particular psychiatric disorder), is conducted in applied settings (clinics, counseling centers, schools), or has a longitudinal focus (intervention research, studies of development) is less easily and hence less often replicated.

indifference because the outcome may be considered as either uninformative or ambiguous. If the results of the original study are successfully replicated, the replication project may be given little attention because it does not add new information to the literature. If the replication study does not yield the same results, the onus implicitly is upon the second investigator to explain and demonstrate why there was a difference across the investigations.

The major reason that replications are not usually viewed with great excitement is that, by definition, they are partly repetitions of experiments that already have been done. Repetition of the experiment at first blush seems undramatic and lacking in originality. Indeed, at cocktail parties with psychologists, one would not want to boast about the fact that his or her research is devoted to replication of work done by other investigators! Yet, a replication experiment should not be viewed as mere repetition of previous work. Rather, replications can be conceptualized either as tests of robustness and generality of the original finding or more careful evaluations of the original hypotheses. This is not merely a terminological change but rather, I believe, a more accurate characterization of the contribution of replications. Replication studies ask whether the relation holds beyond the conditions in place in the original experiment. If the results of a replication do not support the original research, they do not necessarily impugn the original finding. Rather, they may suggest that the relation holds for only a narrow set of conditions or relates to a specific circumscribed set of factors, perhaps some even unspecified in the original report. The original finding may be veridical and not the result of experimental biases or artifacts, but still insufficiently robust to have wide generality.

Replications as tests of generality are particularly important in clinical psychology where research and application are so intertwined. Tests of generality partially address the applied value of many findings and have implications for decisions about treatment. Researchers and clinicians alike wish to know how widely the results of a given treatment can be applied or, indeed, whether the results can be applied at all beyond a very narrow set of experimental conditions. We are rarely surprised when an experienced investigator reports results that treatment is effective and, indeed, even has dramatic effects (e.g., for delinquency [Henggeler et al. 1998] and anxiety disorders [Kendall & Treadwell, 1996]). When these studies are replicated by the same investigator in different settings and with a different sample (Henggeler, 1999; Henggeler et al., 1998) or replicated by a different team of investigators with variations in the treatment (Barrett, 1998; Barrett, Dadds, & Rapee, 1996; Dadds et al., 1999), we can have increased faith in the original findings and in the generality of the results.

Direct and systematic replications add to knowledge in different ways. Replications that closely approximate the conditions of the original experiment increase one's confidence that the original finding is reliable and not likely to have resulted from chance or a particular artifact. Replications that deviate from the original conditions suggest that the findings hold across a wider range of conditions. Essentially, the greater the divergence of the replication from the conditions of the original experiment, the greater the generality of the relation.

Several replication attempts may reveal findings that show the original relation to be evident across a wide range of laboratory and even field conditions. On the other hand, several unsuccessful replication attempts may reveal findings that show the original relation not to be present anywhere. The original finding then may be viewed as trivial in the sense that it is narrowly restricted to a very specific set of circumstances. Alternatively, the original finding may have resulted from uncontrolled factors or biases not evident in the original report or simply from "chance" (Type I error).

Obviously, replication attempts do not invariably produce the same results as the original experiment. Examples may be plentiful, but they are difficult to find because replication studies and "negative results" are infrequently published; they also require the passage of considerable time to allow for the replications to accumulate. One example of a failure to replicate was evident in a single-case experiment. In a study completed several years ago, self-instruction training was used to alter the behavior of three Head Start children who were highly disruptive in class (Bornstein & Quevillon, 1976). Training was conducted for two hours outside of the classroom, where the children and a trainer worked on tasks to develop problem-solving skills. The skills were intended to alter their on-task behavior in the classroom. The children were directed to administer instructions to themselves—first aloud, then in a whisper, and finally without sound (covertly). Self-instruction training was administered and evaluated in a multiple-baseline design across children. The results indicated marked increases in on-task behavior in the classroom for each of the children. Moreover, the markedly improved classroom performance was maintained several weeks after treatment. Several investigators have since tried to repeat this demonstration with little or no success (Bryant & Budd, 1982; Friedling & O'Leary, 1979), including a direct replication that closely followed the procedures (Billings & Wasik, 1985). Clearly, questions are raised about the original findings and the conditions under which they apply. Some of the ambiguities have prompted different types of studies to understand when and how self-instruction training can alter child behavior. The failures to replicate the original findings lend emphasis to the importance of routine replication studies.

If one thinks that replication of positive effects is not rewarded professionally, consider the lack of respect for replication of so-called negative (no-difference) findings. Psychology is a little harsh on this point. In other fields with applied areas of research or where implications affect the public, replication of studies to show no difference is more commonly accepted. This is evident in the cell phone example noted above, but many other examples can be found. For example, there is a great deal of concern about the short- and long-term psychological effects among women having an abortion. Understandably, one might expect all sorts of consequences after abortion, including, but not limited to, depression and posttraumatic stress disorder. Several studies have replicated the effect that women who have obtained an abortion, up to 2 years later do not suffer social, emotional, and other problems more than control women without the experience (Adler, 2000; Major et al., 2000). Does abortion have deleterious psychological consequences on women? Probably yes for some women, but replication of the no-difference finding has been informative. In short, replication of no differences is quite helpful, indeed, when the question is of such importance to the health and well being of human (or animal) life.

The nature of publication practices undoubtedly fosters biases about the information disseminated in the literature. The journal review process favors "positive effects" (i.e., group differences) and systematically excludes similar studies (replications) that find no differences. Thus, when there is a chance finding (Type I error), it is more likely to enter the literature. Failures to replicate are less likely to be published. The paucity of replication research may obscure the number of findings that can be confidently embraced as robust. The notion of the *file-drawer problem*, mentioned previously, refers to the prospect that many nonpublished papers may not have shown the finding and are relegated to the investigator's "file drawer." Those that are published are more likely to be the chance findings (5 in 100 for p = .05) if the study were conducted many times and the null hypothesis is false. Computations can be completed to estimate how many unpublished findings without significant effects (the "file drawer") would be required for the finding in the literature to be challenged (see Rosenthal, 1984; Rosenthal, 1991). For example, at least a couple of thousand studies attest to the effects of psychotherapy (Durlak et al., 1995; Kazdin, 2000; Smith, Glass, & Miller, 1980; Weisz & Weiss, 1993). It would take several thousands of studies with no effects in some file drawer to contest this basic finding. Consequently, it is not very plausible that the effects in the published studies are due to chance or biased reporting. As a general rule, of course, as more studies support a particular finding, the less likely that any unpublished findings would negate the overall relationship that has been found.

From the standpoint of a prospective investigator, replication work is important to consider as a research strategy, particularly at the inception of one's work in an area, when it is important to ensure that the phenomenon can be reproduced. After a phenomenon has been reproduced, it can be analyzed and elaborated in subsequent research. Although replication research is advocated in the present text as an important focus, it would be naive to neglect the point noted earlier that simple replication may conflict with professional rewards. The rewards are for "original experimentation" or for something that has not been done before. (In some areas any well-controlled research would meet this latter criterion.) Yet, replications are not necessarily mere repetitions of studies; often they provide much more careful evaluations of the hypothesis studied in the original experiment and study the topic in a slightly new way. Indeed, one practice is to place in the title of a replication study the subheading "A replication and extension" (Flack et al., 2000; Stoeber, 2000). This conveys that there is new information and a bridge from a prior finding to new knowledge. Even without a new twist, replications may repeat that original experiment with additional control conditions and provide a methodological and theoretical advance.

The value of replication efforts can depend on a number of factors. Replications early in the development of an area of research are particularly important as the bedrock of the theory and empirical phenomena are established. Replications conducted by persons other than the original investigator and with variations in some of the methods and procedures (subjects, settings, and tasks) are also particularly important. An excellent strategy is to include in one's investigation a partial replication of previous research; for example, an investigator could include conditions that closely resemble those in a previous experiment. In addition, conditions can be included that conceptually extend the experiment and the experimental conditions. Essentially, this strategy includes an attempt to combine direct and systematic replication strategies in a single experiment. The results of such research allow one to comment on not only the reliability of the phenomenon, but also the generality of the findings as well, all within the same experiment. Also, the researcher may be able to predict an interaction indicating the conditions across which the original findings may hold.

General Comments

Replication and negative results, two topics treated separately, are related in important ways. In the usual situation we say that a finding is replicated if the original (first) study and the next study both show a significant effect. We say that a finding is not replicated when the first study finds a significant effect, but one or more subsequent studies do not. However, as illustrated in the previous chapter, statistical significance is not a flawless basis for reaching conclusions about the results of the experiment. Statistical significance is a function of many factors (e.g., N, the test used). An example was provided in the previous chapter in which identical findings from two hypothetical studies, as measured by effect size, may lead to rejection of the null hypothesis in one situation and acceptance in another study, purely as a function of power. Thus, seeming failures to replicate occasionally may be artifacts of the methods used to analyze the data.

Although the importance of replication has been advocated for decades, the impact on research practices in psychology has been limited—the same story that was noted for power. The emergence of meta-analysis within the past 25 years has been helpful as a way of evaluating and integrating related studies that may vary in degree to which they replicate each other. By combining multiple studies, the meta-analysis can give an estimate of the true effects in the population and confidence limits about that effect. Also, one can analyze whether characteristics of the study (e.g., methodological features) make a difference in relation to the strength of the effects that were obtained. The ability to combine multiple studies and to analyze characteristics of the studies that may influence (moderate) the effect have served some of the key purposes of replication research.

SUMMARY AND CONCLUSIONS

Three areas related to data interpretation were discussed in this chapter: interpretation of the results of a research study, negative results, and replication. In discussing the results of one's study, little inferential leaps are often made that can misrepresent or overinterpret what actually was found in the data analyses. Common examples from clinical research were mentioned, such as stating something more than one is entitled to say based on statistical or clinical significance or based on the relation demonstrated in the study (e.g., use of the term "predictor"). The concepts discussed are basic, but it is surprising how often the investigator's interpretations of the data make little leaps that the findings do not warrant. Discussion of one's results requires and, indeed, demands going beyond the data, and hence one has to be vigilant in one's own work and in the works of others. The issue is not trivial but has to do with the fundamentals of scientific epistemology—what do we know from this study, what can we say as a result?

Another topic critical to data interpretation is the notion of negative results, a concept that has come to mean that no statistically significant differences were found in the experiment. The concept has received attention because the putative importance of a given study and its publishability often depend on whether statistically significant results are obtained. Unfortunately, such an emphasis has detracted considerably from other considerations, that is, whether the conclusions can be accepted because of the theoretical or empirical importance of the question and quality of the research design, independently of statistical significance. Hence, methodologically weak studies with statistically significant results are more likely to be published, and methodologically sound studies—or studies at least as sound as those published—without statistically significant effects often go unpublished.

Related to the topic of "negative" results is the notion of replication or repetition of a previously conducted study. Replications can vary in similarity to the original experiment. Direct replications attempt to mimic the original experiment, whereas systematic replications purposely attempt to vary the conditions of the original experiment. Replication research may lead to negative results, which can bring into question the basis for the results of the original experiment or the generality of the original findings. Replication research is exceedingly important because it is the most reliable test of whether the finding is veridical. The logic of statistical analyses suggests that occasionally statistical significance will be achieved even when there are no group differences in the population, that is, findings significant by "chance" alone. Since these are likely to be published because of the bias for "positive" findings, there could well be a great many findings that would not stand up under any replication conditions. Thus, to distinguish those findings in the field that have a sound basis requires replication research. Replications need not merely repeat a previous experiment but can address nuances of the original experiment as well as entirely new questions, such as the conditions under which the relation is or is not likely to hold.

KEY CONCEPTS AND TERMS

Direct Replication	Replication
File-Drawer Problem	Systematic Replication
Negative Results	

FOR FURTHER READING

Fagley, N.S. (1985). Applied statistical power analysis and the interpretation of nonsignificant results by research consumers. *Journal of Counseling Psychology, 32,* 391–396.

Jaccard, J., Turrisi, R., & Wan, C.K. (1990). *Interaction effects in multiple regression.* Newbury Park, CA: Sage.

Kratochwill, T.R., Callan-Stoiber, K., & Gutkin, T.B. (2000). Empirically supported interventions in school psychology: The role of negative results in outcome research. *Psychology in the Schools, 37,* 399–413.

Neuliep, J.W. (Ed.) (1991). *Replication research in the social sciences.* Newbury Park, CA: Sage.

Rosnow, R.L., & Rosenthal, R. (1989). Definition and interpretation of interaction effects. *Psychological Bulletin, 105,* 143–146.

Ethical Issues and Guidelines for Research

In prior chapters I have tried to underscore the distinction between methodological practices and the underlying issues they reflect. Too much of methodology training focuses on specific practices (assigning cases randomly to conditions, comparing groups statistically) rather than on the underlying issues these practices address (ruling out major threats to validity, determining if there is a reliable effect). Understanding the underlying issues and purposes of the practices increases the options for designing

497

research. Perhaps there is no aspect of methodology where the distinction between practices and underlying issues has been neglected in research training as much as in the area of ethics. For the researcher, ethical issues often appear reduced to a few practices (developing consent forms, obtaining formal approval of these forms through the shoals of a university review committee, and then having subjects actually sign them.) There are weighty issues underlying these practices that reflect values, morals, law, and social policy and hence greatly affect us as scientists and as citizens.

This chapter raises a number of ethical issues and highlights contemporary guidelines for ethical research practices and professional obligations in the conduct and reporting of research. The focus of the chapter is on those issues primarily in the context of research with human participants. Ethical and practical issues pertaining to infrahuman species are no less significant. Indeed, the increased concern of animal rights, conditions for the care of animals, and sacrificing animals in research and classroom educational programs (e.g., routinely killing frogs in high school biology classes) reflect an increased sensitivity to ethical issues and perhaps reverence for life. The vast majority of research in clinical, counseling, school, and related areas is with human participants. Similarly, many ethical issues related to the practice of psychology (in the context of delivering therapy or consulting) are not addressed in light of the focus of this book on research. Not detailing these latter issues here is not a commentary on their significance. Rather, the core issues that relate to the conduct of research are sufficiently weighty to narrow the focus of this chapter (see Further Readings for broader sources).

CONTEMPORARY CONTEXT AND SCOPE OF THE ISSUES

Highlighting changing views about the role of values in science can convey the context for the significance of ethical issues. Occasionally, a salient view has characterized science as the pursuit of knowledge that is largely value free. The search for knowledge and the methods used in that search often are considered to be ethically neutral. That is, findings from research may be misused, but science itself is sort of above it all. The neutrality view is easily challenged. The development and deployment of weapons for war (atomic bomb, radar, rocket launchers) are feats of science, and scientists have played a central role. The neutrality view, perhaps rarely tenable, is clearly recognized to be at odds with contemporary work. This is due, in part, to many of the topics of research (e.g., developing treatments that can be used throughout the world, genetic engineering of foods, animals, and people) and the globalization of research, which I shall illustrate in a moment. Prominent scientists and prominent publications have made clear that science is laden with values, whether this reflects the focus of research, the conclusions one reaches, or implications that one draws (Erlich, 2000). Strong claims have been made to convey the point, such as noting that the amoral attitude of the scientist—that is, the neutrality view I have mentioned—is "actually immoral, because it eschews personal responsibility for the likely consequences of one's action" (Rotblat, 1999, p. 1475).

Emphasis on the role of values in contemporary research has not emerged ex nihilo but rather reflects the result of many instances in which value-laden decisions have been made, conflicts of interest have emerged, and abuses are evident. This, in turn, has led to the view, advocated here, that ethics is not an ancillary part of research but is a precondition and a foundation for research. Personal integrity, concerns about socially responsible ways of conducting research, and individual responsibility are central to the entire scientific enterprise. All of this sounds too abstract at this early point in the chapter. Let me move to more concrete examples.

Increased attention to ethical issues has resulted from research in public view, in which there have been clashes between the immediate benefits to individual participants, and knowledge or long-term benefits to yet-to-be-identified persons. Also, attention has been mobilized in response to dramatic abuses of trust (fraud, conflict of interest) and tragic events. Beyond these rare events, many standard methodological practices are challenged because of the values they reflect. In some ways, many of the critical issues are not new. However, the global scale of science, the visibility of science in the media, and increased activism and scrutiny of science by the public have placed a microscope on precisely what is going on and why. Dramatic and tragic cases in the news have focused attention on ethical guidelines and practices. Among these was the tragic death of an 18-year-old patient with a disease who was treated in a gene-therapy study. Evaluation indicated that the research departed from a number of guidelines supposedly in place to direct features of the project (Friedmann, 2000). This tragedy helped to galvanize government oversight, university accountability, and new directives for research.

The value issues are easily illustrated by examples from the treatment of HIV. In more than one project, HIV patients have been assigned (randomly) to a control (no-treatment) group or to a placebo group. Some of the research has been conducted in developing countries (South Africa, Thailand, Ivory Coast). Some researchers have argued that standard treatment in the United States, already known to help HIV, is not likely to be the standard treatment in developing countries because it is too expensive or simply unavailable. Thus, a more appropriate control is no treatment, which *is* the standard care in these countries. Needless to say, this position is quite controversial and has generated extensive discussion, led to guidelines for research, and raised ethical issues of research on a worldwide scale (see http://bioethics.gov).

Alas, the problems do not stem just from control groups. In one clinical trial sponsored by the United Nations, 700 prostitutes from several countries were assigned to one of two interventions, a placebo or a vaginal cream that was expected to lower HIV infection. (Prior research had suggested that an ingredient in the spermicide would block the transfer of HIV.) All subjects received condoms and were encouraged to have their clients use them. Use of a placebo in such studies raises one issue, but consider another issue that emerged. Data analyses ended the study early because 100 prostitutes in the treatment (not placebo!) group contracted HIV at a higher rate. That is, the placebo appeared to be doing better (Brannigan, 2000). (One possible explanation is that the spermicide caused lesions and increased vulnerability to HIV.) The design of such studies, even leaving aside the results, raises major issues and brings into sharp focus ethics of research and underlying guidelines and principles. Often subjects, patient groups, and scientists have mobilized to address critical issues involving subject rights or major ethical issues more generally. Assigning patients with a serious medical or psychiatric condition to various control groups is one such issue, but there are more. The use of stem cells is one such issue. Stem cells have the potential of developing into all sorts of other cells and can, in principle, be used to regenerate organs and save human life. Obtaining these cells from fetuses raises all sorts of critical issues (e.g., abortion, right to life) that draw attention to ethical issues more broadly.

Many of the issues seem only tangentially relevant to psychology. They are directly relevant because they generate guidelines, laws, and university review criteria that govern all research and place into the limelight subject rights and privileges more generally. Clearly, assigning subjects to various control conditions in intervention research falls more squarely in the domain of psychology. If it is plausible to reduce suffering by an intervention, why subject patients to conditions known not to work or expected not to work very well (placebo)? Of course, the ivory tower, academic, and methodological answer is easy to generate; one must extol the virtues of randomized controlled clinical trials, throw in a few threats to internal validity that these trials rule out, mention some utilitarian philosophy that conveys the long-term benefit for future generations, and give an example from the past about how some critical research finding in an unrelated area, saved the universe. The arguments are cogent, but answers on a different plane remove the issues from the realm of intellectual debate. These can be summarized—not logically but importantly—by asking the investigator or person who makes the speech just one question, namely, would you want your daughter or son to be assigned to the control condition in this study? For laboratory psychology experiments in which working memory, persuasion, or perception is studied, the question is not one of great weight. But in much of research, especially in health and medicine, the question is a matter of life and death.

Ethical concerns from research extend to social sciences and also entail life and death. A salient example is work in anthropology, in which a conflict emerges between the search for knowledge and the rights of individuals or a larger group. For example, excavating burial grounds of indigenous people, analyzing DNA from bones, and removing artifacts from religious sites are constantly occurring. The rights of those who claim the sites or artifacts must be considered, and the search for knowledge must be balanced against the rights of others. The subject has many rights, and these have been accorded increased recognition over time.[1]

Most psychological experiments do not involve matters of life and death. However, the context for ethical issues and sensitivities is all research of the kind I have highlighted here. The rights of individuals and groups of individuals are central, and they emerge in many different lines of research and have received global attention. Laws and guidelines that govern research are general and pertain to the entire scientific enterprise of which psychology is a part. I mention this at the outset to convey the importance and salience of ethical issues in general.

---

[1]The rights of subjects are reflected in the many guidelines for research, but in other ways as well. As mentioned previously, efforts have been made to alter the ways in which we conceive of persons who serve in research. The change in preferred terminology from "subjects" to "participants" (APA, 2001) reflects this thrust. Also mentioned previously, I have retained "subjects" as the primary term, in part because it has been critical to distinguish among investigators, experimenters, and subjects, all of whom are participants.

Focusing specifically on psychological research makes it easy to identify the situations that routinely raise ethical issues and dilemmas. To begin with, experiments require manipulation of variables, which often may subject participants to experiences that are undesirable or even potentially harmful, such as stress, failure, and frustration. Second, implementing many experimental manipulations may require withholding information from the subject. The experimental question may address how subjects respond without being forewarned about exactly what will happen or the overall purpose. Third, experimentation requires assessment or observation of the subject. Many dependent measures of interest pertain to areas that subjects may consider private, such as views about themselves, beliefs about important social or political issues, and signs of adjustment or maladjustment. One of the most private sources of information (believe it or not) in clinic and community samples is family income. This seemingly simple descriptive information from the sample may raise concerns that the information might be publicly disclosed and have untoward implications (for collection of social assistance, payment of income taxes, custody support). In my own clinic work it is much easier to find out information about who is abusing whom in the home, what parent is taking what illicit substance, and who has a criminal record than it is to obtain accurate information about income. Clearly, issues pertaining to invasion of privacy and violation of confidentiality are raised by assessment, and even by assessment that may not appear to be very weighty. Fourth, the methodological requirements of psychological experiments also raise ethical issues that are particularly acute in intervention research. For example, assigning clients randomly to one of several treatment (or prevention) or control conditions entails an ethical decision favoring experimental design, rather than the seeming appropriateness of one condition over another for the client's problem. Also, whether treatment should ever be withheld reflects an ethical decision made by an investigator.

Ethical issues are also raised by the relationship between the investigator or experimenter and the subject. The difference in the power and status of the experimenter and access to information (about procedures, goals, and likely outcomes) allows for potential abuses of the rights of the individual participant. Without equality along these dimensions, the subject is not an equal in making informed choices about participation or about alternatives (e.g., if in a treatment study). Research participants, particularly in clinical research, often are disadvantaged or dependent by virtue of their age, physical and mental condition, captive status, educational level, or political and economic position. Samples often studied in clinical research include children and adolescents, psychiatric patients, the elderly, prisoners, persons in need of (and maybe desperate for) treatment, and individuals who cannot pay for services in the usual way because they do not have insurance or health coverage. These subjects might be more readily induced into research and have, or at least feel they have, relatively little freedom to refuse or discontinue participation in light of their options.

The status of the investigator is sustained by several factors. The investigator structures the situation in which the subject participates. He or she is seen as an expert and as justified in determining the conditions for performance. The legitimacy, prestige, and importance of scientific research all place subjects in an inferior position. Although subjects can withdraw from the research, this may not be seen as a realistic or very likely option, given the status differential. Subjects may see themselves as lacking both the capacity and right to question the investigator and what is being done. Subjects are at a disadvantage in terms of the information about the experiment at their disposal, the risks that are taken, and the limited means for counteracting objectionable aspects of the treatment.

In current research, subjects are usually informed of the goals of the study and any risks and benefits that might accrue. Written consent is obtained to confirm that subjects understand the study and their rights not to participate and to withdraw. Both legal codes (e.g., for universities receiving any federal funds) and ethical codes (from professional organizations) guide the process of disclosing information to, and obtaining consent from, the subjects. The codes and practices that follow from them ensure that the rights of the individual subject are protected and are given the highest priority in research.

CRITICAL ISSUES IN RESEARCH

Although many ethical issues can be identified, a few seem particularly salient; using deception in experiments, informing participants about the deception after the experiment is completed, invading the subject's privacy, and obtaining informed consent. Whether the research is laboratory based (e.g., college students completing an experiment task), clinic based (e.g., intervention research with clinic samples), or something in between, these issues can easily emerge.

Deception

Deception may take many different forms and often refers to quite different operations. At one extreme, deception can refer to entirely misrepresenting the nature of an experiment. At the other extreme, deception can also refer to being ambiguous about the experiment or not specifying all or many important details. The extent to which these various active (e.g., misrepresentation) or passive (e.g., failure to mention specific details) forms of deception are objectionable, in part depends upon the situations in which they are used and the effects they are likely to have on the participants (Koocher & Keith-Spiegel, 1998). Misleading the participant may not be very objectionable in many experimental arrangements. For example, when participants perform a memory task involving lists of words or syllables, they may be told initially that the purpose is to measure the way in which individuals memorize words. In fact, the purpose may be to assess the accuracy of recall as a function of the way in which the words are presented. In this situation there seems to be little potential harm to the participants or their evaluations of themselves. Alternatively, participants may be placed under psychological stress or led to raise important questions about themselves. For example, participants may be told they have latent adjustment or sexual problems or are odd in the way they think. The goal may be to evaluate these induced states on some other area of functioning.

An illustration of deception in psychological research is provided by the well-known experiments of Stanley Milgram (1933–1984), who conducted research on obedience to authority. The context for the research was the Nazi war crimes and Nuremberg War Criminal trials in which many who were involved in acts of genocide noted that they engaged in horrible acts because they were just following orders, that is, were being obedient. Milgram conducted laboratory experiments in which subjects were recruited. They did not know they were the subjects and were called "teachers" who were going to help others who were "learners." The teachers were given a fictitious story that the experiment was intended to explore the effects of punishment on learning. The learners actually were confederates, that is, actors working as part of the experiment, and it was the teachers who were really the subjects. The teachers were asked and encouraged to increase shocks, including intense shocks to punish the learner. In fact, no actual shocks were given, but the teachers (subjects) did not know this. The results essentially showed that many—in fact, over 60 percent—of the teachers (subjects) administered high doses of the shock (see Milgram, 1974). The results convey the high level of obedience to authority. Many interesting features of this research can easily be found on the Web (search "Stanley Milgram" on most search engines). I mention the example here because of the multiple sources of deception reflected in this experiment. Such deception would not be possible under current research guidelines.

Deception is still possible in contemporary studies of psychology. The ethical dilemma lies in deciding whether deception is justified in a given experiment and whether the possible risks to the participant outweigh the potential benefits in the knowledge the study is designed to yield. Both the risks to the participant and potential benefits usually are a matter of surmise, so the decision is not at all straightforward. The dilemma is particularly difficult because the risks to the individual subject are weighed against the benefits to society. In most psychological experiments the benefits of the research are not likely to accrue to the participant directly. In all honesty, in so many cases, the benefits to society are not so clear either. Weighing potential benefits to society against potential risks to the individual subject is difficult. The safest way to proceed is to minimize or eliminate risk to the subject by not using active forms of deception.

The potential harm that deception may cause for the individual subject certainly is a major ethical objection to its use. Moreover, aside from its direct harmful consequences, the act of deception has been objected to because it violates a value of honesty between individuals, in this case the investigator and subject. Investigators engage in deceptive practices that would not be condoned outside of the experimental setting because they violate the basic rights of individuals. Thus, deception fosters a type of behavior that is objected to on its own grounds independently of its other consequences. Alternatively, it may not be the deceptive behaviors in which investigators may engage as much as the context in which these behaviors occur. Many forms of deception occur in everyday life, and individuals occasionally object to these as well (e.g., surprise parties). The problem with forms of deception and surprises in an experiment is that the professional context of an experiment may lead people to expect full disclosure, candor, and respect for individual rights.

Actually, deception in clinical, counseling, and related areas of research rarely involves efforts to mislead subjects. The central issue for research is the extent to which subjects should be aware of the purpose and procedures of the experiment. Ideally, investigators would fully disclose all available information about what will take place. Complete disclosure would entail conveying to subjects the nature of all of the procedures, even those to which the subjects in any particular condition will not be exposed, and revealing the investigator's view and expectations about what the results might yield. In most psychological experiments with human subjects, full disclosure of available information may not be realistic. If the subject knows the purpose, hypotheses, and procedures, this information could influence or alter the results. Full knowledge about the experiment could raise all of the problems associated with demand characteristics and subject roles, as discussed earlier. These influences are much more likely to occur when subjects are aware of the purpose of the experiment.

The effects of disclosing the purpose and hypotheses to the subjects were demonstrated in the 1970s when the issue of disclosure began to be mandated. In a seminal study, college students participated in a verbal conditioning experiment in which their selection of pronouns in a sentence-construction task was reinforced by the experimenter by saying "good" or "okay" (Resnick & Schwartz, 1973). Some subjects (informed group) were told that the purpose was to increase their use of "I" and "we" pronouns in order to determine whether telling subjects the purpose of the experiment affected the results. These subjects were told the true purpose (to evaluate the effects of full disclosure). Other subjects (uninformed group) were told that the experiment was designed to study verbal communication. They were not informed of the real purpose of the experiment. Subjects in both groups constructed sentences and received approval when "I" or "we" pronouns were used in the sentences. As expected, the uninformed subjects increased in their use of the target pronouns that were reinforced over their base rates in a practice (nonreinforced) period, a finding shown many times in the verbal conditioning literature. In contrast, the informed subjects decreased in their use of target pronouns relative to their initial practice rates. Thus, disclosing information about the purposes of the experiment greatly influenced the findings.

The results suggest that informing subjects about the purposes and expected results of an experiment might dictate the specific relation that is obtained between the independent and dependent variable. Of course, one might view the results in another way, namely, that not telling subjects about the experiment dictates a specific relation as well and one that is not more or less "real" or informative than results obtained under informed circumstances. Yet, a major goal of psychology is to study behavior and to extrapolate findings to those circumstances in which individuals normally behave. That is, most of the theories we develop about human functioning are not intended to account for phenomena evident only in the laboratory situation or under obtrusive and reactive arrangements. Thus, investigators wish to understand how subjects respond to events when subjects are not forewarned about their anticipated effects and the purpose of exposure to these events. Although investigators, in principle, would like to avoid deception, it may be necessary in some form to understand certain behavioral processes.

In general, guidelines for informing subjects are dictated by law and by ethical principles that govern research and informed consent. Such guidelines do not require elaborating all of the views, hypotheses, expectations, and related possibilities to the subjects. Thus, some information invariably is withheld. Of special concern in relation to deception are active efforts to mislead subjects. Such efforts are quite rare in clinical, counseling, and educational research. Research proposals that include efforts to mislead subjects must establish that deception is essential to achieve the research goals and that special procedures to protect subjects are provided to reduce any lingering effects of the experience.

To establish that deception is necessary, at least three criteria must be met. First, the investigator who designs the experiment must make the case to others that deception is justified given the importance of the information that is to be revealed by the experiment. An investigator may not be the best judge because of his or her investment in the research. Hence, review committees involving individuals from different fields of inquiry ordinarily examine whether the proposed procedures are justifiable. The committees, formally developed in most universities and institutions where research is conducted, follow guidelines for evaluating research and for protecting subjects, as discussed later in the chapter.

Second and related, if there is any deception in the planned experiment, there must be assurances that less deceptive or nondeceptive methods of investigation could not be used to obtain the information. This, too, is difficult to assess because whether similar methods would produce the information proposed in an experiment that uses deception is entirely an empirical matter. Researchers genuinely disagree about the extent to which deception is essential.

Third, the aversiveness of the deception itself bears strongly on the justification of the study. The aversiveness refers to the procedures and degree of deception and the potential for, and magnitude of, harmful effects. Deceptions vary markedly in degree, although ethical discussions usually focus on cases wherein subjects are grossly misled about their own abilities or personal characteristics.

Research begins with the view that individual rights are to be protected. Investigators are to disclose to the extent possible details of the design, purposes, risks, benefits, and costs (monetary or other). The purpose is to permit the subject to make an informed decision regarding participation. If deception is to be used, by either withholding critical information or misrepresenting the study, the onus is on the investigator to show cause at the research proposal stage that this is essential for the benefits of the research. Unless the case can be made to review committees that evaluate such proposals, the work may not be permitted.

In many cases, if deception seems necessary, the investigator's creativity and methodological and statistical skills can provide a path to obtain the information without deception. It is useful to begin with the premise there may be no need to deceive subjects. Alternative experimental procedures may address whether deception is necessary. For example, the investigator may present to different groups varying degrees of information and see if this affects the findings. Alternatively, perhaps the methods used to evaluate demand characteristics, such as the preinquiry or use of simulators, can be explored to evaluate if subjects would be likely to perform differently under different conditions of disclosure. The absence of differences between groups studied in this way are consistent with the view that deception may not be critical to the research findings and methods of study in the area of work. These alternatives are not perfect in providing unambiguous answers that might be obtained with deception. These options may begin to make the case to the investigator that deception will be needed to pursue a particular question. A researcher is usually not entitled to begin with the assumption that deception is fine. Just the opposite, the case has to be made that deception is essential or has such benefits as to outweigh other conceptions.

Debriefing

If there is any deception in the experiment or if crucial information is withheld, the experimenter should describe the true nature of the experiment after it is run. Providing a description of the experiment and its purposes is referred to as *debriefing*. The purpose of debriefing is to counteract or minimize any negative effects that the experiment may have had. By debriefing, the experimenter hopes the subjects will not leave the experiment with any greater anxiety, discomfort, or lowered self-esteem than when they arrived. Apart from overcoming possible deleterious effects of deception, debriefing is often considered to convey educative objectives, such as communicating the potential value of research and acknowledging the subjects' contribution to research (Judd, Kidder, & Smith, 1991). These features focus on conveying the benefits of subject participation in research and are of value in their own right.

Debriefing is usually discussed in the context of overcoming the deleterious effects of deception. The manner in which debriefing is conducted and the information conveyed to the subject vary enormously among experiments. Typically, subjects meet with the experimenter immediately after completing the experimental tasks. The experimenter may inform the subject what the experiment was "really" about and explain the reasons that the stated purpose did not convey this. The importance of debriefing varies with the type of experiment and the nature of the deception. As part of the experiment, subjects may have been told that they have tendencies toward mental illness or an early grave. In such situations, subjects obviously ought to be told that the information was not accurate and that they are "normal." Presumably, such information will be a great relief to the subjects. On the other hand, subjects may be distressed that they were exposed to such a deception or that they were "gullible" enough to believe it.

Debriefing has been assumed to be a procedure that resolves the potentially harmful effects of deception. Yet, debriefing has its own problems and may not achieve its intended purposes. First, subjects may believe that the debriefing session is merely a continuation of the experiment and the deception by the experimenter. Suspiciousness on the part of the subject has a reasonable basis. Although quite rare, before the days of informed consent, examples can be found in which subjects were told that the experiment was over and were then "debriefed," when in truth the debriefing itself involved further deception, and the subject continued unwittingly to serve in the experiment (Festinger & Carlsmith, 1959). Also, in their introductory psychology courses college students invariably read about or view films of "classic" experiments in which quite clear deception was invoked, even though such experiments would not be allowed by current standards, as illustrated previously (Milgram, 1974).

Second, debriefing subjects by providing full information about the deception does not necessarily erase the false impressions (e.g., about subject skills) established during the experiment (Ross, Lepper, & Hubbard, 1975; Walster, Berscheid, Abrahams, & Aronson, 1967). This is roughly analogous to someone lying to you and much later saying he or she had a good reason at the time. The initial lie may place a small stain in the fabric of one's relationship that is not completely erased by stain-removing comments. The fact that the effects of deception may linger even after debriefing provides us with further caveats. If deception is to be considered, it must be clearly justified because of the risks to individual rights and integrity.

Debriefing requires considerable thought in research, particularly where subjects are deliberately misguided about the experiment. Debriefing must convey to the subject what the experiment was about, what the purpose was, and how reactions of the subject were typical. It may be necessary to individualize debriefing to meet questions of the individual subjects. The timing of debriefing may be important as well. Sometimes experimenters wait until all subjects complete the experiment and contact subjects with a printed handout or class announcement. The reasons for this are that information provided early in the experiment might filter to other subjects before they serve in the study. However, delayed debriefing may not be as effective as immediate debriefing. If subjects are potentially harmed by the deception, the experimenter's obligation is to debrief as soon and as effectively as possible.

An investigator using deception should demonstrate that the debriefing procedures effectively eliminate incorrect beliefs induced in the experiment. Whether subjects are debriefed should refer more to the outcome of providing certain kinds of information rather than simply the experience to which subjects are exposed. The effectiveness of a particular debriefing technique could be demonstrated in the experiment itself or as part of pilot work prior to the investigation.

Invasion of Privacy

Invasion of privacy represents a broad concept that encompasses practices extending well beyond research. Generally, invasion of privacy refers to seeking information of a personal nature that intrudes upon what individuals view as private. Information may be sought on such topics as religious preferences, sexual beliefs and behaviors, income, and political views. Individuals vary considerably on the areas they regard as sensitive and private. For example, many years ago one survey reported that married women provided detailed answers to questions about birth control practices, a topic that might be viewed as very sensitive, perhaps even more so in the less open and sexually explicit prehistoric days of the survey (Clark, 1967). The respondents were very cooperative in providing answers until they were asked to reveal their family's income, at which point they refused to answer. This question apparently invaded what subjects thought was private information, presumably because it was not part of the topic they had agreed to discuss. There is no reason to think that this has changed. Surveys assess attitudes on all sorts of personal topics. Beyond surveys, other sources solicit information from individuals—including credit bureaus, investigative and sales agencies, and potential employers. All of these are invasions to some people.

The use of tests that measure psychopathology and personality also raises concerns over invasion of privacy. Test results can reflect directly upon an individual's psychological status, adjustment, and beliefs and uncover personal characteristics that the subject might regard as private. Moreover, the information obtained through psychological testing might be potentially damaging if made public. The threat of personality testing to the invasion of privacy has been a topic of considerable concern. One reason is that measures of psychopathology and personality have been used routinely to screen potential employees in government, business, and industry. Many of the questions asked of prospective employees seemed to be of a personal nature and not clearly related to the tasks for which individuals were being selected.

In psychological research the major issues regarding invasion of privacy pertain to how the information from subjects is obtained and used. Ordinarily, information provided in experiments must be provided willingly. Obviously, there are many kinds of research where consent of the individual is neither possible (in cases of severe psychiatric or neurological impairment) nor especially crucial (in the case of studying archival records for groups of unidentifiable subjects).

Two conditions designed to protect the subject's right to privacy in research are anonymity and confidentiality. *Anonymity* refers to ensuring that the identity of the subjects and their individual performance are not revealed. Subjects who agree to provide information must be assured that their responses are anonymous. Anonymity can be assured at the point of obtaining the data as, for example, when subjects are instructed not to identify themselves on an answer sheet and, after the information is obtained, by separating the names of participants from the measures or any associations with the scores. Typically, data are coded so that participants' names cannot be associated with a particular set of data. Only the investigator may have the information revealing the identity of the subject. In most research, confidentiality is maintained by obtaining the data under conditions of anonymity and/or converting the data through coding or data reduction procedures to a format wherein the individual's identity cannot be discerned. Research with clinic populations or in special settings may require additional safeguards regarding the protection of confidentiality (e.g., clinic records). The reason is that many persons may have special interest in the information obtained as part of the research (employers, relatives, school administrators) and that the nature of the information (measures of adjustment, psychopathology) may be potentially damaging if misinterpreted or misused. Also, there may be additional uses or interest in the data (records requested by the clients or families), so the information cannot be destroyed or completely disassociated from the clients' names.

Invasion of privacy extends beyond the process of obtaining information. Once the information is obtained, participants must be assured that their performance is confidential. *Confidentiality* means that the information will not be disclosed to a third party without the awareness and consent of the participant. Conceivably, situations might arise where confidentiality is violated as, for example, when the information might conceal some clear and imminent danger to an individual or society. For example, clinical psychologists are involved with research on the evaluation, treatment, and prevention of AIDS. Confidentiality about who is participating in the research and about test results for infection is obviously important. The information, if inadvertently made available, can serve to stigmatize research participants and subject them to discrimination in everyday life (employment, housing). In some cases information may emerge that has to be reported even though subjects would choose not to have the information revealed. For example, a study on parenting or child–parent interaction may reveal that there is child abuse in the home. In most states this has to be reported to child services as a matter of law.

Research increasingly is conducted over the Web, and subjects provide their answers to measures that appear on their computer screen. The subjects may identify themselves by password, e-mail address, or by subject and demographic variables (age, sex). In such research there may be assurances that the information will remain confidential. Subjects are appropriately wary because it is usually quite easy to trace information to a particular computer, unless one goes to special lengths to erase one's tracks. Also, businesses that claim the information (credit card number, e-mail, social security number) provided by customers over the Web is confidential already have a few well-publicized lapses in security. We all recognize that information over the Web is not private and, in principle, assurances cannot be given that the information is completely confidential. This concern is more likely to emerge as diagnosis, assessment, and psychotherapy are conducted over the Web.

Invasion of privacy enters into many different areas in clinical research. For example, privacy is an important issue in writing the results of research investigations and treatment applications. Clinical research reports occasionally are prepared for publication where an individual case is involved. In these instances, efforts to maintain confidentiality require the investigator to disguise the ancillary information about the client in such a way that his or her identity could not be recognized. Typically, pseudonyms are used when a case is described in published form. Yet, for many case reports a change in the name may not protect the subject's confidentiality. Cases are often selected for presentation *because* they raise special issues, circumstances, and challenges. If there is any risk that preparation of a research report could reveal the identity of a subject, the subject must be informed of this in advance and provide consent.

Another area in clinical research wherein invasion of privacy is possible is in the use of informants for data collection. Occasionally, treatment research with a client or group of clients may solicit the aid of friends, spouses, neighbors, teachers, or employers. The purpose is to ask these individuals to provide data about the client. The information is used to evaluate the effects of treatment or the severity of the client' s problem, although the client may not be aware of this assessment. Seeking information about the client may violate the client's right to privacy and confidentiality. The client may not want his or her problem widely advertised, and any attempts at unobtrusive assessment may violate this wish. For example, asking employers to assess whether the client's alcoholic consumption interferes with work performance may apprise the employer of a problem of which he or she was unaware.

The opportunities for invasion of privacy perhaps have never been greater than the present, given the information collected and the interest in using this information for research and other purposes. For example, evaluation of the census every 10 years in the United States provides information that is increasingly sophisticated and accessible. Much of the information is publicly available through databases that in prior years were not as readily accessible. The database will be used by advertisers that wish to target specific neighborhoods, based on income, education, ethnicity, and other variables that can be obtained, sometimes on a street-by-street basis. For example, automobile manufacturers have a profile of the type of persons who buy their cars; advertising can be targeted to neighborhoods where such persons live, as revealed by the census. Many will view this as invasion of privacy or as a slippery slope leading to such invasion, despite the fact that they cannot be identified individually. Researchers ought to be sensitive to these issues and to address risk that might be associated with the seemingly innocuous goal of gathering information.

Invasion of privacy is often discussed at the level of the individual subject. However, much larger units are relevant and of deep concern in research. Invasion of privacy of communities and cultural and ethnic groups emerges as well. For example, several years ago a study was designed to survey alcohol use in an Inupiat community in Barrow, Alaska (Foulks, 1987; Manson, 1989). The purpose was to examine cases of alcohol abuse and to evaluate community detention programs for acute alcohol detoxification. A representative sample of persons ($N = 88$) over the age of 15 was drawn from the community and interviewed regarding their attitudes, values, and behavior in relation to alcohol use. Other measures of functioning were assessed as well, including church membership and social and work behavior. So far, the project seems innocent enough. However, this all changed with the results and their dissemination.

The results indicated that 41 percent of the sample considered themselves to be excessive drinkers; over 50 percent said that alcohol use caused problems with their spouse and family; 62 percent said they regularly got into fights when drinking. These and similar types of descriptive statements indicated that alcohol use was a problem in this community. Reports of the findings were viewed by the community as highly objectionable and invasive. The community's view was that alcohol use and associated problems resulted from a new way of life imposed on them rather than on implied deficits, biological or otherwise, or problems inherent to the people. The report was criticized as denigrating, culturally imperialistic, and insensitive to the values of American Indian and Alaskan native culture (Foulks, 1989). Great oversimplification of the findings by the news media (e.g., a byline stating, "Alcohol Plagues Eskimos" in the *New York Times*, January 22, 1980) and emphasis on alcoholism and violence in various articles exacerbated the problem.

The consequences of this study might be used to illustrate many issues, such as the need for much better and different relations with the members of the population of interest in relation to the design and reporting stages of the results, and contact with the media. In relation to invasion of privacy, individual community members could not be identified by the report. Nevertheless, community members, whether or not they served as subjects, viewed their privacy as violated, and objected that they were misrepresented (see Manson, 1989). Such examples convey that investigations do not merely describe relations and report findings of abstract scientific interest. The methods of obtaining information, the reporting of that information, and the way information is and could be used are part of the ethical considerations of research.

Independently of the prior study but certainly related to it, there is increased recognition that communities as well as individuals need to be protected in research. That is, informed consent, discussed later in the chapter, focuses on individual participants. Increasingly, research is conducted on an international scale involving samples of different cultures, religions, and traditions. Guidelines have suggested involving community members in developing the project, conveying consent to participants, actually conducting the research, and overseeing the communication and dissemination of results (see Weijer & Emanuel, 2000). Efforts to increase sensitivity to invasion of privacy at the group and community level represent an important advance, but as yet there are no formal requirements mandated for research.

INFORMED CONSENT

Conditions and Elements

An ethical requirement of research is that investigators obtain *informed consent* before subjects serve in the study. There are occasional exceptions, such as situations in which archival records are used and subjects are no longer living or cannot be identified. Implementing the requirement raises special obstacles. In principle, consent can never be completely informed. Not all possible consequences of the experimental procedures, measures, and participation can be known; hence they cannot be presented to inform the subject. Also, the impact of the experimental manipulation or intervention, however seemingly innocuous, can have multiple effects (direct and side effects) among the subjects. Indeed, even well-established interventions can have horrible side effects. For example, oral polio vaccine is highly effective and is no longer "experimental." Even so, 1 of every 750,000 people who receive it get polio from the vaccine (Greensfelder, 2000). Complete information is not available to tell individuals whether they are likely to contract polio and to use the information in such a way as to reduce the number to zero (i.e., by not giving the vaccine to those persons likely to contract polio from it). In research, new knowledge is the desired outcome. Consequently, all the more is it impossible to provide complete information about the intervention and its effects. Stating the logical status and limits of available information that could be presented to the subject is important as a backdrop for the tasks of the investigator. Information cannot be complete. Yet, the responsibility of the investigator is to provide available information and reasonable statements of the likely repercussions from participation so that the subject can make a rational decision.

Informed consent consists of three major elements: competence, knowledge, and volition, and these are described in Table 17.1. In principle, ensuring competence could be a major issue. In practice there are large segments of research where this is not an issue. For example, in laboratory studies with college students with psychological tasks (listening to tapes of innocuous interactions, reading passages and remembering details), competence is not an issue. Subjects are considered quite capable of making rational decisions to participate on the basis of the information provided, and few would be worried about any deleterious effects of participation. In other cases, where characteristics of the sample may impede decision making (very young or very old subjects; individuals with clinical dysfunction that impedes cognitive functioning), competence is an issue. The competence of others who act in behalf of the client (spouses, parents, other relatives) is then the issue because these persons take over responsibility for decision-making. Obviously, having others make critical decisions can raise its own problems if those who provide consent do not have interests of the subject at heart. (This is another good reason to be very nice to your relatives.) Such circumstances arise in considering invasive or risky medical or psychiatric procedures and do not pertain to the vast majority of research. As these comments imply, decisions about subject competence are in the context of considerations of what could happen in the experiment and whether the intervention or manipulation could interfere with broader rights of the subject (e.g., those recognized by law).

TABLE 17.1.   Three Elements of Informed Consent

Competence

The individual's ability to make a well-reasoned decision and to give consent meaningfully. Are there any characteristics of the subjects or the situation in which they are placed that would interfere with their ability to make thoughtful, deliberative, and informed decisions?

Knowledge

Understanding the nature of the experiment, the alternatives available, and the potential risks and benefits. Is there sufficient information provided to the subject, and can the subject process, utilize, and draw on that information? Competence to use this information is relevant as well.

Volition

Agreement to participate on the part of subject that is provided willingly and free from constraint or duress. Are there pressures, constraints, or special contingencies, whether explicit or implicit, that coerce subjects to serve in the study? Penalties or alternatives that are likely to be viewed as aversive for not participating may be a sign that participation is not completely volitional. Also, subjects must be free to revoke their consent at any time.

Knowledge, the second element of consent, pertains to information about the study. To provide adequate knowledge for informed consent, investigators are obligated to describe all facts, risks, and sources of discomfort that might influence a subject's decision to participate willingly. Not all of the conceivable risks need to be described, but rather only those that might plausibly result from the procedure. The information must be presented to the subject in an easily understandable fashion. In addition, subjects should be allowed to raise questions to clarify all of the issues that might be ambiguous. A colleague of mine designed a study to assess the staff of a psychiatric hospital. The goal was to examine their views of patients, treatment, and hospital care. This was a descriptive study and included a rather large assessment battery (approximately 3 hours of assessment, divided into two sessions). A consent form was required—quite reasonable—but he was also asked to list as a risk factor to the participants the possibility that they might become bored because there were so many measures. Becoming bored might be a little extreme as a side effect to caution subjects about. (I may be a poor judge of this and have been accused of being overreactive. It all started because "becoming bored" kept emerging as a phrase among my dissertation committee members.)

Volition means that the subject agrees to participate without coercion. Participation in the experiment cannot be required to fulfill a class assignment, according to current requirements for consent. For subjects to provide consent, they must have a choice pertaining to their involvement in the investigation. The choice cannot be one in which participation in the experiment is substituted for some aversive or coercive alternative (e.g., completing two extra term papers), although in any given case, this may be difficult to discern. Whether the subject can "freely" choose to participate is sometimes evident from the consequences for not agreeing to participate or from withdrawing once consent has been provided. The absence of any penalty partially defines the extent to which the subject's consent was voluntary.

Competence, knowledge, and volition are not straightforward criteria determining whether consent is informed. Consider a few of the salient issues. Competence to provide consent is a major concern with populations that may be incapable or less than fully capable of providing consent (fetuses, young children, persons with intellectual impairment, comatose patients, and institutionalized populations such as psychiatric patients and prisoners, and some university faculty). Determining whether individuals are competent to provide consent presents many problems in its own right. For individuals regarded as incompetent, parents or guardians may give permission, but in medical research a parent or guardian may not consent to participation of an incompetent person in a treatment that promises no direct therapeutic benefit. Competent guardians may not sign away the rights of their incompetent wards.

Even when consent can be sought and obtained from the persons themselves, it is often unclear whether consent is adequate or meaningful, particularly for special populations where competence may be questioned. When consent guidelines and procedures were first formulated, research showed that following consent procedures as described here may not be sufficient to achieve the goals of actually informing the subjects. For example, in one study with voluntarily admitted psychiatric patients, 60 percent of the patients were unable to recall signing the admission form consenting to hospitalization when they were asked within 10 days after admission (Palmer & Wohl, 1972). Some 33 percent of the patients did not recall or could not recall accurately the content of the form. Some of the patients even denied having signed it. Similarly, an evaluation of biomedical research in the Veterans Administration Hospital system revealed that approximately 28 percent of patients interviewed were not aware that they were participating in a research investigation (Committee on Biomedical Research in the Veterans Administration, 1977). Moreover, at least 20 percent of the individual patients had very little or no idea of what the research was about, even though the patients had received carefully implemented informed consent procedures and had signed the appropriate forms. These investigations raised questions about the competence of the patients or the adequacy of the procedures to secure informed consent. These questions continue today. The capacity to understand and make decisions regarding consent may be limited among patient samples, although intensive efforts to educate the subjects about the research may compensate for these deficits (e.g., Carpenter et al., 2000). The quandary is whether informed consent refers to *procedures* to which subjects are exposed (a speech and consent forms) and/or *an outcome of the procedures* (whether subjects, in fact, know, understand, and fully appreciate all the information the consent procedures were designed to convey).

Ensuring that consent is based on knowledge provided to the subject has its own problems. The risks and potential benefits of treatment are not always well known, particularly for populations that have been refractory to conventional treatments. Last-resort or experimental techniques may be improvised. Hence, the necessary information for making a knowledgeable decision is unavailable. For example, in an extreme instance psychosurgery was recommended to control aggressive behavior of a psychiatric patient. Although the patient consented to the procedure, in a landmark decision the court ruled that consent could not be "informed" because of the nature of the treatment and the lack of available information about its benefits and risks (*Kaimowitz v. Michigan Department of Mental Health*).

Volition also raises special issues. Many studies pay subjects for participating or for completing assessments and sometimes the amount of money is high ($200–$500 for completing the assessment battery) and quite high in light of the income of the participants (individuals on welfare or with income at or below the poverty line). Subject payment is usually framed as reimbursement for time spent, but monetary inducements are clearly a gray area. One can be said to always have a choice of saying yes or no, but I think this is a superficial analysis of choice. If some external (or perhaps internal) influence increases the probability of participating to such a high degree, then the alternative (not participating) approaches zero. This is not the place to analyze the concept of choice.

Perhaps more subtle than monetary inducements, the differences in power and status in the experimental setting between the investigator or experimenter and subjects can militate against voluntary consent. Subjects may not feel they can choose freely to participate or to withdraw because of their position in relation to the investigator. Since the investigator structures the research situation, the subject depends almost completely on the information provided to make choices about participation or continuation in the investigation. Thus, consent at any point in the research may not be completely informed because the subject may not have access to important information.

Whether institutionalized populations can truly volunteer for treatment or research also is a problem. Individuals may agree to participate because they feel compelled to do so. They may anticipate long-term gains from staff and administration whose opinions may be important for status or commodities within the institution or for release from the institution. The lure of release and the involuntarily confined status of many populations for whom treatment is provided may make voluntary consent impossible.

In research and treatment informed consent has become the central issue for ensuring the protection of the individual subject. This does not mean that all facets of an experiment are routinely described to the subject prior to participation. However, it does mean that before the research procedures are delivered to the subject or before the subject completes the first measure, all facets of the study that might affect the subject's willingness to participate are described, and subjects are informed of their rights to information about the experiment. Moreover, subjects are assured that they may terminate their participation at any time if they so desire.

Consent Forms

In advance of placing subjects through any procedures or assessments, a consent form is provided to convey information about the study that the subject needs to know to make an informed decision. Usually, institutional review boards and committees (at colleges, universities, hospitals, prisons) are charged with evaluating the research proposal, consent procedures, and consent form. Members who review the proposal are drawn from diverse disciplines. The research proposal is evaluated to examine the research design, specific procedures, conditions to which the subject will be exposed, and risks and benefits. Evaluation of the research design deserves comment. The general plan of the research must be made clear to permit committee members to determine if the questions underlying the investigation are reasonable and can be answered by the study. If the questions cannot be answered by the study, then the subjects should not be placed at any risk or inconvenience. Methodological scrutiny is not very stringent, but it need not be at this point. The investigator ought to be able to make the case that the study is worth doing and that the ends (the results) justify the means (procedures to which subjects will be exposed). In some cases, of course, the means will not be allowed no matter what ends; in other cases the ends seem trivial, and hence any means (or use of subjects) may not be worthwhile. (In my dissertation proposal, no one could tell if there were ends or means, so my proposal whizzed through the consent committee.)

Most psychological experiments do not involve risk situations and are designated as "minimal" risk. The subjects (e.g., college students), experimental tasks (memorizing lists of words, completing personality measures), and risks (mild boredom if the task continues too long) do not exceed the risks of normal living. Review of such studies is relatively straightforward because concerns about subject rights are not raised by the research paradigm. In many such cases, formal review of the study and informed consent procedures are omitted because the experiment is considered to be in a class of procedures that is innocuous. Essentially, such procedures are given blanket approval. In clinical work several features often extend the situation well beyond "minimal risk" by virtue of the population (e.g., patient samples), focus of assessment or intervention (e.g., suicidal intent, depression), and special ethical dilemmas (e.g., random assignment, delaying treatment), as discussed further below. Understandably, the review of proposals and consent procedures of such studies is more stringent. In many universities separate review committees are available for different types of research. For example, a social sciences review committee often reviews psychological experiments with minimal risk. In contrast, research with clinical populations is likely to be reviewed by a biomedical committee.

Providing consent is operationalized by the subject's completion of the consent form. The overall purpose of the form is to convey information, to do so clearly and simply, and to ensure subjects are aware of what they are entering. Although specific details of the forms vary as a function of the type of research and level of risk, several components are common. The form usually includes several ingredients, such as a description of the purpose of the study and the procedures to be followed and a statement of potential risks as well as any benefits for the subject or for society. Moreover, statements are usually included in the form, indicating that the client was permitted to ask questions of the experimenter and actually received answers to his or her satisfaction, that he or she does give permission to participate, that the information included will remain confidential, and that he or she is free to withdraw from the experiment at any time without penalty. The subject signs the form, indicating that each of the above conditions has been met and that he or she agrees to participate. Table 17.2 lists and highlights several components of consent forms, each of which might be represented by a brief paragraph or two within the form.

Letter and Spirit of Consent

The investigator is required to describe the procedures to the subject and to obtain signed consent. The signed consent form satisfies the research requirements and

TABLE 17.2.   Components of Informed Consent Forms

Section of the Form	Purpose and Contents
Overview	Presentation of the goals of the study, why this is conducted, who is responsible for the study and its execution
Description of procedures	Clarification of the experimental conditions, assessment procedures, requirements of the subjects
Risks and inconveniences	Statement of any physical and psychological risks and an estimate of their likelihood. Inconveniences and demands to be placed on the subjects (how many sessions, requests to do any thing, contact at home)
Benefits	A statement of what the subjects can reasonably hope to gain from participation, including psychological, physical, and monetary benefits
Costs and economic consideration	Charges to the subjects (e.g., in treatment) and payment (for participation or completing various forms)
Confidentiality	Assurances that the information is confidential and will be seen only by people who need to do so for the purposes of research (e.g., scoring and data analyses), procedures to ensure confidentiality (removal of names) if it is possible that sensitive information (psychiatric information, criminal activity) can be subpoenaed
Alternative treatments	In an intervention study, alternatives available to the client before or during participation are outlined
Voluntary participation	A statement that the subject is willing to participate and can say no now or later without penalty of any kind
Questions and further information	A statement that the subject is encouraged to ask questions at any time and can contact an individual (or individuals) (listed by name and phone number) who is (are) available for such contacts
Signature lines	A place for the subject as well as the experimenter to sign

hence follows the "letter" of the rules that govern research and the investigator's responsibilities. In addition, there is a "spirit" of informed consent, which refers more nebulously to the overall intent of the procedures and the goal of ensuring that clients genuinely understand what they are signing, what the study entails, and the risks, costs, and benefits. In most research (e.g., laboratory studies with college students), presentation of the consent information followed by the subject's signing of the form is sufficient for the letter and spirit of the consent procedures.

Research that is in any way service related (e.g., treatment) or that involves personally or physically invasive procedures (obtaining private information that could be solicited by the courts, medical tests with remote albeit genuine risks) or persons who are not, or may not be, competent to represent themselves fully (children, disadvantaged persons) raises special obstacles. Clients may be less likely to understand options, choices, and opportunities to change their minds about participation. In such cases, satisfying the letter of the informed consent requirements may not approach the spirit or intent of these requirements.

Interestingly, there are no formal research requirements that subjects actually understand what is presented to them. Thus, presentation of information and signing of consent forms might be accomplished without genuinely informed consent. For this reason both the spirit as well as the letter of consent are important. The spirit of consent emphasizes the investigator's responsibility to maximize the clients' understanding of the investigation and refers to the investigator's "best effort" to convey the purpose, procedures, and risks of participation and generally to meet the consent conditions. It is not a disaster if a prospective subject occasionally refuses to participate. In fact, this may be a good index that the procedures to explain the project are registering. This is not our usual way of thinking about consent in which a subject who refuses may be viewed as recalcitrant or oppositional.

Presentation of the content by repeating significant facets of the study, paraphrasing the consent form, asking questions of the subject at critical points to assess understanding, and similar strategies may help. The time allowed to explain the procedures and to obtain consent may need to be extended to foster the atmosphere required to inform the client. Obviously, protracted consent procedures, clinically *over*sensitive presentations, and ad nauseam requests for feedback on the part of the experimenter ("But do you really understand that you could have nightmares from meeting with such an ugly therapist? O.K., tell me what a nightmare is.") are likely to be inappropriate as a general strategy. This is why the spirit of consent is so important. The rules or letter of consent procedures specify the minimal conditions to be satisfied in discharging responsibilities to the subject. Beyond that, judgment, experience, and common sense are needed to meet the goals of consent and to balance research interests and subject rights.

Different ways of presenting details of the study, as part of the consent procedures, can be identified, varying from perfunctory presentation of the consent form ("Here [consent form is handed to the subject], as soon as you sign this, we can begin"), through lengthy deliberations of individual phrases and concepts ("You are probably wondering what "random" assignment really is and why we do this. Did you ever hear of R.A. Fisher—I didn't, either. . . ."), to overly empathic and mushy understanding ("O.K., how do you feel about all of what I have said so far [about the task of memorizing nonsense syllables]? I'll bet this is a little threatening."). The sample and circumstances of the experiment obviously dictate the letter and spirit of consent and how these are to be achieved.

The spirit of consent is important to underscore for a reason not frequently acknowledged. The investigator often has a conflict of interest in obtaining informed consent. Entry of subjects into the study is the goal, and something critical to the investigator (meeting the demands of a grant, completing a study for a thesis or dissertation, a possible publication that may result) all fall on the side of getting a subject to say "yes" and participate without hesitation. On the other side, there is an obligation to present the information and meet the letter and hopefully the spirit of consent. As consent moves from perfunctory to detailed, more time is required with the subject and the risk or perceived risk on the part of the investigator of losing the subject increases. This is a natural tension for the investigator to be aware of and to combat in order to provide thoughtful explanations of the study.

INTERVENTION RESEARCH ISSUES

In studies of various interventions such as psychotherapy, counseling, and education, additional ethical issues arise or nuances emerge that warrant consideration. Several issues emerge that may vary with the type of intervention (treatment versus prevention), the population (young children, hospitalized adults), and the setting (university, patient services).

Informing Clients about Treatment

An important issue is the information that is provided to the client about the intervention. Outside of the rationale and procedures themselves, the investigator is required to convey the current status of the treatment, assuming that the client is able to understand the information. Whether treatment has been shown to be effective or not in previous applications would seem to be important and routine information. Many treatments are experimental, and the subject normally can be provided with a statement to that effect.

Therapy research raises an interesting dilemma because honesty about the basis of treatment might attenuate some of the therapeutic effects. The processes through which therapy achieves its therapeutic change are not really known. However, mobilization of hope and expectancies for change in the client are among the mechanisms proposed to contribute to, if not largely account for, change (Frank & Frank, 1991; Spiro, 1998). These factors are common to many treatments and hence could explain why many different treatments work and why people get better with attention-placebo conditions and placebo medications. Mentioning the current status of treatment and the possibly important role of hope and belief in the procedures might well attenuate the impact of these factors. What does one say to the prospective client/subject? "Oh, yeah, we do not know that this treatment works or how it works if it does, but hope could be a big factor. That is, it is what you believe as much as, or more than, what we do that could make the big difference. If fact, some experts believe what we do is not too important as long as you are convinced it is something."

Suspicions about treatment efficacy might be raised by full disclosure. In some treatment studies, the independent variable is the expectancy for success conveyed to the subjects. Hence, a treatment is claimed to be very effective or ineffective, depending upon the condition to which the subject is assigned. Disclosure of the current status of the technique would compete with this manipulation.

Information about treatment in an experiment may extend to the treatments the subject will not receive. Conceivably, subjects could be told that there are different treatments, only one of which they will receive. Subjects might want to know whether some treatments are more effective than others and whether they have been assigned to a "control" group. In addition, subjects may show a clear preference for an alternative treatment and react adversely to the condition to which they are assigned. As alternative treatments become known, skepticism about a particular treatment may arise, and therapeutic improvement may be affected.

At the beginning of the study, subjects ought to be told that there are various treatments offered and that assignment to treatment is random, assuming that these are, in fact, the case. Although subjects are rarely pleased to learn that their assignment to treatment will be random, the importance of randomness in assessing the impact of different treatments might be stressed. Only those subjects who agree to the conditions of the investigation can serve as subjects and be assigned to conditions. This does lead to selection of a special group, and that may have implications for the external validity of the results. Often these are the constraints within which most clinical research must work. (This concern is important and often leads to a knee-jerk reaction that samples in research do not represent clinical samples—this is often true. Clinical samples are very special as well, and it is unclear whom *they* represent. For example, most of the people with psychiatric disorders and/or in need of treatment never come to a clinic.)

In passing, it is interesting to note that in research the investigator is expected to convey to the subject what is known about treatment, including any limitations and risks. In contrast, in clinical practice the therapist is not required to clarify the status of the technique or knowledge base. The vast majority of psychotherapy techniques—and there are hundreds and hundreds—have not been subject to empirical evaluation and do not have data attesting to their efficacy. Exacerbating the situation, most clinical practice includes combinations of treatment (eclectic treatment) as the practitioner sees fit in the individual case. The constituent interventions and the combination are rarely subjected to empirical research. Clinical practices often use unevaluated (and hence experimental) treatments in many cases in which there are other treatments with evidence in their behalf. One could argue that much of what is practiced in clinical work is experimental (because of the absence of evidence). Subjects are placed at some risk (cost in money, time, possibly getting worse) insofar as preferred treatment alternatives that the clinician may not know how to implement are not provided. Protection of subjects in research is obviously important; it seems no less important in practice, but that issue is for a very different book.

Withholding the Intervention

Intervention studies often withhold the special treatment or preventive intervention and assign some of the subjects to no-treatment or waiting-list control conditions. Although these control conditions are essential to answer specific research questions, as discussed previously, their use raises obvious ethical questions. Assigning a client to one of these conditions withholds treatment from which a person may benefit. At the very least, treatment for the client is delayed. If the client's condition does not deteriorate, the delay has increased the duration of misery that may have precipitated seeking treatment. At the worst, the client's condition may deteriorate during the period that treatment is withheld.

An investigator is obligated to consider seriously whether a control condition that delays or completely withholds treatment is necessary for the questions addressed in the research. Because of the ethical problems, it may be more appropriate to reserve questions comparing treatment with no treatment to situations where subjects are willing to wait and are unlikely to suffer deleterious consequences. Obviously, volunteer clients solicited from the community may be more appropriate for a study in which a waiting-list group is required than clients who seek treatment at a crisis intervention center. When clients have severe problems and warrant or demand immediate intervention, questions comparing treatment with no treatment are more difficult to justify and to implement.

In some cases, assigning subjects to a waiting-list control group will not really delay treatment. Waiting lists are common at many clinics. A delay before entering treatment may average a few or several months before clients are seen. All subjects who are to serve in the study and who agree to participate can be moved up on the list. Those who are randomly assigned to the intervention condition are treated immediately; those who are assigned to wait can be assessed and then wait the usual delay period of the clinic before receiving treatment. Ethical issues are not eliminated by rearranging one's status on the waiting list. Moving some clients up on the list may delay the treatment of others who are not in the study. Some of the problems of delaying treatment can be alleviated by informing clients at intake of the possibility that they will not be assigned to treatment for a particular (specified) interval. As noted before, the investigation would use only subjects who agree with this stipulation and then randomly assign them to the various treatment and control conditions.

Control Groups and Treatments of Questionable Efficacy

In outcome research some treatments in a given study might be expected to be less effective than others. This expectation may derive from theoretical predictions, previous research, or the nature of the design. For example, in a simple 2×2 factorial design, an investigator may study the effects of such variables as therapist experience (experienced versus inexperienced therapists) and duration of treatment (1 session versus 10 sessions). Subjects in one of the groups resulting from this design will be exposed to inexperienced therapists for one treatment session, a condition likely to be less effective than the others. The use of treatments that have a low probability of being effective raises an ethical issue for the investigator. Is this treatment really needed to address the question of interest? Can the base treatment (the minimal condition provided to the subject) be a standard intervention or one that can be reasonably expected to effect change?

The issue is much clearer in using groups that are designed to control for common treatment factors such as attending treatment sessions, meeting with a therapist, and believing that treatment may produce change. These groups are designed with the express idea that there are few if any components that will actively help the client. Providing a treatment designed to be weak or a control condition designed to be ineffective raises obvious ethical problems. First, the client's problem may not improve or may even become worse without an effective treatment. To withhold a treatment expected to be relatively effective renders these possibilities more salient. Second, clients may lose credulity in the process of psychological treatment in general. Clients expect to receive an effective treatment and to achieve change. If treatment is not reasonable in their judgment and does not produce change, clients may be generally discouraged from seeking help in the future. In general, the control conditions or treatments that may "fill out" the design warrant ethical evaluation by the investigator and review boards. This, of course, applies to any special control condition in which the likelihood of improvement is unexpected or minimal. Other contextual issues—

such as who the clients are (patients seeking treatment, community volunteers) and provisions after the study is completed (e.g., free treatment and care)—may affect evaluation of the issues.

At the beginning of the chapter I mentioned how concerns over placebo controls emerged in the context of research on the treatment of HIV. The concerns have emerged much more broadly and deserve further comment. For example, in the development of medications for depression, there is a controversy about whether placebo controls should be used. The Food and Drug Administration (FDA) in the United States requires a placebo control to identify whether a drug improves upon the often potent effects of placebos in a given sample. Placebos can significantly improve depressive symptoms in 30–50 percent of a clinical sample. One has to show that a medication improves upon this percent. Many medications do, but the increment is surprisingly small (10–20 percent). Can the placebo procedure be justified? Are patients assigned to this condition at special risk for other problems? In partial defense of this policy, meta-analyses of several studies have shown that the risk for suicide is no different for subjects who receive treatment or placebo control conditions. That has not allayed all the concerns. Perhaps the quality of life of the subjects in the placebo group is not as good as those in the treatment group because of the likelihood of continued symptoms and also because of the stress and anxiety of serving in a placebo condition (see Enserink, 2000a).

The matter has extended beyond mere differences in opinions. In considering the issues, the World Medical Association passed a resolution to revise the 1964 Declaration of Helsinki. That declaration addressed research ethics that emerged in response to gruesome medical experiments during the Nazi era. The original version of the Declaration did not preclude use of placebos but was not explicit. The revised version states explicitly that placebos may be used only when there are no other therapies available for comparison. If there is a standard treatment (e.g., an approved medication on the market), any new treatment should be compared to that rather than to a placebo (Enserink, 2000b). This is a major change in research and currently is at odds with FDA requirements in the United States.

Parallels have not been made in research on psychotherapies that involve many disciplines (clinical and counseling psychology, psychiatry, nursing, and social work) where control conditions are used. Direct translation of the policy is not straightforward because many of the treatments that are considered standard (much of psychotherapy) are standard only because they are used a lot and have history and tradition behind them, not because they have evidence in their behalf. With the emergence of evidence-based therapies, perhaps it will be reasonable to extend the stance on placebos to psychotherapy trials. Placebo control conditions might not be justified if there is an evidence-based treatment that could be used for the clinical problem under investigation.

Consent and the Interface with Threats to Validity

Some of the ethical issues in this chapter connect directly with drawing inferences and establishing validity of the experiment. Informed consent procedures illustrate this very nicely. Two issues that have broad implications for drawing inferences from research are randomization and attrition. Mentioned ad nauseum is the use of random assignment for all sorts of reasons, but primarily to make implausible a host of threats to internal validity. Mentioned also was the fact that in any research in which the subject must come back for more than one session (as in treatment and prevention studies, longitudinal studies of development), subjects may dropout. Dropping out can influence all types of experimental validity, as detailed in earlier chapters.

Informed consent raises issues that affect dropping out and threats to validity. Assume that a study compares treatment versus a no-treatment or an attention-placebo control condition. Subjects are informed that they will be assigned to one condition or the other and that the assignment is random. Subjects want to be in the treatment group. After subjects are assigned, they now may evaluate their status and draw inferences about the group they are in. It is likely that more often than not, they will guess correctly, especially if they have any opportunity to chat with other subjects. Subjects might wisely sign the consent form with knowledge that they can withdraw later if they do not get the condition they wish.

How ought the investigator to proceed? One option is to provide consent information, to underscore the importance of participation even if assigned to the no-treatment (waiting-list) or attention-placebo group, and perhaps to convey that if assignment to no treatment may lead to dropping out, it is better to do so now (before being assigned), although of course the subject may drop out at any time. After all subjects agree, then assignment can be made randomly to conditions. This may reduce attrition because dropping out before even being assigned was encouraged. The dilemma is that external validity of the results—that is, the extent to which the results extend to patients—will be challenged further. Those who participate may be more restricted in their characteristics because some effort was made to use only those who really said they would be likely to remain in treatment.

The notion that subjects can change their minds at any time and withdraw consent is an important protection for subjects. As they gain more information (knowledge as a condition for consent), they may decide the intervention is not for them. Dropping out affects experimental validity, and this is something to be aware of. Analyses of dropouts, intent-to-treat analyses of the data, and inducements to the subjects to complete the study are strategies designed to address this issue.

General Comments

The ethical issues raised in intervention research depend upon the precise research question and the control groups that form the basis of the design. Use of no-treatment or waiting-list control groups is essential in research that asks the basic question, "Does this treatment work?" The question usually requires assessing the extent of change without treatment. Similarly, use of a nonspecific treatment control group is important in research that asks the question, "Why does this treatment work?" Such research may require a group to look at the influence of nonspecific or common treatment factors.

The research questions that require ethically sensitive control conditions are fundamental to progress in understanding treatment. The questions themselves cannot be abandoned. However, the conditions under which these questions are examined can be varied to attenuate the objections that normally arise. For example, questions requiring control conditions that withhold treatment or provide nonspecific treatment control groups need not be conducted in settings where clients are in need of treatment and have sought a treatment to ameliorate an immediately felt problem. On the other hand, for situations in which volunteer subjects are solicited and can be informed about the experimental nature of all treatment procedures, a wider range of experimental conditions is more readily justified. In short, when the setting has patient care and service delivery as a high priority, the use of groups that withhold treatment or present "nonspecific" treatments that are expected to produce minimal change is generally unacceptable. When research, rather than service delivery, has the higher priority and clients can be informed of the implications of this priority, the use of such groups may be more readily justified.

Some of the ethical issues of treatment can be ameliorated by providing all subjects with the more (or most) effective treatment in the project after they have completed the treatment or control condition to which they were assigned. After treatment, clients who served as a no-treatment control group also should receive the benefits of treatment. Indeed, this is exactly what the waiting-list control group receives. In studies with several different treatments or a nonspecific control condition, clients who are not completely satisfied with their progress eventually might be given the most effective treatment. Thus, clients may benefit from the project in which they served by receiving the better (or best) treatment. From an experimental standpoint this strategy is useful in further examining the extent of change in clients who continue in the superior treatment. Essentially, there is a partial replication of treatment effects in the design. From an ethical standpoint, providing all subjects with the most effective intervention may attenuate objections against assigning subjects to treatments varying in anticipated effectiveness. Of course, at some point in the research long-term follow-up studies are needed in which we see whether the seemingly effective intervention is better than no treatment over the long term. This might be done in a randomized controlled trial or by creative use of cohort designs in which groups that have not received treatment are followed.

ETHICAL GUIDELINES FOR RESEARCH PRACTICES

Many ethical problems that arise in research seem to be inherent in the research process itself. The use of human subjects often requires weighing alternatives that balance individual rights of the subject against the search for scientific knowledge. Decisions about potential harm, deception, invasion of privacy, withholding of potential beneficial treatment practices, and similar issues have helped stimulate guidelines for research both at the professional and federal levels.

The American Psychological Association has provided a set of principles designed to guide research, practice, consultation, and other activities related to execution of the profession. The guidelines are revised periodically to make refinements, to address emergent issues, and to handle expanding roles of psychologists in daily life (e.g., litigation, consultation) (APA, 2001a). Consider the most recent version of the guidelines (APA, 1992) and, in light of present purposes, the guidelines that pertain specifically to research with human subjects. The guidelines are formulated in such a way as to emphasize the investigator's responsibilities toward individuals who participate in research. The principles are listed in Table 17.3. As guidelines, the principles

TABLE 17.3.   Ethical Principles in the Conduct of Research with Human Participants

Planning Research

(a) Psychologists design, conduct, and report research in accordance with recognized standards of scientific competence and ethical research.

(b) Psychologists plan their research so as to minimize the possibility that results will be misleading.

(c) In planning research, psychologists consider its ethical acceptability under the Ethics Code. If an ethical issue is unclear, psychologists seek to resolve the issue through consultation with institutional review boards, animal care and use committees, peer consultations, or other proper mechanisms.

(d) Psychologists take reasonable steps to implement appropriate protections for the rights and welfare of human participants, other persons affected by the research, and the welfare of animal subjects.

Responsibility

(a) Psychologists conduct research competently and with due concern for the dignity and welfare of the participants.

(b) Psychologists are responsible for the ethical conduct of research conducted by them or by others under their supervision or control.

(c) Researchers and assistants are permitted to perform only those tasks for which they are appropriately trained and prepared.

(d) As part of the process of development and implementation of research projects, psychologists consult those with expertise concerning any special population under investigation or most likely to be affected.

Compliance with Law and Standards

Psychologists plan and conduct research in a manner consistent with federal and state law and regulations, as well as professional standards governing the conduct of research, and particularly those standards governing research with human participants and animal subjects.

Institutional Approval

Psychologists obtain from host institutions or organizations appropriate approval prior to conducting research, and they provide accurate information about their research proposals. They conduct the research in accordance with the approved research protocol.

Research Responsibilities

Prior to conducting research (except research involving only anonymous surveys, naturalistic observations, or similar research), psychologists enter into an agreement with participants that clarifies the nature of the research and the responsibilities of each party.

Informed Consent to Research

(a) Psychologists use language that is reasonably understandable to research participants in obtaining their appropriate informed consent. Such informed consent is appropriately documented.

(b) Using language that is reasonably understandable to participants, psychologists inform participants of the nature of the research; they inform participants that they are free to participate or to decline to participate or to withdraw from the research; they explain the foreseeable consequences of declining or withdrawing; they inform participants of significant factors that may be expected to influence their willingness to participate (such as risks, discomfort, adverse effects, or limitations on confidentiality), and they explain other aspects about which the prospective participants inquire.

(c) When psychologists conduct research with individuals such as students or subordinates, psychologists take special care to protect the prospective participants from adverse consequences of declining or withdrawing from participation.

(d) When research participation is a course requirement or opportunity for extra credit, the prospective participant is given the choice of equitable alternative activities.

(e) For persons who are legally incapable of giving informed consent, psychologists nevertheless (1) provide an appropriate explanation, (2) obtain the participant's assent, and (3) obtain appropriate permission from a legally authorized person, if such substitute consent is permitted by law.

Dispensing with Informed Consent

Before determining that planned research (such as research involving only anonymous questionnaires, naturalistic observations, or certain kinds of archival research) does not require the informed consent of research participants, psychologists consider applicable regulations and institutional review board requirements, and they consult with colleagues as appropriate.

Informed Consent in Research Filming or Recording

Psychologists obtain informed consent from research participants prior to filming or recording them in any form, unless the research involves simply naturalistic observations in public places and it is not anticipated that the recording will be used in a manner that could cause personal identification or harm.

Offering Inducements for Research Participants

(a) In offering professional services as an inducement to obtain research participants, psychologists make clear the nature of the services, as well as the risks, obligations, and limitations.

(b) Psychologists do not offer excessive or inappropriate financial or other inducements to obtain research participants, particularly when it might tend to coerce participation.

Deception in Research

(a) Psychologists do not conduct a study involving deception unless they have determined that the use of deceptive techniques is justified by the study's prospective scientific, educational, or applied value and that equally effective alternative procedures that do not use deception are not feasible.

(b) Psychologists never deceive research participants about significant aspects that would affect their willingness to participate, such as physical risks, discomfort, or unpleasant emotional experiences.

(c) Any other deception that is an integral feature of the design and conduct of an experiment must be explained to participants as early as is feasible, preferably at the conclusion of their participation, but no later than at the conclusion of the research.

Sharing and Utilizing Data

Psychologists inform research participants of their anticipated sharing or further use of personally identifiable research data and of the possibility of unanticipated future uses.

Minimizing Invasiveness

In conducting research, psychologists interfere with the participants or milieu from which data are collected only in a manner that is warranted by an appropriate research design and that is consistent with psychologists' roles as scientific investigators.

Providing Participants with Information about the Study

(a) Psychologists provide a prompt opportunity for participants to obtain appropriate information about the nature, results, and conclusions of the research, and psychologists attempt to correct any misconceptions that participants may have.

(b) If scientific or humane values justify delaying or withholding this information, psychologists take reasonable measures to reduce the risk of harm.

Honoring Commitments

Psychologists take reasonable measures to honor all commitments they have made to research participants.

---

are necessarily ambiguous about concrete research practices. For example, the principles do not say that deception can or cannot be used. Indeed, the thrust of the principles is to point out the obligations of the investigator and to raise those areas in which caution and deliberation are required. The guidelines point to the considerations included in making decisions about whether a given research project should be undertaken. Although it may be difficult to make decisions in any given case, the overriding concern must be given to the protection of the subject. Indeed, the guidelines specify that as the pros and cons of the research are weighed, priority must be given to the subject's welfare. Whether a given investigation adequately protects the rights of subjects usually is decided on the basis of an evaluation of the research by one's colleagues. As mentioned previously, universities and many other institutions where research is conducted rely upon review committees to evaluate the extent to which a proposed investigation provides safeguards for subjects and is consistent with the type of guidelines listed in Table 17.3.

The review process has been mandated by federal regulations for medical and psychological research. Beginning in the mid-1960s the Surgeon General of the Public Health Service required institutions that received federal money for research to establish review committees to consider subjects' rights and to ensure that informed consent was procured for the proposed research. The regulations for research have been revised and elaborated periodically. Current federal regulations are designed to evaluate whether any risks to the subjects are outweighed by the potential benefits to them or by the likely benefits to society in light of the information obtained. In the early 1970s Congress mandated a special commission to draft ethical guidelines for research with human subjects. The National Commission for the Protection of Human Subjects in Biomedical and Behavioral Research was established to examine research and applications in areas where human rights have been or are likely to be violated. The Commission studied and made recommendations for practices in research with fetuses, prisoners, individuals considered for psychosurgery, and children, all of which raise special issues. These guidelines do not apply to the bulk of research in clinical psychology but are important to mention insofar as they reveal Congress' strong interest in ethical issues raised by research with human subjects. (Guidelines continue to emerge to address such special topics as gene therapy and stem-cell research, but also protection of subjects in general; please see the Web site in For Further Readings for links to many different government guidelines.)

To examine the risks and benefits and protection of the subject's welfare, research proposals in a university setting are reviewed by a committee that critically examines the procedures and possible risks to the subjects. The committee is referred to as an Institutional Review Board (or IRB) in the federal codes to protect subjects (United States Department of Health & Human Services [USDHHS], 1983). The committee evaluates whether subjects are provided with the opportunity to give informed consent and made aware of their ability to withdraw consent and terminate participation at any time. Subjects must sign an informed consent form that explains the procedures and purpose in clear and easily understandable language and describes any risks and benefits. Risks are defined broadly to include the possibility of injury—physical, psychological, or social—as a consequence of participation in the experiment. Subjects must also be told that they are free to withhold information (e.g., of a personal nature) and to withdraw from the investigation at any time without penalty. Subjects must be guaranteed that all information they provide will be anonymous and confidential and told how these conditions will be achieved.

Most investigations within psychology include procedures that may be without risk to the subject and hence do not provide problems for review committees to evaluate. Procedures that receive special scrutiny are those projects involving a failure to disclose fully the purpose of the study, deception, the possibility of deleteriously affecting the subject's psychological or physical status, and research involving special populations in which competence to consent is in question (e.g., children). The committee must weigh the merits of the scientific investigation and the advance in knowledge it may provide against possible potential discomfort to the subject.

Ethical responsibility for research cannot be placed solely on the formal review procedures. Ethical guidelines for research encourage investigators to seek advice of others and of diverse perspectives to assess whether procedures are warranted that extend beyond minimal risk (covert observations, invasion of sensitive topics). When weighing scientific merit and the likely benefits of the knowledge against subject rights, the investigator is advised to seek input from colleagues over and above formal review procedures (APA, 1992). In other words, the ultimate ethical responsibility for the integrity of the research falls to the investigator.

It is worth mentioning that different professions have different ethical guidelines, although there is obvious overlap. In many cases these are quite relevant to psychological research because psychology collaborates with investigators of other fields. For example, statisticians are often involved in collaborative arrangements with psychologists. Ethical guidelines for statisticians have been developed by the American Statistical Association (see www.TCNJ.EDU/~ethcstat/start.html). These guidelines underscore important issues regarding the treatment, documentation, analysis, and interpretation of data (ensure data conform with any pledges of confidentiality that were made, collect only the data needed for the purpose of inquiry) and integrity of the statistician (accept no contingency fee arrangements, apply statistical procedures without concern for a favorable outcome). Examination of guidelines from related disciplines is instructive because they raise new issues, provide emphases different from the APA guidelines, and include practices that often help implement existing guidelines.

ETHICAL ISSUES AND SCIENTIFIC INTEGRITY

Ethics in research usually are discussed in relation to the subject and subject rights as illustrated, for example, in the issues raised by informed consent. Professional organizations have guidelines for ethical behavior of their members. The guidelines are intended to outline standards of integrity that pertain to diverse contexts beyond those associated with research and investigator/experimenter and subject interactions (see APA, 1992). Although the full range of ethical standards are not entirely relevant to discussion of methodology and research design (e.g., contacts and relationships with clients in therapy), there are several research-related issues we have neglected. A set of ethical issues might be identified that is essential for maintaining the integrity of science. These issues encompass the obligations and responsibilities of the investigator in relation to one's colleagues, the profession, society, and science more generally.

Fraud in Science

Scientists are not immune to error, deception, and fraud in their work. Historical accounts of science provide a long line of examples in which scientists have made major errors in recording or interpreting their work, have tried to deceive others about their findings, and have altered or faked their data (see Broad & Wade, 1982; Kohn, 1988; Miller & Hersen, 1992). These issues were mentioned briefly in the discussion of sources of artifact and bias in research. In the context of threats to validity, altering and making up data obviously bias research findings and their interpretation; in the context of ethical issues they raise broader issues of great significance.

The distinction between error and fraud in research is major. *Errors* refer to honest mistakes that may occur in some facet of the study or its presentation. The processes entailed by collecting data, scoring measures, transcribing and entering data, and publishing raise multiple opportunities for error and for errors by many different persons. To err is human; to err frequently is careless, and to err in a particular direction (to support a hypothesis), at the very least, is suspicious. The investigator has the responsibility to minimize error by devising procedures to check, monitor, and detect errors and then to rectify them to the extent possible. When errors are detected (as in published reports), investigators are encouraged to acknowledge them. Often journal publications include isolated notes (referred to as errata) where corrections can be written in the same outlet in which the original paper appeared.

Fraud in science refers to explicit efforts to deceive and misrepresent. Of all issues, fraud is the most flagrant because it undermines the foundations of the entire enterprise of scientific research (National Academy of Sciences, 1989). Although fraud is not new in science, recent attention has focused on deliberate efforts of researchers to mislead colleagues and the public. Dramatic instances have come to light in which critical procedures, treatments, or potential breakthroughs could not be replicated or were known by one's colleagues to reflect explicit attempts to misrepresent the actual findings. For example, findings on the effectiveness of a new treatment for a woman whose cancer (a type of leukemia) was advanced were retracted when the investigator confessed to misrepresenting and fabricating the data (Waldholz, 2000). Such acts and their revelations greatly undermine public confidence in the research enterprise.

The most publicized cases of fraud tend to be in the area of health, in which it is not just public confidence but also safety that is involved. For example, a large-scale study (approximately 7000 patients from 13 countries) compared a new medication regimen (combination of medications), aspirin, and placebo for the prevention of recurrent strokes (Enserink, 1996). Aspirin, the generally accepted treatment, was greatly surpassed in effectiveness by the other medication condition. However, the data from one of the sites were reported to be fabricated. Obviously, the extent to which results from such data could influence clinical practice for stroke victims goes beyond undermining public confidence.

Within psychology some topics more than others tend to be in the public light and also highly publicized. The noted psychologist, Sir Cyril Burt (1883–1971), published extensively on the inheritance of intelligence and drew conclusions based on data from identical twins. Posthumous evaluations of his data suggested that the data had been fabricated to support his views. Some evaluations considered the work to be carelessly prepared and hence marked by extensive errors; later evaluations suggested that the scope and direction of the errors were much more suggestive of fraud, a conclusion formally reached by the Council of British Psychology in 1980. Discussion and debate on whether, and the extent to which, fraud was evident continued for sometime even after 1980 (see MacKintosh, 1995).

Evaluations of scientific research have suggested that instances of fraud are likely to be quite rare (National Academy of Sciences, 1989). This does not mean that the status quo is acceptable. The impact and implications of any instance of fraud can be tremendous for the specific area of work (e.g., suggesting a new principle or treatment procedure) as well as for the scientific enterprise in general.

No single or simple cause of fraud is likely to be identifiable. And perhaps fraud does not require a special explanation. I noted at the outset that science is very much a human enterprise, and processes, motivations, and phenomena of human functioning generally (altruism, fraud) can be expected to be found where humans are, even if the base rate is low, there are super protections, and so on. No doubt several influences can conspire to produce fraud, including pressures of investigators to publish for recognition and career advancement, to produce critical breakthroughs, and to obtain funding for seemingly promising avenues of research, to mention a few. Protections to counter fraud include training in the central values of science, emphasis on the importance of the integrity of the investigator in advancing science generally, repeated opportunities in which an individual's work is subjected to review and evaluation by one's colleagues (as part of review processes in advance of the study, when the report is submitted for publication), public access to data records, and efforts to replicate research.

An example conveys the thrust of some of the professional sanctions that loom over research. Early in 1997 a scientific breakthrough was reported, namely, the cloning of an adult mammal. A sheep (named Dolly) was cloned by embryologists in Scotland. Producing another living animal from one cell (Dolly's "mother") was considered to be a remarkable breakthrough because cloning was regarded as not possible given current knowledge and technology. When the finding was first reported, there was some faith in the reliability of the finding, in part because of the reputation of the senior researcher on the project whose years of work and high standards of integrity were known. At the same time, the replicability of the demonstration became very important to ensure this was not a hoax. A quote from one scientist on this point is instructive regarding this discovery. In referring to the research team that made the discovery, the scientist said, "I know and trust them, but if what they did isn't repeatable, they'll pay for it with their careers" (see Waldholz, 1997, p. B1). As it turns out, using a different procedure and a monkey instead of a sheep, cloning was repeated by another research team in the United States a few weeks later; since then many replications have been reported spanning different species. The quote, evident before all of these replications, is noteworthy in conveying the ethos guiding scientific findings as well as consequences for findings that are not replicable and/or are fraudulent.

Apart from sanctions within the professions, there are legal consequences of fraud as well. For example, the use of public funds in research and conduct of research within institutions brings to bear specific laws regarding fraud and oversight boards to monitor scientific integrity, to investigate allegations of fraud, and to pursue through the courts culpability and prosecution. The sanctions and consequences can be personally and professionally devastating. Indeed, being accused and later acquitted in one well-publicized case had very negative consequences from which it was difficult to recover. Notwithstanding the multiple factors to protect against fraud and various forms of sanction, the key remains the ethical commitment and responsibility of the individual investigator to the discipline by conducting studies, reporting data, and preparing reports in as honest and an objective fashion as possible and to train those working under one's charge (e.g., students) in these standards and practices as well.

Allocation of Credit

Another issue related to obligations of the investigator pertains to allocation of credit. Several issues are encompassed, including failure to acknowledge one's sources and reference to other material, and the division of credit among collaborators in research and published projects of that research. Perhaps the most obvious and flagrant issue is that of *plagiarism* or the direct use and copying of material of someone else without providing credit or acknowledgment. The misconduct that plagiarism represents is generally brought to the attention of undergraduate students early in their education. Even so, rare cases emerge among graduate students and seasoned investigators. Special problems and opportunities emerge in science in the circulation of unpublished materials (manuscripts that are reviewed, convention presentations circulated in writing), and this may be exacerbated by posting materials on the Web. A virtue of science is the public nature of the enterprise and the free exchange of ideas. Colleagues are encouraged to exchange ideas, to seek and to provide feedback, and to interact with colleagues to advance research ideas and objectives. The process generally works quite well without repeated claims of plagiarism or theft of ideas.

A more delicate and perhaps less concrete issue pertains to the credit accorded to those involved in research. Projects are usually collaborative. They involve multiple investigators and a team of persons who have responsibility of varying types and in varying degrees for completion of the study. The different components of research and responsibilities from idea to the final published report are numerous. Allocation of credit emerges in such contexts as deciding whom to list as authors on a research article, the order in which they are to appear, the relation between junior and senior scientists or faculty and students, and how the different roles and contributions affect authorship.

Perhaps the most salient issue in allocation of credit in this context is whether a person involved in the project in some way ought to be listed as one of the coauthors on any publication and report. Decisions about allocating credit and authorship are fraught with human frailties related to status, power, greed, ambition, insecurities, anger and revenge, and personality style of the investigators, collaborators, and research assistants. In fact, there is a longstanding rumor that Shakespeare was going to write a play on the interpersonal issues related to scientific discovery, authorship, and publication. He decided against it because it was much too violent and sinister so he settled on lighter plays such as Julius Caesar, MacBeth, and Hamlet.

The human frailties are often heightened in relation to authorship issues, in large part because the stakes of authorship are high or perceived as high. Consequently, concerns about mistreatment or unfair treatment can become quite intense and ruin otherwise good relationships. As to the stakes, publication and the number of publications can have direct implications for tenure, promotion, and salary at many universities. Being an author on another published article moves one closer to these rewards, and hence few researchers early in their academic career would say, "It does not matter whether I am an author; I can be on the next one or the one after that." Apart from the consequences associated with authorship, there is a broader issue, namely, the just allocation and recognition of credit, and this is important independently of other issues. That is, credit ought to be given where credit is due. The difficulty is that once one moves beyond stating such generalities and descends from the high moral ground, chaos can prevail. Individual differences, temperament, personal securities, and other motives noted previously color all of our interpretations about what is a contribution to the study and how much that contribution ought to count toward the final allocation of credit.[2]

A key issue for participation as an author on a paper is evidence that there is a clear contribution to the study. There are no agreed-upon guidelines as to what constitutes a contribution. A contribution is likely to warrant authorship if a person working on the study completes one or more of the following (Fine & Kurdek, 1993):

- Develops the design,
- Writes or prepares portions of the manuscript,
- Integrates or brings together theoretical perspectives,
- Develops novel conceptual views,
- Designs or develops the measures,
- Makes key decisions about the data analyses, and
- Interprets the results.

Guidelines for authorship have been adopted by groups of editors and echo similar criteria as those noted previously. For example, the International Committee of Medical Journal Editors (ICMJE, 1997) have adopted guidelines for biomedical journals. The guidelines note that all three conditions are necessary for authorship. Specifically, anyone designated as an author ought to have made substantial contributions in

- Conceptualizing of the study or the design, or analysis and interpretation of the data,
- Drafting the manuscript or making revisions that are critical to the intellectual content, and
- Providing final approval of the version that is to be published.

---

[2]I recall the animosity I caused on three occasions in which I tried to persuade collaborators that my contribution—completing the Reference section—warranted sole or, my default position, first authorship. My position was invariably weakened by some undergraduate in charge of proofing the footnotes who was making a similar case. Of course, everyone knows that there are usually more references than footnotes, but I still lost out in each case.

The ICMJE guidelines also specify conditions that do *not* warrant authorship. Specifically, merely being the person who acquired the funding for the research (getting the grant), or who collected the data, or who supervised the research group who collected the data, in the ICMJE guidelines are insufficient to be listed as an author. These guidelines are more explicit than one usually sees in discussions of authorship. It is worth noting as well that they have been adopted by over 500 journals (Ducor, 2000).

The ICMJE guidelines are a bit more stringent than the previous set I mentioned because they require that all three of the conditions must be met for authorship. It is easy to envision meeting one of these extremely well (e.g., conceptualizing the entire study) or two and one-half of these (e.g., the first and third by not helping to draft the study). Not meeting all three could easily meet the spirit but miss the letter of the guidelines. This is not a criticism of the guidelines but conveys that weighting the extent to which any one of the criteria has been achieved is an issue.

Indeed, in both sets of guidelines noted here, some of the key points are subject to interpretation. For example, both sets mention contribution to the interpretation of the results or data as a criterion for authorship. What is a contribution to interpretation of the data? An interpretation might range on a continuum from a pithy but brief characterization ("We found nothing, nada!") to integration with cross-disciplinary, intergalactic, neuro-psycho-social-meteorological models. More likely, a graduate student or postdoctoral candidate in the lab of the researcher may have just read an article in a seemingly unrelated area of work. He or she may then convey to the investigator or investigative team a theory that another finding from that other area of research could relate to this study. This information now enters the Discussion section of the article as a possible interpretation of the findings and hence might be regarded by us as a substantial contribution. Yet, whether a contribution is substantial or "really" adds to the interpretation of the results is arguable and can depend on other conditions not noted here (the role it plays in the article, whether it is needed or very helpful, and so on).

Despite the ambiguity, the guidelines help clarify the roles that lobby for authorship. The roles specified by both sets of guidelines can be distinguished from other tasks such as entering data, running the data analyses under direct supervision, typing the manuscript, and preparing ancillary materials (references). These latter tasks might warrant acknowledgment in a footnote, but are not likely to be considered a professional contribution in the sense of the other activities noted previously.

As we work in an area and complete a study, our evaluation of its contribution to the world occasionally is distorted. Perhaps we believe the Nobel committee will want to know who generated the research; the allocation and credit we extend to others may take on unusual proportions. We long for simple rules and guidelines, and one provided by an advisor of mine ("If this study comes out, *I'm* first author; if it does not, *you're* first author.") at least has the advantages of explicitness and clarity. Although the issues of allocation of credit and participation in research can arise in any collaboration, attention has often been accorded faculty–student collaborations because of special features that may impede allocation of credit and communication about that credit (different status, power, expertise) (see Fine & Kurdek, 1993; Goodyear, Crego, & Johnson, 1992).

Investigators, whether faculty and students or multiple colleagues within the profession, are encouraged to discuss these matters explicitly at the inception of research, not merely to address issues of authorship, but also to decide tasks to be completed, responsibility, and credit in relation to all facets of the study. Explicitness is important, but perhaps assumes increasing importance to the extent that there are power, age, status, or other such differences among the investigators and collaborators. The greater the differences, the more assumptions are likely to be made and the less likely such assumptions are to be checked with direct communication. Converse with colleagues, advisors, mentors if you have any interest in subsequent credit.

The degree to which these conversations seem awkward is directly related to their importance in allocating credit. At the same time, in some collaborative arrangements it is difficult to approach a senior collaborator or advisor. Consequently, it is useful to place responsibility on senior investigators for initiating the topic of allocation of credit, to address the matter directly, and to encourage dialogue on the topic. Of course, we know from experience or understanding of human nature that those senior investigators who take the responsibility and begin with open communication about such matters are the collaborators we may need to be least concerned about in relation to allocation of credit. (My own advisors in graduate school served as a model in communicating with me before and after I completed a project with them so I had the benefit of very clear statements. In each occasion, they said they would help me in any way, do much of the work, and write up the project if I promised not to mention them in any way or only by pseudonyms.)

In passing, I ought to mention the notion of order of authorship. That is, once the decision has been made that a given set of authors will be on an article, what ought to be the ordering? This is much fuzzier ground than the authorship issue for all sorts of reasons. Disciplines and areas within a discipline often differ. In some cases the senior author (the person in whose lab the study was completed or who had the greatest role in the study) is listed routinely as the first or last author. It may be widely recognized that this is the research of the person at the beginning or end of the article. Even when there is a tradition, it may be violated if a brand new discovery is made. First authorship becomes important because the finding may be cited frequently, and all authors but the first become lost in the Latin abbreviation, et al. There are no great guidelines for ordering authors in an article. Too often the good graces of the first author seem to dictate without the input of anyone else. The solution is to discuss the matter before the study is completed. (In my own case I almost always insisted on alphabetical ordering of all authors by *first* names. I have been accused of using this because it is "convenient" for me, given that my name is Alan. It is true that in an argument with a chap named Aaron, I switched the criterion to alphabetical order by middle name.)

Sharing of Materials and Data

A central feature of science is the ability to replicate the work of others. Indeed, replication is the primary guarantee of reliability of research findings. Replication is usually discussed in the context of repeating the procedures of a prior investigation. In relation to ethics of research, there is more to it than that. Replication begins with the obligations of an investigator to provide colleagues with the materials to permit them to conduct replications. This might entail providing further descriptions of procedures and specific measures, responding to various questions that facilitate replication of the study, making available special software to present materials to the subjects, or to code, score, or analyze the data.

Often critical features of a study have required years to develop (e.g., treatment manuals) and have important financial implications (software, a new psychological test) that make investigators reluctant or occasionally unwilling to share materials. However, the obligation to share materials begins when the individual enters the role of scientific investigator and places his or her work in the scientific domain (presentation of a paper, publication of a scientific article). At that point the investigator has entered an implied contract with the rest of the scientific community in which he or she will aid in continuation and evaluation of the research. As part of that contract, the scientific community is obligated to provide credit where this is due in relation to the original investigator and to restrict use of the materials to the specific project for which it was requested.

The procedure generally appears to work well, based on the exchange of a great deal of information informally among scientists. The information exchange is often prompted by a published report that helps to establish communication among scientists who begin a dialogue and exchange of materials. There are some formal protections to aid in making research information available. Funding agencies, both federal and private, often include materials in the project proposal and final report, such as measures, detailed descriptions of procedures, and raw data. This information is available by request or as a matter of public record for further scrutiny and use.

One of the most frequently discussed issues pertains to the sharing of data. This, too, is related to replication. Can one obtain the same or similar findings when analyzing the original data that were published? A colleague may believe that the original data were not analyzed correctly or in the most appropriate fashion, or would lead to quite different conclusions if analyzed differently. Data are viewed as part of the public domain and to be shared with others if requested.

There is often reluctance of investigators to share data. One reason is that a given study may be drawn from a larger database. Several other projects may be planned, and the investigator may be unwilling to circulate the data until the projects have been completed, analyzed, and reported. Here, too, once an article has been published in a scientific journal, it is difficult to justify withholding the specific data set on which that article was based. That data set, even if not the entire database, might well be considered to be part of the information available to the scientific community. More than that, it has become law to make raw data available in federally funded research (referred to as the Shelby amendment, passed by Congress in 1998). The law requires that the public (anyone who asks) be given access to data generated by federally funded research. Concern grew from instances in which the government refused access to data, even when the data were used to support controversial policies (e.g., clean air standards set by the Environmental Protection Agency). Parties that might have keen interest in the policy and its rationale (business and industry) ought to have access to the information (data) on which conclusions were drawn. We know as scientists, quite apart from any policy, that the same data set might be subject to different interpretations and, indeed, if analyzed differently might support different or new conclusions. Psychology research has little to do with clean air, but the federal law applies to federally funded research across disciplines.

At first glance the issue may seem to be obvious—of course all data should be shared, and if taxpayer money (federally funded projects) is involved, perhaps there is a special right to public access to these data. Yet, application and interpretation of the law are subject to some debate, in part because investigators have objected to providing unrestricted access to data to others. There are many issues to be resolved, and raising these issues is not the same as stating that investigators are unwilling to share. Table 17.4 lists a number of concerns that have been voiced in sharing data. The concerns reflect rights of the subjects but also have important implications regarding financial loss and gain.

Increasingly in research, databases are made publicly available to other researchers to permit further analyses. For example, in large, federally funded projects, the data may be made available to anyone who wishes to complete further studies. One prominent example was the Epidemiologic Catchment Area (ECA) study, which was a multisite investigation (5 sites) of the prevalence of psychiatric disorders among community and institutionalized adults ($N > 20,000$, 18 years and older) in the United States (Eaton & Kessler, 1985; Regier et al., 1984). The study has led to hundreds of publications elaborating diverse facets of adult disorders. Data were made available to the scientific community, and other studies continue to emerge from the original data.

TABLE 17.4.   Issues and Questions Related to the Sharing of Data and Federal Law Mandating Such Sharing

---

- There is no clear definition of "data," which could range from notebooks to biological material to videotaped interviews.

- There is no clear definition of "publication," which could range from publication in a scholarly journal to a "Power Point" demonstration.

- There is no adequate description of who would be required to pay for the production of data, and the agencies have no administrative structure to oversee this requirement.

- It is not clear how patient privacy and confidentiality of medical records would be maintained.

- The method of enforcement of the measure is unclear as is the method for protection from the misuse of data.

- There are patent, privacy, and intellectual property concerns as well as liability issues.

- Premature release of research findings could be misleading and create many problems in areas of public health and safety. For example, premature disclosure of data could alter the behavior of study participants, thereby significantly impacting the validity of research findings.

Source: Rodin, J., & Barachi, R. (March, 1999). Impacts of the Shelby Amendment: Letters by April 5: To the University's Research Community, *University of Pennsylvania, Almanac,* Volume 45, Number 26 (also available at http://www.upenn.edu/almanac/v45/n26/shelby.html).

Another example is the NIMH Treatment of Depression Collaborative Research Program. In this study, as mentioned earlier, interpersonal psychotherapy, cognitive therapy, and medication (imipramine) were compared for the treatment of adult depression ($N = 250$ cases assigned to treatment, 28 therapists) across multiple sites (3 cities) (Elkin et al., 1985, 1989). Several articles have been completed by the original collaborative team. The database has been made available to the scientific community, and other investigators are now analyzing the results. In both the ECA and the Depression study, publications continue to emerge since the data have been made available.

Placing data within the public domain has obvious advantages for science. A given data set can represent a rich resource. The interests and creativity of a given investigative team that obtained and analyzed the data may not exhaust the knowledge available from that data set. Other investigators with novel hypotheses, varied conceptions of the research issues and underlying theory, and different training or orientations may extract new knowledge. Also, there are "different types" of investigators. We often think of a researcher as someone who collects his or her own data. However, some researchers also supplement this by publishing on the basis of data collected by others (meta-analysts) or drawing from collaborative studies with databases made available. Many creative ideas might be tested among people who either cannot collect original data by virtue of their resources (grants, university position) or are not interested in collecting original data. Access to databases might permit such individuals to contribute more fully to developing the science.

Sharing data might be very useful as a general practice to optimize the knowledge that is gained from any study and the combinations of data sets among interested parties. Indeed, there is a remarkable untapped resource in data that have been collected but have not been fully mined. It would be quite useful if investigators could routinely provide, in some computerized format of the original article, raw data and codes for the variables so the data could be analyzed by others. Inevitably, there would be problems (software incompatibility, incomplete reporting of the codes, and occasional studies and databases that the profession would just as soon forget rather than reanalyze [see my dissertation]). Even so, large-scale studies that in many ways represent once-in-a-lifetime data sets are prime candidates for data sharing in this fashion.

There may be ethical constraints to sharing all data, given that some institutional review committees restrict use of data to the specific purposes outlined in the original proposal and by the investigator who provided that proposal. The purpose is to protect subjects whose consent does not extend to use beyond the original project. Also, investigators are often wary to share data until they have completed their analyses or are protective in general because the ethos for sharing and making data available as a matter of course has yet to be required.

Conflict of Interest

A critical issue that has emerged in scientific research pertains to *conflict of interest* in research. This refers to any situation in which an investigator may have an interest or obligation that can bias, or be perceived to bias, a research project. There are at least three broad variations of conflict to which the researcher must be sensitive, and these include an actual conflict of interest, the perception of a conflict of interest, and lack of communicating information that might reflect either one of these. Conflict of interest emerges in other contexts than research, such as multiple role relations in the context of therapy with clients and faculty–student contacts. These are important, and the reader is referred elsewhere (Koocher & Keith-Spiegel, 1998).

Conflicts of interest in research can emerge in many different ways. Impetus for much of contemporary concern reflects research wherein the investigator may have a financial interest in the results of an investigation. Research findings often have important financial implications for the investigator. For example, investigators, especially in the areas of technology (new software, robotics) and biology (new model of drug action, gene therapy), might begin a company and want the rights for commercial exploitation of the findings. Here the investigators are at once scientists and entrepreneurs, and the roles clearly can conflict. All sorts of potential conflicts can arise, such as whether a faculty member paid by the university should be able to utilize time and resources for an outside commercial interest, and whether students working on research are doing so for their educational experience or to contribute to some financial goal (Cech & Leonard, 2001). These issues are not problematic just at the level of individual investigators. Major research universities often have resources devoted to assisting investigators in launching start-up companies that are for profit. The goal is to utilize findings obtained in research. This transfer of technology has often been completed by business and industry (commercial companies), and universities have entered into this to benefit from the gains.

Conflict of interest can arise from issues wherein money may or may not be involved. For example, research for government agencies or business and industry might require secrecy, perhaps due to national security or to product development, respectively (Kennedy, 2000). The procedures and the results of a study may not be reported because of the agency wish to protect disclosure. Science has as an inherent value in the free flow of information, the availability of previous work that has been completed, any reports and procedures. Practices such as replication of research and scrutiny of findings by one's peers are central to the entire enterprise. Insofar as a researcher enters into arrangements that require withholding the findings or secrecy of any results, there is a broader conflict of interest.

The most widely published instances of conflict of interest have emerged in the areas of biology and health (genetic engineering, development of medications), in which the research is sponsored by foundations or organizations that have a strong commercial interest in the results. For example, an investigator may be evaluating the effects of a medication for obesity and have a grant from a company that produces the medication and, of course, would very much like for that medication to be effective. Effective medications for medical and psychiatric conditions, when successful, can earn a billion dollars a year for a company. This situation could easily represent a conflict of interest for the investigator. The conflict is that science favors careful design of the study and impartial evaluation of the results. That is, the interest is in the evaluation and not in showing that the drug is effective. This is in conflict with the clear agenda of the company that the drug work. If the findings do not "come out" in the way the company wishes, it is likely the results will be believed by the scientific community. If the findings show that the drug is very effective in treating obesity, there might well be some suspicion, and some people will discount the findings. Perhaps one would say, "You would expect this; the research was supported by the foundation that wants the medication to be effective." (Situations like these underscore the critical role of replication of research findings.)

There is a conflict related to support for research and "how the findings come out." A company that funds research and is hoping for a specific result may come into conflict with the investigators and the actual results. I mentioned a large-scale study previously in which a new drug was added to standard treatment to prevent the progression of HIV (Kahn et al., 2000). All patients (> 2,500) from many different sites (77 hospitals) received standard medications designed to lead to lower levels of HIV virus. Some patients also received a new medication; others received a placebo—all in addition to the standard treatment. The study was stopped early because it was clear that the new drug was not helping at all (in deaths and progression of HIV). The investigators published the results of the trial (no-difference finding). This has led to a major conflict and litigation. The drug company that sponsored the trial did not want the results published, does not agree with the results, and stands to lose a great deal by publication of the findings (see Burton, 2000). The investigators say they did not agree to have the company control publication although the company could review the findings before their publication. I do not know what the actual contract from the company to the investigators said about publication rights. The conflict between the company and investigators is not just a minor disagreement; the investigators are being sued for several million dollars for damages due to the study's publication.

The conflict here pertains to who has access to the data and the conflict of interest in publishing the results. How this is addressed in research is decided at the beginning of a study when funds are provided. There is a grant or contract that has fine print about who oversees the results. The investigator must work out the details in advance. As an illustration, I have a "friend" who is a clinical psychology faculty member, looks very much like me and, in fact, is identical in weight, height, thinness of hair, and a few other features. He is currently working on a contract/grant as the principal investigator for a government agency. The contract is redundantly explicit in stating that he cannot publish the data in any form and under any circumstances forever (or maybe even longer) without the explicit written approval of the agency. In the agreement the investigator must sign before the funds were provided, data were defined in many ways (materials developed with the project, reports, charts, drawings, analyses, printouts, notes, and any document finished or unfinished). The contract goes on to convey that all information from this project is the property of the agency, is completely confidential, and cannot be released. In short, the contract is very clear that my friend has no rights with regard to these data and publication.

My friend has described some of the reasons for such restraints on his freedom to publish or report any findings. One of them is government agencies are often judged by the projects in which they are involved, the results of these projects, and whether their use of funds allocated to them has been wise. The data from one little investigation could easily jeopardize all of this. If results were seized upon by the media or some group (advocates for patient rights or some other cause), this all could quickly come to the attention of politicians who oversee funding of the agency. Continued funding of the agency and employment of key personnel at the agency might be threatened. Even if the findings came out as the agency wished, a report by an investigator might easily cast a spin that unwittingly makes the agency look horrible. Consequently, one can readily understand why the agency wants the only say and final say in whether any information can be released. I asked my friend why he agreed to such restrictions. He mentioned that he agreed to all of this because he thought the actual research was very important and that the agency ought to be involved more in this kind of work. He also admitted that getting a grant has several advantages and his interest in funding his research might make him agree to about anything. In any case, here is an instance in which there is a conflict of interest, namely, the practices, interests, and goals of an agency versus the unrestricted dissemination of research findings in science.

In psychological research and perhaps specifically in clinical, counseling, and educational psychology, it is easy to envision conflict of interest. Researchers may own stock in companies that in some way are relevant to their research and their findings. Also, a researcher may serve as a consultant to a company (e.g., that develops software or psychological tests or that publishes books) and receive generous consultation fees for serving as a resource for the company. Serving as someone who gains financially from a company and who conducts research with products that the company may sell could be a conflict of interest or be perceived as a conflict. For example, if a company is developing and publishing treatment manuals, a researcher may be solicited to conduct some type of research on these manuals (surveys of clinicians and what they might like, or treatment outcome studies using the manuals). Finding that the therapy works so it could be promoted in books and workshops might lead to a genuine, or the appearance of, conflict of interest, that is, objective reporting of outcome data by a dispassionate scientist versus reporting of the data by a passionate psychologist who could use or would like the money. Insofar as the researcher stands to gain in financial ways, the research and consultant roles represent a conflict of interest.

Many procedures are in place to address conflict of interest. Professional organizations generally opt for very clear statements by the investigator if there is any possible conflict of interest. Occasionally, the recommendations include stating in the informed consent form any potential association of the investigator that is, or could be conceived as, a conflict. Also, in any research publication, funding sources or possible conflict of interest is to be mentioned, sometimes in the letter of submission to the journal editor, but as well in a footnote in the article itself. Universities that receive federal research funds are mandated to ask faculty to disclose any conflict of interest they may have. Faculty are asked whether they own stock in a company or have a significant financial income from that company (earns more than $10,000 per year, according to current guidelines), or if their research is supported by a company or organization that might provide, or appear to provide, a conflict of interest. Federal policy and guidelines are instructive for conveying the policy and disclosure requirements for individuals and universities involved in federally funded research (see grants.nih.gov/grants/policy/coifaq.html; grants/nih.gov/grants/guide/notice-files/not95-179.html).

There is a dilemma for researchers. Conducting a program of research often requires extensive research funds. It is often the case that one grant or funding source will not support an active research lab. A major task for senior researchers is to maintain funding for staff and students. Several grants may be sought, and any public foundation, resource, or company that funds research is reasonable to pursue. Often companies or businesses that have a vested interest in a specific outcome are viable options to obtain funds. Without mischief on the part of companies or investigators, it is easily the case that funds are provided by the company with the hope of obtaining results that will help the company; investigators may have their own agenda such as complying with that, just doing good science, advancing their careers, or putting themselves in a position where they may obtain more funding. To the extent possible, the commitments and multiple roles of the investigator need to be disclosed. There are broad concerns because disclosure merely makes explicit conflicts or potential conflicts of interest. This is a not a resolution.

Some of the issues may be more readily resolvable than others. For example, a concern is that the investigator may feel pressure to find and report only results that are consistent with the goals of the funding agency and might not be able to publish or disseminate the results freely. At the stage of the grant or award, a contract can be drawn that makes explicit the autonomy of the scientist. This can be accomplished by granting intellectual rights of the findings and by limiting the scientist's role to conducting the research (rather than serving in any other capacities such as a consultant to the company) (see Cech & Leonard, 2001). Next to not being involved in potentially conflicting obligations, contractual arrangements that specify the independence of the researcher in concrete ways may be an excellent strategy for addressing some facets of the conflict of interest in research.

Guiding Principles and Responsibilities

The issues highlighted here are weighty, to say the least, and reflect areas where ambiguity often remains. Obviously, in the case of fraud, the ethical and professional standards and sanctions are relatively clear. Guidelines for allocation of credit, sharing of data, and related matters are actively discussed, and concrete rules cannot easily be provided. Guiding principles have been provided by the American Psychological Association to address these matters and to convey explicitly the ethical obligations of the investigator. Samples of selected principles to cover these obligations are presented in Table 17.5. The guidelines convey important facets of research obligations. In some ways they can be seen to fall beyond the scope of methodology and research design. However, they are pivotal to the use and interpretation of research and the accumulation of findings.

It is clear from the implications of research, that science and scientists are central to society. In many areas (clinical, counseling, and educational psychology; psychiatry; nursing) research may have critical implications that bring researchers into areas of social concern (day care, criminal behavior, child rearing, treatment regimens, custody disputes). Quite apart from the specific line of work and social implications that work may bear, the integrity of each researcher is critical. The guidelines convey that the integrity of the enterprise and obligations of the researcher to maintain these are essential.

Guidelines alone do not ensure adherence to research responsibilities. Consequently, a key issue is how to ensure that persons involved in research are exposed to

TABLE 17.5. Ethical Guidelines for Researchers

Reporting of Results

(a) Psychologists do not fabricate data or falsify results in their publications.

(b) If psychologists discover significant errors in their published data, they take reasonable steps to correct such errors in a correction, retraction, erratum, or other appropriate publication means.

Plagiarism

Psychologists do not present substantial portions or elements of another's work or data as their own, even if the other work or data source is cited occasionally.

Publication Credit

(a) Psychologists take responsibility and credit, including authorship credit, only for work they have actually performed or to which they have contributed.

(b) Principal authorship and other publication credits accurately reflect the relative scientific or professional contributions of the individuals involved, regardless of their relative status. Mere possession of an institutional position, such as Department Chair, does not justify authorship credit. Minor contributions to the research or to the writing for publications are appropriately acknowledged, such as in footnotes or in an introductory statement.

(c) A student is usually listed as principal author on any multiple-authored article that is substantially based on the student's dissertation or thesis.

Sharing Data

After research results are published, psychologists do not withhold the data on which their conclusions are based from other competent professionals who seek to verify the substantive claims through reanalysis and who intend to use such data only for that purpose, provided that the confidentiality of the participants can be protected and unless legal rights concerning proprietary data preclude their release.

Other

(a) *Duplicate Publication of Data:* Psychologists do not publish, as original data, data that have been previously published. This does not preclude republishing data when they are accompanied by proper acknowledgment.

(b) *Professional Reviewers:* Psychologists who review material submitted for publication, grant, or other research proposal review respect the confidentiality of and the proprietary rights in such information of those who submitted it.

Note: These guidelines constitute expectations regarding a much broader set of principles outlined elsewhere and which should be consulted directly. See *Ethical principles of psychologists and code of conduct.* Washington, DC: American Psychological Association. Copyright © 1992 by the American Psychological Association. Reprinted with

guidelines and the key topics. Accreditation of training programs (e.g., in clinical psychology) requires exposure of students to ethical issues and guidelines. More generally, universities involved in federally funded research must ensure that all persons involved in the research (principal investigators, postdoctoral researchers, students and assistants at all levels) are exposed to some university-based instructional program (classroom, Web based) that discusses responsibilities of the researchers, informed consent, conflict of interest, publication practices, authorship, data sharing, and related issues. Instruction has now become a matter of policy for institutions involved in federally funded research (see http://ori.dhhs.gov/html/programs/finalpolicy.asp).

Ethical issues of the researcher in relation to the scientific community are significant. In addressing these, it is important not to lose sight of givens of science. To begin with, scientists are human. Thus, the full panoply of human characteristics, motives, and foibles are likely to be evident. This does not mean that the negative virtues are pervasive or that one ought merely to shrug one's shoulders and say "of course" whenever an instance happens. It does mean that we should not be shocked to hear instances when less-than-desirable samples of humanness are evident, as when researchers argue ad hominem about their theoretical differences, when beliefs are held too tenaciously in the face of seemingly persuasive counterevidence, or when differential standards are applied to interpretation of some kinds of work (mine) rather than other kinds of work (yours). As humans, we are by our very nature limited. We are motivated viewers; we bring subjectivity to our experience and its interpretation. Not only is it true that "seeing is believing," but more critically to our goals, "believing is seeing." Fraud, interests in primary credit, possessiveness of ideas, procedures, and data (as discussed previously) occur and hence always warrant attention.

That scientists are human does not excuse lapses that compete with the very purposes of science. In discussing the lapses, we ought not to lose sight of the other, positive side. Humans have invented sciences and all of the methods, procedures, practices, and values aimed at increasing the objectivity and replicability. There is an enormous commitment, curiosity, and integrity among professionals in all of the sciences to discover, understand, and reveal. Subjectivity, error, and bias cannot be eliminated. Indeed, some of the very methods used to decrease subjectivity introduce their own sources of error, artifact, and bias. For example, statistics are used to provide a criterion to determine if there is a reliable effect; yet chance, in any given case, could explain the difference. As likely in much of research, the absence of differences can be an artifact of weak power. Also, measures are used to permit evaluation of constructs and to provide more objective means of assessment than impressions and personal opinions of the investigator; reactivity of assessment and low validity of the measure are potential limits assessment often introduces. However, these sources of error can be placed within the scientific arena, investigated, and evaluated.

SUMMARY AND CONCLUSIONS

Psychological research raises many ethical issues that are intertwined with methodology. Experimental questions and design options, such as those considered throughout the text, do not always make explicit the need to protect the rights and welfare of the subject. Salient issues pertaining to the rights of subjects include deception and debriefing, invasion of privacy, and informed consent. Deception is a major concern when subjects are misguided about the purpose of the experiment and the misinformation may deleteriously affect their beliefs about themselves or others. Deception is infrequently used or, indeed, permitted in clinical research. If deception is used, subjects must be informed about the true purposes after they complete the experiment. Providing such information, referred to as debriefing, is designed to erase the effects of deception. However, the effects of deception are not invariably erased. Leaving aside the effects of debriefing, many investigators object to deception because of the relationship it fosters between experimenter and subject.

Invasion of privacy is often protected by ensuring that the responses subjects provide are completely anonymous and confidential. Anonymity refers to ensuring that identity of subjects and their individual performance are not revealed. Confidentiality requires that the information will not be disclosed to others without the awareness of the subject. In most research situations anonymity and confidentiality are assured by removing the identity of subjects when the data are evaluated and conveying information publicly (in research reports) only on the basis of group performance. In clinical work, however, threats to invasion of privacy may derive from reports of individual cases in which the individual's identity might be revealed. Also, reports from research may affect large segments of society (ethnic/racial groups) even when the individual identity of the subjects is not at issue.

Informed consent is a central issue that encompasses many ethical concerns and means of protecting subjects in experimentation. Informed consent requires that the subject willingly agree to serve in an experiment and be fully aware of the procedures, risks, and benefits when making the choice to participate. Procuring and interpreting informed consent is not entirely straightforward because the subject must be competent to provide consent, know the relevant information to make a meaningful choice, and consent completely voluntarily. Whether these criteria are met in any given case often is a matter of debate.

Intervention research raises a number of special ethical issues. These include informing the client completely about treatment, withholding treatment, and using treatments of questionable efficacy and placebo control groups. Withholding treatment or using control procedures that may not be therapeutic are ethically objectionable and difficult to justify in situations wherein clients are in need of immediate treatment. Questions requiring these control procedures may be conducted in situations wherein clients are not in immediate jeopardy and agree to the conditions of participation. Some of the ethical issues raised in treatment research can be addressed by providing all clients with the most effective treatment, if they have not achieved marked improvements after participation in a less effective condition.

The many ethical issues raised in research have prompted guidelines designed to protect the rights of individual subjects. The guidelines apprise investigators of their obligations and the priority of ensuring protection of the subject at all times. The guidelines do not necessarily rule out practices that might be objectionable (e.g., deception). However, the onus is upon the investigator to show that there are likely benefits of the research and that these require a departure from full disclosure of the purposes and procedures.

Not all ethical issues and obligations pertain to the relation of the investigator to research subjects. The investigator has obligations to the profession, scientific community, and public more generally. These obligations pertain to the conduct of research. Four issues were discussed to convey concerns in relation to fraud in science, allocation of credit, sharing of materials and data, and conflict of interest. Ethical guidelines also are provided to convey these responsibilities as well.

KEY CONCEPTS AND TERMS

Anonymity	Fraud
Confidentiality	Informed Consent
Conflict of Interest	Invasion of Privacy
Debriefing	Plagiarism

FOR FURTHER READING

American Psychological Association (1992). *Ethical principles of psychologists and code of conduct.* Washington, DC: American Psychological Association. (http://www.apa.org/ethics)

Beauchamp, T., King, N., & Faden, R.R. (1986). *A history and theory of informed consent.* New York: Oxford University Press.

Fine, M.A., & Kurdek, L.A. (1993). Reflections on determining authorship credit and authorship order on faculty–student collaborations. *American Psychologist, 48,* 1141–1147.

Koocher, G.P., & Keith-Spiegel, P. (1998). *Ethics in psychology: Professional standards and cases* (2nd ed.). New York: Oxford University Press.

Miller, D.J., & Hersen, M. (Eds.) (1992). *Research fraud in the behavioral and biomedical sciences.* New York: Wiley & Sons.

Presidential Documents (US President), Executive Order 12975 (October 3, 1995). Protection of Human Research Subjects and Creation of National Bioethics Advisory Commission. *Federal Register, 60* (193), 52063–52065. (also available at http://bioethics.gov)

Rosenthal, R. (1994). Science and ethics in conducting, analyzing, and reporting psychological research. *Psychological Science, 5,* 127–133.

www.nih.gov/sigs/bioethics/conflict.html (This Website provides links for government policy and guidelines for addressing conflict of interest in research.)

www.onlineethics.org (This Website provides a research source for ethical issues in science. The site was designed for engineering but has direct links to key issues applicable to, and discussed in the context of, other sciences [research with children, biomedical applications] and federal guidelines that are directly relevant to psychological research.)

www.TCNJ.EDU/~ethcstat/start.html (ethical guidelines for statistical practice of the American Statistical Association. Many of these guidelines are directly relevant to psychological research.)

Chapter 18

Publication and Communication of Research Findings

CHAPTER OUTLINE

Publication Process: An Overview

Methodologically Informed Manuscript Preparation
Overview
Main Sections of the Article
Questions to Guide Manuscript Preparation
General Comments

Summary and Conclusions

The research process is composed of the design, execution, analysis of the results, and preparation of the report (e.g., journal article). The final step seems straightforward and relatively easy, given the nature and scope of the other steps. In fact, one often refers to preparation of the article as merely "writing up the results." Yet, the implied simplicity of the task belies the significance of the product in the research process. The article is not the final step in this process. Rather, it is an important beginning. The article is often a launching platform for the next study for the authors themselves and for others in the field who are interested in pursuing the findings. Thus, the report is central to the research process.

The article itself not only is a description of what was accomplished, but also conveys the extent to which the design, execution, and analyses were well conceived and appropriate for the conclusions. Recognition of this aspect of the report is why we require proposals for research (e.g., for students pursuing a dissertation and investigators pursuing a grant). At the proposal stage we can examine the thought processes, design, planned execution, and data analyses and make the necessary changes in advance. Even so, writing the full article at the completion of the study raises special issues, many of which could not be completely anticipated at the proposal stage. At that point the authors evaluate critical issues, see the shortcomings of the design, and struggle with any clashes or ambiguities of the findings in light of the hypotheses.

In previous chapters methodology has been discussed from the standpoint of specific strategies in planning, designing, and implementing research. At a broader level methodology can be conceived of as an approach toward thinking and problem solving. The approach considers specific types of obstacles to knowledge. These obstacles are codified in various ways under such rubrics as threats to validity, biases, and artifacts. The skill of the investigator in addressing these obstacles is often reflected in the quality of the design. The quality of a given investigation is invariably a matter of degree and is evaluated both in relation to the criteria for experimental validity and to the constraints placed on the research setting. In relation to manuscript preparation, the task is to convey the rationale for method and design decisions. This chapter discusses publication and communication of the results of research. The chapter emphasizes those facets of manuscript preparation and publication that pertain to methodology and research design. The task of the author is to translate methodological, design, and evaluation issues raised in previous chapters into a rational and readable manuscript, usually for publication in a professional journal. The publication process serves as a backdrop for many of the demands placed on the author in writing up the findings and hence is highlighted next.

PUBLICATION PROCESS: AN OVERVIEW

After an investigation or set of investigations is completed, the results are often published so that they can be disseminated to the scientific community and become part of the accumulated knowledge base. Publication and communication of the research findings involve a process with many decision points and steps. For examples, the investigator decides whether to publish the paper, what to publish (e.g., when a large database may need to be subdivided in some way), where to publish (journal article, chapter, book), and when to publish (e.g., in an ongoing longitudinal study when interim segments of the data may be of interest). Also, authorship, responsibilities for completion and preparation of the paper, obligations to the scientific community in executing and reporting research, and making information and data available raise central issues. The many components of publication and communication are of keen interest because publications address both academic issues (e.g., development of the science) and personal issues (e.g., career advancement) and because these issues span diverse scientific disciplines. Within psychology and other scientific disciplines, professional journals serve as the primary publication outlet for research. This chapter focuses on preparing papers for journal publication, although the remarks may apply to other formats (conference presentations, chapters and books in which research is described).

The publication process is usually conceived as beginning with preparation of a manuscript for journal submission. The process might be traced to a much earlier point. Indeed, decisions made at the design stage, including the focus of the study, the type of question, the strength of the planned design, and events throughout the investigation may govern or restrict the eventual publication choices. However, in discussing the publication process, I shall begin with the assumption of a completed study that contributes to the area of investigation in some substantive way and adds important knowledge. Inherent in this assumption is that the study is sufficiently well designed to generate experimentally valid conclusions. This assumption does not invariably mean that a study will end in a published report of the findings. Not all studies that are begun are completed; of those completed, not all are prepared for publication; of those prepared for publication, not all are submitted to journals for review and evaluation; and of those that are submitted, not all are accepted and published.[1]

After completion of the study, the author(s) prepare a written version of the paper in a very special format. This format in psychology is specified by the American Psychological Association (2001b) but used and illustrated in many journals beyond the discipline of psychology. Once the manuscript is prepared, it is submitted to a journal the author has selected as a desirable and suitable publication outlet. Selection of the journal is based on any of several criteria, including the relevance of the journal in relation to the topic, the prestige value of the journal in an implicit hierarchy of journals in the field, the likelihood of acceptance, the breadth and number of readers or subscribers, and the discipline and audience one wishes to address (psychology, psychiatry, medicine, social work, health, education). Several hundred journal outlets are available in the behavioral and social sciences. Journals in psychology within the English language have been described for purposes of aiding authors in the selection of appropriate outlets for their manuscripts (APA, 1997; http://www.apa.org/journals). Also, the Internet has excellent sites that search for journals in given areas (e.g., clinical psychology) and provide (at this writing) access to over 1800 journals (http://www.psycline.org/journals/psycline.html). These sources provide information that includes the editorial policy, content area or domain, type of paper (investigations, literature reviews, case studies), guidelines for manuscript preparation for each of the journals, and tables of contents of current and past issues.

Once the manuscript is submitted, the journal editor usually sends the paper to two or more reviewers. The reviewers are usually selected because of their knowledge and special expertise in the area of the study or because of familiarity with selected features of the study (e.g., novel methods of data analyses). Some reviewers are consulting editors who review often for the journal and presumably have a perspective of the type and quality of papers the journal typically publishes; other reviewers are ad hoc reviewers and are selected less regularly than consulting editors. Both consulting editors and ad hoc reviewers are often experts and active researchers in the specific area of the study and can evaluate the contribution. Reviewers are asked to evaluate the substance and methods of the study. They evaluate specific details, including those features we have discussed under the rubrics of threats to internal, external, construct, and statistical conclusion validity. The reviewers are instructed to evaluate the paper critically and to offer opinions about its merit.

Once the paper is reviewed, the editor evaluates the manuscript and the comments of the reviewers. In some cases the editor may provide his or her own

---

[1]Not all manuscripts that are accepted for publication are published. In my own career, such as it is, there have been two separate occasions in which I have had a manuscript accepted for publication, entered into production, and noted officially as "in press." Before these manuscripts appeared in print, each journal went out of business and stopped publishing. A coincidence? Maybe. But my acupuncturist, who specializes in rejected authors, feels otherwise. When you pin him down (not easy to do), he says that acceptance of one of my papers definitely places a journal at risk for demise!

independent review of the paper; in other cases he or she may not review the paper at all but defer to the comments and recommendations of the reviewers. The editor writes the author and notes the editorial decision. Usually, one of three decisions is reached: the manuscript is accepted pending a number of revisions that address points of concern in the reviewers' comments; the manuscript is rejected and will not be considered further by the journal; or the manuscript is rejected but the author is invited to resubmit an extensively revised version of the paper for reconsideration.

The *accept* decision usually means that the overall study provides important information and was well done. However, reviewers and the editor may have identified several points for further clarification and analysis. The author is asked to revise the paper to address these points. The revised paper would be accepted for publication. Occasionally, several revisions may be needed as the author and editor work toward achieving the final manuscript.

The *reject* decision means that the reviewers and/or editor considered the paper to include flaws in conception, design, or execution or that the research problem, focus, and question did not address a very important issue. For the journals with high rejection rates, papers are usually not rejected because they are flagrantly flawed in design. Rather, the importance of the study, the suitability of the methods for the questions, and specific methodological and design decisions conspire to serve as the basis for the decision. In many of these cases preparation of the manuscript in ways that emphasize the rationale for methodological practices selected by the investigator might readily lead to different reactions on the part of reviewers.

The *reject–resubmit decision* may be used if several issues emerged that raise questions about the research and the design. In a sense the study may be viewed as basically sound and important, but many significant questions preclude definitive evaluation. The author may be invited to prepare an extensively revised version that includes further procedural details, additional data analyses, clarification of many decision points pivotal to the findings and conclusions, and other changes. The revised manuscript may be entered into the review process anew to reach an accept or reject decision.

Of the three letters, clearly a rejection letter is the most commonly received. Journals often publish their rejection rates, that is, proportion of submitted manuscripts that are rejected, and this figure can be quite high (70–90 percent). Often the prestige value of the journal is, in part, based on the high rejection rate. (If this same criterion were invoked in judging careers, the rejection rate for my manuscripts—now approaching 99.99 percent—would place me in a rather elite group.)

No individual study can address all concerns (or threats to validity). Consequently, the task of the reviewer is to assess what has been done and to judge whether the benefits and knowledge yield warrant publication in the journal. Concretely, reviewers examine such general issues as whether

- the question(s) is (are) important for the field,
- the design and methodology are appropriate to the question,
- the results are suitably analyzed,
- the interpretations follow from the design and findings, and
- the knowledge yield contributes in an incremental way to what is known already.

In noting these criteria, one cannot help but be struck by the judgments reviewers are asked to make. The judgments require a subjective, as well as an objective, evaluation of the study. Science is an enterprise of people and hence cannot be divorced from subjectivity and judgment. In noting subjectivity in the manuscript review and evaluation process, there is a false implication of arbitrariness and fiat. Quality research often rises to the top, and opinions of quality over time are not idiosyncratic.

Focus on the reviewers makes the author appear as playing a passive role in the review process. Just the opposite—the author has the advantage insofar as there is much that can be done in preparation of the manuscript to address the issues that will inevitably emerge. Whether these issues are addressed and how well they are addressed will contribute greatly to the outcome of the journal review process.

Apart from the role of the reviewers and the author, characteristics of the journal are also critical contextual factors that influence the outcome. Individual journals can vary widely in their base rates of acceptance and the types of studies they are likely to accept. A given article might be reviewed quite differently as a function of the journal. Indeed, it is not rare for the same reviewers to provide different recommendations for the same manuscript as a function of the journal for which they are reviewing. For example, a reviewer might say, "This is a fine study, but not extraordinary and up to the standards of this journal." I mention this point not to demoralize potential authors, but to convey that evaluation of a study is always in context. That context includes the other research in the area but also the outlet and audience who will read the study.

Although beyond our purpose, the review process deserves passing comment. The entire process of manuscript submission, review, and publication has been heavily lamented, debated, and criticized. The imperfections and biases of peer review, the lack of agreement among reviewers of a given paper, the influence of variables (prestige value of the author's institution, number of citations of one's prior work within the manuscript) on decisions of reviewers, and the control that reviewers and editors exert over authors have been and continue to be vigorously discussed (Bailar & Patterson, 1985; Cicchetti, 1991; Lindsay, 1988). Of special concern are the review process and the manner in which authors are treated, although there are many ways authors can prepare themselves.[2]

Understanding the review process can be aided by underscoring the one salient characteristic that authors, reviewers, and editors share, to wit, they are all human. This means that they (we) vary widely in skills, expertise, sensitivities, motives, and abilities to communicate. Consequently, the content, quality, and other features of manuscripts, comments of reviewers, and editorial decision letters vary in multivariate ways. As new investigators begin to enter into the journal publication process, they quickly develop a set of stories about irrational features of the process and unreasonable judgments against one of their own studies. Yet, the hurdles of the

---

[2]Excellent readings are available to prepare the author for the journal review process: *The Trial* by Kafka, *The Myth of Sisyphus* by Camus, and *Inferno* by Dante. Also, within clinical psychology, various conceptual views (e.g., learned helplessness), clinical disorders (e.g. posttraumatic stress disorder), and intervention strategies (e.g., stress management, anger control training) are helpful in understanding and preparing oneself for negotiating its shoals. Stress inoculation training and career counseling are often used to help authors who have been traumatized by the review process.

review process can be traversed with only minor assaults to one's self-esteem when one is armed with a perspective on how to design research and to communicate the design and findings to others. (Heavy psychotropic medication can help as well.)

METHODOLOGICALLY INFORMED MANUSCRIPT PREPARATION

Overview

In psychology one's initial introduction to manuscript preparation often occurs at the undergraduate level in a course devoted to a topic within experimental psychology (learning, cognition, motivation) in which research design is also taught. The goal at this early stage of development is to encourage descriptive and objective scientific writing. Understandably, a particular view is fostered to distinguish the style of scientific writing from other forms in which opinion, subjectivity, and description are appropriately intertwined (a literary style where the full range of experience, emotions, and views are central). The style of science writing is to be descriptive and to convey what was actually done so that the methods and procedures can be replicated. Concrete, specific, operational, tangible, objective, precise, and impersonal are some of the characteristics that capture the introduction to writing and scientific papers in the tradition of quantitative research. The effort to describe research in concrete and specific ways is critically important. However, the task of the author goes well beyond description.

Preparation of the report for publication involves three interrelated tasks that I refer to as description, explanation, and contextualization. Failure to appreciate or to accomplish these tasks serves as a main source of frustration for authors, as their papers traverse the process of manuscript review toward journal publication. *Description* is the most straightforward task and includes providing details of the study. Even though this is an obvious requirement of the report, basic details often are omitted in published articles (sex and race of the participants, means, standard deviations) (see Shapiro & Shapiro, 1983; Weiss & Weisz, 1990).

Explanation is slightly more complex insofar as this refers to presenting the rationale of several facets of the study. The justification, decision-making process, and the connections between the decisions and the goals of the study move well beyond description. There are numerous decision points in any given study, most of which can be questioned. The author is obliged to make the case to explain why the specific options elected are well suited to the hypotheses or the goals of the study.

Finally, *contextualization* moves one step further away from description of the details of the study and addresses how the study fits in the context of other studies and in the knowledge base more generally. This latter facet of the article preparation reflects such lofty notions as scholarship and perspective, because the author places the descriptive and explanatory material into a broader context. Essentially, the author is making the case for the study based on the knowledge base. Relatively vacuous claims (e.g., this is the first study of this or the first study to include this or that control condition or measure) are rarely a strong basis for the study. Without context, any "first" is not very important by itself. Indeed, it is easy to be first for a topic that is not very important and has been purposely neglected.

Description, explanation, and contextualization are essential. These elements are used to convey the story, that is, the problem or question of interest and what is known about the problem. The author's task is to provide a cohesive statement of current knowledge and then to convey how the proposed study will redress a critical element to clarify or complete a facet of the story. If the author can tantalize or entice the reader to convey the need for the study and do so in a clear fashion, the manuscript is likely to be favorably reviewed. Admittedly, most of us are not engaging writers. (I offer as proof all prior pages of this book.)

The extent to which description, explanation, and contextualization are accomplished increases the likelihood that the report will be viewed as a publishable article and facilitates integration of the report into the knowledge base. Guidelines provided below emphasize these tasks in the preparation and evaluation of research reports. The guidelines focus on the logic of the study; the interrelations of the different sections; the rationale for specific procedures and analyses; and the strengths, limitations, and place in the knowledge base. Consider main sections of the manuscript that are prepared for journal publication and how these components can be addressed.

Main Sections of the Article

Title.   Well, certainly the title is *not* a "main section" of the article, but it is not trivial either. At least a passing comment is warranted. Usually, one attempts to address the key variables, focus, and population with an economy of words. If the study focuses on diagnosis, assessment, treatment, or prevention, one of these words or variations might well be included. Similarly, if a specific disorder (e.g., depression), personality characteristic (e.g., repression-sensitization), treatment technique (e.g., structural family therapy), or sample (e.g., infants, elderly) is critical, the pertinent terms are likely to be integrated into the title.

Occasionally, one has a hint toward methodology in the title. Key terms are included, perhaps in the form of subtitles, to alert us to methodological points. Terms like "a pilot study" or "preliminary report" may have many different meanings, such as the fact that this is an initial or interim report of a larger research program. These words could also be gently preparing readers for some methodological surprises that threaten experimental validity and telling us not to expect too much from the design. (My dissertation coined the subtitle: "A pre-preliminary, tentative, exploratory pilot study©.") In some cases terms are added to the study such as, "A Controlled Investigation," which moves our expectation in the other direction, namely, that the present study is somehow well conducted and controlled, and perhaps by implication stands in contrast to other studies in the field (or in the author's repertoire). Usually, words noting that the investigation is controlled are not needed unless this is truly a novel feature of research in this area. (Similarly, in the cases of review papers, rather than empirical articles, the use of the subtitle "A review" is usually unnecessary.)

Abstract.   Two features of the Abstract make this section quite critical. First, the Abstract is likely to be read by many more people than is the article. The Abstract probably will be entered into various databases and be accessible through Internet and on-line library searches. Also, most journals list the tables of contents for their issues and provide free access on the Web to Abstracts of articles. Consequently, the Abstract is the only information that most readers will have about the study. Second, for reviewers of the manuscript and readers of the journal article, the Abstract is the first impression of what the author studied and found. Ambiguity, illogic, and fuzziness here are ominous. Thus, the Abstract is sometimes the first or only impression one may have about the study. What is said is critically important.

Obviously, the purpose of the Abstract is to provide a relatively brief statement of goals, methods, findings, and conclusions of the study. Critical methodological descriptors pertain to the participants and their characteristics, experimental and control groups or conditions, design, and major findings. Often space is quite limited; indeed, a word limit (100- or 120-word maximum) may be placed on the Abstract by the journals. It is useful to deploy the words to make substantive statements about the characteristics of the study and the findings, rather than to provide general and minimally informative comments. Similarly, it is advisable to omit vacuous statements ("Implications of the results were discussed." or "Future directions for research were suggested.") and to replace them with comments about the findings or one or two specific implications and research directions ("The findings raise the prospect that there is a Tiny 2 rather than a Big 5 set of personality characteristics.").

Introduction.   The Introduction is designed to convey the overall rationale and objectives. The task of the author is to convey in a crisp and concise fashion why this particular study is needed and the current questions, void, or deficiency the study is designed to address. The section should not review the literature in a study-by-study fashion, but rather convey issues and evaluative comments that set the stage for the study that is to follow. It is in this section that the task of contextualization becomes critically important. Placing the study in the context of what is and is not known and the essential next step in research in the field requires mastery of the pertinent literature, apart from reasonable communication skills. Saying that the study is important (without systematically establishing the context) or noting that no one else has studied this phenomenon (e.g., measure, sample) often are viewed as feeble attempts to short-circuit the contextualization of the study.

It may be relevant to consider limitations of previous work (threats to internal, external, construct, and statistical conclusion validity) and how those limitations can be overcome. These statements build the critical transition from an existing literature to the present study and the rationale for design improvements or additions in relation to those studies. It is important to emphasize that "fixing limitations" of prior work is not necessarily a strong basis for publishing a study. The author must convey that the limitations of prior work are central to a key building block in theory or the knowledge base and cannot be surmounted by the weight of evidence available. Alternatively, the study may build along new dimensions to extend the theory, hypotheses, and constructs to a broader range of domains of performance, samples, settings, and so on. The rationale for the specific study must be very clearly established.

In general, the Introduction will move from the very general to the specific. The very general refers to the opening of the Introduction that conveys the area, general topic, and significance of a problem. For example, in studies of diagnosis, assessment, treatment, or prevention of dysfunction, the Introduction invariably includes a paragraph to orient the reader about the seriousness, prevalence or incidence, and economic and social costs of the disorder. Reviewers of the manuscript are likely to be specialists in the area of the study and hence know the context very well. Yet, many potential readers would profit from a statement that conveys the significance, interest, and value of the main focus of the study.

After the initial material, the Introduction moves to the issues that underlie this particular study. Here the context that frames the specific hypotheses of the study are provided and reflect theory and research that are the impetus for the investigation. Essentially, the author is making a case for conducting the study. Extended paragraphs that are background without close connections to the hypotheses of the study serve as a common weakness of rejected papers. The reviewers appear to "wonder as they wander" through the circuitous path leading to the hypotheses.

The Introduction does not usually permit us to convey all of the information we wish to present. In fact, the limit is usually 2–4 manuscript pages. A reasonable use of this space is in brief paragraphs or implicit sections that describe the nature of the problem, the current status of the literature, the extension to theory and research this study is designed to provide, and how the methods to be used are warranted. The final paragraph, or close to the end, of the Introduction usually includes a statement of the purpose of the study and the specific hypotheses and predictions. By the time the reader reaches this paragraph or set of paragraphs, it should be very clear that these hypotheses make sense, are important, and address a critical issue or need in the knowledge base. In short, the Introduction must establish that the variables are of some interest and that this study addresses a central issue. The extent to which the author conveys a grasp of the issues in the area and can identify the lacunae that the study is designed to fill governs the quality of the report and the chances of acceptance for journal publication.

Method.   This section of the paper encompasses several points related to who was studied, why, and how. The section not only describes critical procedures, but also provides the rationale for methodological decisions. Initially, the subjects or clients are described. From a method and design standpoint, information beyond basic descriptors can be helpful. Why was this sample included, and how is this appropriate to the substantive area and question of interest? In some cases the sample is obviously relevant because they have the characteristic or disorder of interest (e.g., parents accused of child abuse) or is in a setting of interest (nursing home residents). In other cases, samples are included merely because they are available. Such *samples of convenience* may include college students or a clinic population recruited for some purpose other than this study. The rationale for the sample should be provided to convey why *this* sample provides a good test of the hypotheses and whether any special features may be relevant to the conclusions. Subject selection, recruitment, screening, and other features warrant comment. The issue for the author and reviewer is whether features of the subject-selection process could restrict the conclusions in some unique fashion—or worse, in some way represent a poor test, given the purpose of the study.

The design is likely to include two or more groups that are treated in a particular fashion. From the standpoint of methodology and design, the precise purpose of each group and the procedures to which they are exposed should be clarified. Control groups should not merely be labeled as such with the idea that the name is informative.

The author should convey precisely what the group(s) is (are) designed to control, in terms of threats to validity. It is possible that some control procedures are not feasible under the circumstances of the study. Why and how the threats will be addressed should be clarified. Reviewers often criticize a study because certain control conditions were not included. After the paper is rejected by the journal, authors retort in an understandably frustrated way that the control procedure recommended by reviewers was not feasible, that the threats were not plausible anyway, and so on. Generally, the responsibility here lies with the author. The author is advised to identify the critical threats in the area and to convey how these are controlled in the design. Plausible threats that are uncontrolled deserve explicit comment to arrest the reasonable concerns of the reviewers.

Several measures are usually included in the study. Why the constructs were selected for study should be clarified in the Introduction. The specific measures and why they were selected to operationalize the constructs should be presented in the Method section. Information about the psychometric characteristics of the measures is often highlighted. This information relates directly to the credibility of the results. Apart from individual assessment devices, the rationale for including or omitting areas that might be regarded as crucial (multiple measures, informants, settings) deserves comment. The principle here is similar to other sections, namely, the rationale for the author's decisions ought to be explicit.

Occasionally, ambiguous statements may enter into descriptions of measures. For example, measures referred to as "reliable" or "valid" in previous research may be part of the rationale for use in the present study. There are, of course, many different types of reliability and validity. It is important to identify those characteristics of the measure found in prior research that are relevant to the present research. For example, high internal consistency (reliability) in a prior study may not be a strong argument for use of the measure in a longitudinal design where the author hopes for test–retest reliability. Even previous data on test–retest reliability (e.g., over 2 weeks) may not provide a sound basis for test–retest over annual intervals. The information conveys the suitability of the measure for the study and the rationale of the author for selecting the measure in lieu of alternative strategies.

Results.   It is important to convey why specific analyses were selected and how a particular test or comparison addresses the hypotheses or purposes presented earlier in the paper. It is often the case that analyses are reported in a rote fashion in which, for example, the main effects are presented and then interactions for each measure. The author presents the analyses in very much the same way as the computer output. Similarly, if several dependent measures are available, a particular set of analyses is automatically run (e.g., omnibus tests of multivariate analyses of variance followed by univariate analyses of variance for individual measures). The tests may not relate to the hypotheses, predictions, or expectations outlined at the beginning of the paper (Wampold, Davis, & Good, 1990). Knowledge of statistics is critical for selecting the analysis to address the hypotheses of interest and conditions met by the data. In presentation of the Results it is important to convey why specific tests were selected and how these serve the specific goals of the study. I personally find it useful to consider the results and data analysis in relation to the paragraph or statement of the specific purposes or hypotheses (usually, the final paragraph of the Introduction). A useful exercise is for the investigator to read that paragraph about hypotheses and predictions from the Introduction and then immediately start reading the Results section. The results ought to speak directly to and flow from that prior narrative statement.

It is often useful to begin the Results by presenting basic descriptors of the data (such as means, standard deviations for each group or condition) so the reader has access to the numbers themselves. The main body of the Results is to test the hypotheses or to evaluate the predictions. Organization of the Results (subheadings) or brief statements of hypotheses before the analyses are often helpful to prompt the author to clarify how the statistical test relates to the substantive questions.

Several additional or ancillary analyses may be presented to elaborate the primary hypotheses. For example, one might be able to reduce the plausibility that certain biases may have accounted for group differences based on supplementary or ancillary data analyses. Ancillary analyses may be more exploratory and diffuse than tests of primary hypotheses. Manifold variables can be selected for these analyses (sex, race, height differences) that are not necessarily conceptually interesting in relation to the goals of the study. The author may wish to present data and data analyses that were unexpected, were not of initial interest, and were not the focus of the study. The rationale for these excursions and the limitations of interpretation are worth noting. From the standpoint of the reviewer and reader, the results should make clear what the main hypotheses were, how the analyses provide appropriate and pointed tests, and what conclusions can be reached as a result. In light of our prior discussion of statistical evaluation, it would be advisable to move beyond tests of statistical significance and to include measures of magnitude of effects.

Discussion. The Discussion consists of the conclusions and interpretations of the study and hence is the final resting place of all issues and concerns. Typically, the Discussion includes an overview of the major findings, integration or relation of these to theory and prior research, limitations and ambiguities and their implications for interpretation, and future directions. Accomplishing this in a brief space (2–5 manuscript pages) is to the author's advantage.

Description and interpretation of the findings invariably raise a tension between what the author wishes to say about the findings and their meaning versus what can be said in light of how the study was designed and evaluated. It is in the Discussion that one can see the interplay of the Introduction, Methods, and Results sections. For example, the author might draw conclusions that are not quite appropriate, given the method and findings. The Discussion conveys flaws, problems, or questionable methodological decisions within the design that were not previously evident. They are flaws only in relation to the Introduction and Discussion. That is, the reader of the paper can now state that if these are the types of statement the author wishes to make, the present study (design, measures, sample) is not well suited. The slight mismatch of interpretative statements in the Discussion and the methodology is a common, albeit tacit, basis for not considering a study as well conceived and executed. A slightly different study may be required to support the specific statements the author makes in the Discussion; alternatively, the Discussion might be more circumscribed in the statements that are made. (For my dissertation, my committee commended me on the Introduction and Discussion but felt that omission of the Method and Results sections was a rather serious limitation.)

It is usually to the author's credit to examine potential limitations or sources of ambiguity of the study because he or she is in an excellent position by familiarity with procedures and expertise to understand the area. A candid, nondefensive, appraisal of the study is very helpful. Here, too, contextualization may be helpful because limitations of a study are also related to the body of prior research, what other studies have and have not accomplished, and whether a finding is robust across different methods of investigation. Although it is to the author's credit to acknowledge limitations of the study, there are limits on the extent to which reviewers grant a pardon for true confessions. At some point, the flaw is sufficient to preclude publication, whether or not the author acknowledges it. For example, the author of the study might note, "A significant limitation of the present study is the absence of a suitable control group. We are aware that this might limit the strength of the conclusions." Although awareness may have its own intrinsic value, in this case reviewers may not view this as sufficient to bolster the experimental validity of the findings.

At other points, acknowledging potential limitations conveys critical understanding of the issues and directs the field to future work. For example, in explaining the findings, the author may note that, although the dependent measure is useful or valid, there are many specific facets of the construct of interest that it omits. Thus, the results may not extend to different facets of the construct as measured in different ways. This latter use of acknowledgment augments the contribution of the study and the likelihood of favorable evaluation by readers.

Finally, it is useful in the Discussion to contextualize the results to continue the story line that began in the Introduction. With the present findings, what puzzle piece has been added to the knowledge base, what new questions or ambiguities were raised, what other substantive areas might be relevant for this line of research, and what new studies are needed? From the standpoint of contextualization, the new studies referred to here are those that not merely overcome methodological limitations of the present study, but rather focus on the substantive foci of the next steps for research.

Questions to Guide Manuscript Preparation

The section-by-section discussion of the content of an article is designed to convey the flow or logic of the study and the interplay of description, explanation, and contextualization. The study ought to have a thematic line throughout, and all sections ought to reflect that in a logical way. The thematic line consists of the substantive issues guiding the hypotheses and decisions of the investigator (with regard to procedures and analyses) that are used to elaborate these hypotheses.

A more concrete and hence, perhaps, more helpful way of aiding preparation of the manuscript is to consider our task as authors as that of answering many questions. There are questions for the authors to ask themselves or, on the other hand, questions reviewers and consumers of the research are likely to ask as they read the manuscript. These questions ought to be addressed suitably within the manuscript. Table 18.1 presents questions that warrant consideration. They are presented according to the different sections of a manuscript. The questions emphasize the descriptive information, as well as the rationale for procedures, decisions, and practices in the design and execution. The set of questions is useful as a way of checking to see that many important

TABLE 18.1. Major Questions to Guide Journal Article Preparation

Abstract

What are the main purposes of the study?
Who was studied (sample, sample size, special characteristics)?
How were participants selected?
To what conditions, if any, were participants exposed?
What type of design was used?
What are the main findings and conclusions?

Introduction

What are the background and context for the study?
What in current theory, research, or clinical work makes this study useful, important, or of interest?
What is different or special about the study in focus, methods, or design to address a need in the area?
Is the rationale clear regarding the constructs (independent and dependent variables) to be assessed?
What specifically are the purposes, predictions, or hypotheses?
Are there ancillary or exploratory goals that can be distinguished as well?

Method

Participants

Who are the participants, and how many of them are there in this study?
Why was this sample selected in light of the research goals?
How was this sample obtained, recruited, and selected?
What are the subject and demographic characteristics of the sample (sex, age, ethnicity, race, socioeconomic status)?
What, if any, inclusion and exclusion criteria were invoked, that is, selection rules to obtain participants?
How many of those subjects eligible or recruited actually were selected and participated in the study?
Was informed consent solicited? How and from whom (e.g., child and parent), if special populations were used?

Design

What is the design (e.g., group, true experiment), and how does the design relate to the goals?
How were participants assigned to groups or conditions?
How many groups were included in the design?
How are the groups similar and different?
Why are these groups critical to address the questions of interest?

Procedures

Where was the study conducted (setting)?
What measures, materials, equipment, or apparatus were used?
What is the chronological sequence of events to which participants were exposed?
What intervals elapsed between different aspects of the study (assessment, treatment, follow-up)?
If assessments involved novel measures created for this study, what data can be brought to bear regarding pertinent types of reliability and validity?
What checks were made to ensure that the conditions were carried out as intended (treatment integrity procedures, measures)?
What other information does one need to know to understand how participants were treated and what conditions were provided?

(*continued*)

TABLE 18.1.   *(continued)*

Results

What are the primary measures and data upon which the hypotheses or predictions depend?

What analyses are to be used and how specifically do these address the original hypotheses and purposes?

Are the assumptions of the data analyses met?

If multiple tests are used, what means are provided to control error rates (increased likelihood of finding significant differences in light of using many tests)?

If more than one group is delineated (through experimental manipulation or subject selection), are they similar on variables that might otherwise explain the results (diagnosis, age)?

Are data missing due to incomplete measures (not filled out completely by the participants) or due to loss of subjects? If so, how are these handled in the data analyses?

Are there ancillary analyses that might further inform the primary analyses or exploratory analyses that might stimulate further work?

Discussion

What are the major findings of the study?

Specifically, how do these findings add to research and support, refute, or inform current theory?

What alternative interpretations, theoretical or methodological, can be placed on the data?

What limitations or qualifiers are necessary, given methodology and design issues?

What research follows from the study to move the field forward?

Specifically, what ought to be done next (next study, career change of the author)?

---

facets of the study have not been overlooked. As a cautionary note, the questions alert one to the parts rather than the whole; the manuscript in its entirety or as a whole is evaluated to see how the substantive question and methodology interrelate and how decisions regarding subject selection, control conditions, measures, and data analyses relate in a coherent fashion to the guiding question.

General Comments

Preparation of an article often is viewed as a task of describing what was done. With this mind set, authors often are frustrated at the reactions of reviewers. In reading the reactions of reviewers, the authors usually recognize and acknowledge the value of providing more details (further information about the participants, or procedures). However, when the requests pertain to explanation and contextualization, authors are more likely to be baffled or defensive. This reaction may be reasonable because graduate training gives much less attention to these facets of preparing research reports. Also, reviewers' comments and editorial decision letters may not be explicit about the need for explanation and contextualization. For example, some of the more general reactions of reviewers are often reflected in comments such as "Nothing in the manuscript is new," "I fail to see the importance of the study," or "This study has already been done in a much better way by others."[3] In fact, the characterizations may be true. Authors (e.g., me) often feel like they are victims of reviewers who have barely read the manuscript, did not grasp the point, and have no grasp of the literature. Occa-

---

[3]Thanks to my dissertation committee for letting me quote from their comments.

sionally, this is true. As often as not, it is the reviewers who might more appropriately give the victim speech. The author has not made the connections among the extant literature and this study and has not integrated the substantive, methodological, and data-analytic features of this study in a cohesive and thematic way. Reviewers' comments and less-than-extravagant praise often reflect the extent to which the author has failed to contextualize the study to mitigate these reactions.

The lesson for preparing and evaluating research reports is clear. Describing a study does not *eo ipso* establish its contribution to the field, no matter how strongly the author feels that the study is a first. Also, the methodological options for studying a particular question are enormous. For example, the research question(s) could have been studied with many different samples, different constructs and measures, and data-analytic methods. The author ought to convey why a particular set of options was chosen.

In some cases authors select options (measures, control groups) because they were used in prior research. That warrant alone may be weak, because objections levied at the present study may also be appropriate to some of the prior work as well. The author will feel unjustly criticized for a more general flaw in the literature. Yet, if a key methodological decision was based solely on the argument that "others have done this in the past," that is very weak as a rationale, unless the purpose of the study is to address the value of the option as a goal of the study. Also, it may be that new evidence has emerged that makes the past practice more questionable. Over time, the standards and permissible methods may change, and measures and controls once viewed as innovative or even acceptable are viewed as mundane or flawed.

In general, it is beneficial to the author and to the scientific community more generally to convey the thought processes underlying methodological and design decisions. This information will greatly influence the extent to which the research effort is appreciated and viewed as enhancing knowledge. The author is not advised to write a persuasive appeal about how important the study is and how this or that way was the best way to study the phenomenon. Yet, it is useful to convey that decisions were thoughtful and that they represent reasonable choices among the alternatives for answering the questions that guide the study. The contextual issues are no less important. As authors, we often expect the brilliance of the study to shine through and to be self-evident. Any negative review or failure to grasp this is viewed as a sign the reviewer was wearing a sleep mask when he or she read the paper. Yet, the contribution of a study is a judgment call. From the perspective of the author, it is advantageous to be very clear on how and where the study fits in the literature, what it adds, and what questions and research the study prompts.

SUMMARY AND CONCLUSIONS

Publication and communication of results of research represent a complex process involving many issues beyond methodology and research design. Diverse abilities are taxed, beginning with the author's skills in identifying and selecting critical substantive questions and culminating with skills in communicating the results. Methodology and design play major roles throughout the processes of planning, conducting, and communicating research results.

Three interrelated tasks are involved in preparing a manuscript for journal publication. These were described as description, explanation, and contextualization of the study. The writing we are routinely taught in science focuses on description, but the other portions are central as well and determine whether a study not only appears to be important but also, in fact, actually is. Recommendations were made in what to address and how to incorporate description, explanation, and contextualization within the different sections of a manuscript (Introduction, Method). In addition, questions were provided to direct the researcher to the types of issues reviewers are likely to ask about a manuscript.

In preparing the manuscript, the author invariably wishes to make a statement (conclusion). The strength of that conclusion is based on the extent to which the study addresses issues highlighted in prior chapters. It is important for the author to convey the focus and goals of the study clearly and concisely. The design decisions and the rationale for these decisions, when presented clearly, greatly augment the manuscript.

KEY CONCEPTS AND TERMS

Contextualization   Explanation

Description

FOR FURTHER READING

American Psychological Association (1997*). Journals in psychology: A resource listing for authors* (5th ed.). Washington, DC: Author.

American Psychological Association (2001). *Publication manual of the American Psychological Association* (5th ed.). Washington, DC: Author.

Baumeister, R.F., & Leary, M.R. (1997). Writing narrative literature reviews. *Review of General Psychology, 1*, 311–320.

Kupfer, D.J., Kraemer, H.C., & Bartko, J.J. (1994). Documenting and reporting the study results of a randomized clinical trial (spicy meatballs, not pabulum). In R.F. Prien & D.S. Robinson (Eds.), *Clinical evaluation of psychotropic drugs* (pp. 237–260). New York: Raven Press.

Maher, B.A. (1978). A reader's, writer's, and reviewer's guide to assessing research reports in clinical psychology. *Journal of Consulting and Clinical Psychology, 46*, 835–838.

Sternberg, R.J. (1992). *Psychological Bulletin's* top 10 "hit parade." *Psychological Bulletin, 112*, 387–388.

Wilkinson, L. & the Task Force on Statistical Inference, APA Board of Scientific Affairs (1999). Statistical methods in psychology journals: Guidelines and explanations. *American Psychologist, 54*, 594–604.

http://www.apa.org/journals

http://www.psycline.org/journals/psycline.html

(These Websites, and many others, provide access to journal descriptions and can guide the authors in selecting possible outlets for their research.)

Closing Comments

Methodology in Perspective

We have covered several topics central to the design and execution of research. The goal of the book has been to describe diverse methodological practices and options, to convey the rationale for their use, and to relate methodological practices to the process of designing, executing, and evaluating research. The investigator must attend to many aspects to complete a methodologically sound study. In addition, an investigator is asked to complete a study that is important or novel and to communicate the findings in a way that is coherent. These are heavy demands, and methodological issues and concerns infuse each part of the process. In these final comments it is worth returning to key issues and discussing the relationship of methodology to substantive issues that guide research. Also, in a world of *fast* food, *instant* communication, and *rapid* transit, is there something I can provide that will help the interested reader, investigator, and new scientist quickly design a methodologically wonderful study? I thought you would never ask. This chapter ends with one such aid.

GOALS OF METHODOLOGY

Methodology, somewhat like statistics, is often taught in a way that focuses on a cookbook approach. That is, there are special ingredients, and they can be combined in various ways:

- add 1 or 2 hypotheses;
- select lots of subjects, obtain informed consent, and mix thoroughly (but randomly);
- add 3 or more assessment devices;
- collect, score, and enter the data from the completed measures;
- allow to cook for a few nanoseconds, depending on the chip in one's computer;

- generate F or t tests and maybe a regression analysis or two;
- describe the study in a cryptic style (the write-up); and
- allow to sit for 1–2 years (the review and publication process).

No doubt the art and science of methodology make cooking a reasonable metaphor, but not terrifically helpful. Clearly, there are ingredients that can characterize sound studies, but it is better to move away from the ingredients a bit to understand the task and goals at a broader level.

There is much the investigator ought to understand because strategies are required at each stage of the investigation to ensure high-quality research. Before the study is run, the investigator can ensure that threats to internal validity and other types of validity particularly relevant to the study (e.g., construct validity) are addressed, power is high so that differences can be detected, the experimental conditions are planned so that if there is an effect it is likely to be evident in this study (by the conditions or groups that are used), the constructs of interest are well represented (e.g., multiple measures), and the measures are sound in relation to the demands of the study (are reliable, valid, and sensitive to the predictions). During the study the investigator can ensure that the conditions (intervention, manipulation) are administered carefully and consistently, experimenters retain their level of performance (across experimenters and over time for a given experimenter), subjects are treated in a way that is likely to generate minimally biased data, loss of subjects is likely to be minimal, and data are collected with great care to ensure they are complete. After the study and when the data are in, the investigator can complete data analyses to address various influences that can be ruled out or made implausible through careful statistical evaluation (to control for, partial out, and examine the relations of various influences that might interfere with interpretation). These are only some of the strategies, but they convey that methodology is more than putting a few ingredients together—but, of course, so is cooking.

As noted in prior chapters, methodology is a way of thinking and approaching substantive issues. Occasionally, in prior chapters I have used questions that investigators can ask themselves to help guide the consideration of specific methodological practices. The questions were designed to be very specific and hence optimally helpful, but the specificity risks implying that there is a checklist feature of methodology—that is, cover these questions and one is all set. Ultimately, of course, the task of the research is to address broad questions and to utilize all one knows about the substantive topic and methodology to address the questions well. Consider four questions to convey the task:

1. What is the best available and feasible way to test my theory, idea, or hypothesis?
2. If the study were completed as designed, what would be the salient threats to validity or sources of bias that could interfere with drawing valid inferences?
3. Before, during, and after the study is run, what can I do to reduce the plausibility of alternative interpretations of the findings?
4. Are the purposes (e.g., hypotheses), design, methods of data analysis, and discussion coherent—that is, are they addressing the same key issues, do they speak to the same questions, and are they aligned so that what one says about results can legitimately be stated?

These questions are the critical guideposts for research and underscore the task of the investigator. The prior chapters described practices to address these questions and explained the rationale for these practices. In the context of clinical psychology and other areas where research is often conducted outside of the laboratory, grasping the rationale for methodological practices is particularly crucial. Luxuries of research, such as random assignment, a large or virtually unlimited subject pool of homogeneous and cooperative subjects from which to draw, quick studies with one or two lab sessions, no loss of subjects through attrition, and other such features are not always available. Methodology alerts one to the range of factors that compete with interpretation of the results and some of the practices that can be used. Ingenuity in addressing the four questions may be especially important when the ideal circumstances cannot be applied. Indeed, the challenge is to attend to the questions rather than to slavishly draw on any particular methodological practice. I have covered the fact that even time-honored practices (random assignment, significance testing) that are standard fare of methodology and research design raise their own problems. This is not a call to abandon traditional methodology but rather to underscore the fact that methodological practices are designed to aid inferences, and it is the inferences we are about rather than the practices.

SUBSTANTIVE CONTRIBUTION OF METHODOLOGY

A point that has not been conveyed in prior chapters provides a critical perspective on the contribution of methodology to the research enterprise. Practices related to the design of research, assessment, and data evaluation are not merely means toward an end, but in many ways contribute to the end. More specifically, methodological practices contribute to the substantive conclusions we reach in our theories and about the phenomena we study. Because methodology is the lens through which we view phenomena empirically, it dictates directly what we see. Changes in the lens, such as advances in methodology, also change what is revealed and advances in theory and substantive findings. For example, methodological and statistical advances within the past 25 years, such as meta-analyses and structural equation modeling, provided tools to evaluate questions that have been of interest for some time (effects of psychotherapy, causal sequences leading to different forms of psychopathology). The advances were not only new or different ways of answering the same questions of prior methods, but also ways of addressing and hence raising entirely new questions. This is illustrated by meta-analysis, which permits a quantitative, rather than a qualitative or narrative, review of a body of literature. When meta-analysis first emerged, it was touted (appropriately) as a better way of accomplishing the task of reviewing the literature. Yet, meta-analysis is not merely a way of reviewing a literature in a quantitative fashion, but also a way of asking questions about many different variables alone and in combinations from a body of research. Novel questions can be asked about a topic (psychotherapy, education, social programs and interventions) that cannot be easily or, in fact, ever addressed by an individual investigation. This is accomplished in part by coding studies along new variables (therapist characteristics, type of methodology, conceptual views of the investigator) and seeing their impact on treatment. Consequently, new substantive conclusions emerged from the approach to methodology.

Substantive advances also emerge from new methods of assessment. A dramatic example is neuroimaging, which refers to diverse and evolving methods of brain scanning. The advances resulting from neuroimaging are not merely a better way to assess brain activity. The method generates entirely new views about the nature of brain function, circuitry, and brain-behavior relations and permits evaluation of processes (e.g., during performance of various tasks) that could not be observed otherwise. In relation to more familiar psychological inventories, development of a new measure (of self-efficacy, helplessness, personality characteristics) permits investigation of constructs that can elaborate our understanding of human functioning in novel ways.

Methodology is always evolving. The present text has focused on many of the standard practices and issues that are important to master as a foundation. Many of the traditional methodological practices have become traditional, in part, because they successfully address threats to validity and sources of bias. Adhering to traditional methodologies alone, while obviously useful, can also be constraining. For example, in clinical psychology there is a long tradition of using self-report inventories to measure all sorts of constructs. Major advances have been made using self-report, and we depend on such reports to understand key topics in relation to the individual (self-esteem, feelings of helplessness and hopelessness) and society at large (rates of crime, substance use, utilization of health services). At the same time, integrating these measures with novel assessment modalities (e.g., social impact and unobtrusive measures) can give new perspectives and reveal new facets of the relations of interest.

A better example reverts to a topic from the beginning of the book. Most of the statistics in use in psychology are based on linear models, that is, a particular view about how variables relate to each other. There is no reason to think that the world or the world of interest to us as investigators is linear, and, in fact, evidence suggests otherwise in many situations (Haynes, 1992; Kazdin & Kagan, 1994). Science is guided by a revered tenet of parsimony, which refers to selection of an interpretation, among alternative interpretations, that makes the fewest assumptions. That is, the simplest explanation possible to account for the data is the one to be preferred. However, parsimony does not promote simplicity for its own sake. If more complex models can better account for the evidence, then the simpler model should be abandoned. Linear models, main effects, and bivariate relations often explain relations very well. Yet, one might also look for nonlinear models, interactions, and multivariate relations to explain more complex ways that variables can relate to each other and to outcomes of interest. The goal is to explore new ways of looking at phenomena of interest and, in the process, of identifying new phenomena.

Conceptual paradigms that affect the way we see substantive topics also influence methodologies to study them. For example, overarching conceptual views are influencing the study of many topics (the weather, earthquakes, physiology). These conceptual approaches give increased attention to nonlinear, dynamic, and reciprocal relations among independent and dependent variables. More concretely, the tradition of research often considers single variables and unidirectional influences. For example, much of clinical research focuses on the effects of x on y (where x may equal maternal depression, attachment, parenting practices and where *y* may equal child development, school adjustment, adult relationships). That is fine, but there is much to be gained by considering the possibility of mutual, reciprocal, interactive, and dynamic influences of *x* and *y*. Dynamic models, chaos theory, fuzzy logic, and novel ways of looking at causal relations reflect broad changes in thinking about phenomena that transcend many disciplines and will require new methodologies not yet exploited in psychology (Barton, 1994; Hanson, 1995; Haynes, 1992; Robertson & Combs, 1995). Many relations we care about are bidirectional, and any arrows to represent the relations may point both ways. For example, I mentioned that depression is a risk factor for heart attack, but also heart attack is a risk factor for depression, and both together are a risk factor for death. Less morbid, it is not only the case that poor or harsh parenting predicts or contributes to child deviance, but also that child deviance contributes to harsh parenting practices. We have been raised on simple questions, such as "Which came first, the chicken *or* the egg?" or "Why did someone do that, is it free will *or* determinism?" The questions are too simplistic and determine a restricted set of answers.

Advances in computerization also will permit new levels of analyses (integration of multiple variables and models that permit larger chunks of reality to enter into models, predictions, and empirical tests). The complex models will permit evaluation of more intricate relations. The tradition of methodology has been to isolate variables so their influence can be studied free from confounds and other factors that could compete with drawing inferences. Some of this has been dictated by the lack of available methods to handle variables that are not easily isolated, that is, the impact of *x* and *y* (as noted above), in the context and background of *a, b, c,* and *d*. Understanding how variables operate, rather than isolation per se, is the goal, and novel models and methods can bring us new ways of understanding.

The reader is encouraged to explore different ways of looking at the data in individual studies and different and novel methodologies. This can be accomplished in many ways. One way is to explore one's own data sets well beyond the goals of a particular study. First, in a study where two or more groups are studied, some guiding hypothesis may be supported. Let us say that the prediction was that group A would be better on some set of measures than group B and that this was found. It is likely that not all subjects show this effect, even if the group difference was significant. Some further data analyses might be very interesting. What are the subjects like who did not respond in the predicted way? Are there some interesting differences that might suggest other variables that might be important to consider (moderators). For example, I mentioned that the work of our group has shown that children and families who drop out of therapy have much worse outcomes than those who remain in and complete therapy. This is mundane, mildly interesting, and predictable (but has surprisingly little data in its behalf). Peeking at the individuals who violate the prediction is more intriguing. There are patients who complete treatment who do not get better or change appreciably and patients who drop out very early and who are doing wonderfully. How can this be, why, and for whom? Trying to understand exceptions or departures is one of many useful strategies to augment understanding. There is a rigidity that methodology, or at least methodological practices, might unwittingly foster—that is the cookbook view of methodology. Yet, the goal is to understand, and different ways of looking at the data, and especially finding out the conditions and persons for whom predictions do and do not hold, can be extremely helpful.

Second, application of novel data analyses or not-so-novel analyses with different default assumptions (divide the sample with very different cutoff points to define groups; add other variables to make more complex subgroups, such as individuals who show other characteristics in addition to being high versus low on the main variable of interest) can help discover and generate hypotheses. (Remember when other researchers do this with their data, this is called a fishing expedition, but when one does this with one's own data, this is referred to as the process of hypothesis generation and discovery.) The yield from a data set can go well beyond a test of the original hypotheses and can be used to develop conceptual models and hypotheses for the next study.

Third, another way to explore novel methodologies is to enter into collaborative arrangements with investigators from other disciplines (public health, psychiatry, genetics, statistics). Different disciplines have conceptual approaches that are likely to vary from those of psychology. Also, the different disciplines often have quite different views about methods of data analyses that have implications for substantive views about reality. These methods can provide new perspectives on the substantive questions of interest and greatly enrich the yield from research.

At the highest level of mastery, methodology and substantive knowledge merge in the investigator. That is, knowledge of how to draw inferences combines in a seamless way with knowledge of what inferences are possible, likely, and worthwhile, given what is known or remains to be known about the phenomenon. The importance of methodology is not merely to design experiments well but also to sensitize one to different ways of viewing the world and generating, as well as testing, hypotheses. A goal of the book was to provide initial stages in developing this level of mastery and fostering a broader appreciation of the contribution of methodology to the substantive topics of our research.

FINAL WORD: ABBREVIATED GUIDELINES FOR A WELL-DESIGNED STUDY

The comments about methodology refer to central underlying principles and what they are designed to accomplished. While these are lofty and even important, they have the potential of not helping the reader sufficiently well to design and complete a study right now. The reader who has arrived at this point might identify lingering practical questions that have not been answered or answered very well, namely,

- How do I design my study now?
- Where do I begin? and,
- What are the issues to which I have to attend?

The answers are in the previous chapters, but perhaps they have to be mined to find a few gems hidden in tons of rocks. Methodology can be simplified to aid the reader with the practical questions.

I have mentioned that designing and completing a study and communicating the results is very much like a story. There are beginning, middle, and ending parts. They convey a theme and bring the story line to a conclusion but also to some yet-to-be-resolved future outcome. The idea of a story can help the researcher plan, execute, and write up a study. In that spirit, I end with an aid to help the interested reader in concrete ways to move rapidly from pages of methodology to a study.

Table 19.1 presents a story outline for you to use. Here is the recommended use. Take the story outline (the table) into a room where there is privacy and you can talk out loud without being threatened with hospitalization or heavy medication. (Although I have no data, personal experience suggests that using this in public places has rather odd interpersonal consequences, so the usual recommendation—"do not try this at home"—does not apply here; home may be the only place to try this.) As you talk, merely complete the multiple-choice questions (circle the choices in parentheses) or fill-in the options (as indicated by a blank space underlined in the text) to complete the story. When you complete the story, you ought to have a well-designed study! See how simple methodology can be? Makes one wonder why I did not just begin the book with this story outline and leave the rest as an appendix.

TABLE 19.1.   Guidelines for Developing a Well-Designed Study

Directions: The story is designed to be read aloud by the investigator in a private setting. Read each sentence slowly and complete the questions. There are multiple-choice questions, indicated by parentheses, where you are required to circle or underline one of the options, and fill-in questions, indicated by a blank underline, where you are required to write in what you will do. Years of use of these guidelines have shown that the quality of the final study is deleteriously affected if the answer format is violated (if the investigator writes in answers for the multiple-choice parts and circles the blank underlines). Please begin reading slowly and mellifluously now.

Well, I am finally going to begin a study. This is going to be an important study because other studies that even come close to this have not _____(fill-in). Probably, this study, if I ever get it done, will contribute to (the knowledge base, science, humanity, my career [circle one]) in at least two ways 1) _____ and 2) _____, and I know I am being modest. The field is really fortunate to have me to do this study. I am a pretty amazing (gal, guy, person with an identity problem). Basically, I have these (two, three, four) (predictions, hypotheses) and they are

1) _____

2) _____ (add 3, 4 as needed)

I even imagine how I shall analyze the data to test these. Probably, to test these, I shall use _____ (list some statistical tests or analysis). Of course, this is just tentative, but I am pretty cool to even think of the data analyses at this point.

The subjects for this study are going to be _____. I chose this sample, neither because they are just convenient nor because my advisor or colleague has them around—everyone does that and I actually was tempted. But hey, no, not me, *these* subjects are important because _____. I am going to use lots of subjects and, in fact, my sample size—God willing—will be _____. Of course, I did not pull this number out of the air. I looked at a book on power. The first book (*The Power Broker*) did not help, but one on statistics did. I estimate I will need a sample of this size to have a chance to find differences if they exist. To be honest, I hope this sample helps me find differences even if they don't exist. A big sample can't hurt either of these goals. For the subjects to be

included they have to meet these (two, three, four) criteria: 1) _____, 2) _____, and 3) _____. I will *exclude* them if they meet these (two, three, four) criteria: 1)

_____, 2) _____, and 3) _____ or have an "attitude problem." To measure these criteria, I will look at them, ask them a few questions, or give them these measures

_____.

Speaking about measures, I am going to use a lot. Actually, I care about these constructs:

_____; _____ (add _____ as needed). For the first construct

these measures will be used _____; for the second construct these measures will

be used _____ (etc.). I am also throwing in this (these) measures because they (are interesting, are used a lot in this area, may explain why the results come out the way they will, are being pushed by my advisor [colleague, mother]).

The main treatment I will be using is _____. I will be using (guidelines, manual, book on treatment) that I (got from a researcher who developed this treatment, obtained from a credible imitator, invented myself). This is a reasonable version of the treatment.

Treatment will be given to participants for a period of _____ hour(s), for

_____ weeks at about _____ sessions per week. I am going to train the therapists, establish criteria to decide when they are trained, and then monitor the delivery of treatment during the study. How am I going to do the monitoring? Well, I plan to

_____ and _____. I will get some measures of treatment integrity to see that my efforts are not in vain and to see if I or anyone else ought to believe the results. I

plan on a measure that consists of _____.

Oh. I almost forgot. This will be a (between-groups study, single-case study), and I

plan on having (fill in #) _____ (groups or subjects). As applicable if a group

study: The treatment groups include _____. There will be (zero, one, two) control

groups, and these include _____ _____. Many people just throw in a control group without being clear as to why. Not me. My control groups are designed to

control for threats to _____ validity and, of course, are essential to test the hypotheses.

Here is what happens to a subject when he or she comes to this project. First, we give a big (interview, welcoming speech, assessment battery), then, of course, seek informed consent. Yes, the ethics committee has already approved my study, and I have the consent forms finally resolved to pass muster. Getting the wording right and obtaining final approval for the consent forms were (bizarre, no picnic, a breeze because I copied my advisor's forms). Then the subject will (complete, come back for) the assessments. I will then assign subjects (randomly, as the heart may prompt) to conditions. Treatment begins, is then completed, and then followed by posttreatment assessment (right after the last session, on the same day, within one week).

As is my style, I shall probably analyze the data with every statistic I have ever learned and no doubt click my mouse on a few that I have no idea about. Hey—how can one learn without trying new things? But I shall provide very, very specific tests of my hypotheses with focused statistical tests and present these so the reader can see the hypotheses, the tests, and my conclusions. Clarity is not my forte, and people have been on me for that. If the results show anything else interesting—including possible confounds—I shall present that, too, but probably sequester that (whatever that means) from the section that gives the main findings. The reader will be confused if I am, too.

There will be so much richness and depth to my study, and my work in general, that I probably ought to begin my discussion of the results with a brief overview or statement of the main findings. Then I shall try to (describe, explain) a key finding or two in more detail. As soon as I can, I shall make comments about how (this relates to, builds on) other work. If there is any (theory, other area of research outside my topic) to which I can relate the study, I shall (toss, squeeze) that in as well.

I also will make a few comments about the limitations of my study. Given how I have designed this study and my own personal skills, this could be a very brief section. But no study is perfect, and real limitations are always present. In writing this section, I shall try not to get too (defensive, righteous) about how I chose to design the study. In the remote chance that there *are* serious limitations of the study, more likely than not I shall (blame my advisor, remind readers of my difficult childhood, use a small font when this section is run off on my printer).

Finally, if space allows, I shall talk about the next study that ought to be done to build on my work. This future work ought to be an important study and not merely a test of generality to a different sample or setting. Something really (meaty, inspiring, conceptually interesting) in this paragraph will suggest a new "story" that needs to be told. Who knows, maybe I'll even (do that study, rest on my laurels) after completing this study.

Glossary

ABAB Design   A single-case experimental design in which the performance of a subject or group of subjects is evaluated over time across baseline (A) and intervention (B) conditions. A relation is demonstrated between the intervention and performance if performance changes in each phase in which the intervention is presented and reverts to baseline, or near baseline, levels when it is withdrawn. Also called Reversal Design.

Accelerated, Multicohort Longitudinal Design   A prospective, longitudinal study in which multiple groups (two or more cohorts) are studied. Each group covers only a portion of the total time frame of interest. The groups overlap in ways that permit the investigator to discuss the entire development period in a special way.

Acceptability of Treatment   See Treatment Acceptability.

Alpha (α)   The probability of rejecting a hypothesis (the null hypothesis) when that hypothesis is true. This is also referred to as a Type I error.

Alternate-Form Reliability   The correlation between different forms of the same measure when the items of the two forms are considered to represent the same population of items.

Analogue Research   Research that evaluates a particular condition or intervention under conditions that only resemble or approximate the situation to which one wishes to generalize.

Anecdotal Case Study   Intensive study of the individual in which there is no systematic or objective assessment. The "data" (information) is based on reports of the client and therapist without checks on their reliability or validity. See Case Study and Single-Case Experimental Designs.

Anonymity   Ensuring that the identity and performance of the subjects in an investigation are not revealed and cannot be identified.

Archival Records   Institutional, cultural, or other records that may be used as unobtrusive measures of performance.

Artifact   An extraneous influence in an experiment that may threaten validity, usually construct validity.

Attention-Placebo Control Group   A group in treatment research that is exposed to common factors associated with treatment, such as attending treatment sessions, having contact with a therapist, and hearing a logical rationale that describes the genesis of one's problem.

Attrition   Loss of subjects in an experiment. The loss of subjects can threaten all facets of experimental validity.

Baseline Assessment   Initial observations used in single-case designs that are obtained for multiple occasions (e.g., several days) prior to the intervention.

Baseline Phase   The initial phase of most single-case experimental designs in which performance is observed on some measure for several occasions (e.g., days) prior to implementing the experimental condition or intervention.

Behavioral Measures   Assessment that focuses on overt performance in laboratory or everyday settings. The performance attempts to sample directly the behavior of interest.

Beta (β)   The probability of accepting a hypothesis (the null hypothesis) when it is false. This is also referred to as a Type II error.

Birth-Cohort Study   A prospective, longitudinal study in which a group of subjects is identified at birth and followed for an extended period (e.g., through early adulthood).

Blind   Denotes a procedure in which the experimenter and others associated with the investigation (staff, assessors) are kept naive with respect to the hypotheses and experimental conditions. Because of the confusion of the term with loss of vision and the pejorative reference to that condition, terms other than "blind" (masked, experimentally naive) are preferred.

Bonferroni Adjustment   A procedure designed to control for experiment-wise error rate when multiple statistical tests or comparisons are to be made. Although there are several variations, in the most commonly used method the alpha (e.g., $p \leq .05$) is divided by the number of statistical tests that are to be completed. Each individual test is evaluated as statistically significant or not based on whether it meets the p level obtained by this division. For all the tests, the overall rate of alpha is still $p < .05$.

Buffer Items   Items or content of a scale or measure that are intended to disguise or dilute the focus of interest evident in the measure. For example, items related to hobbies or physical health in a self-report scale on psychopathology might be added to serve as buffer or filler items.

Carryover Effect   In multiple-treatment designs the impact of one treatment may linger or have impact on a subsequent treatment. This is equivalent to multiple-treatment interference.

Case-Control Design   An observational research design in which the characteristic of interest is studied by selecting individuals to form groups. The groups vary on that characteristic (e.g., depressed versus not depressed). Once the groups are formed, other current or past characteristics (family relations, personality) are studied. Minimally, two groups are included, namely, those who show the characteristic of interest (cases) and those who do not (controls).

Case Study   An intensive evaluation and report of an individual subject. See Anecdotal Case Study and Single-Case Experimental Designs.

Ceiling Effect   Refers to a limit in the range of scores of a measure. The limit may preclude the ability to show differences among alternative groups or conditions. The effect may be especially likely in multiple-treatment designs. As treatments are added or as the client has changed from a prior treatment, there may be little room (on the measure) to reflect incremental benefits of treatment. Ceiling or floor effect is used as a term, depending on whether the upper or lower limit of the scale provides the restriction.

Changing-Criterion Design   A single-case experimental design that demonstrates the effect of an intervention by showing that performance changes in increments to match a performance criterion.

Checking on the Manipulation   Evaluating whether or the extent to which the independent variable (intervention, experimental manipulation) was delivered correctly and received by the subject.

Clinical Significance   The extent to which the effect of an intervention makes an "important" difference to the clients or has practical or applied value.

Cohort   A group of subjects followed over time.

Cohort Designs   An observational research design in which the investigator studies an intact group or groups over time, that is, prospectively. The design is also referred to as a prospective, longitudinal study.

Comparison Methods   Methods of comparing clients with others, such as a normative sample as a means of evaluating the clinical significance of the changes achieved with an intervention.

Completer Analysis   A way of analyzing the results of a study that includes only those subjects who have completed treatment in a clinical trial. Subjects who have not completed the measures (who dropped out of treatment before posttreatment or follow-up assessment) are omitted from the data analysis. Contrast with Intent-to-Treat Analysis.

Concurrent Validity   The correlation of a measure with performance on another measure or criterion at the same point in time.

Confederate   A person who works as an accomplice in the investigation, although he or she appears to be another subject or part of the natural arrangement of the setting (e.g., someone in a waiting room).

Confidence Interval   A range of values within which the true differences between groups are likely to lie. The formula is : CIs = m ± $z_\alpha s_m$ where m = the mean score; z_α = the z score value (two-tailed) under the normal curve, depending on the confidence level (e.g., z = 1.96 and 2.58 for p = .05 and p = .01); and s_m = the standard error of measurement, i.e., the estimate the standard deviation of a sampling distribution of means or the standard deviation divided by the square root of N (s_m = s$\sqrt{N}$).

Confidentiality   Refers to the practice of not disclosing information obtained from a subject in an experiment without the awareness and consent of the participant. Disclosure would be to a third party (e.g., relative, friend, social service agency, other subjects, courts). There are exceptions where confidentiality is not assured in an investigation, as, for example, when the information might conceal some clear and imminent danger to an individual or society.

Confirmability   A criterion invoked to evaluate data in qualitative research; refers to the extent to which an independent reviewer could conduct a formal audit and reevaluation of the procedures and generate the same findings.

Conflict of Interest   In relation to research, any situation in which the investigator may have more than one role, incentive, or relationship to the procedures or goals of the project. A conflict would be evident, for example, if the investigator were interested in evaluating the impact of the intervention (role of the scientist) and at the same time were interested in the success of the intervention in light of possible financial gain (role of the entrepreneur). When an investigator holds stock in a business that may gain from the findings, or when the findings might be used now or in the future for some financial gain, conflict is evident. Conflict of interest, and the appearance of a conflict of interest, are central issues in the ethics of conducting research.

Confound   A factor, other variable, or influence that covaries with the experimental condition or intervention.

Construct Validity   In the context of experimental design this refers to a type of experimental validity that pertains to the interpretation or basis of the effect that was demonstrated in an experiment. In the context of psychological assessment the term refers to the extent to which a measure has been shown to assess the construct (e.g., intelligence) of interest.

Content Validity   Evidence that the content of the items of a measure reflect the construct or domain of interest. The relation of the items to the concept underlying the measure.

Continuous Assessment   A feature of single-case experimentation in which observations of client functioning are obtained repeatedly (e.g., daily) over time.

Convergent Validity   The correlation between measures that are expected to be related. The extent to which two measures assess similar or related constructs. The validity of a given measure is suggested if the measure correlates with other measures with which it is expected to correlate. Contrast with Discriminant Validity.

Counterbalanced   A method of arranging conditions or tasks for the subjects so that a given condition or task is not confounded by the order in which it appears.

Credibility   A criterion invoked to evaluate data in qualitative research; it reflects whether the methods and subjects are appropriate to the goals and are likely to represent the sample of interest.

Criterion Validity   Correlation of a measure with some other criterion. This can encompass concurrent or predictive validity. In addition, the notion is occasionally used in relation to a specific and often dichotomous criterion when performance on the measure is evaluated in relation to selected groups (e.g., depressed versus nondepressed patients).

Crossover Design   A design in which two interventions are presented to each subject at different points in time. Halfway through the investigation, each subject is shifted to the other intervention or condition. The intervention is evaluated by comparing subject performance under the separate conditions.

Cross-Sectional Design   The most commonly used version of a case-control design in clinical psychology in which subjects (cases and controls) are selected and assessed in relation to current characteristics. This is to be distinguished from studies that are designed to evaluate events or experiences that happened in the past (retrospective studies) or the future (prospective studies).

Debriefing   Providing a description of the experiment and its purposes to the subject after the investigation when deception was used or information was withheld about the investigation. The purpose is to counteract or minimize any lingering negative effects of the experimental manipulation.

Deception   Presentation of misleading information or not disclosing fully procedures and details of the investigation.

Demand Characteristics   Cues of the situation associated with the experimental manipulation or intervention that may seem incidental but may contribute to, or even account for, the results.

Dependability   A criterion invoked to evaluate data in qualitative research; it pertains to the reliability of the conclusions and data evaluation leading to these conclusions.

Dependent Variable   The measure designed to reflect the impact of the independent variable, experimental manipulation, or intervention. Contrast with Independent Variable.

Diffusion or Imitation of Treatment   The inadvertent administration of treatment to a control group, which diffuses or obscures the impact of the intervention. More generally, any unintended procedure that may reduce the extent to which experimental and control conditions are distinct.

Direct Replication   Repetition of an experiment under conditions that are identical to or very closely resemble the conditions of the original experiment. The conditions may entail population of subjects, setting manuals, measures, and procedures. See Systematic Replication.

Discriminant Validity   The correlation between measures that are expected not to relate to each other. The validity of a given measure is suggested if the measure shows little or no correlation with measures with which it is expected not to correlate because the measures assess dissimilar or unrelated constructs. Contrast with Convergent Validity.

Disseminablity of Treatment   The extent to which treatment evaluated in research can be extended to new settings, clients, and services beyond those in which treatment effects were demonstrated. This may include extending treatment to those individuals who select treatments for their clientele (e.g., social service agencies, insurance providers, health care systems), provide treatment in direct services (therapists), and who seek treatment (clients).

Double-Blind Study   A procedure often used in medication trials in which the patients (subjects) and those who administer the drugs (physicians or nurses) are not informed of whether they are receiving the medication or a placebo. The goal is to reduce the likelihood that expectancies or knowledge of the condition, rather than the effects of medication, could influence or account for the results.

Effect Size   A measure of the strength or magnitude of an experimental effect. Also, a way of expressing the difference between conditions (treatment versus control) in terms of a common metric across measures and studies. The method is based on computing the difference between the means of interest on a particular measure and dividing this by the standard deviation (pooled standard deviation of the conditions).

Effectiveness   The impact of treatment in the context of clinical settings and clinical work, rather than well-controlled conditions of the laboratory. In effectiveness studies, treatment is evaluated in clinical settings, with clients referred for treatment and therapists who usually provide services, and without many of the rigorous controls of research. Effectiveness and efficacy studies can be considered to reflect a continuum of experimental control over several dimensions that may affect external validity of the results. Contrast with Efficacy.

Efficacy   The impact of treatment in the context of a well-controlled study conducted under conditions that depart from exigencies of clinical settings. Usually, in efficacy studies there is careful control over the selection of cases, therapists, and administration and monitoring of treatment. Contrast with Effectiveness.

Environmental Variables   Variables that consist of the environmental or situational conditions that are manipulated within an experiment. Alternative conditions (e.g., treatments) or tasks provided to subjects are classified here as environmental variables. Contrast with Subject Variables.

Experimenter   The person who conducts the experiment, runs subjects, or administers the conditions of research. See also Investigator.

Experimenter Expectancies   Hypotheses, beliefs, and views on part of the experimenter that may influence how the subjects perform. Expectancy effects are a threat to construct validity if they provide a plausible rival interpretation of the effects otherwise attributed to the intervention.

Experiment-Wise Error Rate   The probability of a Type I error for all of the comparisons in the experiment, given the number of tests. Contrast with Per-Comparison Error Rate.

External Validity   The extent to which the results can be generalized or extended to persons, settings, times, measures, and characteristics other than those in this particular experimental arrangement.

Face Validity   The extent to which a measure appears to assess the construct of interest. This is not regarded as a formal type of validation or part of the psychometric development or evaluation of a measure.

Factorial Designs   Group designs in which 2 or more variables are studied concurrently. For each variable 2 or more levels are studied. The designs include the combinations of the variables (e.g., 2×2 design, which would encompass 4 groups) so that main effects of the separate variables as well as their combined effect (interactions) can be evaluated.

File-Drawer Problem   The possibility that the published studies represent a biased sample of all studies that have been completed for a given hypothesis. The published studies may reflect those that obtained statistical significance (the 5 percent at the $p < .05$ level). There may be many more studies (the other 95 percent somewhere in a file drawer) that did not attain significance and were never published.

Follow-up Assessment   Evaluation of performance after posttreatment assessment.

Fraud   In the context of science, this refers to explicit efforts to deceive and misrepresent. Examples of fraud include making up (fabricating) the data instead of running the investigation or changing aspects of the results.

Global Ratings   A type of measure that quantifies impressions of somewhat general characteristics. Such measures are referred to as "global" because they reflect overall impressions or summary statements of the construct of interest.

Grounded Theory Hypotheses and explanations that emerge from intensive observations of the phenomenon, i.e., theory comes from and is grounded in observation. The term is used in qualitative research.

History A threat to internal validity that consists of any event occurring in the experiment (other than the independent variable) or outside of the experiment that could account for the results.

Independent Variable The construct, experimental manipulation, intervention, or factor whose impact will be evaluated in the investigation. Contrast with Dependent Variable.

Informants Persons in contact with the client such as a spouse, peers, roommates, teachers, employers, friends, colleagues, and others who might be contacted to complete assessments, or to provide information.

Informed Consent Agreement to participate in research with full knowledge about the nature of treatment, the risks, benefits, expected outcomes, and alternatives. Three elements are required for truly informed consent, namely, competence, knowledge, and volition.

Instructional Variables A specific type of environmental or situational manipulation in which the investigator varies what the subjects are told or are led to believe through verbal or written statements in the experiment.

Instrumentation A threat to internal validity that refers to changes in the measuring instrument or measurement procedures over time.

Intent-to-Treat Analysis A way of analyzing the results of a study that includes all subjects originally assigned to groups or conditions. This analysis usually arises in the context of how to handle dropouts or missing data. All subjects are included, and the missing data usually are estimated by using the last (most recent) data the subject provided before dropping out of treatment. The primary benefit of intent-to-treat analysis is to preserve the random composition of groups and hence to avoid selecting biases that loss of subjects provides. Contrast with Completer Analysis.

Interaction Also called Statistical Interaction. The combined effect of two or more variables as demonstrated in a factorial design. Interactions signify that the effect of one variable (e.g., sex of the subject) depends on the level of another variable (e.g., age).

Internal Consistency The degree of consistency or homogeneity of the items within a scale. Different reliability measures are used (split-half reliability, Kuder–Richardson 20 Formula, coefficient alpha).

Internal Validity The extent to which the experimental manipulation or intervention, rather than extraneous influences, can account for the results, changes, or group differences.

Interrater (or Interscorer) Reliability The extent to which different assessors, raters, or observers agree on the scores they provide when assessing, coding, or classifying subjects' performance.

Invasion of Privacy Seeking information of a personal nature that intrudes on what individuals or a group may view as private.

Investigator The person who is responsible for designing and planning the experiment.

Ipsative Comparison A comparison of the individual with himself or herself. Comparison of scores from the same individual. Contrast with Normative Comparison.

Latin Square The arrangement of experimental conditions in a multiple-treatment design in which each of the conditions (task, treatments) occurs once in each ordinal position. Separate groups are used in the design, each of which receives a different sequence of the conditions.

Longitudinal Study Research that seeks to understand the course of change or differences over time by following (assessing) a group or groups over time, often involving several years. Contrast with Cross-Sectional Design.

Loose Protocol Effect   Refers to the failure of the investigator to specify critical details of the procedures that guide the experimenter's behavior, including the rationale, script, or activities of the investigation.

Magnitude of Effect   A measure of the strength of the experimental effect or the magnitude of the contribution of the independent variable to performance on the dependent variable.

Main Effect   The main effect is equivalent to an overall effect of an independent variable. In a factorial design, main effects are the separate and independent effects of the variables in the design, and are distinguished from interactions. See Interaction.

Masked   Sometimes used instead of "blind" to denote a procedure in which the experimenter and others associated with the investigation (staff, assessors) are kept naive with respect to the hypotheses and experimental conditions. The term "blind" is retained in this book because it continues to be the more frequent term and as a key word in searching resources on methodology. See Blind.

Matching   Grouping subjects together on the basis of their similarity on a particular characteristic or set of characteristics that is known, or presumed, to be related to the independent or dependent variables.

Maturation   Processes within the individual, reflecting changes over time that may serve as a threat to internal validity.

Measurement Sensitivity   The capacity of a measure to reflect systematic variation, change, or differences in response to an intervention, experimental manipulation, or group composition (as in a case-control study).

Mediator   The process, mechanism, or means through which a variable produces a particular outcome. Beyond knowing that A may cause B, the mechanism elaborates precisely what happens (psychologically, biologically) that explains how B results.

Meta-Analysis   A quantitative method of evaluating a body of research in which effect size is used as the common metric. Studies are combined so that inferences can be drawn across studies and as a function of several of their characteristics (e.g., types of interventions).

Methodology   Refers to the diverse principles, procedures, and practices that govern research.

Mismatching   A procedure in which an effort is made to equalize groups that may be drawn from different samples. The danger is that the sample might be equal on a pretest measure of interest but regress toward different means upon retesting. Changes due to statistical regression might be misinterpreted as an effect due to the experimental manipulation.

Moderator   A variable that influences the relationship of two variables of interest. The relationship between the variables (A and B) changes or is different as a functioning of some other variable (sex, age, ethnicity).

Multiple-Baseline Design   A single-case experimental design strategy in which the intervention is introduced across different behaviors, individuals, or situations at different times. A causal relation between the intervention and performance on the dependent measures is demonstrated if each behavior (individual or situation) changes when and only when the program is introduced.

Multiple Comparisons   The number of comparisons or statistical tests in an experiment.

Multiple Operationism   Defining a construct by several measures or in several ways. Typically, researchers are interested in a general construct (depression, anxiety) and seek relations among variables that are evident beyond any single operation or measure to define the construct. Contrast with Single Operationism.

Multiple-Treatment Designs   Designs in which two or more different conditions or treatments are presented to each subject. In most multiple-treatment designs in clinical research, separate groups are used so that the different treatments can be presented in different orders.

Multiple-Treatment Interference A potential threat to external validity when subjects are exposed to more than one condition or treatment within an experiment. The impact of a treatment or intervention may depend on the prior conditions to which subjects were exposed.

Multitrait–Multimethod Matrix The set of correlations obtained from administering several measures to the same subject. These measures include two or more constructs (traits or characteristics), each of which is measured by two or more methods (self-report, direct observation). The purpose of the matrix is to evaluate convergent and discriminant validity and to separate trait from method variance.

My Dissertation Committee A group of eminent scholars whose identity is completely protected because they entered the DCWPP immediately after my dissertation orals. (DCWPP stands for Dissertation Committee Witness Protection Program that provides a change of identity, relocation, and a gift certificate for plastic surgery. Wherever you are, thank you again for your help.)

Negative Results Commonly refers to a pattern of experimental results in which the differences or findings are not statistically significant.

No-Contact Control Group A group that does not receive the experimental condition or intervention; subjects do not know they are participating in the research.

Nonequivalent Control Group A group used in quasi-experiments to rule out or make less plausible specific threats to internal validity. The group is referred to as nonequivalent because it is not formed through random assignment in the investigation.

Nonmanipulated Variables Variables that are studied through selection of subjects or observation of characteristics imposed by nature.

Nonoverlapping Data In single-case designs the data points from one phase (e.g., in an ABAB design) may not share any values so that there is no "overlap" in the graph when the data are plotted. This pattern is often evident when there are changes in means, slope, and level across phases, and the latency of change is rapid, all criteria that are used for nonstatistical evaluation of the data in single-case research.

Nonspecific-Treatment Control Group See Attention-Placebo Control Group.

Nonstatistical Evaluation A method of data evaluation based on visual inspection criteria. Characteristics of the data (changes in means, slopes, and level, and the latency of change) are used to infer reliability of the impact of the experimental manipulation.

Normative Comparison A comparison of the individual with others, especially with a group of individuals who are functioning adequately in everyday life. Contrast with Ipsative Comparison.

Normative Range A range of performance among a nonreferred, community sample that is used as a point of reference for evaluating the clinical significance of change in intervention studies.

No-Treatment Control Group A group that does not receive the experimental condition or intervention.

Novelty Effects A potential threat to external validity when the effects of an intervention may depend in part upon their innovativeness or novelty in the situation. The effects are genuine (i.e., nonchance), but occur because of the context in which they are studied.

Nuisance Variables Characteristics of subjects (age, sex, ethnicity) that are not of interest to the investigator but that may vary systematically across groups and bias the results. In experimental research random assignment of subjects to conditions or groups is a way of ensuring that such variables will be distributed unsystematically across groups. In this way variables are not likely to threaten validity (e.g., by selection).

Null Hypothesis (H_0) The hypothesis that specifies that there is no difference between conditions or groups in the experiment on the dependent measures of interest.

Observational Research   A type of research design in which the relations among variables are observed but not manipulated. Typically, the focus is on characteristics of different subjects or the relations among nonmanipulated variables.

Obtrusive Measures   Any measure or measurement condition in which subjects are aware that some facet of their performance is assessed. See Reactivity.

Operational Definition   Defining a concept by the specific operations or measures that are to be used in an experiment. The specific way the construct will be defined for inclusion in the investigation.

Order Effects   In multiple-treatment designs, the impact of a treatment may depend on whether it appears first (or in some other place) among the treatments presented to the subjects. If the position of the treatments influences the results, this is referred to as an order effect. See also Sequence Effects.

***p* Level or Value**   A value associated with the statistical test (t or F test) that reflects the probability that a value as extreme as, or more extreme than, the one observed would arise by chance alone if the study were repeated a large number of times.

Parsimony   An accepted principle or heuristic in science that guides our interpretations of data and phenomena of interest. The principle refers to selecting the simplest version or account of the data among the competing views or interpretations that are available. If a phenomenon can be explained equally well in multiple ways, one adopts the interpretation that is most economical, that is, uses the fewest constructs. Other names of the principle include the principle of economy, principle of unnecessary plurality, principle of simplicity, and Occam's razor.

Patched-Up Control Group   see Nonequivalent Control Group.

Per-Comparison Error Rate   The probability of a Type I error for a specific comparison or statistical test of differences when several comparisons are made. Contrast with Experiment-Wise Error Rate.

Physical Traces   Unobtrusive measures that consist of selective wear (erosion) or the deposit (accretion) of materials.

Pilot Work   A preliminary test of the procedures of an investigation before running the full-fledged study. Usually, the goals of pilot work are to see if procedures (equipment, recruitment methods) "work," are feasible, and are having the effect (on the manipulation check or even dependent measures). Pilot work is usually conducted in a small scale merely to provide the information the investigator wishes to ensure that the study can be conducted.

Placebo   A substance that has no active pharmacological properties that would be expected to produce change in the condition to which it is applied.

Placebo Effect   Changes in an outcome due to receipt of and participation in a treatment. The changes are due to attention that subjects receive or beliefs and expectations among those who receive or administer the treatment. In the context of drug research, an inert substance may produce an effect that resembles or is identical to the outcomes evident with a genuine medication. This effect is a placebo effect.

Plagiarism   The direct use and copying of material of someone else without providing credit or acknowledgment.

Plausible Rival Hypothesis   An interpretation of the results of an investigation that competes with (rivals) the interpretation the investigator wishes to draw. An alternative interpretation of the data that is plausible in light of the research design.

Postexperimental Inquiry   A method of evaluating whether demand characteristics could account for the results by asking the subjects after the experiment about their perceptions of the purpose of the experiment, what the experimenter expected from them, and how they were supposed to respond.

Posttest-Only Control Group Design   An experimental design (with a minimum of two groups) in which no pretest is given. The effect of the experimental condition across groups is assessed on a postintervention measure only.

Posttest Sensitization   Administration of the posttest may alter the influence of the experimental condition that follows.

Power   The probability of rejecting the null hypothesis (that there are no differences) when, in fact, that hypothesis is false. Alternatively, detecting a difference between groups when, in fact, a difference truly exists.

Predictive Validity   The correlation of a measure at one point in time with performance on another measure or criterion at some point in the future.

Preinquiry   A method of evaluating whether demand characteristics could account for the results by conveying information to the subjects about the experiment without actually running them through the conditions. Subjects are also asked to complete the dependent measures to see if their performance yields the expected results.

Pretest–Posttest Control Group Design   An experimental design with a minimum of two groups. Usually, one group receives the experimental condition and the other does not. The essential feature of the design is that subjects are tested before and after the intervention.

Pretest Sensitization   Administration of the pretest may alter the influence of the experimental condition that follows.

Probability Pyramiding   The error rate or risk of a Type I error that comes from conducting multiple comparisons (e.g., *t* tests) in an experiment.

Projective Techniques   A class of measures that assess facets of personality based on the presentation of ambiguous tasks or materials. Subjects respond with minimal situational cues or constraints.

Prospective Design   A case-control design used to draw inferences about some antecedent condition that results in or is associated with the outcome. Subjects are identified and followed over time to identify who eventually do and do not show the outcome of interst.

Psychobiological (or Psychophysiological) Measures   Assessment techniques designed to quantify biological events as they relate to psychological states.

Psychometric Characteristics   A general term that encompasses diverse types of reliability and validity evidence in behalf of a measure.

Qualitative Research   An approach to research that focuses on narrative accounts, description, interpretation, context, and meaning. The goal is to describe, interpret, and understand the phenomena of interest and to do so in the context in which experience occurs. The approach is distinguished from the more familiar Quantitative Research.

Quantitative Research   The dominant paradigm for empirical research in psychology and the sciences more generally, involving the use of operational definitions, careful control of the subject matter, efforts to isolate variables of interest, quantification of constructs, and statistical analyses. This is distinguished from Qualitative Research.

Quasi-Experimental Design   A type of design in which the conditions of true experiments are only approximated. Restrictions are placed on some facet of the design, such as the assignment of cases randomly to a condition that affects the strength of the inferences that can be drawn.

Random Assignment   Allocating or assigning subjects to groups in such a way that the probability of each subject appearing in any of the groups is equal. This is usually accomplished by determining the group to which each subject is assigned by a table of random numbers.

Random Selection   Drawing subjects from a population in such a way that each member of the population has an equal probability of being drawn.

Randomized Controlled Clinical Trial   A treatment outcome study in which clients with a particular problem are randomly assigned to various treatment and control conditions. This type of study is recognized to be the best and most definitive way of demonstrating that an intervention is effective.

Randomized Controlled Trial   See Randomized Controlled Clinical Trial.

Reactivity   Performance that is altered as a function of subject awareness (of the measurement procedures, of participation in an experiment).

Regression Effect   See Statistical Regression.

Reliability   The extent to which the measures assess the characteristics of interest in a consistent fashion. In relation to measures, consistency may refer to internal consistency (how the items relate to each other), consistency between different parts or alternate forms of the same measure, and consistency in performance on the measure over time (test-retest for a given group of subjects). There are many different types of reliability.

Replication   Repetition of an experiment or repetition of the findings of an experiment.

Research Design   The plan or arrangement that is used to examine the question of interest; the manner in which conditions are planned so as to permit valid inferences.

Response Shift   Changes in a person's internal standards of measurement. The shift reflects a change in values, perspective, or criteria that leads to evaluation of the same or similar situations, behaviors, states, in a different way. The threshold or standards a person invokes have changed although the actual instrument or measure remains the same.

Retrospective Design   A case-control design designed to draw inferences about some antecedent condition that has resulted in, or is associated with, the outcome. Subjects are identified who already show the outcome of interest (cases) and are compared with those who do not show the outcome (controls). Assessment focuses on some other characteristic in the past.

Reversal Phase   A phase or period in single-case designs in which the baseline (nonintervention) condition is reintroduced to see if performance returns to or approximates the level of the original baseline.

Risk Factor   A characteristic that is an antecedent to, and increases the likelihood of, an outcome of interest. A "correlate" of an outcome of interest in which the time sequence is established.

Sample Size   The number of subjects or cases included in a study. This can refer to the overall number of subjects in the study (*N*) or the number of subjects within a group (*n*).

Samples of Convenience   Subjects included in an investigation that appear to be selected merely because they are available, whether or not they provide a suitable or optimal test of the hypotheses or conditions of interest.

Self-Report Inventories   Questionnaires and scales in which the subjects report on some facet of their functioning (personality, cognitions, opinions, behaviors).

Sequence Effects   In multiple-treatment designs, several treatments may be presented to the subject. A series of treatments is provided (treatment A, B, then C for some subjects and B, C, then A for other subjects, and so on for other combinations). If the sequence yields different outcomes, this is referred to as sequence effects. See Order Effects.

Significance Level   See Alpha.

Simulators   A method of estimating whether demand characteristics could explain the findings. Subjects are asked to act as if they received the treatment or intervention even though they actually do not. These simulators are then run through the assessment procedures of the investigation by an experimenter who is "blind" as to who is a simulator and who is a real subject.

Single Operationism   Defining a construct by a single measure or one operation. Contrast with Multiple Operationism.

Single-Case Experimental Designs   Research designs in which the effects of an intervention can be evaluated with the single case, that is, one subject.

Social Impact Measures   Measures in outcome research that are important in everyday life or to society at large (truancy, arrest records, utilization of health services).

Solomon Four-Group Design   An experimental design that is used to evaluate the effect of pretesting. The design can be considered as a combination of the pretest–posttest control group design and a posttest-only design in which pretest (provided versus not provided) and the experimental intervention (treatment versus no treatment) are combined.

Stable Rate   Performance obtained from continuous observations over time, as in single-case designs, in which there is little or no variability in the data.

Statistical Conclusion Validity   The extent to which a relation between independent and dependent variables can be shown, based on quantitative and statistical considerations of the investigation.

Statistical Evaluation   Applying statistical tests to assess whether the obtained results are reliable or can be considered to be sufficient to reject the null hypothesis.

Statistical Power   See Power.

Statistical Regression   The tendency of extreme scores on any measure to revert (or regress) toward the mean of a distribution when the measure is administered a second time. Regression is a function of the amount of error in the measure and the test–retest correlation.

Statistical Significance   A criterion used to evaluate the extent to which the results of a study (e.g., differences between groups or changes within groups) are likely to be due to genuine rather than chance effects. A statistically significant difference indicates that the probability level is equal to or below the level of confidence selected (e.g., $p < .05$), that is, if the experiment were conducted repeatedly, the finding would occur 5/100 on a chance basis.

Subject Roles   Alternative ways of responding that subjects may adopt in response to the cues of the experiment.

Subject Variables   Those variables that are based on features within the individual or circumstances to which they were exposed. These variables are usually not manipulated experimentally.

Subjective Evaluation   A method of evaluating the clinical significance of an intervention outcome by assessing the opinions of clients themselves, individuals who are likely to have contact with the client, or persons in a position of expertise. The question addressed by this method of evaluation is whether changes in treatment have led to differences in how the client is viewed by others or how the client views herself or himself.

Subject-Selection Biases   Factors that operate in selection of subjects or selective loss or retention of subjects over the course of the experiment that can affect experimental validity. Primary examples would be selection, recruitment, or screening procedures that might restrict the generality (external validity) of the findings and loss of subjects that might alter group composition and lead to differences that would be mistaken for an intervention effect (internal validity).

Systematic Replication   Repetition of an experiment under conditions that deliberately depart from or only approximate the conditions of the original experiment. An effort is made to test whether similar results will be obtained when some of the conditions (e.g., type of subject, way of manipulating the independent variable) depart from the original results. See Direct Replication.

Test Sensitization   Alteration of subject performance due to administration of a test before (pretest) or after (posttest) the experimental condition or intervention. The test may influence (e.g., augment) the effect of the experimental condition. This is a potential threat to external validity if the effect of the experimental condition may not generalize to different testing conditions.

Testing A threat to internal validity that consists of the effects of taking a test on repeated occasions. Performance may change as a function of repeated exposure to the measure rather than to the independent variable or experimental condition.

Test–Retest Reliability The stability of test scores over time; the correlation of scores from one administration of the test with scores on the same instrument after a particular time interval has elapsed.

Threats to Construct Validity Those features associated with the experimental condition or intervention that interfere with drawing inferences about the basis for the difference between groups.

Threats to External Validity Characteristics of the experiment that may limit the generality of the results.

Threats to Internal Validity Factors or influences other than the independent variable that could explain the results.

Threats to Statistical Conclusion Validity Considerations within the investigation that undermine the quantitative evaluation of the data.

Transferability A criterion invoked to evaluate data in qualitative research that pertains to whether the data are limited to a particular context (are context bound) and that is evaluated by looking at any special characteristics (unrepresentativeness) of the sample.

Treatment Acceptability The extent to which clients or consumers judge the intervention as one that is reasonable, appropriate, and fair. An evaluation of the treatment procedures rather than the outcome or effects of the treatment.

Treatment Differentiation The demonstration showing that two or more treatments were distinct along predicted dimensions. This complements but is distinguishable from Treatment Integrity.

Treatment Integrity The fidelity with which a particular treatment is rendered in an investigation.

Triangulation The extent to which data from separate sources converge to support the conclusions. Also used as a criterion to evaluate data in qualitative research.

True Experiment A type of research in which the arrangement permits maximum control over the independent variables or conditions of interest. The investigator is able to assign subjects to different conditions on a random basis, to include alternative conditions (treatment and control conditions) as required by the design, and to control possible sources of bias within the experiment that permit the comparison of interest.

Trustworthiness A criterion used to evaluate data in qualitative research. The criterion includes multiple components, namely, credibility, transferability, dependability, and confirmability of the data.

Type I Error See Alpha.

Type II Error See Beta.

Unobtrusive Measures Those measures that are outside of the awareness of the subject.

Validity The extent to which a measure assesses the domain of interest. This encompasses the relation of performance on a measure to performance on other measures at the same time or in the future and to other criteria (e.g., school achievement, occupational status, psychiatric diagnosis). There are many different types of validity.

Visual Inspection A method of data evaluation commonly used in single-case research, based on examining the pattern of change (means, level, slope, latency of change) over phases.

Waiting-List Control Group A group that is designed to control for threats to internal validity. The experimental condition or intervention is not provided during the period that experimental subjects receive the intervention. After this period, subjects in this control group receive the intervention.

Yoked Control Group   A group or control condition designed to ensure that groups are equal with respect to potentially important but conceptually and procedurally irrelevant factors that might account for group differences. Yoking refers to equalizing the groups on a particular variable that might systematically vary across conditions.

References

Achenbach, T.M. (1991). *Integrative guide for the 1991 CBCL/4-18, YSR, and TRF profiles*. Burlington, VT: University of Vermont, Department of Psychiatry.

Adam, K.S., Sheldon-Keller, A.E., & West, M. (1996). Attachment organization and history of suicidal behavior in clinical adolescents. *Journal of Consulting and Clinical Psychology, 64*, 264–272.

Adams, H.E., Wright, L.W., Jr., & Lohr, B.A. (1996). Is homophobia associated with homosexual arousal? *Journal of Abnormal Psychology, 105*, 440–445.

Adams, J.L. (1990). *Conceptual blockbusting: A guide to better ideas* (3rd ed.). Cambridge, MA: Perseus.

Addis, M.E. (1997). Evaluating the treatment manual as a means of disseminating empirically validated psychotherapies. *Clinical Psychology: Science and Practice, 4*, 1–11.

Adler, N.E. (2000). Abortion and the null hypothesis. *Archives of General Psychiatry, 57*, 785–786.

Adler, N.E., Boyce, T., Chesney, M.A., Cohen, S., Folkman, S., Kahn, R.L., & Syme, S.L. (1994). Socioeconomic status and health: The challenge of the gradient. *American Psychologist, 49*, 15–24.

Agency for Health Care Policy and Research. (1999). *Treatment of depression—Newer pharmacotherapies* (Publication No. 99–E014), Evidence Report/Technology Assessment No. 7, Rockville, MD: Author.

Aiken, L.R. (1996). *Rating scales and checklists: Evaluating behavior, personality, and attitude*. New York: Wiley and Sons.

Aiken, L.S., West, S.G., Sechrest, L., & Reno, R.R. (1990). Graduate training in statistics, methodology, and measurement in psychology: A survey of PhD programs in North America. *American Psychologist, 45*, 721–734.

Aldarondo, E., & Sugarman, D.B. (1996). Risk marker analysis of the cessation and persistence of wife assault. *Journal of Consulting and Clinical Psychology, 64*, 1010–1019.

Alden, L. (1989). Short-term structured treatment for avoidant personality disorder. *Journal of Consulting and Clinical Psychology, 57*, 756–764.

Allinder, R.M., & Oats, R.G. (1997). Effects of acceptability on teacher's implementation of curriculum-based measurement and student achievement in mathematics computation. *Rase: Remedial and Special Education, 18*, 113–120.

Alter, C., & Evens, W. (1990). *Evaluating your practice: A guide to self-assessment*. New York: Springer.

American Psychiatric Association. (1994). *Diagnostic and statistical manual of mental disorders*. (4th ed. Revised). Washington, DC: Author.

American Psychiatric Association. (2000). Practice guidelines for the treatment of patients with major depressive disorder (Revision). *American Journal of Psychiatry, 157*, 1–45.

585

American Psychological Association. (1992). *Ethical principles of psychologists and code of conduct.* Washington, DC: American Psychological Association. (http://www.apa.org/ethics).

American Psychological Association. (1997*). Journals in psychology: A resource listing for authors* (5th ed.). Washington, DC: Author.

American Psychological Association. (2001a). Ethical principles of psychologists and code of conduct: Draft for comment. *Monitor in psychology, 32* (2), February, 77–89.

American Psychological Association. (2001b). *Publication manual of the American Psychological Association* (5th ed.). Washington, DC: Author.

Anderson, C.A., Lindsay, J.J., & Bushman, B.J. (1999). Research in the psychological laboratory: Truth or triviality? *Current Directions in Psychological Science, 8,* 3–9.

Aneshensel, C.S., & Stone, J.D. (1982). Stress and depression: A test of the buffering model of social support. *Archives of General Psychiatry, 39,* 1392–1396.

Angoff, W.H. (1988). Validity: An evolving concept. In H. Wainer & H.I. Braun (Eds.), *Test validity.* (pp. 19–32). Hillsdale, NJ: Erlbaum.

Arndorfer, R.E., Allen, K.D., & Aljazireh, L. (1999). Behavioral health needs in pediatric medicine and the acceptability of behavioral solutions: Implications for behavioral psychologists. *Behavior Therapy, 30,* 137–148.

Austin, N.K., Liberman., R.P., King, L.W., & DeRisi, W.J. (1976). A comparative evaluation of two day hospitals: Goal attainment scaling of behavior therapy vs. milieu therapy. *Journal of Nervous and Mental Disease, 163,* 253–262.

Azrin, N.H., Hontos, P.T., & Besalel-Azrin, V. (1979). Elimination of enuresis without a conditioning apparatus: An extension by office instruction of the child and parents. *Behavior Therapy, 10,* 14–19.

Azrin, N.H., Naster, B.J., & Jones, R. (1973). Reciprocity counseling: A rapid learning-based procedure for marital counseling. *Behaviour Research and Therapy, 11,* 365–382.

Baekeland, F., & Lundwall, L. (1975). Dropping out of treatment: A critical review. *Psychological Bulletin, 82,* 738–783.

Baer, D.M. (1977). "Perhaps it would be better not to know everything." *Journal of Applied Behavior Analysis, 10,* 167–172.

Bailar, J.C. III., & Patterson, K. (1985). Journal of peer review: The need for a research agenda. *New England Journal of Medicine, 312,* 654–657.

Bakan, D. (1966). The test of significance in psychological research. *Psychological Bulletin, 66,* 423–437.

Balter, M. (1996). New hope in HIV disease. *Science, 274,* 1988.

Bandura, A. (1978). On paradigms and recycled ideologies. *Cognitive Therapy and Research, 2,* 79–103.

Banken, D.M., & Wilson, G.L. (1992). Treatment acceptability of alternative therapies for depression: A comparative analysis. *Psychotherapy, 29,* 610–619.

Barber, J.G., Bradshaw, R., & Walsh, C. (1989). Reducing alcohol consumption through television advertising. *Journal of Consulting and Clinical Psychology, 57,* 613–618.

Barbar, J.P., Connolly, M.B., Crits-Christoph, P., Gladis, L., & Siqueland, L. (2000). Alliance predicts patients' outcome beyond in-treatment change in symptoms. *Journal of Consulting and Clinical Psychology, 68,* 1027–1032.

Barber, T.X. (1976). *Pitfalls in human research: Ten pivotal points.* Elmsford, NY: Pergamon.

Barkham, M., Rees, A., Stiles, W.B., Shapiro, D.A., Hardy, G.E., & Reynolds, S. (1996). Dose–effect relations in time-limited psychotherapy for depression. *Journal of Consulting and Clinical Psychology, 64,* 927–935.

Barlow, D.H., Reynolds, J., & Agras, W.S. (1973). Gender identity change in a transsexual. *Archives of General Psychiatry, 29,* 569–576.

Barnett, P.A., & Gotlib, I.H. (1988). Psychosocial functioning and depression: Distinguishing among antecedents, concomitants, and consequences. *Psychological Bulletin, 104,* 97–126.

Baron, R.M., & Kenny, D.A. (1986). The moderator–mediator variable distinction in social psychological research: Conceptual, strategic, and statistical considerations. *Journal of Personality and Social Psychology, 51,* 1173–1182.

Barrett, P.M. (1998). Evaluation of cognitive-behavioral group treatments for childhood anxiety disorders. *Journal of Clinical Child Psychology, 27,* 459–468.

Barrett, P.M., Dadds, M.R., & Rapee, R.M. (1996). Family treatment of childhood anxiety: A controlled trial. *Journal of Consulting and Clinical Psychology, 64,* 333–342.

Barthel, C.N., & Holmes, D.S. (1968). High school yearbooks: A nonreactive measure of social isolation in graduates who later became schizophrenic. *Journal of Abnormal Psychology, 73,* 313–316.

Barton, S. (1994). Chaos, self-organization, and psychology. *American Psychologist, 49,* 5–14.

Battro, A.M. (2001). *Half a brain is enough: The story of Nico.* Cambridge: Cambridge University Press.

Baumeister, R.F., & Leary, M.R. (1997). Writing narrative literature reviews. *Review of General Psychology, 1,* 311–320.

Bearden, M., Pearson, D., Rein, D., Chevaux, K., Carpenter, D., Keen, C., & Schmitz, H. (1999, March). *Potential cardiovascular health benefits of procyanidins present in chocolate and cocoa.* Presented at the 217th meeting of the American Chemical Society, Anaheim, CA.

Beatty, W.W. (1972). How blind is blind? A simple procedure for estimating observer naiveté. *Psychological Bulletin, 78,* 70–71.

Beauchamp, T., King, N., & Faden, R.R. (1986). *A history and theory of informed consent.* New York: Oxford University Press.

Beck, A.T., Rush, A.J., Shaw, B.F., & Emery, G. (1979). *Cognitive therapy of depression.* New York: Guilford.

Beck, A.T., Ward, C.H., Mendelson, M., Mock, J., & Erbaugh, J. (1961). An inventory for measuring depression. *Archives of General Psychiatry, 4,* 53–63.

Beck, A.T., Weissman, A., Lester, D., & Trexler, L. (1974). The measurement of pessimism: The Hopelessness Scale. *Journal of Consulting and Clinical Psychology. 42,* 861–865.

Beidel, D.C., Turner, S.M., & Morris, T.L. (2000). Behavioral treatment of childhood social phobia. *Journal of Consulting and Clinical Psychology, 68,* 1072–1080.

Bell, R. (1992). *Impure science: Fraud, compromise, and political influence in scientific research.* New York: Wiley & Sons.

Beneke, W.N., & Harris, M.B. (1972). Teaching self-control of study behavior. *Behaviour Research and Therapy, 10,* 35–41.

Benjamin, Y., & Hochberg, Y. (1995). Controlling the false discovery rate: A practical and powerful approach to multiple testing. *Journal of the Royal Statistical Society, 57* (series B), 289–300.

Berg, B.L. (2001). *Qualitative research methods for the social sciences* (4th ed.). Needham Heights, MA: Allyn & Bacon.

Bergin, A.E., & Garfield, S.L. (Eds.) (1994). *Handbook of psychotherapy and behavior change* (4th ed.). New York: Wiley & Sons.

Bergin, A.E., & Lambert, M.J. (1978). The evaluation of therapeutic outcomes. In S.L. Garfield & A.E. Bergin (Eds.), *Handbook of psychotherapy and behavior change* (2nd ed., pp. 139–189). New York: Wiley & Sons.

Berkson, J. (1938). Some difficulties of interpretation encountered in the application of the chi-square test. *Journal of the American Statistical Association, 33,* 526–542.

Betancourt, H., & Lopéz, S.R. (1993). The study of culture, ethnicity, and race in American Psychology. *American Psychologist, 48,* 629–637.

Beutler, L.E., Brown, M.T., Crothers, L., Booker, K., & Seabrook, M.K. (1996). The dilemma of factitious demographic distinctions in psychological research. *Journal of Consulting and Clinical Psychology, 64*, 892–902.

Beutler, L.E., Machado, P.P.P., & Neufeldt, S.A. (1994). Therapist variables. In A.E. Bergin & S.L. Garfield (Eds.), *Handbook of psychotherapy and behavior change* (4th ed., pp. 229–269). New York: Wiley & Sons.

Billings, D.C., & Wasik, B.H. (1985). Self-instructional training with preschoolers: An attempt to replicate. *Journal of Applied Behavior Analysis, 18*, 61–67.

Bird, H.R., Yager, T.J., Staghezza, B., Gould, M.S., Canino, G., & Rubio-Stipec, M. (1990). Impairment in the epidemiological measurement of psychopathology in the community. *Journal of the American Academy of Child and Adolescent Psychiatry, 29*, 796–803.

Blackless, M., Charuvastra, A., Derryck, A., Fausto-Sterling, A., Lauzanne, K., & Lee, E. (2000). How sexually dimorphic are we? Review and synthesis. *American Journal of Human Biology, 12*, 151–166.

Bloom, L.J., Weigel, R.G., & Trautt, G.M. (1977). "Therapeugenic" factors in psychotherapy: Effects of office decor and subject–therapist pairing on the perception of credibility. *Journal of Consulting and Clinical Psychology, 45*, 867–873.

Bolgar, H. (1965). The case study method. In B.B. Wolman (Ed.), *Handbook of clinical psychology* (pp. 28–38). New York: McGraw-Hill.

Booth, B.M., Blow, F.C., & Cook, C.A.L. (1998). Functional impairment and co-occurring psychiatric disorders in medically hospitalized men. *Archives of Internal Medicine, 158*, 1551–1559.

Bootzin, R.R. (1985). The role of expectancy in behavior change. In L. White, B. Tursky, G.E. Schwartz (Eds.), *Placebo: Theory, research, and mechanisms* (pp. 196–214). New York: Guilford.

Borkovec, T., & Nau, S. (1972). Credibility of analogue therapy rationales. *Journal of Behavior Therapy and Experimental Psychiatry, 3*, 257–260.

Bornstein, P.H., & Quevillon, R.P. (1976). The effects of a self-instructional package on over-active preschool boys. *Journal of Applied Behavior Analysis, 9*, 179–188.

Botvin, G.J., Baker, E., Filazzola, A.D., & Botvin, E.M. (1990). A cognitive-behavioral approach to substance abuse prevention: One-year follow-up. *Addictive Behaviors, 15*, 47–63.

Bowlby, J. (1969). *Attachment and loss. Vol. I: Attachment.* London: Hogarth Press.

Bozarth, J.D., & Roberts, R. R. (1972). Signifying significant significance. *American Psychologist, 27*, 774–775.

Bracht, G.H., & Glass, G.V. (1968). The external validity of experiments. *American Educational Research Journal, 5*, 437–474.

Bradley, C. (1997). Psychological issues in clinical trial design. *Irish Journal of Psychology, 18*, 67–87.

Bradley, C. (1999). Patient preferences and clinical trial design and interpretation: Appreciation and critique of a paper by Feine, Awad, & Lund. *Community Dentistry and Oral Epidemiology, 27*, 85–88.

Brannigan, M. (2000, June 13). Spermicide made by Columbia Labs fails to stop HIV. *Wall Street Journal*, Vol. CCXXXV, No. 116, p. B10.

Braun, H., Jackson, D.N., & Wiley, D.E. (Eds.) (2000). *The role of constructs in psychological and educational measurement.* Mahwah, NJ: Lawrence Erlbaum.

Braver, M.C.W., & Braver, S.L. (1988). Statistical treatment of the Solomon Four-Group Design: A meta-analytic approach. *Psychological Bulletin, 104*, 150–154.

Brent, D.A., Baugher, M., Birmaher, B., Kolko, D.J., & Bridge, J. (2000). Compliance with recommendations to remove firearms in families participating in a clinical trial for adolescent depression. *Journal of the American Academy of Child and Adolescent Psychiatry, 39*, 1220–1226.

Brent, D.A., Perper, J.A., Allman, C.J., Moritz, G.M, Wartella, M., & Zelenak, J.P. (1991). The presence and accessibility of firearms in the homes of adolescent suicides: A case-control study. *Journal of the American Medical Association, 266,* 2989–2995.

Brestan, E.V., & Eyberg, S.M. (1998). Effective psychosocial treatment of conduct-disordered children and adolescents: 29 years, 82 studies, and 5275 kids. *Journal of Clinical Child Psychology, 27,* 180–189.

Breuer, J., & Freud, S. (1957). *Studies in hysteria.* New York: Basic Books.

Brewin, C.R., Andrews, B., & Gotlib, I.H. (1993). Psychopathology and early experience: A reappraisal of retrospective reports. *Psychological Bulletin, 113,* 82–98.

Briere, J., & Runtz, M. (1988). Post sexual abuse trauma. In G.E. Wyatt & G.J. Powell (Eds.) *Lasting effects of child abuse* (pp. 85–99). Newbury Park, CA: Sage.

Broad, W., & Wade, N. (1982). *Betrayers of truth.* New York: Simon & Schuster.

Brown, J. (1987). A review of meta-analyses conducted on psychotherapy outcome research. *Clinical Psychology Review, 7,* 1–23.

Brown, T.A., Antony, M.M., & Barlow, D.H. (1995). Diagnostic comorbidity in panic disorder: Effect on treatment outcome and course of comorbid diagnoses following treatment. *Journal of Consulting and Clinical Psychology, 63,* 408–418.

Brunswik, E. (1955). Representative design and probabilistic theory in a functional psychology. *Psychological Review, 62,* 193–217.

Bryant, L.E., & Budd, K.S. (1982). Self-instructional training to increase independent work performance in preschoolers. *Journal of Applied Behavior Analysis, 15,* 259–271.

Bucholz, K.K., Marion, S.L., Shayka, J.J., Marcus, S.C., & Robins, L.N. (1996). A short computer interview for obtaining psychiatric diagnoses. *Psychiatry Service, 47,* 293–297.

Budney, A.J., Higgins, S.T., Radonovich, K.J., & Novy, P.L. (2000). Adding voucher-based incentives to coping skills and motivational enhancement improves outcomes during treatment for marijuana dependence. *Journal of Consulting and Clinical Psychology, 68,* 1051–1061.

Burke, K.C., Burke, J.D., Regier, D.A., & Rae, D.S. (1990). Age at onset of selected mental disorders in five community populations. *Archives of General Psychiatry, 47,* 511–518.

Burton, T.M. (2000, November 1). Unfavorable drug study sparks battle over publication of results. *Wall Street Journal,* Vol. CCXXXVI, No. 86, pp. B1, B4.

Butcher, J.N. (Ed.) (1995). Special Issue: Methodological issues in psychological assessment research. *Psychological Assessment, 7,* Whole Issue Number 3.

Butcher, J.N. (Ed). (2000). *Basic sources on the MMPI-2.* Minneapolis, MN: University of Minnesota Press.

Butcher, J.N., Graham, J.R., Williams, C.L., & Ben-Porath, Y.S. (1990). *Development and use of the MMPI-2 content scales.* Minneapolis, MN: University of Minnesota Press.

Butzlaff, R.L., & Hooley, J.M. (1998). Expressed emotion and psychiatric relapse: A meta-analysis. *Archives of General Psychiatry, 55,* 547–552.

Calder, A.J., Keane, J., Manes, F., Antoun, N., & Young, A.W. (2000). Impaired recognition and experience of disgust following brain injury. *Nature Neuroscience, 3,* 1077–1078.

Campbell, D.T., & Fiske, D. (1959). Convergent and discriminant validation by the multitrait-multimethod matrix. *Psychological Bulletin, 56,* 81–105.

Campbell, D.T., & Kenny, D.A. (1999). *A primer on regression artifacts.* New York: Guilford Press.

Campbell, D.T., & Stanley, J.C. (1963). Experimental and quasi-experimental designs for research and teaching. In N.L. Gage (Ed.), *Handbook of research on teaching.* Chicago: Rand McNally.

Carlsmith, J.M., Ellsworth, P.C., & Aronson, E. (1976). *Methods of research in social psychology.* Reading, MA: Addison-Wesley.

Carpenter, W.T., Gold, J.M., Lahti, A.C., Queern, C.A., Conley, R.R., Bartko, J.J., Kovnick, J., & Appelbaum, P.S. (2000). Decisional capacity for informed consent in schizophrenia research. *Archives of General Psychiatry, 57,* 533–538.

Carroll, K.M., Rounsaville, B.J., & Nich, C. (1994). Blind man's bluff: Effectiveness and significance of psychotherapy and pharmacotherapy blinding procedures in a clinical trial. *Journal of Consulting and Clinical Psychology, 62,* 276–280.

Case, L., & Smith, T.B. (2000). Ethnic representation in a sample of the literature of applied psychology. *Journal of Consulting and Clinical Psychology, 68,* 1107–1110.

Caspi, A., Moffitt, T.E., Newman, D.L., & Silva, P.A. (1996). Behavioral observations at age 3, predict adult psychiatric disorders. *Archives of General Psychiatry, 53,* 1033–1039.

Castonguay, L.G. (1993). "Common factors" and "nonspecific variables": Clarification of the two concepts and recommendations for research. *Journal of Psychotherapy Integration, 3,* 267–286.

Cech, T.R., & Leonard, J.S. (2001). Conflicts of interest—Moving beyond disclosure. *Science, 291,* 989.

Charmaz, K. (2000). Grounded theory: Objectivist and constructivist methods. In N.H Denzin & Y.S. Lincoln (Eds.), *Handbook of qualitative research* (2nd ed., pp. 509–535). Thousand Oaks, CA: Sage.

Chassan, J.B. (1967). *Research design in clinical psychology and psychiatry.* New York: Appleton-Century-Crofts.

Christian, N.M. (1995, June 26). Call for bright yellow firetrucks has many firefighters seeing red. *Wall Street Journal,* Vol. CCXXV, No. 123, p. B1.

Church, R.M. (1964). Systematic effect of random error in the yoked control design. *Psychological Bulletin, 62,* 122–131.

Cicchetti, D.V. (1991) The reliability of the peer review for manuscript and grant submissions: A cross-disciplinary investigation. *Behavioral and Brain Sciences, 14,* 119–186.

Clark, K.E. (1967). *Invasion of privacy in the investigation of human behavior.* Paper read at Eastern Psychological Association, Boston, MA.

Clement, P.W. (1999). *Outcomes and incomes: How to evaluate, improve, and market your practice by measuring outcomes in psychotherapy.* New York: Guilford.

Cohen, J. (1965). Some statistical issues in psychological research. In B.B. Wolman (Ed.), *Handbook of clinical psychology* (pp. 95–121). New York: McGraw-Hill.

Cohen, J. (1988). *Statistical power analysis in the behavioral sciences.* (2nd ed.). Hillsdale, NJ: Erlbaum.

Cohen, J. (1992). A power primer. *Psychological Bulletin, 112,* 155–159.

Cohen, J. (1996). Likely HIV cofactor found. *Science, 272,* 809–810.

Committee on Biomedical Research in the Veterans Administration. (1977). *Biomedical research in the Veterans Administration.* Washington, DC: National Academy of Sciences.

Cone, J.D. (2000). *Evaluating outcomes: Empirical tools for effective practice.* Washington, DC: American Psychological Association.

Connor-Smith, J.K., Compas, B.E., Wadsworth, M.E., Thomsen, A.H., & Saltzman, H. (2000). Responses to stress in adolescence: Measurement of coping and involuntary stress responses. *Journal of Consulting and Clinical Psychology, 68,* 976–992.

Consumer Reports (1995, November). Mental health: Does therapy help? 734–739.

Cook, T.D., & Campbell, D.T. (1979). *Quasi-experimentation: Design and analysis issues for field settings.* Chicago: Rand McNally.

Cook, T.D., Cooper, H., Cordray, D.S., Hartmann, H., Hedges, L.V., Light, R.J., Louis, T.A., & Mosteller, F. (1992). *Meta-analysis for explanation: A casebook.* New York: Russell Sage Foundation.

Cooney, N.L., Kadden, R.M., Litt, M.D., & Getter, H. (1991). Matching alcoholics to coping skills or interactional therapies: Two-year follow-up. *Journal of Consulting and Clinical Psychology, 59,* 598–601.

Council of National Psychological Associations for the Advancement of Ethnic Minority Interests (2000). *Guidelines for research in ethnic minority communities.* Washington, DC: American Psychological Association.

Cowles, M., & Davis, C. (1982). On the origins of the .05 level of statistical significance. *American Psychologist, 37,* 553–558.

Cronbach, L.J. (1957). The two disciplines of scientific psychology. *American Psychologist, 12,* 671–684.

Cronbach, L.J. (1975). Beyond the two disciplines of scientific psychology. *American Psychologist, 30,* 116–127.

Cronbach, L.J., & Meehl, P.E. (1955). Construct validity in psychological tests. *Psychological Bulletin, 52,* 281–302.

Crowe, M.J., Marks, I.M., Agras, W.S., & Leitenberg, H. (1972). Time-limited desensitization, implosion and shaping for phobic patients: A crossover study. *Behaviour Research and Therapy, 10,* 319–328.

Crowne, D.P., & Marlowe, D. (1964). *The approval motive: Studies in evaluative dependence.* New York: Wiley & Sons.

Cunningham, C.E., Bremner, R., & Boyle, M. (1995). Large group community-based parenting programs for families of preschoolers at risk for disruptive behaviour disorders: Utilization, cost effectiveness, and outcome. *Journal of Child Psychology and Psychiatry, 36,* 1141–1159.

Cuny, H. (1965). *Ivan Pavlov: The man and his theory.* (P. Evans, translation). New York: Paul S. Eriksson Publisher.

Dadds, M.R., Holland, D.E., Laurens, K.R., Mullins, M., Barrett, P.M., & Spence, S.H. (1999). Early intervention and prevention of anxiety disorders in children: Results at 2-year follow-up. *Journal of Consulting and Clinical Psychology, 67,* 145–150.

Davis, C.E. (1998). Prerandomization compliance screening: A statistician's view. In S. A. Schumaker, E.B. Schron, J.K. Ockene, & W.L. McBee (Eds.), *The handbook of health behavior change* (2nd ed., pp. 485–490). New York: Springer.

Davis, W.E. (1973). The irregular discharge as an unobtrusive measure of discontent among young psychiatric patients. *Journal of Abnormal Psychology, 81,* 17–21.

Dawes, R.M. (1994). *House of cards: Psychology and psychotherapy built on myth.* New York: Free Press.

de Groot, J.C. de Leeuw, F.E., Oudkerk, M., Hofman, A., Jolles, J., & Breteler, M.M.B. (2000). Cerebral white matter lesions and depressive symptoms in elderly adults. *Archives of General Psychiatry, 57,* 1071–1076.

Dehue, T. (2000). From deception trials to control reagents: The introduction of the control group about a century ago. *American Psychologist, 55,* 264–268.

Demo, D.H., Allen, K.R., & Fine, M.A. (Eds.). (2000). *Handbook of family diversity.* New York: Oxford University Press.

Denissenko, M.F., Pao, A., Tang, M., & Pfeifer, G.P. (1996). Preferential formation of benzo[a]pyrene adducts at lung cancer mutational hotspots in P53. *Science, 274.* 430–432.

Denzin, N.H, & Lincoln, Y.S. (Eds.) (2000). *Handbook of qualitative research* (2nd ed.). Thousand Oaks, CA: Sage.

DeProspero, A., & Cohen, S. (1979). Inconsistent visual analysis of intrasubject data. *Journal of Applied Behavior Analysis, 12,* 573–579.

DeVellis, R.F. (1991). *Scale development: Theory and applications.* Newbury Park, CA: Sage.

Dies, R.R., & Greenberg, B. (1976). Effects of physical contact in an encounter group context. *Journal of Consulting and Clinical Psychology, 44,* 400–405.

DiLulio, J.J. (1997, January 8). What the crime statistics don't tell you. *Wall Street Journal,* Vol. CCXXIX, No. 5, p. A22.

Dishion, T.J., & Andrews, D.W. (1995). Preventing escalation in problem behaviors with high-risk young adolescents: Immediate and 1-year outcomes. *Journal of Consulting and Clinical Psychology, 63,* 538–548.

Dishion, T.J., Patterson, G.R., & Kavanagh, K.A. (1992). An experimental test of the coercion model: Linking theory, measurement, and intervention. In J. McCord & R.E. Tremblay (Eds.), *Preventing antisocial behavior* (pp. 253–282). New York: Guilford.

Dodge, K.A., Pettit, G.S., & Bates, J.E. (1994) Socialization mediators of the relation between socioeconomic status and child conduct problems. *Child Development, 65,* 649–665.

Domar, A.D. (1998, October). *The application of mind/body techniques to infertile women.* Meeting of the American Society of Reproductive Medicine, San Francisco, CA.

Donaldson, D., Spirito, A., & Farnett, E. (2000). The role of perfectionism and depressive cognitions in understanding the hopelessness experienced by adolescent suicide attempters. *Child Psychiatry and Human Development, 31,* 99–111.

Drasgow, F., & Olson-Buchanan, J.B. (Eds.) (1999). *Innovations in computerized assessment*: Mahwah, NJ: Lawrence Erlbaum.

Dreyer, N.A., Loughlin, J.E., Rothman, K.J. (1999). Cause-specific mortality in cellular telephone users (letter). *Journal of the American Medical Association, 282,* 1814–1816.

Ducor, P. (2000). Coauhorship and coinventorship. *Science, 289,* 873, 875.

Dukes, W.F. (1965). N = 1. *Psychological Bulletin, 64,* 74–79.

Durlak, J.A., Wells, A.M., Cotten, J.K., & Johnson, S. (1995). Analysis of selected methodological issues in child psychotherapy research. *Journal of Clinical Child Psychology, 24,* 141–148.

Eaton, W.W., & Kessler, L. (Eds.). (1985). *Epidemiologic field methods in psychiatry: The NIMH Epidemiologic Catchment Area Program.* NY: Academic Press.

Edwards, A.L. (1957). *The social desirability variable in personality assessment and research.* New York: Dryden.

Eisner, D.A. (2000). *The death of psychotherapy: From Freud to alien abductions.* Westport, CT: Praeger.

Elkin, I., Parloff, M.B, Hadley, S.W., & Autry, J.H. (1985). NIMH Treatment of Depression Collaborative Research Program: Background and research plan. *Archives of General Psychiatry, 42,* 305–316.

Elkin, I., Shea, M.T., Watkins, J.T., Imber, S.D., Sotsky, S.M., Collins, J.F., Glass, D.R., Pilkonis, P.A., Leber, W.R., Docherty, J.P., Fiester, S.J., & Parloff, M.B. (1989). NIMH Treatment of Depression Collaborative Research Program: General effectiveness of treatments. *Archives of General Psychiatry, 46,* 971–982.

Elliott, D.S., Dunford, F.W., & Huizinga, D. (1987). The identification and prediction of career offenders utilizing self-reported and official data. In J.D. Burchard & S.N. Burchard (Eds.), *Preventing delinquent behavior* (pp. 90–121). Newbury Park, CA: Sage.

Ellis, A. (1957). Outcome of employing three techniques of psychotherapy. *Journal of Clinical Psychology, 13,* 344–350.

Endler, N.S. (1990). *Holiday of darkness: A psychologist's personal journal out of his depression* (revised ed.). Toronto: Wall and Thompson.

Enserink, M. (1996). Fraud and ethics charges hit stroke drug trial. *Science, 274,* 2004.

Enserink, M. (2000a). Are placebo-controlled drug trials ethical? *Science, 288,* 416.

Enserink, M. (2000b). Helsinki's new clinical rules: Fewer placebos, more disclosure? *Science, 290,* 418–419.

Epstein, M.H., Kutash, K., & Duchnowski, A.J. (Eds.) (1998). *Outcomes for children and youth with emotional and behavioral disorders and their families: Programs and evaluation best practices*. Austin, TX: Pro-Ed.

Erdberg, P. (1990). Rorschach assessment. In G. Goldstein & M. Hersen (Eds.), *Handbook of psychological assessment* (2nd ed., pp. 387–399). Elmsford, NY: Pergamon.

Erdman, H.P., Klein, M.H., & Greist, J.H. (1985). Direct patient computer interviewing. *Journal of Consulting and Clinical Psychology, 53*, 760–773.

Erlich, P.R. (2000). Evolution of an advocate (Letter). *Science, 287*, 2159.

Esser, G., Schmidt, M.H., & Woerner, W. (1990). Epidemiology and course of psychiatric disorders in school-age children: Results of a longitudinal study. *Journal of Child Psychology and Psychiatry, 31*, 243–263.

Esteller, M., Garcia-Foncillas, J., Andion, E., Goodman, S.N., Hidalgo, O.F., Vanaclocha, V., Baylin, S.B., & Herman, J.G. (2000). Inactivation of the DNA-repair gene MGMT and the clinical response to gliomas of alkylating agents. *New England Journal of Medicine, 343*, 1350–1354.

Exner, J.E. (1995). Comment on "Narcissism in the comprehensive system for the Rorschach." *Clinical Psychology: Science and Practice, 2*, 200–206.

Eysenck, H.J. (1952). The effects of psychotherapy: An evaluation. *Journal of Consulting Psychology, 16*, 319–324.

Eysenck, H.J. (1995). The outcome problem in psychotherapy: What have we learned? *Behaviour Research and Therapy, 32*, 477–495.

Fagley, N.S. (1985). Applied statistical power analysis and the interpretation of nonsignificant results by research consumers. *Journal of Counseling Psychology, 32*, 391–396.

Farrington, D.P. (1991). Childhood aggression and adult violence: Early precursors and later life outcomes. In D.J. Pepler & K.H. Rubin (Eds.), *The development and treatment of childhood aggression* (pp. 5–29). Hillsdale, NJ: Erlbaum.

Farrington, D.P. (1992). The need for longitudinal-experimental research on offending and antisocial behavior. In J. McCord & R.E. Tremblay (Eds.), *Preventing antisocial behavior: Interventions from birth through adolescence* (pp. 353–376). New York: Guilford.

Faulkner & Gray Health Care Information Center (1997). *The 1997 behavioral outcomes and guidelines sourcebook*. New York: Faulkner & Gray.

Feldman, J.J., Hyman, H., & Hart, C.W. (1951). A field study of interviewer effects on the quality of survey data. *Public Opinion Quarterly, 15*, 734–761.

Feldman, R.A., Caplinger, T.E., & Wodarski, J.S. (1983). *The St. Louis conundrum: The effective treatment of antisocial youths*. Englewood Cliffs, NJ: Prentice-Hall.

Festinger, L., & Carlsmith, J.M. (1959). Cognitive consequences of forced compliance. *Journal of Abnormal and Social Psychology, 58*, 203–210.

Fine, M.A., & Kurdek, L.A. (1993) Reflections on determining authorship credit and authorship order on faculty–student collaborations. *American Psychologist, 48*, 1141–1147.

Fisher, B., Bauer, M., Margolese, R., Poisson, R., Pilch, Y., Redmond, C., Fisher, E., Wolmark, N., Deutsch, M., Montague, E., Saffer, E., Wickerham, I., Lerner, H., Glass, A., Shibata, H., Deckers, P., Ketcham, R., Dishi, R., & Russell, I. (1985). Five-year results of a randomized clinical trial comparing total mastectomy and segmental mastectomy with or without radiation in the treatment of breast cancer. *New England Journal of Medicine, 312*, 665–673.

Fisher, E.R., Costantino, J., Fisher, B., Palekar, A.S., Paik, S.M., Suarez, C.M., & Wolmark, N. (1996). Pathologic findings from the National Surgical Adjuvant Breast Project (NSABP) protocol B-17: Five-year observations concerning lobular carcinoma in situ. *Cancer, 78*, 1403–1416.

Fisher, J.D., Silver, R.C., Chinsky, J.M., Goff, B., Klar, Y., & Zagieboylo, C. (1989). Psychological effects of participation in a large group awareness training. *Journal of Consulting and Clinical Psychology, 57*, 747–755.

Fisher, R.A. (1925). *Statistical methods for research workers*. London: Oliver & Boyd.

Fisher, R.A., & Yates, F. (1963). *Statistical tables for biological, agricultural and medical research*. Edinburgh: Oliver & Boyd.

Fisher, S., & Greenberg, R.P. (Eds.) (1989). *The limits of biological treatments for psychological distress: Comparisons with psychotherapy and placebo*. Hillsdale, NJ: Erlbaum.

Flack, W.F. Jr; Litz, B.T.; Hsieh, F.Y.; Kaloupek, D.G., & Keane, T.M. (2000).Predictors of emotional numbing, revisited: A replication and extension. *Journal of Traumatic Stress, 13*, 611–618.

Flick, S.N. (1988). Managing attrition in clinical research. *Clinical Psychology Review, 8*, 499–515.

Forgatch, M.S. (1991). The clinical science vortex: A developing theory of antisocial behavior. In D.J. Pepler & K.H. Rubin (Eds.), *The development and treatment of childhood aggression* (pp. 291–315). Hillsdale, NJ: Erlbaum.

Foulks, E.F. (1987). Social stratification and alcohol use in North Alaska. *Journal of Community Psychology, 15*, 349–356.

Foulks, E.F. (1989). Misalliances in the Barrow Alcohol Study. *American Indian and Native Alaska Mental Health Research, 2* (3), 7–17.

Foxx, R.M., Bremer, B.A., Schutz, C., Valdez, J., & Johndrow, C. (1996). Increasing treatment acceptability through video. *Behavioral Interventions, 11*, 171–180.

Foxx, R.M., & Rubinoff, A. (1979). Behavioral treatment of caffeinism: Reducing excessive coffee drinking. *Journal of Applied Behavior Analysis, 12,* 335–344.

Frank, E., Johnson, S., & Kupfer, D.J. (1992). Psychological treatments in prevention of relapse. In S.A. Montgomery & F. Rouillon (Eds.), *Long-term treatment of depression* (pp. 197–228). Chichester: Wiley & Sons.

Frank, E., Kupfer, D.J., Perel, J.M., Cornes, C., Mallinger, A.G., Thase, M.E, McEachran, A.B., & Grochocinski, V.J. (1993). Comparison of full-dose versus half-dose pharmacotherapy in the maintenance treatment of recurrent depression. *Journal of Affective Disorders, 27*, 139–145.

Frank, E., Kupfer, D.J., Wagner, E.F., McEachran, A.B., & Cornes, C. (1991). Efficacy of interpersonal psychotherapy as a maintenance treatment for recurrent depression. *Archives of General Psychiatry, 48*, 1053–1059.

Frank, J.D., & Frank, J.B. (1991). *Persuasion and healing* (3rd ed.). Baltimore, MD: Johns Hopkins University Press.

Frank, J.D., Nash, E.H., Stone, A.R., & Imber, S.D. (1963). Immediate and long-term symptomatic course of psychiatric outpatients. *American Journal of Psychiatry, 120*, 429–439.

Franke, G.H. (1999). Effects of computer administration on the Symptom Checklist (SCL-90-R) with a special focus on the item sequence. *Diagnostica, 45*, 147–153.

Frasure-Smith, N., Lesperance, F., & Talajic M., (1993). Depression following myocardial infarction: Impact on 6-month survival. *Journal of the American Medical Association, 270*, 1819–1825.

Freiman, J.A., Chalmers, T.C., Smith, H., & Kuebler, R.R. (1978). The importance of beta, the Type II error, and sample size in the design and interpretation of the randomized control trial. *New England Journal of Medicine, 299*, 690–694.

Freud, S. (1933). *Analysis of a phobia in a five-year-old boy*. In Collected papers (Vol. 3). London: Hogarth Press.

Friedling, C., & O'Leary, S. (1979). Effects of self-instructional training on second and third-grade hyperactive children: A failure to replicate. *Journal of Applied Behavior Analysis, 12*, 211–219.

Friedman, L.M., Furberg, C.D., & DeMets, D.L. (1985). *Fundamentals of clinical trials* (2nd ed.) Littleton, MA: PSG Publishing Company.

Friedmann, T. (2000). Principles for human gene therapy studies. *Science, 287,* 2163–2165.

Frisch, M.B. (1998). *Quality of life therapy and assessment in health care. Clinical Psychology: Science and Practice, 5,* 19–40.

Gabbard, G.L., Lazar, S.G., Hornberger, J., & Spiegel, D. (1997). The economic impact of psychotherapy: A review. *American Journal of Psychiatry, 154,* 147–155.

Galton, F. (1872). Statistical inquiries into the efficacy of prayer. *Fornightly Review, 12,* 125–135.

Gilbert, J.P., Light, R.J., & Mosteller, F. (1975). Assessing social interventions: An empirical base for policy. In C.A. Bennett & A.A. Lumsdaine (Eds.), *Evaluation and experiment: Some critical issues in assessing social programs* (pp. 39–193). New York: Academic Press.

Glesne, C. (1999). *Becoming qualitative researchers: An introduction* (2nd ed.). New York: Addison Wesley Longman.

Goodyear, R.K., Crego, C.A., & Johnson, M.W. (1992). Ethical issues in the supervision of student research: A study of critical incidents. *Professional Psychology: Research and Practice, 23,* 203–210.

Gotlib, I.H., Lewinsohn, P.M., & Seeley, J.R. (1995). Symptoms versus a diagnosis of depression: Differences in psychosocial functioning. *Journal of Consulting and Clinical Psychology, 63,* 90–100.

Gottman, J.M., & Glass, G.V. (1978). Analysis of interrupted time-series experiments. In T.R. Kratochwill (Ed.), *Single-subject research: Strategies for evaluating change.* New York: Academic Press.

Gottschalk, L.A., Bechtel, R.J., Maguire, G.A., Harrington, D.E., Levinson, D.M., Franklin, D.L., & Carcamo, D. (2000). Computerized measurement of cognitive impairment and associated neuropsychiatric dimensions. *Comprehensive Psychiatry, 41,* 326–333.

Graham, J.R. (1990). *MMPI-2: Assessing personality and psychopathology.* New York: Oxford University Press.

Graham, S. (1992). "Most of the subjects were White and middle class:" Trends in published research on African Americans in selected APA journals 1970–1989, *American Psychologist, 47,* 629–639.

Grant, D.A. (1948). The Latin square principle in the design and analysis of psychological experiments. *Psychological Bulletin, 45,* 427–442.

Greenberg, J., & Folger, R. (1988). *Controversial issues in social research methods.* New York: Springer-Verlag.

Greenberg, P.E., Sisitsky, T., Kessler, R.C., Finkelstein, S.N., Berndt, E.R., Davidson, J.R.T., Ballenger, J.C., & Fyer, A.J. (1999). The economic burden of anxiety disorders in the 1990s. *Journal of Clinical Psychiatry, 60,* 427–435.

Greensfelder, L. (2000). Polio outbreak raises questions about vaccine. *Science, 290,* 1867, 1869.

Greenwald, A.G. (1975). Consequences of prejudice against the null hypothesis. *Psychological Bulletin, 82,* 1–20.

Grenier, C. (1985). Treatment effectiveness in an adolescent chemical dependency treatment program: A quasi-experimental design. *International Journal of the Addictions, 20,* 381–391.

Gripp, R.F., & Magaro, P.A. (1971). A token economy program evaluation with untreated control ward comparisons. *Behaviour Research and Therapy, 9,* 137–149.

Groth-Marnat, G. (Ed.) (1997). *Handbook of psychological assessment* (3rd. ed.). New York: Wiley & Sons.

Grundy, C.T., Lunnen, K.M., Lambert, M.J., Ashton, J.E., & Tovey, D.R. (1994). The Hamilton Rating Scale for Depression: One scale or many? *Clinical Psychology: Science and Practice, 1,* 197–205.

Guthrie, R.V. (1997). *Even the rat was white: A historical view of psychology.* Needham Heights, MA: Allyn & Bacon.

Haaga, D.A.F. (2000). Introduction to the special section on stepped-care models in psychotherapy. *Journal of Consulting and Clinical Psychology, 68,* 547–548.

Haase, R.F., & Ellis, M.V. (1987). Multivariate analysis of variance. *Journal of Counseling Psychology, 34,* 404–413.

Haase, R.F., Ellis, M.V., & Ladany, N. (1989). Multiple criteria for evaluating the magnitude of experimental effects. *Journal of Counseling Psychology, 4,* 511–516.

Hackmann, A., & McLean, C. (1975). A comparison of flooding and thought stopping in the treatment of obsessional neurosis. *Behaviour Research and Therapy, 13,* 263–269.

Hagen, R.L., Foreyt, J.P., & Durham, T.W. (1976). The dropout problem: Reducing attrition in obesity research. *Behavior Therapy, 7,* 463–471.

Hallfors, D., Khatapoush, S., Kadushin, C., Watson, K., & Saxe, L. (2000). A comparison of paper vs. computer-assisted self-interview for school alcohol, tobacco, and other drug surveys. *Evaluation and Program Planning, 23,* 149–155.

Hammen, C. (1991). *Depression runs in families. The social context of risk and resilience in children* of depressed mothers. New York: Springer-Verlag.

Hanson, B.G. (1995). *General systems theory: Beginning with wholes.* Washington, DC: Taylor & Francis.

Harmatz, M.G., Well, A.D., Overtree, C.E., Kawamura, K.K., Ockene, I.S., & Rosal, M. (1999, August). *Seasonal variation of depression and other moods: A longitudinal approach.,* Meeting of the American Psychological Association, Washington, D.C.

Hartshorne, H., & May, M.A. (1928). *Studies in the nature of character. I: Studies in deceit.* New York: Macmillan.

Hartshorne, H., May, M.A., & Shuttleworth, F.K. (1930). *Studies in the nature of character. III: Studies in the organization of character.* New York: Macmillan.

Hauser, S.T., Powers, S.I., & Noam, G.G. (1991). *Adolescents and their families: Paths of ego development.* New York: Free Press.

Hawkins, J.D., & Lam, T. (1987). Teacher practices, social development, and delinquency. In J.D. Burchard & S.N. Burchard (Eds.), *Prevention of delinquent behavior* (pp. 241–274). Newbury Park, CA: Sage.

Haynes, S.N. (1992). *Models of causality in psychopathology: Toward dynamic, synthetic, and nonlinear models of behavior disorders.* Needham Heights, MA: Allyn & Bacon.

Haynes, S.N. (2001). Special section: Clinical applications of analogue behavioral observation. *Psychological Assessment, 13,* 3–98.

Heap, R.F., Boblitt, W.E., Moore, C.H., & Hord, J.E. (1970). Behavior-milieu therapy with chronic neuropsychiatric patients. *Journal of Abnormal Psychology, 76,* 349–354.

Henggeler, S.W. (1999). Multisystemic therapy: An overview of clinical procedures, outcomes, and policy implications. *Child Psychology and Psychiatry Review, 4,* 2–10.

Henggeler, S. W., Schoenwald, S.K., Borduin, C. M., Rowland, M.D., & Cunningham, P.B. (1998). *Multisystemic treatment of antisocial behavior in children and adolescents.* New York: Guilford.

Henley, N.M. (1977). *Body politics: Power, sex, and nonverbal communication.* Englewood Cliffs, NJ: Prentice-Hall.

Henry, B., Moffitt, T.E., Caspi, A., Langley, J., & Silva, P.A. (1994). On the "rememberance of things past:" A longitudinal evaluation of the retrospective method. *Psychological Assessment, 6,* 92–101.

Henry, W.P., Strupp, H.H., Schacht, T.E., & Gaston, L. (1994). Psychodynamic approaches. In A.E. Bergin & S.L. Garfield (Eds.), *Handbook of psychotherapy and behavior change* (4th ed., pp. 467–508). New York: Wiley & Sons.

Hewison, J., & Tizard, J. (1980). Parental involvement and reading attainment. *British Journal of Educational Psychology, 50,* 209–215.

Higgs, W.J. (1970). Effects of gross environmental change upon behavior of schizophrenics: A cautionary note. *Journal of Abnormal Psychology, 76,* 421–422.

Hill, J., & Maughan, B. (2001). *Conduct disorders in childhood and adolescence.* Cambridge: Cambridge University Press.

Hoagwood, K., & Hibbs, E. (Eds.) (1995). Special section: Efficacy and effectiveness in studies of child and adolescent psychotherapy. *Journal of Consulting and Clinical Psychology, 63,* 683–725.

Hoagwood, K., Hibbs, E., Brent, D.A., & Jensen, P.J. (1995). Efficacy and effectiveness in studies of child and adolescent psychotherapy. *Journal of Consulting and Clinical Psychology, 63,* 683–687.

Hochberg, Y., & Tamhane, A.C. (1987). *Multiple comparison procedures.* New York: Wiley & Sons.

Hodgson, R., & Rachman, S.H. (1974). Desynchrony in measures of fear. *Behaviour Research and Therapy, 12,* 319–326.

Hoffart, A. (1994). Use of treatment manuals in comparative outcome research: A schema-based model. *Journal of Cognitive Psychotherapy, 8,* 41–54.

Holmbeck, G.N. (1997). Toward terminological, conceptual, and statistical clarity in the study of mediators and moderators: Examples from the child-clinical and pediatric psychology literatures. *Journal of Consulting and Clinical Psychology, 65,* 599–610.

Honig, A. (2000). Depression following a heart infarct and increased risk of death. *Nederlands Tijdschrift voor Geneeskunde, 144,* 1307–1310.

Howard, G.S., Maxwell, S.E., & Fleming, K.J. (2000). The proof of the pudding: An illustration of the relative strengths of null hypothesis, meta-analysis, and Bayesian analysis. *Psychological Methods, 5,* 315–332.

Howard, K.I., Kopta, S.M., Krause, M.S., & Orlinsky, D.E. (1986). The dose–effect relationship in psychotherapy. *American Psychologist, 41,* 159–164.

Howard, K.I., Krause, M.S., & Orlinsky, D.E. (1986). The attrition dilemma: Toward a new strategy for psychotherapy research. *Journal of Consulting and Clinical Psychology, 54,* 106–110.

Howard, K.I., Lueger, R.J., Maling, M.S., & Martinovich, Z. (1993). A phase model of psychotherapy outcome: Causal mediation of change. *Journal of Consulting and Clinical Psychology, 61,* 678–685.

Hsu, L.M. (1989). Random sampling, randomization, and equivalence of contrasted groups in psychotherapy outcome research. *Journal of Consulting and Clinical Psychology, 57,* 131–137.

Hsu, L.M. (1995). Regression toward the mean associated with measurement error and the identification of improvement and deterioration in psychotherapy. *Journal of Consulting and Clinical Psychology, 63,* 141–144.

Hubbard, R., & Ryan, P.A. (2000). The historical growth of statistical significance testing in psychology—And its future prospects. *Educational and Psychological Measurement, 60,* 661–681.

Huberty, C.J., & Morris, J.D. (1989). Multivariate analysis versus multiple univariate analyses. *Psychological Bulletin, 105,* 302–308.

Huey, S. J., Jr., Henggeler, S.W., Brondino, M.J., & Pickrel, S.G. (2000). Mechanisms of change in multisystemic therapy: Reducing delinquent behavior through therapist adherence and improved family and peer functioning. *Journal of Consulting and Clinical Psychology, 68,* 451–467.

Hughes, M. (1998). Turning points in the lives of inner-city men forgoing destructive criminal behaviors: A qualitative study. *Social Work Research, 22,* 143–151.

Hulley, S.B., & Cummings, S.R. (Eds.) (1988). *Designing clinical research: An epidemiologic approach*. Baltimore, MD: Williams & Wilkins.

Ilardi, S.S., & Craighead, W.E. (1994). The role of nonspecific factors in cognitive-behavior therapy for depression. *Clinical Psychology: Science and Practice, 1*, 138–156.

Intagliata, J.C. (1978). Increasing the interpersonal problem-solving skills of an alcoholic population. *Journal of Consulting and Clinical Psychology, 46*, 489–498.

International Committee of Medical Journal Editors (1997). Uniform requirements for manuscripts submitted to biomedical journals. *Annals of Internal Medicine, 126*, 36–47. (Retrieved Nobember 19, 2001 from the World Wide Web: www.acponline.org/journal/annals/01jan97/unlfreqr.htm

Jaccard, J., Turrisi, R., & Wan, C.K. (1990). *Interaction effects in multiple regression*. Newbury Park, CA: Sage.

Jacobson, N.S., & Christensen, A. (1996). Studying the effectiveness of psychotherapy: How well can clinical trials do the job? *American Psychologist, 51*, 1031–1039.

Jacobson, N.S., & Revenstorf, D. (1988). Statistics for assessing the clinical significance of psychotherapy techniques: Issues, problems, and new developments. *Behavioral Assessment, 10*, 133–145.

Jacobson, N.S., Roberts, L.J., Berns, S.B., & McGlinchey, J. (1999). Methods for defining and determining the clinical significance of treatment effects in mental health research: Current status, new applications, and future directions. *Journal of Consulting and Clinical Psychology, 67*, 300–307.

Janik, V.M. (2000). Whistle matching in wild bottlenose dolphins (Tursiops truncatus). *Science, 289*, 1355–1357.

Jensen, P.S., Watanabe, H.K., & Richters, J.E. (1999). Who's up first? Testing for order effects in structured interviews using a counterbalanced experimental design. *Journal of Abnormal Child Psychology, 27*, 439–445.

Jesse, L.C.H., & Obrycki, J.J. (2000). Field deposition of Bt transgenic corn pollen: Lethal effects on the monarch butterfly. *Oceologia, 125*, 241–248.

Johnson, R.B. (1997). Examining the validity structure of qualitative research. *Education, 118*, 282–292.

Jones, M.C. (1924a). A laboratory study of fear: The case of Peter. *Pedagogical Seminary, 31*, 308–315.

Jones, M.C. (1924b). The elimination of children's fears. *Journal of Experimental Psychology, 7*, 382–390.

Judd, C.M., Kidder, L.H., &. Smith, E.R. (1991). *Research methods in social relations* (6th ed.). New York: Holt Rinehart & Winston.

Kadden, R.M., Cooney, N.L., Getter, H., & Litt, M.D. (1989). Matching alcoholics to coping skills or interactional therapies: Posttreatment results. *Journal of Consulting and Clinical Psychology, 57*, 698–704.

Kahn, J.O., Cherng, D.W., Mayer, K., Murray, H., & Lagakos, S. (2000). Evaluation of HIV-1 immunogen, an immunologic modifier, administered to patients infected with HIV having 300 to 549 106/L CD4 cell counts: A randomized controlled trial. *Journal of the American Medical Association, 284*, 2193–2202.

Kaimowitz v. Michigan Department of Mental Health, 42 U.S.L. Week 2063 (Michigan Circuit Court, Wayne City, July 10, 1973).

Kaiser, J. (2000). Panel backs EPA and "Six Cities" study. *Science, 289*, 711.

Kazantzis, N. (2000). Power to detect homework effects in psychotherapy outcome research. *Journal of Consulting and Clinical Psychology, 68*, 166–170.

Kazdin, A.E. (1977). Assessing the clinical or applied significance of behavior change through social validation. *Behavior Modification, 1*, 427–452.

Kazdin, A.E. (1978a). Evaluating the generality of findings in analogue therapy research. *Journal of Consulting and Clinical Psychology, 46*, 673–686.

Kazdin, A.E. (1978b). *History of behavior modification.* Baltimore, MD: University Park Press.

Kazdin, A.E. (1981). Drawing valid inferences from case studies. *Journal of Consulting and Clinical Psychology, 49*, 183–192.

Kazdin, A.E. (1982a). *Single-case research designs: Methods for clinical and applied settings.* New York: Oxford University Press.

Kazdin, A.E. (1982b). Symptom substitution, generalization, and response covariation: Implications for psychotherapy outcome. *Psychological Bulletin, 91*, 349–365.

Kazdin, A.E. (1984). Statistical analyses for single-case experimental designs. In D.H. Barlow & M. Hersen (Eds.), *Single-case experimental designs: Strategies for studying behavior change* (2nd ed., pp. 285–324). Elmsford, NY: Pergamon.

Kazdin, A.E. (1986). Acceptability of psychotherapy and hospitalization for disturbed children: Parent and child perspectives. *Journal of Clinical Child Psychology, 15*, 333–340.

Kazdin, A.E. (1989). Identifying depression in children: A comparison of alternative selection criteria. *Journal of Abnormal Child Psychology, 17*, 437–455.

Kazdin, A.E. (1993). Evaluation in clinical practice: Clinically sensitive and systematic methods of treatment delivery. *Behavior Therapy, 24*, 11–45.

Kazdin, A.E. (1994). Informant variability in the assessment of childhood depression. In W.M. Reynolds & H. Johnston (Eds.), *Handbook of depression in children and adolescents* (pp. 249–271). New York: Plenum.

Kazdin, A.E. (1995). Child, parent, and family dysfunction as predictors of outcome in cognitive-behavioral treatment of antisocial children. *Behaviour Research and Therapy, 33*, 271–281.

Kazdin, A.E. (1996a). Combined and multimodal treatments in child and adolescent psychotherapy: Issues, challenges, and research directions. *Clinical Psychology: Science and Practice, 3*, 69–100.

Kazdin, A.E. (1996b). Dropping out of child therapy: Issues for research and implications for practice. *Clinical Child Psychology and Psychiatry, 1*, 133–156.

Kazdin, A.E. (1997). Parent management training: Evidence, outcomes, and issues. *Journal of the American Academy of Child and Adolescent Psychiatry, 36*, 1349–1356.

Kazdin, A.E. (1999). The meanings and measurement of clinical significance. *Journal of Consulting and Clinical Psychology, 67*, 332–339.

Kazdin, A.E. (2000). *Psychotherapy for children and adolescents: Directions for research and practice.* New York: Oxford University Press.

Kazdin, A.E. (2001a). *Behavior modification in applied settings* (6th ed.). Belmont CA: Wadsworth.

Kazdin, A.E. (2001b). Bridging the enormous gaps of theory with therapy research and practice. *Journal of Clinical Child Psychology, 30*, 59–66.

Kazdin, A.E. (2001c). Almost clinically significant ($p < .10$): Current measures may only approach clinical significance. *Clinical Psychology: Science and Practice, 8*, 455–462.

Kazdin, A.E., & Bass, D. (1989). Power to detect differences between alternative treatments in comparative psychotherapy outcome research. *Journal of Consulting and Clinical Psychology, 57*, 138–147.

Kazdin, A.E., & Crowley, M. (1997). Moderators of treatment outcome in cognitively based treatment of antisocial behavior. *Cognitive Therapy and Research, 21*, 185–207.

Kazdin, A.E., & Kagan, J. (1994). Models of dysfunction in developmental psychopathology. *Clinical Psychology: Science and Practice, 1*, 35–52.

Kazdin, A.E., & Krouse, R. (1983). The impact of variations in treatment rationales on expectancies for therapeutic change. *Behavior Therapy, 14*, 657–671.

Kazdin, A.E., & Wassell, G. (1998). Treatment completion and therapeutic change among children referred for outpatient therapy. *Professional Psychology: Research and Practice, 29*, 332–340.

Kazdin, A.E., & Wassell, G. (1999). Barriers to treatment participation and therapeutic change among children referred for conduct disorder. *Journal of Clinical Child Psychology, 28,* 160–172.

Kazdin, A.E., & Wassell, G. (2000). Therapeutic changes in children, parents, and families resulting from treatment of children with conduct problems. *Journal of the American Academy of Child and Adolescent Psychiatry, 39,* 414–420.

Kazdin, A.E., Esveldt-Dawson, K., Unis, A.S., & Rancurello, M.D. (1983). Child and parent evaluations of depression and aggression in psychiatric inpatient children. *Journal of Abnormal Child Psychology, 11,* 401–413.

Kazdin, A.E., French, N.H., & Sherick, R.B. (1981). Acceptability of alternative treatments for children: Evaluations by inpatient children, parents, and staff. *Journal of Consulting and Clinical Psychology, 49,* 900–907.

Kazdin, A.E., French, N.H., Unis, A.S., Esveldt-Dawson, K., & Sherick, R.B. (1983). Hopelessness, depression and suicidal intent among psychiatrically disturbed inpatient children. *Journal of Consulting and Clinical Psychology, 51,* 504–510.

Kazdin, A.E., Holland, L., & Crowley, M. (1997). Family experience of barriers to treatment and premature termination from child therapy. *Journal of Consulting and Clinical Psychology, 65,* 453–463.

Kazdin, A.E., Holland, L., Crowley, M., & Breton, S. (1997). Barriers to Participation in Treatment Scale: Evaluation and validation in the context of child outpatient treatment. *Journal of Child Psychology and Psychiatry, 38,* 1051–1062.

Kazdin, A.E., Kraemer, H.C., Kessler, R.C., Kupfer, D.J., & Offord, D.R. (1997). Contributions of risk-factor research to developmental psychopathology. *Clinical Psychology Review, 17,* 375–406.

Kazdin, A.E., Mazurick, J.L., & Bass, D. (1993). Risk for attrition in treatment of antisocial children and families. *Journal of Clinical Child Psychology, 22,* 2–16.

Kazdin, A.E., Mazurick, J.L., & Siegel, T.C. (1994). Treatment outcome among children with externalizing disorder who terminate prematurely versus those who complete psychotherapy. *Journal of the American Academy of Child and Adolescent Psychiatry, 33,* 549–557.

Kazdin, A.E., Rodgers, A., & Colbus, D. (1986). The Hopelessness Scale for Children: Psychometric characteristics and concurrent validity. *Journal of Consulting and Clinical Psychology, 54,* 241–245.

Kazdin, A.E., Siegel, T., & Bass, D. (1990). Drawing on clinical practice to inform research on child and adolescent psychotherapy: Survey of practitioners. *Professional Psychology: Research and Practice, 21,* 189–198.

Kazdin, A.E., Siegel, T., & Bass, D. (1992). Cognitive problem-solving skills training and parent management training in the treatment of antisocial behavior in children. *Journal of Consulting and Clinical Psychology, 60,* 733–747.

Kazdin, A.E., Stolar, M.J., & Marciano, P.L. (1995). Risk factors for dropping out of treatment among White and Black families. *Journal of Family Psychology, 9,* 402–417.

Kendall, P.C. (Ed.) (1999). Special section: Clinical significance. *Journal of Consulting and Clinical Psychology, 67,* 283–339.

Kendall, P.C., & Chambless, D.L. (Eds.) (1998). Special section: Empirically supported psychological therapies. *Journal of Consulting and Clinical Psychology, 66,* 3–167.

Kendall, P.C., & Grove, W.M. (1988). Normative comparisons in therapy outcome. *Behavioral Assessment, 10,* 147–158.

Kendall, P.C., & Treadwell, K.R.H. (1996). Cognitive-behavioral group treatment for socially anxious youth. In E.D. Hibbs & P. Jensen (Eds.), *Psychosocial treatment research of child and adolescent disorders: Empirically based strategies for clinical practice* (pp. 23–41). Washington, DC: American Psychological Association.

Kennedy, D. (2000). Science and secrecy. *Science, 289*, 723.

Kenny, D.A., & Kashy, A. (1992). Analysis of the multitrait–multimethod matrix by confirmatory factor analysis. *Psychological Bulletin, 112*, 165–172.

Kessler, R.C., Mroczek, D.K., & Belli, R.F. (1999). Retrospective adult assessment of childhood psychopathology. In D. Shaffer, J. Richters, & C.P. Lucas (Eds.), *Diagnostic assessment in child and adolescent psychopathology* (pp. 256–284). New York: Guilford.

Kiesler, D.J. (1966). Some myths of psychotherapy research and the search for a paradigm. *Psychological Bulletin, 65*, 110–136.

Kiesler, D.J. (1971). Experimental designs in psychotherapy research. In A.E. Bergin & S.L. Garfield (Eds.) *Handbook of psychotherapy and behavior change: An empirical analysis* (pp. 36–74). New York: Wiley & Sons.

Kihlstrom, J. (June 1995). *From the subject's point of view: The experiment as conversation and collaboration between investigator and subject.* Keynote address presented at the meeting of the American Psychological Society, New York, NY.

Killen, J.D., Fortmann, S.P., Kraemer, H.C., Varady, A.N., Davis, L., & Newman, B. (1996). Interactive effects of depression symptoms, nicotine dependence, and weight change on late smoking relapse. *Journal of Consulting and Clinical Psychology, 64*, 1060–1067.

Kiresuk, T.J., & Garwick, G. (1979). Basic Goal Attainment Scaling Procedures. In B.R. Compton & B. Gallaway (Eds.), *Social work processes* (Rev ed., pp. 412–420). Homewood, IL: Dorsey.

Kirk, R.E. (1994). *Experimental design: Procedures for the behavioral sciences* (3rd ed.) Belmont, CA: Wadsworth.

Kirk, R.E. (1996). Practical significance: A concept whose time has come. *Educational and Psychological Measurement, 56*, 746–759.

Kirsch, I., & Sapirstein, G. (1998). Listening to Prozac but hearing placebo: A meta-analysis of antidepressant medication. *Prevention and Treatment, 1.* (electronic journal: www.journals.apa.org/prevention).

Kisker, E.E., & Brown, R.S. (1997). Nonexperimental designs and program evaluation. *Children and Youth Services Review, 19*, 541–566.

Klee, R. (1997). *Introduction to the philosophy of science: Cutting nature at its seams.* New York: Oxford University Press.

Klein, D.F. (1998). Groups in pharmacotherapy and psychotherapy evaluations. *Prevention and Treatment, 1.* (no pages—electronic journal—see *http://journals.apa.org*).

Klerman, G.L., Weissman, M.M., Marakowitz, J.C., Glick, I., Wilner, P.J., Mason, B., & Shear, M.K. (1994). Medication and psychotherapy. In A.E. Bergin & S.L. Garfield (Eds.), *Handbook of psychotherapy and behavior change* (4th ed., pp. 734–782). New York: Wiley & Sons.

Klerman, G.L., Weissman, M.M., Rounsaville, B.J., & Chevron, E. (1984). *Interpersonal psychotherapy of depression.* New York: Basic Books.

Klusman, L.E. (1975). Reduction of pain in childbirth by the alleviation of anxiety during pregnancy. *Journal of Consulting and Clinical Psychology, 43*, 162–165.

Knowles, E.S., & Condon, C.A. (2000). Does the rose still smell as sweet? Item variability across test forms. *Psychological Assessment, 12*, 245–252.

Knowles, E.S., Coker, M.C., Scott, R.A., Cook, D.A., & Neville, J.W. (1996). Measurement induced improvement in anxiety: Mean shifts with repeated assessment. *Journal of Personality and Social Psychology, 71*, 352–363.

Koenig, H.G., Hays, J.C., Larson, D.B., George, L.K., Cohen, H.J., McCullough, M.E., Meador, K.G., & Blazer, D.G. (1999). Does religious attendance prolong survival? A six-year follow-up study of 3,968 older adults. *Journal of Gerontology: Medical Sciences, 54A*, M370–M376.

Kohn, A. (1988). False profits: Fraud and error in science and medicine. New York: Basil Blackwell.

Kolvin, I., Garside, R.F., Nicol, A.E., MacMillan, A., Wolstenholme, F., & Leitch, I.M. (1981). *Help starts here: The maladjusted child in the ordinary school*. London: Tavistock.

Koocher, G.P., & Keith-Spiegel, P. (1998). *Ethics in psychology: Professional standards and cases* (2nd ed.). New York: Oxford University Press.

Kopta, S.M., Howard, K.I., Lowry, J.L., & Beutler, L.E. (1994). Patterns of symptomatic recovery in psychotherapy. *Journal of Consulting and Clinical Psychology, 62*, 1009–1016.

Kraemer, H.C., & Thiemann, S. (1987). *How many subjects? Statistical power analysis in research*. Newbury Park, CA: Sage.

Kraemer, H.C., Kazdin, A.E., Offord, D.R., Kessler, R.C., Jensen, P.S., & Kupfer, D.J. (1997). Coming to terms with the terms of risk. *Archives of General Psychiatry, 54*, 337–343.

Krahn, G.L., Hohn, M.F., & Kime, C. (1995). Incorporating qualitative approaches into clinical child psychology research. *Journal of Clinical Child Psychology, 24*, 204–213.

Kratochwill, T.R., Callan-Stoiber, K., & Gutkin, T.B. (2000). Empirically supported interventions in school psychology: The role of negative results in outcome research. *Psychology in the Schools, 37*, 399–413.

Krishef, C.H. (1991). *Fundamental approaches to single subject design and analysis*. Malabar, FL: Kreiger.

Kroll, L., Harrington, R., Jayson, D., Fraser, J., & Gowers, S. (1996). Pilot study of continuation cognitive-behavioral therapy for major depression in adolescents. *Journal of the American Academy of Child and Adolescent Psychiatry, 35*, 1156–1161.

Krueger, J. (2001). Null hypothesis significance testing: On the survival of a flawed method. *American Psychologist, 56*, 16–26.

Kruglanski, A. W. (1975). The human subject in the psychology experiment: Fact and artifact. In L. Berkowitz (Ed.), *Advances in experimental social psychology* (Vol. 8, pp. 101–147). Orlando, FL: Academic Press.

Krupnick, J.L., Sotsky, S.M., Simmens, S., Moyer, J., Elkin, I., Watkins, J., & Pilkonis, P.A. (1996). The role of the therapeutic alliance in psychotherapy and pharmacotherapy outcome: Findings in the National Institute of Mental Health Treatment of Depression Collaborative Research Program. *Journal of Consulting and Clinical Psychology, 64*, 532–539.

Kuhn, T.S. (1996). *The structure of scientific revolutions* (3rd ed.). Chicago: University of Chicago Press.

Kupfer, D.J., Frank, E., Perel, J.M., Cornes, C., Mallinger, A.G., Thase, M.E., McEachran, A.B., & Grochocinski, V.J. (1992). Five-year outcome for maintenance therapies in recurrent depression. *Archives of General Psychiatry, 49*, 769–773.

Kupfer, D.J., Kraemer, H.C., & Bartko, J.J. (1994). Documenting and reporting the study results of a randomized clinical trial (spicy meatballs, not pabulum). In R.F. Prien & D.S. Robinson (Eds.), *Clinical evaluation of psychotropic drugs* (pp. 237–260). New York: Raven Press.

Kupfersmid, J. (1988). Improving what is published: A model in search of an editor. *American Psychologist, 43*, 635–642.

Kutner, B., Wilkins, C., & Harrow, P.R. (1952). Verbal attitudes and overt behavior involving racial prejudice. *Journal of Abnormal and Social Psychology, 47*, 649–652.

La Greca, A.M., Silverman, W.K., Vernberg, E.M., & Prinstein, M.J. (1996). Symptoms of posttraumatic stress in children after Hurricane Andrew: A prospective study. *Journal of Consulting and Clinical Psychology, 64*, 712–723.

La Piere, R.T. (1934). Attitudes vs. action. *Social Forces, 13*, 230–237.

Ladouceur, R., Freeston, M.H., Gagnon, F., Thibodeau, N., & Dumont, J. (1993). Idiographic considerations in the behavioral treatment of obsessional thoughts. *Journal of Behavior Therapy and Experimental Psychiatry, 24*, 301–310.

Lam, D.H. (1991). Psychosocial family intervention in schizophrenia: A review of empirical studies. *Psychological Medicine, 21*, 423–441.

Lambert, M.J. (1983). Introduction to assessment of psychotherapy outcome: Historical perspective and current issues. In M.J. Lambert, E.R. Christensen, & S.S. DeJulio (Eds.), *The assessment of psychotherapy outcome* (pp. 3–32). New York: Wiley & Sons.

Lambert, M.J., & Bergin, A.E. (1994). The effectiveness of psychotherapy. In A.E. Bergin & S.L. Garfield (Eds.), *Handbook of psychotherapy and behavior change* (4th ed., pp. 143–189). New York: Wiley & Sons.

Lambert, M.J., & Brown, G.S. (1996). Data-based management for tracking outcome in private practice. *Clinical Psychology: Science and Practice, 3*, 172–178.

Land, K.C., McCall, P.L., & Williams, J.R. (1992). Intensive supervision of status offenders: Evidence on continuity of treatment effects for juveniles and a "Hawthorne Effect" for counselors. In J. McCord & R.E. Tremblay (Eds.), *Preventing antisocial behavior: Interventions from birth through adolescence* (pp. 330–349). New York: Guilford.

Lazarus, A.A. (1961). Group therapy of phobic disorders by systematic desensitization. *Journal of Abnormal and Social Psychology, 63*, 504–510.

Levin, J.S. (1994). Religion and health: Is there an association, is it valid, is it causal? *Social Science & Medicine, 38*, 1475–1482.

Levin, J.S. (1996). How religion influences morbidity and health: Reflections on natural history, salutogenesis, and host resistance? *Social Science and Medicine, 43*, 849–864.

Lewinsohn, P.M., & Clarke, G.N. (1999) Psychosocial treatments for adolescent depression. *Clinical Psychology Review, 19*, 329–342.

Lewinsohn, P.M., Clarke, G.N., Hops, H., & Andrews, J. (1990). Cognitive-behavioral treatment for depressed adolescents. *Behavior Therapy, 21*, 385–401.

Lewinsohn, P.M., Solomon, A., Seeley, J.R., & Zeiss, A. (2000). Clinical implications of "subthreshold" depressive symptoms. *Journal of Abnormal Psychology, 109*, 345–351.

Lewinsohn, P.M., Steinmetz, J.L., Larson, D.L., & Franklin, J. (1981). Depression-related cognitions: Antecedent or consequence? *Journal of Abnormal Psychology, 91*, 213–219.

Lewis, K.G., & Moon, S. (1997). Always single and single again women: A qualitative study. *Journal of Marital and Family Therapy, 23*, 115–134.

Lezak, M. (1995). *Neuropsychological assessment* (3rd ed.). New York: Oxford University Press.

Lilienfeld, S., Wood, J.M., & Garb, H.N. (2000). The scientific status of projective techniques. *Psychological Science in the Public Interest, 1*, 27–66.

Lin, K., Poland, R.E., & Nagasaki, G. (Eds.) (1993). *Psychopharmacology and psychobiology of ethnicity*. Washington, DC: American Psychiatric Press.

Lincoln, Y.S., & Guba, E.G. (1985). *Naturalistic inquiry*. Beverly Hills, CA: Sage.

Lindsay, D. (1988). Assessing precision in the manuscript review process: A little better than a dice role. *Sociometrics, 14*, 75–82.

Lindsey, E.W. (1998). The impact of homelessness and shelter life on family relationships. *Family Relations, 47*, 243–252.

Lipman, E.L., Offord, D.R., & Boyle, M.H. (1994). Relation between economic disadvantage and psychosocial morbidity in children. *Canadian Medical Association Journal, 151*, 431–437.

Lipsey, M.W. (1990). *Design sensitivity: Statistical power for experimental research*. Newbury Park, CA: Sage.

Little, R.J.A., & Rubin, D.B. (1987). *Statistical analysis with missing data*. New York: Wiley & Sons.

Lovaas, O.I. (1987). Behavioral treatment and normal educational/intellectual functioning in young autistic children. *Journal of Consulting and Clinical Psychology, 55*, 3–9.

Lovaas, O.I. (1988). *Behavioral treatment of autistic children* (film). Huntington Station, NY: Focus International.

Lowman, R.L. (Ed.) (1996). Special section: What every psychologist should know about assessment. *Psychological Assessment, 8*, 339–368.

Luborsky, L., Crits-Cristoph, P., Mintz, J., & Auerbach, A. (1988). *Who will benefit from psychotherapy? Predicting therapeutic outcomes.* New York: Basic Books.

Luborsky, L., Diguer, L., Seligman, D.A., Rosenthal, R., Krause, E.D., Johnson, S., Halperin, G., Bishop, M., Berman, J.S., & Schweizer, E. (1999). The researcher's own therapy allegiances: A "wild card" in comparisons of treatment efficacy. *Clinical Psychology: Science and Practice, 6,* 95–106.

Luthar, S.S. (1999). *Poverty and children's adjustment.* Thousand Oaks, CA: Sage.

Lykken, D.T. (1968). Statistical significance in psychological research. *Psychological Bulletin, 70,* 151–159.

Lyons, J.S., Howard, K.I., Mahoney, M.T., & Lish, J.D. (1997). *The measurement and management of clinical outcomes in mental health.* New York: Wiley & Sons.

MacKintosh, N.J. (Ed.) (1995). *Cyril Burt: Fraud or framed?* New York: Oxford University Press.

Macmillan, M. (2000). *An odd kind of fame: Stories of Phineas Gage.* Cambridge: MIT Press.

Madriz, E. (2000). Focus groups in feminist research. In N.H Denzin & Y.S. Lincoln (Eds.), *Handbook of qualitative research* (2nd ed., pp. 835–850). Thousand Oaks, CA: Sage.

Magnusson, D., Bergman, L.R., Gudinger, G., & Torestad, B. (1991). *Problems and methods in longitudinal research.* New York: Cambridge University Press.

Maher, B.A. (1978a). Stimulus sampling in clinical research: Representative design reviewed. *Journal of Consulting and Clinical Psychology, 46,* 643–647.

Maher, B.A. (1978b). A reader's, writer's, and reviewer's guide to assessing research reports in clinical psychology. *Journal of Consulting and Clinical Psychology, 46,* 835–838.

Major, B., Cozzarelli, C., Cooper, M.L., Zubek, J., Richards, C.; Wilhite, M., & Gramzow, R.H. (2000). Psychological responses of women after first-trimester abortion. *Archives of General Psychiatry, 57,* 777–784.

Malakoff, D. (1999). Bayes offers a "new" way to make sense of numbers. *Science, 286,* 1460–1464.

Manson, S.M. (Ed.). (1989). *American Indian and Alaska Native Mental Health Research, 2* (whole issue number 3).

Marciano, P.L., & Kazdin, A.E. (1994). Self-esteem, depression, hopelessness, and suicidal intent among psychiatrically disturbed inpatient children. *Journal of Clinical Child Psychology, 23,* 151–160.

Marcus, S., Robins, L.N,, & Bucholz, K. (1991). *Quick Diagnostic Interview Schedule III-R: Version 1.0.* St Louis, MO: Washington University School of Medicine.

Margraf, J., Ehlers, A., Roth, W.T., Clark, D.B., Sheikh, J., Agras, W.S., & Taylor, C.B. (1991). How "blind" are double-blind studies? *Journal of Consulting and Clinical Psychology, 46,* 184–187.

Marks, I.M., Shaw, S., & Parkin, R. (1998). Computer-aided treatments of mental health problems. *Clinical Psychology: Science and Practice, 5,* 151–170.

Marmor, J. (1975). Foreword. In. R.B. Sloane, F.R. Staples, A.H. Cristol, N.J. Yorkston, & K. Whipple, *Psychotherapy versus behavior therapy* (pp. xv–xviii). Cambridge, MA: Harvard University Press.

Marrs, R.W. (1995). A meta-analysis of bibliotherapy studies. *American Journal of Community Psychology, 23,* 843–870.

Martin, J.E., & Sachs, D.A. (1973). The effects of a self-control weight loss program on an obese woman. *Journal of Behavior Therapy and Experimental Psychiatry, 4,* 155–159.

Masling, J.M. (1960). The influence of situational and interpersonal variables in projective testing. *Psychological Bulletin, 57,* 65–85.

Mathalon, D.H., Sullivan, E.V., Lim, K.O., & Pfefferbaum, A. (2001). Progressive brain volume changes and the clinical course of schizophrenia in men: A longitudinal magnetic resonance imaging study. *Archives of General Psychiatry, 58,* 146–157.

Matt, G.E. (1989). Decision rules for selecting effect sizes in meta-analysis: A review and re-analysis of psychotherapy outcome studies. *Psychological Bulletin, 105,* 106–115.

Matt, G.E., & Navarro, A.M. (1997). What meta-analyses have and have not taught us about psychotherapy effects: A review and future directions. *Clinical Psychology Review, 17,* 1–32.

Matthews, D.B. (1986). Discipline: Can it be improved with relaxation training? *Elementary School Guidance and Counseling, XX,* 194–200.

Matthys, W., Walterbos, W., Njio, L., & van Engeland, H. (1989). Person perception in children with conduct disorders. *Journal of Child Psychology and Psychiatry, 30,* 439–448.

Maxwell, J.A. (1996). *Qualitative research design.* Newbury Park, CA: Sage.

Mazumdar, S., Liu, K.S., Houck, P.R., & Reynolds, C.F., III (1999). Intent-to-treat analysis for longitudinal clinical trials: Coping with the challenge of missing values. *Journal of Psychiatric Research, 33,* 87–95.

McCullough, M.E. (1995). Prayer and health: Conceptual issues, research review, and research agenda. *Journal of Psychology and Theology, 23,* 15–29.

McGuire, W.J. (1997). Creative hypothesis generating in psychology: Some useful heuristics. *Annual Review of Psychology, 48,* 1–30.

McGuire, W.J. (1999). *Constructing social psychology: Creative and critical processes.* Cambridge: Cambridge University Press.

Meehl, P. (1978). Theoretical risks and tabular asterisks: Sir Karl, Sir Ronald, and the slow progress of soft psychology. *Journal of Consulting and Clinical Psychology, 46,* 806–834.

Meier, S.T., & Wick, M.T. (1991). Computer-based unobtrusive measurement: Potential supplements to reactive self-reports. *Professional Psychology: Research and Practice, 22,* 410–412.

Mellors, J.W., Rinaldo, C.R., Jr., Gupta, P., White, R.M., Todd, J.A., & Kingsley, L.A. (1996). Prognosis in HIV-1 infection predicted by the quantity of virus in plasma. *Science, 272,* 1167–1170.

Melov, S., Ravenscroft, J., Malik, S., Gill, M.S., Walker, D.W., Clayton, P.E., Wallace, D.C., Malfroy, B., Doctrow, S.R., & Lithgow, G.J, (2000). Extension of life-span with superoxide dismutase/catalase mimetics. *Science, 289,* 1567–1569.

Meltzoff, J., & Kornreich, M. (1970). *Research in psychotherapy.* New York: Atherton.

Meston, C.M., & Frohlich, P.F. (2000). The neurobiology of sexual function. *Archives of General Psychiatry, 57,* 1012–1030.

Meyer, G.J., Finn, S.E., Eyde, L.D., Kay, G.G., Moreland, K.L., Dies, R.R., Eisman, E.J., Kubiszyn, T.W., & Reed, G.M. (2001). Psychological testing and psychological assessment. A review of evidence and issues. *American Psychologist, 56,* 128–165.

Meyer, V. (1957). The treatment of two phobic patients on the basis of learning principles. *Journal of Abnormal and Social Psychology, 55,* 261–266.

Meyers, A.W., Graves, T.J., Whelan, J.P., & Barclay, D. (1996). An evaluation of television-delivered behavioral weight loss program. Are the ratings acceptable? *Journal of Consulting and Clinical Psychology, 64,* 172–178.

Miles, M.B., & Huberman, A.M. (1994). *Qualitative data analysis: An expanded source book.* (2nd ed.). Thousand Oaks, CA: Sage.

Miles, M.B., & Weitzman, E.A. (1994). Appendix: Choosing computer programs for qualitative data analyses. In M.B Miles & A.M. Huberman, (Eds.). *Qualitative data analysis* (2nd ed., pp. 311–317). Thousand Oaks, CA: Sage.

Milgram, S. (1974). *Obedience to authority.* New York: Harper & Row.

Milinki, A.K. (Ed.) (1999). *Cases in qualitative research: Research reports for discussion and evaluation.* Los Angeles: Pyrczak.

Miller, D.J., & Hersen, M. (Eds.) (1992). *Research fraud in the behavioral and biomedical sciences.* New York: Wiley and Sons.

Miller, L. (Ed.) (1999). *Postpartum mood disorders.* Washington, DC: American Psychiatric Press.

Milner, J.S. (1989). Additional cross-validation of the Child Abuse Potential Inventory. *Journal of Consulting and Clinical Psychology, 57,* 219–223.

Moher, D., Dulberg, C.S., & Wells, G.A. (1994). Statistical power, sample size, and their reporting in randomized controlled trials. *Journal of the American Medical Association, 272,* 122–124.

Mohr, L.B. (1985). The reliability of the case study as a source of information. *Advances in Information Processing in Organizations, 2,* 65–93.

Mohr, L.B. (1990). *Understanding significance testing.* Newbury Park, CA: Sage.

Mook, D.G. (1983). In defense of external invalidity. *American Psychologist, 38,* 379–387.

Morgan, D.L. (1998). *The focus group guidebook.* Thousand Oaks, CA. Sage.

Morgan, R.W., Kelsh, M.A., Zhao, K., Exuzides, K.A., Heringer, S., & Negrete, W. (2000). Radiofrequency exposure and mortality from cancers of the brain and lymphatic/hematopoietic system. *Epidemiology, 11,* 118–127.

Moss, M. (1996, September 18). Does annual survey of US drug use give straight dope? *Wall Street Journal,* Vol. CCXXVIII, No. 56, pp. A1, A10.

Mrazek, P.J., & Haggerty, R.J. (Eds.) (1994). *Reducing risks for mental disorders: Frontiers of preventive intervention research.* Washington, DC: National Academy Press.

Multiple Risk Factor Intervention Trial Research Group (1982). Multiple risk factor intervention trial: Risk factor changes and mortality results. *Journal of the American Medical Association, 248,* 1465–1477.

Murberg, T.A., Bru, E., Svebak, S., Tveteras, R., & Aarsland, T. (1999). Depressed mood and subjective health symptoms as predictors of mortality in patients with congestive heart failure: A two-year follow-up study. *International Journal of Psychiatry in Medicine, 29,* 311–326.

Murphy, L.L., Conoley, J.C., & Impara, J.C. (Eds.) (1994). *Tests in print. IV* (Vols. 1 & 2). Lincoln, NE: Buros Institute of the University of Nebraska. Buros Institute of Mental Measurements: University of Nebraska Press.

Nagel, E. (1961). *The structure of science.* New York: Harcourt.

Nathan, P.E., &. Gorman, J.M. (Eds.) (1998). *Treatments that work.* New York: Oxford University Press.

National Academy of Sciences, Committee on the Conduct of Science (1989). *On being a scientist.* Washington, DC: National Academy Press.

Needleman, H.L. (Ed.) (1988). *Low level of lead exposure: The clinical implications of current research.* New York: Raven Press.

Needleman, H.L., & Bellinger, D., (1984). The developmental consequences of childhood exposure to lead: Recent studies and methodological issues. In B.B. Lahey & A.E. Kazdin (Eds.), *Advances in clinical child psychology* (Vol. 7, pp. 195–220). New York: Plenum.

Needleman, H.L., Schell, A.S., Bellinger, D., Leviton, A., & Alldred, E.N. (1990). The long-term effects of exposure to low doses of lead in childhood: An 11-year follow-up report. *New England Journal of Medicine, 322,* 83.

Nelson, L.D. (Ed.) (2000). Special section: Methods and implications of revising assessment instruments. *Psychological Assessment, 12,* 235–303.

Neuliep, J.W. (Ed.) (1991). *Replication research in the social sciences.* Newbury Park, CA: Sage.

Newcomb, M.D., & Bentler, P.M. (1988). *Consequences of adolescent drug use: Impact on the lives of young adults.* Newbury Park, CA: Sage.

Newcomb, M.D., & Bentler, P.M. (1989). Substance use and abuse among children and teenagers. *American Psychologist, 44,* 242–248.

Newman, M.G. (2000). Recommendations for a cost-offset model of psychotherapy allocation using generalized disorder as an example. *Journal of Consulting and Clinical Psychology, 68,* 549–555.

Newman, M.G., Consoli, A., & Taylor, C.B. (1997). Computers in assessment and cognitive behavioral treatment of clinical disorders: Anxiety as a case in point. *Behavior Therapy, 28*, 211–235.

Newman, M.G., Kenardy, J., Herman, S., & Taylor, C.B. (1997). Comparison of palmtop-computer-assisted brief cognitive-behavioral treatment to cognitive-behavioral treatment for panic disorder. *Journal of Consulting and Clinical Psychology, 65*, 178–183.

Neyman, J., & Pearson, E.S. (1928). On the use and interpretation of certain test criteria for purposes of statistical inference. *Biometrika, 294*, 175–240 (Part 1), 263–294 (Part 2).

Nezu, A.M., & Perri, M.G. (1989). Social problem-solving therapy for unipolar depression: An initial dismantling investigation. *Journal of Consulting and Clinical Psychology, 57*, 408–413.

Nezworski, M.T., & Wood, J.M. (1995). Narcissism in the comprehensive system for the Rorschach. *Clinical Psychology: Science and Practice, 2*, 179–199.

Nich, C., & Carroll, K. (1997). Now you see it, now you don't: A comparison of traditional versus random-effects regression model in the analysis of longitudinal follow-up data from a clinical trial. *Journal of Consulting and Clinical Psychology, 65*, 252–261.

Nickerson, R.S. (2000). Null hypothesis significance testing: A review of an old and continuing controversy. *Psychological Methods, 5*, 241–301.

Noll, R.B., Zeller, M.H., Vannatta, K., Bukowski, W.M., & Davies, W.H. (1997). Potential bias in classroom research: Comparison of children with permission and those who do not receive permission to participate. *Journal of Clinical Child Psychology, 26*, 36–42.

Nunnally, J. (1960). The place of statistics in psychology. *Educational and Psychological Measurement, 20*, 641–650.

O'Connell-Rodwell, C.E., Arnason, B., & Hart, L.A. (2000). Seismic properties of elephant vocalizations and locomotion. *Journal of the Acoustical Society of America, 108*, 3066.

O'Donohue, W., Plaud, J.J., & Hecker, J.E. (1992). The possible function of positive reinforcement in home-bound agoraphobia: A case study. *Journal of Behavior Therapy and Experimental Psychiatry, 23*, 303–312.

Offord, D., Boyle, M.H., Racine, Y.A., Fleming, J.E., Cadman, D.T., Blum, H.M., Byrne, C., Links, P.S., Lipman, E.L., MacMillan, H.L., Rae Grant, N.I., Sanford, M.N., Szatmari, P., Thomas, H., & Woodward, C.A. (1992). Outcome, prognosis, and risk in a longitudinal follow-up study. *Journal of the American Academy of Child and Adolescent Psychiatry, 31*, 916–923.

Offord, D., Boyle, M.H., Racine, Y.A., Szatmari, P., Fleming, J.E., Sanford, M.N., and Lipman, E.L. (1996). Integrating assessment data from multiple informants. *Journal of the American Academy of Child and Adolescent Psychiatry, 35*, 1078–1085.

Ogles, B.M., Lunnen, K.M., & Bonesteel, K. (2001). Clinical significance: History, application, and current practice. *Clinical Psychology Review, 21*, 421–446.

OPTAIO™ Provider's desktop (1997). The Psychological Corporation, San Antonio, TX.

Orne, M.T. (1962). On the social psychology of the psychological experiment: With particular reference to demand characteristics and their implications. *American Psychologist, 17*, 776–783.

Orne, M.T. (1969). Demand characteristics and the concept of quasi-controls. In R. Rosenthal & R.L. Rosnow (Eds.), *Artifact in behavioral research* (pp. 143–179). New York: Academic Press.

Orne, M.T., & Scheibe, K.E. (1964). The contribution of nondeprivation factors in the production of sensory deprivation effects: The psychology of the "panic button." *Journal of Abnormal and Social Psychology, 68*, 3–12.

Ouimette, P.C., Finney, J.W., & Moos, R.H. (1997). Twelve-step and cognitive-behavioral treatment for substance abuse: A comparison of treatment effectiveness. *Journal of Consulting and Clinical Psychology, 65*, 230–240.

Paivio, S.C., & Greenberg, L.S. (1995). Resolving "unfinished business": Efficacy of experiential therapy using empty-chair dialogue. *Journal of Consulting and Clinical Psychology, 63*, 419–425.

Palmer, A.B., & Wohl, J. (1972). Voluntary-admission forms: Does the patient know what he's signing? *Hospital and Community Psychiatry, 23,* 250–252.

Parloff, M.B. (1986). Placebo controls in psychotherapy research: A sine qua non or a placebo for research problems? *Journal of Consulting and Clinical Psychology, 54,* 79–87.

Parsonson, B.S., & Baer, D.M. (1978). The analysis and presentation of graphic data. In T.R. Kratochwill (Ed.), *Single-subject research: Strategies for evaluating change* (pp. 101–165). New York: Academic Press.

Patterson, G.R. (1982). *Coercive family process.* Eugene, OR: Castalia.

Patterson, G.R., Chamberlain, P., & Reid, J.B. (1982). A comparative evaluation of a parent-training program. *Behavior Therapy, 13,* 638–650.

Patterson, G.R., Reid, J.B., & Dishion, T.J. (1992). *Antisocial boys.* Eugene, OR: Castalia.

Paul, G.L. (1966). *Insight versus desensitization in psychotherapy: An experiment in anxiety reduction.* Stanford, CA: Stanford University Press.

Paul, G.L. (1967). Outcome research in psychotherapy. *Journal of Consulting Psychology, 31,* 109–118.

Phillips, E.L. (1985). *Psychotherapy revised: New frontiers in research and practice.* Hillsdale, NJ: Erlbaum.

Polkinghorne, J. (1996). *Beyond science: The wider human context.* New York: Cambridge University Press.

Popper, K. (1959). *The logic of scientific discovery.* New York: Basic Books.

Presidential Documents (US President), Executive Order 12975 (October 3, 1995). Protection of Human Research Subjects and Creation of National Bioethics Advisory Commission. *Federal Register, 60* (193), 52063–52065. Retrieved November 19, 2001 from the World Wide Web: http://bioethics.gov

Prinz, R.J., & Miller, G.E. (1994). Family-based treatment for childhood antisocial behavior: Experimental influences on dropout and engagement. *Journal of Consulting and Clinical Psychology, 62,* 645–650.

Rachman, S.J., & Hodgson, R.I. (1974). Synchrony and desynchrony in fear and avoidance. *Behaviour Research and Therapy, 12,* 311–318.

Rachman, S. J., & Wilson, G. T. (1980). *The effects of psychological therapy* (2nd ed.). Oxford: Pergamon.

Reckase, M.D. (1996). Test construction in the 1990s: Recent approaches every psychologist should know. *Psychological Assessment, 8,* 354–359.

Regier, D.A., Myers, J.K., Kramer, M., Robins, L.N., Blazer, D.G., Hough, R.L., Eaton, W.W., & Locke, B.Z. (1984). The NIMH Epidemiologic Catchment Area program: Historical context, major objectives, and study population characteristics. *Archives of General Psychiatry, 41,* 934–941.

Reichardt, C.S., & Gollob, H.F. (1989). Ruling out threats to validity. *Evaluation Review, 13,* 3–17.

Reimers, T.M., Wacker, D.P., Cooper, L.J., & DeRaad, A.O. (1992). Clinical evaluation of the variables associated with treatment acceptability and their relation to compliance. *Behavioral Disorders, 18,* 67–76.

Resnick, J.H., & Schwartz, T. (1973). Ethical standards as an independent variable in psychological research. *American Psychologist, 28,* 134–139.

Robertson, R., & Combs, A. (Eds.) (1995). *Chaos theory in psychology and the life sciences.* Mahwah, NJ: Erlbaum.

Robins, L., Helzer, J., Weissman, M., Orvaschel, H., Gruenberg, E., Bruche, J., & Regier, D. (1984). Lifetime prevalence of specific psychiatric disorders in three sites. *Archives of General Psychiatry, 41,* 949–958.

Rodin, J., & Barachi, R. (1999). Impacts of the Shelby Amendment: Letters by April 5: To the University's Research Community, *University of Pennsylvania, Almanac, 45* (26).

Roediger, H.L., III, & McDermott, K.B. (2000). Tricks of memory. *Current Directions in Psychological Science, 9,* 123–127.

Rogers, C., & Dymond, R. (Eds.) (1954). *Psychotherapy and personality change.* Chicago: University of Chicago Press.

Rosen, G.M. (1993). Self-help or hype? Comments on psychology's failure to advance self-care. *Professional Psychology: Research and Practice, 24,* 340–345.

Rosenthal, R. (1966). *Experimenter effects in behavioral research.* New York: Appleton-Century-Crofts.

Rosenthal, R. (1969). Interpersonal expectations: Effects of the experimenter's hypothesis (pp. 181–277). In R. Rosenthal & R.L. Rosnow (Eds.), *Artifact in behavioral research.* New York: Academic Press.

Rosenthal, R. (1976). *Experimenter effects in behavioral research* (enlarged edition). New York: Irvington.

Rosenthal, R. (1979). The "file drawer problem" and tolerance for null results. *Psychological Bulletin, 86,* 638–641.

Rosenthal, R. (1984). *Meta-analytic procedures for social research.* Beverly Hills, CA: Sage.

Rosenthal, R. (1991). Replication in behavioral research. In J.W. Neuliep (Ed.), *Replication research in the social sciences* (pp. 1–30). Newbury Park, CA: Sage.

Rosenthal, R. (1994). Science and ethics in conducting, analyzing, and reporting psychological research. *Psychological Science, 5,* 127–133.

Rosenthal, R., & Gaito, J. (1963). The interpretation of levels of significance by psychological researchers. *Journal of Psychology, 55,* 33–38.

Rosenthal, R., & Rosnow, R.L. (1969). *Artifact in behavioral research.* New York: Academic Press.

Rosenthal, R., & Rosnow, R.L. (1975). *The volunteer subject.* New York: Wiley & Sons.

Rosenthal, R., & Rosnow, R.L. (1991). *Essentials of behavioral research: Methods and data analysis* (2nd. ed.). New York: McGraw-Hill.

Rosnow, R.L., & Rosenthal, R. (1989). Definition and interpretation of interaction effects. *Psychological Bulletin, 105,* 143–146.

Ross, J.A. (1975). Parents modify thumbsucking: A case study. *Journal of Behavior Therapy and Experimental Psychiatry, 6,* 248–249.

Ross, L., Lepper, M.R., & Hubbard, M. (1975). Perseverance in self-perception and perception: Biased attributional processes in the debriefing paradigm. *Journal of Personality and Social Psychology, 32,* 800–892.

Rossi, J.S. (1990). Statistical power of psychological research: What have we gained in 20 years? *Journal of Consulting and Clinical Psychology, 58,* 646–656.

Rotblat, J. (1999). A Hippocratic oath for scientists. *Science, 286,* 1475.

Roth, A., & Fonagy, P. (1996). *What works for whom: A critical review of psychotherapy research.* New York: Guilford.

Rounsaville, B.J., Chevron, E.S., Prusoff, B.A., Elkin, I., Imber, S., Sotsky, S., & Watkins, J. (1986). The relation between specific and general dimensions of the psychotherapy process in Interpersonal Psychotherapy of depression. *Journal of Consulting and Clinical Psychology, 55,* 379–394.

Rush, A.J., Beck, A.T., Kovacs, M., & Hollon, S. (1977). Comparative efficacy of cognitive therapy and pharmacotherapy in the treatment of depressed outpatients. *Cognitive Therapy and Research, 1,* 17–37.

Rutter, M.B. (1981). Epidemiological/longitudinal strategies and causal research in child psychiatry. *Journal of the American Academy of Child Psychiatry, 20,* 513–544.

Sperry, L., Brill, P., Howard, K.I., & Grissom, G. (1996). *Treatment outcomes in psychotherapy and psychiatric interventions.* New York: Brunner/Mazel.

Spiegel, D., Bloom, J.R., Kraemer, H.C., & Gottheil, E. (1989). Effect of psychosocial treatment on survival of patients with metastatic breast cancer. *Lancet, 2* (8668), 888–891.

Spirito, A., Overholser, J., Ashworth, S., Morgan, J., & Benedict-Drew, C. (1988a). Evaluation of a suicide awareness curriculum for high school students. *Journal of the American Academy of Child and Adolescent Psychiatry, 27,* 705–711.

Spirito, A., Williams, C.A., Stark, L.J., & Hart, K.J. (1988b). The Hopelessness Scale for Children: Psychometric properties with normal and emotionally disturbed adolescents. *Journal of Abnormal Child Psychology, 16,* 445–458.

Spiro, H. (1998). *The power of hope: A doctor's perspective.* New Haven, CT: Yale University Press.

Spitzer, A., Webster-Stratton, C., & Hollinsworth, T. (1991). Coping with conduct-problem children: Parents gaining knowledge and control. *Journal of Clinical Child Psychology, 20,* 413–427.

Stake, R.E. (1995). *The art of case study research.* Thousand Oaks, CA: Sage.

Stanger, C., & Verhulst, F.C. (1995). Accelerated longitudinal designs. In F.C. Verhulst & H.M. Koot (Eds.), *The epidemiology of child and adolescent psychopathology* (pp. 385–405). New York: Oxford University Press.

Stein, J.A., Golding, J.M., Siegel, J.M., Burnam, M.A., & Sorenson, S.B. (1988). Long-term psychological sequelae of child sexual abuse: The Los Angeles Epidemiologic Catchment Area Study. In G.E. Wyatt & G.J. Powell (Eds.), *Lasting effects of child abuse* (pp. 135–154). Newbury Park, CA: Sage.

Sternberg, R.J. (1992). *Psychological Bulletin's* top 10 "hit parade." *Psychological Bulletin, 112,* 387–388.

Stevens, S., Hynan, M.T., & Allen, M. (2000). A meta-analysis of common factor and specific treatment effects across the outcome domains of the phase model of psychotherapy. *Clinical Psychology: Science and Practice, 7,* 273–290.

Stice, E., Barrera, M., Jr., & Chassin, L. (1993). Relation of parental support and control to adolescents' externalizing symptomatology and substance use: A longitudinal examination of curvilinear effects. *Journal of Abnormal Child Psychology, 21,* 609–629.

Stiles, W.B. (1993). Quality control in qualitative research. *Clinical Psychology Review, 13,* 593–618.

Stoeber, J. (2000). Prospective cognitions in anxiety and depression: Replication and methodological extension. *Cognition and Emotion. 14,* 725–729.

Stoff, D.M., Breiling, J., & Maser, J.D. (Eds.) (1997). *Handbook of antisocial behavior.* New York: Wiley & Sons.

Strasburger, V.C. (1995). *Adolescents and the media: Medical and psychological impact.* Thousand Oaks, CA: Sage.

Straus, M.A. (1979). Measuring intrafamily conflict and violence: The Conflict Tactics Scales (CTS). *Journal of Marriage and the Family, 41,* 75–88.

Strauss, A.L., & Corbin, J.M. (1998). *Basics of qualitative research: Techniques and procedures for developing grounded theory.* Thousand Oaks, CA: Sage.

Stricker, G., & Healey, B.J. (1990). Projective assessment of object relations: A review of the empirical literature. *Psychological Assessment, 2,* 219–230.

Strupp, H.H., Hadley, S.W., & Gomes-Schwartz, B. (1977). *Psychotherapy for better or worse: An analysis of the problem of negative effects.* New York: Jason Aronson.

Sue, S. (1999). Science, ethnicity, and bias: Where have we gone wrong? *American Psychologist, 54,* 1070–1077.

Sugden, D.A. & Wright, H.C. (1998). *Motor coordination disorders in children.* Thousand Oaks, CA: Sage.

Suzuki, L.A., Ponterotto, J.G., & Meller, P.J. (Eds.) (2000). *The handbook of multicultural assessment: Clinical, psychological, and educational applications* (2nd ed.). New York: Wiley & Sons.

Swedo, S.E., Allen, A.J., Glod, C.A., Clark, C.H., Teicher, M.H., Richter, D., Hoffman, C., Hamburger, S., Dow, S., Brown, C., & Rosenthal, N.E. (1997). A controlled trial of light therapy for the treatment of pediatric seasonal affective disorder. *Journal of the American Academy of Child and Adolescent Psychiatry, 36,* 816–821.

Szapocznik, J., Rio, A., Murray, E., Cohen, R., Scopetta, M., Rivas-Vasquez, A., Hervis, O., Posada, V., & Kurtines, W. (1989). Structural family versus psychodynamic child therapy for problematic Hispanic boys. *Journal of Consulting and Clinical Psychology, 57,* 571–578.

Tarnowski, K.J., & Simonian, S.J. (1992). Assessing treatment acceptance: The Abbreviated Acceptability Rating Profile. *Journal of Behavior Therapy and Experimental Psychiatry, 23,* 101–106.

Tarrier, N., & Barrowclough, C. (1990). Family interventions for schizophrenia. Special Issue: Recent developments in the behavioral treatment of chronic psychiatric illness. *Behavior Modification, 14,* 408–440.

Thigpen, C.H., & Cleckley, H.M. (1954). A case of multiple personality. *Journal of Abnormal and Social Psychology, 49,* 135–151.

Thigpen, C.H., & Cleckley, H.M. (1957). *Three faces of Eve.* New York: McGraw-Hill.

Thomas, L., & Krebs, C.J. (1997). A review of statistical power analysis software. *Bulletin of the Ecological Society of America, 78,* 126–139.

Thompson, B. (1996). AERA editorial policies regarding statistical significance testing: Three suggested reforms. *Educational Researcher, 25,* 26–30.

Tizard, J., Schofield, W.N., & Hewison, J. (1982). Reading collaboration between teachers and parents in assisting children's reading. *British Journal of Educational Psychology, 52,* 1–15.

Tohen, M., Bromet, E., Murphy, J.M., & Tsuang, M.T. (2000). Psychiatric epidemiology. *Harvard Review of Psychiatry, 8,* 111–125.

Tomarken, A.J. (1995). A psychometric perspective on psychophysiological measures. *Psychological Assessment, 7,* 387–395.

Toro, P.A., Bellavia, C.W., Daeschler, C.V., Owens, B.J., Wall, D.D., Passero, J.M., & Thomas, D.M. (1995). Distinguishing homelessness from poverty: A comparison study. *Journal of Consulting and Clinical Psychology, 63,* 280–289.

Tremblay, R.E., Masse, B., Perron, D., Leblanc, M., Schwartzman, E., & Ledingham, J.E. (1992). Early disruptive behavior, poor school achievement, delinquent behavior, and delinquent personality: Longitudinal analyses. *Journal of Consulting and Clinical Psychology, 60,* 64–72.

Tukey, J.W. (1991). The philosophy of multiple comparisons. *Statistical Science, 6,* 100–116.

Tversky, A., & Kahneman, D. (1971). Belief in the law of small numbers. *Psychological Bulletin, 76,* 105–110.

United States Congress, Office of Technology Assessment. (1991). *Adolescent health.* (OTA-H-468). Washington, DC: US Government Printing Office.

United States Department of Health and Human Services, National Institutes of Health, Office for Protection from Research Risks. (1983). *Code of federal regulations: Part 46: Protection of human subjects.* Washington, DC: US Government Printing Office.

Verhulst, F.C., & Koot, H.M. (1992). *Child psychiatric epidemiology: Concepts, methods, and findings.* Newbury Park, CA: Sage.

Vidich, A.J., & Lyman, S.M. (2000). Qualitative methods: Their history in sociology and anthropology. In N.H. Denzin & Y.S. Lincoln (Eds.), *Handbook of qualitative research* (2nd ed., pp. 37–84). Thousand Oaks, CA: Sage.

Vispoel, W.P. (2000). Computerized versus paper-and-pencil assessment of self-concept: Score comparability and respondent preferences. *Measurement and Evaluation in Counseling and Development, 33,* 130–143.

Vostanis, P., Feehan, C., Grattan, E., & Bickerton, W. (1996). Treatment for children and adolescents with depression: Lessons from a controlled trial. *Child Clinical Psychology and Psychiatry, 1,* 199–212.

Wade, S.L., Taylor, H.G., Drotar, D., Stancin, T., & Yeates, K.O. (1998). Family burden and adaptation during the initial year after traumautic brain injury in children. *Pediatrics, 102,* 110–116.

Waldholz, M. (1997, February 28). How do we know Dolly isn't a hoax? *Wall Street Journal,* Vol. CCXXIX, No. 41, pp. B1, B2.

Waldholz, M. (2000, February 7). Doctor admits faking data on cancer therapy. *Wall Street Journal,* Vol. CCXXXV, No. 27, p. B2.

Walker, A.J. (1996). Couples watching television: Gender, power, and the remote control. *Journal of Marriage and the Family, 58,* 813–823.

Walker, J.G., Johnson, S., Manion, I., & Cloutier, P. (1996). Emotionally focused marital intervention for couples with chronically ill children. *Journal of Consulting and Clinical Psychology, 64,* 1029–1036.

Wallerstein, R.S. (1986). *Forty-two lives in treatment: A study of psychoanalysis and psychotherapy.* New York: Guilford.

Walster, E., Berscheid, E., Abrahams, D., & Aronson, V. (1967). Effectiveness of debriefing following deception experiments. *Journal of Personality and Social Psychology, 6,* 371–380.

Waltz, J., Addis, M., Koerner, K., & Jacobson, J.S. (1993). Testing the integrity of a psychotherapy protocol: Assessment of adherence and competence. *Journal of Consulting and Clinical Psychology, 61,* 620–630.

Wampold, B.E., Davis, B., & Good, R.H.III (1990). Hypothesis validity of clinical research. *Journal of Consulting and Clinical Psychology, 58,* 360–367.

Wannamethee, S.G., & Sharper, A.G. (1999). Type of alcoholic drink and risk of major coronary heart disease events and all-cause mortality. *American Journal of Public Health, 89,* 685–690.

Waterhouse, A., Shirley, R., & Donovan, J. (1996). Antioxidants in chocolate. *Lancet, 348,* 834.

Watkins, C.E., Campbell, V.L., Nieberding, R., & Hallmark, R. (1995). Contemporary practice of psychological assessment by clinical psychologists. *Professional Psychology: Research and Practice, 26,* 54–60.

Watson, J.B., & Rayner, R. (1920). Conditioned emotional reactions. *Journal of Experimental Psychology, 3,* 1–14.

Webb, E.J., Campbell, D.T., Schwartz, R.D., Sechrest, L., & Grove, J.B. (1981). *Nonreactive measures in the social sciences* (2nd ed.). Boston: Houghton Mifflin.

Weber, S.J., & Cook, T.D. (1972). Subject effects in laboratory research: An examination of subject roles, demand characteristics, and valid inference. *Psychological Bulletin, 77,* 273–295.

Webster-Stratton, C. (1996). Early intervention with videotape modeling: Programs for families of children with oppositional defiant disorder or conduct disorder. In E.D. Hibbs & P. Jensen (Eds.), *Psychosocial treatment research of child and adolescent disorders: Empirically based strategies for clinical practice* (pp. 435–474). Washington, DC: American Psychological Association.

Webster-Stratton, C., & Spitzer, A. (1996). Parenting of a young child with conduct problems: New insights using qualitative methods. In T.H. Ollendick & R.J. Prinz (Eds.), *Advances in clinical child psychology* (Vol. 18, pp. 1–62). New York: Plenum Press.

Wehmeyer, M.L., & Palmer, S.B. (1998). Factor structure and construct validity of scores on the Hopelessness Scale for Children with students with cognitive disabilities. *Educational and Psychological Measurement, 58,* 661–667.

Weijer, C., & Emanuel, E.J. (2000). Protecting communities in biomedical research. *Science, 289,* 1142–1144.

Weiner, I.B. (1995). Methodological considerations in Rorschach research. *Psychological Assessment, 7,* 330–337.

Weiss, B., & Weisz, J.R. (1990). The impact of methodological factors on child psychotherapy outcome research: A meta-analysis for researchers. *Journal of Abnormal Child Psychology, 18,* 639–670.

Weiss, G., Minde, K., Douglas, V., Werry, J., & Sykes, D. (1971). Comparison of the effects of chlorpromazine, dextroamphetamine and methylphenidate on the behaviour and intellectual functioning of hyperactive children. *Canadian Medical Association Journal, 104,* 20–25.

Weisz, J.R., & Weiss, B. (1993). *Effects of psychotherapy with children and adolescents.* Newbury Park, CA: Sage.

Weisz, J.R., Walter, B.R., Weiss, B., Fernandez, G.A., & Mikow, V.A. (1990). Arrests among emotionally disturbed violent and assaultive individuals following minimal versus lengthy intervention through North Carolina's Willie M. Program. *Journal of Consulting and Clinical Psychology, 58,* 720–728.

Weisz, J.R., Weiss, B., & Donenberg, G.R. (1992). The lab versus the clinic: Effects of child and adolescent psychotherapy. *American Psychologist, 47,* 1578–1585.

Weisz, J.R., Weiss, B., Han, S.S., Granger, D.A., & Morton, T. (1995). Effects of psychotherapy with children and adolescents revisited: A meta-analysis of treatment outcome studies. *Psychological Bulletin, 117,* 450–468.

Werner, E.E., & Smith, R.S. (1982). *Vulnerable, but invincible: A longitudinal study of resilient children and youth.* New York: McGraw-Hill.

Werner, E.E., & Smith, R.S. (1992). *Overcoming the odds: High risk children from birth to adulthood.* Ithaca, NY: Cornell University Press.

West, R.R. (1995). Cholesterol screening: Can it be justified? *Hospital Update,* May, 219–229.

Wetzler, S., & Sanderson, W.C. (Eds.) (1997). *Treatment strategies for patients with psychiatric comorbidity.* New York: Wiley & Sons.

Widom, C.S., & Shepard, R.L. (1996). Accuracy of adult recollections of childhood victimization: Part 1. Childhood physical abuse. *Psychological Assessment, 8,* 412–421.

Wierzbicki, M., & Pekarik, G. (1993). A meta-analysis of psychotherapy dropout. *Professional Psychology: Research and Practice, 24,* 190–195.

Wiger, D.E. (1999). *The psychotherapy documentation primer.* New York: Wiley & Sons.

Wilkinson, L., & the Task Force on Statistical Inference, APA Board of Scientific Affairs (1999). Statistical methods in psychology journals: Guidelines and explanations. *American Psychologist, 54,* 594–604.

Williams, C.L., Butcher, J.N., Ben-Porath, Y.S., & Graham, J.R. (1992). *MMPI-A Content Scales: Assessing Psychopathology in Adolescent.* Minneapolis, MN: University of Minnesota Press.

Wilson, G.T. (1996). Manual-based treatments: The clinical application of research findings. *Behaviour Research and Therapy, 34,* 295–314.

Windle, C. (1954). Test–retest effect on personality questionnaires. *Educational and Psychological Measurement, 14,* 617–633.

Winer, B.J., Brown, D.R., & Michels, K.M. (1991). *Statistical principles in experimental design* (3rd. ed.). New York: McGraw-Hill.

Winslow, R. (1995, July 14). New pertussis vaccines by 3 companies prove effective in 2 European studies. *Wall Street Journal,* Vol. CCXXV, p. B5C.

Woelk, H. (2000). Comparison of St John's wort and imipramine for treating depression: Randomised controlled trial. *British Medical Journal, 321,* 536–539.

Wolf, M.M. (1978). Social validity: The case of subjective measurement or how applied behavior analysis is finding its heart. *Journal of Applied Behavior Analysis, 11*, 203–214.

Wright, K.M., & Miltenberger, R.G. (1987). Awareness training in the treatment of head and facial tics. *Journal of Behavior Therapy and Experimental Psychiatry, 18*, 269–274.

Wulsin, L.R., Vaillant, G.E., & Wells, V.E. (1999). A systematic review of the mortality of depression. *Psychosomatic Medicine, 61*, 6–17.

www.apa.org/journals

www.infoplease.com/ipa/A0855617.html

www.nih.gov/sigs/bioethics/conflict.html

www.onlineethics.org

www.psycline.org/journals/psycline.html

www.TCNJ.EDU/~ethcstat/start.html

www.upenn.edu/almanac/v45/n26/shelby.html

Wyatt, G.E., & Powell, G.J. (Eds.) (1988). *Lasting effects of child abuse*. Newbury Park, CA: Sage.

Yates, B.T. (1995). Cost-effectiveness analysis, cost–benefit analysis, and beyond: Evolving models for the scientist–manager–practitioner. *Clinical Psychology: Science and Practice, 2*, 385–398.

Ybarra, G.J., Passman, R.H., & Eisenberg, C.S. (2000). The presence of security blankets or mothers (or both) affects distress during pediatric examinations. *Journal of Consulting and Clinical Psychology, 68*, 322–330.

Yeaton, W.H., & Sechrest, L. (1981). Critical dimensions in the choice and maintenance of successful treatments: Strength, integrity, and effectiveness. *Journal of Consulting and Clinical Psychology, 49*, 156–167.

Yin, R.K. (1994). *Case study research: Design and methods* (2nd ed.). Thousand Oaks, CA: Sage.

Zilboorg, G., & Henry, G. (1941). *A history of medical psychology*. New York: W.W. Norton.

Author Index

Subject Index

ABAB design, 280–283, 292–299
alpha, 68–69, 71, 440–450, 454–469
Analogue research, 140–144
Anecdotal case study, 266, 300
Animal research, 37–38, 51, 87, 112, 114, 120,
   140–141, 380, 394, 498
Artifacts, 11, 18, 82–108. *See also* Subject Roles
  data related, 97–101
  experimenter characteristics, 90
  experimenter expectancy effects, 63–64, 87–89
  investigator and experimenter as sources of,
    83–91
  procedures, 83–86
  stages of, 82–83
Assessment, 19, 115, 225–227, 304–306, 324–326,
   355–405. *See also* Follow-up; Multiple
   measures; Reactivity; Reliability; Unobtrusive
   measures; Validity
  clinical practice and, 312–317, 324–325
  computers in, 383–385, 424
  construct validity and, 56fn
  continuous, 274–275, 302, 316–317, 428–429
  developing new measures, 365–367
  direct observations, 377–379
  experimental manipulations and, 225–227
  follow-up, 430–434
  global ratings, 368–372
  interrelationship of different measures, 401–402
  journals devoted to, 115fn
  measurement strategies, 367–387
  obtrusive, 45, 387–389
  projective techniques, 375–377
  psychobiological measures, 380–383
  psychometric characteristics, 358–361
  reactive, 45–46, 226, 387–390
  retrospective, 238–239

  selecting assessment methods, 314–315, 356–362
  self-report inventories, 372–375
  sensitivity of the measure, 360–361
  social desirability in, 373–374
  unreliability of, 75–76
Attention-placebo control group, 191–195. *See also*
   Nonspecific treatment control group
Attrition, 30–31, 105–108, 128–129, 187, 196,
   251–252, 366, 430–431, 451–454
  during follow-up, 106–107, 430–431
  minimizing, 107–108
  threat to validity, 30, 105–106, 251–252
Authorship, 547–549
  allocation of credit, 530–533, 541

Baseline, 274–280, 316
  functions of, 275–276
Bayesian analyses, 468fn
Beta, 68–69
Birth-cohort study, 242–243
"Blind" experimenters, 59–60, 88–89, 93
  checking on, 89
  terminology, 60, 88fn
Bonferroni adjustment, 455–457, 460
Buffer items, 389

Carryover effects, 43–44, 177–178
Case-control designs, 138–139, 235–241
  considerations in using, 239–241
  cross-sectional design, 236–237, 261–262
  retrospective design, 237–239
  strengths and weaknesses of, 239–241
Case study, 111–112, 265–273, 300–312, 318–324
  anecdotal case study, 266, 273
  Anna O., 268, 270
  characteristics of, 267–268